Finally, Gandhi and Fanon come together in strategic dialogue! Not just reprinted words from old masters, but new connections from their militant daughters, granddaughters and new generations of resisters and scholars reimagining their legacies for 21st-century struggles. Marshall and Meyer and *Insurrectionary Uprisings* help us build roads to the future by walking through the best of past movements and thinking sharply about where we need to go. This is a must-read for academics and activists alike, looking to make real change in the years to come.

—**Stellan Vinthagen**, Endowed Chair in the Study of Nonviolent Direct Action and Civil Resistance; Professor of Sociology at University of Massachusetts, Amherst and at University of Gothenburg.

Insurrectionary Uprisings, is a powerful anthology. Their Preface and Introduction alone make a significant contribution to what we – people who want to change the world – need to be thinking about! Near the end of the Intro, they ask: "...if we grasp the extreme urgency of this moment, do we know where to find the wisdom, guidance, and materials we need to build a future?" They then offer us more than 50 pieces from people around the world, facing different realities, across generations that provide insights from a range of perspectives. Not every question can be answered in any one collection, and the editors make no pretence that this collection offers a road map to a better future. But the material in this book must be taken seriously for many reasons, not the least of which is that it will push your ways of thinking, our collective awareness and help us discover new ways to strengthen our connections with one another. This is a book you will want to keep readily accessible as we all struggle through these most challenging of times, this is a book you will want to share with others.

—**Leslie Cagan**, has served as lead organizer of countless US mass mobilizations, from the Vietnam War to nuclear disarmament, from queer liberation to Cuba solidarity, from climate change to social justice; former national coordinator, United for Peace and Justice; former co-chair, Pacifca Radio.

*Insurrectionist Uprisings* is a highly provocative convergence of thoughts on holistic decolonization of peoples and Nature – both of whom have been subverted and abased right from precolonial years. This book should awaken everyone to the call for action in the struggle to birth a just new world. We either we act now in solidarity or we descend deeper into the pit of barbarism. *Insurrectionist Uprisings* is a much-needed ladder for escaping present

toxic, unequal, depraved and exploitative global relations. It is a great feat, an outstanding gift of a library of living texts!

— **Nnimmo Bassey**, Health of Mother Earth Foundation, Right Livelihood Award Laureate.

An amazing collection of thinkers from around the world. It needs to be supplemented from my region beyond the upper castes of India, with more stories and struggles done by so many grassroots Indigenous women activists and others. We must have more practicum and theories on how to exercise our right to resist. We need new thinking on how we do resistance. These are the thoughts that this reader evoked and provoked in me. With this, we should head for the nonviolent insurrection!

— **Binalakshmi Nepram**, Founder, Global Alliance of Indigenous Peoples, Gender Justice, and Peace; Board member of International Peace Bureau (the 1910 Nobel Peace Prize Laureate).

I've often said that actions that grow out of love have the most power. Reading the words of Puerto Rico's Lolita Lebron in her never-before-published letter to Catholic Worker founder Dorothy Day reminded me of this. This powerful book brings together both classic and new works which will help empower future generations in building for peace and decolonization.

— **Oscar Lopez Rivera**, Puerto Rican former political prisoner, named "the Mandela of the Americas" by progressive Latin American heads of state.

# INSURRECTIONARY UPRISINGS

## A Reader in Revolutionary Nonviolence and Decolonization

Edited by

Wende Marshall and Matt Meyer

**Daraja Press**

Published by
Daraja Press
https://darajapress.com
in association with
Zand Graphics Ltd, Kenya
https://zandgraphics.com
2022

ISBN: 9781988832999

Permissions granted for the reproduction of materials incorporated here can be
found in the Acknowledgements (p.399)

Cover image: Nadezda Grapes
Cover design: Kate McDonnell

Library and Archives Canada Cataloguing in Publication

Title: Insurrectionary uprisings : a reader in revolutionary nonviolence and
decolonization / edited by Wende Marshall & Matt Meyer.
Names: Marshall, Wende Elizabeth, 1961- editor. | Meyer, Matt, 1962- editor.
Description: Includes bibliographical references and index.
Identifiers: Canadiana (print) 20210119691 | Canadiana (ebook) 20210119713 |
ISBN 9781988832999 (softcover) | ISBN 9781990263002 (ebook)
Subjects: LCSH: Nonviolence. | LCSH: Passive resistance. | LCSH: Social action.
Classification: LCC HM1281 .I57 2021 | DDC 303.6/1—dc23

# WHEN YOU TIE ROPE AND RIBBON

*for oscar lópez rivera*

you make two knots
so that years and names
can climb up or down

uniting thick and thin threads
simplicities and opacities
tense and resolved dialectics

your eyes are closed fists
that guide your hands
so the ribbon may last centuries
or until we have no need
to unleash forces
or unarm states

Raquel Salas Rivera, 2018


# CUANDO AMARRAS SOGA Y CINTA

*para oscar lópez rivera*

creas dos nudos
para que puedan subir o bajar
años y nombres

uniendo hebras gruesas y finas
simplicidades y opacidades
dialécticas tensas y resueltas

tus ojos son puños cerrados
que guían tus manos
para que la cinta dure siglos
o hasta que no haya necesidad
de desatar fuerzas
y desarmar estados

—Raquel Salas Rivera, 2018

# CONTENTS

# FOREWORD

Joyce Ajlouny

A singular perspective on the intersections of revolution, reform, and nonviolent resistance risks distorting their intricacies and watering down their complexities. Solutions to oppression and conflict manifest in the varied experiences of those who carried the weight and struggled before us. Their stories must be heard, contextualized, and discerned to inspire change in the present. In *Insurrectionary Uprisings*, Marshall and Meyer compellingly make a case for moving beyond the 'one idea' of an expert and instead embracing wisdom directly from the people and their grassroots movements.

This scholarly collection is extraordinary in examining what constitutes viable strategies of resistance; making the case for best practices and lessons learned. It also offers a critical toolbox for peace and justice practitioners. This collection of essays asks us to look beyond our local context, to think of oppressive structures as interlinked. We can't speak of colonialism without speaking of white supremacy and we can't challenge state violence without challenging systemic racism. The shameful global realities presently surrounding vaccine equity put these intersections front and center as we consider corporate greed, power, and our shared security.

Through my exposure to the remarkable work of the American Friends Service Committee as General Secretary, I have found that our strongest work is that which successfully builds on an integrated analysis and brings peace practitioners and activists together to formulate shared solutions towards a more unified, connected peace and justice agenda beyond the single-issue. To illustrate, I saw the intensity of interactions, mutual inspiration and incredible knowledge sharing when we brought together Palestinian liberation activists with members of the Movement of Black Lives, or when immigrant youth in the U.S. collaborated with youth in Latin America. Such intersectional experiences can't be accomplished with theoretical experts in the field alone. The role of nonprofits or academia can only go this far. The vision and lived experiences of the oppressed need to be front and center.

Four years ago, when I was preparing for my role with AFSC, a friend advised me to read Angela Davis' *Freedom Is a Constant Struggle: Ferguson, Palestine, and the Foundations of a Movement*. Davis highlights the interconnectedness of oppression in all its forms and wherever it manifests, from state terror to mass incarceration, drawing lessons from Black feminism, the anti-apartheid struggle in South Africa, and other movements. Davis powerfully and plainly compels us to build the collective movement for human liberation, in many of the same ways *Insurrectionary Uprisings* does today.

Davis' words were extremely helpful as I made the transition from living and working under military occupation in Palestine to leading a global peace and justice organization in the U.S. As I entered the global peace and justice world as a professional, my own lived experience of growing up and raising my children under Israeli occupation informed my vision and my approach to peacebuilding. It is where I derive my unwavering commitment to justice, but also where I find courage to resist and stand by those oppressed wherever they may be.

Being raised Quaker also had a profound impact on me. Quakers believe in letting our 'life speak' as a commitment to action. Quakers open the way for the Spirit to lead and seek 'that of God' in ourselves and everyone, especially those whom we do not agree with. These are the foundations of putting our beliefs and values into practice and letting them 'speak' regardless of consequences.

Being a U.S. citizen since birth allowed me to experience democracy but to also witness its fragility. I have seen, through monumental moments of courage and dissent, how every person has a voice that matters and how that has the power to drive societal change. The intertwined histories of being Palestinian, Quaker and American inspires my vision for justice.

Palestinian liberation has become central to peace and justice in part because it presents transformative manifestations of resistance and popular mobilization that everyone can learn from – including our failures. In nearly every global peace and justice conversation, the Palestine experience finds its place and offers wisdom. From militarism, occupation and apartheid, colonialism, policing and state violence, mass incarceration, collective punishment, uprisings, civil disobedience and nonviolent resistance, peace negotiations and treaties, we can find a myriad of experiences to draw lessons from. Palestinian voices provide a distinctive window as we aspire to build the global movement for human liberation, especially at this time; to revive a global peace agenda with an intersectional lens.

Popular resistance is the staple of the Palestinian lived experience; it's in our DNA. Resistance is in every action we take, in our *Sumoud* (steadfastness), in our perseverance, forbearance, and in our art and music, and in our courage. Resistance does not necessitate an elaborate plan or campaign – it is in our being, in our hearts and souls. My vivid recollection of the two *Intifadas* (uprisings) of the late 1980s and early 2000s are examples of the organic nature of popular mobilization.

I was a young teacher at the Ramallah Friends School, just returning from my studies in Michigan, when the first *Intifada* erupted. Israeli authorities closed all schools and outlawed all gatherings of more than a few people in Occupied Territories. Instead of encouraging violent resistance, the underground Palestinian leadership listened to the wants of communities and guided us through a strategy that we all willingly and excitedly followed. Fliers were disbursed in town at night– they encouraged us to create clandestine classrooms, secretly and seamlessly moving the location from one house to the next where students would gather and we (the teachers) would ensure their education was not interrupted. In addition, we planted neighborhood gardens and shared the produce, we raised chickens on the rooftops and increased our self-sufficiency while boycotting Israeli products. We also created neighborhood watch groups and developed other social services. At the same time, we continued taking to the streets. We protested every day. We were confronted with a belligerent military and many lost their lives. But we persisted for six years until the Oslo Peace Process was underway.

Fast forward, two recent examples include the action that unified Palestinians in the region against home expulsions in Sheikh Jarrah and the police crackdown on youth in Jerusalem and other Palestinian cities inside the Green Line, and the extraordinary weekly Great March of Return mobilization at the Gaza border. Reflecting upon these times, and the persistent and creative nonviolent acts of resistance, I profess that Palestinians, like all oppressed people, understand their oppression. We know how to resist, we don't need politicians to hand us down 'the plan', and we don't need saviors. Instead, we need partners who will walk with us, who will listen and help amplify our narratives, and whose solidarity we can reciprocate.

Drawing on so many other struggles as this anthology does, including the Palestine experience, we can capture and document nonviolent solutions to conflict and systems of oppression, grounding us in and amplifying the community voices of those most affected.

Social and digital media and our virtual platforms enable us to engage and pursue joint action at remarkable scales. The world is seeing a rise in social movements as ordinary people challenge oppressive systems and promote alternative visions. We've seen protests in Lebanon and Bolivia and uprisings overthrowing dictatorships in Algeria and Sudan. And we've seen how the local can impact the global, from the global racial justice movement following the killing of George Floyd, to the #MeToo movement, to when a small-scale local initiative in Sweden moved young people around the world to join a global campaign for climate action. Even in the face of repression or outright war, local social activists and peacebuilders persist in their quest to pursue nonviolent and just solutions.

A new tide of people-powered organic movements are on the rise; they are connecting and sharing knowledge and experiences across oceans; they are challenging power structures in creative ways and energizing each other for action and change. Their connections are powerful, many are unprecedented, and their time is now.

This movement of movements is changing the landscape for nonprofit organizations who need to find new ways to support, empower, and scale up the grassroots mobilization to shift public narratives, influence political processes, and transform systems. Traditional advocacy outfits are sidelined by an upsurge of grassroots organizing. If they stay grounded in the visions and demands of the grassroots, nonprofits can play an important role of convening and coordinating these collective energies and counteracting the fragmentation of civil society actors.

*Insurrectionary Uprisings* provides tools for all of the above. It builds synergies, unites discourses, and creates inspired solutions. From the local to the global, it draws on the rich experiences and varied knowledge of extraordinary contributors and weaves together a thought-provoking menu of drivers and solutions for movements globally.

*Insurrectionary Uprisings* is an essential book. It calls on solidarity activists, nonprofits, advocates, and academicians alike, to walk the talk and be led by the strategies and voices of oppressed people. Our moment calls for urgency, for people-centered, intersectional, and decolonized approaches, for recognizing that our differences are a strength, for courage, and for putting values into action.

Now is the moment to let our lives speak.

# PREFACE: OUTRAGE IS NOT ENOUGH!

Matt Meyer and Wende Marshall

---

*For hundreds of years white men had been telling the people of the Americas to forget the past; but now the white man Marx came along, and he was telling people to remember. The old-time people had believed the same thing: they must reckon with the past because within it lay seeds of the present and future. They must reckon with the past because within it lay this present moment and also the future moment.*

*The stories Marx related, the great force of his words, the bitterness and fury—they had caught hold... This was the end of what the white man had to offer the Americas: poisoned smog in the winter and the choking clouds that swirled off sewage treatment leaching fields and filled the sky with fecal dust in early spring.*
—Leslie Marmon Silko (Laguna Pueblo), from *Almanac of the Dead* (1992)

*In 1976 [following mass collective nonviolent resistance across Palestine, struggling against settler-colonialist land theft], we (Palestinians) discovered ourselves, we discovered the world, and it discovered us.* —Edward Said, *The Question of Palestine* (1977)

*My interest is not in the capture of power, but in the control of power by the people... After years of freedom, people of [India] are wracked by hunger, rising prices, corruption... oppressed by every kind of injustice... It is a Total Revolution we want, nothing less!* —Jayaprakash Narayan (1974)

Outrage is on the rise.

The lessons of 2020 must surely center on the fragility and regeneration of life. Nothing less than a global pandemic, economic crisis, intensified foci on militarized policing and white supremacy, and the challenges of democracy and authoritarianism shook the world in unprecedented ways. The horrors of countless unnecessary deaths were countered by mass mobilizations against police violence and for Black lives; fascist rumblings were met by popular resistance taking diverse tactical, strategic, and ideological forms. New networks, coalitions, and organizations were built, new life returned to small ecosystems which experienced a short-term reprieve from daily super-industrial onslaughts. The billionaires got far richer and the poor more impoverished and ill, but a veil was lifted from those realities which gives hope for new possibilities.

Revolutionaries everywhere, of all stripes and tendencies, are challenged to ask and answer: how do we mold outrage to something more focused and sustainable? Organizers are driven to put into concrete form the everyday acts of resistance and feelings of frustration which make up the seedlings of all effective movements. Peace and justice activists echo all good socialists, communists, anarchists, and others in rephrasing Lenin's pivotal question: What is to be done? Mao teaches us (in reports he wrote before even gaining state power) that revolution is not a concept to be trifled with, neither a dinner party nor even a well-placed, carefully researched, and powerful essay...in fact nothing which can be 'refined, so leisurely and gentle, so temperate, kind, courteous, restrained and magnanimous.' And while we strongly agree with the next line in Mao's famous quote, that 'a revolution is an insurrection,' we are not as certain that the second part of his phrasing—that revolution is definitionally an act of violence—is as well borne out by the hundred years of history which have followed. There is something, for us, in the parallel chorus of Gandhi and Che which adds that all revolutionaries are, at our roots, motivated by love for the people, which creates an additive to Mao's far-reaching vision. A century of neocolonial imperialism and unsuccessful attempts at class struggle in single nation-states suggests that new thinking is needed about the nature of violence itself within our interrogations of philosophy, principles, and practicalities of movement-building. Feminism writ large suggests that the means and the ends have always been more indelibly connected than most radical male theoreticians have given concrete credit to.

We put together this book as dedicated, 21st century revolutionaries, looking to build upon vital texts of the past to formulate new guideposts for future endeavors. As we rebuild the world after every crisis, we are called upon to glean key lessons from the past...and remain struck that the power of creative, unarmed resistance has barely been conceptualized or made practical for contemporary revolutionary struggle. We have failed to develop a praxis whereby revolutionary theory and nonviolent practice can morph into potentially winning ideological or operational frameworks. We are certain that regurgitating the words or work of Gandhi (or for that matter Che) will not bring us where we need to be. We obviously feel that there is much to be gained by investigating the contours of the broadest conceptual definitions of both revolution and nonviolence. This modern 'guide for radicals' asserts no rules (as Alinsky might have liked), but rather a Freirean conceit that with enough of the best thinking and theorizing, we may better name our current realities so that we are collectively in a stronger place to change them.

One word, and a certain type of politics popularly associated with it in recent movement parlance (at least and maybe especially in the extremely under-developed U.S. left) is 'identity.' For us, identity politics as generally understood is a confining space—one that we can neither afford to ignore nor stay too long focused upon. Caucuses and right's campaigns for marginalized peoples are necessary steps in the process of human liberation; being permanently stuck in those spaces of processes can be dead-end reformist at least, counterrevolutionary at worst. Our best understanding of identity has been described by the great Palestinian activist-intellectual Edward Said. In reviewing the many Palestinian perspectives, ideologies, leaders and leading organizations, viewpoints, strategies and tactics, he ultimately asserted that the ground-breaking work built at the grassroots level in the occupied territories—which was largely nonviolent though not philosophically so and not emphasized by the larger movement as such—was crucial in forging a global 'identity' which moved all the people closer to liberation.

In stating 'we discovered ourselves' in the years building up towards the First Intifada and beyond, Said understood that a *liberatory* identity might not automatically win state power or needed concessions but was undeniably a key element in the path towards freedom. For Said and for us, a liberatory identity must be based upon material conditions and liberatory practice, not on demographics.

We are moved by the phrase 'Total Revolution,' developed and utilized by the post-Gandhian Indian militants who wished to couple the old man's multiplicity of teachings about unarmed strategies, tactics, and ways of life with other left elements of the time, including socialism and some of Mao's teachings of how to build it. For Jayakapresh (JP) Narayan and Narayan Desai, Total Revolution meant a revitalized and reinvigorated Gandhianism which built on the most radical elements of satyagraha and focused on economic change, inter-personal change, and a transnational look at world politics which went way beyond India's borders. We can well understand why the official purveyors of mainstream historical revisionism in India, and the architects of the modern Indian nuclear, sub-imperialist, Kashmir-colonizing nation-state, should seek to cauterize the more radical Gandhi, to cement him into an impossible-to-replicate, idolized and saintly 'Mahatma' statue of absolutely no use to social change movement-building. We are more concerned with the all-too-many progressive Mahatma worshipers, who imply that a quasi-religious commitment to actions plans (and lifestyle?) developed over a century ago should be a main model for modern times. We are struck by how very far behind they are, and in their large, corporate-sponsored (or at least status-quo-acceptable) shadow how very constrained they leave the rest of us, from the Totally Revolutionary ideals of JP and others—quite committed to radical nonviolence but unwilling to caste their entire world-changing visions on the shoulders of one man.

We too want nothing less than total revolution, not as copywrite-laden phrases or set ideological constructs, but a fluid, dialectical approach towards making the planet and all its people a place of beauty, justice and liberation for all inhabitants and growing things. We believe that total revolution is both a goal and a method, and that insurrectionary uprisings will be absolutely essential to meeting that goal through those processes.

The essays in this reader suggest that there is much more about unarmed mass mobilizations which need to be understood and developed by those committed to revolution than has been previously admitted. The problem has been especially enshrined by those who rely on a worldview which elevates the tactics of armed, military action to an unerring philosophy that revolution can only be advanced through the barrel of a gun. The famous Mao quote, of course, is that power – not revolution – grows out of the barrel of the gun...but long forgotten is the rest of the Chairman's treatise, that 'the Party commands the gun, the gun must never be allowed to command the Party.' We may disagree that 'war can only be abolished through war,' but feel even more strongly opposed to the diluting of revolutionary thinking which deconstructs everything down to its lowest common denominator. Just as Gandhi and Che agreed about the centrality of love for all revolutionaries, we suggest that at the base of all revolutionary praxis is a commitment to eradicate violence of all kinds inflicted upon the people. Why such reticence, therefore, to explore in fully revolutionary contexts the power of militant nonviolent direct actions?

◊

When one reflects upon the roots of radical nonviolence, before and beyond Gandhi, it becomes clear that puritanism has been one of the major stumbling blocks holding back a revolutionary application of disciplined, mass unarmed resistance strategies. Even those who held closely to what they explicitly credited as Gandhian approaches, such as many in the U.S., Black-led, southern-based freedom movement, understood that basic fact. The dialectics and dynamics of that 'long Sixties' period from the mid-1950's through the late 1970's saw a greater understanding of the nuances and false dichotomies inherent in the splitting debates about nonviolence vs. self-defense or revolutionary armed struggle vs. nonviolent mass organizing in support of revolutionary movements. The more fundamental contradictions, within advanced struggle in Africa, Asia, Latin America, or the Middle East—like the more backwards movements of the U.S. or Europe—has always been between reform and revolution, where our true debates and conflicts should really be located. Those who believe that tiny changes are all that is needed to end oppression, that racialized capitalism, heteropatriarchy, imperialism and other forms of oppression will yield way through a series of slow and small refinements of the current status quo have deeper problems than questions of methodology or nonviolence. Those who cry for peace with no concern about justice shed bitter tears at best.

As the essays between these pages go deeper into contemporary theories of decoloniality and early 21st century practice, we find a growing space for symbiosis between ideologies and revolutionary ideas which have not always found common ground in our organizational practice. Yet the lack of current movements or united fronts with enough force to hold back authoritarian dictators, to stem the tide of an onslaught of fascist organizing, to turn around a climate crisis which threatens life beyond homo-sapiens, seems evidently clear. We can only hope to get closer through the kinds of interrogations we believe Lugones and Quijano point to in their essays about coloniality, power and process. We review with cautionary excitement the extremely new practices of a People's Strike formation in the U.S.A. and continued pushing from the Zapatistas in Mexico and beyond for a grassroots democratic autonomy which breaks with past dogmas and reaches for new revolutionary fusion.

Having gone through these stops on a route examining specific strategies and tactics, what we have learned, what conclusion can we reach? We know that we are called to continue the work of building a heightened praxis which leads us to a more effective set of revolutionary methods designed to win actual struggles. We know that these struggles, and the movements, campaigns, organizations and individuals which lead them cannot fall prey as easily as before to the traps of capitalist reformism, misogyny, white supremacy, coloniality, or militarist fantasies centered around the glory of the gun. We are challenged and motivated to rethink the way arms have been seen as the only vehicle for revolutionary change, and to rethink how some talk of nonviolence shuts down conversations seeking to move short-term, minor changes.

Understanding revolution, now more than ever, must mean understanding dialectics. This means moving far beyond the false dichotomies posited by revisionist history, and refusing to continue, as we have said, 'to fight our grandfather's battles.' It is about understanding the dialectic between philosophy, strategy, and tactics, utilizing the tools of dialectical materialism to study a moment and organize action campaigns and movements based on those moments. What are the differences and what are the interrelations between the strategies, tactics, philosophies, and ideologies we are called upon to study? What are the gemstones of past study and struggle which we need to fuse together to build new praxis for a new future?

A proper dialectical understanding views both nonviolent and armed struggle as *tools*, beyond simple or singular strategies, tactics, or philosophies to be parsed as if they are dividing lines between reform and revolution. Revolutionaries today and tomorrow need nonsectarian access to a highly diversified toolbox, a palette of multiple shades to paint a new world with endless color under a rainbow arc of freedom. We hope that in reviewing this history of Insurrectionary Uprisings and the commentaries which surrounded them, we have set forth some answers as well as questions to the forward-looking query of What is to be Done? We offer no concrete program of action, no organizational model or training module, which we believe will get us to where we need to go. We reject all ideas that a small group who happen to hold 'the right ideas, the correct answers' will hold what we need to build winning people's movements. But we do believe that talk of revolution, study of struggle, the building for mass strikes, development of grassroots cooperatives, cross-border resistance communications, and new radical internationals will all be part of taking us there.

The revolution we need will surely require more reading, writing, and dialogue—some of it in forms much less public than a published book. We can only hope that this effort sets some spaces for these dialogues to take place. The revolution we need will surely require insurrectionary uprisings. We look forward to seeing you in the whirlwind, and in the center of our diverse and swirling struggles.

# INTRODUCTION: INSURRECTIONS, UPRISINGS, AND A SANKOFA LOOK AT THE STRATEGIES WE NEED

Wende Marshall and Matt Meyer

---

The essays in this volume analyze structures of power and violence in the context of half a millennium of bloody Euro-American expansion and imperial rule. While history and empirical evidence have shown on numerous occasions that violence can have short-term efficacy in people's struggles for liberation, it is not a viable route to a society of solidarity, reciprocity, and cooperation.

Violence is the preeminent tool of the master class.

The 'master's tools,' Audre Lorde warned, would 'never dismantle the master's house.' Although they might, she argued, 'temporarily allow us to beat him at his own game,' they would not lead us to the deep, global transformation we must achieve to honor the sanctity of all life on earth. These prophetic words define the theme of *Insurrectionary Uprisings*.

Mark Muhannad Ayyash eloquently argued in 'Building from the Rubble', that 'European colonial projects since the fifteenth century have ravaged the majority of the world's population through slavery, race and racism, and the transfer of massive wealth from the world's colonized spaces' to feed the imperial war-making of Euro-America. Amid the 2021 U.S.-backed, Israeli assault on Palestine, Ayyash was clear that a crumbling Euro-American empire is raining devastation, and that all of us—the world's dominated, enslaved, colonized and dispossessed—are caught in the cross hairs of this cataclysm. We are, Ayyash writes, 'being crushed like rubble under the weight of the world of empire.' But Ayyash asks us to see the potential in the rubble, to transform it and our 'shattered and fragmented selves' into 'a new humanity and a new world.' The new world we seek cannot be produced with the master's tools.

This book presents historic and contemporary writings about the potentially revolutionary power of nonviolence and decolonization. Many of the essays contained herein do not explore or even mention nonviolence, and some of the authors presented here were proponents of armed struggle.

- Robert Franklin Williams (1925-1966), president of the North Carolina NAACP and author of *Negroes with Guns* (1962), asserts in a dialogue with Rev. Dr. Martin Luther King, Jr. and Dave Dellinger that '... Negroes are faced with the necessity of combatting savage violence. The struggle is for mere existence... (and) there is no lawful deterrent against those who would do him violence.'
- Amilcar Cabral (1924-1973), leader of the Guinea-Bissau & Cape Verdean

armed struggle for liberation from Portugal, was a commanding general who also believed that militarism should be subsumed under struggles for decolonization, 'the re-signification of local non-European cultures and the formation of social forms shorn of colonial subconsciousness.'[1]

- Kenneth Kaunda (1924-2021), former president of Zambia and fierce proponent of Southern African liberation, supported the armed struggle of the African National Congress in South Africa, allowing them safe haven in Zambia despite his personal interest in Christian pacifism and pragmatic nonviolence.

The words of Williams, Cabral and Kaunda in this volume remind us of the potential efficacy of revolutionary armed struggle. But the contradiction of armed struggle, as Hannah Arendt and Graça Machel argued in essays in this volume, is that violent means can easily overwhelm the goal of liberation. 'The practice of violence, like all action,' Arendt wrote, 'changes the world, but the most probable change is a more violent world.' While armed struggle can sometimes beat the enemy in some parts of the globe, the record of armed struggle producing societies based on love and cooperation is, indeed, quite slender.

Questions of effective praxis are at the center of our ongoing dialogue. These questions seek neither to divide nor divert from our fundamental goal: figuring out how we can—collectively and expediently and with the greatest tribute to life, healing, and the wisdom of ancestors—build the mass movements and revolutions which will result in lasting peace, justice, and liberation. To grasp the righteous potential of nonviolent insurrection and decoloniality, we must attend to the ways in which our world is saturated with physical, structural, and epistemological violence.

Some essays explore the effects of structural and physical violence in our communities and nations, and people's response to this terror. The piece by Graça Machel, for example, discusses the devastating effects of war on children. As UNICEF's Special Representative for Children and Armed Conflict, Machel reported that more and more of the world had become a 'moral vacuum' in which 'children are slaughtered, raped and maimed... exploited as soldiers... starved and exposed to extreme brutality.' Declaring children as 'zones of peace,' she argued, would allow us to 'recapture our instinct to nurture and protect children.'

Fannie Lou Hamer's testimony before the 1964 Democratic Convention describes the brutality of the police in the Jim Crow South. Held in a cell following her attempt to register to vote, the police told Hamer, 'We are going to make you wish you was dead.' And Rev. Dr. Martin Luther King, Jr.'s powerful sermon, 'Beyond Vietnam,' prophesies against the structural violence of poverty and white supremacy in Vietnam and the U.S. and exhorts pacifists to recognize the U.S. government as 'the greatest purveyor of violence in the world today.'

---

1. 'Cabral, Amilcar,' *Global Social Theory*, https://globalsocialtheory.org/thinkers/cabral-amilcar/.

Each of these essays challenge us to recognize that the U.S. deploys terror daily at home and abroad and demands that we consider whether nonviolent insurrection is a viable means to counter a global order built on bloody brutality and the dangerous fictions of nation, race, and gender. The theorizing of coloniality by the Peruvian sociologist Aníbal Quijano and the Argentine feminist philosopher Maria Lugones is crucial to understanding the depth of what it means to fashion a decolonized world. Placing the colonialist/capitalist world system in the analytic frame of modernity, Quijano and Lugones describe coloniality as the savage imposition of European systems of hierarchy, knowledge and culture on the colonized, which persist even after the formal, political formation of independent states. They theorized that the path to liberation requires a process of epistemological decolonizing that delves deeply into the violent processes through which Indigenous ways of being and knowing are/were violently suppressed and replaced with Euro-American constructs of race, gender, and sexuality.

It is our position that we have much to learn from our ancestors. The legacy of Thoreau, Arendt, Gandhi, Pyarelal, King, Cone, Harding, Baker, Boggs, Hamer, Fanon, Deming, Cabral, Sutherland, Kaunda, Lorde, Lebron, Tillmon, Feinberg, Cáceres, Lugones, Quijano, and Trask, Williams, Day, Lebron, and Pyarelal root us in the long struggles for freedom and justice which strengthen us as we continue to resist and build. It is also our position that the wisdom and praxis of early twenty-first century revolutionaries can be a source of inspiration and insight to those who wish to commit their lives to defeating the Euro-American colonial and imperial beast.

In choosing the content of this volume, we asked ourselves how to best embody the concept of *Sankofa*, an Akan, Twi, and Fante concept that to move forward one must retrieve wisdom and lessons from the past. It is our position that we cannot create a world based on solidarity, collectivity, justice, and liberation without *re-membering* the ethical and material basis of the social worlds that were destroyed by the expansion of Euro/America and the white supremacist, capitalist, heteropatriarchy whose inevitable implosion threatens the entire globe.

## Outline of the Book

We open with what many consider 'the classics,' inspired by a modern contextualization from South African radical Ela Gandhi. Ela's last name reveals her lineage from her grandfather's days in that country but tells less of the story of her own youthful involvement with the African National Congress underground as a militant supporter of the anti-apartheid liberation struggle. Ela inspires and reminds us that even our most basic and familial constructs must be reinvented and made relevant for each new generation. Hannah Arendt teaches us that violence can be an effective, rational, and sometimes necessary but ultimately problematic tool because the means inherently overwhelm the ends. Thoreau spotlights how all nation-states require civil disobedience to remain viable. Thoreau's spin on the Christian notion that suffering can be redemptive is the assertion that prison is 'the only house in a slave-state in which a free man can abide with honor.' It is not just redemptive but also principled to take the risks which will land one behind bars or worse. Thoreau adds: 'Under a government which imprisons any unjustly, the true place for a just man (sic) is also a prison... It is there that the fugitive slave, and the Mexican prisoner on parole, and the Indian come to plead the wrongs of his (sic) race... on that separate, but more free and honorable ground, where the State places those who are not *with* her but *against* her.'

Gandhi is often mis-characterized as promoting 'passive resistance' when in fact he asserts that all nonviolence of his type is 'a more active and real' way of fighting against all 'wickedness.' Furthermore, while Gandhi sees pacifist resistance and civil disobedience as part of his more radical 'Satyagraha,' the more significant aspect of 'Satyagraha' (truth force, soul force, love force) is noncooperation with evil. Pyarelal, Gandhi's official biographer, added that Gandhi believed himself to be a 'better' socialist or communist than those who took on those titles more directly; that he saw his struggles as 'identical' to socialist and communist struggles from an economic, political, and social point of view.

Rai adds, in some ways like U.S. nonviolent academic-strategist Gene Sharp[2] and others before him, that Gandhi was deeply strategic in his thinking and actions. There are two key points here: he understood the importance of cadre organization and he understood that working alongside and in conjunction with armed actions could be important in terms of tactics and timing. Rai notes that armed actions are sometimes 'simpler' partly because 'an armed struggle inevitably involves a small cadre of trained and armed militants, rather than the millions of people who were galvanized and transformed by the mass nonviolent struggle around the Salt March. Frantz Fanon argued the extreme violence of the colonizer inevitably leads the colonized to regain their own humanity through the use of violence.. The tens of thousands who volunteered to be arrested during the salt campaign, and the millions who defied British imperial law, found another way to breach the myth of their inferiority.'

As Roy implies in her writings, if we do not understand or follow these more radical aspects and strategic nuances of Gandhi (and King, and Mandela), his legacy is too easily co-opted and re-written by the powerful forces seeking to maintain their grasp on politics, economics, and history.

Starhawk adds, in a critique and contextualization of the sexism and patriarchy of past leaders including Gandhi, that 'the revolution we need to make includes a profound change in relationship to our experience of being a body. One of the insights of ecofeminism, the convergence of the feminist and ecology movements, is that our destruction of the environment is allowable because of the deep devaluation of nature and the body in the underlying religious and philosophical systems that shape our worldviews.' Well beyond engaging in 'morality plays' of social witness, the question is 'how best can we collectively take power?'

---

2. Sometimes referred to as 'the Machiavelli of nonviolence' and 'the Clausewitz of nonviolent warfare,' Gene Sharp was the founder and director of the Harvard-associated Albert Einstein Institute, and author of numerous books including the iconic three-volume *The Politics of Nonviolent Action* (1973).

XXVI | INSURRECTIONARY UPRISINGS

In the opening to our second section, we see King's 'Beyond Vietnam' as throwing down a gauntlet: struggles against imperialism, capitalism, white supremacy, and militarism—within a nation-state or internationally—can never be separated as unconnected 'issues.' What is needed is revolution— 'a true revolution of values' he proclaimed. Vincent Harding, the first drafter of King's classic anti-war speech, added that King was shaping a new role for himself, that of training an 'army' of 3000 cadre of poor people towards a transformational 'experiment with truth and power.' Harding himself explains: 'Martin was trying to be on time, trying to be faithful, trying to go forward, to create whatever openings towards the future that he could...King was desperately searching for the connections with his past, for the openings to his and our future...Serve the people. Serve humanity. Let the oppressed go free. Let America be born again. A wild and visionary set of ideas!'

Fannie Lou Hamer's experiences bear evidence to these visionary movement-wide plans. Ella Baker provided organizational frameworks for these efforts, noting that genuine leadership is 'the development of the individual to his highest potential for the benefit of the group.' And James Cone reminds us that Minister Malcolm X (El Hajj Malik el-Shabazz) didn't advocate violence, but rather advocated self-defense. He characterizes Malcolm as 'too powerful' even for some of his own followers: 'too profoundly human, transcending race and other reactionary limits.' Our work now is to do as Martin and Malcolm did: 'disciplined thinking about freedom' which is relevant to our times. We would do well to recall that Minister Malcolm's call for social change was 'by any means necessary' and not by armed means solely or primarily.

Grace Lee Boggs concludes that these 'civil rights' era legacies can provide insight regarding 'what true revolutions are about... redefining our relationships with one another, to the Earth and to the world; about creating a new society in the places and spaces left vacant by the disintegration of the old; about hope, not despair; about saying yes to life and no to war; about finding the courage to love and care for the peoples of the world as we love and care for our own families.' Malcolm and Martin, in the process of their lives and continuing growth, developed strategies for transforming narrow struggles for rights into struggles which could 'advance the humanity of everyone in society.'

Boggs' fundamental questions are our own, as resonant as before the day they were written, more prescient now than at any point since: 'Thinking back over these years, I can't help wondering: Might events have taken a different path if we had found a way to infuse our struggle for Black Power with King's philosophy of nonviolence? Is it possible that our relationships with one another today, not only inter- but intra-racially, would be more harmonious if we had discovered how to blend Malcolm's militancy with King's vision of the beloved community? Could such a synthesis have a revolutionary power beyond our wildest dreams? Is such a revolutionary power available to us today?'

The next two sections take us from the late 1950's and the dawning of decolonization through to the heady days of the late 1960's and 1970's, when it seemed that revolution was sweeping across the entire planet and the old orders might give way to more hopeful possibilities. Transitioning from an analysis of early

1960's protest to late 1960's radical trajectories and beyond, we spotlight the assertion that today's revolutionaries need to 'refuse to choose' between the false dichotomies of a Martin King-Malcolm X split. Furthermore, our own understanding of the praxis of those figures and the movements they came to symbolize and inspire is veiled in mythology and revisionist history which obscures their lessons for today. We need to lift the veil and sharpen the lessons we draw from those periods. We need also to both understand the context of radical Black internationalism, which was emerging at that time, and a more poly-centric world of true international depth.

Malcolm, in the last months and days of his life, was clear about his own legacy as well as about the need for international connections between U.S. Black Liberation movements and the global context of struggle; the formation of the Organization of Afro-American Unity based on the newly developed Organization of African Unity was no less a testament to this. 'Dr. King wants the same thing I want,' Malcolm asserted: 'FREEDOM! If you're not ready to die for it, put the word 'freedom' out of your vocabulary... It is a time for martyrs now, and if I am to be one, it will be for the cause of brotherhood.' These ideals, Malcolm believed, were the only things which could save the people from a darker future ahead. His earlier speeches about tactics and strategies, including his famous rejoinder that he'd be 'nonviolent to anyone who is nonviolent to me' became more nuanced and deeper. 'It is criminal,' he wrote, 'to teach a man not to defend himself when he is the constant victim of brutal attacks.' His attempts at assessing a single standard dated back some years prior, when he noted that: 'If it is wrong to be violent defending Black women and Black children and Black babies and Black men, then it is wrong for America to draft us, and make us violent abroad in defense of her. And if it is right for America to draft us and teach us how to be violent in defense of her, then it is right for you and me to do whatever is necessary to defend our own people right here in this country.' More than anything, Malcolm understood that the tactics and even strategies developed over the course of movement-building had to be tested and retested to assess their usefulness and power.

Even before Malcolm's assassination, debates between movement tacticians were taking place which are being repeated now in sometimes less-revealing forms. *Negroes With Guns* author Robert Franklin Williams engaged in an almost-lost dialogue with 'Revolutionary Nonviolence' author Dave Dellinger on what constituted wise strategy in 1960. For his part, Dellinger admitted that 'it is a perversion of nonviolence to identify only with the aggressor and not with his victims. The failure of pacifists with respect to the South has been our failure to identify' with the oppressed people of African descent, not identifying enough 'with the victims to the point where we feel the hurts as if they were our own.' Historian Sally Bermanzohn, herself a survivor of the 1979 Greensboro Massacre where the KKK and local law enforcement in North Carolina murdered anti-Klan demonstrators, summarized that 'the Civil Rights Movement succeeded not because of its nonviolence, but because it was combined with armed self-defense to make the South less violent and more democratic.' And the legacy of organizers such as Ella Baker and Bayard Rustin cannot be undervalued, not so much because of their personal leadership styles but because they fought to steadfastly engage in the hard work of people-to-people community organizing.

The basis of Black Power which saw the Student Nonviolent Coordinating Committee take center stage in positing a new framework for people's struggle laid down a gauntlet in strategic and tactical terms. White people must spend more time working within their own communities, against the racist and fascist onslaught which was already on display. Changing their name to the Student *National* Coordinating Committee, SNCC militant Gwendolyn Zoharrah Simmons makes clear that ultimately the new orientation was never designed to separate people or heighten the differences in methods of struggle, but rather to seek a greater, more human and spiritual unity based on shared work against racism, militarism and materialism. Black Panther political prisoner Russell Maroon Shoatz explains this view in the context of rage and humiliation felt by many (especially men) in fighting for liberation. Our inclusion of the words of Colin Kaepernick and Black Lives Matter activists brings us full circle, noting that 'there has never been a period in the history of America where anti-Blackness has not been an ever-present terror. Racialized oppression and dehumanization is woven into the very fabric of our nation.' Pulley asserts that the Movement for Black Lives and outcry that 'Black Lives Matter' has at its roots a call for an end to the War on Black Lives, especially manifest in urban U.S.A., often with the police taking the role of occupying army. The need, therefore, is to 'reconfigure all livelihood on this land...to take up again the serious and ultimately revolutionary question of what real post-slavery 'reconstruction' would mean.'

Zoharrah Simmons concludes that, despite her years of front-line experience with SNCC and all the other formations she was part of, 'it has taken years for me to really understand and appreciate the significance of this nonviolent revolution in which I was involved.' With rage, impatience at the pace of change, and a lack of faith about the nature of fundamental change, it is not difficult to realize how elusive clarity around strategy and praxis can be. The need for a dialectical analysis of the past and present pitfalls and possibilities continues.

Searching for samplings of that deep analysis in recent history leads easily to the great African liberationist Amilcar Cabral, always concerned with strategy, tactics, and connecting the means and ends. Cabral asserted that Pan-Africanism was simply *a means* to return to the source. For us, in a 21st century context which prioritizes Pan Africanism as a central part of a new internationalism, we must deepen our investigations regarding the sources of the future we are hoping to build. In an oft-forgotten section of Cabral's iconic 'Tell No Lies, Claim No Easy Victories' delivered in his role of commander-in-chief of the armed guerillas of the African Party for the Independence of Guinea and Cape Verde/PAIGC, he warned the combatants that in their undying efforts to be one with the people, *they must be militants but never militarists.*

Understanding that unity is extremely important, but that principled unity is required for true social change, our principles must be built both upon ideals for a future devoid of oppression on all levels as well as on a careful study of the conditions which we continually face. Since the zenith of national liberations struggle which took center stage fifty years ago, we have done well to identify the evils of our unjust societies: imperialism, colonialism, and neocolonialism; patriarchy and sexism; white supremacy and racism; capitalism and neoliberalism; authoritarianism and militarism. We have not fared nearly as well, however, in articulating how to build a new world based on what we have learned about our moment in time.

Cabral noted that 'many times we are confronted with phenomenon that seem to be the same, but political activity demands that we be able to distinguish them...We must deeply analyze each situation to avoid loss of time and energy doing things that we are not to do and forgetting things that we have to do.' In Guinea-Bissau during the war for freedom, Cabral emphasized through study and struggle the lifting of ethnic and cultural subgroups and ultimate forging of a national consciousness among them. The PAIGC stressed the equality and empowerment of women, and even—in a most dialectical manner—critiqued the problem of using guns to win freedom; 'We are not defending the armed fight...it is a violence against even our own people,' wrote Cabral. To what degree have we—so many decades later—come close to doing a similarly careful, dialectical review of what is to be done in this historic period? Have we analyzed and identified what has come before in ways in which praxis, both theory and practice, can benefit from the past so we are not forced to repeat it?

Any review of contemporary African history will reveal that for years Ghana's founding father Kwame Nkrumah was heralded as 'Africa's Gandhi' for his use and defense of 'positive active' as a nonviolent means of bringing independence to his people. Zambia's Kenneth Kaunda, who even more directly considered himself a pacifist and studied with AJ Muste, wrote more directly, however, about the inappropriate and unhelpful choices he seemed forced to make after Zambia was free from British colonial rule. The 'either-or" of absolute adherence to strategies and tactics based on one's principles is an unrealistic measure, he found, for dealing with real-world problems in real time. 'For violence and non-violence,' Kaunda wrote, 'far from being absolute alternatives, are complementary in practice. As a tactic, the effectiveness of non-violence is enhanced when it stands out in sharp relief against a backdrop of imminent actual violence. It has been said that non-violence *needs* violence in the same way stars need the night sky to show them off.'

On the other side of the spectrum, the iconic works of Frantz Fanon—so often misunderstood and/or taken out of context to suggest that violent confrontation was the only way a people could be truly liberated—writes clearly here that 'the violence of the Algerian people is not hatred of peace...neither the conviction that only war may end the colonial regime.' Rather, a unique series of tactics *including some armed* were developed during Algeria's 'savage war of peace.' These words underscore the dialogue which Barbara Deming was attempting in her open letter to Fanon, searching for a dialectic that would end up seeding a fully blossomed 'revolution and equilibrium.'

The dialectic can appear as irony when extracted like single-shot photos from the modern world. In Mozambique, center of one of the most successful armed liberation struggles resulting in a flourishing new government with women's, youth, and workers leadership at the center of post-independence policies, a bloody civil war funded by apartheid South Africa and the U.S. caused havoc and extensive militarism. As that war came to a close, some leaders of the armed struggle—including former Minister of Education and Front for the Liberation of Mozambique (FRELIMO) Central Committee members Graça Machel, who would become South African First Lady some decades later—asserted their profound understandings, not quite pacifist, that the singular emphasis on arms and guns poisoned the younger generation of Mozambicans. As noted, Machel became one of the world's leading authorities on child soldiers and advocates for an end to all use of young people in conflict situations.

In post-apartheid South Africa, these 'ironic' contexts allowed for a leader of the Quaker community to also be a representative of the Communist Party and also be elected to Parliament, becoming Deputy Minister of Defense. Is it ironic that Nozizwe Madlala-Routledge, in this position, helped preside over an end to conscription and forced military service? Is it surprising that she ultimately did not last long in that job? In all of these cases, as we search for a clearer connection to the nuanced work of real people in real-world situations (as opposed to theoreticians and academics far away from actual conflict), is it possible that there are more rich and varied examples of 'revolutionary nonviolence' than we ever had imagined? As Bill Sutherland lived and witnessed it from 1953 through 2010, and as Sutherland and Meyer posited it in 'Guns and Gandhi in Africa,' must we now understand the world not simply in terms of 'black and whites'—the discordant keys on a piano keyboard—but work to play between the cracks?

Two mediations on anger, written a decade apart by Barbara Deming and Audre Lorde, anchor the section on 'Combative Pacifism Against Patriarchy.' Deming explored the role of nonviolence in the struggle for liberation and justice in 'On Anger.' Deming analyzes the role of anger in nonviolent struggle, arguing that productively confronting our own 'raw anger' requires that it be channeled into 'the disciplined anger of the search for change.' Anger at one's own oppression, Deming wrote, is an affirmation of our fundamental worth. Although anger can be violent, it is not inherently so: when anger 'contains both respect for oneself and respect for the other' it becomes a form of communication with the potential to transform oppressive structures and relationships. This transmutation of anger, Deming posits, from affliction to the 'determination to bring about change... might serve as a definition of revolution.'

Audre Lorde's essay 'The Uses of Anger,' written in 1981, explores her rage at white supremacy and the guilt and defensiveness of feminist white women in response to her anger. By failing to engage with the anger of women of color, by fearing it, white feminists, Lorde argues, remain silently trapped in their role of upholding race and class-based oppression. 'To turn aside from the anger of Black women with ...the pretext of intimidation ... is merely another way of preserving racial blindness, [and] the power of unaddressed privilege.' But when women learn to face each other's anger across race and class without denial or guilt, when that anger is 'expressed and translated into action,' it becomes a source of liberatory energy.

Beth Ritchie's essay 'How Anti-Violence Taught Me to Become a Prison Abolitionist,' challenges the lack of intersectional analysis in both movements to end gender-based violence and movements struggling for racial justice. Her disappointment in the lack of attention to gender oppression in racial justice organizing led to her commitment to anti-violence organizing 'against rape, battering, sexual harassment, emotional abuse, and economic exploitation of women and the non-gender conforming.' But her experience in the anti-violence movement led her to perceive the ways in which the lack of structural analysis and understanding of the conjuncture of race, class, and gender leads to a failure to comprehend that the 'criminal legal system is not only racist, [but also] relies on heteropatriarchal assumptions that narrate a kind of social order based on dominion.'

'Welfare as a Women's Issue' is a powerful but little-known essay written by Johnnie Tillmon, a leader of the National Welfare Rights Organization in the late 1960s and 1970s. Tillmon argued that being on welfare was 'like a super sexist marriage. You trade in a man for *the* man. But you can't divorce him if he treats you bad. He can divorce you, of course, cut you off anytime he wants... *The* man runs everything. In ordinary marriage, sex is supposed to be for your husband. On A.F.D.C. [Aid to Families with Dependent Children] you're not supposed to have any sex at all. You give up control of your own body. It's a condition of aid. You may even have to agree to get your tubes tied so you can never have more children... *The* man, the welfare system, controls your money. He tells you what to buy, what not to buy, where to buy it, and how much things cost. If ... rent, for instance, really costs more than he says they do, it's just too bad for you.'

Leslie Feinberg's essay challenged hegemonic heteropatriarchy, positing that transgender is a form of human expression that pre-dates the rise of Christianity, capitalism, and global European power. Citing evidence that trans folk—especially among Indigenous people in the Americas and pre-Roman European peasants—were politically and ritually powerful, and 'respected members of their communities,' Feinberg argued that the rise of private property and class society, along with the male-dominated family severely winnowed the scope of gender expression. The rise of Christian power was the impetus for a targeted war against queer and transgender people, including witch trials and the Inquisition, that continues to this day. Trans folk in the present are confronted with police brutality, discrimination in housing and health care and other forms of quotidian violence. But, Feinberg argued, trans women, men and youth have played a militant role in resisting heteropatriarchy and envisioning a new world.

Nazan Üstündağ's essay describes Rojava, also known as the Autonomous Administration of North and East Syria, as the struggle of the stateless Kurds for liberation from Syria, Turkey, and Iran. Üstündağ's cites the theory of Turkish-born Abdullah Öcalan, founder of the Kurdistan Worker's Party, whose Marxism, feminism and calls for nonviolent revolution have deeply inspired the struggle for liberation and the forming of a new secular, non-ethnic and non-patriarchal society. Öcalan argues that a 'women's revolution in epistemology, ethics and aesthetics' is fundamental to the project of liberation. To protect women from capitalism and patriarchy, the Rojava revolution created gender equal cooperatives and academies, formed women's defense units to respond to gender-based violence, and all-women military units, led by commanders who were women. The

Kurdish struggle and the founding of Rojava illustrate the powerful role of feminist thought in the building of a post-capitalist, post-ethnic and post-patriarchal world.

Other essays in this section by Roy, Skolkin-Smith, and the Women's Pentagon Action join the thinking of Deming, Lorde, Ritchie, Tillmon and Üstündağ, with intersectional analyses that foreground the failures of capitalist heteropatriarchy and challenge the notion that we can 'bomb our way to a feminist paradise.'

To begin to decolonize is to find the basis of the future in the past, before and beyond the imposition of Euro-American ways of being and knowing. This is the emphasis in Section 6, 'Resisting Empire.' To become decolonized is to recognize that epistemology tied to conquest and colonization, to enslavement and genocide and to the creation of races, genders and nations can never be a viable path toward our liberation. The writers in this section argue persuasively that decolonizing (and decoloniality) depends, as Quijano wrote, upon opening the possibility for non-Eurocentric rationalities and 'parallel horizons' of knowing. For Haunani-Kay Trask, learning Hawaiian history meant leaving the library and returning to the land. Planting taro—a traditional Hawaiian staple—led her to 'feel again the spirits of nature.' But more than anything, (re)learning the Hawaiian language was key. 'I had to learn the language like a lover,' she wrote, 'so that I could rock within her and lay at night in her dreaming arms.' For Aimee Rowe, in 'Queer Indigenous Manifesto' remaking relationships to the land, to dispossession and to family are critical steps in defining decolonized activism centered on Indigenous sovereignty and land struggles. At a time when 'the mask of the U.S. settler nation state' has been torn from its hinges, Rowe asserts that it is time to 'decenter the role of the U.S. nation-state in its politics and imaginary' and to 'imagine all-our-relations beyond the limiting liberal politics of nationalism.' As a queer ally of Indigenous struggles, Rowe defines the task as aligning the LBGTQ movement with the fight against settler-colonial expansion.

Analyzing the violence of the experience of colonization and its continued ramification in ostensibly post-colonial societies, Maria Lugones deconstructs Euro-American gender and sexuality constructs and re-members the worldviews of the Indigenous. Lugones dense essay is well worth reading for its brilliant insight into the brutality of (on-going) processes based upon the original colonial dichotomy of human and nonhuman. The aim of the colonizer was/is 'brutal access to people's bodies through unimaginable exploitation, violent sexual violation, control of reproduction and systematic terror.' This 'civilizing' transformation in the lives of the Indigenous resulted in 'the colonization of memory ... of people's senses of self, of intersubjective relation, of their relation to the spirit world, to land, to the very fabric of their conception of reality, identity, and social, ecological and cosmological organization.' For Lugones, resistance is powerfully expressed not in the public sphere of politics, but infra-politically, inwardly as oppressed communities take up the collective task of 'constituting resistant meaning and each other against the constitution of meaning and social organization by power.'

Lugones builds upon the work of Aníbal Quijano, whose seminal contribution to theorizing decoloniality centered on race, makes clear that coloniality remains the form of domination and exploitation undergirding the world capitalist system to this day. In Quijano's analysis, the coloniality of power is built upon the imposition of the racial classification of humans as a form of social and economic control. Racial identity was linked to divisions of labor and the exploitation of colonial capitalism. Coloniality was/is the imposition of Euro-American cultural, economic, and social systems, an epistemology grounded in the degradation of the colonized. In pointing a way forward, Quijano argues that we must free ourselves from the constraints of Eurocentric categories. 'It is time,' he wrote, 'to learn to free ourselves from the Eurocentric mirror where our image is always, necessarily distorted.'

Marshall's analysis of Indigenous Hawaiian decolonization efforts ground the theories of decoloniality in the struggle for autonomy and sovereignty in Mexico and the Pacific. Finally, Berta Cáceres brief but powerful speech upon accepting the Goldman Prize honoring grassroots environmental activism challenges us to wake up and recognize that we are out of time. 'We must shake our conscience free of rapacious capitalism, racism and patriarchy that will only assure our own self-destruction... Our Mother Earth—militarized, fenced-in, poisoned... demands that we take action.'

The final section, 'Revolutionary Nonviolence in the 21st Century,' is a collection of recent essays that begin to define revolutionary nonviolence and decoloniality in a new century and during a pandemic, widespread uprising against police violence and capitalist crisis. John Holloway asserts that we are 'living the fire of capitalist crisis' as our anger, our fear, our hopes, and our determination to end the nightmare of capitalist crisis soar. Nick Estes names resource colonization of Navajo lands as the real pandemic and notes the long, violent U.S. history of 'sacrificing or killing off groups of people—through war or disease or both—in the name of its self-proclaimed destiny.' Estes foregrounds the absurdity of U.S. responses to multiple current crisis. 'When confronted with science ... that deny its mythology, the United States chooses hallucination. It sees Indigenous genocide unfold before its very eyes and blames 'pre-existing conditions.' It sees police murdering and torturing Black people ... and describes that as law and order. It sees global warming coming and does nothing... It sees a pandemic approaching months in advance and chooses not to act.' Like Holloway, Estes is hopeful that a new world is coming into being. From Standing Rock to Minneapolis, when people chant 'water is life' and 'Black lives matter,' they are contesting the degraded colonial meaning of life and legitimacy of capitalist rule. Marshall's essay addresses white people directly arguing that any hope of nonviolent revolution is up to them. She urges white people to confront the multiple ways in which white life in the U.S. is made possible by 'the dead and debilitated bodies of Black, Indigenous and Brown people.' Marshall exhorts white people to 'confront the terror and violence' which undergirds the foundation of white lives. Kali Akuno, interviewed in 'A Deeper Understanding,' argues that nonviolent revolution is feasible if great masses of workers cease to participate in the running of capitalism. Self-defense and revolutionary violence are, Akuno implies, the result of a lack of mass participation in the struggle. Mass organizing at a scale great enough to shut down the ports, the factories, the schools, and the hospitals opens the possibility for nonviolent revolution. Sacajawea Hall, in the same essay, notes that the prevalence of nonprofit social justice organizations with paid staff mitigates against mass uprising. 'The conversation is more about how people get paid to do the work, compared to how we get back to a voluntary responsibility and [learning] to sustain ourselves.' Finally, Mark Ayyash and Insurgent Subcommander Moisés ground us in the struggle of Palestinians and Zapatista peasants. Ayyash points to the decolonial world rising from the rubble of 70 years of vicious Israeli assault. Moisés honors global resistance and rebellion and sees in them 'clues of a humanity that refuses to follow the system in its hasty passage to collapse.'

Moisés communique announces the Zapatista's intention to travel the world:

That various Zapatista delegations, men, women and *others* of the color of our land, we will go out to travel the world, we will walk or sail to remote soils, seas and skies, seeking not difference, not superiority, not affront, much less forgiveness and the pity. We will go to find what makes us equal. Not only humanity that animates our different skins, our different ways, our different languages, and colors. Also, and above all, the common dream that, as a species, we have shared since ... we started walking on the lap of the first woman: the search for freedom that animated that first step ... and that continues to walk.

◊

The violence that saturates our worlds, the terror and brutality that radiates outward (historically and geographically) from Euro-America is evident from every level of the international policy down to every cell in the human organism. There is a straight line from the destruction of the commons of the 1500's to the 55 million people on Earth currently affected by drought. There is a direct connection between the global wildfire crisis—the scorching of even Arctic lands, and the exploitation, degradation, and dispossession of hundreds of millions of people for the profit of a tiny minority. There is a direct connection between the destruction of primary forest lands and agro-industrial production of food, and the epidemics of Covid-19, Diabetes, and HIV.

Is there widespread recognition that we are facing existential threats to our planet and ourselves? Have folks grasped the very perilous position that we, collectively, are in? And, if we grasp the extreme urgency of this moment, do we know where to find the wisdom, guidance, and materials we need to build a future?

To move beyond outrage, to build the roads that will lead us to a dictatorship of solidarity, love, and reciprocity among humans and between humans and the earth, we must delve deeply into herstories to explore the roots of our current contradictions and forge new pathways toward the world we seek to build. We hope that some of the words that follow will light the path forward.

# SECTION I

# 1. CONTEMPORARY ROOTS OF RADICAL NONVIOLENCE: BEFORE AND BEYOND GANDHI

*Though questions regarding the limitations of nonviolence and how radical nonviolent methods could successfully be used goes back to the earliest debates about the nature of change, the 20th Century work of India's Mohandas Gandhi is often seen as a turning point. Considered revolutionary among pacifists of his time who felt him too confrontational and controversial, Gandhi is now seen as the 'great soul' standard of modern-day nonviolence. This opening section to our review of revolution, decoloniality, and nonviolent social change begins with an early militant influence on Gandhi and the massive Indian independence movement he helped lead—Henry David Thoreau. Gandhi's own writings are complemented by Hannah Arendt's classic commentary on the nature of violence, and Gandhi's personal secretary Pyarelal describes a lesser-known economic aspect of the man's philosophy. Critiques of Gandhi have marked the past quarter-century, and the articles by Milan Rai and Arundhati Roy suggest some of the ways in which strict and literal interpretations of the man can lead to some uncomfortable contradictions in the current context. Finally, Starhawk's essay seeks to rescue these roots of radical nonviolence from puritanism which would ultimately destroy any movement.*

*We lead the section off with a brief commentary special for this book from Gandhi's granddaughter Ela, who was born, raised, and works in South Africa, a former Member of Parliament of Nelson Mandela's 1994 government.*

—The editors

# GANDHI AND REVOLUTIONARY NONVIOLENCE

Ela Gandhi

As is now well known, Gandhi's nonviolent action campaigns started in South Africa. In 1906, he began to look at different nonviolent movements and realized that nonviolence is not just the absence of violence: there's much more to nonviolence than just the absence of violence. It is also not a 'passive' resistance, as many people began incorrectly to describe the movement of passive resistance. Gandhi said, 'it's not passive; it's very, very active.' It is an active, nonviolent resistance to injustice wherever we see it, and it doesn't necessarily mean that *satyagraha* always involves a large-scale action. It can be practiced in any situation where there is injustice. If one is opposing that injustice, one can use nonviolent techniques to establish justice.

In looking back at Gandhiji, he had several assumptions and beliefs on which he based his techniques. The first one was that change is possible. People can change, and we have to believe that. Many people refuse to believe that change is possible. We must struggle against this. Personal, **as well as social change, is** possible.

The second assumption that Gandhi made is that people are basically good. The idea that people are basically 'born being good' is a positive and contagious assumption! Some people believe that there are 'natural' criminals, but Gandhi always said that one must criticize the actions, not the person. We must learn to separate the person from the action, as well as the conditions which cause people to act in certain ways. We've got to focus our criticism and struggle against the actions that are unacceptable for us, not against the individuals who are involved. If we don't separate the action from the person, we fall into the notion that we will rid ourselves of our problems if we just get rid of or change the individuals in positions of power. We must realize that it is the action, the condition, and the system which must be eliminated, not the person himself or herself.

The third assumption we base our work on is that we can best bring about goodness in individual human beings within a climate of love. Love is an especially important principle, one which Rev. Dr. Martin Luther King described very well in many books as well as in his Nobel Peace Prize acceptance speech. Hatred and anger must be removed and replaced with a love force. Good news is often suppressed by responses of anger and hatred. Even Nelson Mandela, when he spoke about nonviolent action in South Africa, said that you cannot fight hatred and anger with hatred and anger, you cannot fight violence with violence. One must fight with the opposite of what we're opposing, with love and with nonviolence.

When I have talked about revolutionary nonviolence and what we've seen in the South African situation, we must remember that even as the people who initiated the modern armed struggle—people like Nelson Mandela, Walter Sisulu and many others— also used nonviolent action throughout the anti-apartheid struggle. Also, most of the anti-apartheid solidarity movements developed in other countries were based on nonviolent strategies. We can also look back with respect to the African National Congress leadership before Mandela and Sisulu, men such as Chief Albert Luthuli, another Nobel Peace laureate.

All these leaders—Gandhi, King, Luthuli, and Mandela—have a background with strong spiritual understanding. Spirituality is an important aspect of past and contemporary struggles. Today, the promotion of spirituality is often seen in terms of religious fundamentalism. But was Gandhi a fundamentalist? Clearly No! The same for Mandela, King, and the others. They practiced their religions, but were all open to other faiths, in fact embracing all faiths. They embraced spirituality because of their love of people and belief in the possibility of change. We've seen it in South Africa and in the friendships between Archbishop Desmond Tutu and the Dalai Lama.

We should recognize that revolutionary nonviolence is a great strategic ideal. When we talk about revolutionary nonviolence, everyone has said that Gandhiji was a great strategist. But he didn't just come up with the idea, for instance, of the Salt March—which was one of his biggest and most impactful nonviolent struggles. He didn't just come up with that idea overnight! There was a lot of preparation, and part of the preparation was preparing the initial group: the 67 people who started on the march. He trained them. They were disciplined cadres of the struggle. They were trained first, and then they moved into the struggle.

There were many principles about how we would propagate the idea of the Salt *satyagraha*. The organizers went into the villages throughout India and got the support of the people. It was that patient work that resulted in millions of people participating from across the sub-continent. It couldn't have just happened overnight! It couldn't have just happened with Gandhi doing it alone. He had all these volunteers, who went out into the villages and spoke to the people, had meetings with the people, lived with the people, and got them to understand what the source of the action was about. So, the people became passionate and owned the struggle. *They owned the struggle.* It wasn't Gandhiji's struggle, it was 'my struggle.' And that was the important part of that struggle.

Finally, people on their own would not have been able to do this successfully...even if there were masses of them —which they did. But that alone wouldn't have got them the kind of victory that they had... without international support, without media support, and without having a whole 'marketing' strategy. We use the term 'marketing', and of course, Gandhi didn't talk in those terms. But today, when we talk about principles, we use that mean taking this whole movement to the community, to the people, everywhere in the world. The entire world knew about the mobilizations, about the Salt March, and that can only happen through media. We must remember that at that time, there were no cellphones, there was no internet, there was no WhatsApp and all these social media that we have today! But Gandhi was able to mobilize media through whatever methods he had at his disposal. He used those methods to get the world to know about the campaigns and to get world sympathy.

In my own earlier days of struggle in South Africa of the 1980s, we used these techniques in the United Democratic Front, which comprised many organizations, from many different perspectives and communities throughout the whole country. All these organizations were opposed to the racist apartheid regime. And we got all of them together, which at the time was against the law and very much against government policy—and against the government itself! We were just a small group of revolutionaries who were dissatisfied, working to oppose the suffering and oppression and to break the policy and practice of enforced repression and apathy. When we brought all our organizations together, we were able to articulate that there were millions of people throughout South Africa who would struggle for change. Many young people were in the lead, something we continue to aim for today. Because the need for social change and revolutionary nonviolence is far from over!

# ON THE DUTY OF CIVIL DISOBEDIENCE

Henry David Thoreau

1849[1]

I heartily accept the motto— 'That government is best which governs least;' and I should like to see it acted up to more rapidly and systematically. Carried out, it finally amounts to this, which also I believe— 'That government is best which governs not at all;' and when men are prepared for it, that will be the kind of government which they will have. Government is at best but an expedient; but most governments are usually, and all governments are sometimes, inexpedient. The objections which have been brought against a standing army, and they are many and weighty and deserve to prevail, may also, at last, be brought against a standing government. The standing army is only an arm of the standing government. The government itself, which is only the mode by which the people have chosen to execute their will, is equally liable to be abused and perverted before the people can act through it. Witness the present Mexican war, the work of comparatively a few individuals using the standing government as their tool; for, in the outset, the people would not have consented to this measure.

This American government—what is it but a tradition, though a recent one, endeavoring to transmit itself unimpaired to posterity, but each instant losing some of its integrity? It has not the vitality and force of a single living man; for a single man can bend it to his will. It is a sort of wooden gun to the people themselves; and, if ever they should use it in earnest as a real one against each other, it will surely split. But it is not the less necessary for this; for the people must have some complicated machinery or other, and hear its din, to satisfy that idea of government which they have. Governments show thus how successfully men can be imposed on, even impose on themselves, for their own advantage. It is excellent, we must all allow, yet this government never of itself furthered any enterprise, but by the alacrity with which it got out of its way. *It* does not keep the country free. *It* does not settle the West. *It* does not educate. The character inherent in the American people has done all that has been accomplished; and it would have done somewhat more if the government had not sometimes got in its way. For government is an expedient, by which men would fain succeed in letting one another

---

1. Henry David Thoreau, 'On Civil Disobedience' https://www.ibiblio.org/ebooks/Thoreau/Civil%20Disobedience.pdf [in the public domain]. This is an abridged version of the original

alone; and, as has been said, when it is most expedient, the governed are most let alone by it. Trade and commerce, if they were not made of India rubber, would never manage to bounce over obstacles which legislators are continually putting in their way; and, if one were to judge these men wholly by the effects of their actions, and not partly by their intentions, they would deserve to be classed and punished with those mischievous persons who put obstructions on the railroads.

But, to speak practically and as a citizen, unlike those who call themselves no-government men, I ask for, not at once no government, but *at once* a better government. Let every man make known what kind of government would command his respect, and that will be one step toward obtaining it.

After all, the practical reason why, when the power is once in the hands of the people, a majority are permitted, and for a long period continue, to rule, is not because they are most likely to be in the right, nor because this seems fairest to the minority, but because they are physically the strongest. But a government in which the majority rule in all cases can not be based on justice, even as far as men understand it. Can there not be a government in which the majorities do not virtually decide right and wrong, but conscience?—in which majorities decide only those questions to which the rule of expediency is applicable? Must the citizen ever for a moment, or in the least degree, resign his conscience to the legislator? Why has every man a conscience, then? I think that we should be men first, and subjects afterward. It is not desirable to cultivate a respect for the law, so much as for the right. The only obligation which I have a right to assume is to do at any time what I think is right. It is truly enough said that a corporation has no conscience, but a corporation of conscientious men is a corporation *with* a conscience. Law never made men a whit more just; and, by means of their respect for it, even the well-disposed are daily made the agents of injustice. A common and natural result of an undue respect for the law is, that you may see a file of soldiers, colonel, captain, corporal, privates, powder-monkeys and all, marching in admirable order over hill and dale to the wars, against their wills, aye, against their common sense and consciences, which makes it very steep marching indeed, and produces a palpitation of the heart. They have no doubt that it is a damnable business in which they are concerned; they are all peaceably inclined. Now, what are they? Men at all? or small movable forts and magazines, at the service of some unscrupulous man in power? Visit the Navy Yard, and behold a marine, such a man as an American government can make, or such as it can make a man with its black arts, a mere shadow and reminiscence of humanity, a man laid out alive and standing, and already, as one may say, buried under arms with funeral accompaniment, though it may be

> Not a drum was heard, not a funeral note,
> As his corpse to the ramparts we hurried;
> Not a soldier discharged his farewell shot
> O'er the grave where our hero we buried.

The mass of men serve the State thus, not as men mainly, but as machines, with their bodies. They are the standing army, and the militia, jailers, constables, *posse comitatus,* &c. In most cases, there is no free exercise whatever of the judgment or of the moral sense, but they put themselves on a level with wood and earth and stones, and wooden men can perhaps be manufactured that will serve the purpose as well. Such command no more respect than men of straw, or a lump of dirt. They have the same sort of worth only as horses and dogs. Yet such as these even are commonly esteemed good citizens. Others, as most legislators, politicians, lawyers, ministers, and officeholders, serve the state chiefly with their heads; and, as they rarely make any moral distinctions, they are as likely to serve the devil, without *intending* it, as God. A very few, as heroes, patriots, martyrs, reformers in the great sense, and *men,* serve the State with their consciences also, and so necessarily resist it for the most part; and they are commonly treated by it as enemies. A wise man will only be useful as a man, and will not submit to be 'clay,' and 'stop a hole to keep the wind away,' but leave that office to his dust at least:

> 'I am too high-born to be propertied,
> To be a secondary at control,
> Or useful serving-man and instrument
> To any sovereign state throughout the world.'

He who gives himself entirely to his fellowmen appears to them useless and selfish, but he who gives himself partially to them is pronounced a benefactor and philanthropist.

How does it become a man to behave toward the American government today? I answer that he cannot without disgrace be associated with it. I cannot for an instant recognize that political organization as *my* government which is the *slave's* government also.

All men recognize the right of revolution; that is, the right to refuse allegiance to and to resist the government when its tyranny or its inefficiency are great and unendurable. But almost all say that such is not the case now. But such was the case, they think, in the Revolution of '75. If one were to tell me that this was a bad government because it taxed certain foreign commodities brought to its ports, it is most probable that I should not make an ado about it, for I can do without them: all machines have their friction, and possibly this does enough good to counterbalance the evil. At any rate, it is a great evil to make a stir about it. But when the friction comes to have its machine, and oppression and robbery are organized, I say, let us not have such a machine any longer. In other words, when a sixth of the population of a nation which has undertaken to be the refuge of liberty are slaves, and a whole country is unjustly overrun and conquered by a foreign army, and subjected to military law, I think that it is not too soon for honest men to rebel and revolutionize. What makes this duty the more urgent is the fact, that the country so overrun is not our own, but ours is the invading army.

◊

Practically speaking, the opponents to reform in Massachusetts are not a hundred thousand politicians at the South, but a hundred thousand merchants and farmers here, who are more interested in commerce and agriculture than they are in humanity and are not prepared to do justice to the slave and to Mexico, *cost what it may*. I quarrel not with far-off foes, but with those who, near at home, co-operate with, and do the bidding of those far away, and without whom the latter would be harmless. We are accustomed to say, that the mass of men are unpre-pared; but improvement is slow because the few are not materially wiser or better than the many. It is not so important that many should be as good as you, as that there be some absolute goodness somewhere; for that will leaven the whole lump. There are thousands who are *in opinion* opposed to slavery and to the war, who yet in effect do nothing to put an end to them; who, esteeming themselves chil-dren of Washington and Franklin, sit down with their hands in their pockets, and say that they know not what to do, and do nothing; who even postpone the ques-tion of freedom to the question of free-trade, and quietly read the prices-current along with the latest advice from Mexico, after dinner, and, it may be, fall asleep over them both. What is the price-current of an honest man and patriot today? They hesitate, and they regret, and sometimes they petition, but they do nothing in earnest and with effect. They will wait, well disposed of, for others to remedy the evil, that they may no longer have it to regret. At most, they give only a cheap vote, and a feeble countenance and Godspeed, to the right, as it goes by them. There are nine hundred and ninety-nine patrons of virtue to one virtuous man, but it is easier to deal with the real possessor of a thing than with the temporary guardian of it.

All voting is a sort of gaming, like chequers or backgammon, with a slight moral tinge to it, a playing with right and wrong, with moral questions; and bet-ting naturally accompanies it. The character of the voters is not staked. I cast my vote, perchance, as I think right; but I am not vitally concerned that that right should prevail. I am willing to leave it to the majority. Its obligation, therefore, never exceeds that of expediency. Even voting *for the right* is *doing* nothing for it. It is only expressing to men feebly your desire that it should prevail. A wise man will not leave the right to the mercy of chance, nor wish it to prevail through the power of the majority. There is but little virtue in the action of masses of men. When the majority shall at length vote for the abolition of slavery, it will be because they are indifferent to slavery, or because there is but little slavery left to be abolished by their vote. *They* will then be the only slaves. Only *his* vote can hasten the abolition of slavery who asserts his own freedom by his vote.

I hear of a convention to be held at Baltimore, or elsewhere, for the selection of a candidate for the Presidency, made up chiefly of editors, and men who are politicians by profession; but I think, what is it to any independent, intelligent, and respectable man what decision they may come to, shall we not have the advantage of his wisdom and honesty, nevertheless? Can we not count upon some independent votes? Are there not many individuals in the country who do not attend conventions? But no: I find that the respectable man, so-called, has imme-diately drifted from his position, and despairs of his country when his country has more reasons to despair of him. He forthwith adopts one of the candidates thus selected as the only *available* one, thus proving that he is himself *available* for any purposes of the demagogue. His vote is of no more worth than that of any unprincipled foreigner or hireling native, who may have been bought. Oh, for a man who is a *man*, and, as my neighbor says, has a bone in his back which you cannot pass your hand through! Our statistics are at fault: the population has been returned too large. How many *men* are there to a square thousand miles in the country? Hardly one. Does not America offer any inducement for men to settle here? The American has dwindled into an Odd Fellow—one who may be known by the development of his organ of gregariousness, and a manifest lack of intellect and cheerful self-reliance; whose first and chief concern, on coming into the world, is to see that the alms-houses are in good repair; and, before yet he has lawfully donned the virile garb, to collect a fund for the support of the widows and orphans that may be; who, in short, ventures to live only by the aid of the Mutual Insurance company, which has promised to bury him decently.

It is not a man's duty, as a matter of course, to devote himself to the eradication of any, even the most enormous wrong; he may still properly have other concerns to engage him; but it is his duty, at least, to wash his hands of it, and, if he gives it no thought longer, not to give it practically his support. If I devote myself to other pursuits and contemplations, I must first see, at least, that I do not pursue them sitting upon another man's shoulders. I must get off him first, that he may pursue his contemplations too. See what gross inconsistency is tolerated. I have heard some of my townsmen say, 'I should like to have them order me out to help put down an insurrection of the slaves or to march to Mexico —see if I would go;' and yet these very men have each, directly by their allegiance, and so indirectly, at least, by their money, furnished a substitute. The soldier is applauded who refuses to serve in an unjust war by those who do not refuse to sustain the unjust government which makes the war; is applauded by those whose own act and authority he disregards and sets at naught; as if the State were penitent to that degree that it hired one to scourge it while it sinned, but not to that degree that it left off sinning for a moment. Thus, under the name of Order and Civil Government, we are all made at last to pay homage to and support our own meanness. After the first blush of sin, comes its indifference; and from immoral it becomes, as it were, *un*moral, and not quite unnecessary to that life which we have made.

◊

Unjust laws exist: shall we be content to obey them, or shall we endeavor to amend them, and obey them until we have succeeded, or shall we transgress them at once? Men generally, under such a government as this, think that they ought to wait until they have persuaded the majority to alter them. They think that, if they should resist, the remedy would be worse than the evil. But it is the fault of the government itself that the remedy *is* worse than the evil. *It* makes it worse. Why is it not more apt to anticipate and provide for reform? Why does it not cherish its wise minority? Why does it cry and resist before it is hurt? Why does it not encourage its citizens to be on the alert to point out its faults, and *do* better than it would have them? Why does it always crucify Christ, excommunicate Copernicus and Luther, and pronounce Washington and Franklin rebels?

One would think that a deliberate and practical denial of its authority was the only offence never contemplated by the government; else, why has it not assigned its definite, its suitable and proportionate penalty? If a man who has no property refuses but once to earn nine shillings for the State, he is put in prison for a period unlimited by any law that I know and determined only by the discretion of those who placed him there; but if he should steal ninety times nine shillings from the State, he is soon permitted to go at large again.

If the injustice is part of the necessary friction of the machine of government, let it go, let it go: perchance it will wear smooth—certainly, the machine will wear out. If the injustice has a spring, or a pulley, or a rope, or a crank, exclusively for itself, then perhaps you may consider whether the remedy will not be worse than the evil; but if it is of such a nature that it requires you to be the agent of injustice to another, then, I say, break the law. Let your life be a counter friction to stop the machine. What I have to do is to see, at any rate, that I do not lend myself to the wrong which I condemn.

◊

I do not hesitate to say, that those who call themselves abolitionists should at once effectually withdraw their support, both in person and property, from the government of Massachusetts, and not wait till they constitute a majority of one before they suffer the right to prevail through them. I think that it is enough if they have God on their side, without waiting for that other one. Moreover, any man more right than his neighbors constitutes a majority of one already.

I meet this American government, or its representative, the State government, directly, and face to face, once a year, no more, in the person of its tax-gatherer; this is the only mode in which a man situated as I am necessarily meets it; and it then says distinctly, Recognize me; and the simplest, the most effectual, and, in the present posture of affairs, the indispensablest mode of treating with it on this head, of expressing your little satisfaction with and love for it, is to deny it then. My civil neighbor, the tax-gatherer, is the very man I have to deal with —for it is, after all, with men and not with parchment that I quarrel—and he has voluntarily chosen to be an agent of the government. How shall he ever know well what he is and does as an officer of the government, or as a man, until he is obliged to consider whether he shall treat me, his neighbor, for whom he has respect, as a neighbor and well-disposed man, or as a maniac and disturber of the peace, and see if he can get over this obstruction to his neighborliness without a ruder and more impetuous thought or speech corresponding with his action? I know this well, that if one thousand, if one hundred, if ten men whom I could name—if ten *honest* men only—aye, if *one* HONEST man, in this State of Massachusetts, *ceasing to hold slaves*, were actually to withdraw from this co-partnership and be locked up in the county jail therefor, it would be the abolition of slavery in America. For it matters not how small the beginning may seem to be: what is once well done is done forever. But we love better to talk about it: that we say is our mission. Reform keeps many scores of newspapers in its service, but not one man. If my esteemed neighbor, the State's ambassador, who will devote his days to the settlement of the question of human rights in the Council Chamber, instead of being threatened with the prisons of Carolina, were to sit down the prisoner of Massachusetts, that State which is so anxious to foist the sin of slavery upon her sister—though at present she can discover only an act of inhospitality to be the ground of a quarrel with her—the Legislature would not wholly waive the subject of the following winter.

Under a government which imprisons any unjustly, the true place for a just man is also a prison. The proper place today, the only place which Massachusetts has provided for her freer and less desponding spirits, is in her prisons, to be put out and locked out of the State by her own act, as they have already put themselves out by their principles. It is there that the fugitive slave, and the Mexican prisoner on parole, and the Indian come to plead the wrongs of his race, should find them; on that separate, but more free and honorable ground, where the State places those who are not *with* her but *against* her—the only house in a slave-state in which a free man can abide with honor. If any think that their influence would be lost there, and their voices no longer afflict the ear of the State, that they would not be as an enemy within its walls, they do not know by how much truth is stronger than error, nor how much more eloquently and effectively he can combat injustice who has experienced a little in his own person. Cast your whole vote, not a strip of paper merely, but your whole influence. A minority is powerless while it conforms to the majority; it is not even a minority then; but it is irresistible when it clogs by its whole weight. If the alternative is to keep all just men in prison or give up war and slavery, the State will not hesitate which to choose. If a thousand men were not to pay their tax-bills this year, that would not be a violent and bloody measure, as it would be to pay them, and enable the State to commit violence and shed innocent blood. This is, in fact, the definition of a peaceable revolution, if any such is possible. If the tax-gatherer, or any other public officer, asks me, as one has done, 'But what shall I do?' my answer is, 'If you really wish to do anything, resign your office.' When the subject has refused allegiance, and the officer has resigned his office, then the revolution is accomplished. But even suppose blood should flow. Is there not a sort of bloodshed when the conscience is wounded? Through this wound a man's real manhood and immortality flow out, and he bleeds to an everlasting death. I see this blood flowing now.

◊

Thus, the state never intentionally confronts a man's sense, intellectual or moral, but only his body, his senses. It is not armed with superior wit or honesty, but with superior physical strength. I was not born to be forced. I will breathe after my own fashion. Let us see who is the strongest. What force has a multitude? They only can force me who obey a higher law than I. They force me to become like themselves. I do not hear of *men* being *forced* to live this way or that by masses of men. What sort of life were that to live? When I meet a government which says to me, 'Your money or your life,' why should I be in haste to give it my money? It may be in a great strait, and not know what to do: I cannot help that. It must help itself; do as I do. It is not worth the while to snivel about it. I am not responsible for the successful working of the machinery of society. I am not the son of the engineer. I perceive that, when an acorn and a chestnut fall side by side, the one does not remain inert to make way for the other, but both obey their own laws, and spring and grow and flourish as best they can, till one, perchance, overshadows and destroys the other. If a plant cannot live according to its nature, it dies, and so a man.

◊

I have never declined paying the highway tax, because I am as desirous of being a good neighbor as I am of being a bad subject; and, as for supporting schools, I am doing my part to educate my fellow countrymen now. It is for no particular item in the tax-bill that I refuse to pay it. I simply wish to refuse allegiance to the State, to withdraw and stand aloof from it effectually. I do not care to trace the course of my dollar, if I could, till it buys a man, or a musket to shoot one with—the dollar is innocent—but I am concerned to trace the effects of my allegiance. In fact, I quietly declare war with the State, after my fashion, though I will still make use and get what advantages of her I can, as is usual in such cases.

◊

The authority of government, even such as I am willing to submit to—for I will cheerfully obey those who know and can do better than I, and in many things even those who neither know nor can do so well—is still an impure one: to be strictly just, it must have the sanction and consent of the governed. It can have no pure right over my person and property but what I concede to it. The progress from an absolute to a limited monarchy, from a limited monarchy to a democracy, is progress toward a true respect for the individual. Even the Chinese philosopher was wise enough to regard the individual as the basis of the empire. Is a democracy, such as we know it, the last improvement possible in government? Is it not possible to take a step further towards recognizing and organizing the rights of man? There will never be a really free and enlightened State, until the State comes to recognize the individual as a higher and independent power, from which all its own power and authority are derived and treats him accordingly. I please myself with imagining a State at last which can afford to be just to all men, and to treat the individual with respect as a neighbor, which even would not think it inconsistent with its own repose, if a few were to live aloof from it, not meddling with it, nor embraced by it, who fulfilled all the duties of neighbors and fellow-men. A State which bore this kind of fruit and suffered it to drop off as fast as it ripened, would prepare the way for a still more perfect and glorious State, which also I have imagined, but not yet anywhere seen.

# REFLECTIONS ON VIOLENCE

Hannah Arendt

1969[1]

Violence, being instrumental by nature, is rational to the extent that it is effective in reaching the end which must justify it. And since when we act we never know with any amount of certainty the eventual consequences of what we are doing, violence can remain rational only if it pursues short-term goals. Violence does not promote causes, it promotes neither History nor Revolution, but it can indeed serve to dramatize grievances and to bring them to public attention. As Conor Cruise O'Brien once remarked, 'Violence is sometimes needed for the voice of moderation to be heard.' And indeed, violence, contrary to what its prophets try to tell us, is a much more effective weapon of reformers than of revolutionists. (The often-vehement denunciations of violence by Marxists did not spring from humane motives but from their awareness that revolutions are not the result of conspiracies and violent action). France would not have received the most radical reform bill since Napoleon to change her antiquated education system without the riots of the French students [in May 1968], and no one would have dreamed of yielding to reforms of Columbia University without the riots during the [1968] spring term.

Still, the danger of the practice of violence, even if it moves consciously within a non-extremist framework of short-term goals, will always be that the means overwhelm the end. If goals are not achieved rapidly, the result will not merely be defeat but the introduction of the practice of violence into the whole body politic. Action is irreversible, and a return to the status quo in case of defeat is always unlikely. The practice of violence, like all action, changes the world, but the most probable change is a more violent world.

Finally, the greater the bureaucratization of public life, the greater will be the attraction of violence. In a fully developed bureaucracy, there is nobody left with whom one could argue, to whom one could present grievances, on whom the pressures of power could be exerted. Bureaucracy is the form of government in which everybody is deprived of political freedom, of the power to act; for the rule by Nobody is not no-rule, and where all are equally powerless we have a tyranny without a tyrant. The crucial feature in the students' rebellions around the world is that they are directed everywhere against the ruling bureaucracy. This explains

1. Hannah Arendt, 'On Violence' A Special Supplement: Reflections on Violence by Hannah Arendt | *The New York Review of Books*. This is an abridged version of the original

what at first glance seems so disturbing, that the rebellions in the East demand precisely those freedoms of speech and thought that the young rebels in the West say they despise as irrelevant. Huge party machines have succeeded everywhere to overrule the voice of citizens, even in countries where freedom of speech and association is still intact.

The dissenters and resisters in the East demand free speech and thought as the preliminary conditions for political action; the rebels in the West live under conditions where these preliminaries no longer open the channels for action. The transformation of government into administration, of republics into bureaucracies, and the disastrous shrinkage of the public realm that went with it, have a long and complicated history throughout the modern age; and this process has been considerably accelerated for the last hundred years through the rise of party bureaucracies.

What makes man a political being is his faculty to act. It enables him to get together with peers, to act in concert, and to reach out for goals and enterprises which would never enter his mind, let alone the desires of his heart, had he not been given this gift—to embark on something new. All the properties of creativity ascribed to life in manifestations of violence and power actually belong to the faculty of action. And I think it can be shown that no other human ability has suffered to such an extent by the Progress of the modern age.

For progress, as we have come to understand it, means growth, the relentless process of more and more, of bigger and bigger. The bigger a country becomes in population, in objects, and in possessions, the greater will be the need for administration and with t, the anonymous power of the administrators. Pavel Kohout, the Czech author, writing in the heyday of the Czech experiment with freedom defined a 'free citizen' as a 'Citizen-Co-ruler.' He meant nothing else but the 'participatory democracy' of which we have heard so much in recent years in the West. Kohout added that what the world, as it is today, stands in greatest need of may well be 'a new example' if 'the next thousand years are not to become an era of supercivilized monkeys.'

This new example will hardly be brought about the practice of violence, although I am inclined to think that much of its present glorification is due to the severe frustration of the faculty of action in the modern world. It is simply true that the riots in the ghettos and the rebellions on the campuses make 'people feel they are acting together in a way that they rarely can.' We don't know if these occurrences are the beginnings of something new—the 'new example'—or the death pangs of a faculty that mankind is about to lose. As things stand today, when we see how the superpowers are bogged down under the monstrous weight of their own bigness, it looks as though the 'new example' will have a chance to arise, if at all, in a small country, or in small, well-defined sectors in the mass societies of the large powers.

For the disintegration processes, which may become so manifest in recent years—the decay of many public services, of schools and police, of mail delivery and transportation, the death rate on the highways and the traffic problems in the cities—concern everything designed to serve mass society. Bigness is afflicted with vulnerability, and while no one can say that assurance where and when the breaking point has been reached, we can observe, almost to the point of measuring it, how strength and resiliency are insidiously destroyed, leaking, as it were, drop by drop from our institutions. And the same, I think, is true for the various party systems—the one-party dictatorship in the East as well as the two-party systems in England and the United States, or the multiple party systems in Europe—all of which were supposed to serve to political needs of modern mass societies, to make representative government possible where direct democracy would not do because 'the room will not hold all' (John Selden).

Moreover, the recent rise of nationalism around the globe, usually understood as a worldwide swing to the right, has now reached the point where it may threaten the oldest and best-established nation-states. The Scotch and the Welsh, the Bretons and the Provençals, the ethnic groups whose successful assimilation had been the prerequisite for the rise of the nation-state, are turning to separatism in rebellion against the centralized governments of London and Paris.

Again, we do not know where these developments will lead us, but we can see how cracks in the power structure of all but the small countries are opening and widening. And we know, or should know, that every decrease of power is an open invitation to violence—if only because those who hold power and feel it slipping from their hands have always found it difficult to resist the temptation of substituting violence for it.

# ON SATYAGRAHA

Mohandas K. Gandhi

1938[1]

Non-violence is 'not a resignation from all real fighting against wickedness'. On the contrary, the Non-violence of my conception is a more active and more real fighting against wickedness than retaliation whose very nature is to increase wickedness. I contemplate a mental and therefore a moral opposition to immoralities. I seek entirely to blunt the edge of the tyrant's sword, not by putting up against it a sharper edged weapon but by disappointing his expectation that I would be offering physical resistance. The resistance of the soul that I should offer instead would elude him. It would at first dazzle him and at last compel recognition from him, which recognition would not humiliate him but would uplift him.
—Young India, 8-10-1925, p. 346

Having flung aside the sword, there is nothing except the cup of love which I can offer to those who oppose me. It is by offering that cup that I expect to draw them close to me.
—Young India, 2-4-1931, p. 54

For the past thirty years I have been preaching and practicing *Satyagraha*. The principles of *Satyagraha* as I know it today, constitute a gradual evolution. Satyagraha differs from Passive Resistance as the North Pole from the South. The latter has been conceived as a weapon of the weak and does not exclude the use of physical force or violence for the purpose of gaining one's end, whereas the former has been conceived as a weapon of the strongest and excludes the use of violence in any shape or form.

The term *Satyagraha* was coined by me in South Africa to express the force that the Indian there used for full eight years and it was coined in order to distinguish it from the movement then going on in the United Kingdom and South Africa under the name of Passive Resistance.

Its root meaning is holding on to truth, hence Truth-force. I have also called it Love-force or Soul-force. In the application of *Satyagraha*, I discovered in the earliest stages that pursuit of truth did not admit of violence being inflicted on one's opponent, but he must be weaned from error by patience and sympathy. For what

---

1. Mohandas K. Gandhi, 'What is Satyagraha' https://www.mkgandhi.org/swmgandhi/chap03.htm [in public domain]

appears to be truth to the one may appear to be error to the other. And patience means self-suffering. So, the doctrine came to mean vindication of Truth not by infliction of suffering on the opponent but on oneself.

But on the political field the struggle on behalf of the people mostly consists in opposing error in the shape of unjust laws. When you have failed to bring the error home to the lawgiver by way of petitions and the like, the only remedy open to you, if you do not wish to submit to error, is to compel him by physical force to yield to you or by suffering in your own person by inviting the penalty for the breach of the law. Hence *Satyagraha* largely appears to the public as Civil Disobedience or Civil Resistance. It is civil in the sense that it is not criminal.

The lawbreaker breaks the law surreptitiously and tries to avoid the penalty, not so the civil resister. He ever obeys the laws of the State to which he belongs, not out of fear of the sanctions but because he considers them to be good for the welfare of society. But there come occasions, generally, rare, when he considers certain laws to be so unjust as to render obedience to them a dishonor. He then openly and civilly breaks them and quietly suffers the penalty for their breach. And in order to register his protest against the action of the lawgivers, it is open to hi m to withdraw his co-operation from the State by disobeying such other laws whose breach does not moral turpitude.

In my opinion, the beauty and efficacy of *Satyagraha* are so great and the doctrine so simple that it can be preached even to children. It was preached by me to thousands of men, women and children commonly called indentured Indians with excellent results.

*Satyagraha* is literally holding on to Truth and it means, therefore, Truth-force. Truth is soul or spirit. It is, therefore, known as soul force. It excludes the use of violence because man is not capable of knowing the absolute truth and, therefore, not competent to punish. The word was coined in South Africa to distinguish the non-violent resistance of the Indians of South Africa from the contemporary 'passive resistance' of the suffragettes and others. It is not conceived as a weapon of the weak.

Passive resistance is used in the orthodox English sense and covers the suffragette movement as well as the resistance of the Non-conformists. Passive resistance has been conceived and is regarded as a weapon of the weak. Whilst it avoids violence, being not open to the weak it does not exclude its use if, in the opinion of a passive resister, the occasion demands it. However, it has always been distinguished from armed resistance and its application was at one time confined to Christian martyrs.

Civil Disobedience is civil breach of unmoral statutory enactments. The expression was, so far as I am aware, coined by Thoreau to signify his own resistance to the laws of a slave State. He has left a masterly treatise on the duty of Civil Disobedience. But Thoreau was not perhaps an out-and-out champion of non-violence. Probably, also, Thoreau limited his breach of statutory laws to the revenue law i.e. payment of taxes. Whereas the term Civil Disobedience as practiced in 1919 covered a breach of any statutory and unmoral law. It signified the resister's outlawry in a civil, i.e., non-violent manner. He invoked the sanctions of the law and cheerfully suffered imprisonment. It is a branch of *Satyagraha*.

Non-co-operation predominantly implies withdrawing of co-operation from the State that in the non-cooperators view has become corrupt and excludes Civil Disobedience of the fierce type described above. By its very nature, non-co-operation is even open to children of understanding and can be safely practiced by the masses. Civil Disobedience presupposes the habit of willing obedience to laws without fear of their sanctions. It can, therefore, be practiced only as a last resort and by a select few in the first instance at any rate. Non-co-operation, too, like Civil Disobedience is a branch of *Satyagraha* which includes all non-violent resistance for the vindication of Truth.

# GANDHIJI'S COMMUNISM

Pyarelal

1946[1]

Gandhiji has often claimed in the course of his discussions with Communist and Socialist friends that he is a better Communist or a Socialist than they. Their goal is identical. The difference in regard to the means and the technique employed is however fundamental. Changing the structure of society through violence and untruth has no attraction for him because he knows that it will not benefit the dumb millions of India. During the period of his detention in the Aga Khan Palace, he studied Communist literature. He has a scientific mind and the knowledge of Communism and Socialism picked up from his talks with friends and casual reading did not satisfy him. He read Das Capital and went through some of the other writings of Marx as also of Engels, Lenin and Stalin. He read some books about the Reds in China too and at the end of it was convinced more than ever that Communism of his conception was the only thing that could bring relief to suffering humanity.

In his Ashram and the institutions that are being run under his guidance and inspiration, the ruling principle is: 'To each according to his need, from each according to his capacity.' His Ashrams are thus themselves experiments in Communism based on nonviolence and Indian village conditions. In Sevagram Ashram the dictum is followed that the inmates are there only on the sufferance of the village people. A cantankerous fellow felled some Ashram trees for his use as fuel though he had no title to them. Another encroached upon the right of way through his field although he had accepted compensation for it. No legal redress was applied for. An announcement was made that the Ashram people were there only for the service of the village folk and that they would go away elsewhere if the latter did not want them. Ultimately the troublemakers were persuaded by their fellow villagers to behave reasonably. In Sabarmati Ashram the women inmates not only merged their domestic kitchens into the communal kitchen and continued to run it but were even persuaded not only to take children other than their own into their families and to look after them like their own but also to let their children be looked after by others. Here was an experiment of pulling down of the walls and emancipation of women without the disintegration of family life, a veritable revolution less the anarchy.

1. *Harijan*, 31-3-1946

But as a friend humorously remarked after dining in the common kitchen of the Talimi Sangh, which feeds more than a hundred individuals, 'Gandhiji' calls it a rasoda (kitchen) and It sounds commonplace; the Communists would call it a 'Commune' and everybody would be impressed by it.' Did not the good old knight of Addison wonder how a certain play could be a tragedy since there was not a line in it, but he could understand?

# TAKING GANDHI WITH A PINCH OF SALT

Milan Rai

2015[1]

*It is no service to the man and damaging to us today as we struggle with similar problems of liberation, if we turn Gandhi into a saint and an icon, removing him from history and sandpapering off his strange edges.*

A few days ago, I learned that a common insult among young boys playing video games is: 'Who taught you to fight? Gandhi?' There's a certain logic to the insult. While Gandhi was dedicated to suicidal self-sacrifice, which can be honoured on the battlefield, he was equally committed to not physically harming his opponents, which has its limitations in military strategy, whether the conflicts are real-world or virtual.

At the same time, Gandhi was a proponent of what we might call nonviolent militarism, referring to himself as the 'general' of the Indian independence struggle, and asking for obedience from his footsoldiers. In May 1930, in his weekly newspaper Navajivan, Gandhi quoted these lines from Tennyson, honouring the virtues of British soldiers in the Crimean War:

Theirs not to make reply,
Theirs not to reason why,
Theirs but to do and die.

The Mahatma ('great soul') commented: 'I feel that this is as it should be'. Those considering becoming part of the independence struggle should use their rational faculties in deciding whether or not to join the movement, but, having joined, they should put aside their own thoughts and obey their leaders (ultimately, Gandhi himself) unquestioningly.

For many of us looking back, these sentiments (which Gandhi repeated often) jar with the picture of Gandhi we have inherited. This airbrushed picture has been constructed by Gandhi's devoted followers and by a political and social mainstream that prefers to tame figures such as Gandhi or Martin Luther King Jr rather than engage with their complexity and their radicalism.

---

1. Source: https://www.telesurenglish.net/opinion/Taking-Gandhi-with-a-Pinch-of-Salt-20150126-0017.html

If there is a single iconic Gandhian act, it is the Salt March of 1930, a campaign Gandhi led that triggered a national nonviolent uprising that led to the arrest of over 60,000 people.

The bare facts of the campaign, as usually recounted, run as follows. Starting on 12 March 1930, Gandhi marched 220 miles from his ashram to the sea, and once there he made salt from seawater on 6 April, encouraging people all over the country to publicly defy the British Salt Act which forbade Indians from collecting or selling salt. After Gandhi was arrested on 5 May, he escalated the campaign from prison by ordering a nonviolent assault on the Dharasana Salt Works on 21 May 1930. Some 2,500 Indian men marched on the works and allowed themselves to be brutally beaten (two died) without retaliating. After months of massive civil disobedience, in 1931, Gandhi was released from prison and he subsequently negotiated an end to the campaign face-to-face with the British viceroy Lord Wavell. Gandhi was acclaimed by the people of India for his victory.

There are troubling omissions at several points in what we may call 'the standard account'. (We should note that the Tennyson quotation and Gandhi's injunction to obey nationalist leaders unquestioningly comes precisely as the salt campaign was heating up in May 1930.)

Let's take the start of the Salt March. One important fact about Gandhi's departure from his ashram – with 78 of his followers – is that it violated his own principles. Gandhi had written less than a year earlier in June 1929, that while he did not believe in vaccination against diseases such as smallpox, he recognised that 'No one has the right to endanger society through his obstinacy'. He went on: 'Hence, when smallpox spreads in a community which believes in vaccination, those who do not believe in it should, in addition to observing the rules of sanitation, segregate themselves voluntarily from that society.' Gandhi did not follow this injunction to segregate himself and his fellow ashramites in March 1930, instead setting off on a long march through a string of villages. This was despite the fact that smallpox had just struck in his ashram, killing three unvaccinated children by 9 March 1930, just three days before Gandhi set off for the sea.

There may have been good strategic or tactical reasons for Gandhi not to have delayed his march to the sea. There may have been good strategic or tactical reasons for him to have kept secret the existence of smallpox in the ashram as he led the next phase of the Indian independence struggle. These are matters that can be debated. What is not debatable is that leaving out this significant aspect of genesis of the Salt March distorts our picture of a man who dedicated himself to Truth with a capital 'T'.

The next major turning point moment in the salt campaign was the march on the Dharasana Salt Works. What is generally omitted in accounts of this extraordinary action is the interrelationship between Gandhi's salt campaign and the armed campaign of another wing of the Indian nationalist movement.

After Gandhi made salt on 6 April, but before he was arrested on 5 May (there was a month-long pause by the sea), there was a daring raid on the government armoury at Chittagong in Bengal on 18 April, when 50 young men and women shot sentries and set one of the buildings on fire. A large number of the raiders were later killed in gunfights with the police. This much-admired action was followed by violent riots in Madras in the south-east. In Peshawar in the north-west, a riot on 24 April turned into a rebellion that overthrew British rule in the city for 10 days.

Gandhi's biographer Kathryn Tidrick writes that the decision to march on the Dharasana Salt Works 'was clearly made with the Chittagong raid in mind': 'The Dharsana raid would be its non-violent equivalent in courage and its spiritual antidote.'

The Chittagong attack is an important part of the story of the Salt March and Gandhi's somewhat desperate decision-making regarding Dharasana. By erasing the impact of the Chittagong raid, the standard account of the Salt March diminishes Gandhi's humanity, and elevates him into an untroubled strategic guru removed from history, escalating his campaign at the strategically appropriate moment.

Gandhi was an extraordinary political force, a scarcely-believable example of what nonviolence can accomplish. Speaking personally, no figure had more impact on me as I came to consciousness than Mohandas Karamchand Gandhi, and I've no doubt I would have been an unquestioningly obedient devotee if I'd ever met him. Nevertheless, it is no service to the man, and damaging to us today as we struggle with similar problems of liberation, if we turn Gandhi into a saint and an icon, removing him from history and sandpapering off his strange edges.

On the day he was arrested, 5 May 1930, Gandhi wrote to the British viceroy condemning the 'reign of terrorism' of the British and disowning responsibility for the violent actions of other nationalists. He added: 'the question of responsibility apart, I dare not postpone action on any cause whatsoever, if non-violence is the force the seers of the world have claimed it to be and if I am not to belie my own extensive experience of its working'. Gandhi went on: 'If you say, as you have said, that the civil disobedience must end in violence, history will pronounce the verdict that the British Government, not bearing because not understanding non-violence, goaded human nature to violence which it could understand and deal with.'

The then British Secretary of State for India, William Wedgewood Benn (Tony Benn's father), said before Gandhi's arrest: 'if Gandhi is arrested and disorder followed, it [the civil disobedience campaign] would become merged in the terrorist organization and thereby strengthen it'. Benn added that if the independence struggle became simply a terrorist movement, at least it would be 'a straight fight with the revolver people, which is a much simpler and much more satisfactory job to undertake'.

Simpler partly because an armed struggle inevitably involves a small cadre of trained and armed militants, rather than the millions of people who were galvanised and transformed by the mass nonviolent struggle around the Salt March. Frantz Fanon argued that the colonised must use violence against their oppressors to free themselves psychologically from their internalised oppression, created by centuries of imperial violence. The tens of thousands who volunteered to be arrested during the salt campaign, and the millions who defied British imperial law, found another way to breach the myth of their inferiority.

The final turning point of the Salt March campaign was its end. The standard account glosses over the fact that Gandhi's personal handling of the negotiations with Wavell in early 1931 led to this massive national convulsion ending without any advance for the independence movement. Those who had been arrested during the struggle were freed, and land that had been confiscated and not yet sold was returned to its former owners. The campaigners' most passionately-advanced demand, that there be a government inquiry into police action during the protest campaign, was not granted. The Salt Law itself, at the centre of the storm, remained law. Gandhi naively believed he had converted the viceroy, and he allowed all these concessions to the British without gaining any concrete advantage for his people in return. And yet Gandhi was acclaimed by the ordinary people wherever he went in India for his victory.

Winston Churchill identified the nature of Gandhi's victory, saying of his negotiations with Wavell: 'It is alarming and also nauseating to see Mr. Gandhi, a seditious Middle Temple lawyer of the type well-known in the East, now posing as a fakir, striding half naked up the steps of the Viceregal palace to parley on equal terms with the representative of the King-Emperor.' Gandhi's assertion of equality with the viceroy, his counter-power based purely on articulating the feelings of the Indian people, was a subtle yet devastating strategic blow to British imperialism. Perhaps he did know something about fighting.

# WHEN THE SAINTS GO MARCHING OUT: THE STRANGE FATE OF MARTIN, MOHANDAS, AND MANDELA

Arundhati Roy

2003[1]

We're coming up to the fortieth anniversary of the March on Washington, when Martin Luther King Jr. gave his famous "I Have a Dream" speech. Perhaps it's time to reflect—again—on what has become of that dream.

It's interesting how icons, when their time has passed, are commodified and appropriated (some voluntarily, others involuntarily) to promote the prejudice, bigotry, and inequity they battled against. But then in an age when everything's up for sale, why not icons? In an era when all of humanity, when every creature of God's earth, is trapped between the IMF chequebook and the American cruise missile, can icons stage a getaway?

Martin Luther King is part of a trinity. So it's hard to think of him without two others elbowing their way into the picture: Mohandas Gandhi and Nelson Mandela. The three high priests of nonviolent resistance. Together they represent (to a greater or lesser extent) the twentieth century's nonviolent liberation struggles (or should we say "negotiated settlements"?): of colonized against colonizer, former slave against slave owner.

Today the elites of the very societies and peoples in whose name the battles for freedom were waged use them as mascots to entice new masters.

Mohandas, Mandela, Martin.
India, South Africa, the United States.
Broken dreams, betrayal, nightmares.
A quick snapshot of the supposedly "Free World" today.

---

1. Source: This text is an expanded version of an essay originally broadcast by BBC Radio 4, August 25, 2003. By request of the BBC, which had determined that copyright restrictions prohibited it from broadcasting direct quotations from King's public speeches, the original used only paraphrases of King's words. In this version, direct quotations have been used. The text here is from Arundhati Roy: *My Seditious Heart: Collected Nonfiction*, Chicago: Haymarket Books, 2019, 273-82. for which permission to reproduce was granted by Arundhati Roy & Haymarket Books.

Last March in India, in Gujarat—Gandhi's Gujarat—right-wing Hindu mobs murdered two thousand Muslims in a chillingly efficient orgy of violence. Women were gang-raped and burned alive. Muslim tombs and shrines were razed to the ground. More than a hundred fifty thousand Muslims have been driven from their homes. The economic base of the community has been destroyed. Eyewitness accounts and several fact-finding commissions have accused the state government and the police of collusion in the violence.[2] I was present at a meeting where a group of victims kept wailing, "Please save us from the police! That's all we ask ..."

In December 2002, the same state government was voted back to office. Narendra Modi, who was widely accused of having orchestrated the riots, has embarked on his second term as chief minister of Gujarat. On August 15, 2003, Independence Day, he hoisted the Indian flag before thousands of cheering people. In a gesture of menacing symbolism, he wore the black RSS cap—which proclaims him as a member of the Hindu nationalist guild that has not been shy of admiring Hitler and his methods.[3]

One hundred thirty million Muslims—not to mention the other minorities, Dalits, Christians, Sikhs, Adivasis—live in India under the shadow of Hindu nationalism.

As his confidence in his political future brimmed over, Narendra Modi, master of seizing the political moment, invited Nelson Mandela to Gujarat to be the chief guest at the celebration of Gandhi's birth anniversary on October 2, 2002.[4] Fortunately, the invitation was turned down.[5]

And what of Mandela's South Africa? Otherwise known as the Small Miracle, the Rainbow Nation of God? South Africans say that the only miracle they know of is how quickly the rainbow has been privatized, sectioned off, and auctioned to the highest bidders. In its rush to replace Argentina as neoliberalism's poster child, it has instituted a massive program of privatization and structural adjustment. The government's promise to redistribute agricultural land to twenty-six million landless people has remained in the realm of dark humor.[6] While more than 50 percent of the population remains landless, almost all agricultural land is owned by sixty thousand white farmers.[7] (Small wonder that George Bush on his recent visit to South Africa referred to Thabo Mbeki as his "point man" on the Zimbabwe issue.)

Post-apartheid, the income of the poorest 40 percent of Black families has diminished by about 20 percent.[8] Two million have been evicted from their

2. See "Democracy: Who Is She When She's at Home?" Arundhati Roy: *My Seditious Heart: Collected Nonfiction*, Chicago: Haymarket Books, 2019: 160–76.
3. "Cong[ress Party] Ploy Fails, Modi Steals the Show in Pain," *Indian Express*, August 16, 2003.
4. Government Invite," August 4, 2003; "Guj[arat]–Mandela," Press Trust of India, August 5, 2003; and "Battle for Gujarat's Image Now on Foreign Soil," *Times of India*, August 7, 2003.
5. Agence France-Presse, "Relax, Mandela Isn't Coming, He's Working on a Book," August 5, 2003.
6. Michael Dynes, "Mbeki Can Seize White Farms under New Law," *Times* (London), January 31, 2004, 26.
7. Ibid.
8. Patrick Laurence, "South Africa Fights to Put the Past to Rest," *Irish Times*, December 28, 2000, 57.

homes.[9] Six hundred die of AIDS every day. Forty percent of the population is unemployed, and that number is rising sharply.[10] The corporatization of basic services has meant that millions have been disconnected from water and electricity.[11] A fortnight ago, I visited the home of Teresa Naidoo in Chatsworth, Durban. Her husband had died the previous day of AIDS. She had no money for a coffin. She and her two small children are HIV-positive. The government disconnected her water supply because she was unable to pay her water bills and her rent arrears for her tiny council flat. The government dismisses her troubles and those of millions like her as a "culture of non-payment."[12]

In what ought to be an international scandal, this same government has officially asked the judge in a US court case to rule against forcing companies to pay reparations for the role they played during apartheid.[13] Its reasoning is that reparations—in other words, justice—will discourage foreign investment.[14] So South Africa's poorest must pay apartheid's debts, so that those who amassed profit by exploiting Black people during apartheid can profit even more from the goodwill generated by Nelson Mandela's Rainbow Nation of God. President Thabo Mbeki is still called "comrade" by his colleagues in government. In South Africa, Orwellian parody goes under the genre of Real Life.

What's left to say about Martin Luther King's America? Perhaps it's worth asking a simple question: Had he been alive today, would he have chosen to stay warm in his undisputed place in the pantheon of Great Americans? Or would he have stepped off his pedestal, shrugged off the empty hosannas, and walked out on to the streets to rally his people once more?

On April 4, 1967, one year before he was assassinated, Martin Luther King spoke at the Riverside Church in New York City. That evening he said: "I could never again raise my voice against the violence of the oppressed in the ghettos without having first spoken clearly to the greatest purveyor of violence in the world today—my own government."[15]

Has anything happened in the thirty-six years between 1967 and 2003 that would have made him change his mind? Or would he be doubly confirmed in his opinion after the overt and covert wars and acts of mass killing that successive governments of his country, both Republican and Democrat, have engaged in since then?

9. Anthony Stoppard, "South Africa: Water, Electricity Cutoffs Affect 10 Million," Inter Press Service, March 21, 2002.
10. Henri E. Cauvin, "Hunger in Southern Africa Imperils Lives of Millions," New York Times, April 26, 2002, A8; James Lamont, "Nobody Says 'No' to Mandela," Financial Times (London), December 10, 2002, 4; and Patrick Laurence, "South Africans Sceptical of Official Data," Irish Times, June 6, 2003, 30
11. See Ashwin Desai, We Are the Poors: Community Struggles in Post-Apartheid South Africa (New York: Monthly Review Press, 2002).
12. South African Press Association, "Gauteng Municipalities to Target Service Defaulters," May 4, 1999; Alison Maitland, "Combining to Harness the Power of Private Enterprise," Financial Times (London), August 23, 2002, survey: "Sustainable Business," 2.
13. Nicol Degli Innocenti and John Reed, "SA Govt Opposes Reparations Lawsuit," Financial Times (London), May 19, 2003, 15.
14. South African Press Association, "S Africa Asks US Court to Dismiss Apartheid Reparations Cases," BBC Worldwide Monitoring, July 30, 2003.
15. Martin Luther King, Jr., A Testament of Hope: The Essential Writings and Speeches of Martin Luther King, Jr., ed. James M. Washington (New York: HarperCollins, 1991), 233.

Let's not forget that Martin Luther King Jr. didn't start out as a militant. He began as a Persuader, a Believer. In 1964 he won the Nobel Peace Prize. He was held up by the media as an exemplary Black leader, unlike, say, the more militant Malcolm. It was only three years later that Martin Luther King publicly connected the US government's racist war in Vietnam with its racist policies at home.

In 1967, in an uncompromising, militant speech, he denounced the American invasion of Vietnam. He said:

> *We have been repeatedly faced with the cruel irony of watching Negro and white boys on TV screens as they kill and die together for a nation that has been unable to seat them together in the same schools. So we watch them in brutal solidarity burning the huts of a poor village, but we realize that they would never live on the same block in Detroit.*[16]

The *New York Times* had some wonderful counter-logic to offer the growing antiwar sentiment among Black Americans: "In Vietnam," it said, "the Negro for the first time has been given the chance to do his share of fighting for his country."[17]

It omitted to mention Martin Luther King Jr.'s remark that "there are twice as many Negroes dying in Vietnam as whites in proportion to their size in the population."[18] It omitted to mention that when the body bags came home, some of the Black soldiers were buried in segregated graves in the Deep South.

What would Martin Luther King Jr. say today about the fact that federal statistics show that African Americans, who account for 12 percent of America's population, make up 21 percent of the total armed forces and 29 percent of the US Army?[19]

Perhaps he would take a positive view and look at this as affirmative action at its most effective?

What would he say about the fact that having fought so hard to win the right to vote, today 1.4 million African Americans, which means 13 percent of all voting-age Black people, have been disenfranchised because of felony convictions?[20]

To Black soldiers fighting in Vietnam, Martin Luther King Jr. said, "As we counsel young men concerning military service we must clarify for them our nation's role in Vietnam and challenge them with the alternative of conscientious objection."[21]

---

16. Ibid., 233.
17. "Men of Vietnam," *New York Times*, April 9, 1967, Week in Review, 2E. Quoted in Mike Marquesee, *Redemption Song: Muhammad Ali and the Spirit of the Sixties* (New York: Verso, 1999), 217
18. King, *Testament of Hope*, 245.
19. David M. Halbfinger and Steven A. Holmes, "Military Mirrors a Working-Class America," *New York Times*, March 30, 2003, A1; Darryl Fears, "Draft Bill Stirs Debate over the Military, Race, and Equity," *Washington Post*, February 4, 2003, A3.
20. David Cole, "Denying Felons Vote Hurts Them, Society," *USA Today*, February 3, 2000, 17A; "From Prison to the Polls," editorial, *Christian Science Monitor*, May 24, 2001, 10.
21. King, *Testament of Hope*, 239.

In April 1967, at a massive antiwar demonstration in Manhattan, Stokely Carmichael described the draft as "white people sending Black people to make war on yellow people in order to defend land they stole from red people."[22]

What's changed? Except of course, the compulsory draft has become a poverty draft—a different kind of compulsion. Would Martin Luther King Jr. say today that the invasion and occupation of Iraq and Afghanistan are in any way morally different from the US government's invasion of Vietnam? Would he say that it was just and moral to participate in these wars? Would he say that it was right for the US government to have supported a dictator like Saddam Hussein politically and financially for years while he committed his worst excesses against Kurds, Iranians, and Iraqis—in the 1980s when he was an ally against Iran? And that when that dictator began to chafe at the bit, as Saddam Hussein did, would he say it was right to go to war against Iraq, to fire several hundred tons of depleted uranium into its fields, to degrade its water supply systems, to institute a regime of economic sanctions that resulted in the death of half a million children, to use UN weapons inspectors to force it to disarm, to mislead the public about an arsenal of weapons of mass destruction that could be deployed in a matter of minutes, and then, when the country was on its knees, to send in an invading army to conquer it, occupy it, humiliate its people, take control of its natural resources and infrastructure, and award contracts worth hundreds of millions of dollars to American corporations like Bechtel?

When he spoke out against the Vietnam War, Martin Luther King Jr. drew some connections that many these days shy away from making. He said, "The problem of racism, the problem of economic exploitation, and the problem of war are all tied together. These are the triple evils that are interrelated."[23] Would he tell people today that it is right for the US government to export its cruelties—its racism, its economic bullying, and its war machine—to poorer countries?

Would he say that Black Americans must fight for their fair share of the American pie and the bigger the pie, the better their share—never mind the terrible price that the people of Africa, Asia, the Middle East, and Latin America are paying for the American Way of Life? Would he support the grafting of the Great American Dream onto his own dream, which was a very different, very beautiful sort of dream? Or would he see that as a desecration of his memory and everything that he stood for? The Black American struggle for civil rights gave us some of the most magnificent political fighters, thinkers, public speakers, and writers of our times. Martin Luther King Jr., Malcolm X, Fannie Lou Hamer, Ella Baker, James Baldwin, and of course the marvelous, magical, mythical Muhammad Ali.

Who has inherited their mantle?

Could it be the likes of Colin Powell? Condoleezza Rice? Michael Powell?

They're the exact opposite of icons or role models. They *appear* to be the embodiment of Black people's dreams of material success, but in actual fact, they

---

22. Quoted in Marqusee, *Redemption Song*, 218.
23. King, *Testament of Hope*, 250.

represent the Great Betrayal. They are the liveried doormen guarding the portals of the glittering ballroom against the press and swirl of the darker races. Their role and purpose is to be trotted out by the Bush administration looking for brownie points in its racist wars and African safaris.

If these are Black America's new icons, then the old ones must be dispensed with because they do not belong in the same pantheon. If these are Black America's new icons, then perhaps the haunting image that Mike Marqusee describes in his beautiful book *Redemption Song*—an old Muhammad Ali, afflicted with Parkinson's disease, advertising a retirement pension—symbolizes what has happened to Black Power, not just in the United States but the world over.[24]

If Black America genuinely wishes to pay homage to its real heroes, and to all those unsung people who fought by their side, if the world wishes to pay homage, then it's time to march on Washington. Again. Keeping hope alive—for all of us.

---

24. Marqusee, *Redemption Song*, 1–4, 292.

# RECLAIMING NONVIOLENCE FROM GANDHIAN PURITANISM

Starhawk

---

2002[1]

Does Gandhi's Sex Life Matter? Gandhi and King were not the only influences on the development of movements grounded in nonviolence. In the United States and in England, Quakers have long been in the forefront of struggles for social justice. Their religious pacifism influenced the course of liberation movements from the antislavery campaigns of the 1800s to the antinuclear campaigns of the 1980s.

Women pioneered many of the tactics used by Gandhi and King. Alice Paul revitalized the suffrage movement in the U.S. when she brought back from England the tactics of direct action. In England, suffragists demanding women's right to vote chained themselves to lamp posts and broke shop windows in an earlier version of the property-damage controversy. They filled the jails and went on hunger strikes, withstanding enormous suffering when they were forcibly fed. In the U.S., women marched, chained themselves to the White House fence, and challenged President Wilson over the hypocrisy of fighting for democracy abroad while denying it to women at home. Nevertheless, it is Gandhi and King who again and again are cited as the authors of the nonviolent philosophy, whose pictures are carried in demonstrations, whose works are quoted. Many pacifists call themselves Gandhians; I know of no one, not even any woman, who calls herself a Paulian or Pankhurstian or Ella Bakerian or Rosa Parksian. It may be a measure of the internalized sexism even among people in the movement that we still look to men as moral authorities and erase the contributions of women. But for that very reason, we need to examine their legends and legacies.

For Gandhi nonviolence was not just strategic, it was deeply moral, and it went far beyond eschewing violence. Satyagraha, truth force or soul force, was an energetic force that could only be marshaled by long and deep preparation, much as certain yogis employ special techniques and diets in order to command special powers. It was part of a way of life that required forms of self-discipline few of today's activists are interested in undertaking: most notably, giving up sex altogether.

---

1. Source: https://gandhiserve.org/e/activities/events/2006/pw.pdf

While no one I know of is proposing abstinence as a requirement for joining a direct-action campaign, for Gandhi it was indispensable. Satyagraha could not be mobilized without brahmacharya, a comprehensive self-discipline that included sexual abstinence. And not just abstinence outside of marriage. Gandhi actually went beyond the Pope in viewing even marital sex as a sign of lack of self-control. A man's progeny were living proof of his inability to control his lusts.

Satyagraha, for Gandhi, was also not about low-risk cross-the-line actions. He waged satyagraha campaigns infrequently, and each campaign required a pledge from his followers to be willing to die before giving up. Gandhi used all his moral authority and the weapons of guilt and shame on his followers to get them to live up to his ideals.

And Gandhi was no anti-authoritarian. He was a Mahatma, a religious leader in an authoritarian religious tradition that included a level of veneration and obedience unlikely to appeal to most of us today. His near-deification by many pacifists lies firmly within that tradition.

King was also a religious leader, a minister, functioning in a milieu in which ministers were venerated and strong leadership was expected. King held a deeply religious, Christian moral commitment to nonviolence. In the Birmingham campaign of 1963, the very first pledge required of activists was to meditate on the life of Jesus every day and to pray. Three of the ten pledges involved Christ.

But King was also a fallible mortal being who, we now know, carried on a long-standing secret extramarital affair. We can't begrudge him the comfort and solace he must have needed to sustain the tensions and dangers of his work. But we can point out that he follows the pattern of male spiritual and political leaders from New Age gurus to Jim Baker to Clinton, who publicly preach a strict sexual morality while privately indulging their own needs and desires.

Does Gandhi's sex life matter? Does King's? On the one hand, no, their flaws shouldn't undercut our respect for their philosophy, their courage, their real contributions to human liberation and political struggle.

But from a woman's point of view, from an anarchist viewpoint, and from the perspective of earth-based spirituality, yes, it does. Gandhi's rejection of sexuality, of the body, leaves us firmly in the world view of patriarchy, split between body and spirit, venerating Gods that transcend the flesh, and suffering the inevitable degradation of those of us who bring that flesh into the world. That worldview is a comfortable fit with Christianity as well (although certainly within both Christianity and Hinduism, strands can be found that do value nature, the erotic, and women).

The revolution we need to make includes a profound change in relationship to our experience of being a body. One of the insights of ecofeminism, the convergence of the feminist and ecology movements, is that our destruction of the environment is allowable because of the deep devaluation of nature and the body in the underlying religious and philosophical systems that shape our worldviews. And the devaluation of women — the violence, rape, and destruction perpetrated on female bodies around the globe — is also supported by the same philosophical and religious systems that identify women with nature and the body, and assign them both low value.

That essential mind/body split is the basis of all systems of domination, which function by splitting us off from a confidence in our inherent worth and by making integral parts of ourselves —our emotions, our sexuality, our desires — bad and wrong.

When we are bad, we deserve to be punished and controlled. Punishment systems lie at the root of violence. Marshall Rosenberg, a teacher of nonviolent communication, describes how violence is justified by the split between the deserving and undeserving: 'You have to make violence enjoyable for domination systems to work ... You can get young people to enjoy cutting off the arms of other young people in Sierra Leone because of the thinking that you are giving people what they deserve.... When you can really justify why people are bad, you can enjoy their suffering.' And so we see people who deplore the violence of the attacks on the World Trade Towers, who empathize and suffer with the victims, gleefully demanding that we bomb Afghanistan back to the stone age because the Afghanis have been defined as deserving of punishment.

As human beings, we always have a somewhat problematic relationship to our body. The body is the source of pleasure — it is life itself. But it is also the source of pain, need, discomfort, and deprivation, and ultimately it suffers death. A liberated world, a world that could come into balance with the natural systems that sustain life, a world that values women, must also value life, embodiment, physicality, flesh, sex.

## Nonviolence and Suffering

Both King and Gandhi believed in the transcendent value of suffering. Now, a certain asceticism is helpful if you are asking people to risk physical discomfort, injury, imprisonment, or even death. A belief in the value of suffering is a useful thing to have when you are voluntarily putting yourself in a position in which you are likely to suffer.

But embracing suffering is problematic for women, who have always been taught to suffer and sacrifice for others. Conditioned to swallow our anger, to not strike back, we have not had a choice about accepting blows without retaliation. Nonviolence puts a high moral value on those behaviors, encourages men to practice them, and develops them as a political strategy. Yet women's empowerment involves acknowledging our anger, owning our rage, allowing ourselves to be powerful and dangerous as well as accommodating and understanding.

And from the perspective of an earth-based spirituality, which values pleasure, the erotic, the beauty and joy of this life, suffering is sometimes inevitable but never desirable. We can learn from it; if we are truly going to change the world, we probably can't avoid it — but we don't seek it or venerate it. Instead, we share it as much as possible through solidarity with each other.

One of Gandhi's strong principles was that we accept the suffering and the consequences of our actions, that we don't try to avoid or evade punishment but welcome it. That position creates a powerful sense of freedom and fearlessness. If we accept the inevitability of punishment, if part of the power of our action is to voluntarily go to jail, we move beyond fear and beyond the system's ability to use our fear to control us. But often the way this principle plays out is that the focus becomes the arrest rather than the action.

There's something to be said for doing a strong action and getting away with it. There's even more to be said for conceiving of an action that does not derive its impact from an arrest, but from what it actually is and does. And if we do choose an arrest strategy, let's do it for a purpose we've thought about and clearly defined, not just by default.

## Authority and Virtue

The underlying moralism in Gandhi's formulation of nonviolence is a subtle thread, but it encourages other moralisms that contribute to the worthy/sexy dichotomy. If we hold a punitive relationship to the body's needs, we assume a posture of internal violence toward the self that extends to other strong emotions and passions. And we become judgmental toward others, rigid in our thinking and viewpoints. Any behavior that does not fit our model is seen as 'violent,' and violent people are seen as deserving of punishment. So our very 'nonviolence' puts us into an authoritarian, dominating mode. Gandhi and King both exemplified religious authority and top-down styles of leadership. They were good, benevolent father figures (although how good they were to their own children is another issue), but dependence on any sort of father figure is not a route to empowerment for women, nor for anyone who wants to function as a liberated, full human being. Anti-authoritarians rightly criticize that model of leadership as keeping us all childlike, released from true responsibility for our lives.

Nonviolence does not have to be practiced in an authoritarian manner. The Quaker tradition of consensus and non-hierarchical organization is a counterbalancing force in nonviolent movements. The Quaker-influenced Movement for a New Society, which introduced affinity groups, consensus, and horizontal power structures to the antinuclear movement in the seventies and eighties, pioneer an empowering model of organizing.

But at times the Quaker influence in the nonviolence movement also contributed to the drift toward morality plays. Quaker pacifism involves a process of deep discernment, of constant self-questioning, of asking, 'Are my actions in alignment with my values? Does my conscience allow me to participate in this act or comply with this procedure?' This process of deep self-examination imparts a clarity and purity to actions, and can serve as an important inner compass.

But if the main measure of an action's success becomes how closely it allows us to conform to our personal moral values, we can lose sight of whether or not it is actually effective. When our actions again and again are ignored or seem to have little immediate impact on the wrongs we protest, we can unconsciously give up hope of actually winning.

There are many different modes of a politics of despair. We usually associate that phrase with the secret, militant cells of the seventies that carried out political bombings and robberies in a last desperate hope that the extremity of their acts would spark a revolution. But it could equally be applied to those who act simply to be virtuous in the face of doom and lose sight of the possibility of victory.

Such actions may be admirable and inspirational. But our time and attention can become focused on the minutia of moral choices in an action: Should I stand up or sit down when the police come? Should I walk with them or go limp? Should I voluntarily place my hand on the pad to be fingerprinted or make them pick it up and place it there? It's not that those questions shouldn't be asked, they can be valuable in helping us define our goals and limits.

But when we don't go beyond them to ask, 'What is the objective of this action? How does each of my choices further that objective?' then we undercut our chances of being effective. And they reinforce the system's focus on individuals as isolated actors instead of encouraging us to ask, 'How do we collectively take power?'

# SECTION II
# 2. ROOTS OF THE US BLACK-LED FREEDOM MOVEMENT

*Throughout the world, the U.S. so-called 'civil rights' movement is often seen as the methodological inheritor of Gandhi's nonviolent practice. And while it can hardly be argued that the Rev. Dr. Martin Luther King, Jr. was deeply influenced by his Indian elder, there are many other influencers of that era deserving of our attention and careful study. For one, scholar and activist Vincent Harding, who helped author MLK's 'Beyond Vietnam' speech, also urged the generations which followed not to use the term 'civil rights' but rather to understand the period of a great U.S. movement for democracy—a southern-based, Black led series of campaigns and coalitions fighting for jobs and justice. An excerpt of one of Harding's own essays is included here, as is an excerpt of theologian James Cone's classic juxtaposition of MLK and Minister Malcolm X, noting the importance of those two leaders' similarities as opposed to emphasizing their differences. Our emphasis is on the voices of women leaders from this period—Ella Baker and Fannie Lou Hamer—who understood that a few reformist legal rights were at best the tip of a much larger block of needed social change. Grace Lee Boggs, a renowned Detroit-based organizer and author, frames how community-building today could learn from the work of this period.*

*Early Student Nonviolent Coordinating Committee activist Ruby Sales leads off this section off with some of her own history, confronting hatred and extreme violence in the 1960's South. As someone who has never waivered in her support for people's rights and liberation, Sales' commentary looks at the 'soul' of 21st Century U.S.A. and the nature of change as we look toward the future.*

—The editors

# AND SO IT IS NOW.

Ruby Sales

---

'They are bringing drugs and sending their criminals.'
'Go back to where you come from.'
'Go back to your crime ridden neighborhoods.'

The nation heard former President Trump spit these perniciously racist and divisive words out with repetitive and unrepentant self-righteous rage and malicious intent. He followed these statements with other racist diatribes, telling a cheering audience of teenaged White conservatives that 'Representative Talib is a lunatic.'

Although these racist phrases by a still-popular president disturb our moral equilibrium, we must view them as more than single events. We must understand them as part of a historical pattern of hate speech that continues a long White supremacist history of demonization, criminalization, degradation and fragmentation of the body and lives of Black and Brown peoples.

As troubling as this charge sounds, it is not hyperbolic. Nor am I spreading secondhand gossip to gin up racial controversy or angst. Rather and sadly, mine is a first-hand account. I speak from the deep throated voice of a survivor of an attempted assassination by a White supremacist segregationist in the light of day in Lowndes County, Alabama during the Southern Freedom Movement. I owe my survival and breath to Jonathan Daniels' generous and loving instincts and actions. Jon, as we called him, was my dear White freedom fighter seminarian brother from the Episcopal Divinity School. He pushed me down and took the bullet that saved my life! My soul is a witness.

The hate speech that the White male assassin used when he attempted to kill me and when he assassinated Jonathan were not the words of a single and lone crazy southern White man. Rather, his words echoed the common White anti-Black hate speech that hung like a dangerous and menacing cloud over the South during the Movement. Larry Hancock and Stuart Wexler remind us in their book, *The Awful Grace of God: White Religious Terrorism, White Supremacy, and the Unsolved Murder of Martin Luther King Jr.* of the deadly consequences of the marriage of White hate speech with state sanctioned violence during the Southern Freedom Movement. According to them, J.R. Stoner and the Reverend Charles Lynch told a packed church of White southerners that 'the four young girls who died in the Birmingham bombing were not children, but little niggers ... and if there's four less niggers tonight then I say Good for whoever planted the bomb.'

As a Black woman who grew up in the segregated South, I first heard the terrifying sounds of White anti-Black speech coming from the police, ordinary White people, ministers and mobs when I was a young adolescent Tuskegee Institute college student during my first demonstration. The White hate noises grew louder and more strident when I left college to work as a member of SNCC in 'Bloody Lowndes County' Alabama.

The city of my childhood although in the South differed vastly from rural Black Belt Alabama. It was located near one of the largest Army posts in the United States and was filled with Black men on active duty as well as Black veterans who fought in World War II and the Korean War. Many of them bore the visible and enduring scars of fighting for the ideals of democracy in a country where the guardians of Whiteness stripped them of their citizenship, made them sit on the back of the bus, lynched them, and subjected them to police terror in bars, buses, jails and streets of America even when they wore the green and brown uniforms gleaming with brass buttons for bravery or outstanding service. After miraculously escaping death in foreign lands, they came home to a political death. Yet, they never gave up on this country or democracy — both of which they loved and served but which did not love or serve them.

My father was one of those men. Even though he bore the battle scars of southern White supremacy, he kept faithful to the ideals of democracy. He was a part of a generation of Black women and men who were hopeful pragmatists. They clearly saw and experienced all the ugliness of White supremacy and the hatred that saturated it. Yet, they refused to grovel in cynicism and non-redemptive anger, hatred or bitterness.

It was their pragmatic optimism and agape that my generation brought to the Southern Freedom Movement. Our mothers and fathers could not pass on to us the rites of citizenship or a guaranteed future. However, they bequeathed to us the belief that we had a charge to keep to upbuild democracy. So as did our fathers, we became freedom fighters for a country that we loved and wanted to serve but one which did not love us or want to serve us. We embarked on a journey of faith to help our nation to live up to its promise even though it did not see any promise in us.

We were not alone. Even during a long history of racism, White America produced—out of its better and most ideal self—a generation of White daughters and sons who believed their mothers and fathers that despite its documented history of racism America was large enough for everyone. Therefore, as did generations of their ancestors before them, they courageously broke with a culture of Whiteness to upbuild a counterculture of democracy.

During this exhilarating and high-spirited season of hope, young Black and White people walked across hundreds of years of segregated walls to find each other. We engineered a new moment of intimacy and community where we became our brothers' and sisters' keepers united in a common vision and common struggle.

It was not easy. Daily we faced torrents of White hate speech. Our lives were constantly at risk from White men in pickup trucks who chased us at ninety miles an hour with their shotguns dancing out the windows or visibly displayed on gun racks. We sat in quiet fear as the drivers tried to outrun us often on country dirt roads where they were determined to terrorize us, shoot us, or run us off the road. Our fates lay in the hands of young drivers barely out of their teens who suddenly had four or five lives in their hands. In our duty as freedom fighters on the front line, we learned the art of survival by staying on full alert to every sound and signal that resonated danger.

We learned early that hate speech is not benign without context or consequences. The realities of our lives taught us that hate speech is a preamble to White anti-Black state sanctioned and vigilante violence. Despite our youthful idealism, we grasped the hard and dangerous American truth that a White person's first amendment right to speak hate can mean the mark of death for Black and Brown peoples.

This truth stared us in the face on a hot summer day in August when SNCC members joined local Black youth who organized a protest where they courageously and lovingly took on the predatory system of sharecropping on behalf of their elders. On the day of our protest, an angry mob of White men of all ages hurled hate speech at us. They armed themselves with guns, baseball bats, garbage can-tops, and any other weapon they could find. They surrounded us and threatened to kill us while yelling, 'nigger, monkey, bitches, go back to Africa or wherever you come from.' The presence of our two White companions who walked the picket line with Black demonstrators further escalated their anger. With voices hardened by years of misplaced grievances and internalized self-hatred for their failure to economically achieve what they were told was their birthright as White men, they lashed out with venom yelling, 'nigger lovers' and 'outside agitators, communists, traitors.' I am convinced that if the sheriff had not arrested us, these White men raving with hate speech learned from the lips of slick race baiting politicians, teachers and preachers would have tortured and murdered us as they did Viola Luzzio, Jimmy Lee Jackson, Medgar Evers and the four little Black Birmingham girls.

In jail, we endured growing anxiety from the menacing threats and psychological terrorism of the armed White deputy sheriff who promised to make us drink toilet water and to make Black male prisoners rape my three female cell companions and me. We could hardly breathe from the stench and smell of rancid food and broken unflushed toilets.

On the 6th day the White sheriff forced us under gun point and hate speech to leave jail. He would not let us alert anyone that he was releasing us. We hesitated to leave because all of us knew the story of the young freedom fighters Goodman, Chaney and Schwerner whom a gang of White men murdered on June 21, 1964, after the sheriff forcibly released them from a Mississippi jail in the deep darkness of a Southern rural night.

In the Alabama summer heat of the day and because we refused to eat for six days while in jail out of fear for our safety, we were thirsty and hungry. The group designated Jonathan Daniels, Father Richard Morrisroe, a White young Catholic priest from Chicago, Joyce Bailey, an 18-year-old local Black youth and me, to get drinks for everyone.

When we reached the front door of Cash Store where the White female owner had always graciously served us without incident, a White man stood in the door waving a shotgun at me when my foot touched the first step leading to the door. His words, 'bitch I will blow your goddamned brains out' greeted me. Before I could react or even process the danger right in front of my face, Jonathan swiftly and instinctively pulled me back. I fell backwards to the ground, and Jonathan's action placed him straight in the line of fire. I heard the loud roar of the blast that sent his body flying into the air, dead as it hit the ground.

I lay stiff on the ground thinking that I was dead, and dead meant that one could see and hear but could not move. Out of the edge of my eyes, I saw Father Morrisroe holding Joyce's hand, protecting her by refusing to let her go as they ran for their lives. The assassin whose voice dripped with the poisonous breath of hate speech aimed his gun and hit Father Morrisroe in the back. He fell from the blow and begged for water.

We later found out that the White man's name was Tom Coleman who appointed himself as a deputy that day so that he could kill under the cover of law. He had a reputation for hating Black people. Rumor had it that he had previously murdered several Black men. Despite his lethal carnage that day, his anger and blood lust were insatiable. Like a madman guarding his prey, he stood over Father Morrisroe's body wildly waving his shotgun at Jimmy Rogers and Gloria Larry who rushed to Morrisroe to comfort him and to quench his thirst. Richard later told us that White men put him in a hearse where they placed Jonathan's dead body dripping blood in a rack on top of him. At the hospital White doctors refused to attend to him and called him a 'nigger lover.' A White army general finally agreed to attend to Father Morrisroe. The doctor's intervention and care saved Richard's life. However, the trauma and physical devastation did not end that day. They remain today as a constant reminder of the hate that nearly killed him.

Every one of us who witnessed Tom Coleman's bloody rampage never shook off the residue of trauma. Additionally, our daily experiences in the crucible of White nationalist violence as freedom fighters in the southern valley of death buttressed by hate speech would abide in our minds and hearts forevermore.

Every August I still hear the vile racist hate speech that Tom Coleman flung at me that accompanied his shooting rampage. I still hear the voice of the White man who shouted 'bitch, I will cut your throat' as I walked into the courtroom to testify at the murder trial of the State of Alabama vs. Tom Coleman. An all-White jury found Tom Coleman not guilty of the murder of Jonathan Daniels. When interviewed twenty-five years later when he was an old man, Tom Coleman said if he had it to do over, he would do it again.

More than fifty-five summers later, I tell my story during a blistering national heat wave of White supremacy, hate speech and White state sanctioned and vigilante violence at the borders, in sites of terror called detention centers and in public spaces throughout the country. Once again Black and Brown communities—whether citizens, immigrants, migrants or refugees—face a White supremacist reign of terror. Under Trump and still true for too many White citizens, hate speech is the official state language. It is disguised as populism and national security.

Today I sit on my front porch, looking through the lens of history with hindsight, insight and foresight. I have the eerie and unsettling feeling of historical *deja vu*. I remember how police tortured Black children with high-speed water hoses that took the bark off trees. I also witnessed White police who commanded German Shepherd dogs to attack the delicate throats of Black children. I witnessed White police beating and stomping the stomachs of pregnant Black women.

Although I have not allowed the events of that August to capture my soul or to encase me in anger and bitterness, I am especially reminded, as we face modern, virulent seasons of White supremacy, of how the currents of White violence and hate speech traumatize us despite the life jackets that we wear. Because we are fully human, these assaults leave us all spiritually wounded and hurt.

Contrary to the claims of politicians, pundits and social critics who contend that Trump's hate speech and White nationalism are distractions that steer us away from focusing on urgent and more important bread and butter issues, it is from my vantage point in history that I strongly disagree. To them I offer both a strong rebuke and my unequivocal dissent. To them I say that they are enablers when they refuse to take seriously the mark of death that hate speech places on Black and Brown peoples. It is the enduring reality that Rima L. Vesely-Flad astutely observed in *Racial Purity and Dangerous Bodies; Racial Pollution and Black Lives, and the Struggle for Justice* (Fortress Press 2017) that 'Black people are constructed as internal enemies that threaten the moral foundations of white, Christian, democratic, capitalist nations.' I agree with her observation.

Given her observation, America must ask the following questions. What is more important than the efficacy of Black lives and bodies and our right to life, liberty and access to the rites of citizenship? What is more important than the right of our children to grow up without the state seeing them as enemy combatants who threaten the future of White power and the culture of Whiteness? Finally, we must resolve the questions of White supremacy that have been on the table since the Doctrine of Discovery and enslavement. Who owns the bodies and lives of Black and Brown people? Was Chief Justice Taney right when he ruled in the Dred Scott Decision that Black people have no rights that White men are bound to uphold?

These are more than transactional questions. They are transcendent ones that determine the soul of America. How we finally resolve these issues as a nation will determine whether democracy dies a premature death or whether we will create an outward world where we continue to labor to build in the words of Vincent Harding 'an America that is yet to be born.'

The White supremacist massacre in El Paso carried out by a White man against Latinx people underscores the urgency of the moment. We face a similar choice that Martin Luther King Jr. faced when White liberals, moderates, and conservatives as well as members of the media demanded that he slow down the wheels of the Southern Freedom Movement. His answer in a letter from a Birmingham jail recorded in his book, *Why We Can't Wait*, is still appropriate today. 'For years now I have heard the word 'Wait!' It rings in the ear of every Negro with piercing familiarity. This 'Wait' has almost always meant 'Never.' We must come to see, with one of our distinguished jurists, that 'justice too long delayed is justice denied.''

So, it was then, and so it is now.

# BEYOND VIETNAM

Martin Luther King, Jr

1967[1]

Mr. Chairman, ladies and gentlemen, I need not pause to say how very delighted I am to be here tonight, and how very delighted I am to see you expressing your concern about the issues that will be discussed tonight by turning out in such large numbers. I also want to say that I consider it a great honor to share this program with Dr. Bennett, Dr. Commager, and Rabbi Heschel, some of the most distinguished leaders and personalities of our nation. And of course it's always good to come back to Riverside Church. Over the last eight years, I have had the privilege of preaching here almost every year in that period, and it's always a rich and rewarding experience to come to this great church and this great pulpit.

I come to this magnificent house of worship tonight because my conscience leaves me no other choice. I join you in this meeting because I am in deepest agreement with the aims and work of the organization that brought us together, Clergy and Laymen Concerned About Vietnam. The recent statements of your executive committee are the sentiments of my own heart, and I found myself in full accord when I read its opening lines: 'A time comes when silence is betrayal.' That time has come for us in relation to Vietnam.

The truth of these words is beyond doubt, but the mission to which they call us is a most difficult one. Even when pressed by the demands of inner truth, men do not easily assume the task of opposing their government's policy, especially in time of war. Nor does the human spirit move without great difficulty against all the apathy of conformist thought within one's own bosom and in the surrounding world. Moreover, when the issues at hand seem as perplexing as they often do in the case of this dreadful conflict, we are always on the verge of being mesmerized by uncertainty. But we must move on.

Some of us who have already begun to break the silence of the night have found that the calling to speak is often a vocation of agony, but we must speak. We must speak with all the humility that is appropriate to our limited vision, but we must speak. And we must rejoice as well, for surely this is the first time in our nation's history that a significant number of its religious leaders have chosen to move beyond the prophesying of smooth patriotism to the high grounds of a firm dissent based upon the mandates of conscience and the reading of history. Perhaps a new spirit is rising among us. If it is, let us trace its movement, and pray

---

1. Source: https://www.crmvet.org/info/mlk_viet.pdf

that our inner being may be sensitive to its guidance. For we are deeply in need of a new way beyond the darkness that seems so close around us.

Over the past two years, as I have moved to break the betrayal of my own silences and to speak from the burnings of my own heart, as I have called for radical departures from the destruction of Vietnam, many persons have questioned me about the wisdom of my path. At the heart of their concerns, this query has often loomed large and loud: 'Why are you speaking about the war, Dr. King? Why are you joining the voices of dissent?' 'Peace and civil rights don't mix,' they say. 'Aren't you hurting the cause of your people?' they ask. And when I hear them, though I often understand the source of their concern, I am nevertheless greatly saddened, for such questions mean that the inquirers have not really known me, my commitment, or my calling. Indeed, their questions suggest that they do not know the world in which they live. In the light of such tragic misunderstanding, I deem it of signal importance to state clearly, and I trust concisely, why I believe that the path from Dexter Avenue Baptist Church—the church in Montgomery, Alabama, where I began my pastorate—leads clearly to this sanctuary tonight.

I come to this platform tonight to make a passionate plea to my beloved nation. This speech is not addressed to Hanoi or to the National Liberation Front. It is not addressed to China or to Russia. Nor is it an attempt to overlook the ambiguity of the total situation and the need for a collective solution to the tragedy of Vietnam. Neither is it an attempt to make North Vietnam or the National Liberation Front paragons of virtue, nor to overlook the role they must play in the successful resolution of the problem. While they both may have justifiable reasons to be suspicious of the good faith of the United States, life and history give eloquent testimony to the fact that conflicts are never resolved without trustful give and take on both sides. Tonight, however, I wish not to speak with Hanoi and the National Liberation Front, but rather to my fellow Americans.

Since I am a preacher by calling, I suppose it is not surprising that I have seven major reasons for bringing Vietnam into the field of my moral vision. There is at the outset a very obvious and almost facile connection between the war in Vietnam and the struggle I and others have been waging in America. A few years ago there was a shining moment in that struggle. It seemed as if there was a real promise of hope for the poor, both black and white, through the poverty program. There were experiments, hopes, new beginnings. Then came the buildup in Vietnam, and I watched this program broken and eviscerated as if it were some idle political plaything on a society gone mad on war. And I knew that America would never invest the necessary funds or energies in rehabilitation of its poor so long as adventures like Vietnam continued to draw men and skills and money like some demonic, destructive suction tube. So I was increasingly compelled to see the war as an enemy of the poor and to attack it as such.

Perhaps a more tragic recognition of reality took place when it became clear to me that the war was doing far more than devastating the hopes of the poor at home. It was sending their sons and their brothers and their husbands to fight and to die in extraordinarily high proportions relative to the rest of the population. We were taking the black young men who had been crippled by our society and sending them eight thousand miles away to guarantee liberties in Southeast

Asia which they had not found in southwest Georgia and East Harlem. So we have been repeatedly faced with the cruel irony of watching Negro and white boys on TV screens as they kill and die together for a nation that has been unable to seat them together in the same schools. So we watch them in brutal solidarity burning the huts of a poor village, but we realize that they would hardly live on the same block in Chicago. I could not be silent in the face of such cruel manipulation of the poor.

My third reason moves to an even deeper level of awareness, for it grows out of my experience in the ghettos of the North over the last three years, especially the last three summers. As I have walked among the desperate, rejected, and angry young men, I have told them that Molotov cocktails and rifles would not solve their problems. I have tried to offer them my deepest compassion while maintaining my conviction that social change comes most meaningfully through nonviolent action. But they asked, and rightly so, 'What about Vietnam?' They asked if our own nation wasn't using massive doses of violence to solve its problems, to bring about the changes it wanted. Their questions hit home, and I knew that I could never again raise my voice against the violence of the oppressed in the ghettos without having first spoken clearly to the greatest purveyor of violence in the world today: my own government. For the sake of those boys, for the sake of this government, for the sake of the hundreds of thousands trembling under our violence, I cannot be silent.

For those who ask the question, 'Aren't you a civil rights leader?' and thereby mean to exclude me from the movement for peace, I have this further answer. In 1957, when a group of us formed the Southern Christian Leadership Conference, we chose as our motto: 'To save the soul of America.' We were convinced that we could not limit our vision to certain rights for black people, but instead affirmed the conviction that America would never be free or saved from itself until the descendants of its slaves were loosed completely from the shackles they still wear. In a way we were agreeing with Langston Hughes, that black bard of Harlem, who had written earlier:

> O, yes, I say it plain,
> America never was America to me,
> And yet I swear this oath
> —America will be!

Now it should be incandescently clear that no one who has any concern for the integrity and life of America today can ignore the present war. If America's soul becomes totally poisoned, part of the autopsy must read 'Vietnam.' It can never be saved so long as it destroys the deepest hopes of men the world over. So it is that those of us who are yet determined that 'America will be' are led down the path of protest and dissent, working for the health of our land.

As if the weight of such a commitment to the life and health of America were not enough, another burden of responsibility was placed upon me in 1954.[2] And I cannot forget that the Nobel Peace Prize was also a commission, a commission to work harder than I had ever worked before for the brotherhood of man. This is a calling that takes me beyond national allegiances.

But even if it were not present, I would yet have to live with the meaning of my commitment to the ministry of Jesus Christ. To me, the relationship of this ministry to the making of peace is so obvious that I sometimes marvel at those who ask me why I am speaking against the war. Could it be that they do not know that the Good News was meant for all men—for communist and capitalist, for their children and ours, for black and for white, for revolutionary and conservative? Have they forgotten that my ministry is in obedience to the one who loved his enemies so fully that he died for them? What then can I say to the Vietcong or to Castro or to Mao as a faithful minister of this one? Can I threaten them with death or must I not share with them my life?

Finally, as I try to explain for you and for myself the road that leads from Montgomery to this place, I would have offered all that was most valid if I simply said that I must be true to my conviction that I share with all men the calling to be a son of the living God. Beyond the calling of race or nation or creed is this vocation of sonship and brotherhood. Because I believe that the Father is deeply concerned, especially for His suffering and helpless and outcast children, I come tonight to speak for them. This I believe to be the privilege and the burden of all of us who deem ourselves bound by allegiances and loyalties which are broader and deeper than nationalism and which go beyond our nation's self-defined goals and positions. We are called to speak for the weak, for the voiceless, for the victims of our nation, for those it calls 'enemy,' for no document from human hands can make these humans any less our brothers.

And as I ponder the madness of Vietnam and search within myself for ways to understand and respond in compassion, my mind goes constantly to the people of that peninsula. I speak now not of the soldiers of each side, not of the ideologies of the Liberation Front, not of the junta in Saigon, but simply of the people who have been living under the curse of war for almost three continuous decades now. I think of them, too, because it is clear to me that there will be no meaningful solution there until some attempt is made to know them and hear their broken cries.

They must see Americans as strange liberators. The Vietnamese people proclaimed their own independence in 1954—in 1945 rather—after a combined French and Japanese occupation and before the communist revolution in China. They were led by Ho Chi Minh. Even though they quoted the American Declaration of Independence in their own document of freedom, we refused to recognize them. Instead, we decided to support France in its reconquest of her former colony. Our government felt then that the Vietnamese people were not ready

---

2. King says '1954,' but most likely means 1964, the year he received the Nobel Peace Prize..

for independence, and we again fell victim to the deadly Western arrogance that has poisoned the international atmosphere for so long. With that tragic decision we rejected a revolutionary government seeking self-determination and a government that had been established not by China—for whom the Vietnamese have no great love—but by clearly Indigenous forces that included some communists. For the peasants this new government meant real land reform, one of the most important needs in their lives.

For nine years following 1945 we denied the people of Vietnam the right of independence. For nine years we vigorously supported the French in their abortive effort to recolonize Vietnam. Before the end of the war we were meeting eighty percent of the French war costs. Even before the French were defeated at Dien Bien Phu, they began to despair of their reckless action, but we did not. We encouraged them with our huge financial and military supplies to continue the war even after they had lost the will. Soon we would be paying almost the full costs of this tragic attempt at recolonization.

After the French were defeated, it looked as if independence and land reform would come again through the Geneva Agreement. But instead there came the United States, determined that Ho should not unify the temporarily divided nation, and the peasants watched again as we supported one of the most vicious modern dictators, our chosen man, Premier Diem. The peasants watched and cringed and Diem ruthlessly rooted out all opposition, supported their extortionist landlords, and refused even to discuss reunification with the North. The peasants watched as all of this was presided over by United States influence and then by increasing numbers of United States troops who came to help quell the insurgency that Diem's methods had aroused. When Diem was overthrown they may have been happy, but the long line of military dictators seemed to offer no real change, especially in terms of their need for land and peace.

The only change came from America as we increased our troop commitments in support of governments which were singularly corrupt, inept, and without popular support. All the while the people read our leaflets and received the regular promises of peace and democracy and land reform. Now they languish under our bombs and consider us, not their fellow Vietnamese, the real enemy. They move sadly and apathetically as we herd them off the land of their fathers into concentration camps where minimal social needs are rarely met. They know they must move on or be destroyed by our bombs.

So they go, primarily women and children and the aged. They watch as we poison their water, as we kill a million acres of their crops. They must weep as the bulldozers roar through their areas preparing to destroy the precious trees. They wander into the hospitals with at least twenty casualties from American firepower for one Vietcong-inflicted injury. So far we may have killed a million of them, mostly children. They wander into the towns and see thousands of the children, homeless, without clothes, running in packs on the streets like animals. They see the children degraded by our soldiers as they beg for food. They see the children selling their sisters to our soldiers, soliciting for their mothers.

What do the peasants think as we ally ourselves with the landlords and as we refuse to put any action into our many words concerning land reform? What do they think as we test out our latest weapons on them, just as the Germans tested out new medicine and new tortures in the concentration camps of Europe? Where are the roots of the independent Vietnam we claim to be building? Is it among these voiceless ones?

We have destroyed their two most cherished institutions: the family and the village. We have destroyed their land and their crops. We have cooperated in the crushing of the nation's only noncommunist revolutionary political force, the unified Buddhist Church. We have supported the enemies of the peasants of Saigon. We have corrupted their women and children and killed their men.

Now there is little left to build on, save bitterness. Soon the only solid physical foundations remaining will be found at our military bases and in the concrete of the concentration camps we call 'fortified hamlets.' The peasants may well wonder if we plan to build our new Vietnam on such grounds as these. Could we blame them for such thoughts? We must speak for them and raise the questions they cannot raise. These, too, are our brothers.

Perhaps a more difficult but no less necessary task is to speak for those who have been designated as our enemies. What of the National Liberation Front, that strangely anonymous group we call 'VC' or 'communists'? What must they think of the United States of America when they realize that we permitted the repression and cruelty of Diem, which helped to bring them into being as a resistance group in the South? What do they think of our condoning the violence which led to their own taking up of arms? How can they believe in our integrity when now we speak of 'aggression from the North' as if there was nothing more essential to the war? How can they trust us when now we charge them with violence after the murderous reign of Diem and charge them with violence while we pour every new weapon of death into their land? Surely we must understand their feelings, even if we do not condone their actions. Surely we must see that the men we supported pressed them to their violence. Surely we must see that our own computerized plans of destruction simply dwarf their greatest acts.

How do they judge us when our officials know that their membership is less than twenty-five percent communist, and yet insist on giving them the blanket name? What must they be thinking when they know that we are aware of their control of major sections of Vietnam, and yet we appear ready to allow national elections in which this highly organized political parallel government will not have a part? They ask how we can speak of free elections when the Saigon press is censored and controlled by the military junta. And they are surely right to wonder what kind of new government we plan to help form without them, the only real party in real touch with the peasants. They question our political goals and they deny the reality of a peace settlement from which they will be excluded. Their questions are frighteningly relevant. Is our nation planning to build on political myth again, and then shore it up upon the power of a new violence?

Here is the true meaning and value of compassion and nonviolence, when it helps us to see the enemy's point of view, to hear his questions, to know his assessment of ourselves. For from his view we may indeed see the basic weaknesses of our own condition, and if we are mature, we may learn and grow and profit from the wisdom of the brothers who are called the opposition.

So, too, with Hanoi. In the North, where our bombs now pummel the land, and our mines endanger the waterways, we are met by a deep but understandable mistrust. To speak for them is to explain this lack of confidence in Western worlds, and especially their distrust of American intentions now. In Hanoi are the men who led this nation to independence against the Japanese and the French, the men who sought membership in the French Commonwealth and were betrayed by the weakness of Paris and the willfulness of the colonial armies. It was they who led a second struggle against French domination at tremendous costs, and then were persuaded to give up the land they controlled between the thirteenth and seventeenth parallel as a temporary measure at Geneva. After 1954 they watched us conspire with Diem to prevent elections which could have surely brought Ho Chi Minh to power over a unified Vietnam, and they realized they had been betrayed again. When we ask why they do not leap to negotiate, these things must be considered.

Also, it must be clear that the leaders of Hanoi considered the presence of American troops in support of the Diem regime to have been the initial military breach of the Geneva Agreement concerning foreign troops. They remind us that they did not begin to send troops in large numbers and even supplies into the South until American forces had moved into the tens of thousands.

Hanoi remembers how our leaders refused to tell us the truth about the earlier North Vietnamese overtures for peace, how the president claimed that none existed when they had clearly been made. Ho Chi Minh has watched as America has spoken of peace and built up its forces, and now he has surely heard the increasing international rumors of American plans for an invasion of the north. He knows the bombing and shelling and mining we are doing are part of traditional pre-invasion strategy. Perhaps only his sense of humor and of irony can save him when he hears the most powerful nation of the world speaking of aggression as it drops thousands of bombs on a poor, weak nation more than eight hundred, or rather, eight thousand miles away from its shores.

At this point I should make it clear that while I have tried to give a voice to the voiceless in Vietnam and to understand the arguments of those who are called 'enemy,' I am as deeply concerned about our own troops there as anything else. For it occurs to me that what we are submitting them to in Vietnam is not simply the brutalizing process that goes on in any war where armies face each other and seek to destroy. We are adding cynicism to the process of death, for they must know after a short period there that none of the things we claim to be fighting for are really involved. Before long they must know that their government has sent them into a struggle among Vietnamese, and the more sophisticated surely realize that we are on the side of the wealthy, and the secure, while we create a hell for the poor.

Surely this madness must cease. We must stop now. I speak as a child of God and brother to the suffering poor of Vietnam. I speak for those whose land is being laid waste, whose homes are being destroyed, whose culture is being subverted. I speak for the poor in America who are paying the double price of smashed hopes at home, and dealt death and corruption in Vietnam. I speak as a citizen of the world, for the world as it stands aghast at the path we have taken. I speak as one who loves America, to the leaders of our own nation: The great initiative in this war is ours; the initiative to stop it must be ours.

This is the message of the great Buddhist leaders of Vietnam. Recently one of them wrote these words, and I quote:

Each day the war goes on the hatred increased in the hearts of the Vietnamese and in the hearts of those of humanitarian instinct. The Americans are forcing even their friends into becoming their enemies. It is curious that the Americans, who calculate so carefully on the possibilities of military victory, do not realize that in the process they are incurring deep psychological and political defeat. The image of America will never again be the image of revolution, freedom, and democracy, but the image of violence and militarism.

If we continue, there will be no doubt in my mind and in the mind of the world that we have no honorable intentions in Vietnam. If we do not stop our war against the people of Vietnam immediately, the world will be left with no other alternative than to see this as some horrible, clumsy, and deadly game we have decided to play. The world now demands a maturity of America that we may not be able to achieve. It demands that we admit we have been wrong from the beginning of our adventure in Vietnam, that we have been detrimental to the life of the Vietnamese people. The situation is one in which we must be ready to turn sharply from our present ways. In order to atone for our sins and errors in Vietnam, we should take the initiative in bringing a halt to this tragic war.

I would like to suggest five concrete things that our government should do to begin the long and difficult process of extricating ourselves from this nightmarish conflict:

Number one: End all bombing in North and South Vietnam.

Number two: Declare a unilateral cease-fire in the hope that such action will create the atmosphere for negotiation.

Three: Take immediate steps to prevent other battlegrounds in Southeast Asia by curtailing our military buildup in Thailand and our interference in Laos.

Four: Realistically accept the fact that the National Liberation Front has substantial support in South Vietnam and must thereby play a role in any meaningful negotiations and any future Vietnam government.

Five: Set a date that we will remove all foreign troops from Vietnam in accordance with the 1954 Geneva Agreement. [*sustained applause*]

Part of our ongoing [*applause continues*], part of our ongoing commitment might well express itself in an offer to grant asylum to any Vietnamese who fears for his life under a new regime which included the Liberation Front. Then we must make what reparations we can for the damage we have done. We must provide the medical aid that is badly needed, making it available in this country if necessary. Meanwhile [*applause*], meanwhile, we in the churches and synagogues have a continuing task while we urge our government to disengage itself from a disgraceful commitment. We must continue to raise our voices and our lives if our nation persists in its perverse ways in Vietnam. We must be prepared to match actions with words by seeking out every creative method of protest possible.

As we counsel young men concerning military service, we must clarify for them our nation's role in Vietnam and challenge them with the alternative of conscientious objection. [*sustained applause*] I am pleased to say that this is a path now chosen by more than seventy students at my own alma mater, Morehouse College, and I recommend it to all who find the American course in Vietnam a dishonorable and unjust one. [*applause*] Moreover, I would encourage all ministers of draft age to give up their ministerial exemptions and seek status as conscientious objectors. [*applause*] These are the times for real choices and not false ones. We are at the moment when our lives must be placed on the line if our nation is to survive its own folly. Every man of humane convictions must decide on the protest that best suits his convictions, but we must all protest.

Now there is something seductively tempting about stopping there and sending us all off on what in some circles has become a popular crusade against the war in Vietnam. I say we must enter that struggle, but I wish to go on now to say something even more disturbing.

The war in Vietnam is but a symptom of a far deeper malady within the American spirit, and if we ignore this sobering reality [*applause*], and if we ignore this sobering reality, we will find ourselves organizing 'clergy and laymen concerned' committees for the next generation. They will be concerned about Guatemala and Peru. They will be concerned about Thailand and Cambodia. They will be concerned about Mozambique and South Africa. We will be marching for these and a dozen other names and attending rallies without end unless there is a significant and profound change in American life and policy. [*sustained applause*] So such thoughts take us beyond Vietnam, but not beyond our calling as sons of the living God.

In 1957 a sensitive American official overseas said that it seemed to him that our nation was on the wrong side of a world revolution. During the past ten years we have seen emerge a pattern of suppression which has now justified the presence of U.S. military advisors in Venezuela. This need to maintain social stability for our investments accounts for the counterrevolutionary action of American forces in Guatemala. It tells why American helicopters are being used against guerrillas in Cambodia and why American napalm and Green Beret forces have already been active against rebels in Peru.

It is with such activity that the words of the late John F. Kennedy come back to haunt us. Five years ago he said, 'Those who make peaceful revolution impossible will make violent revolution inevitable.' [*applause*] Increasingly, by choice or by accident, this is the role our nation has taken, the role of those who make peaceful revolution impossible by refusing to give up the privileges and the pleasures that come from the immense profits of overseas investments. I am convinced that if we are to get on to the right side of the world revolution, we as a nation must undergo a radical revolution of values. We must rapidly begin [*applause*], we must rapidly begin the shift from a thing-oriented society to a person-oriented society. When machines and computers, profit motives and property rights, are considered more important than people, the giant triplets of racism, extreme materialism, and militarism are incapable of being conquered.

A true revolution of values will soon cause us to question the fairness and justice of many of our past and present policies. On the one hand we are called to play the Good Samaritan on life's roadside, but that will be only an initial act.

One day we must come to see that the whole Jericho Road must be transformed so that men and women will not be constantly beaten and robbed as they make their journey on life's highway. True compassion is more than flinging a coin to a beggar. It comes to see that an edifice which produces beggars needs restructuring. [*applause*]

A true revolution of values will soon look uneasily on the glaring contrast of poverty and wealth. With righteous indignation, it will look across the seas and see individual capitalists of the West investing huge sums of money in Asia, Africa, and South America, only to take the profits out with no concern for the social betterment of the countries, and say, 'This is not just.' It will look at our alliance with the landed gentry of South America and say, 'This is not just.' The Western arrogance of feeling that it has everything to teach others and nothing to learn from them is not just.

A true revolution of values will lay hand on the world order and say of war, 'This way of settling differences is not just.' This business of burning human beings with napalm, of filling our nation's homes with orphans and widows, of injecting poisonous drugs of hate into the veins of peoples normally humane, of sending men home from dark and bloody battlefields physically handicapped and psychologically deranged, cannot be reconciled with wisdom, justice, and love. A nation that continues year after year to spend more money on military defense than on programs of social uplift is approaching spiritual death. [*sustained applause*]

America, the richest and most powerful nation in the world, can well lead the way in this revolution of values. There is nothing except a tragic death wish to prevent us from reordering our priorities so that the pursuit of peace will take precedence over the pursuit of war. There is nothing to keep us from molding a recalcitrant status quo with bruised hands until we have fashioned it into a brotherhood.

This kind of positive revolution of values is our best defense against communism. [*applause*] War is not the answer. Communism will never be defeated by the use of atomic bombs or nuclear weapons. Let us not join those who shout war and, through their misguided passions, urge the United States to relinquish its participation in the United Nations. These are days which demand wise restraint and calm reasonableness. We must not engage in a negative anticommunism, but rather in a positive thrust for democracy [*applause*], realizing that our greatest defense against communism is to take offensive action in behalf of justice. We must with positive action seek to remove those conditions of poverty, insecurity, and injustice, which are the fertile soil in which the seed of communism grows and develops.

These are revolutionary times. All over the globe men are revolting against old systems of exploitation and oppression, and out of the wounds of a frail world, new systems of justice and equality are being born. The shirtless and barefoot people of the land are rising up as never before. The people who sat in darkness have seen a great light. We in the West must support these revolutions.

It is a sad fact that because of comfort, complacency, a morbid fear of communism, and our proneness to adjust to injustice, the Western nations that initiated so much of the revolutionary spirit of the modern world have now become the arch antirevolutionaries. This has driven many to feel that only Marxism has a revolutionary spirit. Therefore, communism is a judgment against our failure to make democracy real and follow through on the revolutions that we initiated. Our only hope today lies in our ability to recapture the revolutionary spirit and go out into a sometimes hostile world declaring eternal hostility to poverty, racism, and militarism. With this powerful commitment we shall boldly challenge the status quo and unjust mores, and thereby speed the day when 'every valley shall be exalted, and every mountain and hill shall be made low [*Audience:*] *(Yes)*; the crooked shall be made straight, and the rough places plain.'

A genuine revolution of values means in the final analysis that our loyalties must become ecumenical rather than sectional. Every nation must now develop an overriding loyalty to mankind as a whole in order to preserve the best in their individual societies.

This call for a worldwide fellowship that lifts neighborly concern beyond one's tribe, race, class, and nation is in reality a call for an all-embracing and unconditional love for all mankind. This oft misunderstood, this oft misinterpreted concept, so readily dismissed by the Nietzsches of the world as a weak and cowardly force, has now become an absolute necessity for the survival of man. When I speak of love I am not speaking of some sentimental and weak response. I'm not speaking of that force which is just emotional bosh. I am speaking of that force which all of the great religions have seen as the supreme unifying principle of life. Love is somehow the key that unlocks the door which leads to ultimate reality. This Hindu-Muslim-Christian-Jewish-Buddhist belief about ultimate reality is beautifully summed up in the first epistle of Saint John: 'Let us love one another (Yes), for love is God. (Yes) And every one that loveth is born of God and knoweth God. He that loveth not knoweth not God, for God is love... If we love one another, God dwelleth in us and his love is perfected in us.' Let us hope that this spirit will become the order of the day.

We can no longer afford to worship the god of hate or bow before the altar of retaliation. The oceans of history are made turbulent by the ever-rising tides of hate. History is cluttered with the wreckage of nations and individuals that pursued this self-defeating path of hate. As Arnold Toynbee says: 'Love is the ultimate force that makes for the saving choice of life and good against the damning choice of death and evil. Therefore the first hope in our inventory must be the hope that love is going to have the last word.' Unquote.

We are now faced with the fact, my friends, that tomorrow is today. We are confronted with the fierce urgency of now. In this unfolding conundrum of life and history, there is such a thing as being too late. Procrastination is still the thief of time. Life often leaves us standing bare, naked, and dejected with a lost opportunity. The tide in the affairs of men does not remain at flood—it ebbs. We may cry out desperately for time to pause in her passage, but time is adamant to every plea and rushes on. Over the bleached bones and jumbled residues of numerous civilizations are written the pathetic words, 'Too late.' There is an invisible book of life that faithfully records our vigilance or our neglect. Omar Khayyam is right: 'The moving finger writes, and having writ moves on.'

We still have a choice today: nonviolent coexistence or violent coannihilation. We must move past indecision to action. We must find new ways to speak for peace in Vietnam and justice throughout the developing world, a world that borders on our doors. If we do not act, we shall surely be dragged down the long, dark, and shameful corridors of time reserved for those who possess power without compassion, might without morality, and strength without sight.

Now let us begin. Now let us rededicate ourselves to the long and bitter, but beautiful, struggle for a new world. This is the calling of the sons of God, and our brothers wait eagerly for our response. Shall we say the odds are too great? Shall we tell them the struggle is too hard? Will our message be that the forces of American life militate against their arrival as full men, and we send our deepest regrets? Or will there be another message—of longing, of hope, of solidarity with their yearnings, of commitment to their cause, whatever the cost? The choice is ours, and though we might prefer it otherwise, we must choose in this crucial moment of human history.

As that noble bard of yesterday, James Russell Lowell, eloquently stated:

> Once to every man and nation comes a moment to decide,
> In the strife of truth and Falsehood, for the good or evil side;
> Some great cause, God's new Messiah offering each the gloom or blight,
> And the choice goes by forever 'twixt that darkness and that light.
> Though the cause of evil prosper, yet 'tis truth alone is strong
> Though her portions be the scaffold, and upon the throne be wrong
> Yet that scaffold sways the future, and behind the dim unknown
> Standeth God within the shadow, keeping watch above his own.

And if we will only make the right choice, we will be able to transform this pending cosmic elegy into a creative psalm of peace. If we will make the right choice, we will be able to transform the jangling discords of our world into a beautiful symphony of brotherhood. If we will but make the right choice, we will be able to speed up the day, all over America and all over the world, when justice will roll down like waters, and righteousness like a mighty stream. [*sustained applause*]

# MARTIN AND MALCOLM ON NONVIOLENCE AND VIOLENCE

James Cone

2001[1]

No issue has been more hotly debated in the African American community than violence and nonviolence. No two persons symbolize this debate more than Martin Luther King, Jr., and Malcolm X. They represent two radically different responses to nonviolence and violence in the black freedom movement during the 1960s. Their perspectives are still widely discussed and debated today but seldom understood. Martin King's followers frequently misrepresent Malcolm X's views, referring to him as a 'messiah of hate' and a 'black Ku Klux Klan of racial extremists.' Malcolm X's followers distort Martin King's views, often calling him a 'twentieth century religious Uncle Tom pacifist'—the best weapon of whites who want to brutalize black people. Any view can be discredited by simplifying it to the level of caricature.

In this essay, I will present a brief analysis of Martin and Malcolm's views on nonviolence and violence, beginning with Martin's view because Malcolm's perspective was developed largely as a critical response to the white and black media's presentation of Martin's views as normative for the African American community.

Martin Luther King, Jr., was a pastor and civil rights leader and is arguably not only America's most distinguished theologian but also the most influential American in the twentieth century. He was named *Time*'s 'Man of the Year' in 1963 and awarded the Nobel Peace Prize in 1964. He is the only American with a national holiday in his name alone. With the support of many ordinary people in the black freedom movement, King's practice and thought radically transformed America's understanding of itself and inspired liberation movements around the world. One can hardly go anywhere and not encounter his moral influence.

Martin King is best known as America's preeminent advocate of nonviolence. From the time of the yearlong, triumphant Montgomery, Alabama, bus boycotts (1955-56) to his tragic assassination in Memphis, Tennessee (April 4, 1968), Martin King embraced nonviolence absolutely. For King, nonviolence was not only an effective strategy of social change; it was the heart of his philosophy of life. There was no limit to his advocacy of nonviolence in conflict situations. He contended

---

1. Source: *Phylon*, V. 49, No. 3 and 4, Autumn/Winter 2001: 173-183.

that nonviolence was the most potent weapon for both blacks in the U.S. Civil Rights movement and for other oppressed peoples struggling for justice throughout the world. Nonviolence was not only the best tool for solving conflicts within nations; it could also resolve differences between nations. For King, the acquisition of nuclear weapons by several nations created the situation in which 'the choice is no longer between nonviolence and violence. It is either nonviolence or nonexistence.'

The roots of Martin King's journey to nonviolence lie in Atlanta, Georgia, where he was born on January 15, 1929. As the son of the Reverend Martin Luther King, Sr., who was pastor of the prestigious Ebenezer Baptist Church, young Martin was nurtured in the black Baptist tradition of the Christian faith. He followed his father into the ordained ministry in his late teens. The Christian idea of love, as expressed in Jesus' Sermon on the Mount and his sacrificial death on the cross, was the hallmark of the black religious experience that shaped King's perspective. He combined Christian love with the accommodative and protest philosophies of Booker T. Washington and the NAACP. Together these ideas provided the religious and political resources for King to develop a militant nonviolent philosophy of social change in the context of the black struggle for racial justice in America.

The development of Martin King's philosophy of nonviolence was a gradual process. Initially, his unpleasant childhood experiences with racial segregation had a profoundly negative effect on his attitudes toward whites. He was introduced to racial prejudice at the early age of five when the father of his white friend told young Martin that his son could no longer play with him because he was colored. This and other encounters with white prejudice shook King deeply, and thereby made it difficult to love whites as he was taught at home and church. At one point during his early years, he was determined to hate all whites.

Martin King's negative attitude toward whites started to change through the influence of religion, education, and personal encounters with moderate whites in an intercollegiate organization and later at Crozer Theological Seminary (Chester, Pennsylvania) and Boston University School of Theology. At Morehouse College, he read Henry David Thoreau's 'Essay on Civil Disobedience' and was introduced to a wide range of political and religious philosophies that supported the integration of Negroes into the mainstream of American society. In graduate school, King not only met liberal whites as teachers and fellow students; he also encountered progressive theological and philosophical ideas that reinforced his beliefs bout justice and love, integration, and the beloved community. He read books and essays about and by Mahatma Gandhi, Walter Rauschenbusch, and Reinhold Niebuhr at Crozer. At Boston, under the tutelage of Edgar Sheffield Brightman and L. Harold DeWolf, King acquired a sophisticated knowledge of Personalism—a philosophy that accented the infinite value of the human person.

A year prior to his completion of doctoral studies, Martin King accepted the call to become the pastor of Dexter Avenue Baptist Church in Montgomery, Alabama—a middle-class church whose membership included many professors and administrators of Alabama State University. When Rosa Parks was arrested (December 1, 1955) because she refused to give up her bus seat to a white man, the black community was enraged. In protest, they initiated a boycott of the city buses (December 5) and asked King to be their leader.

Martin King was not committed to nonviolence at the beginning of the bus protest. As white violence became increasingly focused on King personally through police harassment, the bombing of his house, volumes of hate mail, and frequent telephone threats of harm, King, seeking to protect himself and his family from white violence, applied for a gun permit which, of course, was rejected. The threat of violence was so real that armed blacks took turns guarding King's home. King also kept a loaded gun in his house which Bayard Rustin of the War Resistance League nearly sat on during a visit.

The most important factors that influenced Martin King to reject self-defense and adopt nonviolence was his personal appropriation of the faith of his parents and the black church. The decisive point occurred a few weeks after the inauguration of the Montgomery Bus boycott, January 27, 1956. He received a nasty phone call about midnight: 'Listen, nigger, we've taken all we want from you; before next week you'll be sorry you ever came to Montgomery.' Though he was accustomed to receiving about forty threats daily, for some reason that one stunned him, preventing him form going back to sleep. Martin began to realize, as he often said later in his sermons, that his wife and newly born baby daughter could be taken from him or he from them at any moment. He got out of bed and went to the kitchen to heat some coffee, hoping it would provide some relief. None came. He reflected back on the theologies and philosophies he had studied in graduate school, searching for a way to cope with the problem of evil and suffering but they provided no help in his moment of distress. He was 'ready to give up' and tried to think of a way to remove himself from the leadership of the boycott without looking like a coward. Exhausted, he had lost his courage. King decided to take his problem to the Gd his parents told him about—the One they and other black Christians said could 'make a way out of no way.' 'With my head in my hands,' King recalled, 'I bowed over the kitchen table and prayed... 'I am here taking a stand for what I believe is right. But now I'm afraid. The people are looking to me for leadership, and if I stand before them without strength and courage, they will falter. I am at the end of my powers. I have nothing left. I've come to the point where I can't face it alone.'

It was in the midst of this crisis of faith that Martin King felt an inner voice saying to him: 'Stand up for righteousness, stand up for justice, stand up for truth, and lo, I will be with you always.' After that revelatory experience, he said: 'I was ready to face anything.'

Three nights later, Martin King's house was bombed and people were amazed how calm he was. After finding out that his wife and baby were safe, he walked on his porch to face and angry black crowd with weapons of violence, ready to return and eye for an eye. 'Don't let us get panicky,' King said. He pleaded with then to get rid of their weapons because 'we can't solve this problem through retaliatory violence.' On the contrary, 'We must meet violence with nonviolence.' Turning to the most persuasive authority in the black Christian experience, King reminded blacks of the words of Jesus' 'Love your enemies; bless them that curse you; pray for them that despitefully use you.' We must love our white brothers ... no matter what they do to us.'

These are difficult words for any person or community, especially for an oppressed black community, which has lived under the psychological and physical brutalities of white supremacy for nearly four centuries. Black people get tired of turning the other cheek in the face of white brutality. Montgomery blacks accepted King's appeal because he connected it with their belief that there was a divine power in the world greater than the forces of white supremacy.

It was one thing to love individual whites personally but quite another to use love as a political instrument of social change. It was Gandhi who provided Martin King with the philosophical and political insight of nonviolent direct action. With a deeper knowledge of Gandhi's philosophy of nonviolence and its application in South Africa and India, King became a firm believer and astute defender of nonviolence. Jesus Christ defined the center of King's religious understanding of love and Gandhi showed him how to use love as an instrument to transform society.

King's commitment to nonviolence was also informed by his knowledge of liberal Protestant theology and the philosophy of Personalism, both of which emphasized the oneness and infinite value of humanity. King combined these intellectual resources with black faith and Gandhi, and from these three sources created a distinctive and persuasive perspective on nonviolence.

Martin King not only preached nonviolence during the Montgomery bus boycott, he founded a national organization, Southern Christian Leadership Conference, in order to demonstrate the power of nonviolence to achieve justice in every segment of American life. The officers were mostly ministers and its motto was 'to redeem the soul of America.'

For King, love was the most powerful force in the world, and nonviolence was love expressed politically. Because nonviolence was widely thought of by many people as 'doing nothing,' King repeatedly emphasized the active dimensions of nonviolence. It was only passive in the sense of refusing to inflict physical harm on others. Nonviolence, therefore, was not a method for cowards—people afraid to suffer for the cause of justice. Nonviolence resists evil but it refuses to commit evil. Even the enemy is a person and must be treated as such. The nonviolent activist does not insult or seek to destroy the opponent but rather seeks to make the enemy a friend. However, even if nonviolence fails to convert the enemy to a friend, it eliminates hate from the hearts of those who are committed to it. Nonviolence bestows courage and self-respect to oppressed people who were once consumed by fear and low self-esteem.

King believed that only moral means could achieve moral ends, because 'the end is preexistent in the means.' Violence, therefore, was 'both impractical and immoral.' As a ten-percent minority on the richest and most powerful nation in the world, it was ludicrous to think that blacks could achieve freedom through violence. Even though most blacks were not morally committed to nonviolence, King persuaded them to adopt it as their best strategy for achieving justice.

The practical arguments for nonviolence were for those who could not accept it morally. From the Montgomery bus boycott (1955) to the Selma March (1965),

Martin King inspired African Americans to hold firmly to nonviolence in their struggle for justice. The success of the student sit-ins (1960), the Freedom Rides (1961), Birmingham demonstrations (1963) and the March on Washington (1963) provided King with the opportunity to demonstrate the power of nonviolence in destroying legal segregation in American life. The triumphant march from Selma to Montgomery was the climax of the first phase of the Civil Rights Movement. The Civil Rights Act (1964) and the Voting Rights Act Bill (1965) were its major political achievements.

It was much easier to advocate nonviolence when there were concrete victories and few serious challenges to its advocacy. Malcolm X was the most effective critic of King and nonviolence. But he was a marginal figure in the southern-based Civil Rights Movement. After the Watts riots in Los Angeles (August, 1965) and the rise of Black Power (June, 1966), King's views on nonviolence were seriously challenged by young movement activists who became disillusioned with the relevance of nonviolence for bestowing self-esteem and eliminating poverty in the black community of the urban ghettoes of the North. They turned to Malcolm X's Black Nationalist self-defense philosophy as an alternative to Martin King.

Martin King was forced to defend nonviolence among critics who were captivated by the legacy of Malcolm X powerfully expressed in the rise of Black Power. King met his critics head-on and challenged them to prove that Black Power was more effective than nonviolence in achieving real results. Though many black militants rejected King's views on nonviolence and integration, they admired his courage and respected his commitment to principle.

Martin King's stature in the white community continued to increase as long as he persuaded blacks to hold firmly to nonviolence. But they rejected him when he applied his view to America as a nation. King's opposition to America's war in Vietnam won him few friends in government and the society at large. Most whites acknowledged that King was an expert on civil rights as long as he urged blacks to be nonviolent in their struggle for justice. They told King to stick to civil rights and leave peace issues between nations to the elected politicians and their advisors. The idea that a black preacher's views on America's foreign policy should be taken seriously was ludicrous to most whites, especially to President Lyndon B. Johnson who saw himself as the Negro's best friend in government. What right did King have to criticize America and its President when they have done so much for the Negro?

Between 1966 and 1968, King struggled against an American public who resisted further advances in civil rights and resented his claim that America was 'the greatest purveyor of violence in the world today.' King's political optimism in the early phase of the of the Civil Rights Movement was transformed into a tough religious hope, derived from his deep belief that 'unearned suffering is redemptive.'

King's faith in nonviolence was first and foremost an unshakeable religious commitment. Although he preached the strategic value of nonviolence, the essence of King's belief was his acceptance of it as a way of life, 'because of the sheer morality of its claim.' Thus, even in defeat, nonviolence still wins. This is so because the universe is moving toward justice. No person or nation can prevent its ultimate realization. This faith sustained the later King in his struggles to achieve economic justice for garbage workers in Memphis as he was preparing for the Poor People's Campaign to pressure the federal government to withdraw from the war in Vietnam and to intensify instead the War on Poverty. An assassin's bullet ended King's life while he was standing on the balcony of the Lorraine Motel in Memphis. But his hope still lives on in those who today fight for justice.

When we turn to Malcolm X, we hear a different voice from that of Martin King, one that whites, and some blacks found most disturbing to their religious and political sensibilities. Malcolm X was a Muslim minister and Black Nationalist leader, who was the most formidable race critic in American history. More effectively than anyone else, he exposed the racist hypocrisy of American democracy and the ethical contradictions of white Christianity. His unrelenting and uncompromising critique of America and Christianity was bold and devastating. Few people could listen to him and not be challenged by the cogency of his analysis.

Malcolm focused his criticism on the failure of white people to treat black people as human beings. That and that alone was at the heart of his critique. There was nothing fancy or sophisticated about it. Just plain talk—telling the truth about the crimes against blacks that whites did not want to hear about, and few blacks had the courage to confront.

Whites enslaved blacks for 244 years, segregated then for another 100, and lynched them all along the way whenever and wherever whites had a mind to demonstrate their absolute power over blacks. How could American whites exclude blacks and other people of color from the political process and yet say that this nation is the land of the free? How could white Christians treat blacks as brutes, and still claim love as their central religious principle? With rage, humor, and devastating logic, Malcolm had a field day exposing these political and religious contradictions.

Malcolm's articulation of the gap between the American creed and deed angered many whites because he spoke forcefully and bluntly, refusing to sugarcoat the truth about the crime whites committed against blacks. He not only spoke out passionately against the brutality and cowardice of the Ku Klux Klan but also against the structural and hidden violence of the American government. 'Stop talking about Mississippi,' he railed. 'American is Mississippi!' To understand Malcolm's perspective on violence, it is necessary to view it within the political and religious context of America's nearly four centuries of racist violence against blacks and its white Christian justification and tolerance.

Born in Omaha, Nebraska, May 19, 1925, Malcolm lived when American was defined by overt racist violence. Segregation was the law of the land, the KKK was marching, lynching was commonplace, and the government, educational institutions, and churches routinely practiced and openly taught that blacks were inferior—both mentally and physically. No black person could escape the physical and psychological violence of white supremacy.

Malcolm's father Earl Little, a Baptist preacher and follower of the Black Nationalist Marcus Garvey, was a special target of white hate groups. While Malcolm was still in his mother's womb, the KKK paid the Little family a visit and forced their move from Omaha to Lansing, Michigan, where at the age of four Malcolm witnessed the burning down of their home by a white hate group called the Black Legionnaires. Malcolm called the event 'the nightmare night in 1929.' Two years later, Malcolm claimed that the same group killed his father, leaving the family fatherless and soon penniless. Unable to cope, Malcolm's mother, Louise Little, had a mental breakdown and was hospitalized in Kalamazoo.

The Little children were placed in foster homes. After Malcolm's eighth grade teacher told him that a lawyer was 'no realistic goal for a nigger,' he became disillusioned, despite being at the top of his class. He dropped out of school and went to Boston and then to New York where he became a dealer in drugs, prostitution, numbers running, and con games. He described himself as 'a predatory animal' who 'deliberately invited death.' Before he reached his twenty-first birthday, Malcolm was arrested for armed robbery and sentenced to eight to ten years at a Massachusetts prison in February 1946.

While in prison, Malcolm had two profound conversations: intellectual and spiritual. Through the example of an inmate, he discovered the power of the intellect. He became a voracious reader, disciplined thinker, and skilled debater. In 1948, under the influence of his family, Malcolm became a member for Elijah Muhammad's Nation of Islam (NOI) and its most effective recruiter and articulate defender. The NOI reversed the value-system of white America by making everything black good and everything white evil. It substituted black supremacy for white supremacy. While Malcolm accepted the theology of the NOI, it was its Black Nationalist philosophy, emphasizing black self-respect and self-defense, which inspired his intellectual imagination and fueled his religious commitment. He enjoyed giving whites the same medicine they dished out to blacks. Unlike Martin who had no taste for violence in any form, Malcolm viewed retaliatory violence as a necessary response to criminal acts. That is the only language criminals understand, he contended. To love someone who hates you is to speak a language they do not understand, like speaking French to a person who only knows German. Malcolm learned this eye-for-an-eye principle on the streets of Boston and New York where survival depended on doing to others before they did it to you. He also learned it from reading American history, which is replete with genocidal acts against Native people of the land and wherever this nation decided to raise the American flag. That was why Malcolm said that the white man made the mistake of letting me read history books.

Malcolm was released from prison in August 1952 and quickly became the most influential minister in the NOI—second only to the Messenger, the Honorable Elijah Muhammad, as Malcolm and other followers called him. Malcolm was appointed to head the prestigious Temple Number 7 in New York and became the NOI's national spokesperson, lecturing and debating white and black intellectuals at America's most prestigious universities. He distinguished himself as the most feared, controversial, and articulate race critic in America. Since the overt racist violence of the southern conservatives was obvious and effectively exposed in the media by Martin Luther King, Jr., and the Civil Rights Movement, Malcolm X focused his critique on the covert racist violence of northern white liberals.

Malcolm's attack on white liberal was persistent and brutal. He exposed their link to the creation of the urban black ghetto where drugs, poverty, crime, unemployment, and bad housing are its defining characteristics. While Martin King praised white liberals for their support, Malcolm castigated them for their hypocrisy—professing to be for integration while creating de facto segregation in schools, housing, and other segments of American life. When blacks manage to move into a white community, the liberals are the first to leave.

No issue angered Malcolm X more than what whites said about violence and nonviolence in the Civil Rights Movement. They urged blacks to follow Martin King—embrace nonviolence and reject violence in any form. Malcolm could hardly contain his rage as he pointed out the contradictions between what whites advised blacks to do to get their freedom and what they did to attain their own. Patrick Henry did not practice the virtues of nonviolence. George Washington was no pacifist. When whites feel that their rights have been violated, they do not advocate turning the other cheek or kneeling down to pray. Because whites did not apply to themselves the same moral logic they urged on blacks, Malcolm regarded them as the worst hypocrites on the planet.

Malcolm did not advocate violence; he advocated self-defense. He believed that the right of self-defense is an essential element in the definition of humanity. Whites have always recognized this principle for themselves but not for blacks. This kind of racist thinking infuriated Malcolm. If whites have the right to defend themselves against their enemies, why not blacks? Malcolm used provocative language to express his rage. 'If you want to know what I'll do, figure out what you'll do. I'll do the same thing—only more of it.' He contended that blacks should use 'any means necessary' to get their freedom and whites should be prepared for 'reciprocal bleeding.' He did not regard such language as violent. He called it intelligence. 'A black man has the right to do whatever is necessary to get his freedom that other human beings have done to get their freedom.'

Malcolm regarded nonviolence as a ridiculous philosophy, one that whites would never embrace as their own. He never understood why Martin King adopted it. How could blacks be regarded as human beings if they do not defend themselves? Everything in creation has a right to defend itself except the American Negro. It pained Malcolm to see black women, men, and children being beaten, kicked, and attacked by dogs. If the government does not protect black people, they are within their right to protect themselves, he contended.

In contrast to the portrayal of Martin King as a promoter of love and nonviolence, the media portrayed Malcolm as a preacher of hate and violence. They also, along with the FBI, were effective in creating dissension within the NOI, especially between Malcolm and Muhammad. In December 1963, Muhammad suspended Malcolm purportedly for saying that the assassination of President Kennedy was a case of the 'chickens coming home to roost.'

Three months later, Malcolm bolted from the NOI. He made a pilgrimage to Mecca, became a Sunni Muslim, adopted the name El-Hajj Malik El-Shabazz, and rejected the racist ideology of the NOI.

Malcolm also went to Africa to connect the black freedom movement in the U.S. with liberation movements around the world. 'It is incorrect to classify the revolt of the Negro as simply a racial conflict of blacks against whites, or as a purely American problem,' he said at Barnard College. 'Rather we are today seeking a global rebellion of the oppressed against the oppressor, the exploited against the exploiter.'

While Malcolm's separation from the NOI and subsequent experience in Mecca and Africa had a profound effect on his philosophy of freedom, causing him to reject the racist ideology of Elijah Muhammad, he did not relinquish his self-defense philosophy and his radical critique of white supremacy. For Malcolm white America remained a racist nation and Christianity white nationalism.

The animosity between Malcolm and the NOI deepened. They firebombed Malcolm's house one week before a team of assassins murdered him, as he was about to speak at the Audubon Ballroom, February 21, 1965. It was widely said that Malcolm died by the violence he fomented. But it is more accurate to say that he died while exposing white violence and fighting for the freedom of African Americans and other oppressed peoples throughout the world.

Both Martin and Malcolm were thirty-nine when they were assassinated. Ironically, the blacks Malcolm loved killed him. They could not tolerate Malcolm's truth. It was too powerful, too profoundly human, transcending race and other reactionary limits.

A lone gunman killed Martin. He symbolized white America's inability to tolerate any black person who refuses to stay in his/her place. Staying in an assigned place is something that neither Martin nor Malcolm could do. Their spirits were too powerful to be contained or restrained. In this sense, Martin and Malcolm followed the path of Jesus the Galilean whose rebellion against the place assigned to him led to the cross.

Most theologians, especially in the U.S., find their assigned places quite comfortable. They stay in their places and write essays and books about this and that but say very little if anything about the inhuman places this society assigns to the poor and people of color. They are like the learned of Jesus' time. They get bogged down in things that may be intellectually interesting for their group but hardly matter when considered in the light of what the gospel demands of us today.

We need theologians and preachers like Martin and Malcolm to show us the way so we will be able to make the gospel of Jesus so plain that no one will be able to claim they did not know what it demands of us.

We today have much to learn from Martin and Malcolm as we seek to create a community, nation, and world that are both just and peaceful. They were both disciplined thinkers and responsible activists. Though their views on nonviolence and violence were different, they complemented and corrected each other, showing us that an abstract, absolutist, and uncritical commitment to violence or nonviolence, to Martin or Malcolm is wrongheaded.

We do not need to choose between Martin and Malcolm but rather to acknowledge the value in both.

Our primary task is to do today what Martin and Malcolm did in theirs. We must not simply adopt Martin or Malcolm or both and think that we have the answers to our racial problems. We should stand on their intellectual and spiritual foundation. But their thought cannot serve as a substitute for our own thinking.

We have to think for ourselves because we have problems that Martin and Malcolm never faced. We should use them as the springboard for our creative thinking and militant action.

Our reflective task is not easy, and it will take a lot of hard, disciplined thinking about freedom—what it means and how to achieve it. Martin's and Malcolm's life and writings give us theoretical ideas and practical examples to work with. They remind us that we are part of a great African American intellectual tradition that stretches back to Ida B. Wells and W. E. B. Du Bois, Sojourner Truth and Frederick Douglass, Fannie Lou Hamer and Ella Baker, Nelson Mandela and Steve Biko. With these revolutionary resources, we have enough intellectual and spiritual power to move into the twenty-first century—ready to face anything that hinders our freedom. If we stand together as proud, disciplined thinkers and militant acting people, the movement for justice will not be contained.

I hope we will not let our differences destroy our much-needed unity. We can learn from Martin and Malcolm about how to be different and yet work together for the same cause. I only hope that we can sustain our struggle for freedom, keep on keeping on so that our children and our children's children will be able to live in a clean and safe environment and a just and peaceful world.

# SO MUCH HISTORY, SO MUCH FUTURE: MARTIN LUTHER KING, JR. AND THE SECOND COMING OF AMERICA

Vincent Harding

1979[1]

It was impossible for King—or any other single individual to understand, much less command all the tendencies now set loose in the black communities of the land (of course, he knew that he was being falsely identified as an 'Uncle Tom' by many northern black rhetoricians of revolution who had never once risked their lives as King had done so many times in the cause of his people's freedom). At the same time, Martin was trying to understand where the real, critical centers of power lay in American society, trying to understand how he could tackle the powerful forces which supported war, racism, poverty and the internal subversion of the freedom movement's many parts.

No easy task. Still, King seemed convinced that he would be unfaithful to the history he had already made with others, untrue to his forebears and his children in the struggle for justice, unless he followed what appeared to be the logic of the movement. For him, that logic, that history, that sense of integrity pressed him towards a more radical challenge than he had ever mounted before, one which would leave him more naked to his enemies than ever before. Very little that he had learned in all the dangerous campaigns of the south had prepared him for the task of striking towards the heart of America's real political, economic and social structures of oppression, exploitation and greed. Not even the bitter Chicago experience had been lived with long enough to help him build the kind of analysis, organization and strategy which were needed. Yet, moving as much as anything else on the power of his deep sense of compassion and courage, he determined to go in that direction, tried to fashion a two-pronged attack on the center of America's foreign and domestic policies of repression, co-optation, and de-humanization. He had concluded that there could be no black freedom, no true freedom for anyone without such a challenge being raised, and he knew that

---

1. Source: https://is.cuni.cz/studium/predmety/index.php?do=download&did=77732&kod=JMM606

he could no longer assume that the federal government would even be a reluctant ally. No, that government and its policies was now the prime target.

First, King decided to try to respond fully to the unspeakable agony, the terrible crime of Vietnam, defying all his critics and many of his friends, from the White House to members of his own organization and his own family. On April 4, 1967, at Riverside Church in New York City, the struggling leader searcher addressed a major meeting sponsored by Clergy and Laymen Concerned About Vietnam. Near the beginning of his vibrant presentation, King admitted that he had not spoken clearly and early enough, but vowed that he would never make that mistake again. Justifying the connection he saw among the struggles for equal rights and economic justice in America and the demand for an end to American military involvement in Vietnam, King placed them all within the context of his commission as a minister of Jesus Christ and a Nobel Peace Prize awardee. Unflinchingly, he identified America as the essential aggressor in the war and called his nation 'the greatest purveyor of violence in the world'.

Attempting to give voice to the many millions of the voiceless of the world whose 'movement' towards freedom he now felt he was representing, Martin called to the American nation, to President Lyndon Johnson, to men and women everywhere and said,

Somehow this madness must cease. We must stop now, I speak as a child of God and brother to the suffering poor of Vietnam. I speak for those whose land is being laid waste, whose homes are being destroyed, whose culture is being subverted. I speak for the poor of America who are paying the double price of smashed hopes at home and death and corruption in Vietnam. I speak as a citizen of the world, for the world as it stands aghast at the path we have taken. I speak as an American to the leaders of my own nation. The great initiative in this war is ours. The initiative to stop it must be ours.

The black struggle for freedom had served to inspirit and inspire the rapidly mounting American anti-war movement. Now King was urgently placing himself into the center of this force which he had helped to create, calling for conscientious objection, even draft resistance, following the earlier examples of such SNCC leaders as Bob Moses, Jim Forman and Stokely Carmichael, as well as James and Diane Bevel of his own staff. But King was still ahead of most of SCLC, its board and its staff, and some persons within his organization were seriously opposed to so forceful a move into the anti-Vietnam war arena. Indeed, this was one of Martin's major difficulties through much of the post 1965 period: the vision that he was trying to fashion, the history he was trying to make, was often beyond the capacities, the aspirations, the politics and the imagination of most of the men and women who made up SCLC, his only real organizational base.

At the same time, of course, as head of the organization, he had to accept at least some of the blame for its political backwardness. Still, King drove forward, was driven forward by all the explosive forces around him, by all the history he had helped to make, and soon he turned from Riverside Church to forge the second prong of his militant challenge to white American power.

In the summer of 1967, after two of the decade's most deadly urban uprisings—in Newark and Detroit—had stunned the nation, after a national Black

Power Convention had done much to stamp that variously-defined slogan in the minds of black folks everywhere, King announced his plans for a major attack on America's internal structures of inequality and injustice.

On August 16, 1967, the *New York Times* carried a story from SCLC's tenth annual convention in Atlanta, a story which began, 'The Rev. Martin Luther King, Jr. said today that he planned to 'dislocate' Northern cities with massive but nonviolent demonstrations of civil disobedience before Congress adjourns its current session.' According to the reporter, Martin had said, 'That he had decided on the step to provide an alternative to rioting and to gain large federal spending for impoverished Negroes.'

It was a version of the non-violent army again, now surfacing at a far more volatile, confused, and dangerous moment in the nation's history and in King's own career. There was much unclarity and disagreement within the ranks of SCLC and among the many-faceted freedom movement organizations, but by the end of 1967, King and his staff had again decided to focus this potentially revolutionary challenge in Washington, D.C., fully aware of the ugly, angry, and unreceptive mood at work in the White House and elsewhere.

At his radical best, King was determined to press the logic of his position, the movement of his people's history. Having attacked the nation's anti-liberationist overseas actions, he now intended to move on to the heart of the government, demanding a response to the suffering of its own semi-colonized peoples. (Nor was King paving a way of welcome for his move by saying late in 1967: 'I am not sad that black Americans are rebelling; this was not only inevitable but eminently desirable. Without this magnificent ferment among Negroes, the old evasions and procrastinations would have continued indefinitely'. He was not paving a way, but he was indicating his own way, his own movement in the vortex of 'this magnificent ferment'.)

Martin was trying to be on time, trying to be faithful, trying to go forward, to create whatever openings towards the future that he could. Jamming his life against the advice of many of his black and white movement supporters, defying the angry warnings of Lyndon Johnson, King searched for his new role, for the new role of his people. In an America which seemed at times on the edge of armed racial warfare, an America increasingly torn over the Vietnam war, an America unresponsive to the deepest needs of its own people, especially its poor—in the midst of this history King was desperately searching for the connections with his past, for the openings to his and our future.

By December 1967, Martin had at least temporarily taken his new, powerful and dangerous position. In a series of broadcasts for Canadian Public Radio, he said, 'Negroes...must not only formulate a program; they must fashion new tactics which do not count on government goodwill.' Instead, he said the new tactics must be those which are forceful enough, 'to compel unwilling authorities to yield to the mandates of justice.' But here at the end, at the beginning, at the end, in his last major published document, King was not talking about Blacks alone: the movement had grown; there was no way to 'overcome' without taking on much more than we had ever taken on before. Thus, he said,

The dispossessed of this nation—the poor, both white and Negro—live in a cruelly unjust society. They must organize a revolution against that injustice, not against the lives of the persons who are their fellow citizens, but against the structures through which society is refusing to take the means which have been called for, and which are at hand, to lift the load of poverty.

Martin King was talking about a non-violent revolution in America, to transform the entire society on behalf of its poorest people, for the sake of us all. Martin King was moving towards an experiment with truth and power, and he was calling for 3,000 persons to join him for three months of intensive training to begin that revolution at the seat of America's political power, Washington, D.C. Martin King was shaping a new role for himself, leader of a non-violent revolutionary army/movement, one which he also saw connecting with the oppressed peoples of other nations.

For some time, he had been talking about the need for 'a revolution of values' within America which would deal with the needs of our own exploited and dehumanized peoples and place us at the side of all men and women struggling for justice and liberation throughout the world. Now, at the end, at the beginning, the words were clearer, sharper, harsher, no longer the vague 'revolution of values', Martin King, who had begun twelve years before as the spokesman for a people who wanted to be treated with dignity on a segregated city bus, was now calling for non-violent revolution against all the 'structures' of injustice in America. He had declared non-violent war against all the political, economic, and social structures which denied dignity, hope and the opportunities for the fullest self-development to all the black, white, red and brown brothers and sisters of those early pilgrims towards freedom in Montgomery. Although the seed for such a development was present in every fundamental black challenge to the racist powers of the society, surely no one in Montgomery—including Martin Luther King, Jr.—ever imagined that a dozen years later the history they and others had made, the future which their opponents had fought to deny, would now lead King to call for non-violent revolution in America.

In 1967, no one, including King, really knew what such a revolution would mean, how it would really be organized and mounted, what its concrete, programmatic goals might be; but he was determined to move forward. At Riverside Church, precisely one year before his assassination, Martin had proclaimed the fullness of time, declaring,

Now let us begin. Now let us re-dedicate ourselves to the long and bitter–but beautiful–struggle for a new world... The choice is ours, and though we might prefer it otherwise, we *must* choose in this crucial moment of human history.

For him, the non-violent army of revolution was his own choice, his own contribution to the world-wide struggle of the oppressed. Here, again, almost no one on his staff was ready for this, ready to move directly against the ruthless, brutal power of white America's most deeply vested military, political, economic, and racial self-interests. Unclear, often afraid, everyone, including Martin, tended to drag their feet through the winter of 1967-68, the winter of preparation. All the while, they were taking harsh criticisms on every hand, palpably sensing the dangers of this new, more radical direction mounting all around then, dangers from within and without.

Perhaps Martin King had seen and felt more than he was able to accomplish. Perhaps he could not ever be ready for this new role. Perhaps in the violent climate of America, it was impossible to be ready for such a campaign of revolutionary, non-violent civil disobedience without an organization that was fully prepared for all the dangers, all the opportunities and all the long, hard, preparatory work. SCLC was not that organization. Nevertheless, ready, or not, King appeared to be trying to get ready—facing toward Washington, D.C.

But first there were garbage collectors to help in Memphis, and there were powerful forces at every level of American society who were determined that Martin Luther King would never be ready for the kind of revolution he had now announced. As a result, Martin never made it to Washington, never found out if he was ready or not.

When the word of his death vas flashed to the black communities of America, they sent up their requiem screams of anguish and rage. When they heard that the King was dead, they lighted great fires everywhere, especially in Washington. Were these simply continuations of the long, hot summers, the burning of the dream? Were they no more than angry, flaming protestations? Were they funeral pyres for the King, for the hope, for the dream? Or were they, possibly, just possibly, torches, torches of continuing hope, searching for a way to the future, a way to that future that Martin King did not have a chance to make?

If they were flaming searchlights, then after the fires, after the screams, the search seemed to be dramatically intensified. All the tendencies towards inner and outer rebellion, towards black questioning of America's very nature, towards the search for black identity, all the outrage and the passion were poured into a thousand projects, conferences, caucuses, organizations, in countless strident demands upon existing institutions. (And all the attempts at official subversion were also intensified, of course.) Black students, Black welfare mothers, Black preachers, Black lawyers, Black policemen, Black congressmen, Black psychologists, Black priests and nuns, Black elected officials—all these and many more were driven toward each other, at least temporarily, seeking to touch, to hold and to organize and make demands as never before. For a while, a powerful thrust of solidarity seemed to pull together many who had been fragmented, seemed to energize others who had been apathetic.

At the same time, over the years immediately following King's death, many other diverse persons and groups had taken up the torches, searching for their own new way. The revived force of the Black movement helped stimulate new groupings and revitalize older ones in the women's movement, among Native Americans, Chicanos, Latinos and white ethnics. The various splintered Marxist movements in America gained new courage and new converts. The homosexuals formed a 'liberation' movement. The prisoners across the country (mostly black, of course) fought for rights long denied them, fought and died, with Attica, 1971, as the symbol of all these struggles for new levels of freedom, justice and dignity behind prison bars. Meanwhile, the anti-war movement grew in force and breadth; draft resistance became almost respectable; then after terrible final crimes of destruction, American forces were finally pushed pulled out of Vietnam, ending at an embassy wall, with one last mad, American-like scramble of each man and woman for themselves, seeking to escape the judgment of history. Later, across the globe in South Africa, the children of Soweto, inspired by the children of Malcolm and Martin, raised their fists in defiance and hope, were beaten and shot down, but will rise again, with the judgment of history.

Martin King was part of it all. He had helped to create this history, in his life and in his death. Indeed, it is likely fair to say that this man who grew from a spokesperson for his people's search for simple dignity in a medium-sized southern city to become a giant symbol of the search for justice across the globe–this man, with all of his weaknesses, all of his flaws, all of his blind spots and all of his creative, courageous greatness, made all the history he could make. Perhaps of even more importance to us here and now, we are able to see that he helped force open the way to the possibility of a new vision, a second coming of America, an America in which justice, compassion and humanity prevail.

Now, largely as a result of the movement King represented, as a result of the significant developments since his death, the old America has been cracked, wedged open, cannot be the same again. Now, the forces which were absent from the first official beginning of America, in the days following July 4, 1776—the blacks, the women, the Native Americans, the Chicanos, the students, and many more—all who were then pressed aside are now present, are all more aware of themselves, of ourselves, than ever before. King helped create the possibility that all of us might break beyond our own individual and group interests and catch a vision of a new America, create a vision of a new common good in a new future which will serve us all. He saw that our needs were economic and spiritual, political and moral, social and personal, and as the end, the beginning approached, he was groping his way towards a new integration—one which had very little to do with the legalities of Brown v. The Board of Education.

But in the midst of this struggle, this groping, this searching, King learned some things, and the message he left was the message he learned, the message he had been given by the earlier generations of our freedom-striving people: Freedom is a constant struggle. The message he left was that a new America cannot be created without an even more difficult, radical, and dangerous struggle than we have known up to now. The message he left is that black people can no longer make any separate peace with America, that our needs are the needs of other millions of Americans, that the entire society must be challenged with the force of revolutionary change in all of its political, economic, social and psychic structures.

The message he left for those who would create a new future was that we cannot find the jobs we need, we cannot find the education we need, we cannot find the health care we need, we cannot find the physical and psychic security and development we need, we cannot find the creative male-female relationships we need, we cannot build the mutually nurturing relationship to our environment that we need, we cannot create the nonexploitative relationship to the raw-producers of the world we need, we cannot develop the fraternity with the freedom lovers everywhere we need–we cannot find/create these things in an America as it is presently structured, in an America that makes financial profits and personal prestige 'the bottom line.'

Thus, like King, we must be driven, we must press forward towards revolutionary transformation of ourselves and of our nation, for the good of all its people. The bottom line (if ever there is such a thing) must become compassion and the attention to human needs, which has no bottom, no end. The message he left, then, was that for all who would create a future which is at once worthy of our past struggles and capable of moving us far beyond those struggles, we must be prepared to move forward as never before. And this time, I am sure he would urge us to know that we cannot wait for a messiah, not even a black one. No, only many groupings of serious, disciplined, organized and self-confident men, women and children can bring about the transformation that we now need.

At Riverside Church he called us: 'Now let us re-dedicate ourselves to the long and bitter–but beautiful–struggle for a new world'. Closely examined, we realize that King's Riverside statement is no different than the last testament of Frantz Fanon, especially if we substitute King's 'America' for Fanon's 'Europe':

Humanity is waiting for something other from us than... imitation...if we want humanity to advance a step further, if we want to bring it up to a different level than that which (America) has shown it, then we must invent and we must make discoveries... For (America), for ourselves and for humanity, comrades, we must turn over a new leaf, we must work out new concepts and try to set afoot a new (being).

Yes, that is essentially the message King left as he made all the history he could, as he opened the future for us to make, to re-make. Serve the people. Serve humanity. Let the oppressed go free. Let America be born again. A wild and visionary set of ideas, of course, but our struggle for freedom, like all struggles of freedom, has been wild and visionary from the very beginning. (Remember, once it was wild and visionary to believe that such words as these would ever be spoken at the University of Mississippi and published by its press!)

So I am not afraid to be wild and visionary, with Martin, brother, comrade and friend. And I dare, with him to believe, to hope, to risk the charge of madness and super-subjectivity. Indeed, I dare to believe that somewhere, perhaps everywhere, Martin and Chairman Mao, Martin and Malcolm, Martin and Fanon, Martin and Fannie Lou, Martin and Medgar, Martin and A.J. Muste, Martin and Tom Merton, Martin and Emma Goldman, Martin and Clarence Jordan, Martin and Ida B Wells-Barnett, Martin and Slater King, Martin and Ralph Featherstone, Martin and Ruby Doris Saith, Martin and Bertha Gober, Martin and all those folks and many more; indeed Martin and Jesus of Nazareth—all of them, I believe all of them, somewhere, perhaps everywhere, are having a grand time discovering, re-discovering themselves, each other, moving ever more deeply into that ultimate, overwhelming light of freedom out of which we all came. And I dare to believe that they are hoping for us, hoping that we will find again, within ourselves, that we will dredge out from all its dark and hidden places, that infinite capacity to hope and struggle which is stored up like a great light within us all.

I dare to believe that they are hoping that we will dare to believe that we can do the impossible, that we will, dare to believe that we can do the impossible, that we will, that we can make America a new society for all of its people. I dare to believe that they are hoping for us, believing that we can, that we shall continue overcoming–overcoming today, overcoming tomorrow, overcoming the fears, overcoming the complacency, overcoming the desire for nothing more than security and safety. I dare to believe that Martin is hoping, knowing that the power to continue overcoming is within us as it was within him, within all of them, wherever they are. And I dare to believe that Bertha is still singing her song, somewhere, everywhere, still singing our song, our special Mississippi song, our American song, our world-wide song, for us, for them, for everyone:

> We've been 'buked and we've been scorned,
> We've been talked about, sure as you're born.
> But we'll never turn back, no,
> we'll never turn back,
> Until we've all been freed, and we have equality

# BIGGER THAN A HAMBURGER

Ella Baker

1960[1]

*Ella Baker (1903—1986) played an instrumental role in the development of the civil rights movement of the 1950s and 1960s. Baker was born in Norfolk, Virginia, and grew up in rural Littleton, North Carolina. After graduating from Shaw University, she organized consumer cooperatives in New York and worked on consumer affairs for the Works Progress Administration (WPA). In the 1940s Baker became a national field secretary of the NAACP, traveling throughout the country organizing branches and developing membership drives. Increasingly, Baker became disaffected with the NAACP's leadership, because decision-making occurred primarily in the national office rather than in the branch organizations. In 1957 Baker joined King to help found the SCLC. She directed the SCLC national office and was instrumental in coordinating major civil disobedience actions. She became critical of the SCLC because of its emphasis on charismatic leadership. In 1960 Baker was the principal organizer in helping student protesters establish the SNCC. She solicited funds for SNCC and assisted in planning strategies for voter registration drives and desegregation campaigns. Baker eventually broke with the SCLC after she disagreed with ministers who felt that SNCC should simply be an arm of the SCLC, rather than an independent organization. Although she pre-ferred working behind the scenes to playing a public leadership role, she is widely regarded by scholars as one of the central leaders in the Black Freedom movement.*

The Student Leadership Conference made it crystal clear that current sit-ins and other demonstrations are concerned with something much bigger than a hamburger or even a giant-sized Coke.

Whatever may be the difference in approach to their goal, the Negro and white students, North and South, are seeking to rid America of the scourge of racial segregation and discrimination—not only at lunch counters, but in every aspect of life.

In reports, casual conversations, discussion groups, and speeches, the sense and the spirit of the following statement that appeared in the initial newsletter of the students at Barber-Scotia College, Concord, N.C., were re-echoed time and again:

1. Source: http://www.historyisaweapon.com/defcon1/bakerbigger.html

We want the world to know that we no longer accept the inferior position of second-class citizenship. We are willing to go to jail, be ridiculed, spat upon, and even suffer physical violence to obtain First Class Citizenship.

By and large, this feeling that they have a destined date with freedom, was not limited to a drive for personal freedom, or even freedom for the Negro in the South.

Repeatedly it was emphasized that the movement was concerned with the moral implications of racial discrimination for the 'whole world' and the 'Human Race'.

This universality of approach was linked with a perceptive recognition that 'it is important to keep the movement democratic and to avoid struggles for personal leadership.'

It was further evident that desire for supportive cooperation from adult leaders and the adult community was also tempered by apprehension that adults might try to 'capture' the student movement. The students showed willingness to be met on the basis of equality, but were intolerant of anything that smacked of manipulation or domination.

This inclination toward *group-centered leadership*, rather than toward a *leader-centered group pattern of organization*, was refreshing indeed to those of the older group who bear the scars of the battle, the frustrations and the disillusionment that come when the prophetic leader turns out to have heavy feet of clay.

However hopeful might be the signs in the direction of group-centeredness, the fact that many schools and communities, especially in the South, have not provided adequate experience for young Negroes to assume initiative and think and act independently accentuated the need for guarding the student movement against well-meaning, but nevertheless unhealthy, over-protectiveness.

Here is an opportunity for adult and youth to work together and provide genuine leadership—the development of the individual to his highest potential for the benefit of the group.

Many adults and youth characterized the Raleigh meeting as the greatest or most significant conference of our period.

Whether it lives up to this high evaluation or not will, in a large measure, be determined by the extent to which there is more effective training in and understanding of non-violent principles and practices, in group dynamics, and in the re-direction into creative channels of the normal frustrations and hostilities that result from second-class citizenship.

# THE BELOVED COMMUNITY OF MARTIN LUTHER KING

Grace Lee Boggs

2004[1]

In the 1960s I didn't pay much attention to Martin Luther King, Jr. My own social change activities unfolded in the inner city of Detroit. So I identified more with Malcolm X than with Martin. Like most Black Power activists, I viewed King's notions of nonviolence and beloved community as somewhat naïve and sentimental.

Neither was I involved in the 15-year campaign launched in 1968 by Detroit's Congressman John Conyers to declare King's birthday a national holiday. I held back, concerned that it would turn King into an icon, obscure the role of grassroots activists, and reinforce the tendency to rely on charismatic leaders.

Thirty-five years have now passed since King was killed, decades during which I have been continuously involved in the struggle to free our communities of the crime and violence that escalated in the wake of the urban rebellions of the late 1960s and the de-industrialization of Detroit. In the 20 years since President Reagan signed into law the King holiday, we seem to have drifted further from anything like a beloved community in this nation.

Thinking back over these years, I can't help wondering: Might events have taken a different path if we had found a way to infuse our struggle for Black Power with King's philosophy of nonviolence? Is it possible that our relationships with one another today, not only inter- but intra-racially, would be more harmonious if we had discovered how to blend Malcolm's militancy with King's vision of the beloved community? Could such a synthesis have a revolutionary power beyond our wildest dreams? Is such a revolutionary power available to us today?

These are the times that try our souls. I cannot recall any previous period when the challenges have been so basic, so interconnected, and so demanding, not just to specific groups but to everyone living in this country, regardless of race, ethnicity, class, gender, age, or national origin.

As I have read and re-read King's speeches and writings from the last two years of his life, it has become increasingly clear to me that King's prophetic vision is now the indispensable starting point for 21st-century revolutionaries.

---

1. Source: https://www.yesmagazine.org/issue/hope-conspiracy/2004/05/21/the-beloved-community-of-martin-luther-king

# King's new kind of revolution

Viewing Martin Luther King, Jr., as a revolutionary is in sharp contrast to the official view of him as simply an advocate for the rights of African Americans within the current system. In the last two years of his life, confronted with problems that required more complex solutions than visions of Black and White children marching hand in hand, King began to explore a new kind of revolution, one that would challenge all the values and institutions of our society and combine the struggle against racism with a struggle against poverty, militarism, and materialism.

'The black revolution,' he insisted, 'is much more than a struggle for rights for Negroes. It is exposing evils that are deeply rooted in the whole structure of our society.'

'The war in Vietnam,' he said, 'is a symptom of a far deeper malady within the American spirit. Material growth has been made an end itself. Our scientific power has outrun our spiritual power.'

This is what we should be talking about as we celebrate King's 75th birthday this year.

The Montgomery Bus Boycott of 1955–56, which provided King with his first experience in movement leadership, was a watershed because it created a theory and practice of revolutionary struggle very different from that which prevailed in the first half of the 20th century under the influence of the 1917 Russian Revolution. In those days most radicals, including myself, conceived of revolutionary struggle as an insurrection, a seizure of power by the oppressed from their oppressors, by the victims from the villains.

By contrast, the Montgomery Bus Boycott was a year-long, nonviolent, disciplined, and ultimately successful boycott by an African-American community, struggling against their dehumanization, not as angry victims or rebels, but as new men and women, representative of a new more human society. Using methods that transformed them, they triggered the human identity and ecology movements that over the last 40 years have been creating a new civil society in the United States.

As a Baptist preacher and philosopher, King played a pivotal role in helping the bus boycotters in Montgomery, Alabama, create the new paradigm of nonviolent transformative struggles, which over the next nine years forced Congress to pass the 1964 Civil Rights Act and the 1965 Voting Rights Act.

## Self-transforming, structure-transforming

King was a movement activist for only 13 years, from his participation in the Montgomery Bus Boycott to his assassination in April 1968. But the dialectical development of his thinking during those turbulent years is unmistakable.

In June 1965, the rebellion in Watts, California, confronted King with the reality that civil and voting rights legislation had little to offer black youth living desperate lives in northern ghettoes. So in 1966 he went to Chicago to meet with these young people.

Reflecting on these meetings and on the mounting resistance to the Vietnam War, King concluded that the crisis of black youth was rooted in structural questions that required going beyond both civil rights and Black Power. 'One unfortunate thing about Black Power,' he said, 'is that it gives race a priority precisely at a time when the impact of automation and other forces have made the economic question fundamental for blacks and whites alike.'

As a result, in his major writings and speeches in the last two years of his life (Where Do We Go From Here: Community or Chaos? and Time to Break Silence), King began to project a new kind of radical revolution that would begin the shift from a 'thing-oriented society to a person-oriented society.'

He rejected the dictatorship of technology, which, he said, diminishes people because it eliminates their sense of participation. 'Enlarged material powers,' he warned repeatedly, 'spell enlarged peril if there is no proportionate growth of the soul.' 'When machines and computers, profit motives and property rights are considered more important than people,' he said, 'the giant triplets of racism, materialism, and militarism are incapable of being conquered.'

Instead, King had a vision of people at the grassroots and community level participating in creating new values, truths, relationships, and infrastructures as the foundation for a new society. He called for programs that would involve young people in 'self-transforming and structure-transforming' direct actions 'in our dying cities.' He called for a radical revolution in values and a new social system that goes beyond both capitalism, which he said is 'too I-centered, too individualistic,' and communism, which is 'too collective, too statist.'

The catastrophe of the Vietnam War also inspired him to project a new concept of global citizenship that we now urgently need to practice as we grapple with the catastrophe of our current occupation of Iraq. 'Every nation,' he said, 'must now develop an overriding loyalty to mankind as a whole in order to preserve the best in their individual societies.'

'Disinherited people all over the world,' he said, 'are bleeding to death from deep social and economic wounds.' In order for the United States to get on the right side of this world revolution, we must 'undergo a radical revolution in values.'

King's reasons for opposing a war against communism could be applied almost verbatim to the current war against terrorism. 'Poverty, insecurity and injustice,' he explained, 'are the fertile soil in which the seed of communism grows. A positive revolution of values is our best defense against communism.'

## Giving birth to a new society

It is difficult to imagine a set of projections that go more to the roots of our current crisis. In fact, I venture to say that if, over the nearly 40 years since MLK's assassination, we had been building a movement to make the revolution that he projected, September 11th might have been avoided.

As the Bush administration continues to exploit popular fears to carry out its agenda of military buildup, cutbacks in social programs, and suppression of dissent, we need to tap into King's revolutionary spirit. By internalizing and sharing his concept of love as the readiness to go to any length to restore community, we can help more Americans recognize that the best way to insure our peace and security is not by warring against the 'axis of evil' but through a revolution in our own values and practice. That revolution must include a concept of global citizenship in which the life of an Afghan, Iraqi, North Korean, or Palestinian is as precious as an American's.

Hopeful signs are popping up in cities and communities throughout the country. More than 100 U.S. cities and 400 more around the world have defied the Bush administration's abandonment of the Kyoto Treaty on global warming by devising local initiatives to meet the treaty's goals. Local groups are organizing programs to reduce our dependence on global capitalism by creating more self-reliant economies, including local currencies like the Ithaca dollar and urban agriculture programs. Experiments in education for our young people, such as Detroit Summer and KIDS (Kids Involved in Direct Service), are pioneering self-transforming and structure-transforming community-building programs in our schools from kindergarten through high school.

King constantly pointed out to those in the freedom movement that their refusal to respond in kind to the violence and terrorism of their opponents was increasing their own strength and unity. He reminded them and the world that their goal was not only the right to sit at the front of the bus or to vote, but to give birth to a new society based on more human values. In so doing, he not only empowered those on the front lines, but in the process developed a strategy for transforming a struggle for rights into a struggle that advances the humanity of everyone in the society and thereby brings the beloved community closer to realization. This is what true revolutions are about. They are about redefining our relationships with one another, to the Earth and to the world; about creating a new society in the places and spaces left vacant by the disintegration of the old; about hope, not despair; about saying yes to life and no to war; about finding the courage to love and care for the peoples of the world as we love and care for our own families. King's revolutionary vision is about each of us becoming the change we want to see in the world.

# TESTIMONY BEFORE THE CREDENTIALS COMMITTEE, DEMOCRATIC NATIONAL CONVENTION

Fannie Lou Hamer

1964[1]

*Fannie Lou Hamer's life took a dramatic turn the day she showed up for a mass meeting to learn about voting. It was August 1962 and Hamer, who was forty-four years old, wasn't even sure what a 'mass meeting' was. 'I was just curious to go, so I did,' she said.[2] The meeting was organized by the Student Nonviolent Coordinating Committee (SNCC) and Hamer was told something she'd never heard before: black people had the right to vote.*

*One of twenty children born to a family of sharecroppers in the Mississippi Delta, Hamer grew up picking cotton and cutting corn and attended school through the sixth grade. She married a fellow sharecropper and the two scratched out a living doing hard, menial work on a plantation near Ruleville, Mississippi.*

*According to biographer Sina Dubovoy, when Hamer heard SNCC's presentation, she asked herself, 'What did she really have? Not even security.' A lynching in a nearby town in 1904 had terrorized blacks then, and the ever-present KKK still kept them quiet. As Dubovoy notes, 'The Mississippi Delta was the world's most oppressive place to live if you were black.'[3] Hamer decided on the spot to register to vote. On August 31, 1962, she boarded a bus to Indianola with seventeen others to try to register to vote. The next day she was kicked off the plantation where she had lived and worked for eighteen years. Her husband lost his job, too.*

*Hamer immediately went to work as a field organizer for SNCC. Returning home from a training workshop in June 1963, Hamer's bus was intercepted by policemen. She and two others were taken to jail in Winona, Mississippi, and mercilessly beaten. Hamer suffered permanent damage to her kidneys. After recovering from her injuries, she traveled across the U.S. telling her story. With her genuine, plainspoken style, Hamer raised more money for SNCC than any other member.*

1. Source: https://americanradioworks.publicradio.org/features/sayitplain/flhamer.html
2. Sina Dubovoy, *Civil Rights Leaders: American Profiles.* New York: Facts on File Books, 1997) p. 101.
3. Ibid., 101-12.

*In 1964, with the support of the Mississippi Freedom Democratic Party (MFDP), Hamer ran for Congress. The incumbent was a white man who had been elected to office twelve times. In an interview with the Nation, Hamer said, 'I'm showing the people that a Negro can run for office.' The reporter observed: 'Her deep, powerful voice shakes the air as she sits on the porch or inside, talking to friends, relatives and neighbors who drop by on the one day each week when she is not campaigning. Whatever she is talking about soon becomes an impassioned plea for a change in the system that exploits the Delta Negroes. 'All my life I've been sick and tired,' she shakes her head. 'Now I'm sick and tired of being sick and tired.'⁴ But the MFDP's bid to win a seat at the Atlantic City convention still failed. At the Democratic National Convention in Chicago four years later the MFDP succeeded. On that occasion, Dubovoy recounts, 'Hamer received a thunderous standing ovation when she became the first African American to take her rightful seat as an official delegate at a national-party convention since the Reconstruction period after the Civil War, and the first woman ever from Mississippi.'⁵*

Mr. Chairman, and to the Credentials Committee, my name is Mrs. Fannie Lou Hamer, and I live at 626 East Lafayette Street, Ruleville, Mississippi, Sunflower County, the home of Senator James O. Eastland, and Senator Stennis.

It was the 31st of August in 1962 that eighteen of us traveled twenty-six miles to the county courthouse in Indianola to try to register to become first-class citizens.

We was met in Indianola by policemen, Highway Patrolmen, and they only allowed two of us in to take the literacy test at the time. After we had taken this test and started back to Ruleville, we was held up by the City Police and the State Highway Patrolmen and carried back to Indianola where the bus driver was charged that day with driving a bus the wrong color.

After we paid the fine among us, we continued on to Ruleville, and Reverend Jeff Sunny carried me four miles in the rural area where I had worked as a time-keeper and sharecropper for eighteen years. I was met there by my children, who told me that the plantation owner was angry because I had gone down to try to register.

---

4. Jerry DeMuth, 'Tired of Being Sick and Tired,' Nation, 1 June 1964. Reprinted in *Reporting Civil Rights: Part II: American Journalism 1963-1973*. New York: Penguin, 2003), pp. 99-106./footnote]

    *SNCC had formed the MFDP to expand black voter registration and challenge the legitimacy of the state's all-white Democratic Party. MFDP members arrived at the 1964 Democratic National Convention intent on unseating the official Mississippi delegation or, failing that, getting seated with them. On August 22, 1964, Hamer appeared before the convention's credentials committee and told her story about trying to register to vote in Mississippi. Threatened by the MFDP's presence at the convention, President Lyndon Johnson quickly preempted Hamer's televised testimony with an impromptu press conference. But later that night, Hamer's story was broadcast on all the major networks.*

    *Support came pouring in for the MFDP from across the nation.*[footnote]Clayborne Carson, In *Struggle: SNCC and the Black Awakening of the 1960s*. Cambridge: Harvard University Press, 1981, 124-25.

5. Dubovoy, Op. Cit., 108

After they told me, my husband came, and said the plantation owner was raising Cain because I had tried to register. Before he quit talking the plantation owner came and said, 'Fannie Lou, do you know - did Pap tell you what I said?'

And I said, 'Yes, sir.'

He said, 'Well I mean that.' He said, 'If you don't go down and withdraw your registration, you will have to leave.' Said, 'Then if you go down and withdraw,' said, 'you still might have to go because we are not ready for that in Mississippi.'

And I addressed him and told him and said, 'I didn't try to register for you. I tried to register for myself.'

I had to leave that same night.

On the 10th of September 1962, sixteen bullets was fired into the home of Mr. and Mrs. Robert Tucker for me. That same night two girls were shot in Ruleville, Mississippi. Also Mr. Joe McDonald's house was shot in.

And June the 9th, 1963, I had attended a voter registration workshop; was returning back to Mississippi. Ten of us was traveling by the Continental Trailway bus. When we got to Winona, Mississippi, which is Montgomery County, four of the people got off to use the washroom, and two of the people—to use the restaurant—two of the people wanted to use the washroom.

The four people that had gone in to use the restaurant was ordered out. During this time I was on the bus. But when I looked through the window and saw they had rushed out I got off of the bus to see what had happened. And one of the ladies said, 'It was a State Highway Patrolman and a Chief of Police ordered us out.'

I got back on the bus and one of the persons had used the washroom got back on the bus, too.

As soon as I was seated on the bus, I saw when they began to get the five people in a highway patrolman's car. I stepped off of the bus to see what was happening and somebody screamed from the car that the five workers was in and said, 'Get that one there.' When I went to get in the car, when the man told me I was under arrest, he kicked me.

I was carried to the county jail and put in the booking room. They left some of the people in the booking room and began to place us in cells. I was placed in a cell with a young woman called Miss Ivesta Simpson. After I was placed in the cell I began to hear sounds of licks and screams, I could hear the sounds of licks and horrible screams. And I could hear somebody say, 'Can you say, "yes, sir", nigger? Can you say "yes, sir"?'

And they would say other horrible names.

She would say, 'Yes, I can say "yes, sir".'

'So, well, say it.'

She said, 'I don't know you well enough.'

They beat her, I don't know how long. And after a while she began to pray, and asked God to have mercy on those people.

And it wasn't too long before three white men came to my cell. One of these men was a State Highway Patrolman and he asked me where I was from. I told him Ruleville and he said, 'We are going to check this.'

They left my cell and it wasn't too long before they came back. He said, 'You are from Ruleville all right,' and he used a curse word. And he said, 'We are going to make you wish you was dead.'

I was carried out of that cell into another cell where they had two Negro prisoners. The State Highway Patrolmen ordered the first Negro to take the blackjack.

The first Negro prisoner ordered me, by orders from the State Highway Patrolman, for me to lay down on a bunk bed on my face.

I laid on my face and the first Negro began to beat. I was beat by the first Negro until he was exhausted. I was holding my hands behind me at that time on my left side, because I suffered from polio when I was six years old.

After the first Negro had beat until he was exhausted, the State Highway Patrolman ordered the second Negro to take the blackjack.

The second Negro began to beat and I began to work my feet, and the State Highway Patrolman ordered the first Negro who had beat me to sit on my feet - to keep me from working my feet. I began to scream and one white man got up and began to beat me in my head and tell me to hush.

One white man - my dress had worked up high - he walked over and pulled my dress - I pulled my dress down and he pulled my dress back up.

I was in jail when Medgar Evers was murdered.

All of this is on account of we want to register, to become first-class citizens. And if the Freedom Democratic Party is not seated now, I question America. Is this America, the land of the free and the home of the brave, where we have to sleep with our telephones off the hooks because our lives be threatened daily, because we want to live as decent human beings, in America?

Thank you.

# 3. SELF-DETERMINATION, SELF-DEFENSE, AND THE RISE OF BLACK POWER

*With the rise of 'Black Power' globally—and the devasting losses of the U.S.-based Black Liberation leadership of iconic figures Minister Malcolm X, Rev. Dr. Martin Luther King, Jr., and many others, questions of self-defense and the long-term feasibility of nonviolence came to the fore in more heated and divisive ways than in previous eras. Much confusion about those divisions, however, continues to confuse organizers and diffuse the power of alternative movements of all tactics, strategies and ideologies. This section's lead piece, however—written by Truth-Telling Project founder David Ragland along with Natalie Jeffers and Matt Meyer—proclaims that the time is now to put 'our grandfathers battles' behind us; there is no reasonable need to choose between Martin and Malcolm, or between the differences they have come to represent which, according to James Cone's essay in the previous section was growing less and less every year. The vital nuances of the late 1960's through 1980's are poignantly explored by those who lived and worked within those forgotten spaces, including Gwendolyn Zoharrah Simmons of the Student Nonviolent Coordinating Committee's influential Atlanta chapter, which first asserted the need for Black leadership in greater specificity; Sally Bermanzohn's historical review about the realities and legacies of violence and nonviolence in the 'civil rights' context; an article on the often conflictual roles of Bayard Rustin; and a little-known exchange between 'Negroes with Guns' author and New Afrikan militant Robert Franklin Williams, Dr. King, and white war resistance leader Dave Dellinger. The section speeds forward to the present day, with commentary from Colin Kaepernick, a dialogue with political prisoner Russell Maroon Shoatz, and a look at the Black Lives Matter and Movement for Black Lives platform work.*

*To get us started, however, is brief commentary from Marielle Fanon, the distinguished daughter of Frantz Fanon—arguably the most important anti-colonial internationalist whose work in psychiatry is often cited as the basic rationale for why the use of violence on the part of the oppressed is a prerequisite for victory. Understanding Frantz Fanon's actual views from an 'insider' perspective, Marielle reflects upon more radical resistance and the need to carefully redefine what the touchstone words of the past mean for our future work ahead.*

—The editors

# THE NEED FOR RADICAL MUTATIONS

Mireille Fanon Mendès-France

I can't really say what Gandhi and Fanon might discuss if they had met today!

But if we consider the strategy characterized as Gandhian, it is one of a peaceful 'resilience.' Whatever the conditions in which one is living, whatever the aggression or domination and suffering one is facing, if one works in peace and with a lot of resilience, it is considered good. For me, it is a liberal way of looking at the world, one more example of the capitalist way of controlling the world. They ask for resilience, and when the imperial power invades Iraq or Afghanistan, their advice to the rest of us is to live in peace! Then they want to teach us what resilience is! I think it is a most aggressive way of thinking about the world, just another application of the 'New World Order'.

At the time of Gandhi, some spoke of 'passive resistance' but now they don't agree. Under the capitalist system, if the people are using resistance, they break the movement and harass those people who are using these methods. That is why I think it is now more a matter of resilience, a new word adopted for a new form of oppression against people fighting for liberation and emancipation.

There are two emblematic cases, the first one from Palestine. After the Second Intifada, all Palestinian activities were labelled as terrorists, and all supporters were asked to change the way they resist. Asking the Palestinians to learn about resilience and not to fight against oppression suggested that resisting oppression was illegitimate and illegal, in a context in which thousands of Palestinians were imprisoned. There was a shift from what we long considered international law, which gives people a right to resist. This desire for 'resilience' over resistance is in some ways an actual violation of international law.

The other example is Haiti, and we can add to that Venezuela and the blockades against Cuba as well. Instead of condemning colonial governments for their theft, former colonies are being asked to pay illegitimate debts. Haiti is emblematic of this: they've had to pay these international 'debts' which is the cause of the current crisis. Haiti is in the hands of gangs and there is no functioning state. The international elite has decided to not support Haiti: 'this country is not important for us, they don't count.' There was no one country asking for restitution of the illegal debt.

If we don't recognize that capitalism was founded on slavery, then we can't understand anything about where we are right now and why peoples of Africa and African descent are marginalized and discriminated against all around the world. Without this fundamental element, you miss the most important thing.

The Trans-Atlantic slave trade and enslavement of Africans was the foundation of the modern capitalist system, as well as of globalization.

We should remember that Black bodies were considered as if we were furniture, property! Even now, Black bodies are still considered as nothing. We can see that particularly in certain countries, but also in the ways in which migrants and immigrants are treated by the former colonizers. In reality, the international community just continues to consider Black, Brown and Asian bodies as 'furniture'—they just make sure that the people have the bare minimum for living and nothing more. This is exactly what they want to have happen in Cuba, Venezuela, etc. Haiti is a perfect example of the paradigm of domination, which is the same Eurocentric domination we have seen all through history. It has been led by modernity and the hierarchy of race.

Even if struggles for independence are mostly behind us, all that people fought for liberation has not fully been achieved. I think that now we are on the agenda to get full emancipation—not just an end to colonial control—and it *has* to be achieved. Therefore, we must think about how not to sacrifice our own emancipation in any way, and if that means it is necessary to use some violence, we have to be very prudent. We are still in the conditions when the United Nations made their resolutions regarding violence and freedom movements regarding the rights of people under colonial (and now we might say neocolonial) control, in order to be fully free. These include the rights to self-defense, to defense of one's land, in some cases to take up arms. We are still in this momentum and movement where, if it is necessary to use a certain kind of violence, we do so by asking for the respect of these UN resolutions.

If one gets an end to colonialism, it does not necessarily mean that the people are all free. Some people still need full liberation, for example with the Palestinian people; they need to get their territorial liberation from the settler-colonial Israel. We must also remember what Fanon said in *The Wretched of the Earth* about the national bourgeoisie. He wrote that if, after independence, you just go forward under and endorse the European model, then you are not free! Freedom and emancipation need a radical decolonial rupture. And this fully decolonial rupture has never been allowed to take place. When this rupture began in some places, the imperial powers came in to destroy it—as in the cases of Lumumba in the Congo, Sankara in Burkina Faso, Biko in South Africa and so on.

So, what now? How to redefine resistance and revolution and decolonization at this moment?

Perhaps we should think more about radical mutations. We must have a complete rupture from the Eurocentric models, for the imperialist order, and these changes cannot be achieved without the liberation and full freedom of all peoples. It cannot be achieved without an end to structural racism and the complete freedom of the African continent. It cannot be achieved without an end to white supremacy and the liberation of all people of African and Indigenous descent everywhere. There must be integration of African people throughout the Diaspora and on the continent. Only then can we hope to break these paradigms of domination and—through radical mutations and rupture from past oppression—build a beautiful world for the future.

# REFUSING TO CHOOSE BETWEEN MARTIN AND MALCOLM: FERGUSON, BLACK LIVES MATTER, AND A NEW NONVIOLENT REVOLUTION

David Ragland; Matt Meyer; and Natalie Jeffers

2016[1]

The triple-threat crisis of racism, militarism and materialism continues to define the American empire: unprecedented levels of racially-biased incarceration, increasingly disempowering and divided educational systems based on race and class, and statistics which show that Blacks are 9 times more likely to be killed by police. Despite a President (in an extraordinary act of self-denial) proclaiming in his final major address that there is no Black America, the evidence suggests that we are living in a particularly dangerous period of time, particularly if you are or know a young person of African descent.

2015 was not only a year of fear, brutality and injustice, it was a year of sustained resistance that honoured not only a strong national Black radical politics of organising, but also helped cultivate a new and thriving, nonviolent international movement for Black Liberation. As we enter 2016, the Movement for Black Lives must navigate itself in uncharted territory and hazardous spaces, but is accompanied by a vigourous knowledge of self, a thriving and committed community of activists and organizers who are cognizant of the need for guiding principles and the creation of a Black Radical national policy platform.

The Movement is malleable – to be shaped and reshaped depending on the needs of both specific moments and long-term, community-based goals. At the core will remain three essential demands: divestment from racist systems and investment in Black communities; community self-control and community-centered decision making; and the creation of alternative Institutions and radical spaces which express and reflect one's right to live freely. These principles are inspired by a re-imagination of what it means to build radical democracy, laid

1. Source: *Counterpunch*. January 18, 2016. https://www.counterpunch.org/2016/01/18/refusing-to-choose-between-martin-and-malcolm-ferguson-black-lives-matter-and-a-new-nonviolent-revolution/

down by a generation of youth organisers like Martin Luther King Jr and Malcolm X, Ella Baker and Fannie Lou Hamer, Kwame Ture and Angela Davis, and so many others.

It is fitting that on Dr. King's 2016 birthday weekend, an intergenerational, intersectional movement of Black radicals and their allies are collectively organising to reclaim the moment, using MLK's tools of nonviolent civil disobedience and direct action to launch a 'Year of Resistance and Resilience.' Coordinated actions taken across the U.S. and the world will ensure that this birthday weekend is understood as a time for visible resistance to current injustices, not simply celebratory affirmations of past victories.

## Building an Affirmation

Black Lives Matter is an ideological and political intervention in a world where Black lives are systematically and intentionally targeted for demise. It is an affirmation of Black folks as human, and an affirmation of our contributions to society, humanity, resilience, and resistance in the face of deadly oppression.

At the root of this movement is a critique of violence. At times this past year, it seemed that the empire commonly known as the U.S.A. has rarely been so divided. Alongside of the social divisions, however, it seems that the rising new movements may, at last, be in the process of uniting different struggles working across the many landscapes of oppression, and uniting philosophical approaches too often used to divide us.

The current movement emerging from the Ferguson uprising, #BlackLivesMatter and other Black Liberation formations have learned from the leaderfocused movements of the past not to rely on single, charismatic, too-often-male leaders that centralize, mainstream or silo organizational life, principles or culture(s). Nevertheless, even though some youth organisers will say 'This Ain't Yo Daddy's Civil Rights Movement,' the philosophical specter of past generations echo through modern debates about strategy and tactics. These include real differences of styles and preferences, including the efficacy of reform versus radical demands, the power of mass civil resistance and nonviolence versus the legitimacy and need for armed self-defense, and the different roles which solidarity and alliance-building can take. These differences, however, have too often been posited as do-or-die dichotomies, falsely suggesting that there is only one path to effective and lasting social change.

## X Vs Jr

The images of Rev. Martin Luther King, Jr. and Minister Malcolm X are rolled out by the movement and their critics in equal measure. They swiftly and elegantly deliver historical visions which slot conveniently into particular, not-always accurate, not-often-useful, historical narratives. One is the Pro-Violence and Revolutionary, the other is Pacifist and Reformist.

We are too often instructed to forget the intersections where their actions, movements and messages met, and there is good reason why we are distracted from connecting these dots: to connect is to find new meaning in cooperation and collaboration between organising groups. Yet, there is much evidence we can draw from that bridge the gap between Martin and Malcolm, including one bright, smiling, brotherly, moment captured when the two men met and shook hands across the divides of their times. That moment – with two men committed to both racial justice and human rights for all, committed to an internationalism which understood the U.S. empire and the struggle of Black folks in a global context, committed to an understanding that tactical differences should never stand in the way of principled unity – beckons us to a 21st Century imperative.

We must REFUSE TO CHOOSE between Martin and Malcolm. This time is our time to reimagine and practice revolutionary nonviolence.

## Rejecting and Accepting the Past

While rejecting the representation of two myopic heteronormative male narratives of liberation, Malcolm and Martin offer a recognizable context to begin a critical conversation about what our Black Liberation past has inspired, and what popular culture can diminish.

Scholarship and common sense have already laid down most of what we need to know. As each of those two giants engaged with the world outside the U.S. borders, they grew in understanding that the problem of the 'Black' world within the U.S. could not be solved merely through U.S. legislative or political remedies, nor through a single ideological or tactical approach. They clearly understood that the reforms of their earlier days would not be sufficient in ridding the U.S. or the world of white supremacy which lay at its very foundation; a revolution – whether of values or of arms or of a combined social resistance – would be needed for true emancipation on a Global, diasporic scale.

There is, of course, a dualism here which we shouldn't simply avoid: armed and nonviolent approaches suggest different types of tactical considerations with likely different results. Missing, though, in almost all past tactical debates, but present in the #BlackLivesMatter movement is the creation of spaces that develop a revolutionary and militant nonviolence mindset and discipline, borne of highly organized mass civil disobedience and resistant direct actions to 'shut down and completely disrupt 'Business as Usual', dismantle racist systems, and transform institutions through acts of self-determination and reparations.

Most historians agree that Malcolm and Martin were killed for beginning to make transnational, strategic, and philosophical connections, and that the FBI's Counter-Intelligence Program which hunted them both continues to this day, though in different names and forms. It continues to seek to 'expose, disrupt, misdirect, discredit, or otherwise neutralize the activities' of all those struggling for Black Liberation.

The U.S. National security state went to outright war against the Black Panthers, their allies, and others who came after, but the spirit of the Panthers marches strong in the minds and on the t-shirts of youth organisers bearing such slogans as 'Assata Taught Me.' It is also in the present, intergenerational radical learning spaces created to facilitate dialogue with the elders of past struggles.

By anchoring to the traditions of Black radical politics, the movement builders of today refuse to perpetuate the continued assassination of Dr. King, burying him in a soft-focused, nostalgic and 'dreamy' 1963. We refuse to end King's story with 'I Have a Dream,' as if he never was a young radical who was imprisoned, beaten and discredited, as if he never grew into a powerful movement leader defying many advisors and funders by speaking out sharply against the war in Vietnam and in favor of economic justice for all. We refuse to go along with state-sponsored attempts to bury Black radicals behind bars as U.S. political prisoners, or in exile with bounties on their heads, and so spotlight the words – sent from Cuba – of Black Liberation Army leader Assata Shakur. Her most recent writing implores us to remember that 'this is the 21st century and we need to redefine r/evolution. this planet needs a people's r/evolution. a humanist r/evolution. r/evolution is not about bloodshed or about going to the mountains and fighting... the fundamental goal of r/evolution must be peace...r/evolution is love.'

In August 1963, as hundreds of thousands were marching on Washington DC to assert that 'jobs and freedom' were still necessary for the descendants of enslaved Africans one hundred years after the end of the Civil War, Martin declared that America had offered Black folks 'a bad check,' one marked 'insufficient funds' in the areas of liberty and justice. On that day, when Malcolm was suggesting that the march itself was a sell-out, a conscious person wanting to take action would have had to make a logistical choice: to go to DC or stay home. A few months later, in Malcolm's 'Message to the Grassroots,' he clarified his differences with the civil rights leadership, and sharpened his own definition of revolution. 'The Black revolution,' he stated, 'is world-wide in scope and in nature. The Black revolution is sweeping Asia, sweeping Africa, rearing its head in Latin America...Revolution overturns and destroys everything that gets in its way...Revolution is based on land.'

More than fifty years since those thunderous messages, we no longer need to make a choice. The mainstream history textbooks would like to freeze-frame Martin in 1963, having his dream and nothing more. They would like to cut Malcolm out altogether, or else freeze him in some internal extremist, Muslim-based, fratricidal debacle. Martin came closer to Malcolm in his concern for what might be described as reparations or redistribution of wealth. Malcolm's attempt to take the U.S. to the United Nations for its violation of human rights offers a glimpse into his strategic, peaceful, coalition thinking, similar to King's gathering of international support and cross-movement, interfaith work.

## New Moments, Nuances, New Movements

Theologian James Cone taught us to look beyond the white-washed images of Malcolm-versus-Martin. Student activist Ashoka Jegroo told us that today's movements need not dichotomize those men as opposing sentinels. Charles

Cobb and Akinyele Umoja and Sally Bermanzohn and others have provided detailed works showing the nuances involved in the real movements of the 1950s, 60s, and 70s, suggesting that today we can and must go beyond false dichotomies.

In 2016, we must do more than simply acknowledge that we need not choose between Martin and Malcolm. To be effective, we must actively engage in the texts of Baldwin and Fanon; Dellinger and Braden; Lee-Boggs, Butler and Lorde; as well as hooks and Abu-Jamal and West. We must learn from a diasporic history of resistance and rebellion, from Haiti, Trinidad and Jamaica; Ghana, Guinea Bissau and Mozambique; Chile, Costa Rica, and Brazil; India, East Timor, and Vietnam, and – yes – the streets of San Juan and Brixton. We must interweave, interconnect and intersect nuanced arguments, achievements and concerns, and be willing to critique and challenge one another as we reimagine society and explore our universe for new suns.

There is much debate about what makes for effective and transformative move-ment-building – on local, national, or transnational scales. This much at least, from the last half-century of history, seems clear: a merger of ideological and tech-nical thinking will be needed, along with full access to and (re)distribution of all natural, material, and human resources. A revolutionary nonviolent praxis will require:

- A combination of reform and more radical measures, leading up to fully transformative and lasting change
- A multiplicity of intersectional strategy and tactics that expand what we consider as nonviolence
- A disciplined understanding and preparation for the fact that casualties and bloodshed occur in all revolutions, and that militarism on the part of revolutionaries is always a costly error
- Massive training for mass organising between social, economic, political and environmental movements, by imaginative, creative, resistance-ori-ented means
- Concrete, grassroots constructive programs, that seek to build new societies and alternative institutions, and that invest in Black communities and the communities of other historically oppressed peoples and nations
- Explicit programs to eradicate white supremacy and hetero-normative patriarchy, with the goal of liberation for all people.

This is not to say that the U.S. today, despite the ebullient mood on some cam-puses, is – to use a favorite phrase of Kwame Ture (aka Stokely Carmichael) – 'ready for revolution.' It IS to say that radicals today, across different struggles and movements, might do well to step carefully around the dividing lines of past decades. We must find intersections and opportunities that exist in these new spaces, building unity where our elders could not. As the U.S. empire shows grow-ing signs of decline, lashing out and closing ranks at anything beyond the 1% rul-ing elite, opportunities for radical change – as well as for vicious backlash and repression – will emerge with growing frequency. Let us not allow our people's movements to be divided, co-opted, or conquered – especially not along historic fault lines so clearly set up to divide and conquer us.

Liberation educator Paulo Freire noted that 'violence is the tool of the master,' and feminist poet Audre Lorde reminded us that 'You cannot dismantle the Master's House with the Master's Tools' So, let us reimagine new ways to build a society where Black people can live freely and dream, and let's find, as Barbara Deming implored, 'equilibrium' in our revolutionary process.

Constantly the hegemonic status quo re-equips to co-opt, capture, and destroy our dissent. Today's movements must not seek to be 'brought into the fold.' The fold can only hold a few, and we no longer want the morphine of acceptance. Let us speak Truth to Empire, like the people of Ferguson and like U.S. political prisoners have been trying to do. It is time to refuse to fight our grandfather's battles, and refuse to be limited by unnecessary past choices and false dichotomies.

It is time to build power, unite, and win!

# POSITION PAPER: THE BASIS OF BLACK POWER

Student Nonviolent Coordinating Committee

---

1966[1]

The myth that the Negro is somehow incapable of liberating himself, is lazy, etc., came out of the American experience. In the books that children read, whites are always 'good' (good symbols are white), blacks are 'evil' or seen as savages in movies, their language is referred to as a 'dialect,' and black people in this country are supposedly descended from savages.

Any white person who comes into the movement has the concepts in his mind about black people, if only subconsciously. He cannot escape them because the whole society has geared his subconscious in that direction.

Miss America coming from Mississippi has a chance to represent all of America, but a black person from either Mississippi or New York will never represent America. Thus the white people coming into the movement cannot relate to the black experience, cannot relate to the word 'black,' cannot relate to the 'nitty gritty,' cannot relate to the experience that brought such a word into existence, cannot relate to chitterlings, hog's head cheese, pig feet, ham hocks, and cannot relate to slavery, because these things are not a part of their experience. They also cannot relate to the black religious experience, nor to the black church, unless, of course, this church has taken on white manifestations.

## White Power

Negroes in this country have never been allowed to organize themselves because of white interference. As a result of this, the stereotype has been reinforced that blacks cannot organize themselves. The white psychology that blacks have to be watched, also reinforces this stereotype. Blacks, in fact, feel intimidated by the presence of whites, because of their knowledge of the power that whites have over

---

their lives. One white person can come into a meeting of black people and change the complexion of that meeting... People would immediately start talking about 'brotherhood,' 'love,' etc.; race would not be discussed.

If people must express themselves freely, there has to be a climate in which they can do this. If blacks feel intimidated by whites, then they are not liable to vent the rage that they feel about whites in the presence of whites—especially not the black people whom we are trying to organize, i.e., the broad masses of black people. A climate has to be created whereby blacks can express themselves. The reasons that whites must be excluded is not that one is anti-white, but because the effects that one is trying to achieve cannot succeed because whites have an intimidating effect. Ofttimes, the intimidating effect is in direct proportion to the amount of degradation that black people have suffered at the hands of white people.

## Roles of Whites and Blacks

It must be offered that white people who desire change in this country should go where that problem (racism) is most manifest. The problem is not in the black community. The white people should go into white communities where the whites have created power for the express purpose of denying blacks human dignity and self-determination. Whites who come into the black community with ideas of change seem to want to absolve the power structure of its responsibility for what it is doing, and saying that change can only come through black unity, which is the worst kind of paternalism. This is not to say that whites have not had an important role in the movement. In the case of Mississippi, their role was very key in that they helped give blacks the right to organize, but that role is now over, and it should be.

People now have the right to picket, the right to give out leaflets, the right to vote, the right to demonstrate, the right to print.

These things which revolve around the right to organize have been accomplished mainly because of the entrance of white people into Mississippi, in the summer of 1964. Since these goals have now been accomplished, whites' role in the movement has now ended. What does it mean if black people, once having the right to organize, are not allowed to organize themselves? It means that blacks' ideas about inferiority are being reinforced. Shouldn't people be able to organize themselves? Blacks should be given this right. Further, white participation means in the eyes of the black community that whites are the 'brains' behind the movement, and that blacks cannot function without whites. This only serves to perpetuate existing attitudes within the existing society, i.e., blacks are 'dumb,' 'unable to take care of business,' etc. Whites are 'smart,' the 'brains' behind the whole thing.

How do blacks relate to other blacks as such? How do we react to Willie Mays as against Mickey Mantle? What is our response to Mays hitting a home run against Mantel performing the same deed? One has to come to the conclusion that it is because of black participation in baseball. Negroes still identify with the

Dodgers because of Jackie Robinson's efforts with the Dodgers. Negroes would instinctively champion all-black teams if they opposed all white or predominantly white teams. The same principle operates for the movement as it does for baseball: a mystique must be created whereby Negroes can identify with the movement.

Thus an all-black project is needed in order for the people to free themselves. This has to exist from the beginning. This relates to what can be called 'coalition politics.' There is no doubt in our minds that some whites are just as disgusted with this system as we are. But it is meaningless to talk about coalition if there is no one to align ourselves with, because of the lack of organization in the white communities. There can be no talk of 'hooking up' unless black people organize blacks and white people organize whites. If these conditions are met, then perhaps at some later date—and if we are going in the same direction—talks about exchange of personnel, coalition, and other meaningful alliances can be discussed.

In the beginning of the movement, we had fallen into a trap whereby we thought that our problems revolved around the right to eat at certain lunch counters or the right to vote, or to organize our communities. We have seen, however, that the problem is much deeper. The problem of this country, as we had seen it, concerned all blacks and all whites and therefore if decisions were left to the young people, then solutions would be arrived at. But this negates the history of black people and whites. We have dealt stringently with the problem of 'Uncle Tom,' but we have not yet gotten around to Simon Legree. We must ask ourselves, who is the real villain—Uncle Tom or Simon Legree? Everybody knows Uncle Tom, but who knows Simon Legree? So what we have now in SNCC is a closed society, a clique. Black people cannot relate to SNCC because of its unrealistic, nonracial atmosphere; denying their experience of America as a racist society. In contrast, the Southern Christian Leadership Conference of Martin Luther King, Jr., has a staff that at least maintains a black facade. The front office is virtually all black, but nobody accuses SCLC of being racist.

If we are to proceed toward true liberation, we must cut ourselves off from white people. We must form our own institutions, credit unions, co-ops, political parties, write our own histories.

To proceed further, let us make some comparisons between the Black Movement of the early 1900s and the movement of the 1960s—i.e., compare the National Association for the advancement of Colored People with SNCC. Whites subverted the Niagara movement (the forerunner of the NAACP) which, at the outset, was an all-black movement. The name of the new organization was also very revealing, in that it presupposed blacks have to advanced to the level of whites. We are now aware that the NAACP has grown reactionary, is controlled by the black power structure itself, and stands as one of the main roadblocks to black freedom. SNCC, by allowing the whites to remain in the organization, can have its efforts subverted in much the same manner, i.e., through having them play important roles such as community organizers, etc. Indigenous leadership cannot be built with whites in the positions they now hold.

These facts do not mean that whites cannot help. They can participate on a voluntary basis. We can contract work out to them, but in no way can they participate on a policy-making level.

## Black Self-Determination

The charge may be made that we are 'racists,' but whites who are sensitive to our problems will realize that we must determine our own destiny.

In an attempt to find a solution to our dilemma, we propose that our organization (SNCC) should be black-staffed, black-controlled, and black-financed. We do not want to fall into a similar dilemma that other civil rights organizations have fallen into. If we continue to rely upon white financial support we will find ourselves entwined in the tentacles of the white power complex that controls this country. It is also important that a black organization (devoid of cultism) be projected to our people so that it can be demonstrated that such organizations are viable.

More and more we see black people in this country being used as a tool of the white liberal establishment. Liberal whites have not begun to address themselves to the real problem of black people in this country—witness their bewilderment, fear, and anxiety when nationalism is mentioned concerning black people. An analysis of the white liberal's reaction to the word 'nationalism' alone reveals a very meaningful attitude of whites of an ideological persuasion toward blacks in this country. It means previous solutions to black problems in this country have been made in the interests of those whites dealing with these problems and not in the best interests of black people in the country. Whites can only subvert our true search and struggles for self-determination, self-identification, and liberation in this country. Reevaluation of the white and black roles must *now* take place so that white no longer designate roles that black people play but rather black people define white people's roles.

Too long have we allowed white people to interpret the importance and meaning of the cultural aspects of our society. We have allowed them to tell us what was good about our Afro-American music, art, and literature. How many black critics do we have on the 'jazz' scene? How can a white person who is not part of the black psyche (except in the oppressor's role) interpret the meaning of the blues to us who are manifestations of the song themselves?

It must be pointed out that on whatever level of contact blacks and whites come together, that meeting or confrontation is not on the level of the blacks but always on the level of the whites. This only means that our everyday contact with whites is a reinforcement of the myth of white supremacy. Whites are the ones who must try to raise themselves to our humanistic level. We are not, after all, the ones who are responsible for a genocidal war in Vietnam; we are not the ones who are responsible for neocolonialism in Africa and Latin America; we are not the ones who held a people in animalistic bondage over 400 years. We reject the American dream as defined by white people and must work to construct an American reality defined by Afro-Americans.

# White Radicals

One of the criticisms of white militants and radicals is that when we view the masses of white people we view the overall reality of America, we view the racism, the bigotry, and the distortion of personality, we view man's inhumanity to man; we view in reality 180 million racists. The sensitive white intellectual and radical who is fighting to bring about change is conscious of this fact, but does not have the courage to admit this. When he admits this reality, then he must also admit his involvement because he is a part of the collective white America. It is only to the extent that he recognizes this that he will be able to change this reality.

Another common concern is, how does the white radical view the black community, and how does he view the poor white community, in terms of organizing? So far, we have found that most white radicals have sought to escape the horrible reality of America by going into the black community and attempting to organize black people while neglecting the organization of their own people's racist communities. How can one clean up someone else's yard when one's own yard is untidy? Again we feel that SNCC and the civil rights movement in general is in many aspects similar to the anticolonial situations in the African and Asian countries. We have the whites in the movement corresponding to the white civil servants and missionaries in the colonial countries who have worked with the colonial people for a long period of time and have developed a paternalistic attitude toward them. The reality of the colonial people taking over their own lives and controlling their own destiny must be faced. Having to move aside and letting the natural process of growth and development take place must be faced.

These views should not be equated with outside influence or outside agitation but should be viewed as the natural process of growth and development within a movement; so that the move by the black militants and SNCC in this direction should be viewed as a turn toward self-determination.

It is very ironic and curious that aware whites in the country can champion anticolonialism in other countries in Africa, Asia, and Latin America, but when black people move toward similar goals of self-determination in this country they are viewed as racists and anti-white by these same progressive whites. In proceeding further, it can be said that this attitude derives from the overall point of view of the white psyche as it concerns the black people. This attitude stems from the era of the slave revolts when every white man was a potential deputy or sheriff or guardian of the state. Because when black people get together among themselves to workout their problems, it becomes a threat to white people, because such meetings were potential slave revolts.

It can be maintained that this attitude or way of thinking has perpetuated itself to this current period and that it is part of the psyche of white people in this country whatever their political persuasion might be. It is part of the white fear-guilt complex resulting from the slave revolts. There have been examples of whites who stated that they can deal with black fellows on an individual basis but become threatened or menaced by the presence of groups of blacks. It can be maintained that this attitude is held by the majority of progressive whites in this country.

## Black Identity

A thorough re-examination must be made by black people concerning the contributions that we have made in shaping this country. If this re-examination and re-evaluation is not made, and black people are not given their proper due and respect, then the antagonisms and contradictions are going to become more and more glaring, more and more intense, until a national explosion may result.

When people attempt to move from these conclusions it would be faulty reasoning to say they are ordered by racism, because, in this country and in the West, racism has functioned as a type of white nationalism when dealing with black people. We all know the habit that this has created throughout the world and particularly among nonwhite people in this country.

Therefore any re-evaluation that we must make will, for the most part, deal with identification. Who are black people, what are black people, what is their relationship to America and the world?

It must be repeated that the whole myth of 'Negro citizenship,' perpetuated by the white elite, has confused the thinking of radical and progressive blacks and whites in this country. The broad masses of black people react to American society in the same manner as colonial peoples react to the West in Africa and Latin America, and had the same relationship—that of the colonized toward the colonizer.

# TRULY HUMAN: SPIRITUAL PATHS IN THE STRUGGLE AGAINST RACISM, MILITARISM, AND MATERIALISM

Gwendolyn Zoharah Simmons

2011[1]

The situation facing people of color, poor people, people without power and influence in the United States and around the world is a deteriorating one that continues to grow worse—in spite of all the talk of progress and technological greatness that we are being bombarded with ... each and every day of our lives. We are facing in our nation tremendous forces of greed, avarice, racism, a disregard for people's lives, growing class disparities, and undisguised rampant militarism. We are facing a dire situation, the likes of which we may never have seen before. Since the beginning of this new century, with the events of 9/11 as the initial catalyst, our government and transnational corporations have raided the U.S. treasury, taken away our civil liberties and civil rights, and bankrupted the nation in the name of 'national security.'

Our country is the largest arms manufacturer in the world, and the largest seller of weapons in the world. Every year, a larger percent of the tax share falls on the people of the middle- and lower-income tax brackets, while service and benefits to these people are destroyed. No other 'democratic' country takes as large a portion of its revenue from working people at the lower ends of the spectrum, and as little from persons who have property or high incomes as does the United States: 54 percent of the U.S. budget was spent on the military in 2009, a fact that is often camouflaged by the government and the media and hidden from the public.

What is often hidden from the public's view is the fact that the United States is an imperialist empire maintained by over 150 bases and military installations whose aims are not only military but are there to promote the economic and political objectives of U.S. capitalism. They target countries where there are pop-

1. Simmons, G.Z. 'Truly Human: Spiritual Paths in the Struggle Against Racism, Militarism, and Materialism'. in *We Have Not Been Moved: Resisting Racism and Militarism in 21st Century America.* New York: War Resisters League, pp. 347-360

ular resistance movements directed against U.S. interests. The Pentagon owns 854,441 different buildings and equipment spread over thirty million acres, making it one of the largest landowners in the world. It takes 1,332,300 persons to run all the Pentagon's military bases and instillations. When we hear the phrase, 'the U.S. is the sole superpower,' we must understand what this means. Among other things it means that the United States has control over most UN member governments, and the conquest, control or supervision of the various regions of the world which fall under one of its several military command centers located both inside the United States and at several sites around the world. The United States has built fourteen new bases in seven countries in and around the Persian Gulf since 9/11. Additionally, the government has constructed twenty installations in Iraq including the largest embassy in the world in Baghdad. Out of sight of most citizens, the government is expanding or building bases or installations in Algeria, Australia, Brazil, Czech Republic, Djibouti, France, Ghana, Italy, Kirghizstan, Mali, Morocco, Poland, Tajikistan, and Uzbekistan. Overall, the plan is to have a string of installations located in a west-to-east corridor extending from Colombia in South America to North Africa, the Near East, Central Asia to the Philippines. To pay for all this military might, our government spends more than $1.2 trillion a year.

We can see that Dr. Martin Luther King's statement that the United States has become the 'greatest purveyor of violence in the world' is more prophetic than ever.

It has become clearer than ever that those of us who oppose the role our government is playing in the world must work harder than ever before to change its course. We must organize peace and justice movements stronger than any we have built in the past. In order to alter the path of our country, we must change our country and ourselves. We must affirm that we have no desire to continue as the sole superpower in the world at such a horrific cost to our citizens and others. We oppose using military might to bend the world to the dictates of the monied elites who are the beneficiaries of U.S. imperial projections of power. We must work for true peace, which requires both institutional justice and individual spiritual change. It is from this framework that I will explain some of my own journey, as a Muslim peace and justice activist and academic.

◊

I first became involved in the student sit-in movement in 1962, as a freshman at Spelman College in Atlanta, Georgia. In 1964, I joined with a thousand other mostly college-aged volunteers who journeyed to Mississippi to participate in the Mississippi Summer Project. That summer finally put Mississippi on the nation's radar screen as one of the worst—if not the worst—state in the union for African American people. We volunteers, most of whom were white and middle class, made our country acknowledge what had been largely ignored by the politicians and business leaders in this, the mythical 'land of the free and home of the brave.' Our nation, that shining beacon of democracy, had some dirty little secrets that the Project exposed to the world during the summer of 1964. Those secrets included the denial of the franchise to Black Americans, the literal entrapment of thousands of Blacks in a sharecropping system (which was just a bit better than slavery), and the daily fear and terror under which Blacks lived (caused by lynching, beatings, cross burnings, false arrests and the like). As fate would have it, I became one of a very few female project directors that summer when I was unexpectedly appointed director of the Laurel, Mississippi Project. A veteran Student Nonviolent Coordinating Committee (SNCC) field worker, Lester McKinney, had been assigned the task but was arrested shortly after our small crew of three arrived in Laurel and set up the Project, leaving me and my first-time-in-the-South comrade, James Garrett, to continue our work.

Neither of us had ever set foot in Mississippi before, but at least I was from the South (Memphis, Tennessee), and there was a saying when I grew up: that the Mississippi Delta began on the main street in Memphis, Tennessee. Plus, SNCC folks in Atlanta knew me. I had been one of the student agitators from the Atlanta University complex, had served on SNCC's Coordinating Committee, and had been to jail a few times. But this was hardly a resume for leading a project in Mississippi, where everyone's life was literally on the line twenty-four hours a day, seven days a week. Nonetheless, James Forman—the executive director of SNCC—didn't have anyone else to replace McKinney, so he told me to hold down the fort until he could send a more seasoned field worker to take over. Given that I was already scared to death by just being in Mississippi, I was not happy to be given the assignment. By the grace of God, Garrett and I, along with the twenty-three other volunteers who joined us that summer, survived the summer alive and accomplished the Project goals in spite of the frequent attacks from the white establishment and the Ku Klux Klan types who dogged our steps at every turn. Six of us remained in Laurel for another thirteen months after the summer ended. We continued our Freedom Schools, as well as our organizing of the Laurel chapter of the Mississippi Freedom Democratic Party and held mock voter registrations and mock elections in support of the Project's efforts to get the federal government to ensure the vote for Black Mississippians.

During my time in Laurel, some of the SNCC women from across the South began to challenge the authoritarian male leadership and rampant sexism in SNCC and the other civil rights organizations. I joined these women in several gatherings and was exposed for the first time to feminist thought. While the theory was new, the beliefs and actions were not. I realized that my grandmother, Rhoda Bell Douglass who raised me, and my closest aunts, Jessie Neal Hudson and Ollie B. Smith, were feminists—as were many of the strong women in the church of my upbringing, the Gospel Temple Missionary Baptist Church. It was from them that I had learned so many of the organizational and leadership skills that would be necessary in my future life. These women stood up for themselves against so many odds. They had respect for themselves and their abilities to make a way out of no way. They were the backbone of our churches and our communities; without them the Black community would not have survived.

After leaving my work as project director in Laurel, Mississippi, I became a participant in and architect of the Black Power wing of SNCC as a founding member of its Atlanta Project—the organization's first truly urban field project.

The beginnings of a theory and rationale for Black Power were first developed in the Atlanta Project. We wrote 'A Position Paper on Race,' which we presented to the whole organization (and which appeared, in full, in the *New York Times*—labeled as SNCC's position paper for Black Power). The following is a brief excerpt from the position paper, in which we explained our Call for SNCC to become an all-Black organization. This was, one should remember, post–Mississippi Summer, when SNCC had become a much more racially integrated organization as several summer volunteers opted not to return home effectively becoming SNCC field staff. The Atlanta office staff was at least half white at the time we issued our paper.

> [We] believe that the form of white participation as practiced in the past is now obsolete.
>
> Some of our reasons are as follows:
>
> ○ The inability of whites to relate to the cultural aspects of Black society;
> ○ Attitudes that whites consciously or unconsciously bring to Black communities about themselves (Western superiority) and about Black people (paternalism);
> ○ [White] inability to shatter white-sponsored community myths of Black inferiority and self-negation;
> ○ The unwillingness of whites to deal with the roots of racism that lie within the white community;
> ○ Whites, though individually liberal, are symbols of oppression to the Black community—due to the collective power that whites have over Black lives.
>
> Because of these reasons ... we advocate a conscious change in the role of whites, which will be in tune with the developing self-consciousness and self-assertion of the Afro-American people.

Many of our white colleagues saw this statement as a slap in the face; a number of the Black members also disagreed, thus causing the organization to practically split in two over the issue of the role of whites in SNCC. Tangential to this issue was the development of the Black power thrust within SNCC, which was enunciated by Stokely Carmichael while on a demonstration in Mississippi. The phrase caught on like wildfire and was later embraced as the future thrust and direction of the organization by a slim majority. This was announced to the press—and the rest is history. SNCC's embrace of Black Power caused it to lose much of its white liberal financial support, leading ultimately to its untimely and unfortunate demise.

My formal entry into the peace movement began when SNCC staff's consciousness about the injustice and immorality of the Vietnam War became a major topic of discussion within the organization. SNCC issued a bold statement against the war that all of us who worked in Atlanta took part in drafting. This is an excerpt from that statement:

We believe the United States government has been deceptive in claims of concern for the freedom of the Vietnamese people... We know for the most part that elections in this country in the North as well as in the South, are not free... We question then the ability and even the desire of the U.S. government to guarantee free elections abroad. We maintain that our country's cry of 'preserve freedom in the world' is a hypocritical mask behind which it squashed liberation movements which are not bound and refuse to be bound by the expediency of the U.S. cold war policy.

The statement encouraged people of conscience to resist the draft and work instead to bring freedom and democracy to Black and poor people in this nation. SNCC was the first major civil rights organization to issue a public statement against the Vietnam War. After this statement was issued, I became very involved in the anti-war movement, and with my Atlanta Project co-workers began developing a Black anti-draft effort in Georgia.

SNCC began to falter for many reasons, including dwindling financial support due to its Black Power stance, its anti–Vietnam War position, and the growing tensions within the organization over the role of whites. During this period, several of the Atlanta Project members and I joined the Nation of Islam, under the leadership of the Honorable Elijah Muhammad. I did so out of my growing rage with white America and my evolving belief that white America would never give African Americans justice or equality no matter how much we marched and protested. I had seen so much white hatred, so much local government collusion with the Klan and other white supremacists; I had witnessed up close the federal government's stalling and reneging on promises made, as well as the racism and paternalism of my white liberal colleagues. My belief in Dr. King and his message of 'love your enemy' and 'turn the other cheek' had faltered. At that time, I thought that the only solution was the separation of the races and for America to give African Americans the economic reparations as called for by the Nation. These demands included five contiguous southern states and the necessary funds to build a viable and independent Black nation. I sadly thought at that time that reconciliation between Blacks and whites was an impossibility; the wounds were just too deep. I felt that whites would never admit their wrongs, much less make restitution for their past and current wrongdoings. I really believed at the time that it was only through the separation of the races with reparations could there ever be a just reconciliation between our two communities.

These were some of the major events that shaped my early years in the struggle for racial justice, women's rights, and an end to U.S. imperialism. These events have, of course, played a large part in shaping my current worldview. Much of my knowledge regarding social action and organizing was largely formed through my involvement in these great efforts to right the historic wrongs of our nation and to reshape our nation's collective consciousness of it true history, the good, the bad and the ugly of it. It had been my great fortune to know and work with human rights and peace luminaries as well as the largely unknown lieutenants and foot soldiers such as myself. These included Dr. Martin Luther King Jr., Mrs. Fannie Lou Hamer, Congressman John Louis, Miss Ella Baker, Stokely Carmichael, Howard Zinn, Staughton Lynn, Vincent Harding, Bob Moses, James Foreman, Ruby Doris Robinson, the Honorable Elijah Muhammad, and Minister Louis Farrakhan, to name just a few. The list of those who helped to shape and mold me in these crucibles of struggle is long, and I am grateful to have been touched by them all.

While I turned my back on the civil rights movement and the theories of nonviolent direct action that undergird it for a time, my post–civil rights experiences have led me back to the teachings of Mahatma Gandhi and Martin Luther King Jr. as the only way out of the cycles of violence and revenge fueling so much of the turmoil in our world today. It has taken me years to truly comprehend the importance of this movement and what it was able to do with a minimum amount of bloodshed and loss of life. It has only been since growing older and being exposed to the many struggles for justice in our world that I have been truly able to appreciate not only the gains but the methodology of the civil rights movement. This was a movement of our time, during the era of violent overthrows of governments, when a minority group that had been racially oppressed and stigmatized for centuries was able to change racist, sexist, anti-people policies and institutions in a region of the country steeped in prejudice, ignorance, tyranny, and violence. Using nonviolent social protests and grassroots organizing, poor people—many of whom were illiterate—took on their state governments, the White Citizens Councils, the Ku Klux Klan, their employers on the plantations and in the mills, and ultimately the federal government. These poorest of the poor, these most despised ones, confronted the mighty institutions of entrenched hatred and oppression armed only with love and faith in God, with a conviction in the justice of their cause and a steadfast determination to change their own lives (and thereby the lives of their oppressors as well). Against all odds, these folks emerged victorious; they changed things and they changed themselves in the process. Most of us who were in that movement can never forget it, because—for a brief time—we experienced a Beloved Community in those towns and hamlets where we worked with people who loved God, loved themselves, and were determined to bring about a change in their own lives and the life of this nation.

It has taken years for me to really understand and appreciate the significance of this nonviolent revolution in which I was involved. I was blinded earlier by my rage and my impatience with the pace of change, and my lack of faith that fundamental change could occur through nonviolent means and the will of the people to overcome oppression. It has taken me many years to see the superiority of change brought about nonviolently versus change engendered through force and violence.

Most of the time, I am thankful to have been born a Black female in the Jim Crow South. Of course, it has taken me a long time to appreciate this fact and even now—given the persistence of racism and sexism in our world—I still feel sad to have to experience the prejudices that come to a person born Black and female in this, the twenty-first century. But when I am in my best mind, I can appreciate my life story because of what I have learned from my personal experiences. It is not the theory of nonviolent direct action that makes the difference for me. It is the practical lessons learned from the experiences of that time. I have seen incredible changes occur in the U.S. South, as well as in other parts of our nation. I teach a class in African American religious traditions, in which we focus on the liberatory role of religion in the African American sojourn from slavery to freedom. It amazes me that none of my students—who are Black, white, Latino, and Asian—can believe that less than forty years ago African American people could not vote in many places in the South, could not eat in white restaurants, or go into the front door of theatres, visit museums, libraries, zoos, amusement parks, or art galleries (except on that one day of the week set aside for 'Coloreds'). They cannot believe that there were white and colored toilets, white and colored water fountains, that Blacks sat in the backs of buses, with 'colored only' and 'white only' cars on trains, that there were segregated and unequal white and colored hospitals and that their beloved University of Florida was all-white by law, or that it was illegal for Blacks and whites to marry or date. It pleases me that they find this information so shocking, so awful, 'so stupid,' as they would say. This shows that the cataclysmic changes caused by the civil rights movement are now an ingrained part of this society, normalized for many if not most of us. It is unthinkable for most Southerners—Black or white—to advocate a return to the overt racism of the past. That would be as unthinkable as reinstituting slavery.

Now, I do not want to suggest that we have reached a racial nirvana in the South, or anywhere else here in the United States. A significant percentage of these same students, most expressly the white ones, oppose affirmative action—believing that it is 'reverse discrimination.' Most, if not all, oppose the idea of reparations for African Americans for past wrongs. But I wanted to point out the positives that grew out of the civil rights struggles, because there are many positives in my own life and in the collective life of our nation. We must hold onto these realities even as we confront the many negatives in our world today. There are huge issues confronting us, which threaten us individually and collectively. Especially since 9/11, for example, an anti-Muslim hysteria has been spreading in a way that harkens back to the bad old days—such that I myself thought long and hard before I informed my neighbors that I was a Muslim.

The second great influence on my own life, beyond my time in the Black-led freedom movement, has been my time as a student, a disciple, and a devotee of the contemporary Sufi Master Sheikh Muhammad Raheem Bawa Muhaiyadeen. It was Bawa (which means father) who initiated me into Sufism, the mystical path in Islam. My years with him radically altered my life—but in a different way than did my work in the civil rights movement. My social justice activist work—then and now—focuses on the needed external changes in the material world. My work on the Sufi path is directed at the internal changes that I need to address if my life is to reach its true destiny. This is the work of becoming *a true human being.* It took me a while to see the relationship between the needed internal changes and the external changes that I had focused upon in my youth. Initially, I even saw the two paths as being in conflict. How could I continue my social change work if I needed to focus all my attention on spiritual development, and changing my inner self from that of an animal in human form to that of a spiritually enlightened person, as mysticism teaches? Sufism teaches us that the true destiny of the human being is to reach a highly exalted state of consciousness, which they refer to as becoming 'God-man/man-God.' My own teacher taught his students that to merge with God, so that one's base qualities are erased and only the qualities of God remain, is the destiny for all of us who have been born in human form. To become a purified human person is our true birthright; this is the belief that Bawa and all Sufis before him taught. It was my duty and the duty of everyone who receives 'the inner call to become truly human' to achieve this state of spiritual consciousness in the time allotted us on this earth.

As we build for nonviolent revolution and the creation of beloved communities, if we are to understand how we can develop peace with justice, we must examine closely the process by which persons, groups, and even nations can become peaceful, harmonious, and restored to equanimity. We must understand how our religious and spiritual beliefs can help to guide us in this process. Of course, we know that there are gruesome things being done by some people to others all the time in our world today. Most of these are the attacks of the powerful against the weak, and many of them invoke religion as the basis for inequity and hate. It's hard not to feel rage about these things.

In addition to the struggles with my government for justice here at home, I have been to some of the hot spots of our world, during or immediately after violent conflict over the last thirty years. I visited Vietnam, Cambodia, and Laos at the end of the Vietnam War and saw the horrific devastation caused by our bombs, our napalm, and our other weapons of destruction we rained down on the people and the infrastructure of those countries. I visited the Cambodian 'killing fields' and saw the mountains of skulls and skeletons interspersed with the deceased's clothing dotted across that devastated and almost empty land—thanks to Pol Pot and his Khmer Rouge soldiers turned into killing machines, many of whom were children under the age of fifteen. I have traveled and lived in the Middle East, and have spent time in Israel and Palestine, and seen the fear and anxiety of the Israelis in Tel Aviv, Haifa, Jerusalem, and in the settlements in the West Bank and Gaza. I have traveled on the 'Settlers Only' roads in an armor-plated Israeli bus, looked at the Israeli 'apartheid wall' crisscrossing and swallowing up Palestinian farmland—built in the name of security, but bringing only more insecurity for the Israelis and hardships for the Palestinians. I have spent time in Palestinian towns and villages—Gaza, Ramallah, Hebron, Bethlehem, and others—waiting at the checkpoints and watching the humiliation of old Palestinian men and women at the hands of Israeli children in the military who police these checkpoints. I have scrambled over barricades made of huge concrete blocks, mounds of dirt and stones blocking vehicle and pedestrian entrances to Palestinian villages. I have waited for hours at the checkpoint in Ramallah trying to enter during the Israeli enforced curfew which locked the town down. I have been in Bethlehem just after the curfew of a week or more has been lifted and watched the men, women, and children dash around madly through the streets in the two or three hour window they had been given to do their shopping, run errands to the pharmacy, see the doctor, or visit a sick relative or friend before the curfew descended again and they are locked in their homes with no idea when they will be permitted to leave again. I have slept in Gaza while the Israeli military planes and helicopters flew overhead, shining menacing spotlights down on the people. I have seen the devastation and disruption of Palestinian life and lands at the hands of the Israeli military caused by brutal Occupation.

Given my own experiences in the U.S. with violence and oppression, I am not interested in some sappy so-called reconciliation that does not change the power dynamics between the rich and poor, the oppressed and the oppressor. I am not interested in a 'reconciliation' which enables the powerful to issue a verbal apology for what they have done, feel good about themselves for confessing without giving up any of their power or making social, political or economic restitution for their misdeeds. These so-called reconciliation processes let things continue pretty much as they did before the reconciliation process occurred and therefore the violence of the status quo is left intact—no fundamental change occurs and therefore no real healing occurs, and no real beloved community can be built on a sham.

The first thing that always comes to mind when I hear the people in power say that they long for or even demand peace from those challenging their power and the status quo is 'if you want peace, you must work for justice.' But what is peace; what is justice? As I wanted to share more than my own understanding on this matter, I consulted the words of Gandhi, Martin King, Howard Zinn, Elise Boulding, and others who have written perceptively about this issue to see what guidance they could give.

The inclusion of both parties to the conflict is a must. A peace agreement cannot be reached when one party has little or no respect for their opponent.

It was, after all, Gandhi himself who said: 'I am a man of peace. I believe in peace. But I do not want peace at any price. I do not want the peace that you find in stone; I do not want the peace that you find in the grave; but I do want the peace which you find embedded in the human breast, which is exposed to the arrows of the whole world, but which is protected from all harm by the power of almighty God.'

Physical violence often grows in a culture of sexual and emotional violence; it goes hand and hand with the abuse of alcohol or other drugs. There are violent upheavals caused by industrial strife. Rape and pillage of the land continues unabated; racial prejudice and other forms of ethnic violence present another form of violence. What causes this violence, which is so ubiquitous in many places in the world today? Howard Zehr, the internationally known Mennonite writer whom some call a prophet of restorative justice has noted that 'at the heart of most violence is disrespect.' I certainly agree with this given my experiences with racial violence in the South. During the civil rights struggle, it was evident that those white officials and laypersons who attacked us not only hated us with a vengeance but also held us in contempt. They had no respect for us as fellow citizens or even as human beings. Any effort to enact a culture of peace and the building of beloved communities requires respect for other peoples, respect for their and our own forebears and future generations, respect for other ways of thinking, respect for creation, and self-respect.

As we analyze the anti-justice and anti-peace forces in our world today, many of us feel like Karen Horst Cobb—who spoke out against the nurturance of revenge and vengeance, often promoted in the name of Christianity in our country. In her article 'No Longer a Christian,' Cobb cited Ephesians 6:12, saying, 'We are not wrestling against flesh, but against powers and principalities and spiritual wickedness in high places.' Bawa describes these powers and principalities in this way:

These evil qualities are our only enemy if we truly understand things. Sufism teaches that one cannot find peace within until one engages in this war within. What I have learned is that while I am fighting the internal demons within I must also labor in my neighborhood, my community, my nation, and in my world to change the social and economic injustices and to work for peace and to build beloved communities in my neighborhood and lend to its building in our world. Our physical survival is at stake.

Dr. King would agree. He said in a sermon:

> I do not minimize the complexity of the problems that need to be faced in achieving disarmament and peace. But I am convinced that we shall not have the will, the courage, and the insight to deal with such matters unless in this field we are prepared to undergo a mental and spiritual reevaluation, a change of focus which will enable us to see that the things that seem most real and powerful are indeed unreal and have come under a sentence of death. It is not enough to say, 'We must not wage war.' It is necessary to love peace and sacrifice for it. We must concentrate not merely on the eradication of war but on the affirmation of peace.

My friend and colleague Dr. Farid Esack, a South African Qur'anic scholar and progressive Muslim, has written a wonderful book, *On Being a Muslim*. In it, Farid asks: 'How does our faith manifest itself in socially relevant terms?' Is our religion a Sunday-only affair if you are a Christian, or a Friday-only religion if you are Muslim? He also asks, 'How can we be witnesses for God in an unjust society? How do we join with others in our religious communities in a commitment to establish a just order on earth?' Esack believes that God's goal, according to the teachings of Islam, is nothing less than the creation of a nonracist, nonsexist, noneconomic exploitative society. And Dr. King might add: 'Any religion that professes to be concerned with the souls of men and is not concerned with the slums that damn them, the economic conditions that strangle them, and the social conditions that cripple them is a dry as dust religion. Such a religion is . . . an opiate of the people.'

We people who seek peace and the building of beloved communities must intensify our actions right now. On February 4, 1968, only two months before King was gunned down by an assassin's bullets, he gave the sermon at Ebenezer Baptist Church titled *The Drum Major Instinct* in which he condemned racism, economic exploitation, and militarism as the interrelated triple evils that face all contemporary seekers of justice. Dr. King knew that in order to eliminate one of these triple evils, it was necessary to eliminate them all. We must remember that at the end of his life, King called for an economic Bill of Rights of the Disadvantaged; his final Poor People's Campaign would have united African American, Native American, Latinos, and poor Euro-Americans. Today, Farid Esack urges all people of faith to be committed to struggling against everything that works against the dignity of all people—including racism, sexism, homophobia, and poverty. If we truly believe that God created all human beings in his/her image, then we should be committed to eliminating those things that dehumanize. In Islam, there is the belief that men and women are vicegerents (deputies) of God who were given an *amanah* (trust) by God to care for ourselves and the entire creation. Each human and all of nature have been put into each of our trust by God to be the caretakers over this magnificent creation.

When we change ourselves, we change the world. Personal transformation is a necessary element in our ability to fundamentally change the injustices in our world. As peace studies pioneer and Quaker Elise Boulding said, if we cannot imagine a peaceful world, then we cannot work to bring it into existence. Bawa, in his book *Islam and World Peace*, wrote on the prerequisites for establishing peace and ending conflict. He stated:

> We must remove all the differences that separate us from God and our fellow humans.
> ... We must fight against our tendencies toward separations of my race/your race, my country/your country/my religion/your religion. We must wage a holy war against our own evil qualities.'

And what, then, must we work for? We have to stop the elites from using the race card against us. We have to struggle together for a just peace, which must include:

- Universal health care for all, which must include full medical and dental coverage;
- An end to homelessness by any means necessary, including massive construction programs for low-cost, decent housing, subsidized housing, housing vouchers, or other innovative ways of providing housing for all;
- A guaranteed living wage for all workers, with government-subsidized quality day care for all children, and an end to all unemployment; and
- Quality public education for all, not just the wealthy, including culturally competent curriculum, critical inquiry, skills-based learning environments with respect, and protected rights for students, teachers, parents, and community members.

These are the major issues that I would like to see a reinvigorated people's movement fight for and win!

Finally, the best shield against war, terrorism, and violence in general is economic justice for all the peoples of the world. The United States, Europe, and all the multinational corporate fat cats everywhere must share the wealth and technology with the people of the global South. After all, the foundation for that wealth was built on the stealing of Indigenous land, the Atlantic Slave Trade, and the theft of the material resources of Africa, Asia and the Pacific, South America and the Caribbean, and the Middle Eastern world. Never have the armies of the North brought peace, prosperity or democracy to people of Africa, Asia, or Latin America. If, as Dr. King wrote, justice is really 'love in application,' then surely it is time to muster up the spiritual love we so easily talk about in our own religious and social inner circles and forge a unified love-force powerful enough to end the triple evils of our era.

# ARE PACIFISTS WILLING TO BE NEGROES? A DIALOGUE ON FIGHTING RACISM AND MILITARISM, USING NONVIOLENCE AND ARMED STRUGGLE

Dave Dellinger; Robert Franklin Williams; Martin Luther King, Jr; and Dorothy Day

1960[1]

## Dave Dellinger:

Robert F. Williams makes a strong case for a negative answer to the question many Negroes are asking these days: can Negroes afford to be nonviolent? The Montgomery bus protest, which was once hailed as a portent of greater victories to come, is fast becoming an icon for pacifist devotions. In Alabama and Mississippi, in North Carolina and Virginia, in Little Rock and Tallahassee, the organized movement for liberation is almost at a standstill. In almost any southern town, the individual Negro who dares to assert his dignity as a human being in concrete relationships of everyday life rather than in the sanctuary of the pulpit is in danger of meeting the fate of Mack Parker or Emmett Till.

In such a situation, it would be arrogant for us to criticize Robert Williams for arming in defense of himself and his neighbors. Gandhi once said that although nonviolence is the best method of resistance to evil, it is better for persons who have not yet attained the capacity for nonviolence to resist violently than not resist at all. Since we have failed to reach the level of effective resistance, we can hardly condemn those who have not embraced nonviolence. Nonviolence without resistance to evil is like a soul without a body. Perhaps it has some meaning in heaven but not in the world we live in. At this point, we should be more

1. Martínez, Elizabeth 'Betita', Matt Meyer and Mandy Carter. Eds. 2012. *We Have Not Been Moved: Resisting Racism and Militarism in 21st Century America*. Oakland, CA: PM Press: 21-33.

concerned with our own failure as pacifists to help spread the kind of action undertaken in Montgomery than with the failures of persons like Williams who, in many cases, are the only ones who stand between an individual Negro and a marauding Klan.

When nonviolence works, as it sometimes does against seemingly hopeless odds, it succeeds by disarming its opponents. It does this through intensive application of the insight that our worst enemy is actually a friend in disguise. The nonviolent resister identifies so closely with his opponent that he feels his problems as if they were his own, and is therefore unable to hate or hurt him, even in self-defense. This inability to injure an aggressor, even at the risk of one's own life, is based not on a denial of the self in obedience to some external ethical command, but on an extension of the self to include one's adversary. 'Any man's death diminishes me.'

But it is a perversion of nonviolence to identify only with the aggressor and not with his victims. The failure of pacifists with respect to the South has been our failure to identify with a 'screaming Mack Parker' or with any of the oppressed and intimidated Negroes. Like the liberals, we have made a 'token' identification to the point of feeling indignant at lynching and racist oppression, but we have not identified ourselves with the victims to the point where we feel the hurts as if they were our own. It is difficult to say what we would be doing now if Emmett Till had been our own son, or if other members of our family were presently living in the south under the daily humiliation suffered by Negroes. But it is a good bet that we would not be in our present state of lethargy. We would not find it so easy to ask them to be patient and long-suffering and nonviolent in the face of our own failure to launch a positive nonviolent campaign for protection and liberation. The real question today is not can Negroes afford to be pacifists, but are pacifists willing to be Negroes?

This question is particularly pointed in the South, and those of us who live in the North should not feel overconfident as to how we would act if we lived there. But the tragic fact is that in the South, the bulk of the members of the Society of Friends and of other pacifist groups live down to the rules of segregation much as other people do... So long as this pattern is maintained, a temporary absence of overt violence only means the appearance of peace when there is no peace. Human beings must love one another, or they will learn to hate one another. Segregation is incompatible with love. Sooner or later, segregation must erupt into violence, and those white persons who conform to the practice of segregation are as surely responsible as those of either color who bring out the guns.

Robert Williams makes a bad mistake when he implies that the only alternative to violence is the approach of the 'cringing, begging Negro ministers,' who appealed to the city for protection and then retired in defeat. The power of the police, as the power of the F.B.I., the courts, and the federal government is rooted in violence. The fact that the violence does not always come into bloody play does not alter the fact that the power of the government is not the integrating power of love but the disintegrating power of guns and prisons. Unfortunately, too many of those who hailed the precedent of the Montgomery bus protest have turned away from its example and have been carrying on the fight in the courts or by appeals to legislators and judges.

In Montgomery, it was Rosa Parks, Martin King and their comrades who went to jail, not the segregationists. The power of the action lay partly in the refusal of the participants to accept defeat when the power of the local government was stacked against them, partly in their refusal to cooperate with the evil practice (riding the segregated buses) and partly in the spirit of dignity and love expressed in the words and actions of King.

Those of us who are white will never experience the indignities that are imposed from birth to burial on our colored brothers. But the least we can do while working for another Montgomery is to refuse to conform to segregation wherever we are… These simple acts of identification and decency could turn out to be more revolutionary than we dare hope.

## Robert Franklin Williams:

In 1954, I was an enlisted man in the U.S. Marine Corps. As a Negro in an integrated unit that was overwhelmingly white, I shall never forget the evening we were lounging in the recreation room watching television as a news bulletin flashed on the screen. This was the historic Supreme Court decision that segregation in the public schools is unconstitutional. Because of the interracial atmosphere, there was no vocal comment. There was for a while complete silence. I never knew how the Southern white boys felt about this bulletin. Perhaps I never will, but for myself, my inner emotions must have been approximate to the Negro slaves' when they first heard about the Emancipation Proclamation. Elation took hold of me so strongly that I found it very difficult to refrain from yielding to an urge of jubilation. I learned later that night that other Negroes in my outfit had felt the same surge of elation.

On this momentous night of May 17, 1954, I felt that at last the government was willing to assert itself on behalf of first-class citizenship, even for Negroes. I experienced a sense of loyalty that I have never felt before. I was sure that this was the beginning of a new era of American democracy. At last, I felt that I was a part of America and that I belonged. That was what I had always wanted, even as a child.

I returned to civilian life in 1955 and the hope I had for Negro liberation faltered. I had returned to a South that was determined to stay the hand of progress at all cost. Acts of violence and words and deeds of hate and spite rose from every quarter. An attitude prevailed that Negroes had a court decree from the 'Communist inspired court,' but the local racist had the means to initiate the old law of the social jungle called Dixie. Since the first Negro slaves arrived in America, the white supremacists have relied on violence as a potent weapon of intimidation to deprive Negroes of their rights. The Southerner is not prone to easy change; therefore the same tactics that proved so successful against Negroes through the years are still being employed today. There is open defiance to law and order throughout the South today. Governor Faubus and the Little Rock campaign was a shining example of the Southern racists' respect for the law of the land and constituted authority.

The State of Virginia is in open defiance of federal authority. States like my native state of North Carolina are submitting to token integration and openly boasting that this is the solution to circumvention of the Supreme Court decisions. The officials of this state brazenly slap themselves on the back for being successful in depriving great numbers of their colored citizens of the rights of first-class citizenship. Yes, after having such short-lived hope, I have become disillusioned about the prospect of a just, democratic-mined government motivated by politicians with high moral standards enforcing the Fourteenth Amendment without the pressure of expediency.

Since my release from the Marine Corps, I could cite many cases of unprovoked violence that have been visited upon my people . . . The Southern brute respects only force. Nonviolence is a very potent weapon when the oppressed is civilized, but nonviolence is no match or repellent for a sadist. I have great respect for the pacifist, that is, for the pure pacifist. I think a pure pacifist is one who resents violence against nations as well as individuals and is courageous enough to speak out against jingoistic governments (including his own) without an air of self-righteousness and pious moral individuality. I am not a pacifist and I am sure that I may safely say that most of my people are not. Passive resistance is a powerful weapon in gaining concessions from oppressors, but I venture to say that if Mack Parker had had an automatic shotgun at his disposal, he could have served as a great deterrent against lynching.

Rev. Martin Luther King is a great and respected leader of our race. The Montgomery bus boycott was a great victory for American democracy. However, most people have confused the issues facing the race. In Montgomery the issue was a matter of struggle for human dignity. Nonviolence is made to order for that type of conflict. While praising the actions of those courageous Negroes who participated in the Montgomery affair, we must not allow the complete aspects of the Negro struggle throughout the South to be taken out of their proper perspective. In a great many localities in the South Negroes are faced with the necessity of combatting savage violence. The struggle is for mere existence. The Negro is in a position of begging for life. There is no lawful deterrent against those who would do him violence. An open declaration of nonviolence, or turn-the-other-cheekism is an invitation that the white racist brutes will certainly honor by brutal attack on cringing, submissive Negroes. It is time for the Negro in the South to reappraise his method of dealing with his ruthless oppressor.

In 1957, the Klan moved into Monroe and Union County (North Carolina). In the beginning we did not notice them much. Their numbers steadily increased to the point wherein the local press reported as many as seventy-five hundred racists massed at one rally. They became so brazen that mile-long motorcades started invading the Negro community. These hooded thugs fired pistols from car windows, screamed, and incessantly blew their automobile horns. On one occasion they caught a Negro woman on the street and tried to force her to dance for them at gun point. She escaped into the night, screaming and hysterical. They forced a Negro merchant to close down his business on direct orders from the Klan. Drivers of cars tried to run Negroes down when seen walking on the streets at night. Negro women were struck with missiles thrown from passing vehicles. Lawlessness was rampant. A Negro doctor was framed on a charge of performing an abortion on a white woman. This doctor, who was vice-president of the NAACP, was placed in a lonely cell in the basement of a jail, although men prisoners are usually confined upstairs. A crowd of white men started congregating around the jail. It is common knowledge that a lynching was averted. We have had he usual threats of the Klan here, but instead of cowing, we organized an armed guard and set up a defense force around the doctor's house. On one occasion, we had to exchange gunfire with the Klan. Each time the Klan came on a raid they were led by police cars. We appealed to the President of the United States to have the Justice Department investigate the police. We appealed to Governor Luther Hodges. All our appeals to constituted law were in vain. Governor Hodges, in an underhanded way, defended the Klan. He publically made a statement, to the press, that I had exaggerated Klan activity in Union County—despite the fact that they were operating openly and had gone so far as to build a Klan clubhouse and advertise meetings in the local press and on the radio.

A group of nonviolent ministers met the city Board of Aldermen and pleaded with them to restrict the Klan from the colored community. The city fathers advised these cringing, begging Negro ministers that the Klan had constitutional rights to meet and organize in the same way as the NAACP. Not having been infected by turn-the-other-cheekism, a group of Negroes who showed a willingness to fight caused the city officials to deprive the Klan of its constitutional rights after local papers told of dangerous incidents between Klansmen and armed Negroes. Klan motorcades have been legally banned from the City of Monroe.

The possibility of tragedy's striking both sides of the tracks has caused a mutual desire to have a peaceful coexistence. The fact that any racial brutality may cause white blood to flow as well as Negro is lessening racial tension. The white bigots are sparing Negroes from brutal attack, not because of a new sense of morality, but because Negroes have adopted a policy of meeting violence with violence.

I think there is enough latitude in the struggle for Negro liberation for the acceptance of diverse tactics and philosophies. There is need for pacifists and nonpacifists. I think each freedom fighter must unselfishly contribute what he has to offer. I have been a soldier and a Marine. I have been trained in the way of violence. Self-defense to a Marine is a reflex action. People like Rev. Martin Luther King have been trained for the pulpit. I think they would be as out of place in a conflict that demanded real violent action as I would be in a pulpit praying for an indifferent God to come down from Heaven and rescue a screaming Mack Parker or Emmett Till from an ungodly howling mob. I believe if we were going to pray, we ought to pass the ammunition while we pray. If we are too pious to kill in our own self-defense, how can we have the heart to ask the Holy God to come down to this violent fray and smite down our enemies?

As a race, we have been praying for three hundred years. The NAACP boasts that it has fought against lynching for fifty years. A fifty year fight without victory is not impressive to me. An unwritten anti-lynch law was written overnight in Monroe. It is strange that so-called Negro leaders have never stopped to think why a simple thing like an anti-lynch law in a supposedly democratic nation is next to impossible to get passed. Surely every citizen in a republic is entitled not to be lynched. To seek an anti-lynch law in the present situation is to seek charity. Individuals and governments are more inclined to do things that promote the general welfare and well-being of the populace. A prejudiced government and a prejudiced people are not going to throw a shield of protection around the very people in the South on whom they vent pent-up hatreds as scapegoats. When white people in the South start needing such a law, we will not even have to wait fifty days to get it.

On May 5, 1959, while president of the Union County branch of the NAACP, I made a statement to the United Press International . . . and I said then what I say now. I believe that Negroes must be willing to defend themselves, their women, their children, and their homes. They must be willing to die and to kill in repelling their assailants. There is no Fourteenth Amendment, no equal protection under the law. Negroes *must* protect themselves . . . The Negro on the street who suffers most is beginning to break out of the harness of the nonviolent race preachers. The fact that the NAACP had to issue a statement saying, 'The NAACP has never condoned mob violence but it firmly supports the right of Negroes individually and collectively to defend their person, their homes and their property from attack' is a strong indication of the sentiment among the masses of Negroes. How can an individual defend his person and property without meeting violence with violence? What the NAACP is advocating now is no more than I had advocated in the first place. I could never advocate that Negroes attack white people indiscriminately. Our branch of the NAACP in Union County is an interracial branch.

It is obvious that the Negro leadership is caught in a terrible dilemma. It is trying to appease both white liberals who want to see Negro liberation given to us in eye-dropper doses and the Negro masses, who are growing impatient and restive under brutal oppression. There is a new Negro coming into manhood on the American scene and an indifferent government must take cognizance of this fact. The Negro is becoming more militant, and pacifism will never be accepted wholeheartedly by the masses of Negroes so long as violence is rampant in Dixie. Even Negroes like King who profess to be pacifists are not pure pacifists and speak proudly of the Negro's role of violence in this violent nation's wars. In a speech at the NAACP convention, he said, 'In spite of all our oppression, we have never turned to a foreign ideology to solve our problems. Communism has never invaded our ranks. And now we are simply saying we want our freedom, we have stood with you in every crisis. For you, America, our sons died in the trenches of France, in the foxholes of Germany, on the beachheads of Italy and in the islands of Japan. And now, America, we are simply asking you to guarantee our freedom.' King may not be willing to partake in expeditions of violence, but he has no compunction about cashing in on the spoils of war. There are too many Negro leaders who are afraid to talk violence against the violent racist and are too weak-kneed to protest the warmongering of the atom-crazed politicians of Washington.

Some Negro leaders have cautioned me that if Negroes fight back, the racist will have cause to exterminate the race. How asinine can one get? This government is in no position to allow mass violence to erupt, let alone allow twenty million Negroes to be exterminated. I am not half so worried about being exterminated as I am about my children growing up under oppression and being mentally twisted out of human proportions.

We live in perilous times in America, and especially in the South. Segregation is an expensive commodity, but liberty and democracy too have their price. So often the purchase check of democracy must be signed in blood. Someone must be willing to pay the price, despite the scoffs from the Uncle Toms. I am told that patience is commendable and that we must never tire of waiting, yet it is instilled at an early age that men who violently and swiftly rise to oppose tyranny are virtuous examples to emulate. I have been taught by my government to fight, and if I find it necessary I shall do just that. All Negroes must learn to fight back, for nowhere in the annals of history does the record show a people delivered from bondage by patience alone.

## Rev. Dr. Martin Luther King Jr. on the Social Organization of Nonviolence:

Paradoxically, the struggle for civil rights has reached a stage of profound crisis, although its outward aspect is distinctly less turbulent and victories of token integration have been won in the hard-resistance areas of Virginia and Arkansas.

The crisis has its origin in a decision rendered by the Supreme Court more than a year ago, which upheld the pupil placement law. Though little noticed then, this decision fundamentally weakened the historic 1954 ruling of the Court. It is imperceptibly becoming the basis of a *de facto* compromise between the powerful contending forces.

The 1954 decision required for effective implementation resolute Federal action supported by mass action to undergird all necessary changes. It is obvious that Federal action by the legislative and executive branches was half-hearted and inadequate. The activity of Negro forces, while heroic in some instances, and impressive in other sporadic situations, lacked consistency and militancy sufficient to fill the void left by government default. The segregationists were swift to seize these advantages, and unrestrained by moral or social conscience, defied the law boldly and brazenly.

The net effect of this social equation has led to the present situation, which is without clear-cut victory for either side. Token integration is a developing pattern. This type of integration is merely an affirmation of a principle without the substance of change.

It is, like the Supreme Court decision, a pronouncement of justice, but by itself does not insure that the millions of Negro children will be educated in conditions of equality. This is not to say that it is without value. It has substantial importance. However, it fundamentally changes the outlook for the whole movement, for it raises the prospect of long, slow change without a predictable end. As we have seen in Northern cities, token integration has become a pattern in many communities and remained frozen, even though environmental attitudes are substantially less hostile to full integration than in the South.

This then is the danger. Full integration can easily become a distant or mythical goal—major integration may long be postponed, and in the quest for social calm a compromise firmly implanted in which the real goals are merely token integration for a long period to come.

The Negro was the tragic victim of another compromise in 1878, when his full equality was bargained away by the Federal Government and a condition somewhat above slave status but short of genuine citizenship became his social and political existence for nearly a century.

There is reason to believe that the Negro of 1959 will not accept supinely any such compromise in the contemporary struggle for integration. His struggle will continue, but the obstacles will determine its specific nature. It is axiomatic in social life that the imposition of frustrations leads to two kinds of reactions. One is the development of a wholesome social organization to resist with effective, firm measures any efforts to impede progress. The other is a confused, anger-motivated drive to strike back violently, to inflict damage. Primarily, it seeks to cause injury to retaliate for wrongful suffering. Secondarily, it seeks real progress. It is punitive—not radical or constructive.

The current calls for violence have their roots in this latter tendency. Here one must be clear that there are three different views on the subject of violence. One is the approach of pure nonviolence, which cannot readily or easily attract large masses, for it requires extraordinary discipline and courage. The second is violence expressed in self-defense, which all societies, from the most primitive to the most cultured and civilized, accept as moral and legal. The principle of self-defense, even involving weapons and bloodshed, has never been condemned, even by Gandhi, who sanctioned it for those unable to master pure nonviolence. The third is the advocacy of violence as a tool of advancement, organized as in warfare, deliberately and consciously. To this tendency many Negroes are being tempted today. There are incalculable perils in this approach. It is not the danger of sacrifice of physical being which is primary, though it cannot be contemplated without a sense of deep concern for human life. The greatest danger is that it will fail to attract Negroes to a real collective struggle, and will confuse the large, uncommitted middle group, which as yet has not supported either side. Further, it will mislead Negroes into the belief that this is the only path and place them as a minority in a position where they confront a far larger adversary than it is possible to defeat in this form of combat. When the Negro uses force in self-defense he does not forfeit support—he may even win it, by the courage and self-respect it reflects. When he seeks to initiate violence he provokes questions about the necessity for it, and inevitably is blamed for its circumstances. It is unfortunately true that however a Negro acts, his struggle will not be free of violence initiated by his enemies, and he will need ample courage and willingness to sacrifice to defeat this manifestation of violence. But if he seeks it and organizes it, he cannot win. Does this leave the Negro without a positive method to advance? Mr. Robert Williams would have us believe that there is no effective and practical alternative.

He argues that we must be cringing and submissive or take up arms. To so place the issue distorts the whole problem. There are other meaningful alternatives.

The Negro people can organize socially to initiate many forms of struggle, which can drive their enemies back without resorting to futile and harmful violence. In the history of the movement for racial advancement, many creative forms have been developed—the mass boycott, sit-down protests and strikes, sit-ins, refusal to pay fines and bail for unjust arrests, mass marches, mass meetings, prayer pilgrimages, etc. Indeed, in Mr. Williams's own community of Monroe, North Carolina, a striking example of collective community action won a significant victory without use of arms or threats of violence. When the police incarcerated a Negro doctor unjustly, the aroused people of Monroe marched to the police station, crowded into its halls and corridors, and refused to leave until their colleague was released. Unable to arrest everyone, the authorities released the doctor and neither side attempted to unleash violence. This experience was related by the doctor who was the intended victim.

There is more power in socially organized masses on the march than there is in guns in the hands of a few desperate men. Our enemies would prefer to deal with a small, armed group rather than with a huge, unarmed but resolute mass of people. However, it is necessary that the mass-action method be persistent and unyielding. Gandhi said the Indian people must 'never let them rest,' referring to the British. He urged them to keep protesting daily and weekly, in a variety of ways. This method inspired and organized the Indian masses and disorganized and demobilized the British. It educates its myriad participants, socially and morally. All history teaches us that like a turbulent ocean beating great cliffs into fragments of rock, the determined movement of people incessantly demanding their rights always disintegrates the old order.

In this form of struggle—noncooperation with evil through mass actions—'never letting them rest'—which offers the more effective road for those who have been tempted and goaded to violence. It needs the bold and the brave because it is not free of danger. It faces the vicious and evil enemies squarely. It requires dedicated people, because it is a backbreaking task to arouse, to organize, and to educate tens of thousands for disciplined, sustained action. From this form of struggle more emerges that is permanent and damaging to the enemy than from a few acts of organized violence.

Our present necessity is to cease our internal fighting and turn outward to the enemy, using every form of mass action yet known—create new forms—and resolve never to let them rest. This is the social lever, which will force open the door to freedom. Our powerful weapons are the voices, the feet, and the bodies of dedicated, united people, moving without rest toward a just goal. Greater tyrants than Southern segregationists have been subdued and defeated by this form of struggle. We have not yet used it, and it would be tragic if we spurn it because we have failed to perceive its dynamic strength and power.

I am reluctant to inject a personal defense against charges by Mr. Williams that I am inconsistent in my struggle against war and too weak-kneed to protest nuclear war. Merely to set the record straight, may I state that repeatedly, in public addresses and in my writings, I have unequivocally declared my hatred for this most colossal of all evils and I have condemned any organizer of war, regardless of his rank or nationality. I have signed numerous statements with other Americans condemning nuclear testing and have authorized publication of my name in advertisements appearing in the largest circulation newspapers in the country, without concern that it was then 'unpopular' to so speak out.

## Dorothy Day (writing in 1962):

The first people who came to see me the day I arrived in Cuba were Robert and Mabel Williams, exiles from the United States, and wanted by the FBI... Robert Williams came to the attention of the public some years ago as local representative of the NAACP, when he urged that the Negroes arm themselves and use man's natural right to defend himself. His lawyer, Conrad Lynn, is an old friend of the *Catholic Worker* and well known in legal circles for his defense of the Puerto Rican Nationalists. Conrad was the first lawyer to come to our defense when the first twenty-eight pacifists were arrested in 1955 for refusing to take shelter during an air raid drill, on the grounds that such drills are acts of psychological warfare. In the late 1940s, he had defended a group that included Irene Mary Naughton, one of our editors, when they were arrested at Palisades Park, New Jersey, where Negroes were not permitted to use the swimming pool.

Williams's case has interested me from the beginning, because I have felt that he was merely advocating what the Catholic Church in its theology permitted: 'the right of a man to defend his life,' an argument which is used in all debates about pacifism. (But all Catholics as well as others become pacifists of a kind in regard to racial and class war and it is a false patriotism and nationalism, which plunge them into armed resistance.) Williams keeps pointing out that since the colored have armed themselves under his leadership in Union County, there has been no violence, no lynching, as there have been in other parts of the South.

While we talked, he showed me two news releases from the Student Nonviolent Coordinating Committee of Atlanta, Georgia, distributed by the Southern Conference Educational Fund of Louisville, Kentucky. The first story was a protest against the killing of an unidentified Negro discovered in Goodman, Mississippi, on September 13 of this year in the Big Black River, his body in a sack weighted down with one hundred pounds of rocks . . . In Ruleville, Mississippi, the second news release told of two young Negro women active in registering Negroes to vote who were shot in the head, arms, and legs by bullets from a shotgun fired from a speeding car. (I was shot in this way at Koinonia Farm, Americus, Georgia in the mid-fifties, when a few editors of the *Catholic Worker* took turns going down to visit the Christian interracial community started by Clarence Jordan some years ago.)

Williams's contention is that a man has a right and a duty to defend himself, and that if it is known that a Negro will defend the life of his family and himself by shooting, there will be fewer attacks instigated by the White Citizens Council and the Ku Klux Klan...

There is no racial discrimination in Cuba, where 35 percent of the population is Negro and there has always been intermarriage. Negroes have held high political office and rank in the army, even when they were not accepted socially. There were kinds of discrimination, in the past, probably based on degree of color, education, and financial status. But with the revolution, the accent is on 'all men are brothers.'

The case of Williams became a *cause celebre* in the Negro press in the United States and also in the Cuban press, and the family was offered occupation and hospitality at the Hotel Capri, one of the largest hotels of Cuba, in the Vedado district. Here they have two big rooms, overlooking the ocean. On a clear day they can see on the horizon, four miles out, the American warship *Oxford*, and sometimes others. People are always gazing from stone walls that border the Malecon, which is the drive along the ocean, and pointing out to one another the ever present American threat four miles out of the harbor.

I talked to the Williams in their two-room apartment all one afternoon, on another occasion. He is a big man with a beard and he has a soft and gentle face. It was hard to think of him harboring hatred. But the present situation has been building up for many years. He has been in Havana now for more than one year. The Hotel Capri is an expensive place, but I am sure they long for their own home. The children are going to a special school, a boarding school that is run outside Havana for the children of repatriates born in the United States who speak English and have little knowledge of Spanish. Cuba is a paradise for children, where everyone is thinking of them and their needs. Mabel is studying Spanish, but Robert is finding it hard to learn a new tongue. He is filled with his own work besides, which takes a good deal of his time, getting out an exile's edition of the *Crusader*, a little paper which he used to mimeograph in Monroe, North Carolina, but is now printed in Havana and which he is having a hard time circulating in the United States.

William Worthy, the journalist from the *Baltimore Afro-American*, who was recently sentenced to three months in jail for visiting Cuba without a U.S. passport, and is currently out on bail, had given me a shopping bag filled with Afro-American papers and gifts of toilet articles, medicines and candy for his friend Williams. We exchanged news, mine being about Bill Worthy whom I had seen a few days before at dinner, the night before I sailed, and Williams telling me of his difficulties getting his paper out.

I have the greatest admiration for Robert Williams, the exile, forced out of his own country with threats against his life merely because he was asserting man's essential dignity, and his right to defend his life. It is a natural right, as taught by the Church, and it is only because of the life of grace, opened to us by the coming of Jesus, that we hold to our pacifist stand throughout race war, class war and every other type of war. As a pacifist, and my pacifism is based on the teachings of the Sermon on the Mount, I must accept the supernatural point of view and the idea that absolute pacifism is to be aimed at.

The teaching of the Church has always been that man has a natural right to defend his life. Many are called but few are chosen, one might say, to turn the other cheek in such a way that it mitigates wrath rather than increases it. Few can love even their brothers, their closest associates, without the help of grace. Everyone speaks of the ease with which we can love the masses, the people, and be hostile or indifferent to our neighbor, pass on the other side as the priest and Levite did. 'And how can we love God whom we don't see if we do not love our brother whom we do see?' It seems to me that this is the whole teaching of the Church, and the working out of love of brother in the building up of a new social order.

We have long been confronted with the problem of pacifism in such a social order as the one we live in with its race prejudices. Certainly it does not work out unless we are getting down to the roots, trying to change all those things that make for war—poverty, class hatred, race hatred. Pacifism is impossible unless we are ready to give up our lives in order to save them. 'For he who would save his life will lose it; but he who loses his life for my sake will save it. For what doth it profit a man if he gain the whole world, but ruin or lose himself?' (Luke 9.24.)

Williams is, or rather he was, a Unitarian; and his wife Mabel was a Catholic. Neither profess any religion now. Those who said 'Lord, Lord' also had tried to kill them, and they have had a lifetime of seeing their brothers discriminated against, scorned, insulted, tortured.

The battle is still raging about integration, and from his exile Williams listens to the American broadcasts, publishes his little paper the *Crusader* which he tries to get into the States, writes for Cuban magazines and thinks of nothing but his life's battle. He is truly an exile, safe for the time, but his eyes always seem to be on his own country with love and hate and longing.

# BAYARD RUSTIN: A UNIQUE, CLANDESTINE AND ENDURING QUEER LEADER OF THE CIVIL RIGHTS MOVEMENT

Mel Paisley

2018[1]

It feels disingenuous to write less than a novel about Bayard Rustin and call it his life's story.

He was the chief architect of the 1963 March on Washington, integrated all-white labor unions, and helped streamline the logistics for activating non-violence into a formidable protest strategy in the mid-20th Century.

A sharp, intense, and glaringly brilliant man, Rustin had to balance his immense talent for organization and advocacy with the threat that if he were too visible, his homosexuality, pacifist draft-dodging during WWII, and youthful proximity to the Communist Party would be used by detractors to smear or discredit the Civil Rights Movement. Some of his contemporaries felt that respectability politics made him a liability to the causes he supported, so he worked in the background with little mainstream recognition, sidelined from textbooks and grade school discussions about heroes of the time.

Raised a Quaker by his NAACP Affiliated grandmother, Rustin was exposed to both a conviction for non-violence and a slew of revolutionary activists and thinkers at a young age, via house visits from figures such as Mary McLeod Bethune and W. E. B. Du Bois himself. He joined the Young Communists League while at university in the 1930s, then revoked his allegiance to it in 1941 when they dropped racial equality from their roster of priorities.

He worked as an organizer for the Congress of Racial Equality (CORE) and the Fellowship of Reconciliation (FOR) in the early 1940s, then spent two years in prison as a conscientious objector refusing to fight in the second World War. He was imprisoned again on a grueling North Carolina chain gang with other members of CORE in 1947 after testing out a Supreme Court ruling which claimed

1. Source: Paisley, Mel. "Bayard Rustin: A Unique, Calndestine and Enduring Queer Leader of the Civil Rights Movement." *Wussy.* January 3, 2018. https://www.wussymag.com/all/2018/1/3/bayard-rustin-a-unique-clandestine-and-enduring-queer-leader-of-the-civil-rights-movement

to ban segregation laws on interstate travel. He would serve a third sixty day jail term in 1953 on 'lewd vagrancy' and moral indecency charges after being found having sex with two men in a parked car on a warm Pasadena night.

## Organizing the March on Washington

After their correspondence during the Montgomery Bus Boycotts, Martin Luther King Jr. took on Rustin as a deeply intimate collaborator, friend, and invaluable advisor.

Despite virulent pushback from a minority of other leaders gathered in Harlem's Roosevelt Hotel to discuss the inception of the March on Washington, Rustin was selected as the man to spearhead the organizational effort—so long as he stayed out of the limelight. He had decades of experience in organization, an undeniable mastery of mobilizing activists, and had traveled abroad to work with West African Independence movements in the 1950s. Pulling dizzying hours in a rented out former Harlem church on the corner of West 130th and Lenox Avenue. Rustin was charged to pull together countless threads of logistics, communication, and organizational manpower in the span of two months.

## Relationship to Queer Liberation

A fantastically busy man constantly sidelined for potentially endangering the causes he championed the on basis of his sexuality, it's not surprising that Bayard Rustin didn't become a vocal gay rights activist until the 1980s.

While he was never ashamed of his orientation, according to his partner upon his death, Rustin did decline an invitation to be included in a book about the struggles of out black gay activists, because he felt that he didn't contribute enough to gay rights while he was in the prime of his career in activism, and that he didn't publicly 'come out' so much as was outed involuntarily in the semi-public eye. In 1986, he testified on the behalf of a New York City queer civil liberties law, stating that at that point in his life and experience in human liberties, gay rights had become the new barometer for social change and progress.

# VIOLENCE, NONVIOLENCE AND THE CIVIL RIGHTS MOVEMENT

Sally Bermanzohn

2010[1]

Violence was central to politics during the civil rights era (1950s-1960s) in the United States. For a century following the Civil War, Ku Klux Klan terror and lynch-mob murders had bolstered Southern segregation, and the role of brutality continued during the Civil Rights Movement. Between 1956 and 1966, white supremacists committed more than 1000 documented violent incidents aimed at stopping integration, including bombing, burning, flogging, abduction, castration, and murder. The criminal justice system from the local to the federal government punished few of these crimes. But at the height of the Civil Rights Movement in the mid-1960s, Congress passed significant civil rights laws and the FBI finally acted against the KKK. Violent racists went underground.

How did a grassroots movement achieve such success? Did pure morality win the battle? What was the dynamic between violence, nonviolence and civil rights?

Many historical accounts portray Martin Luther King, Jr. as a saint, and the Civil Rights Movement as a biblical struggle. Coretta Scott King portrayed her slain husband as 'an instrument of a Divine plan and purpose.' Pulitzer prize-winning biographies emphasized biblical themes through their titles, which compared King to Christ (Bearing the Cross by Garrow) and Moses (Parting the Waters by Branch). In contrast, this article analyzes King as a master politician who deeply understood the use of terror by Southern racists, and who developed nonviolent resistance as a practical strategy.

King was not a pure pacifist. As a young man in divinity school he thought that an armed revolt was the only way to end segregation. As an adult he wrote that sometimes violence could be justified if it was the only means of resisting tyranny. In the last years of his life, he spoke out against the U.S. War in Vietnam and in support of (armed) national liberation movements.' King deplored violence for moral reasons, but also because the power structure of the South meant that when violent conflicts occurred, blacks inevitably lost. King knew that gaining the moral upper hand was a practical necessity to gain white liberals' support of the black movement. King and other civil rights leaders skillfully utilized

1. Source: Bermanzohn, Sally Avery. 2000. 'Violence, Nonviolence and the Civil Rights Movement'. *New Political Science*. V. 21. N. 1: 31-48.

the unique factors that were favorable at that time, including the Cold War and spread of television. Understanding the practical side of King allows activists today to learn from him as a strategist.

Many historical accounts belittle the role of violence and ignore one of the Civil Rights Movement's greatest achievements: forcing the state to combat racist violence. For example, the Encyclopedia Britannica fails to mention violence at all in its description of the Civil Rights Movement as

> ... a mass movement starting in the late 1950s that, through the application of nonviolent protest action, broke the pattern of racially segregated public facilities in the South and achieved the most important breakthrough in equal-rights legislation for blacks since the Reconstruction period.'

In contrast, Piven and Cloward in *Poor People's Movements* argue that thwarting racist brutality was the most significant victory of the Civil Rights Movement. They state: 'in the South the deepest meaning of the winning of democratic rights is that the historical primacy of terror as a means of social control has been substantially diminished.' And they criticize scholars, including leftists, for 'the tendency to ignore this gain.'

Getting the state to protect black lives and punish racist murderers dominated the efforts of civil rights groups for most of the 20th century. Ida B. Wells-Barnett told an audience in 1909, 'lynching is color-line murder ... it is a national crime and requires a national remedy.'' That same year, blacks and whites founded the National Association for the Advancement of Colored People (NAACP) which campaigned for federal anti-lynching legislation for six decades. Anti-lynching bills passed the House of Representatives in 1922, 1937, and 1940, but Senate filibusters by Southern Democrats defeated each of them. In 1951, 94 African Americans signed We Charge Genocide, a petition to the United Nations based on the 1948 Genocide Convention. In the 1950s, the Ku Klux Klan grew, as did violence against blacks acting on their constitutional rights. During the Montgomery bus boycott Martin Luther King, Jr. developed nonviolent resistance as a way 'to continue our struggle while coping with the violence it aroused.' A breakthrough occurred in the mid-1960s, at the height of the Civil Rights Movement. In 1964, after the Ku Klux Klan murdered three civil rights activists, President Lyndon Baines Johnson finally ordered the FBI to combat the Klan. In 1968, federal civil rights legislation finally made racist assaults a federal crime. Federal action rippled through state and local law enforcement, in a battle for equal protection.

As Robert Williams wrote in 1962, 'in a civilized society the law is a deterrent against the strong who would take advantage of the weak, but the South is not a civilized society.'

# I. White Violence, Government Complicity, and Black Self-Defense

Until the mid-1960s, the U.S. government allowed racist terror to exist in the South. Lynching is mob murder in defiance of law and established judicial procedures, and after Reconstruction it became commonplace in the South. Between 1882 and 1968, newspapers reported 4742 lynch murders in the U.S.. Seventy-three percent of the victims (3445 individuals) were black. Eighty-one percent (3848) occurred in 12 Southern states.' A lynch tradition cannot exist without the complicity of authorities. Local and state officials, including police, jailers, mayors, and others, often facilitated, or at least did not impede, racist mobs. The U.S. Congress failed to pass anti-lynching legislation. Federal authorities maintained a hands-off policy, viewing racist violence as a matter for Southern states to handle.

The structure of violence varied from place to place, varying by tradition and personality of the authorities. In Southern cities, blacks developed their own institutions, including churches and civic organizations that were independent of whites. In the rural South, however, many blacks were economically dependent on whites, and terror continued.

Many southern whites abhorred violence. Thirty thousand women joined the Southern Women for the Prevention of Lynching in the 1930s. Many business leaders opposed lynching because it created a 'bad business climate' and spurred Blacks to migrate to the north. Some political leaders with concerns about their national reputations spoke out against violence but nevertheless allowed it to continue. Whites who advocated for equality of the races could themselves become targeted. Violence threatened everyone who violated the social order.

Washington set the tone of the country's official response to violence. Presidents occasionally spoke out deploring a particular atrocity, but the federal government maintained a hands-off policy from the fall of Reconstruction until 1964. The terror against blacks was considered by national leaders as a problem for state and local authorities.

## Black Self-Defense

Defending one's life is a fundamental human instinct. When government fails to protect people, they will do what they can to protect themselves. Rural African Americans' recourse was self-reliance, defending themselves. Many blacks in the rural South used weapons to hunt and to defend their homes and families. People did not openly discuss armed self-defense, but they widely practiced it. James Forman, a 1960s civil rights leader, wrote about the prevalence of 'self-defense—at least of one's home.' Forman noted that in rural areas 'there was hardly a black home in the South without its shotgun or rifle.'

To analyze the dynamics of violence and armed self-defense, I interviewed African Americans who grew up poor in the rural South before civil rights. Ronnie Johnson, Willena Cannon, and Thomas Anderson gave detailed descriptions of the impact of violence on the lives of their families. Ronnie Johnson comes from a large family in southern Mississippi. He explained that 'behind the front door of every house was a couple of shotguns and rifles. A drawer had shells in it. In the bedroom was another shotgun.' Johnson discussed the elaborate measures his family took to protect themselves:

For my family, the greatest fear was a surprise attack by a group, by the Klan, that would have overwhelming force and drag people from the house. To protect themselves, families like mine tried to have a lot of sons and teach them how to use weapons. My kinfolk lived in houses that were within shouting distance of each other, so they could gather in time of need. Our house was at the end of a long road that led off the main highway, and everyone kept dogs in the yard. By the time anyone got down that road, everybody knew who they were, what they were, and why they were coming. This close network provided a common defense for ordinary occasions. But if a concerted effort came against one family, then it could be a shoot-out.

Blacks' possession of arms deterred white violence. Yet the possession of firearms could not always protect African Americans from violence. A surprise attack by a mob of whites could leave blacks powerless to defend themselves. Willena Cannon grew up in Mullins, South Carolina in the 1940s-1950s, in a share-cropping family. As a child she witnessed the Klan murder of her neighbor. White men lynched her neighbor by trapping him in a barn and setting it on fire. The black man's 'crime' was dating a white woman, a consensual relationship that was well known in the area. Willena, her family and neighbors watched in horror as the white men stopped anyone from saving the man in the barn. As smoke engulfed the building, adults carried Willena and the other small children away. The incident terrorized Willena for years. Thomas Anderson, for his part, made sure that everyone in the county, white and black, knew that he was an expert marksman. His philosophy was 'armed self-defense. You don't go after nobody. But if they come after you, you protect yourself.'

## Tensions Mount in the 1950s

The tensions between racist violence and civil rights increased throughout the 1950s. Black servicemen had fought and died for the U.S. in World War II, yet state laws and terror continued to disenfranchise Southern blacks. As the United States emerged as a global power, it became harder for the federal government to maintain its 'hands-off' policy towards the South. Racist violence and segregation became embarrassing for U.S. foreign policy. In 1954 the Supreme Court found segregated education unconstitutional in a case argued by the NAACP. The unanimous Brown v. Board of Education decision placed the Constitution squarely on the side of black political rights. But the Southern power structure yielded nothing. Across the South, political leaders declared they would defy the Court rather than implement integration. 'Constitution or no Constitution, we will keep segregation in Mississippi,' Governor Ross Barnett declared defiantly. 'I call on every official in the state of Mississippi, every citizen, to use every Constitutional and legal means ...' Then he paused, took a breath, and added emphatically, 'every possible way ...'

Encouraged by the actions of state political leaders, white violence became more audacious. In 1955, two white men in Mississippi killed a 14-year-old boy for 'talking fresh to a white woman.' Unaware of Mississippi's social order, Emmett Till made a fatal error. He was a young teen from Chicago, vacationing with relatives in Mississippi. He told his cousins about his integrated school, and about his friends, including white girls. Then he said 'bye, baby' to a white woman in Mississippi. That night two men took Till from his uncle's home, beat him and threw his battered body into the river. Despite overwhelming evidence, a Mississippi jury (all white men) let the murderers free. The murder of Emmett Till sent shock, fury, and fear through black communities. Ronnie Johnson recalled, 'I never will forget the day they pulled Emmett Till's body out of the river. They found him about a half a mile from where we lived. That night all my aunts and uncles came over to our house. The fear, the whispers, the anticipation: what should we do?'

Till's young age and mild nature of his offense shocked the Johnson family. A few days later, Ronnie's teenage uncle came home from his gas station job covered with blood. A local white man didn't like the way he pumped gas, jumped out of the car, and hit him in the face, breaking his nose. Ronnie's father and uncle grabbed weapons and went to revenge the attack. They knew who the white man was and where he lived but couldn't find him that night. Despite the family network and elaborate methods of self-defense, Mississippi had become too dangerous for Ronnie Johnson's father and mother. Quickly, they picked up and left the state.

The inaction of local and state authorities encouraged the Ku Klux Klan, whose ranks swelled to 50,000 in the early 1960s. Wherever civil rights activity developed, Klan violence followed. Bombing became the weapon of choice, as violent racists targeted the homes of scores of 'uppity' blacks and 'moderate' whites, as well as churches, synagogues, integrated schools, and local government offices. The bomb that killed four little girls in a Birmingham church in 1963 was the 21st bomb in eight years detonated against blacks in that city alone, which became known to many as 'Bombingham.'

As opposition to the KKK grew, white segregationists developed new organizations that attracted more middle-class membership. White Citizens Councils sprang up across the South in the 1950s, holding rallies of up to 10,000 people. Though the Citizens Councils claimed to use economic pressure to stop integration, rather than violence, often their membership and activities overlapped with the Klan (for example, the Alabama Klansmen who castrated the black man were also members of the Citizens Council). Some referred to the Councils as the 'uptown KKK.'

State governments established state agencies dedicated to maintaining segregation. The Mississippi State Sovereignty Commission, from 1956 through 1977, 'used spy tactics, intimidation, false imprisonment, jury tampering and other illegal methods ... to maintain segregation at all costs.' The Commission gathered intelligence on 60,000 people, one out of every 37 people in Mississippi. Arkansas, Louisiana, Alabama and Florida created similar state investigative commissions. In Mississippi, none of the documents released in 1998 showed a direct connection between the Sovereignty Commission and the deaths of civil rights advocates. But the documents do include plans for using violence. For example, there were multiple discussions of 'taking care of' individuals who tried to integrate Mississippi colleges, including having their cars hit by a train or engineering an accident on the highway.

Hovering above the state government efforts to thwart African Americans' civil rights was the FBI. Since its origin in 1908, the FBI had been active in the South, as in the rest of the country. But J. Edgar Hoover, who in headed the Bureau from 1919 to 1972, interpreted his mission as hunting down Communists, weeding out anti-American activity, and not protecting civil rights. In 1939, after 4692 people had died in documented lynchings, Hoover directed the FBI in 1939 to carry out formal investigations of mob murders. However, he opposed federal anti-lynching legislation in a 1956 confidential report to President Eisenhower, because he did not see violence against blacks as a significant problem, and he saw the Civil Rights Movement as led by subversives. Thus the FBI gathered information on violence, but punishment required action by local authorities. Racist violence was not Hoover's concern, and he repeatedly dismissed it as a 'local issue.'

James Forman expressed the view of many activists in the South: 'the FBI was a farce. It wasn't going to arrest any local racists who violate any and all laws on the statute books. Instead it would play a game of taking notes and pictures."

Although no African American was immune to violence, activists received the most threats. Many individual NAACP leaders and lawyers responded by carrying revolvers. Daisy Bates, head of the Arkansas NAACP who led the Little Rock High School desegregation, carried a handgun in her car, and displayed it to scare off white adolescents who threatened her. NAACP lawyers J. L. Chestnut and Orzell Billingsley wore guns as they pursued legal cases in rural Alabama. Vernon Dahmer, president of the Hattiesburg, MS NAACP, died using a shotgun to defend his family and home, after the KKK firebombed it.

When Martin Luther King, Jr. emerged as a leader during the 1955 Montgomery bus boycott, he received the typical response to civil rights activists. His life was threatened, and his home bombed. And in the tradition of the South, after whites firebombed his house, blacks armed themselves and surrounded King's house to protect him.

## II. Martin Luther King, Jr. Developed Nonviolence as a Practical Strategy

How does one fight for equal rights when any action, any small gesture, risks brutal retaliation? Blacks rallied against the Klan in Harlem in 1949, but in the South similar tactics were suicidal. In this fearful environment, NAACP court cases dominated the fight for racial justice. But by the mid-1950s, as Southern politicians flagrantly defied the Supreme Court, many blacks questioned the effectiveness of the legal strategy. For example, Connie Lane, a lifelong resident of Greensboro, North Carolina, was 22 years old when the Court overturned segregation in 1954. But nothing changed for her, and she felt great frustration towards the NAACP, which she described as 'this grand organization, something for the bourgeoisie black folks, the doctors, the lawyers—not for ordinary people, not for me.' She and other African Americans argued over tactics. Was there an alternative to the NAACP's legal strategy? What was the best way to gain equal rights? How could blacks avoid violence directed against them? Anger and fear vied for the upper hand. There were no easy answers.

Martin Luther King, Jr. described the debate in the black community:

> During the fifties, many voices offered substitutes for the tactics of legal recourse. Some called for a colossal blood bath to cleanse the nation's ills ... But the Negro of the South in 1955 assessing the power of the force arrayed against him, could not perceive the slightest prospect of victory in this approach. He was unarmed, unorganized, untrained, disunited, and most important, psychologically and morally unprepared for the deliberate spilling of blood. Although his desperation had prepared him to die for freedom if necessary, he was not willing to commit himself to racial suicide with no prospect of victory.

King grew up in the South, fearful of the Klan and lynch murders. The first time police arrested King, which was during the Montgomery bus boycott, 'panic seized him ... King gave in to visions of nooses and lynch mobs.' King appreciated that blacks' own institutions, their churches, civic groups, schools, were weak compared to the coercive powers arrayed against them. Even where blacks made up a substantial part, or even a majority, of the population, they faced what Morris termed 'the iron fist of Southern government.'

At first, King assumed violence was needed to win equal rights. He wrote, 'when I was in theological school I thought the only way we could solve our problem of segregation was an armed revolt.'' He met pacifists, but felt they had 'an unwarranted optimism concerning man.' He felt many were self-righteous, and he never joined a pacifist organization. Instead, he was searching for a 'realistic pacifism.' Mahatma Gandhi's philosophy sparked King's interest because of his efficacy. According to Gandhi, 'the moral appeal to the heart and conscience is, in the case of human beings, *more effective* than an appeal based on threat of bodily pain or violence.' Gandhi criticized passive nonviolence and advocated aggressive resistance. King felt that Gandhi's philosophy was 'the only *morally and practically* sound method open to oppressed people in their struggle for freedom.' He described Gandhi's nonviolent resistance as 'one of the most potent weapons available.'

It is one thing to study Gandhi in school, and quite another to apply the principles to a different time place and circumstance. Blacks in the American South faced very different conditions than the anti-colonial struggle in India. Would nonviolence work? Or would it just subject black people to more violence? Tactics were a matter of life and death for activists. Many blacks saw nonviolence as passive and ineffectual, as acceptance of the status quo. On the other hand, they realized that any use of arms could be used as an excuse for increased white violence against them. In college and divinity school, King determined through lengthy discussions with his classmates that support from white liberals was possible, if it could be mobilized. Placing the freedom movement on the high moral ground was necessary to gain support outside the black community.

When the Montgomery Bus Boycott put theory to the test, King advocated nonviolence, not passivity. King often used the word 'militant' or 'coercion' to describe their tactics. In one speech, for example, he stated 'not only are we using the tools of persuasion—but we've got to use the tools of coercion.'' He was aggressive in negotiations with the white city leaders, breaking a historical pattern of black leaders caving in because of fear. The boycott continued for a year, and the unity of the black community was remarkable. Unlike court battles that depended on a few brave plaintiffs and their lawyers, the boycott depended for its success on black working people, the maids, the day laborers, every day for a year finding ways other than the bus to get to work.

King struggled deeply within himself to provide nonviolent leadership. He knew that as a leader, he was a target for violent whites. His home was assaulted three times, and people protected him with arms. There were weapons inside King's home. Civil rights leader Bayard Rustin visited King in the middle of the boycott and saw guns in the King household. At one point, Rustin 'shouted to stop someone from sitting on a loaded pistol that was lying on the couch.' Reverend Glenn Smiley, a follower of Gandhi who visited King to advise him on nonviolent resistance, advised King to 'get rid of the guns around his house.' King talked intensely to Smiley, describing his fears about violence. King told Smiley, 'don't bother me with tactics ... I want to know if I can apply nonviolence to my heart.'

King knew that nonviolent resistance was a strategy that could fail and lead to great bloodshed. John Keane points out that 'renunciation of violence' can sometimes result in 'tragic annihilation.' As a leader, King felt responsible if a demonstration provoked violence against the demonstrators. Mass leaders often face moral dilemmas as they make choices on how to proceed, and King criticized people who saw nonviolent resistance as a pure and simple moral stand. He said, 'I came to see the pacifist position not as sinless.' King criticized self-righteous advocates of peace, stating that 'the pacifist would have a greater appeal if he did not claim to be free from the moral dilemmas that the Christian non-pacifist confronts.'

In 1963 in Birmingham police used billy clubs, firehouses, and German shepherds against civil rights demonstrators. Eight ministers published a letter blaming King for the violence, stating that grievances should be pursued only in courts, not in the street. King responded in a letter from Birmingham City Jail, declaring:

> ... the white power structure of this city left the Negro community with no other alternative ... Its ugly record of police brutality is known in every section of this country. Its unjust treatment of Negroes in the courts is a notorious reality. There have been more unsolved bombings of Negro homes and churches in Birmingham than any city in this nation.

King's nonviolent strategy caught on because it was effective, spurring millions into action and rallying support from around the country and the world. It was the most practical method to deal with racist violence. Some civil rights activists followed King's strategy, even though they themselves personally disagreed with nonviolence. Ella Baker, a leader who worked NAACP in the 1940s and with King in the 1950s, was not a pacifist. She explained, 'I frankly could not have sat and let someone put a burning cigarette on the back of my neck ... If they hit me, I might hit them back.' Connie Lane, Greensboro activist, explained that she disagreed with King's philosophy. 'I never could get into all this passive resistance, somebody hits you, you fall down on your knees and start praying.' She paused, then added, 'but I appreciated what Dr. King was doing.'

A major challenge to King's strategy came from Robert Williams of Monroe, North Carolina. Williams served in the army in World War II and the Marines in the Korean War. When he returned home to North Carolina, the local NAACP chapter elected him their president. In 1957, a Klan motorcade attacked the house where the Monroe NAACP was meeting, and Williams and others shot at them. The KKK backed off. Williams' NAACP chapter led a variety of civil rights struggles, including a campaign to free two boys, ages seven and nine, who were incarcerated for playing a children's kissing game with white girls.

In 1959, Williams helped a black woman bring a suit against a white man who assaulted her, tore off her clothing, and tried to rape her. Williams' frustration rose to the boiling point when the all-white-male jury quickly acquitted the white man. It was yet another example of the double standard of the South. In the name of protecting white women, white men lynched black men and boys, and at the same time felt entitled to violate black women. Just after the verdict, a furious Williams declared on the courthouse steps, 'the Negro in the South cannot expect justice in the courts. He must convict his attackers on the spot. He must meet violence with violence, lynching with lynching.' For this statement, Williams was kicked out of the NAACP.'

An intense debate ensued on the strategy of Robert Williams versus that of Martin Luther King, Jr. In the *Southern Patriot* in 1961, King stressed nonviolent resistance as aggressive action against segregation. In an opposing article, Williams advocated armed self-defense, stating:

> ... in a civilized society the law is a deterrent against the strong who would take advantage of the weak, but the South is not a civilized society; the South is a social jungle; it had become necessary for us to create our own deterrent ... we would defend our women and our children, our homes and ourselves with arms.

Williams' words reflected the sentiment of many. But Williams had crossed an unwritten rule about armed self-defense: he publicly advocated it. James Forman pointed out that 'self-defense was something people should do and not proclaim.' Williams' phrase 'meeting violence with violence, lynching with lynching' was roundly criticized, because it could be interpreted as a strategy of violence, a justification for blacks lynching whites. The NAACP and King wanted to clearly demarcate themselves from that view. But while criticizing Williams, both the NAACP and King affirmed the right of self-defense. As they removed Williams from membership, the NAACP stated, 'we do not deny but reaffirm the right of an individual and collective self-defense against unlawful assaults.' King blasted Williams for the 'advocacy of violence as a tool of advancement, organized as in warfare, deliberately and consciously.' He saw it as an approach with 'incalculable perils,' whereas nonviolent mass action was a constructive alternative. But King defended the right of self-defense, stating it was accepted as 'moral and legal' by all societies. And he acknowledged that pure nonviolence 'cannot readily or easily attract large masses, for it requires extraordinary discipline and courage.' King's nonviolent strategy won the public debate. But nonviolent resistance continued to coexist with armed self-defense.

King was a 'practical pacifist,' not a 'pure' one. In 1967-1968, he spoke out against the Vietnam War, saying 'these are revolutionary times. All over the globe men are revolting against old systems of exploitation and oppression ... The shirt-less and barefoot people of the earth are rising up as never before.' He sympa-thized with the national liberation movements who were using force of arms.

## The Movement Forces the Federal Government Off the Fence

In the early 1960s, civil rights activists continued to face violence, and the federal government continued its 'hands-off' policy. In 1961, black and white Freedom Riders rode on public buses though the South, integrating public facilities. The FBI knew that the Klan planned a 'baseball bat greeting' for the Freedom Riders in Alabama but failed to protect them from a brutal beating. The FBI also stood by while police beat people trying to exercise their right to vote. In 1962, Fanny Lou Hamer, a 45-year-old Mississippi-country woman who would become a nationally recognized civil rights leader, tried to register at the county court-house. She was arrested, evicted from her home, and shot at.

But violence did not stop the movement, as sit-ins, marches, and voter regis-tration drives spread across the south.

Pressure on Washington to end segregation and violence mounted. On the one hand, the failure of the government to protect the exercise of constitutionally protected rights became increasingly embarrassing in the context of the Cold War. The Soviet Union used the South's brutality to batter the U.S. image abroad. On the other hand, American national interests found King's nonviolence useful in international relations. The U.S. promoted King's leadership as an alternative to the armed national liberation struggles in Africa and other parts of the world. For example, the United States Information Agency made a video of the 1963 March on Washington which they showed around the world as evidence of peace-ful progress in race relations in the U.S.. But that required that there be progress. Such progress depended on the federal government doing something it had failed to do for almost a century: dismantle the stranglehold of white supremacy on local and state government and punish racist violence.

The mounting pressure came to a head in June 1964. Civil rights activists orga-nized Freedom Summer, attracting Northern white and black students to come

South to work on voter registration and other issues. In June, the Ku Klux Klan lynched three young civil rights workers, James Chaney, Andrew Goodman, and Michael Schwerner, in Neshoba County, Mississippi. A deputy sheriff drove one of the two cars of the Klansmen. The murders of the young men, one black and two white, became international news. Finally, a president took action: President Johnson directly ordered J. Edgar Hoover to stop the Klan. As a result, the FBI added a counterintelligence program (COINTELPRO) against the Klan to its programs against civil rights activists, the Black Panthers, and Vietnam War protesters. It was the only COINTELPRO initiated under pressure from outside the Bureau and the only one directed at rightwing groups.

Thus in 1964, as the Ku Klux Klan marked its 98th year of working to undermine the U.S. Constitution, the FBI determined that the Klan was 'essentially subversive.' The Bureau's 'war on the Klan' lasted until 1971, when it was disbanded along with the other COINTELPROs. The FBI focused on infiltrating Klan organizations, and by the late 1960s, there were 2000 FBI informants in racist hate groups, comprising perhaps 20% of total Klan membership. Sometimes it was unclear whose side the informants were on. One man on the FBI payroll talked about murdering all black people. Another informant was part of the carload of Klansmen who murdered civil rights worker Viola Liuzzo. Federal involvement, despite its serious shortcomings, was decisive in cutting the link in many places between vigilantes and local law enforcement. There were exceptions, including police complicity with Klan murders in Greensboro in 1979, and police brutality that continues to plague the country to this day. But the Civil Rights Movement, by forcing authorities to punish violent racists, had taken a major step in breaking the white supremacist grip on power.

## Conclusion

Nonviolent resistance combined with armed self-defense in the Civil Rights Movement to force the government to do its job: protect people's rights regardless of race. Government actions curtail or encourage violence. In the U.S., from Reconstruction until the height of the Civil Rights Movement, the federal policy of 'hands off' towards the South had fostered violence against blacks. Even in the late 1950s and 1960, whites could brutalize blacks and get away with it. The lynch-mob murders of Emmett Till in 1955, Mack Charles Parker in 1959, and Goodman, Chaney, and Schwerner in 1964 went unpunished. Particularly in rural Southern counties, African Americans often had no recourse to government protection. Some used arms to defend themselves and their homes, but the effectiveness was limited, because violent whites had the power of local and state institutions behind them.

African Americans bent on civil rights coped with the violence used against them in various ways. Many activists routinely carried handguns to protect themselves, as they faced harassment and sometimes murder. When the Montgomery bus boycott launched massive protest action, Martin Luther King, Jr. argued for the boycotters to be nonviolent to differentiate themselves from the tactics of the Ku Klux Klan and White Citizens Council, and to win the support of white liberals. King gradually developed nonviolence into a strategy in the late 1950s and early 1960s, a strategy which helped the Civil Rights Movement grow in size and effectiveness. Pacifism coexisted with armed self-defense: both King and the NAACP officially upheld the right of self-defense.

During the Cold War in the new medium of television, massive nonviolent resistance galvanized national and international attention, as the Civil Rights Movement demanded that the Constitution be enforced throughout the country. U.S. leaders found King's nonviolent strategy useful in foreign diplomacy because it could be promoted as an alternative to armed national liberation movements. In the 1960s, faced with both international pressure and the growing size and scope of the Civil Rights Movement, the federal government finally acted to thwart racist violence in the South. In a dramatic policy shift, LBJ in 1964 ordered J. Edgar Hoover to use the FBI to undermine the Ku Klux Klan, not just gather information on it. The federal government thus began to break the link between violent racists and Southern local and state government, a central victory for civil rights.

John Keane suggests that strategies of social change may be evaluated based on whether they create or strengthen pluralistic peaceful society. Sometimes the use of arms can be constructive, as it was in the American Revolution. Pacifism, too, can be effective or counterproductive based on how it is practiced. Sometimes it has disarmed people who then face increased bloodshed. On the other hand, Keane finds that Gandhi's movement in India 'used nonviolence as a means of contesting illegitimate power, for the purpose of strengthening civil society." In the same way, King's nonviolent resistance forced the U.S. government to guarantee civil rights. The Civil Rights Movement succeeded, not because of its nonviolence, but because it was combined with armed self-defense to make the South less violent and more democratic.

# WE WILL CREATE OUR FREEDOM: THE IMPORTANCE OF THE MOVEMENT FOR BLACK LIVES PLATFORM

Aislinn Pulley

2016[1]

There is a movement rumbling through the streets of this country. There is sustained organizing, national and local collaborations that are enduring the grueling work of refusing to allow extrajudicial Black death to continue to be hushed up, accepted as normal.

There is debate occurring, and at times, rigorous examination of the current conditions that have produced outrage and misery. We are collectively grappling with the hypocrisy at the root of what it is to be 'American' and what it is to be Black on the soil of this settler colonial land. The continued onslaught of death forces into view the chasm between the myth of American exceptionalism and the reality of our blood-stained streets.

In Chicago, the Let Us Breathe Collective is continuing to lead an occupation across the street from the notorious police torture site, Homan Square, where over 7,000 people have been disappeared. Today marks Day 21 of the uprising against Homan Square, aptly called #FreedomSquare.

Today also marks the 31st day that Black Lives Matter activists in Los Angeles have occupied LA's City Hall, calling for the firing of Charlie Beck for leading the most murderous police force in the United States.

In this historic moment, we are challenged as a movement to define what systemic change could actually look like. What are the steps necessary to permanently end the police and state violence that will undoubtedly continue to produce death and misery?

New York City's response to protesters of police violence earlier this month sheds light on these questions. On the second day of an occupation of City Hall Park, coordinated by the anti-police violence organization, Millions March NYC,

---

1. Source: Pulley, Aislinn. 'We Will Create Our Freedom: The Importance of the Movement for Black Lives Platform'. *Truthout.* August 11, 2016. https://truthout.org/articles/we-will-create-our-freedom-the-importance-of-the-movement-for-black-lives-platform/

New York Police Department Commissioner Bill Bratton announced his resignation. Immediately, Mayor Bill de Blasio named his successor, NYPD veteran, James P. O'Neall, and vowed a seamless transition. This situation both exemplifies the pressure police forces are facing nationwide to respond to increasing public demands to end police violence, and also reflects the superficial nature of municipal governments' response to this outcry. Merely replacing figureheads does not get to the root of the problem of police violence, such as Chicago's replacement of Police Superintendent Garry McCarthy with Eddie Johnson. The victory lies only in the fact that the state has been forced to act as a result of persistent public pressure. It is not, however, evidence of systemic change in any form or fashion.

The easiest thing the state can do is replace figureheads and call that change. Officials will do this, however reluctantly, while providing a counter-narrative stating that the relationship between the community and police is mending. They are also avidly working to create false equivalencies in order to end public resistance. For example, some officials claim that police are 'also under attack' and therefore, need hate crime legislation—an argument which posits that there is a historic oppression linked to policing — which is, of course, absurd.Policing is a profession. Police officers take off their uniforms and badges when their shift is over, like doctors, or nurses, or Starbucks baristas. They are not an oppressed class of people.

The police, in their current formation, will not stop killing us. The Baltimore police killed a 23-year-old mother, Korryn Gaines, in her house and shot her 5-year-old son on August 1. A few days prior, Chicago police had shot and killed 18-year-old Paul O'Neal. Reportedly, witnesses have claimed that they saw police officers turn off their cameras before shooting him; however, official reports state that the body cameras simply 'didn't work.' And the family of 16-year-old Pierre Lourry, whom the Chicago police shot on April 11, 2016, has still not received the police report about the shooting.

The police will continue to murder us extrajudicially because that is how the police in the United States are currently organized to function. They are taught to shoot first. They are taught to operate as if they are at war with the Black and Brown communities,immigrants, the poor, the unemployed, the sick and anyone who does not immediately lie down into a form of submission they deem acceptable. And they are protected heavily by the collective bargaining agreements brokered by the Fraternal Order of Police.

US policing will remain violent and continue to be militarized until a movement large and powerful enough forces the state into restructuring. Currently, the Obama administration is preparing to re-authorize the military weaponry to local police departments that was halted after the Ferguson uprising. The weaponry will include grenade launchers and armored tracked vehicles. There is no doubt that there will be more Philandos, more Korryns, more Pauls. The violence of the state will not end by way of the next election cycle. Only the collective power of the people can force an end to this violence — the collective power of our very selves forging a movement capable of stopping the violent apparatus that continues to wage war on our lives.

The Movement for Black Lives platform, released by over 50 organizations on August 1, 2016, seeks to set forth clear demands to enable Black life to be lived without threat of state terror, murder or subjugation. It advocates for the intentional restructuring of society to end the system's most brutal current components. With six categories, the platform expands the definition of freedom to encompass a vision of a future that addresses historical oppressions rooted in the founding of the United States as not only a white supremacist, capitalist patriarchy, but also as an imperialist settler colonial nation. These definitions are important because they make visible the traumas that maintain the status quo: those of continued Indigenous subjugation and invisibilization, the international exploitation of our diasporic family abroad, and the role of U.S. imperialism in maintaining global power. We can never forget that the populations killed at the highest rates by U.S. police are our Indigenous brothers and sisters. This continued murder and exploitation must be seen within the continuum of genocide that is constantly erased and ignored as a necessary function of settler colonialism and legitimization of the American empire.

The Movement for Black Lives platform provides a necessary contribution to how we, as members of this movement, can focus our fight on toppling the oppressive structures and systems that made possible the murder of Korryn Gaines inside her own home, under the excuse that she had outstanding traffic warrants.

When we say that the police are waging 'war' on our communities, it may be a bit misleading. 'War' presupposes a time of peace that existed within this paradigm and suggests an alternative normal mode of functioning. We know that there has never existed an alternate safe epoch of Black life under U.S. capitalism. Black wage theft, terror, murder and rape under slavery; the white supremacist violence used to destroy Reconstruction; the subjugation enforced under Jim Crow; and the current policing and prison nation under which we now exist all speak to the evolution of Black subjugation at the hands of the American empire. Therefore, to 'End the War on Black Lives,' as the Movement for Black Lives platform states, is really to completely reconfigure Black livelihood and by proxy, all livelihood on this land. It is to take up again the serious and ultimately revolutionary question of what real post-slavery 'Reconstruction' would mean. This is a vital and necessary task and the only way we will begin to craft a future on this land that does not necessitate the murder, death and misery of the many in order to benefit the few.

We refuse disillusionment at the pathetic farce of democracy the national elections attempt to portray. It is by our own hands and our own minds that we will have to study, create, debate and fight to figure out how we will make a world and a country that enable our existence to flourish. Our resilience has never been in question.

What remains important and undetermined is whether we will build a movement capable of understanding the details of how our current system works to maintain itself—and capable of working to dismantle the system's nooses from our necks.

It's important to study the Movement for Black Lives policy platform—to discuss and debate it. We should view this as a living document with which we can build, edit, explore and/or create other proposals.

This means that the increasing number of us who are called to be a part of the fight to end Black oppression in this country will have to challenge ourselves to make connections with other parts of our community that we have not yet connected with or have not yet been called to actively organize. We will have to enter into conversation and struggle with everyone in our community. That means being in the factories talking to workers, being in fast food restaurants with employees fighting for a livable wage, being on the corner, on the block, in the hood, in the laundromat, in the barber shop. We must build a mass movement that encompasses the reality of who we are, that contains class consciousness and deepens our understanding of how class oppression combined with white supremacy is the deadliest beast we have historically fought against. We must make these connections intentionally, in order to politically understand the social forces necessary to achieve the ultimate goal of ending the current policing system, and by necessary inclusion, the system that demands that such violent state apparatus exist.

We are creating our future together, and we are rejecting all preconceived notions of what we can and can't do. We built up this country's infrastructure through our blood, sweat, tears and death and, we will create our freedom. We are striving to create the world in which our children and children's children will be able to live without threats of police murder, poverty, unemployment and lack of access to education and health care.

We have no choice but to resist because we cannot breathe, and we cannot live in this current state. Ours is an actual fight for the right to live. We are the true right-to-life movement. Our lives matter, and we have the right to exist on this land unmarred, unthreatened and free of terror.

# AMNESTY INTERNATIONAL AMBASSADOR OF CONSCIENCE AWARD SPEECH

Colin Kaepernick

2018[1]

It is only fitting that I have the honor of Eric Reid introducing me for this award. In many ways, my recognition would not be possible without our brotherhood. I truly consider him to be more than a friend—Eric, his wife, his children...they are all a part of my family.

Not only did he kneel by my side during the national anthem throughout the entire 2016 NFL season, but Eric continued to use his platform as a professional football player to protest systemic oppression, specifically police brutality against Black and brown people.

Eric introducing me for this prestigious award brings me great joy.

But I am also pained by the fact that his taking a knee, and demonstrating courage to protect the rights of Black and brown people in America, has also led to his ostracization from the NFL when he is widely recognized as one of the best competitors in the game and in the prime of his career.

People sometimes forget that love is at the root of our resistance.

My love for Eric has continually grown over the course of our ongoing journey. His brotherhood, resilience, and faith have shined brightly in moments of darkness. My love for my people serves as the fuel that fortifies my mission. And it is the people's unbroken love for themselves that motivates me, even when faced with the dehumanizing norms of a system that can lead to the loss of one's life over simply being Black.

History has proven that there has never been a period in the history of America where anti-Blackness has not been an ever-present terror. Racialized oppression and dehumanization is woven into the very fabric of our nation–the effects of which can be seen in the lawful lynching of Black and brown people by the police, and the mass incarceration of Black and brown lives in the prison industrial complex. While America bills itself as the land of the free, the receipts show that the U.S. has incarcerated approximately 2.2 million people, the largest prison population in the history of humankind.

1. Source: https://www.amnesty.org/en/latest/news/2018/04/colin-kaepernick-ambassador-of-conscience/

As police officers continue to terrorize Black and brown communities, abusing their power, and then hiding behind their blue wall of silence, and laws that allow for them to kill us with virtual impunity, I have realized that our love, that sometimes manifests as Black-rage, is a beautiful form of defiance against a system that seeks to suppress our humanity–A system that wants us to hate ourselves.

I remind you that love is at the root of our resistance.

It is our love for 12-year-old Tamir Rice, who was gunned down by the police in less than two seconds that will not allow us to bury our anger. It is our love for Philando Castille, who was executed in front of his partner and his daughter, that keeps the people fighting back. It is our love for Stephon Clark, who was lynched in his grandma's backyard that will not allow us to stop until we achieve liberation for our people.

Our love is not an individualized love—it is a collective love. A collective love that is constantly combating collective forms of racialized hate. Chattel slavery, Jim Crow, New Jim Crow, massive plantations, mass incarcerations, slave patrols, police patrols, we as a collective, since the colonization of the Americas have been combating collective forms of systemic racialized hate and oppression.

But I am hopeful. I am inspired.

This is why we have to protest. This is why we are so passionate. We protest because we love ourselves, and our people.

It was James Baldwin who said, to be Black in America, 'and to be relatively conscious is to be in a rage almost all the time.' My question is, why aren't all people? How can you stand for the national anthem of a nation that preaches and propagates, 'freedom and justice for all', that is so unjust to so many of the people living there? How can you not be in rage when you know that you are always at risk of death in the streets or enslavement in the prison system? How can you willingly be blind to the truth of systemic racialized injustice? When Malcolm X said, 'I'm for truth, no matter who tells it. I'm for justice, no matter who it is for or against. I'm a human being, first and foremost, and as such I'm for whoever and whatever benefits humanity as a whole'. I took that to heart.

While taking a knee is a physical display that challenges the merits of who is excluded from the notion of freedom, liberty, and justice for all, the protest is also rooted in a convergence of my moralistic beliefs, and my love for the people.

Seeking the truth, finding the truth, telling the truth and living the truth has been, and always will be what guides my actions. For as long as I have a beating heart, I will continue on this path, working on behalf of the people.

Again...Love is at the root of our resistance.

Last but certainly not least; I would like to thank Amnesty International for *The Ambassador of Conscience Award*. But in truth, this is an award that I share with all of the countless people throughout the world combating the human rights violations of police officers, and their uses of oppressive and excessive force. To again quote Malcolm X, when he said that he, 'will join in with anyone—I don't care what color you are—as long as you want to change this miserable condition that exists on this earth', I am here to join with you all in this battle against police violence.

# RAGE, HUMILIATION, TESTOSTERONE, YOUTH AND THE POLITICS OF LIBERATION

Russell Maroon Shoatz and Steve Bloom

2017[1]

Steve Bloom, a comrade and veteran activist, asked me several questions regarding... aspects of our political struggle against oppression back in the 1960s and '70s and are still pressing concerns.

**Steve**: Today, looking back almost 50 years, what do you think of the idea that in the 1960s 'revolution had come' and it was 'time to pick up the gun?' What is your present-day assessment of the choice by a wing of the Panthers and the BLA (Black Liberation Army) to engage in an armed offensive against the established state power in the U.S.A., starting in the last half of the 1960s? What were the consequences? What was achieved? What failures or setbacks were suffered as a result? What balance sheet would you draw for us today?

What would you say to me today about the manner in which the Oakland Panthers chose to announce that decision to the world?

**Maroon**: From my vantage point as an individual who joined what Malcolm X defined as the struggle for human rights, 50 years ago, in 1967, I co-founded Philadelphia's Black Unity Council, an organization that merged with Philly's Panthers in 1969. That led to me being forced underground for a year and a half in the ranks of the BLA. Captured in 1972, I have subsequently been a political prisoner, serving multiple 'natural life' death-by-incarceration sentences due to my political activities.

My expressions here are of a deeply felt personal nature, but time, reflection and study has allowed me to recognize how our politics of the struggle for human rights, more often than not, is intertwined with rage, humiliation, testosterone (amongst males) and a youthful lack of clarity.

---

1. Shoatz, Russell Maroon. 'Rage, Testosterone, Youth, and the Politics of Liberation.' *San Francsico Bayview*. May 29, 2017. **http://sfbayview.com/2017/05/russell-maroon-shoatz-rage-humiliation-testosterone-youth-and-the-politics-of-liberation/** Copyright © 2017 Pampata. Send our brother some love and light: Russell Maroon Shoats/z, AF-3855, SCI Graterford, P.O. Box 246, Rte 29, Graterford PA 19426.

In my case, from the age of 5 until I was 34, I was consumed with a smoldering sense of rage, fed by feelings of humiliation.

I was born in Philadelphia, Pennsylvania, in 1943 – my parents, my siblings and I in a mostly Black working class neighborhood known as 'The Black Bottom.' Tiny row houses, treeless and narrow streets and trash clogged empty lots is what I most remember about my early years.

All symbols of power and authority there were white: white corner store owners, bill collectors, cops and later school teachers.

The only white family I knew of was the Pfifers, with their little girl who would beg for bread and their 'crazy' son Paul.

At the same time, at 5 years of age, I had never heard anyone discuss anything in racial terms, or how white skin privilege operated to form my world.

Seared in my memory is an event that twisted my personality into knots for decades. Something I witnessed at the age of 5. My father and I were gazing out our tiny living room window, watching two white cops brutally beat and drag a Black man to their parked patrol car, directly across the narrow street from where we stood.

At that age, I had never witnessed such violence – not in our home or my small world of vacant, trash filled lots, alleyways or on the one lane streets that I was allowed to play on.

My emotions revolved around wide-eyed unasked questions that can be summed up in one word: Why? Though everything came back to that one word, my young mind really wanted to know why were those cops beating and using such loud, forceful sounding words against that guy?

Why was my father standing so still, while I peered up to see his reactions to what we were witnessing with my questioning eyes – that never caught his attention? Why were the neighbors, who I could see across the narrow street, all watching from their own doorways and windows and themselves as well seemingly frozen in their movements and not even talking loud enough to be heard through our open summer evening window?

I felt no fear, but my young mind could sense fear in my father and the neighbors. I just wanted someone to tell me why?!

Once the cops got the Black guy in their car, one of them turned and blurted: 'Any of you other niggers want some of this?' And I saw our neighbors begin to shut their doors and withdraw from their windows, while my father took my hand and pulled me away from our window as well.

Right then, at the age of 5, I determined that what had occurred was wrong. And I also immediately passed judgment on my father and those neighbors: They were afraid to do anything about that wrong, and that caused me to lose respect for all of them.

Entering elementary school the following year marks another experience that added to the warping of my character.

During one of my first classes, I failed to follow a white female teacher's instructions on some forgotten matter, and that caused her to sharply smack me across my face, and then force me into the cramped well beneath her desk, and I had to remain there for quite some time.

I had never been slapped or otherwise beaten. My parents did not believe in or practice beating their children, nor had I ever witnessed any fighting between the two of them. In fact, aside from the two cops beating of the Black guy the year before, the only violence I ever saw was during a rare trip to the movies; and our family, relatives or neighbors had no TVs to watch such things.

Thus, the slap stunned and confused me, causing me to start crying. Not from the pain, but from the frustrating realization that the teacher had displayed – like the two cops – that she also had the ability to exercise a power that was hard to resist.

My tears that day were from a powerless rage that even as a 6-year-old I knew was based in a deep feeling that something in the universe had to be out of place in order for me to be experiencing such emotions. A rage that I would harbor for decades to come, fed by a seemingly unending cavalcade of examples that I would face, or become aware that even my untutored mind had no problem in determining were simply wrong and unjust. A rage that for many years was misdirected.

In time, adding to my rage was my witnessing or learning of many other Black people suffering abuse in many ways. And my inability or efforts to resist such things caused me to expand the loss of respect for my father and neighbors into feelings of humiliation about myself and Black people in general.

And it is important to point out that once my family and neighbors began to rent, share and buy TVs in the early 1950s, the demeaning ways Blacks were depicted on the small screen: 'Mammies,' buffoons and characters whose roles were designed to debase Blacks and afford whites a sense of inflated self-worth left me feeling more humiliated.

Rage and humiliation fed on each other.

In my mind, Blacks were essentially cowards. I did not place myself in that category, but it subsequently provoked a decades-long quest to prove to myself and the entire world that I was justified in not placing myself amongst such cowards.

Along the way I ran into the gang culture of the middle 1950s. And from 13 to 20 years of age, the gangs of Philly were my instrument and stage that facilitated my search for a form of recognition and a level of respect that could not be denied by anyone.

The young males who were in my gang and our counterparts in rival gangs were undoubtedly harboring similar feelings of rage and humiliation, though the fratricide amongst us left little time to reflect on such things. Our male dominated gangs were as testosterone driven as ancient gladiator arenas.

Unlike youth groups in better-off communities, our Black gangs never had any real adult guidance or supervision. We had our 'old heads,' who were always older former gang members, but they too held firmly to the gang culture, and that never elevated beyond placing a premium on the search for recognition and respect – even after the old heads began devoting more time and energy to marriage and children.

In Philly, the young Black women of that era generally displayed less of a desire to try to keep up with the testosterone driven competition, though some did participate as a means to wrestle with their own feelings of rage and their humiliation that was compounded by the overarching cultural practices that were more oppressive and abusive towards women.

Malcolm's 'By any means necessary!' approach to the human rights struggle changed everything.

Adding a new approach to the heroic civil rights struggle that was based in the South, a primarily nonviolent effort that caused me to reexamine my belief about Blacks being cowards. Still, nonviolence held little appeal for many who saw Malcolm's teachings as more suited to serving to rid us of our humiliation and redirect our rage away from our Black-on-Black violence: seeking both our humanity and political, economic and social changes.

Some said revolutionary change was needed. Followers of that doctrine emerged to form the Black Panther Party in Oakland, California – albeit earlier Black Panther formations were already in motion in the South, amongst the urban based Revolutionary Action Movement (RAM) and elsewhere. RAM, in particular, was heavily influenced by Robert F. Williams and his North Carolina NAACP chapter, who had practiced armed self-defense extensively in the 1950s and early 1960s.

The coming together of the 'any means necessary' doctrine and an ever increasingly political strata of young Black men, who were full of rage and feelings of humiliation, proved to be a powerful formula for recruiting Black youth who remained unmoved by the nonviolent methods of the early civil rights struggles.

It is very important to recognize that Black women also harbored feelings of rage and humiliation. Given the history of the U.S.A., Black women had to be experiencing even more rage and humiliation than most Black men! And the already mentioned heroic civil rights struggles that had been taking place in the South propelled to the world's attention the now iconic Rosa Parks, Gloria Richardson, Ella Baker, Fannie Lou Hamer and quite a larger number. And in the urban areas, untold numbers of lesser known women would populate and distinguish themselves, not only amongst the Black Panthers, but amongst the ranks and leadership of hundreds of forgotten formations.

Still, the testosterone-fueled men usually smothered or pushed to the background those female contributions, especially in the urban areas, which were essentially youth movements that allowed, encouraged and elevated the mystique of 'the bad motherfucker.' At the same time, the women, who did more than their share to establish and sustain all these groups, placed more value on working to solve the mountain of problems and difficulties being given voice to.

The women's closer connections to the children left them with little appetite for the usual 'king of the mountain, last man standing' syndrome that the raging, testosterone 'drunk' men were practicing. And unlike the Southern civil rights struggles, the urban youth in question lacked a mass of older people who they trusted, who could afford them with a wealth of learned experiences the leading urban youth could weigh while making important decisions.

Even on matters concerning armed self-defense, only practiced on the margins of the usual nonviolent Southern struggle, people like Robert F. Williams and the Deep South's Deacons for Defense and some lesser known local formations had quite a number of professionally trained military veterans, who went forward to use their training to organize and lead the defense of the civil rights struggle against both the police and Ku Klux Klan. The urban formations only sporadically produced such effective armed self-defense.

After the Southern civil rights struggle succeeded in winning major reforms in voting rights, public accommodations etc., that arena of our struggle became preoccupied with consolidating those gains, while Malcolm's human rights struggle evolved into the Black Power/Black Liberation struggle – revolutionary doctrines and political, economic and social programs that were almost always led by youthful Black urban men.

When I joined that urban struggle in 1967, rage, humiliation, testosterone, youth and politics had all come together, and I found a movement dominated by kindred spirits. Our philosophies, ideologies, doctrines, programs, strategies, tactics and practice were always overshadowed by those elements.

We idolized Che Guevara, the Tupamaro urban guerrilla group of Uruguay; we doggedly held on to Mao Tse Tung's quote, 'Political power grows from a barrel of a gun.' We trained and practiced armed self-defense against the police, FBI and any others we believed were enemies. 'The Mini Manual of Urban Guerrilla Warfare' and Panther Field Marshal Don Cox instructed on 'Forming Self Defense Forces.' Later his urban guerrilla writings in his 'For the Liberation of America' reached us from exile.

By 1971, not only the Panthers, but scores of other 'bad motherfuckers' across the U.S. had taken on the police and FBI in defense of their offices, homes and persons. They robbed banks to fund the struggle, highjacked planes to seek exile in foreign countries, staged retaliatory attacks against the police drug suppression measures, escaped after capture, and developed an extensive and effective underground system that may never be properly exposed because of actions that could still endanger the freedom of many.

Malcolm X had been assassinated by then, but our actions paid homage to him for teaching us how to channel our rage and humiliation against those who were oppressing us.

The youthful male testosterone was stoked in other ways. Elaine Brown, who would become the only female to lead the Black Panther Party, made a record album where she crooned, 'Believe it, my friend, for this silence to end, we'll just have to get guns and be men.'

Before the Los Angeles Panther head Bunchy Carter was assassinated, he wrote a powerful poem for his mother that we reworked into an oath for new recruits: 'If I should fall, weapon in hand, you'll be free, and I a man. For a slave of natural death who dies cannot balance two dead flies. If I should fail to follow our goal, may burning cancer torment my soul.'

Those of us who went underground wound up on a 'run and gun' mission, and that, coupled with our rage and humiliation, further distanced us from the political programs that kept us connected to the Black community. And since that community was not ready to join or adequately support our urban guerrilla activities, and our youthful minds could not find any way forward except more of what we were doing. Our fate was death, injury, prison or exile, and those who suffered those fates have still not been determined.

Freedom ain't free!

We raged on. Every blow struck lessened our burden of suffering humiliation in silence. And those of us who survived found time to read 'The Wretched of the Earth,' where the author and veteran of the Algerian war of national liberation in the 1950s and early 1960s, who was a psychiatrist who had a chance to study both sides of the conflict, discovered that often in liberation struggles the overarching political goals are sidetracked by the powerful needs of many amongst the oppressed to lash out against their oppressors in order to simply regain their feelings of being human.

In my case, I distinctly remember the exact moment that occurred with me – when I again started feeling fully human since suffering the trauma of a confused, defenseless 5-year-old, watching my father and our neighbors all being forced to stand by while the two white cops beat and arrested the Black guy, then hurl humiliating threats our way on departure.

After my 1972 capture, by 1976 I had been transferred to the state prison at Huntingdon due to unsuccessful escape attempts from two other prisons. Huntingdon at that time was known as the 'breakin' camp' because of its brutality. It was there in 1977 that four comrades and I took over a cell block, held the guards hostage, and then were able to escape into the surrounding mountains and forest of Central Pennsylvania.

To make a long story short, one comrade got trapped inside, another was killed on a mountainside, two others were captured that night, while I was chased through the mountains and woods for a month before being recaptured.

Once returned to the prison, I was viciously beaten and, since I had been beaten by guards previously and that was what they would do to try to break prisoners' spirits 'normally,' I expected as much.

Within a couple days I was taken outside the prison to a court hearing, and the police presence was so large, I suspected the different agencies and departments that had obviously come together after our initial escape and during the month long hunt were all trying to get in on 'the picture,' as it were. And the press did show up in large numbers – reporters with their microphones, notebooks and cameras.

The court was a long way from Philly or Pittsburgh, where most of my family and supporters lived. Still I could see five of them surrounded by a lot of the cops and prison guards.

That hearing didn't last long, and I was not allowed to say anything to my people, but was besieged by the press and gawking cops, while my handlers were frantically trying to force a way through the crowd to the waiting cars.

The reporters were firing questions my way, while I rummaged through my brain for something that would make an impact. My capture had forced me out of my run-and-gun posture, back into the political arena where words are weapons.

When the cops got to the cars, before they could get me secured inside, I turned and blurted as loud as I could: 'Tell everybody the slave got caught and is going back to the plantation.' That caused the cops to slam me against the car they were forcing me into. Apparently, they were embarrassed by my continuing defiance, even after the epic, month-long chase through the mountains and words they no doubt hunted in. They thought a 'nigger' from the city would head for the first fast food place to try to rob someone, get a burger, fries and coke, then head for the city, not come within a day or two of the 'hunters' throwing in the towel.

Once back in the prison isolation cell, I began to ponder what had happened before, during and after my escape: my refusal to accept the natural life (death-by-incarceration) sentence, my earlier unsuccessful escape attempts, my growing awareness of how massive the search for me had been, and just how shook-up the angry cops and prison guards remained.

That's when it happened! The humiliation I had been suffering all those years seemed to lift from my shoulders and land directly on that faceless mass of oppressors and authorities who were represented by the cops who packed my hearing, and who all had been out of their minds by how much it took to capture a single implacable rebel!

I stood up, out of earshot of anyone, and as loud as I could shouted: 'That's right. I'm a bad motherfucker!' Then I gently laughed to myself and lay down on my bunk with a 'knowing' smile on my face.

The rage and humiliation simply disappeared. I had forced the world to recognize me as a human being; and I knew it.

Since then I have again felt rage at injustices and due to personal wrongs I've suffered. But the burning, overpowering rage never again returned.

I have also been forced into degrading and humiliating situations during decades of imprisonment since that time, but nothing has been able to take away the dignity I discovered as a human being, now knowing that I am as much as anyone, and more than most.

I remain committed to the struggle for human rights for all of humanity. Since I'm wiser and understand more now, I can better weigh the socioeconomic and sociopolitical as well as the historic factors that preceded their formations. Absent the rage and not suffering the humiliation that once tormented me, I can better help formulate and carry out what is decided about the kinds of far reaching changes that are needed.

When I recognize rage in younger people, I understand how that can dominate their thinking. The same with the humiliation they cannot easily escape or avoid, while the testosterone and its ability to cause a hard to control exuberance amongst young males, in particular, are factors I advise others to always factor in while moving forward.

My story is closer to what untold numbers of highly motivated 1960s and 1970s 'revolutionaries' usually don't write about or discuss nowadays. And I believe I have answered comrade Steve Bloom's earlier questions, if one sets aside the usual self-congratulatory narratives related to how the Black Panther Party, BLA and other related groups and formations served the communities, though they did do some of that as well.

Younger activists, and oppressed people in general, can benefit more from the veterans of the struggles from earlier generations working even closer than when our veterans spend so much time on fine tuning their ideological, philosophical positions and worldviews. The looming threats that could very well lead to the next 10 or 20 years!

Straight Ahead!

# 4. REVOLUTIONARY NONVIOLENCE IN AFRICA: PLAYING BETWEEN THE CRACKS

*In this section we begin to truly plunge into the nexus/praxis between revolutionary armed struggle and revolutionary nonviolence—such that those two ideas are thought about in the most useful tactical ways (as we struggle to remain principled even in the midst of potential debate).*

*Africa World/Red Sea Press co-founder Kassahun Checole, a dedicated Pan African elder who continues to help grow progressive publishing efforts throughout the world, writes our section introduction beginning from his own very personal experiences as a young militant in the Eritrean independence struggle. Mozambique's Graça Machel, Guinea-Bissau's Amilcar Cabral, South Africa's Nozizwe Madlala-Routledge, and Zambia's Kenneth Kaunda all contribute insights based on their forefront experiences trying to make the connections which seem both most needed and most elusive. How one could be a contemporary Deputy Minister of Defense and also a Quaker-based pacifist; how one could defend one's own borders from overt attack when one wishes to adhere to the best nonviolence practices; how one could maintain what U.S. radical feminist termed a 'revolutionary equilibrium...are all discussed in these pages, focusing on a continent 'off the radar' but central for decades in the development of some of the most ingenious, effective, and potentially replicable campaigns which run the political gamut from small, local, grassroots affinity groups to massive, multinational, formal settings.*

*—The editors*

# REVOLUTIONS AND THEIR OUTCOMES

Kassahun Checole

When we talk about revolutions and their outcomes—what they do, where they go, what happens to them—it is hard not to start with my own history, engaged in revolutionary action since I was 15 years old in a small country called Eritrea, at that time a part of Ethiopia. My initial involvement in Pan Africanism was a cultural and literary engagement, but I moved on to more active, militant participation in both the Marxist movement and the Ethiopian student movement, and the Marxist and political aspects of the Eritrean liberation movement. During that journey, I was also involved with the independence movement of East Timor, the anti-apartheid movement, and the anti-colonial struggles all over Africa. So, my range of interest goes through the last 50 years of struggle.

I have begun in the last years to question our ways—our methods of doing the actions that we've done. Where are we going? How come we have not arrived at where we thought we would be? These are deep-rooted questions—for all of us but also for myself; I'm not blaming anybody or accusing anyone. Since I was a participant, however, it is right to reflect on the fact that my role, limited or small as it was, may not have been as good as it should have been.

We must first look at the early independence movement that began in the 1940s and 1950s. This wave resulted in almost half of Africa becoming independent from colonialism. Interestingly, however, the decolonization process in Africa was almost immediately co-opted, enjoined, or controlled by those who were our original colonizers. They managed to create structures and the means of controlling the newly independent countries throughout the continent. They've done it very well. What Kwame Nkrumah labeled neocolonialism, a colonialism without direct European presence, controls the apparatus of a country's economy, society, cultural and other structures. All the systems that we were creating and trying to create were corrupted in the name of democracy, in the name of freedom.

A second problem which is part of the neocolonial dynamic became especially jarring in what I call the second wave of African revolutions. That also began in the late 1950s, but matured in the 1970s and 1980s, from Algeria and Ghana to Guinea Bissau, Mozambique, Angola, Cape Verde, and up to the South African struggles against the racist apartheid regime. These movements were led not just by the practical activity of decolonizing the country, but also with the theoretical vision of challenging a significant social order that would change from the traditions, challenges the modern western modern model along economic, cultural, and other lines. But while armed with a clear ideological mission that governments and societies would have to change in radical ways, the second wave itself has now failed, with a group of people who are thinking more about their pockets than the people.

In Angola, the former President and his daughter have now become billionaires. The daughter is so rich that she lends money to the Portuguese government, Angola's former colonial rulers! She owns the airlines of Portugal and the major hotels. Yet, when you go to Angola, you will see the depths of poverty, the lack of health facilities which should have been built there for the billions of dollars that the oil and the diamonds of Angola bring out. There and elsewhere, some of our earlier leaders have become paternalistic and patronizing. And they have remained in power for decades—some of them up to the up to the present. They refuse to leave the space for younger, innovative people. They think, as fathers (and they're mostly men, fathers), that they have a special role to play. Some of them were at a time engaged in positive work. But the failure of their legacy is also very vivid, very clear.

My notion is not to blame the west too much. Because the policies and self-interests of the west are a given. The history is based on modern empires. They do what empires do; we should take that for granted. We can't expect any charity or mercy from the west. The question for us then is: How is it that we did not do what was necessary to make sure that the west did not dominate our economies and societies?

Too often our leaders have felt that they cannot rely on the people; that most of our people were not ready to deal with the power which true democracy should provide. We are faced with a generational divide, which does give some space for hope. We have what I call 'the visionary children of Africa'—the majority of Africa is young people, and many are simply fantastic. The reason why I travel throughout Africa is because these young people give me hope.

In Kenya, for example, there is a group which is revisioning the whole banking system, such that top economists are suggesting that the rest of the world is now ten years behind this Kenyan model. 10 years behind! There is some young scientist in South Africa who created an airplane that can fly without the nasty petrol which we have normally used all these decades. There is extraordinary innovation! Too many of our young people however, including those creators, have no access to power.

We must reconcile to the fact that we brought some of our current problems by our own means. And now, in our old age, we cannot think about solutions. We must deepen our exploration of how to bring about change through peaceful means, because we have learned what violence can lead to. We must work towards a future based on ethical thinking, and new leadership based on creating new systems based on the power of the people.

# THE IMPACT OF ARMED CONFLICT ON CHILDREN

Graça Machel

1996[1]

## Introduction

### The attack on children

Millions of children are caught up in conflicts in which they are not merely bystanders, but targets. Some fall victim to a general onslaught against civilians; others die as part of a calculated genocide. Still other children suffer the effects of sexual violence or the multiple deprivations of armed conflict that expose them to hunger or disease. Just as shocking, thousands of young people are cynically exploited as combatants.

In 1995, 30 major armed conflicts raged in different locations around the world.

1. All of them took place within States, between factions split along ethnic, religious or cultural lines. The conflicts destroyed crops, places of worship and schools. Nothing was spared, held sacred or protected – not children, families or communities. In the past decade, an estimated two million children have been killed in armed conflict. Three times as many have been seriously injured or permanently disabled, many of them maimed by landmines.
2. Countless others have been forced to witness or even to take part in horrifying acts of violence.

These statistics are shocking enough, but more chilling is the conclusion to be drawn from them: more and more of the world is being sucked into a desolate moral vacuum. This is a space devoid of the most basic human values; a space in which children are slaughtered, raped, and maimed; a space in which children are exploited as soldiers; a space in which children are starved and exposed to extreme brutality. Such unregulated terror and violence speak of deliberate victimization. There are few further depths to which humanity can sink.

---

1. Source: https://childrenandarmedconflict.un.org/1996/08/1996-graca-machel-report-impact-armed-conflict-children/

The lack of control and the sense of dislocation and chaos that characterize contemporary armed conflicts can be attributed to many different factors. Some observers point to cataclysmic political upheavals and struggles for control over resources in the face of widespread poverty and economic disarray. Others see the callousness of modern warfare as a natural outcome of the social revolutions that have torn traditional societies apart. The latter analysts point as proof to many African societies that have always had strong martial cultures. While fierce in battle, the rules and customs of those societies, only a few generations ago, made it taboo to attack women and children.

Whatever the causes of modern-day brutality towards children, the time has come to call a halt. The present report exposes the extent of the problem and proposes many practical ways to pull back from the brink. Its most fundamental demand is that children simply have no part in warfare. The international community must denounce this attack on children for what it is – intolerable and unacceptable.

Children can help. In a world of diversity and disparity, children are a unifying force capable of bringing people to common ethical grounds. Children's needs and aspirations cut across all ideologies and cultures. The needs of all children are the same: nutritious food, adequate health care, a decent education, shelter and a secure and loving family. Children are both our reason to struggle to eliminate the worst aspects of warfare, and our best hope for succeeding at it.

Violent conflict has always made victims of non-combatants. The patterns and characteristics of contemporary armed conflicts, however, have increased the risks for children. Vestiges of colonialism and persistent economic, social and political crises have greatly contributed to the disintegration of public order. Undermined by internal dissent, countries caught up in conflict today are also under severe stress from a global world economy that pushes them ever further towards the margins. Rigorous programmes of structural adjustment promise long-term market-based economic growth, but demands for immediate cuts in budget deficits and public expenditure only weaken already fragile States, leaving them dependent on forces and relations over which they have little control. While many developing countries have made considerable economic progress in recent decades, the benefits have often been spread unevenly, leaving millions of people struggling for survival. The collapse of functional Governments in many countries torn by internal fighting and the erosion of essential service structures have fomented inequalities, grievances and strife. The personalization of power and leadership and the manipulation of ethnicity and religion to serve personal or narrow group interests have had similarly debilitating effects on countries in conflict.

All of these elements have contributed to conflicts, between Governments and rebels, between different opposition groups vying for supremacy and among populations at large, in struggles that take the form of widespread civil unrest. Many drag on for long periods with no clear beginning or end, subjecting successive generations to endless struggles for survival.

Distinctions between combatants and civilians disappear in battles fought from village to village or from street to street. In recent decades, the proportion of war victims who are civilians has leaped dramatically from 5 per cent to over 90 per cent. The struggles that claim more civilians than soldiers have been marked by horrific levels of violence and brutality. Any and all tactics are employed, from systematic rape, to scorched-earth tactics that destroy crops and poison wells, to ethnic cleansing and genocide. With all standards abandoned, human rights violations against children and women occur in unprecedented numbers. Increasingly, children have become the targets and even the perpetrators of violence and atrocities.

Children seek protection in networks of social support, but these have been undermined by new political and economic realities. Conflict and violent social change have affected social welfare networks between families and communities. Rapid urbanization and the spread of market-based values have also helped erode systems of support that were once based on the extended family.

Unbridled attacks on civilians and rural communities have provoked mass exoduses and the displacement of entire populations who flee conflict in search of elusive sanctuaries within and outside their national borders. Among these uprooted millions, it is estimated that 80 per cent are children and women.

Involving children as soldiers has been made easier by the proliferation of inexpensive light weapons. Previously, the more dangerous weapons were either heavy or complex, but these guns are so light that children can use them and so simple that they can be stripped and reassembled by a child of 10. The international arms trade has made assault rifles cheap and widely available so the poorest communities now have access to deadly weapons capable of transforming any local conflict into a bloody slaughter. In Uganda, an AK-47 automatic machine gun can be purchased for the cost of a chicken and, in northern Kenya, it can be bought for the price of a goat.

Moreover, the rapid spread of information today has changed the character of modern warfare in important ways. While the world surely benefits from ready access to information, it will pay a price if it fails to recognize that information is never entirely neutral. International media are frequently influenced by one or another of the parties to a conflict, by commercial realities and by the public's degree of interest in humanitarian action. The result of these influences are depictions that can be selective or uneven, or both. Whether a story is reported or not may depend less on its intrinsic importance than on subjective perceptions of the public's appetite for information and on the expense of informing them. For example, while coverage of the conflicts in Bosnia and Herzegovina and Somalia was extensive, very little has been reported about the conflicts in Afghanistan and Angola. The media is capable of effectively galvanizing international public support for humanitarian action, as it did for Indo-Chinese refugees in the late 1970s and for Somalia in 1992. The threat of adverse international publicity may also be positive, holding the potential for keeping some gross violations of human rights in check. Ultimately, however, while reports of starving children or overcrowded camps for displaced persons may be dramatic, they do little to support efforts for long-term reconstruction and reconciliation.

# Mitigating the Impact of Armed Conflict on Children

Armed conflicts across and between communities result in massive levels of destruction; physical, human, moral and cultural. Not only are large numbers of children killed and injured, but countless others grow up deprived of their material and emotional needs, including the structures that give meaning to social and cultural life. The entire fabric of their societies – their homes, schools, health systems and religious institutions – are torn to pieces.

War violates every right of a child – the right to life, the right to be with family and community, the right to health, the right to the development of the personality and the right to be nurtured and protected. Many of today's conflicts last the length of a 'childhood', meaning that from birth to early adulthood, children will experience multiple and accumulative assaults. Disrupting the social networks and primary relationships that support children's physical, emotional, moral, cognitive and social development in this way, and for this duration, can have profound physical and psychological implications.

In countless cases, the impact of armed conflict on children's lives remains invisible. The origin of the problems of many children who have been affected by conflicts is obscured. The children themselves may be removed from the public, living in institutions or, as is true of thousands of unaccompanied and orphaned children, exist as street children or become victims of prostitution. Children who have lost parents often experience humiliation, rejection and discrimination. For years, they may suffer in silence as their self-esteem crumbles away. Their insecurity and fear cannot be measured.

## Child soldiers

One of the most alarming trends in armed conflict is the participation of children as soldiers. Children serve armies in supporting roles, as cooks, porters, messengers and spies. Increasingly, however, adults are deliberately conscripting children as soldiers. Some commanders have even noted the desirability of child soldiers because they are 'more obedient, do not question orders and are easier to manipulate than adult soldiers'.

A series of 24 case studies on the use of children as soldiers prepared for the present report, covering conflicts over the past 30 years, indicate that government or rebel armies around the world have recruited tens of thousands of children. Most are adolescents, though many child soldiers are 10 years of age or younger. While the majority are boys, girls also are recruited. The children most likely to become soldiers are those from impoverished and marginalized backgrounds and those who have become separated from their families.

## Recruitment

Child soldiers are recruited in many different ways. Some are conscripted, others are press-ganged or kidnapped and still others are forced to join armed groups to defend their families. Governments in a few countries legally conscript children under 18, but even where the legal minimum age is 18, the law is not necessarily a safeguard. In many countries, birth registration is inadequate or non-existent and children do not know how old they are. Recruiters can only guess at ages based on physical development and may enter the age of recruits as 18 to give the appearance of compliance with national laws.

Countries with weak administrative systems do not conscript systematically from a register. In many instances, recruits are arbitrarily seized from the streets or even from schools and orphanages. This form of press ganging, known in Ethiopia as 'afesa', was prevalent there in the 1980's, when armed militia, police or army cadres would roam the streets picking up anyone they encountered. Children from poorer sectors of society are particularly vulnerable. Adolescent boys who work in the informal sector, selling cigarettes or gum or lottery tickets, are a particular target.

In Myanmar, whole groups of children from 15 to 17 years old have been surrounded in their schools and forcibly conscripted. Those who can subsequently prove they are under-age may be released, but not necessarily. In all conflicts, children from wealthier and more educated families are at less risk. Often, they are left undisturbed or are released if their parents can buy them out. Some children whose parents have the means are even sent out of the country to avoid the possibility of forced conscription.

In addition to being forcibly recruited, youth also present themselves for service. It is misleading, however, to consider this voluntary. While young people may appear to choose military service, the choice is not exercised freely. They may be driven by any of several forces, including cultural, social, economic or political pressures.

One of the most basic reasons that children join armed groups is economic. Hunger and poverty may drive parents to offer their children for service. In some cases, armies pay a minor soldier's wages directly to the family. Child participation may be difficult to distinguish as in some cases whole families move with armed groups. Children themselves may volunteer if they believe that this is the only way to guarantee regular meals, clothing or medical attention. Some case studies tell of parents who encourage their daughters to become soldiers if their marriage prospects are poor.

As conflicts persist, economic and social conditions suffer and educational opportunities become more limited or even non-existent. Under these circumstances, recruits tend to get younger and younger. Armies begin to exhaust the supplies of adult manpower and children may have little option but to join. In Afghanistan, where approximately 90 per cent of children now have no access to schooling, the proportion of soldiers who are children is thought to have risen in recent years from roughly 30 to at least 45 per cent.

Some children feel obliged to become soldiers for their own protection. Faced with violence and chaos all around, they decide they are safer with guns in their hands. Often such children join armed opposition groups after experiencing harassment from government forces. Many young people have joined the Kurdish rebel groups, for example, as a reaction to scorched earth policies and extensive human rights violations. In El Salvador, children whose parents had been killed by government soldiers joined opposition groups for protection. In other cases, armed forces will pick up unaccompanied children for humanitarian reasons, although this is no guarantee that the children will not end up fighting. This is particularly true of children who stay with a group for long periods of time and come to identify it as their protector or 'new family'.

In some societies, military life may be the most attractive option. Young people often take up arms to gain power and power can act as a very strong motivator in situations where people feel powerless and are otherwise unable to acquire basic resources. In many situations, war activities are glorified. In Sierra Leone, the expert met with child soldiers who proudly defended the number of 'enemies' they had killed.

The lure of ideology is particularly strong in early adolescence, when young people are developing personal identities and searching for a sense of social meaning. As the case of Rwanda shows, however, the ideological indoctrination of youth can have disastrous consequences. Children are very impressionable and may even be lured into cults of martyrdom. In Lebanon and Sri Lanka, for example, some adults have used young people's immaturity to their own advantage, recruiting and training adolescents for suicide bombings. However, it is important to note that children may also identify with and fight for social causes, religious expression, self-determination or national liberation. As happened in South Africa or in occupied territories, they may join the struggle in pursuit of political freedom.

## How child soldiers are used

Once recruited as soldiers, children generally receive much the same treatment as adults – including the often brutal induction ceremonies. Many start out in support functions which entail great risk and hardship. One of the common tasks assigned to children is to serve as porters, often carrying very heavy loads of up to 60 kilograms including ammunition or injured soldiers. Children who are too weak to carry their loads are liable to be savagely beaten or even shot. Children are also used for household and other routine duties. In Uganda, child soldiers have often done guard duty, worked in the gardens, hunted for wild fruits and vegetables and looted food from gardens and granaries. Children have also been used extensively in many countries as lookouts and messengers. While this last role may seem less life-threatening than others, in fact it puts all children under suspicion. In Latin America, reports tell of government forces that have deliberately killed even the youngest children in peasant communities on the grounds that they, too, were dangerous.

Although the majority of child soldiers are boys, armed groups also recruit girls, many of whom perform the same functions as boys. In Guatemala, rebel groups use girls to prepare food, attend to the wounded and wash clothes. Girls may also be forced to provide sexual services. In Uganda, girls who are abducted by the Lord's Resistance Army are 'married off' to rebel leaders. If the man dies, the girl is put aside for ritual cleansing and then married off to another rebel.

A case study from Honduras illustrates one child's experience of joining an armed group:

> At the age of 13, I joined the student movement. I had a dream to contribute to make things change, so that children would not be hungry... Later I joined the armed struggle. I had all the inexperience and the fears of a little girl. I found out that girls were obliged to have sexual relations 'to alleviate the sadness of the combatants'. And who alleviated our sadness after going with someone we hardly knew? At my young age I experienced abortion. It was not my decision. There is a great pain in my being when I recall all these things... In spite of my commitment, they abused me, they trampled my human dignity. And above all, they did not understand that I was a child and that I had rights.

While children of both sexes might start out in indirect support functions, it does not take long before they are placed in the heat of battle.

Here, their inexperience and lack of training leave them particularly exposed.

The youngest children rarely appreciate the perils they face. A number of case studies report that when the shelling starts the children get over-excited and forget to take cover. Some commanders deliberately exploit such fearlessness in children, even plying them with alcohol or drugs. A soldier in Myanmar recalls: 'There were a lot of boys rushing into the field, screaming like banshees. It seemed like they were immortal, or impervious, or something, because we shot at them but they just kept coming.'

The progressive involvement of youth in acts of extreme violence desensitizes them to suffering. In a number of cases, young people have been deliberately exposed to horrific scenes. Such experience makes children more likely to commit violent acts themselves and may contribute to a break with society. In many countries, including Afghanistan, Mozambique, Colombia and Nicaragua, children have even been forced to commit atrocities against their own families or communities.

## Gender-based violence: a weapon of war

Rape poses a continual threat to women and girls during armed conflict, as do other forms of gender-based violence including prostitution, sexual humiliation and mutilation, trafficking and domestic violence. While abuses such as murder and torture have long been denounced as war crimes, rape has been downplayed as an unfortunate but inevitable side effect of war. Acts of gender-based violence, particularly rape, committed during armed conflicts constitute a violation of international humanitarian law. When it occurs on a massive scale or as a matter of orchestrated policy, this added dimension is recognized as it was at the most recent International Conference of the Red Cross and Red Crescent, as a crime against humanity. Recent efforts to prosecute rape as a war crime, however, have underscored the difficulties in applying international human rights law and humanitarian law.

Women of all ages may be victims of violence in conflict, but adolescent girls are particularly at risk for a range of reasons, including size and vulnerability. Their vulnerability is even greater in some localities where they are considered less likely to have sexually transmitted diseases and the HIV/AIDS virus. Characteristics such as ethnicity, class, religion or nationality may be factors that determine which women or girls are subjected to violence. Women and girls are at risk in all settings whether in the home, during flight or in camps to which they have fled for safety. Children affected by gender-based violence also include those who have witnessed the rape of a family member and those who are ostracized because of a mother's assault.

Most child victims of violence and sexual abuse are girls, but boys are also affected and cases of young boys who have been raped or forced into prostitution are under-reported. In Bosnia and Herzegovina, sons and fathers have been forced to commit sexual atrocities against each other. In some cases, boys traumatized by violence have also subsequently been the perpetrators of sexual violence against girls.

Rape is not incidental to conflict. It can occur on a random and uncontrolled basis due to the general disruption of social boundaries and the license granted to soldiers and militias. Most often, however, it functions like other forms of torture and is used as a tactical weapon of war to humiliate and weaken the morale of the perceived enemy. During armed conflict, rape is used to terrorize populations or to force civilians to flee.

Often, gender-based violence is practised with the intent of ethnic cleansing through deliberate impregnation. The Special Rapporteur on the situation of human rights in the territory of the former Yugoslavia found that this was the case in Bosnia and Herzegovina and in Croatia. The thousands of Korean women forced to serve as military sexual slaves during the Second World War is another example of rape being used as a weapon of war.

## Child victims of prostitution and sexual exploitation

Poverty, hunger and desperation may force women and girls into prostitution, obliging them to offer sex for food or shelter, for safe conduct through the war zone or to obtain papers or other privileges for themselves and their families. Children have been trafficked from conflict situations to work in brothels in other countries, transported from Cambodia to Thailand, for example, and from Georgia to Turkey. In refugee camps in Zaire, the expert heard numerous reports of girls who had been pressured by their families to enter prostitution. Similarly, some parents among the internally displaced communities in Guatemala have been forced to prostitute their children. Other girls have done so in the hope of securing greater protection. In Colombia, for example, there have been reports of girls as young as twelve submitting themselves to paramilitary forces as a means of defending their families against other groups.

With time, different forms of gender-based violence experienced during armed conflicts become institutionalized, since many of the conditions that created the violence remain unchanged. Young girls who have become victims of prostitution for armies, for example, may have no other option but to continue after the conflict has ceased. In Phnom Penh, the number of child victims of prostitution continues to escalate with an estimated 100 children sold into prostitution each month for economic reasons.

Children may also become victims of prostitution following the arrival of peacekeeping forces. In Mozambique, after the signing of the peace treaty in 1992, soldiers of the United Nations Operation in Mozambique (ONUMOZ) recruited girls aged 12 to 18 years into prostitution. After a commission of inquiry confirmed the allegations, the soldiers implicated were sent home. In 6 out of 12 country studies on sexual exploitation of children in situations of armed conflict prepared for the present report, the arrival of peacekeeping troops has been associated with a rapid rise in child prostitution.

Sexual exploitation has a devastating impact on physical and emotional development. Unwanted and unsafe sex is likely to lead to sexually transmitted diseases and HIV/AIDS, which not only affect immediate health but also future sexual and reproductive health and mortality. In Cambodia, according to a study prepared for the present report, it is estimated that 60 to 70 per cent of the child victims of prostitution are HIV positive. Adolescent girls may nonetheless suffer in silence after the trauma of sexual exploitation; they often fear reprisals from those who attacked them or rejection by their families, not to mention the sheer personal humiliation and anguish which causes so many of them to withdraw into a shell of pain and denial. WHO has found that among rape victims the risk of suicide is high.

When a pregnancy is forced, the determination about whether it will be carried to term depends on many local circumstances, including access to and the safety of abortion, community support systems and existing religious or cultural mores. In Rwanda, the expert heard conflicting reports about the numbers of pregnancies that had been terminated or brought to term, abandoned or adopted.

All women and young girls who give birth during conflict must contend with the unexpected economic and psychosocial consequences of raising a child without adequate systems of support. The deterioration of public health infrastructure reduces access to reproductive health services, such as family planning, treatment for sexually transmitted diseases and gynaecological complications, and pre- and post-natal care.

Complications in pregnancy and delivery are especially likely for children who have children. Owing to their physical immaturity, many pregnant adolescents experience infection as a result of unsafe or incomplete abortion.

Victims of repeated rape and young girls who give birth in the absence of trained birth attendants and in unhygienic conditions are at greater risk of chronic pelvic inflammatory diseases and muscle injury that can result in incontinence. Without sensitive, timely and adequate medical care, many of these victims die. Some commit suicide because of the humiliation and embarrassment they suffer.

# Reconstruction and Reconciliation

## Reconstruction

The task of rebuilding war-torn societies is a huge one that must take place not only at the physical, economic, cultural and political, but also at the psychosocial level. Reconstruction must relate to the child, the family, the community and the country. Rebuilding need not simply mean returning to the way things were, but can offer opportunities to leap into the future rather than follow a slow but steady path of progress. Programmes designed during reconstruction can lay foundations for child protection and strengthen social infrastructures, particularly in relation to health and education. Children are rarely mentioned in reconstruction plans or peace agreements, yet children must be at the centre of rebuilding.

Part of putting children at the centre means using youth as a resource. Young people must not be seen as problems or victims, but as key contributors in the planning and implementation of long-term solutions. Children with disabilities, children living or working in the streets and children who are in institutions as a result of conflict should all become essential participants in post-conflict planning and reconstruction. In countries emerging from conflict, agencies such as ILO have a key role to play through skills and entrepreneurship training programmes that address youth. The international community has an important responsibility for sharing technical skills and knowledge as well as financial resources.

The challenges facing communities attempting to rebuild are enormous. As a consequence of scorched-earth policies, communities often have little from which to reconstruct. In many countries, landmines restrict the use of roads and agricultural lands. 'Donor pullout' can leave populations struggling to survive, particularly if humanitarian assistance has been structured in ways that encourage dependency rather than build family and community strength and integrity. For these reasons, the seeds of reconstruction should be sown even during conflict. Particularly for children, emergency aid – investment that secures their physical and emotional survival – will also be the basis for their long-term development. In this sense, emergencies and development should never be arbitrarily or artificially separated.

As daunting as reconstruction is the task of restoring family livelihood. UNHCR and others have developed a form of reintegration assistance known as 'quick impact projects'. These are simple, small-scale projects designed to act as bridges between returnees and residents while bringing immediate, tangible economic and social benefits. They involve the beneficiary community in determining priorities and implementation. One version of the quick impact projects gives female-headed households special consideration and provides loans and credits to enable them to form cooperatives and open small businesses. Before the conflict, women may have been less involved than men in economic activity, but armed conflicts can change this pattern dramatically. These projects have been particularly successful in Central America. However, not all quick impact projects have managed to involve local communities meaningfully, and some have been criticised for offering quick fix approaches which fail to benefit the community in the long term.

Such bridging programmes are crucial in providing a more formalized transition from the emergency phase to the longer-term reconstruction phase. In Cambodia, the expert was told that the phasing out of UNHCR has left a gap in support for many children and families. Agency staff argue that more defined programming, using development principles for a transitional rehabilitation phase would promote the rebuilding of a cohesive, caring social network supportive of women and children. The memoranda of understanding recently agreed between agencies such as UNHCR and UNICEF should be of help in establishing clearer directives for transition planning between agencies, but such planning needs to involve a variety of agencies and NGOs.

Education for children must be a priority in all reconstruction. For refugee children, it is important that their home countries recognize the schooling they have undertaken in the country of asylum. To facilitate this process, students should be provided with appropriate documentation of courses and qualifications. The recovery and reintegration of children will affect the success of the whole society in returning to a more peaceful path. To some extent, returning to non-violent daily activities can start the process of healing and national reconciliation, but communities must also take positive steps that signal to children the break with the violence of the past. In the demilitarization of communities, eroding the cultures of violence that conflict has engendered must be an important priority. Women's groups, religious groups and civil society all play key roles in this area.

## Reconciliation

Truth commissions, human rights commissions and reconciliation groups can be important vehicles for community healing. To date, 16 or more countries in transition from conflict have organized truth commissions as a means of establishing moral, legal and political accountability and mechanisms for recourse. In South Africa and Guatemala, the commissions are aimed at preserving the memory of the victims, fostering the observance of human rights and strengthening the democratic process. In Argentina, where there was an assumption that offenders would receive punishment, there have subsequently been amnesties to the consternation of the human rights community.

It is difficult, if not impossible, to achieve reconciliation without justice. The expert believes that the international community should develop more systematic methods for apprehending and punishing individuals guilty of child rights abuses. Unless those at every level of political and military command fear that they will be held accountable for crimes and subject to prosecution, there is little prospect of restraining their behaviour during armed conflicts. Allowing perpetrators to benefit from impunity can only lead to contempt for the law and to renewed cycles of violence.

In the case of the gravest abuses, including but not limited to genocide, international law can be more appropriate than national action. In view of this, the Security Council has established International Tribunals to punish perpetrators of war crimes and crimes against humanity committed in the former Yugoslavia and Rwanda. The expert welcomes these tribunals, but is concerned that they may have neither the resources nor the powers to fulfil their objectives. They deserve greater financial support and more determined political backing. The expert supports the proposed creation of an international criminal court, which would have a permanent prosecutor's office to try cases of genocide and other violations of international law.

One of the most disturbing and difficult aspects of children's participation in armed conflict is that, manipulated by adults, they may become perpetrators of war crimes including rape, murder and genocide. As of June 1996 in Rwanda, 1,741 children were being held in detention in dreadful conditions. Of these, approximately 550 were under 15 years, and therefore beneath the age of criminal responsibility under Rwandan law. The Government of Rwanda has transferred responsibility for the cases of young people who were under the age of 15 at the time of the genocide from the Ministry of Justice to the Ministry of Labour and Social Affairs. They were subsequently released into newly established juvenile or community detention facilities. For the estimated 1,191 children who are in detention and deemed criminally responsible, UNICEF, through the Ministry of Justice, provides legal assistance for their defence. It is also advocating special provisions for the trial of these adolescents. The dilemma of dealing with children who are accused of committing acts of genocide illustrates the complexity of balancing culpability, a community's sense of justice and the 'best interests of the child'.

The severity of the crime involved, however, provides no justification to suspend or to abridge the fundamental rights and legal safeguards accorded to children under the Convention on the Rights of the Child. States Parties should establish a minimum age below which children are presumed not to have the capacity to infringe penal law. While the Convention does not mention a specific age, the United Nations Standard Minimum Rules for the Administration of Juvenile Justice (The Beijing Rules) stress that this age shall not be fixed at too low a level, bearing in mind the child's emotional, mental and intellectual maturity. The Committee on the Rights of the Child states that the assessment of the children's criminal responsibility should not be based on subjective or imprecise criteria, such as the attainment of puberty, age of discernment or the child's personality. Those children who have been deemed criminally responsible should, as article 40 of the Convention asserts, be treated with dignity, and have their social reintegration taken into account. Children should, inter alia, be given the opportunity to participate in proceedings affecting them, either directly or through a representative or an appropriate body, benefit from legal counselling and enjoy due process of law. Deprivation of liberty should never be unlawful or arbitrary and should only be used as a measure of last resort. In all instances, alternatives to institutional care should be sought.

## Conflict prevention

> 'Children are dropping out of childhood. We must envision a society free of conflict where children can grow up as children, not weapons of war.'

Much of the present report has focused on methods by which children can be protected from the worst impacts of armed conflict. However well such measures are implemented, clearly the most effective way to protect children is to prevent the outbreak of armed conflicts. The international community must shatter the political inertia that allows circumstances to escalate into armed conflict and destroy children's lives. This means addressing the root causes of violence and promoting sustainable and equitable patterns of human development. All people need to feel that they have a fair share in decision-making, equal access to resources, the ability to participate fully in civil and political society and the freedom to affirm their own identities and fully express their aspirations. Such ideas have been eloquently expressed, with analytic power that cannot be attempted here, in such texts as *The Challenge to the South: The Report of the South Commission* and the report of the Commission on Global Governance entitled *Our Global Neighbourhood*.

Preventing conflicts from escalating is a clear responsibility of national Governments and the international community, but there is also an important role for civil society. Religious, community and traditional leaders have often been successful at conflict management and prevention, as have scholars and NGOs involved in mediation and capacity building. Women's organizations, too, have been very influential, promoting the presence of women at the negotiating table, where they can act as their own advocates and agents for peace. One example is African Women in Crisis, a UNIFEM programme working to strengthen the capacity of women's peace movements throughout Africa. The statement of the Third Regional Consultation on the Impact of Armed Conflict on Children in West and Central Africa recommends that peace missions, reconciliation forums and all peace-building efforts should incorporate women as key members of negotiating teams. The expert agrees.

## Education for peace

All sectors of society must come together to build 'ethical frameworks', integrating traditional values of cooperation through religious and community leaders with international legal standards. Some of the groundwork for the building of 'ethical frameworks' can be laid in schools. Both the content and the process of education should promote peace, social justice, respect for human rights and the acceptance of responsibility. Children need to learn skills of negotiation, problem solving, critical thinking and communication that will enable them to resolve conflicts without resorting to violence. To achieve this, a number of countries have undertaken peace education programmes. In Lebanon, the expert visited the education for peace programme, jointly undertaken in 1989 by the Lebanese Government, NGOs, youth volunteers and UNICEF and now benefiting thousands of children nationally. In Liberia, the student palaver conflict management programme employs adolescents as resources in peer conflict resolution and mediation activities in schools. In Northern Ireland, the expert was informed about initiatives aimed at the universal inclusion of peace education elements in school curricula. Similarly in Sri Lanka, an education for conflict resolution programme has been integrated into primary and secondary school education. An innovative element is the programme's use of various public media to reach to out-of-school children and other sectors of the community. While such initiatives are not always successful, they are indispensable to the eventual rehabilitation of a shattered society.

The statement of the Second Regional Consultation on the Impact of Armed Conflict in the Arab Region called for a comprehensive review of the content, process and structure of peace education programmes (sometimes called 'global education' or 'education for development' programmes). The review was to include an assessment of best practice and coordination, the promotion of effective evaluation techniques and an exploration of stronger methods of involving and responding to local needs, aspirations and experiences. The consultation also emphasized the importance of integrating peace education principles, values and skills into the education of every child.

Adults are just as much in need of conflict management skills and human rights education as children and youth. Here, the most difficult challenge is to achieve tolerance not just between individuals, but also between groups. The media can play an important role by helping readers and viewers to enjoy diversity and by promoting the understanding that is needed for peaceful co-existence and the respect that is required for the enjoyment of human rights. The media's role as mediator has been explored in South Africa, where some journalists have been trained to use their access to both sides of conflict in order to help bring about national consensus on divisive issues.

## Demilitarization

In addition to pursuing equitable patterns of development, Governments can lower the risk of armed conflict by reducing levels of militarization and by honouring the commitments made at the World Summit for Social Development to support the concept of human security. Towards that end, Governments must take firm action to shift the allocation of resources from arms and military expenditures to human and social development. Sub-Saharan Africa, for example, is heavily militarized: between 1960 and 1994, the proportion of the region's gross domestic product (GDP) devoted to military spending rose from 0.7 per cent to 2.9 per cent. The region's military expenditure is now around $8 billion, despite the fact that 216 million people live in poverty. South Asia is another region that spends heavily on arms. In 1994, it spent $14 billion on the military although 562 million South Asians live in absolute poverty. Governments worldwide should take uncompromising steps to demilitarize their societies by strictly limiting and controlling access to weapons.

At the international level, Governments must exercise the political will to control the transfer of arms to conflict zones, particularly where there is evidence of gross violation of children's rights. The United Nations must adopt a much firmer position on the arms trade, including a total ban on arms shipments to areas of conflict and determined efforts to eliminate the use, production, trade and stockpiling of anti-personnel landmines. The United Nations Register of Conventional Arms should be expanded to include more types of weapons and mandatory reporting should be required.

Donors and development agencies should give priority to programmes that include conflict prevention components designed to help manage diversity and reduce economic disparities within countries. Economic development in itself will not resolve conflicts. However, unless the reduction of economic disparities becomes an essential ingredient in all programmes, human development will be constantly thwarted by violent conflict. Donors should make stronger efforts to ensure that a greater percentage of their funding is aimed directly at social infrastructures and programmes for children.

## Conclusion

'We want a society where people are more important than things, where children are precious; a world where people can be more human, caring and gentle.'

The present report has set forth recommendations for the protection of children during armed conflict. It has concentrated on what is practical and what is possible, but this cannot be enough. In considering the future of children, we must be daring. We must look beyond what seems immediately possible and find new ways and new solutions to shield children from the consequences of war and to directly address the conflicts themselves.

There is a clear and overwhelming moral case for protecting all children while seeking the peaceful resolution of wars and challenging the justification for any armed conflict. That children are still being so shamefully abused is a clear indication that we have barely begun to fulfil our obligations to protect them. The immediate wounds to children, the physical injury, the sexual violence, the psychosocial distress, are affronts to each and every humanitarian impulse that inspired the Convention on the Rights of the Child. The Convention commits States to meet a much broader range of children's rights, to fulfil the rights to health, to education and to growth and development within caring and supportive families and communities.

The report has shown how all rights to which children are entitled are consistently abused during armed conflict. Throwing a spotlight on such abuses is one small step towards addressing them. Exposure challenges perpetrators to face up to their actions and reminds defenders of children's rights of the enormity of the task ahead. The only measure by which the present report can be judged is the response it draws and the action it stimulates. To some extent, both are already under way: the report has in many ways broken new ground, focusing not just on the debate or resolution that form the final product, but on a process of consultation and cooperation among Governments, international agencies, NGOs and many other elements of civil society. Above all, the report has engaged families and children in explaining their situations and asserting their rights.

The present report's mobilization work is ongoing. Commitments have already been made, at national and regional levels, to hold meetings that will begin to implement the report's conclusions. Further publications are planned, including a book, a series of research papers, information kits and a popular version of the report. In the preparation of the report, there were many other issues that could not be covered in the time available, and that demand further investigation. These include: operational issues affecting the protection of children in emergencies; child-centred approaches to the prevention of conflict and to reconstruction and development; the treatment of child rights violations within existing human rights mechanisms; the role of the military in protecting child rights; child rights issues in relation to peace and security agendas; special programming for adolescents in conflict situations, and particularly child-headed households; the role of women in conflict prevention, management and resolution; community and regional approaches to humanitarian relief; and the development of effective training programmes in the area of child rights for all actors in conflict situations. In following up the present report, it is recommended that each of these issues be pursued through research and other means.

The flagrant abuse and exploitation of children during armed conflict can and must be eliminated. For too long, we have given ground to spurious claims that the involvement of children in armed conflict is regrettable but inevitable. It is not. Children are regularly caught up in warfare as a result of conscious and deliberate decisions made by adults. We must challenge each of these decisions and we must refute the flawed political and military reasoning, the protests of impotence, and the cynical attempts to disguise child soldiers as merely the youngest 'volunteers'.

Above all else, the present report is a call to action. It is unconscionable that we so clearly and consistently see children's rights attacked and that we fail to defend them. It is unforgivable that children are assaulted, violated, murdered and yet our conscience is not revolted nor our sense of dignity challenged. This represents a fundamental crisis of our civilization. The impact of armed conflict on children must be everyone's concern and is everyone's responsibility; Governments, international organizations and every element of civil society. Each one of us, each individual, each institution, each country, must initiate and support global action to protect children. Local and national strategies must strengthen and be strengthened through international mobilization.

Let us claim children as 'zones of peace'. In this way, humankind will finally declare that childhood is inviolate and that all children must be spared the pernicious effects of armed conflict. Children present us with a uniquely compelling motivation for mobilization. Universal concern for children presents new opportunities to confront the problems that cause their suffering. By focusing on children, politicians, Governments, the military and non-State entities will begin to recognize how much they destroy through armed conflict and, therefore, how little they gain. Let us take this opportunity to recapture our instinct to nourish and protect children. Let us transform our moral outrage into concrete action. Our children have a right to peace. Peace is every child's right.

# WHY WE USE VIOLENCE

Frantz Fanon

1960[1]

## Context (by Timur Uçan)

**The conference:** The following discourse has been pronounced in Accra in
April 1960 during an international conference. Little information is available concerning the conference itself: (i) Its name: some sources name this
conference the 'Accra Conference on Peace and Security in Africa' *('Con-
férence d'Accra sur la paix et la sécurité en Afrique')*, but probably its exact
name was 'Conference on the positive action for peace and security in
Africa' *('Conference de l'action positive pour la paix et la sécurité en Afrique')*
(cf. Matt Meyer—http://www.wri-irg.org/node/22754 ). (ii) Its exact date:
it has been probably held on 4th of April 1960, as Fanon refers to the
Sharpeville Massacre in his discourse, about which he says that it happened two weeks before. (iii) Its composition: the discourse of Fanon starts
with a reference to an earlier discourse made during the same conference
by Kwame N'krumah. Also Bill Sutherland reported to Matt Meyer that
he attended this conference with Reverend Abraham Johannes Muste and
Reverend Ralph Abernathy.

**On Fanon during this period:** Fanon became the chief-doctor of a division
of the psychiatric hospital of Blida-Joinville in Algeria in 1953. From the
beginning of the Algerian war in 1954 he secretly joined the National Liberation Front (FLN) of Algeria. He resigned from his job in 1956 and was
expelled from Algeria by the French in 1957. He then rejoined the FLN in
Tunis and started working in its newspaper 'El Moudjahid'. During this
period, he escaped several murder attempts commanded by the French
government, notably during his hospitalizations for Leukemia in Italy and
Morocco. In March 1960, less than a month before the present conference he was appointed ambassador for the Provisional Government of the
Algerian Republic (GPRA) based in Ghana. In this sense, 'Why We Use
Violence' may be seen as one of the first occasion at which Fanon would

---

1. Note: Please do not share or quote without permission of the translator (Timur Uçan), as the translation needs yet to be
finalized. The footnotes are mine and the terms between square brackets are original French terms of Fanon's discourse, which have been quoted to mark explicitly translation choices. Attention has been paid during the translation to
convey the original peculiarities of the author's style which are often at odds with idioms of contemporary English.

officially exercise his ambassadorial function. In this sense, this discourse constitutes a major document to evaluate the kind of political stance he took to be compatible with his thought.

A crucial year in the process of decolonization of Africa was 1960, during which 17 countries obtain their independence out of which 14 were totally or partially under French rule. Twelve of those countries would proclaim their independence between April and December 1960. It matters to see that Fanon's discourse has been written just before the official acknowledgment by the French government of the collapse of its colonial empire in Africa. It can be argued that from the perspective of the French government, the main incentive for the acceptance of the emancipation of these countries was (i) negatively: the fear of the reproduction of the Algerian case which had led the 4th French Republic to its end in 1958 (something Fanon alludes to in his discourse) and (ii) positively: firstly, the taking of the political initiative in order to retain some power on the newly decolonized countries; and secondly, to fight against Communism (Fanon will later denounce and criticize this in 1961 in his *The Wretched of the Earth*, 'On Violence', 30-34. What can also be seen as the founding act of the French neo-colonialist and secret policy in Africa, a policy named by the militant François-Xavier Verschave 'Françafrique' in an eponymous book (1999), turned into a documentary in 2002).

## Why we use Violence

I think that all the worries which inhabit Africa today have been tackled with mastery and clear-sightedness by the discourse of Doctor N'Krumah.

Today, I would like to inform you of reflections aroused by certain passages [of this discourse]. The problem of violence and of racism in African States will be questioned today, which I would like to fraternally debate with you.

Today, I do not want, as you might imagine, to proceed with a criticism of the colonial system. I do not want, me that I am a colonized, talking to colonized,[2] to demonstrate that the colonial State is an abnormal State, inhuman and condemnable. It would be grotesque on my part to wish to convince you of the unacceptable character of colonial oppression. However, I would like to center my reflections on violence consubstantial to colonial oppression.

## A regime founded on violence

The colonial regime is a regime established by violence. It is always by force that the colonial regime implanted itself. It is against the will of peoples that other

---

2. Fanon uses 'colonized' to refer to persons native to colonized lands.

peoples[3] more advanced in destructive techniques or numerically more powerful imposed themselves.

I say that such a system established by violence can logically only be faithful to itself and its duration in time depends on [est function de] the maintenance of violence.

But the violence which is here questioned is not an abstract violence, it is not only a violence deciphered by the spirit, it is also a violence of the daily behavior of the colonizer towards the colonized: *apartheid* in South Africa, forced labor in Angola, racism in Algeria. Despise, hatred politics, such are the manifestations of a very concrete and very painful violence.

Colonialism, nevertheless, does not satisfy itself with this violence in respect to the present. The colonized people is ideologically presented as one people stopped in its evolution, impermeable to reason, incapable to lead its own affairs, requiring the permanent presence of a direction.[4] The history of colonized peoples is transformed into meaningless agitation and, therefore, we have quite the impression that for these peoples humanity started with the arrival of these valorous colonizers. Violence in daily behavior, violence with respect to the past which is emptied from any substance, violence with respect to future, as the colonial regime presents itself [se donne] as needing to be eternal. We thus see that the colonized people, taken within a network of a tridimensional violence, the meeting point of multiple, diverse, reiterated and cumulative violence, is quite rapidly led to logically pose to itself the problem of ending [d'une fin] the colonial regime by any means.

This violence of colonial regime is not only lived on a spiritual level, but also on the one of muscles and blood. This violence which wills itself violent,[5] which becomes more and more disproportionate, irremediably provokes the birth of an internal violence in the colonized people and a just anger arises and seeks to express itself.

The role of the political party which takes charge of the destinies of this people is to contain this violence and to channel it by assuring a pacific platform and a constructive ground as, for the human spirit which contemplates the unfolding of history and which attempts to remain on the ground of the universal, violence must be first fought against with the language of truth and reason. But it happens, alas – and there cannot be men who do not deplore this historical necessity -, it

---

3. 'People' is the best translation of the French term 'Peuple', but note that it only partially corresponds to the ordinary English uses: less than a plural term for 'persons' as in 'some people might think that x', the use of Fanon involves or connotes some singular form of cultural or political unity as in 'the Algerian people', etc.
4. 'Direction' may be used - in French as in English – both to indicate a way to a destination (as in 'turn left in direction of x' and to refer to one or several managers or rulers ('the direction decided that x').
5. This characterization of colonial violence by Fanon is *not* a mere pleonasm. Indeed by a violence which does not *will* itself violent one can both qualify violent acts perpetrated by persons who are trying to hide the violent character of their operation (as in some secret military operations), or violent acts in which violence is not taken as an end but only as a means (cf. the contrast between intending to murder and murdering someone and killing someone in self-defense, i.e. without premeditation). Fanon addresses here an aspect of violence proper to its political instrumentalization within the colonial context: a 'violence which *wills itself violent*' should probably be understood here as a violence which is being publicly perpetrated and assumed as such in order to found or maintain a colonial state and the respect of the colonizer/colonized distinction consubstantial to it.

happens, I say, that in some enslaved lands the violence of the colonized becomes simply a manifestation of its properly animal existence. I say animal and I speak as a biologist, as such reactions are, on the whole, only defense reactions translating [traduisant] an absolutely commonplace instinct of conservation.

And the acquisition of the Algerian revolution is precisely to have grandiosely culminated and to have provoked the mutation of the conservation instinct in value and truth. For the Algerian people, the only solution was this heroic combat at the heart of which he had to crystallize its national consciousness and deepen its quality of African people.

And no one may deny that all this blood spilt in Algeria will eventually be the yeast of the grand African nation.

In some colonies, the violence of the colonized is the last gesture made by the tracked man, willing thereby to signify that he is ready to defend his life. There are colonies which fight for freedom, independence, for the right to happiness. In 1954, the Algerian people took up arms because the colonialist jail was becoming so oppressing that it was not bearable anymore, that the hunting of Algerians, in the streets and in the countryside was definitively open and because, finally, it was not for him a question anymore of giving sense to his life but of giving one to his death.

## Racism in Algeria and in British Colonies

... The millions of Europeans which are in Algeria pose particular problems. Colonizers in Algeria fear the Algerian Nation. Physical fear, moral fear. And this double fear is translated [se traduit] through aggression and highly homicidal conducts. At the basis of this behavior we find: (1) a highly powerful culpability complex. 'If the Algerians, they say, would one day lead Algeria, they would probably do what us, the colonizers, have done, and would make us pay for our crimes'; (2) there is also a particular Manicheist conception of humanity which would always be divided between oppressors and oppressed.

... We Africans are not racists and the honorable Dr. N'Krumah is right when he says: 'The concept of Africa to Africans does not mean that other races are excluded from it. It means solely that Africans who are naturally the majority in Africa must themselves rule their own countries. We struggle for the future and it is one of the most important struggles'.

The colonizer in Algeria says that Algeria belongs to him. We, Algerians, we say: 'All right, Algeria belongs to all, let's build it on democratic bases and together let's build an Algeria which is at the scale of our ambition and our love'.

Colonizers answer us that they do not will a modified Algeria. That what they want is an Algeria which perpetuates itself eternally in its actual state. In reality, the French colonizer does not live in Algeria, he rules there and every attempt to modify the colonial status elicits highly murderous reactions in the colonizer.

Fourteen days ago our brothers from South Africa were manifesting their hostility to laws promulgated by the racist government of the Union. 200 deaths have been numbered.[6] We cry for our brothers [nous pleurons nos frères] from South Africa, we criticize the South African government and we say that this international moral pressure is a major asset in the struggle for African freedom.

## The massacres

But on 8th of May 1945, almost fifteen years ago, the Algerian people were marching in Algeria's main streets in order to reclaim the liberation of some political prisoners and the application of human rights on national territory. At the end of the day 45 000 Algerians were buried.[7]. These numbers which revolt consciousness are the numbers recognized by the government of the French Republic[8]. To date, not one French has been sued to answer for one of those 45 000 deaths.

What we say is that we must close ranks. Our voice must be powerful not only by its tone but also through concrete measures which could be taken against such and such colonial State.

African comrades, that never one day arises where one could see in twenty-four hours 45 000 citizens swept by colonialist Barbary!

We must make the white colonizers and the nations which support them truly hesitant.

In Angola where 200 000 Portuguese spread terror. In Rhodesia where the monstrous face of Racism shows itself with an unmatched violence. In Kenya where our valorous brother Jomo Kenyata rots in prison and where the colonizers do not despair to give a last victorious battle.

The colonizer as we find him in Algeria, in Angola, in Kenya, in Rhodesia, in South African Union, is obstinately hostile to any attempts on his supremacy.

We do not say to the colonizer: 'you are a stranger, go away'. We do not say to him: 'we are going to take the lead of the country and make you pay for your crimes and those of your ancestors'. We do not say to him that against the past hatred of the Black we will oppose compete with the present and future hatred of the White. We say to him: 'we are Algerians, let's banish from our soil any racism, any form of oppression and let's work for mankind, for the flourishing and the enrichment of mankind'.

The colonizer answers us, and the French government supports him: 'Algeria is French'. In Angola: Angola is Portuguese. In South-African Union: South African Union is a white State. To the statement of the Algerian Prime Minister, Ferhat Abbas, in which he solemnly appeals to the Europeans of Algeria as Algerian citizens—a statement whose elevated thought and moving terms have struck the most pro-French Occidental countries—the general De Gaulle has answered,

6. Allusion to the Sharpeville massacre of the 21st of March 1960 in the region of Transvaal, South Africa which led to the radicalization of the struggle against Apartheid later on. Today, only 69 victims of this massacre are officially recognized.
7. Allusion to the massacres of Setif, Guelma and Kherrata, Algeria. Contemporary researches estimate this number to be between five and ten thousands.
8. That such number had been officially recognized by France at that time is highly improbable, as in 1945, only 1165 victims had been recognized.

under the pressure of the colonizers and the army, that any idea of an Algerian nation ought to be destroyed. Instead of recognizing the Algerian national sovereignty, the French government has preferred changing of government six times and one time of Republic. And the Fifth Republic put in place by the general De Gaulle faces [connaît], despite the atomic bombs thrown in the Algerian Sahara, increasingly difficult moments because of the lasting of Algerian war [par suite du prolongement de la guerre d'Algérie].

In our underground military hospitals, the Algerian wounded made prisoners by the French are well often cowardly, savagely slaughtered in their beds. We heal tortured Algerians. We heal Algerian women who became insane after rapes and tortures. And by dozens [vingtaines] we bury Algerians shot in the back. And the valorous Yugoslav people welcome at an accelerated cadency amputated, dismembered, blinded Algerians and I say that if wrath does not submerge the one who assists to such things, it is that he lacks a dimension.

Besides, it must be pointed [signalé] that it is firstly [d'abord] this wrath, this immense repulsion for French atrocities that has led to our ranks the biggest part of the European Algerians who are today members of the FLN. Sometimes it is the own children of police officers who during the nights are obsessed with the shouts of the tortured. And you understand now why some Christians, some priests also militate within the FLN. Why today there are Europeans of Algeria, descendents of the colonizers who die under the French bullets in the ranks of the brave Algerian National Liberation Army.

## The Unique Solution

No the violence of the Algerian people is not hatred of peace and rejection of human contact, neither the conviction that only war may end the colonial regime in Algeria.

The Algerian people has chosen the unique solution which was left to him and this choice we will maintain [et ce choix nous nous y maintiendrons].

The general de Gaulle says: 'we must break the Algerian people'. We answer him: 'Let's negotiate, find a solution which is at the scale of contemporary history. But know that if you want to break the Algerian people, you will have to accept to see your armies get shattered against the wall of the glorious Algerian soldiers'.

So many Africans are dead in order to defend the sovereignty of European states, that today it is worth that some Africans accept to die for the freedom of Africa. And my presence here in Ghana as an official representative of the GPRA, the Algerian flag floating on Accra, proves that the government and the people of Ghana supports the Algerian people, base an unconditional hope on its victory and have a fraternal and warm regard for the glorious soldiers of the Algerian army.

My presence here testifies that Algeria is with you, that you make its suffering yours and that in a very precise way, a big step is done in the path of unity and African greatness.

# ON REVOLUTION AND EQUILIBRIUM

Barbara Deming

1971[1]

*What we want to do is to go forward all the time . . . in the company of all men. But can we escape becoming dizzy?* —Frantz Fanon in *The Wretched of the Earth*

'Do you want to remain pure? Is that it?' a black man asked me, during an argument about nonviolence. It is not possible to act at all and to remain pure; and that is not what I want, when I commit myself to the nonviolent discipline. There are people who are struggling to change conditions that they find intolerable, trying to find new lives; in the words of Frantz Fanon in *The Wretched of the Earth*, they want 'to set afoot a new man.' That is what I want, too; and I have no wish to be assigned, as it were, separate quarters from those who are struggling in a way different from mine—segregated from my companions rather as, several years ago in Birmingham at the end of a demonstration, I found myself segregated in the very much cleaner and airier white section of the jail. I stand with all who say of present conditions that they do not allow men to be fully human and so they must be changed—all who not only say this but are ready to act.

At a recent conference about the directions the American Left should take, a socialist challenged me: 'Can you call degrading the violence used by the oppressed to throw off oppression?' When one is confronted with what Russell Johnson calls accurately 'the violence of the *status quo*'—conditions which are damaging, even murderous, to very many who must live within them—it is degrading for all to allow such conditions to persist? And if the individuals who can find the courage to bring about change see no way in which it can be done without employing violence on their own part—a very much lesser violence, they feel, than the violence to which they will put an end—I do not feel that I can judge them. The judgments I make are not judgments upon men but upon the means open to us—upon the promise these means of action hold or withhold. The living question is: What are the best means for changing our lives—for really changing them?

The very men who speak of the necessity of violence, if change is to be accomplished, are the first, often, to acknowledge the toll it exacts among those who use

1. Barbara Deming, *Revolution and Equilibrium*, New York: Grossman Publishers, 1971

it—as well as those it is used against. Frantz Fanon has a chapter in *The Wretched of the Earth* entitled 'Colonial war and Mental Disorders' and in it he writes, 'We are forever pursued by our actions.' After describing, among other painful disorders, those suffered by an Algerian terrorist—who made friends among the French after the war and then wondered with anguish whether any of the men he had killed had been men like these—he comments, 'It was what might be called an attack of vertigo.' Then he asks a poignant question: 'But can we escape becoming dizzy? And who can affirm that vertigo does not haunt the whole of existence?'

'Vertigo'—here is a word, I think, much more relevant to the subject of revolutionary action than the word 'purity.' No, it is not that I want to remain pure; it is that I want to escape becoming dizzy. And here is exactly the argument of my essay: we can escape it. Not absolutely, of course; but we can escape vertigo in the drastic sense. It is my stubborn faith that if, as revolutionaries, we will wage battle without violence, we can remain very much more in control—of our own selves, of the responses to us which our adversaries make, of the battle as it proceeds, and of the future we hope will issue from it.

The future—by whom will it be built? By all those whom the struggle has touched and marked. And so the question of how it marks them is not irrelevant. The future will be built even, in part, by those who have fought on the losing side. If it is a colonial struggle, of course, a good many of the adversaries can be expected to leave at the end of a successful revolution; but if it is a civil struggle, those who have been defeated, too, will at least help to make the new society what it is. How will the struggle have touched them? How will it have touched the victors?

Carl Oglesby, in *Containment and Change*, quotes a Brazilian guerilla: 'We are in dead earnest. At stake is the humanity of man.' Then he asks, 'How can ordinary men be at once warm enough to want what revolutionaries say they want [humanity], cold enough to do without remorse what they are capable of doing [cutting throats], and poised enough in the turbulence of their lives to keep the aspiration and the act both integrated and distinct? How is it that one of these passions does not invade and devour the other?'

Oglesby would seem to answer that, generally speaking, one cannot expect the rebel to have the poise he describes. 'He is an irresponsible man whose irresponsibility has been decreed by others. ... He has no real views about the future ... is not by *type* a Lenin, a Mao, a Castro. ... His motivating vision of change is at root a vision of something absent—not of something that *will* be there ... a missing landlord, a missing mine owner, a missing sheriff...' Ultimately, says Oglesby, he must *become* responsible. But how? It is in the midst of the struggle that he must at least begin to be, isn't it? And so the very means by which we struggle, and their tendency either to give us poise or to leave us dizzy, is surely, again, relevant.

I think of the words with which Fanon opens the final chapter of *The Wretched of the Earth*: 'Come then, comrades; it would be as well to decide at once to change our ways.' I quote Fanon often—because he is eloquent, but also because he is quoted repeatedly these days by those who plead the need for violence. It is my conviction that he can be quoted as well to plead for nonviolence. It is true that he declares: 'From birth it is clear ... that this narrow world, strewn with prohibitions, can only be called in question by absolute violence.' But I ask all those who are readers of Fanon to make an experiment: Every time you find the word 'violence' in his pages, substitute for it the phrase 'radical and uncompromising action.' I contend that with the exception of a very few passages this substitution can be made, and that the action he calls for could just as well be nonviolent action.

He writes for example: Violence alone, violence committed by the people, violence organized and educated by its leaders, makes it possible for the masses to understand social truths and gives the key to them. Without that struggle, without that knowledge of the practice of action, there's nothing but a fancy-dress parade ... a few reforms at the top ... and down there at the bottom an undivided mass ... endlessly marking time.' 'Knowledge of the practice of action'—*that* is what Fanon seems to be absolutely necessary, to develop in the masses of people an understanding of social truths, accomplish that 'work of clarification,' 'demystification,' 'enlightening of consciousness' which is the recurring and the deepest theme of his book. This action could be nonviolent action; it could very much better be nonviolent action—if only that action is bold enough.

Here is Fanon as he argues the necessity for 'mere rebellion'—which Oglesby has described—to become true revolution: 'Radicalism and hatred and resentment—'a legitimate desire for revenge'— cannot sustain a war of liberation. Those lightning flashes of consciousness which fling the body into stormy paths or which throw it into an almost pathological trance where the face of the other beckons me on to giddiness, where any blood calls for the blood of the other ... that intense emotion of the first few hours falls to pieces if it is left to feed on its own substances. ...You'll never overthrow the terrible enemy machine, and you won't change human beings if you forget to raise the standard of consciousness of the rank-and-file.'

The task involves the enlightening of consciousness. But violence 'beckons me on to giddiness.' I repeat Fanon's words: 'It would be as well to decide at once to change our ways.' Another man with whom I was arguing the other day declared to me, 'You can't turn the clock back now to nonviolence!' turn the clock back? The clock has been turned to violence all down through history. Resort to violence hardly marks a move forward. It is nonviolence which is in the process of invention, if only people would not stop short in that experiment. Fanon again: 'If we want humanity to advance a step further, if we want to bring it up to a different level than that which Europe has shown it, then we must invent and we must make discoveries.' It is for that spirit of invention that I plead. And again I would like to ask something of all readers of Fanon. Turn to that last chapter of *The Wretched of the Earth* and read it again. Is he not groping here visibly for a way that departs from violence?

He writes, 'We today can do everything, so long as we do not imitate Europe.' And earlier in the book he has reported, 'The argument the native chooses has been furnished by the seller. ... The native now affirms that the colonialist understands nothing but force.' He writes, 'We must leave our dreams. ... And earlier he has written, 'The native is an oppressed person whose permanent dream is to become the persecutor.' He writes, 'Leave this Europe where they are never done talking of Man, yet murder men everywhere they find them, at the corner of every one of their own streets, in all the corners of the globe. ... Europe has ... set her face against all solicitude and all tenderness. ... So, my brother, how is it that we do not understand that we have better things to do than to follow that same Europe. ... When I search for Man in the technique and the style of Europe, I see only a succession of negations of man, and an avalanche of murders. ... Let us combine our muscles and our brains in a new direction. Let us try to create the whole man, whom Europe has been incapable of bringing to triumphant birth. All the elements of a solution .. have, at different times, existed in European thought. But the action of European men has not carried out the mission which fell to them. We must try to set afoot a new man.' And he writes, 'It is simply a very concrete question of not dragging men toward mutilation. ... The pretext of catching up must not be used to push men around, to tear him away from himself or from his privacy, to break and kill him. No, we do not want to catch up with anyone. What we want to do is to go forward all the time, night and day, in the company of Man, in the company of all men.'

*But how in the company of all men if we are willing to kill?* In the passages I have quoted does Fanon not warn us again and again against murder, warn us that murder cannot possibly bring to birth the new man—that it was precisely Europe's propensity for murder that kept her from carrying out the mission we now inherit? What really but radical nonviolence is he here straining to be able to imagine? We must 'vomit up' the values of Europe, he has written. Is it not above all the value that Europe and America have put upon violence that we must vomit up? He writes, 'It is simply a very concrete question of not dragging men toward mutilation.' Yes, very concrete, I urge because it comes down to the means by which we struggle, comes down to a choice of *which* 'practice of action' we are going to study.

At this point suddenly I can hear in my head many voices interrupting me. They all say: 'Who among us likes violence? But nonviolence has been tried.' It has *not* been tried. We have hardly begun to try it. The people who dismiss it now as irrelevant do not understand what it could be. And, again, they especially do not understand the very much greater control over events that they could find if they would put this 'practice of action,' rather than violence, to a real test.

What most people are saying just now of course is that nonviolence gives us no control at all over events. 'After years of this,' says Stokely Carmichael, 'we are at almost the same point.' Floyd McKissick expresses the same disillusion: all the nonviolent campaigns have accomplished essentially nothing for black people. They have served to integrate a token few into American society. Even those few cannot be said to have been absorbed into the mainstream; they still are not allowed to forget the color of their skins. And the great majority of black people are actually worse off than before. He declares, with reason, 'We are concerned about the aspirations of the 90 percent down there'—those of whom Fanon spoke, the many 'endlessly marking time.'

I won't try to pretend that progress has been made that has not been made. Though I would add to the picture these two men and others paint that there is one sense in which things hardly can be said to be at the same point still. If one speaks of psychological forces that will make a difference—the determiniation of black people not to accept their situation any longer, the determination of some white people not to accept it either, and a consciousness on the part of other white people that changes are bound to come now, doubts about their ability to prevent them—in these terms all has been in constant motion. And these terms—Fanon for one would stress—are hardly unimportant. Literally, yes, one can speak of gains that seem to mock those who have nearly exhausted themselves in the struggle for them. But I think one has to ask certain questions. Have gains been slight because nonviolent tactics were the wrong tactics to employ—or did many of those leading the battle underestimate the difficulties of the terrain before them? Did they lack at the start a sufficiently radical vision? Can those who have now turned from reliance upon nonviolence say surely that resort to violence over those same years would have brought greater gains?

There are those who are implying this now. One observer who implies it strongly is Andrew Kopkind, writing in The *New York Review of Books* in August about the uprisings in the ghettos. He writes, 'Martin Luther King and the 'leaders' who appealed for nonviolence, CORE, the black politicians, the old S.N.C.C. *are all* beside the point. Where the point is is in the streets. ... The insurrections of July have done what everyone in America for thirty years has thought impossible; mass action has convulsed the society and brought smooth government to a halt.' He itemizes with awe: they caused tanks to rumble through the heart of the nation's biggest cities, brought out soldiers by the thousands, destroyed billions of dollars worth of property. This violence (or as Dave Dellinger better names it, this counterviolence of the victimized) certainly called out the troops. One thing violence can be counted on to do is bring the antagonist forth in battle dress. The question that hasn't been answered yet is: Did this gain the rebels an advantage? It gained them many casualties. The powers-that-be paid their price, too, as Kopkind points out. But it is one thing to be able to state the price the antagonist paid, another to be able to count your own real gains. Kopkind gives us the heady sense of an encounter really joined at last, of battle lines drawn. But in the days of Birmingham, too, people had the excited sense of an engagement entered. Kopkind himself grants, 'It is at once obvious that the period of greatest danger is just beginning.'

I have slighted, however, one pint that he is making, and a very central point: 'Poor blacks,' he writes, 'have stolen the center stage from the liberal elites ... their actions indict the very legitimacy of [the] government.' Yes, this is a fact not to overlook: the people of the ghettos have thrown down a challenge to government that is radical. But Kopkind is writing about two things: the offering of radical challenge and resort to violence. And he writes clearly as though he assumes that such a challenge can only be offered violently. It is with this assumption that I argue.

It is an assumption many share. Carl Oglesby seems to share it. In *Containment and Change* he criticizes 'the politics of the appeal to higher power ... the same thing as prayer ... a main assumption of which is that [the higher power] is not bad, only misinformed.' He appears to see all nonviolent action as covered by this definition. 'This way of thinking brought the peasants and priests to their massacre at Kremlin Square in 1905. ... It rationalized the 1963 March on Washington for Jobs and Freedom. The Freedom Rides, the nonviolent sit-ins, and the various Deep South marches were rooted in the same belief: . . . The Vietnam war demonstrations are no different. ... The main idea has always been to persuade higher authority... to do something. Far from calling higher authority into question, these demonstrations actually dramatize and even exaggerate its power.'

He goes on then to describe how the 'whimsical' hopes that are entertained about the powerful evaporate: 'Sometimes mass-based secular prayer has resulted in change. But more often it has only shown the victim-petitioner that the problem is graver and change harder to get than [he] had imagined. ... It turns out that the powerful know perfectly well who their victims are .... and that they have no intention of changing anything. This recognition is momentous, no doubt the spiritual low point of the emergent revolutionary's education. He finds that the enemy is not a few men but a whole system whose agents saturate the society. ... He is diverted by a most realistic despair. But this despair contains within itself the omen of that final reconstitution of the spirit which will prepare [him] . . . for the shift to insurgency, rebellion, revolution. ... At the heart of his despair lies the new certainty that there will be no change which he does not produce himself.'

With this description I do not ague at all. It is a very accurate description of the education those protesting in this country have been receiving. May more and more read the lesson. I argue with the contention that nonviolent action can only be prayerful action—must by its nature remain naïve. Too often in the past it has confined itself to petition, but there is no need for it to do so—especially now that so many have learned 'change [is] harder to get than they had imagined.' As Kopkind writes, 'all that has come until now is prologue.' But this does not mean that our alternatives have suddenly been reduced. There have always been those in the nonviolent movement who called for radical action. The pressure that nonviolent moves could put upon those who are opposing change, the power that could be exerted this way, has yet to be tested.

I have introduced the word 'power' deliberately. When the slogan 'Black Power' was first taken up, the statements immediately issued, both for and against it, all seemed to imply that 'power' was a word inconsistent with a faith in nonviolence. This was of course the position taken by Stokely Carmichael: 'we had to work for power because this country does not function by morality, love and nonviolence, but by power. For too many years, black Americans marched and had their heads broken and got shot. They were saying to the country, 'Look, you guys are supposed to be nice guys and we are only going to do what we are supposed to do. Why ... don't you give us what we ask?... We demonstrated from a position of weakness. We cannot be expected any longer to march and have our heads broken in order to say to whites: Come on, you're nice guys. For you are not nice guys. We have found you out.'

Carmichael gives us: the humble appeal to conscience on the one hand, the resort to power on the other. If the choice were really this, anyone who wanted change would certainly have to abandon nonviolent action. For as Bradford Lyttle comments in a paper on Black Power, no, most people are not nice guys. 'It isn't necessary to be hit over the head to learn this. ... Some Christians call the un-niceness of people 'original sin.' It's Freud's 'ego.' Naturalist Konrad Lorenz studies it as aggressiveness and argues convincingly that it's instinctive with men. Whatever the un-niceness may be, it is part of all of us, and our job is to minimize it.'

The trouble is that advocates of nonviolence themselves often write in terms that seem to corroborate the picture Carmichael paints. When they actually engage in direct action, they pay great attention to other than moral pressures that can be and have to be placed on those with whom they are struggling. But on paper they tend again and again to stress only the appeal that can be made to conscience. Lyttle, in his paper on Black Power, notes: 'Carmichael's vision isn't limited to Negroes. Machiavelli had it: ... 'A man who wishes to make a profession of goodness in everything must necessarily come to grief among so many who are not good. Therefore it is necessary ... to learn how not to be good.' Then he pleads that to put one's faith in coercive power is tragic, and his argument is: 'Throughout history, those who have most deeply touched the hearts of hardened men have been the ones who chose not to defend themselves with violence.' He, too, seems here to pose a narrow choice: resort to power (learning how not to be good) or appeal to conscience (learning, Carmichael would put it, to do only what we are supposed to do). But the choice is very much wider than this (as Lyttle of course knows); and the distinctions that seem to have been set up here are unreal. To resort to power one need not be violent,[2] and to speak to conscience one need not be meek. The most effective action both resorts to power *and* engages conscience. Nonviolent action does not have to beg others to 'be nice.' It can in effect force them to consult their consciences—or to pretend to have them. Nor does it have to petition those in power to do something about a situation. It can face the authorities with a new fact and say: Accept this new situation which *we* have created.

If people doubt that there is power in nonviolence, I am afraid that it is due in part to the fact that those of us who believe in it have yet to find for ourselves an adequate vocabulary. The leaflets we pass out tend to speak too easily about love and truth—and suggest that we hope to move men solely by being loving and truthful. The words do describe our method in a kind of shorthand. But who can read the shorthand? It is easy enough to recommend 'love.' How many, even among those who like to use the word, can literally feel love for a harsh opponent—not merely pretending to while concealing from themselves their own deepest feelings? What is possible is to act toward another human being on the assumption that all men's lives are of value, that there is something about any man to be loved, whether one can *feel* love for him or not.[3] It happens that, if one

---

2. Although those in the Movement who issued critical statements against use of the slogan 'Black Power' seemed almost always to imply that 'power' was an improper word, I couldn't help noticing that just that word had a way of slipping into their own publicity releases—an S.C.L.C. release, for example, repudiating the slogan but speaking the next moment of the 'political power' they sought through pushing voter registration.
3. Sometimes, if one disciplines oneself to act upon this assumption, the feeling of love for one's enemy enters one, taking one by surprise—a kind of grace. Some readers may ask: Why should one want to feel love for one's enemy? But I note that Fanon in *Black Skin, White Masks* writes, 'I, the man of color, want only this: ...That it be possible for me to discover and to love man, wherever he may be.'

does act on this assumption, it gives one much greater poise in the situation. It is easy enough to speak about truth; but we had better spell out how, in battle, we rely upon the truth. It is not simply that we pay our antagonist the human courtesy of not lying to him. We insist upon telling him truths he doesn't want to hear—telling what seems to us the truth about the injustice he commits. Words are not enough here. Gandhi's term for nonviolent action was 'satyagraha'—which can be translated as 'clinging to the truth.' What is needed is this—to *cling* to the truth as one sees it. And one has to cling with one's entire weight. One doesn't simply say, 'I have a right to sit here,' but acts out that truth—and sits here. One doesn't just say, 'If we are customers in this store, it's wrong that we're never hired here,' but refuses to be a customer any longer. One doesn't just say, 'I don't believe in this war,' but refuses to put on a uniform. One doesn't just say, 'The use of napalm is atrocious,' but refuses to pay for it by refusing to pay one's taxes. And so on and on. One brings what economic weight one has to bear, what political, social, psychological, what physical weight. There is a good deal more involved here than a moral appeal. It should be acknowledged both by those who argue against nonviolence and those who argue for it that we, too, rely upon force.

If greater gains have not been won by nonviolent action it is because most of those trying it have, quite as Oglesby charges, expected too much from 'the powerful'; and so, I would add, they have stopped far too short of really exercising their peculiar powers—those powers one discovers when one refuses any longer simply to do another's will. They have stopped far short not only of widespread nonviolent disruption but of that form of noncooperation which is assertive, constructive—that confronts those who are 'running everything' with independent activity, particularly independent economic activity. There is leverage for change here that has scarcely begun to be applied.

To refuse one's cooperation is to exert force. One can, in fact, exert so very much force in this way that many people will always be quick to call noncooperation violent. How, then, does one distinguish nonviolent from violent action? It is not that it abstains from force, to rely simply upon moral pressure. It resorts even to what can only be called physical force—when, for example, we sit down and refuse to move, and we force others to cope somehow with all these bodies. The distinction to make is simply that those committed to a nonviolent action is as bold as it must be in any real battle for change, some at least of those resisting the change are bound to *feel* that injury has been done them. For they feel it as injury to be shaken out of the accustomed pattern of their lives. The distinction remains a real one. Perhaps there is another way it could be put. The man who acts violently forces another to do *his* will—in Fanon's words, he tears the other away from himself, pushes him around, often willing to break him, kill him. The man who acts nonviolently insists upon acting out his own will, refuses to act out another's—but in this way, only, exerts force upon the other, not tearing him away from himself but tearing from him only that which is not properly his own, the strength which has been loaned to him by all those who have been giving him obedience.

But the distinction I have just made is a little too neat. In almost any serious nonviolent struggle, one has to resort to obstructive action. When we block access to buildings, block traffic, block shipments, it can be charged that we go a little further than refusing obedience and impose upon the freedom of action of others. There is some justice to the charge. I nevertheless think it appropriate to speak of nonviolent obstruction, and I would revert to my original description as the definitive one: the person committed to nonviolent action refuses to injure the antagonist. It is quite possible to frustrate another's action without do him injury.[4] And some freedoms are basic freedoms, some are not. To impose upon another man's freedom to kill, or his freedom to help to kill, to recruit to kill, is not to violate his person in a fundamental way.[5]

But I can imagine the impatience of some of my readers with these various scruples. What, they might say, has this to do with fighting battles—battles which are in dead earnest? How can we hope to put any real pressure upon an adversary for whom we show such concern?

This is the heart of my argument: We can put *more* pressure on the antagonist for whom we show human concern. It is precisely solicitude for his person *in combination with* a stubborn interference with his actions that can give us a very special degree of control (precisely in our acting both with love, if you will—in the sense that we respect his human rights—and truthfulness, in the sense that we act out fully our objections to his violating *our* rights). We put upon him two pressures—the pressure of our defiance of him and the pressure of our respect for his life—and it happens that in combination these two pressures are uniquely effective.

One effect gained is to 'raise the level of consciousness' for those engaged in the struggle— those on both sides. Because the human rights of the adversary are respected, though his actions, his official policies are not, the focus of attention becomes those actions, those policies, and their true nature. The issue cannot be avoided. The antagonist cannot take the interference with his actions personally, because his person is not threatened, and he is forced to begin to acknowledge the reality of the grievance against him. And those in rebellion—committed to the discipline of respect for all men's lives, and enabled by this discipline to avoid that 'trance' Fanon describes, 'where the face of the other beckons me on to giddiness,' is enabled to see more and more clearly that (as Oglesby says) 'the enemy is not a few men but a whole system,' and to study that system.

---

4. It is possible, but not always simple. When we stage an act of massive obstruction in a city, for example, there is always the risk that we will prevent some emergency call from being answered—prevent a doctor's car from getting through, perhaps,. One has obviously to anticipate such situations and be ready to improvise answers to the human problems raised.

5. I am uneasy, however, at the way Carl Davidson of S.D.S. words his defense of obstruction. He writes in New Left Notes of November 13, 1967: 'The institutions our resistance has desanctified and delegitimized, as a result of our action against their oppression of others, have lost all authority and hence all respect. As such, they have only raw coercive power. Since they are without legitimacy in our eyes, they are without rights. Insofar as individuals such as recruiters, continue to remain in association with those institutions, they run the risk of being given the same treatment. ... We can assert the Nuremberg decisions and other past institution and individuals associated with that institution have lost their legitimacy and their rights.' Can one give individuals the same treatment that one gives institutions—and deny them all respect? If he means that we need not grant individuals the right to oppress others, I am in agreement. But if he means that when we can identify an individual as an oppressor, then we need not treat him as though he had any human rights—he alarms me. This formulation would seem to me to lead into grim territory.

The more the real issues are dramatized, and the struggle raised above the personal, the more control those in nonviolent rebellion begin to gain over their adversary. For they are able at one and the same time to disrupt everything for him, making it impossible for him to operate within the system as usual, and to temper his response to this, making it impossible for him simply to strike back without thought and with all his strength. They have as it were two hands upon him—the one calming him, making him ask questions, as the other makes him move.

In any violent struggle one can expect the violence to escalate. It does so automatically, neither side being really able to regulate the process at will. The classic acknowledgment of this fact was made by President Kennedy when he saluted Premier Khrushchev for withdrawing nuclear missiles from Cuba. 'I welcome this message,' he said, because 'developments were approaching a point where events could have become unmanageable.' In nonviolent struggle, the violence used against one may mount for a while (indeed, if one is bold in one's rebellion, it is bound to do so), but the escalation is no longer automatic; with the refusal of one side to retaliate, the mainspring of the automation has been snapped and one can count on reaching a point where de-escalation begins. One can count, that is, in the long run, on receiving far fewer casualties.

Nothing is more certain than this and yet, curiously, nothing is less obvious. A very common view is that nonviolent struggle is suicidal. This is, for example, Andrew Kopkind's view: 'Turn-the-other-cheek was always a personal standard, not a general rule: people can commit suicide but peoples cannot. Morality, like politics, starts at the barrel of a gun.' (A surprising sentence, but by morality he means, no doubt, the assertion of one's rights.) The contention that nonviolent struggle is suicidal hardly stands up under examination. Which rebels suffered more casualties—those who, under Gandhi managed to throw the British out of India or the so-called Mau Mau who struggled by violence to throw the British out of Kenya? The British were certainly not 'nice guys' in their response to the Gandhians. They, and the Indian troops who obeyed their orders, beat thousands of unarmed people, shot and killed hundreds. In the Amristar Massacre, for example, they fired into an unarmed crowd that was trapped in a spot where no one could escape and killed 379 people, wounding many more. There was a limit, nevertheless, to the violence they could justify to themselves—or felt they could justify to the world. Watching any nonviolent struggle, it is always startling to learn how long it can take the antagonist to set such limits; but he finally does feel constrained to set them—especially if his actions are well publicized. In Kenya, where the British could cite as provocation the violence used against them, they hardly felt constrained to set any limits at all on their actions, and they adopted tactics very similar to those the Americans are using today against eh Vietnamese. In that struggle for independence, many thousands of Africans fighting in the forest and many thousands of their supporters and sympathizers on the reserves were killed. Many were also tortured.[6]

One can, as I say, be certain if one adopts the discipline of nonviolence that in the long run one will receive fewer casualties. And yet very few people are able to see that this is so. It is worth examining the reasons why the obvious remains unacknowledged. Several things, I think, blind people to the plain truth.

First, something seems wrong to most people engaged in struggle when they see more people hurt on their own side than on the other side. They are used to reading this as an indication of defeat, and a complete mental readjustment is required of them. Within the new terms of struggle, victory has nothing to do with their being able to give more punishment then they take (quite the reverse); victory has nothing to do with their being able to punish the other at all; it has to do simply with being able, finally to make the other move. Again, the real issue is kept in focus. Vengeance is not the point; change is. But the trouble is that in most men's minds the thought of victory and the thought of punishing the enemy coincide. If they are suffering casualties and the enemy is not, they fail to recognize that they are suffering fewer casualties than they would be if they turned to violence.

Actually, something seems wrong to many people, I think, when—in nonviolent struggle—they receive any casualties at all. They feel that if they are not hurting anybody, then they shouldn't get hurt themselves. (They shouldn't, but it is not only in nonviolent battle that the innocent suffer.) It is an intriguing psychological fact that when the ghetto uprisings provoked the government into bringing out the troops and tanks—and killing many black people, most of them onlookers—observers like Kopkind decided that the action had been remarkably effective, citing as proof precisely the violence of the governments' response. But when James Meredith was shot, just for example, any number of observers editorialized: 'See, nonviolence doesn't work.' Those who have this reaction overlook the fact that nonviolent battle is still battle, and in battle of whatever kind, people do get hurt. If personal safety had been Meredith's main concern, he could, as the saying goes, have stayed at home.

Battle of any kind provokes a violent response—because those who have power are not going to give it up voluntarily. But there is simply no question that—in any long run—violent battle provokes a more violent response and brings greater casualties. Men tend not to think in long-run terms, of course; they tend to think in terms of isolated moments. There will always be such moments that one can cite, in which a particular man might have been safer if he had been armed. If Meredith had been carrying a loaded pistol, he might well have shot his assailant before the man shot him. (He might also well have been ambushed by still more men.) Whatever one can say about overall statistics, some men will always feel

---

6. See *Mau Mau from Within: The Story of the Kenya Land and Freedom Army* by Donald Barnett and Karari Njama, New Edition from Daraja Press, 2021, https://darajapress.com/publication/mau-mau-from-within-land-freedom-army

safer when armed—each able to imagine himself the one among many who would always shoot first.

To recognize that men have greater, not less control in the situation when they have committed themselves to nonviolence requires a drastic readjustment of vision. And this means taking both a long-range view of the field and a very much cooler, more objective one. Nonviolence can inhibit the ability of the antagonist to hit back. (If the genius of guerilla warfare is to make it impossible for the other side really to exploit its superior brute force, nonviolence can be said to carry this even further.) And there is another sense in which it gives one greater leverage—enabling one both to put pressure upon the antagonist and to modulate this response to that pressure. In violent battle the effort is to demoralize the enemy, to so frighten him that he will surrender. The risk is that desperation and resentment will make him go on resisting when it is no longer even in his own interest. He has been driven beyond reason. In nonviolent struggle the effort is of quite a different nature. One doesn't try to frighten the other. One tries to undo him—tries, in the current idiom, to 'blow his mind'—only in the sense that one tries to shake him out of former attitudes and force him to appraise the situation now in a way that takes into consideration your needs as well as his. One is able to do this—able in a real sense to change his mind (rather than to drive him out of it)—precisely because one reassures him about his personal safety all the time that one keeps disrupting the order of things that he has known to date. When—under your constant pressure—it becomes to his own interest to adapt himself to change, he is able to do so. Fear for himself does not prevent him. In this sense a liberation movement that is nonviolent sets the oppressor free as well as the oppressed. ...

What has very clearly worked, in the evolution of animals, to preserve and advance the life of each species, has been a particular *balance* of two instincts. The one, as it were, asserts the individual's right to exist. This is the so-called evil instinct. Lorenz names it 'aggression.' But just as I would substitute another word for Fanon's 'violence,' I would substitute another word here—and rename 'aggression' 'self-assertion.' The second instinct restrains the first when it endangers another's right to exist. In human terms, the first amounts to respecting one's own person, the second to respecting the person of the other. Lorenz points out, by the way, that the only animals capable of love are those that are 'aggressive.' One can, it seems, *only* love another 'as one loves oneself.'

This life-saving balance—this equilibrium between self-assertion and respect for others—has evolved among animals on the physiological plane. In human beings it can be gained only on the plane of consciousness. And the plea this essay makes is precisely that we make the disciplined effort to gain it—all those of us who hope really to change men's lives, who, in Fanon's words, 'want humanity to advance a step further,' want to 'set afoot a new man.' My plea is that the key to a revolution that would 'go forward all the time . . . in the company of Man, in the company of all men,' lies in discovering within ourselves this poise. But it calls equally for the strengthening of *two* impulses—calls both for assertion (for speaking, for acting out 'aggressively' the truth, as we see it, of what our rights are) and for restraint toward others (for the acting out of love for them, which is to say of respect for their human rights). May those who say that they believe in nonviolence learn to challenge more boldly those institutions of violence that constrict and cripple our humanity. And may those who have questioned nonviolence come to see that one's rights to life and happiness can only be claimed as inalienable if one grants, in action, that they belong to all men.

# MESSAGE TO THE PEOPLE OF PORTUGAL

Amilcar Cabral

1969[1]

The Khartoum Conference marks for us a new stage in our struggle in relation to international public opinion. We have never before had a meeting of this kind, with the objective of informing the representatives of anti-colonialist opinion, particularly in Europe and America, about the advance of our struggles, about the concrete situations in our countries, and about the negative and even criminal attitude of the Portuguese colonialist government.

We are convinced that the Conference will fulfill its purpose. From now on, international public opinion, being better informed, will be able to take more concrete measures to show its solidarity with the struggle of the African peoples of the Portuguese colonies.

On the question of the freeing of prisoners-of-war by the PAIGC, I would like to say that for our people in Guinea and Cabo Verde and for our combatants in general, the freeing of three more Portuguese prisoners-of-war at Christmas does not constitute anything new, and is in line with our policy. We have always clearly proclaimed that we never confuse the people of Portugal with Portuguese colonialism. In March 1968 we freed three prisoners-of-war, and in the context of Christmas we considered it worthwhile to free three more. This gesture towards the Portuguese people also proves to the world that the Portuguese colonialist government is lying when it claims that we are bandits, terrorists and a savage people.

We expressed to the three freed prisoners our desire that they should rejoin their families and speak to them about us, so that in this way, despite the crimes of the colonialist government, the links between our people and the people of Portugal should be maintained.

Obviously when a government faces the situation in which the Portuguese government finds itself, it has to lie, and lie a lot. This we understand but can never accept.

If the war communiqués of the fascist government, in an attempt to conceal the existence of prisoners, claim that soldiers have died or disappeared and these soldiers then 'miraculously' appear, only one conclusion can be drawn from such

1. Source: https://marxists.architexturez.net/subject/africa/cabral/1969/mpp.htm

lies, namely that the Portuguese government has no consideration either for its own people, to whom it tells gross lies, or for the young men who, at the cost of sacrifices and of their own lives, are fighting without glory in a criminal war in our country.

We consider that a prisoner-of-war deserves respect, because he is giving his life, whether or not the cause he is fighting for is just. For this reason we call on the people and patriots of Portugal to force the government to respect the people it governs and to respect the minimum of international norms regulating the situation of prisoners-of-war.

Many people thought that the political eclipse of Salazar would mean at the very least some modifications by the Portuguese government with regard to respect for international laws and above all with regard to the defence of the interests of the Portuguese people.

Salazar, whose mind was obstinately closed to the realities of the world today, carried out a policy which dragged him into the enormous pit of colonial war. But Marcelo Caetano was not obliged to fall into the same pit; his continuing of Salazar's colonial policy is conscious and truly criminal. To justify his attitude. Marcelo Caetano has to invent 'historias do arco-da-velha',[2] as they say in Portugal.

The story that we are fighting in order to create in Guinea a base from which to attack Cabo Verde and hand it over to the Communists means that Marcelo Caetano thinks he can still deceive the Portuguese people. We are certain that the Portuguese people will not let themselves be deceived, and we and the patriots of Portugal are here today to put things in their proper perspective.

We are fighting to effectively liberate Guinea and Cabo Verde, in order that our peoples may have the possibility of determining their own destinies. If we took up arms to fight against Portuguese colonialism, against foreign domination in our country, it was not so that we could then hand our country over to somebody else. We repeat what we have already proclaimed many times: we want to liberate our country in order to create in it a new life of work, justice, peace and progress, in collaboration with all the peoples of the world, and most of all with the people of Portugal.

What Marcelo Caetano fears is that the Portuguese people will know that Guinea and Cabo Verde will be part of a free and independent Africa, willing to collaborate openly and loyally with the Portuguese people. While fighting for the total liberation of our country, we do not lose sight of an objective which we consider important for our own people, namely fraternal collaboration and co-operation with the people of Portugal.

When Marcelo Caetano says that Guinea must be defended whatever the price, the price he is thinking of is the life Of the young Portuguese whom he is going to send to their deaths like the many who have already been killed or mutilated. We know that the Portuguese colonialist government is going to send to our country

---

2. An expression peculiar to Portuguese, meaning a fairytale or long, fantastic story. Ed.

a further 10 or 15 thousand men, or even 20 thousand as they are beginning to say. However many they send, the Portuguese government will just be sending them to their death. This is why the Portuguese people must oppose this, and demand the return of its sons who are dying for an unjust cause while their own country lacks young hands to work the land, to build Portugal and, as the poets say, to rediscover their own country.

We know (and I speak as a technician) that Portugal has the means of offering a dignified life to all its sons. That is to say that it is their own country which the Portuguese must defend and build with their efforts and sacrifices, and in a certain future they will collaborate with us of Guinea and Cabo Verde, and we will all link hands fraternally, on the basis of history, of friendship and of all the ties that unite us.

In relation to the demonstrations against the colonial wars which have recently taken place in Portugal, we must say that we appreciate them greatly and are following them very attentively. We have always said to our people, to our combatants, that the Portuguese people is a worthy people which in the course of history has already made an outstanding contribution to the evolution of humanity.

We wish to affirm to you that the attitude of the students and people in their recent demonstrations, both at the church of S. Domingos and on the occasion of the funeral of Antonio Sergio, should be a source of encouragement to you and above all a confirmation of the fact that no contradictions exist between the people of Portugal and our people, that there is not, has never been, and will never be any conflict to separate them, and that whatever crimes the colonialists may commit, in the future our people will join hands in fraternal collaboration.

Marcelo Caetano, when he took over from Salazar, could have ended the colonial wars, but did not want to. We are certain that this mission will be accomplished by the Portuguese people, by their workers and peasants, by their young people, by their progressive and anti-colonialist intellectuals, in fact by all those who truly respect and love Portugal and who know that to fight against the colonial war is to save Portugal from the suffering, ruin and danger for their own independence which this war creates.

# THE FUTURE OF REVOLUTION, NONVIOLENCE, AND ARMED STRUGGLE IN AFRICA

Bill Sutherland and Matt Meyer

2000[1]

*As regards the final stage of Positive Action, namely nation-wide, nonviolent, sit-down-at-home strikes, boycotts, and non-cooperation, they will constitute the last resort. We had no guns, but even if we had, the circumstances were such that nonviolent alternatives were open to us, and it was necessary to try them before resorting to other means.*
—Kwame Nkrumah, On the Power of Positive Action (in the struggle for the independence of Ghana)

We have long lost count of the number of times when pacifists have accused us of being dupes of the advocates of armed struggle, defending their right to arms more than our own commitment to nonviolence. Conversely, some of those involved in liberation movements—and more commonly, their allies in the north—have accused us of being soft in our commitment to the cause, unwilling to fully embrace the only true path to change. These criticisms, more than anything, have assured us that, in fact, a certain unity of purpose exists which has long been overlooked.

Buried in a false dichotomy of tactical and strategic purity, a true and clear analysis of the pros and cons of both armed struggle and nonviolent direct action has been lost, losing along with it the chance for a dialectical revolutionary perspective that brings people together rather than pulling them apart. Such a perspective might mean the giving up of long-held puritanical beliefs in search of a philosophy of revolution that includes the spiritual as well as the strategic, that connects the means and the ends, and that understands the constant, ongoing, multi-leveled efforts required for lasting, radical, mass-based social change.

Fundamentally, we believe that it is up to each movement and each people to determine their own ideologies and methods of struggle. As internationalists,

1. Source: excerpted from the concluding chapter of *Guns and Gandhi in Africa*, Bill Sutherland and Matt Meyer, Africa World Press, 2000

however, we do believe that there are some common lessons to be learned, and as grassroots practitioners we certainly know that people can and do affect conditions and circumstances, and can shift a given dynamic of struggle by the methods used-whatever the social conditions of the moment. We are frustrated when our own long-term colleagues from the north and the south-and from both sides of the nonviolence/armed struggle debate-find it unfashionable to speak of the need for one group to learn from the other. Those of us who believe that there are more points of commonality than difference, it would seem, must be missing something important. The methodology, to these people, represents the revolutionary cause itself.

On the contrary, we believe that these distinct groupings of progressive people not only can study and work together-but must do so. There are greater technological possibilities than ever before for the south-north divide to be shattered. But economic injustices and long-held prejudices still prevent meaningful communication from taking place. The business world, out of abject necessity, has begun to understand the opportunistic merits of a multicultural and multinational approach, albeit skewed towards power remaining in the hands of the few. For those seeking to turn these power imbalances on their head-to make revolution-it is imperative that we all take appropriate responsibility for building bridges. Appropriate responsibility, for our part, does not mean pretending that we are all equal partners coming together with equal resources. Some groupings—even within our low-budget grassroots movements—must be willing to give up some power and resources, while others must be ready to take on leadership positions. First and foremost, our movements must be willing to take a critical and realistic look at history and be willing to learn some hard lessons across dogmatic ideological lines.

A summary of the themes of our dialogues, and of the methods used to bring about peace and justice in modern-day Africa, shows that, in several countries, there was a conscious use of Gandhian nonviolence as the principal means of struggle. In Ghana, Nkrumah changed the name to Positive Action, but credited Gandhi in his writings and speeches. In Zambia, Kaunda was the most explicit in his use of nonviolent action. The first experiments by Gandhi, and the influence of Nobel laureate Albert Luthuli, were evidence that nonviolence in South Africa had some considerations beyond simple pragmatism. In these cases, as well as Tanzania and Namibia, where Nyerere and Nujoma engaged in nonviolence on a pragmatic basis, the example of India's struggle was an inspiration. This was also because there had been a connection between the Pan-African movement leaders, such as George Padmore, and the leaders of the Free India movement in London.

Most countries that turned to armed struggle, earlier had engaged in some form of nonviolent action. This was true of Algeria, South Africa, Namibia, Mozambique, Zimbabwe, and in Kenya's Mau Mau experiences. Even after being committed to armed struggle, nonviolent actions proved to be quite effective. We recall that the FLN in Algeria was losing militarily when its nonviolent response to Red Hand action kept world pressure on France. It was Black Consciousness action and the United Democratic Front in the 1980s that gave focus to the external support afforded the anti-apartheid freedom fighters. External support-the pressure of worldwide public opinion-has always been an essential element in successful nonviolent action, and certainly played a major role as northern powers used newly independent African nations as pawns in the Cold War game. People-to-people solidarity, against political and economic domination, is the foundation for a positive globalization.

So often, in societies which have undergone dramatic change, the structures which brought about the changes were disbanded because people felt that they had achieved their goal, whether political independence or socialist revolution. History indicates that once leaders take state power, divisions often develop between the ruling party and the People. This has been true in countries that have followed Western capitalist Eastern socialist, and non-aligned political models. Nyerere's Ujamaa, Kaunda's humanism, South Africa's Freedom Charter-all attempted innovative changes and faced with difficulty the traps set by the neo-colonial and neo-liberal northern powers. There has, throughout the world, been a gulf between radical theory and practice; the question now is how to work the system between a rock and a hard place.

In looking at strategies for the future, several points stand out:

First, the most effective forms of struggle have always involved mass participation. This is true whether the struggles are nonviolent or armed, whether based on mass action (as in Ghana or South Africa) or on people's armies (as in Algeria or Zimbabwe).

Secondly, no struggle has ever been entirely nonviolent or military in nature, and support for revolutionary movements must not be contingent on these elements.

Finally, it must be understood that, in one sense, the matrix for revolution is never peace; it is static violence. Colonialism in Africa and segregated society in the U.S. constituted classic examples of static violence, of basic social injustice where peace could not be possible. It should be no surprise, then, that the primary agents for change were fundamentally inter-related, with Malcolm X and Martin Luther King having their effects on one another as they did on African society, even while Lumumba, Nkrumah, Haile Selassie, and Nyerere were having their effect upon movements in the United States and the rest of the Diaspora.

In a world of globalization, the Pan-African movement must also be global. As it continues to work for the unity of people of African descent throughout the world, it must also unite with other movements seeking peace and justice. Connections between Pan-Africanists must be made with environmentalists, feminists, human rights advocates, and those seeking economic justice. No struggle is won without allies. Our movements must learn not simply to unite or merge, but to build cooperation through parallel action.

In a world of institutionalized militarism as well as war, where there is an inextricable mix of physical, psychological, and spiritual violence, one may well find more love and creativity in people engaged in armed struggle than in those who refuse to risk violence yet remain inactive in the face of injustice. But while nonviolent resisters must not be rigid in promoting their method of struggle, we do not accept that the tragedy of taking life—even in the struggle for a just cause—is somehow cathartic or without negative social consequences. The connectedness between the means and the ends, like the links between the personal and the political, suggests that nonviolence must be a leading part of any constructive social movement.

In a world of turmoil and reevaluation, we have been looking for answers from our positions on Pan-Africanism and Gandhian nonviolence. We have tried to redefine 'soul force' to encompass both spiritual power and the original African American definition of soul: breathing genuine warmth and human feeling into western materialism and eastern asceticism. In our theory of nonviolent revolution, the goal is a society with structures that will encourage and promote maximum opportunities for individual as well as group expression. It recognizes that no governmental system can be responsible for individual motivation and choice but relies upon the creativity that comes from voluntary group associations. By spirit and soul, we do not seek to push a theological, religious, or New Age agenda; we refer to the very source of human strength for continual creative struggle, for lasting social change.

What 'soul force' means for each of us, or how it can and should be appropriately used, is indeed a unique and personal proposition. As we struggle for unity across yesterday's ideological and strategic lines, it seems to us that this question—the quest to find a mix of the spiritual and the political, the means and the ends—is key to addressing tomorrow's hurdles. Revolutions don't have clear beginnings or endings. The more we try to finalize our definitions or strategies or tactics—putting simple prescriptions for complex situations—the less we seem to understand about the building for truly revolutionary change. In the meantime, as we stumble together through high times and low, our own simple suggestion is to not get trapped by our own rhetoric or dogmas. We must better understand the gray areas, with no set or simple answers based on theories of the past. Our experiences suggest complexities beyond white and the black, like the shadows and the cracks between the keys on a piano.

Now is the time to write new tunes for a new tomorrow. When and wherever possible, we must try to play in the cracks.

# UBUNTU AND THE WORLD TODAY

Nozizwe Madlala-Routledge

2017[1]

Ubuntu is a concept present here in Africa. But I also believe it is present in all human beings if it is allowed to thrive and prosper.

Ubuntu is a concept of sharing. It suggests that if there is something I can give to you, even if it may be is something that I need, it would benefit me to give it to you. I give it to you, there is a relationship we create, and a better understanding between us which will benefit us both.

There are examples from traditions throughout Africa. If, for example, I have five cows which I need for their milk, but there is a possibility that I could give a little calf to a neighbor, that is something which should be done. My neighbor could bring up that calf, would now have their own milk, and the community will benefit from the gift that I gave them. There is also a tradition, called iLima in isiZulu, where people come together to help one person to build their house. There is a feeling that we all belong together. This is true when we grow food together, sow seeds together, when a whole village enjoys and supports itself from sharing. For us, it has been a way of coexistence.

Of course, with urbanization we have lost some of these practices of Ubuntu. But we are trying to bring them back. So a child who grows up and gets educated does not seek to accumulate only for themselves, especially if a child next to them doesn't have a bed to sleep on or even basic shelter. In South Africa following the end of apartheid, we have encouraged everyone to participate in the rebuilding and governing of the country.

It is not enough for people vote, to choose the people through voting who will represent us in parliament. It is just as important, in the spirit of Ubuntu, to experience what the poorest in the community experience. We have a very good example of one former top Minister spent a night in a shack just so he would know what the people who live there go through. You can't know what people's needs are if you don't live with them and share their experiences.

I also want to emphasize that we've got to make these realities part of our present-day experience, especially in the contexts of globalization and modernity. All

---

1. Source: compiled by Matt Meyer from collected speeches and presentations of Nozizwe Madlala-Routledge, 2008-2017

of these concepts and values of the past have to co-exist. One vital among those values is looking after the planet, which has long been critical to our survival and coexistence. We can't leave behind that behind or see it as a thing of the past. When we pass on the planet to the next generation, we have to leave it in the condition that is positive for them.

To experience peace and freedom, to enjoy nature, we have a responsibility given to us by nature itself, to carry forth these positive ideas about sharing. The issue of gender relations is also a part of it. Even as women are getting into areas previously occupied only by men, it is important that women continue to value the history of collective decision-making and sharing power. Hoarding power is what has lead to conflict and war. So these Ubuntu values which have been lost or eroded because of modernization have to be brought back into our modern life.

I really do believe that we do have it in all of us to thrive with Ubuntu. If a developed country spends its scientific knowledge on the creation of weapons and arms, for example, and if those arms get sold to poor countries, we live in a cycle of death. What actually happens is that the resources of the poor country get diverted from the basics of life: health, education, housing. A lot of the conflicts which happen on our continent are due to this. We don't manufacture small arms here–the weapons come from and the money goes to benefit people in the Global North! They are responsible for killing people here!! This is the opposite of Ubuntu.

A more positive example is this: If the world had looked away from South Africa, we may not have achieved the peace and freedom we achieved when the world condemned apartheid. We would not have achieved an end to the racist regime as quickly as we did. When the world declared apartheid 'a sin against humanity', the conflict was brought much closer to being solved. Just like that, it is still possible to fight the problems of the world—led by the peoples of individual countries on the front lines. In this way, we can come together and work together, and win: if we unite as we did in the South African Mass Democratic Movement.

We are not calling for a situation where democracy or other values are imposed. We can support the causes which individuals and citizen have taken up themselves. In South Africa, the issue of international solidarity called for a boycott...and they did this with our support from within the country. We said: 'even though we are suffering now with the boycott, divestment will help us change our country'. That is the type of cooperation and working together which the world needs today. Ubuntu is not just for Africa.

# THE RIDDLE OF VIOLENCE

Kenneth Kaunda

1981[1]

It was according to the principles of non-violence on the Gandhi model that the final stages of the freedom struggle in Zambia were conducted. The doctrine became the official policy of the United National Independence Party and apart from a few regrettable lapses, it was honoured by the masses, whose discipline in the face of grave provocation was remarkable. Almost as hard to beat as the aggressive tactics of the police and army were the sneers of our opponents who thought all the exhortations to non-violence were at best hypocrisy and at worst weakness. But had we acted on the basis of a blow for blow, the history of the last days of Northern Rhodesia and the first days of Zambia would have been written in blood.

But it was another Indian, Kasterbhai Narayan who in the early sixties long before the freedom struggle was over, unwittingly sowed in my mind the seeds of some disquieting thoughts about non-violence. They have since germinated to surplant the strong, simple concepts of classical *satyagraha* with more ambiguous, complex and not altogether satisfactory ideas. Not that Mr Narayan had any doubts about the efficiency of *satyagraha*. He was in Dar es Salaam as a member of the Reverend Michael Scott's International Peace Brigade—a task force of pacifists which aimed to march south from Tanzania in order to liberate Northern Rhodesia (as it was then) from the Central African Federation using only the weaponry of the Spirit. They would be armed solely with the sacred scripture of whatever religion they avowed, go to prison in droves and bring key centres of the country to a halt by lying or sitting down in main roads and across railway tracks. Sir Roy Welensky, the Federal Prime Minister, would then resign in exasperation and hand the country over to its rightful owners. That was the theory.

I fell to talking with Mr Narayan who was very pleased to learn that I was a disciple of Mahatma Gandhi and committed to the doctrine of *satyagraha*. He seemed to feel however, that I was in danger of polluting the purity of my pacifist vocation by getting mixed up in a nationalist movement whose aims were political. Just as Gandhi resigned from the Indian National Congress n 1936 and choose to go it alone, so Mr Narayan appealed to me to resign all political offices and take up the family trade—my father having been a travelling evangelist—and spread the gospel of *satyagraha* by preaching and example.

1. Kenneth Kaunda, *The Riddle of Violence*. Harper Collins, New York, 1981

Kasterbhai Narayan is a man of great holiness and I have always believed that God sends holy men and women across our path with messages it is foolish to ignore. So I was thrown into great confusion and went through days of mental torment, questioning my motives for political leadership.

In the nicest possible way Mr Narayan was in effect accusing me of betraying my idol, Gandhi, for the fake but glittering prizes of political power. Whether he knew it or not, he had touched a most sensitive nerve. I had, and still have, mixed feelings about public office. One part of me, and a big part at that, shrinks from the necessary antics of the political circus, the lure of the publicity trap and the will to domination every leader must, however regretfully, develop. The temptation to become a wilderness saint, living on the Zambian equivalent of locusts and wild honey and refining my spirit by punishing my body, was very attractive to me.

At that time, the hard days of the freedom struggle still lay ahead, and if there was one thing I feared more than any suffering I might have to endure myself it was the possibility I should prove to be a false shepherd and lead my fellow countrymen to their doom. I could not see much light at the tunnel's end. And I did not need to be a prophet, only a student on the newspapers to guess that my immediate future must be taken up with still more strife, more imprisonment, more disruption of home and family life—more of everything, in fact, that had made my life almost unbearable.

After a couple of sleepless nights, I decided that Mr Narayan was mistaken. Or at least ... if indeed he had brought a message from God for me, it must somehow have got jumbled up on the way. The people had asked me to lead them and I had taken them into the depths of a very dark and frightening wood. I did not see how I could abandon them, only to appear again as the servant of a higher destiny, urging them to try a more excellent way as they milled about in confusion. The first thing to do was get out of the wood. At the people's urging, I had just parted company with my old boss and comrade, Harry Nkumbula because I had reluctantly decided that he was tired, drained of ideas and without any clear sense of direction. It hardly seemed wise to leave the people to get through the wilderness following one blind guide, Nkumbula,–the other, me, having perversely plucked out his eyes in obedience to some inner voice. That at least is how I saw things. Obviously, Mr Narayan must follow his star and I mine.

That meeting with Mr Narayan taught me a lesson or two about non-violence which took a long time to permeate my system. And in the years since, life, like a can-wagging schoolmaster, has dinned into me the salient points whenever I was in danger of forgetting them. From time to time, other Narayans have crossed my path and invited me to abandon my chosen trade as a journeyman-politician for a better one. I do not know why it is that I seem to be thrown into contact constantly with *gurus*, priests and philosophers with a passionate desire to save me from my worst self and recruit me for the cause. I am frequently told, for the good of my soul, that I am too religious to be a political leader. I suspect that deep down, they think I am too inept at *my* trade but might make out at *theirs*. I like the company of these mystics, seers and assorted saints and enjoy arguing with them, but I have no immediate plans to take holy orders.

...Mr Narayan... was inviting me, as others have done since, to make an either-or choice between an uncompromising stand on the issue of non-violence and pushing ahead with a political career which must lead me occasionally to do things at odds with my convictions. I could never see the issue in such stark either-or terms. Take, for instance, the case of the very movement Mr Narayan was representing, the Reverend Michael Scott's International Peace Brigade. In the event, the Brigade never marched. That is no disgrace. At least its members cared enough about our plight to do something about it. The reasons why the Peace Brigade disbanded are history now and need not concern us. But supposing it *had* marched, infiltrated Northern Rhodesia and fetched up in the streets of Lukasa, and suppose the Governor or Sir Roy Welensky had obligingly lowered the flag and handed over the instruments of power. What then? The politicians having been urged to abandon their trade and join the ranks of the moralists, who would have done all the sordid things needed to build good government and ensure the survival of the nation?

This is the problem of all protest movements which set their targets very high and claim to succeed where the politicians have failed. They hope to bridge the gap between warring factions by the appeal to a common interest that lies beyond conflict. And so long as they are stating broad though obvious truths at a time when people are sick of violence, they will have success as they are able to fire the public imagination and meet the mood of the moment. But when the marching stops, where do you go from there? Once the general mood has to become earthed, as it were, in practical action, then the movement's unity becomes shaky and political party loyalties revive. Party divisions are not always or even usually manufactured by politicians, though these wily birds may exploit them; parties generally reflect deep conflicts of human interest which can only be dealt with head-on. They will not go away like a marauding leopard scared off by the beating of drums and the waving of flags.

I have sworn never to fish in the troubled waters of someone else's country, having myself often been on the receiving end of unasked-for advice. But the Peace Movement of Northern Ireland seems to illustrate my point well. As a humanitarian, I have a great concern for its success, and as a practical politician I have stood where its members now stand—in No Man's Land between hostile armies. Racism or sectarianism—the stakes are the same, the survival of the nation as a human rather than sub-human enterprise. The courage, hope and love of the Peace People are beyond praise. But as they know better than I, they have reached a point where the marching has to stop and the perplexing question faced: what do we do now? No matter how disillusioned they may be with governments and politicians, they will find that politics is the only effective way of getting certain things done. Earnest dialogue alone will not heal deep divisions centuries old. The options are stark. The movement can keep its unity of purpose by turning its attention to uncontroversial projects in the field of education, community affairs and so on, and leave politics to the politicians—hardly a congenial idea since it was out of a conviction the old politics are dead that the movement came into being. Or else the movement will change into being a political party with a good chance that all the deep wounds of sectarian division will open up again.

I have no wish to sell short movements such as the Peace People. At the very least they help to create a climate in which people allow themselves to think about the hitherto unattainable. I simply want to make the point that politics will out, and therefore the either-or thinking of Mr Narayan, if taken seriously, would rob political life of its idealists without affecting the need for politicians as such. If the good man in politics quits the field, he leaves the more cynical of the breed to do as they like.

As I reflect now upon my experiences during Zambia's freedom struggle, I realize that non-violence is an exercise in public relations. It is often much else as well—a philosophy of life, a willingness to make heroic sacrifice, a religious vocation—but as a tactic its success or failure hangs on whether the offending regime can be shamed or spurred by outraged public opinion into putting its house in order. Thus a free press and all the gadgetry of the television age are as vital to the protest as the protesters themselves.

In one way, the Mahatma Gandhi and I were equally fortunate in facing a colonial power which fell far short of being a ruthless tyranny. Britain has always been very sensitive to public opinion—that is one of the glories. So the Viceroy who allowed reporters and even film cameramen into Gandhi's cell was inadvertently contributing to the effectiveness of the Mahatma's campaign of passive resistance. I too knew that all that happened to myself and my comrades during our non-violent struggle was shown within hours on British TV and reported over the radio and in the newspapers. I was able in this way to state my case not only throughout Zambia but also in London at the heart of empire. Had our struggles been in the Republic of South Africa or Salazaar's Portuguese African colonies, it might have been a different story. For every Steve Biko whose terrible fate gets world headlines, hundreds of his comrades vanish off the face of the earth, disciples of Gandhi and believers in armed struggle alike. By the eyes of God their courage and sacrifice are seen and noted, but politically, what the world does not know, it does not get worked up about.

◊

It is not pleasant for the disciple of non-violence to be patronized by supercilious opponents nor does he enjoy being written off as a fool and a weakling by some of his comrades, but these things he can put up with. What he finds truly agonizing is the realization that try as he will to distance himself from all the violence in thought and deed, he cannot. For violence and non-violence, far from being absolute alternatives, are complementary in practice. As a tactic, the effectiveness of non-violence is enhanced when it stands out in sharp relief against a backdrop of imminent of actual violence. It has been said that non-violence *needs* violence in the same way stars need the night sky to show them off.

My own experience bears out this truth. In the early days of the nationalist movement when I was trying to impress on our followers the importance of learning and practicing the methods of non-violent struggle, my speeches were reported by the press in a semi-humorous way and I was lampooned as 'The Preacher'. I suppose I was regarded by those in power as a harmless crackpot. But then as things got bogged down and it looked as though Sir Roy Welensky and his Federal Government would succeed in holding off our nation's independence indefinitely, sections of the Party's Youth Brigade lost patience. Instead of putting up quietly with all the provocation and racial taunts that were their daily lot, they retaliated and there were some very nasty incidents. Editorials in national newspapers argued that Kaunda was losing control of the Party and there was much gloom and doom talk about the prospect of civil war. And the same people who had earlier dismissed my advocacy of non-violence as silly sermonizing then turned around and reviled me for failing to get the Party to heed my preaching.

But official attitudes towards me changed radically. Whist the Party was following instructions and avoiding violent confrontation I was shrugged aside as irrelevant; when widespread violence became a real possibility, I was suddenly seen as a rational alternative to the so-called 'men of violence'. By 'rational' of course the white settlers meant the black opponent least likely to cause them anxiety or threaten their privileged position. Martin Luther King noted similar change in attitude on the part of the U.S. Government following the black riots in Detroit and elsewhere. From being a localized nuisance he became something of a national hero because it is easier to cope with bus boycotts than the burning down of city ghettos. And I suspect that Gandhi and his *satyagraha* policy became much more attractive to the British Government when Nehru's National Congress began rioting in the streets. It is the stars and the dark night again—the play and counterplay of violence and non-violence. Just as the stars do not stop shining when the night has gone, so non-violence has its own validity quite apart from violence. Nonetheless, it is not wise for the pacifists to be too self-righteous about the 'men of violence'—their very existence often guarantees his effectiveness.

The other aspect of the dilemma of the political leader who chooses the way of non-violence concerns his relationship with his followers. The people want results, especially when they have been suffering oppression and the denial of their rights for years past. Indeed, had their impatience not reached the boiling point the mass movement would probably not have come into existence at all. Western observers of Africa have a curious tendency to equate such impatience with immaturity. They claim that a more civilized people would possess their souls in patience whatever the provocation. Europe's recent history does not furnish very convincing evidence of this principle—was not Prime Minister Chamberlain reviled as the Great Appeaser for advocating just this sort of patience after Munich?

For years, right-wing politicians in Britain combined condemnation of black 'terrorist' action in Rhodesia with exhortations to the black population to bids their time until their betters decide they were ready for and deserving of basic human rights. I cannot imagine that great hero of British right-wing politicians, Sir Winston Churchill, telling the occupied people's of Europe in 1940 to be patient and trust the Nazis to restore their freedom one day—maybe not in their own lifetime nor that of their children, but one day. Such patience would be neither noble nor civilized but the mark of a happy slave.

Once oppressed peoples wake up to the fact that it is not the law of God nor the nature of the universe that they should be treated as a second-class human beings, then a single day of continued servitude becomes insupportable, let alone a lifetime of it. And even those too old to benefit much by self-determination themselves become impatient for it on behalf of their children and future generations yet unborn.

If to this impatience in the face of injustice is added the commonsense perception that the powerful never willingly give up power—it has to be taken from them, it is obvious that the mind of the a people on the brink of a freedom struggle is not very hospitable to *any* long-term strategies, least of all those of non-violence, which mean delayed results and the suppression of honest feelings. So the leader of a mass movement, whatever path he chooses to follow, is living on borrowed time—he must get results before his followers' frustration explodes and he is swept aside. And if he is committed to a policy of non-violence, his political lifespan depends upon both his supports *and* his opponents—his supporters, because there is a limit to the amount of knocking about without retaliation they are prepared to take from security forces who are not themselves committed to non-violence; and his opponents, in that they must be wise enough to make concessions willingly before they are compelled to do so. If, lulled into complacency by the apparent docility of the freedom movement, those in power refuse to make significant concessions, then the movement's leader will almost certainly fall and be replaced by someone pledged to get quick results at whatever cost in human life.

The problem with this line of argument is obvious—any ruling power which is wise enough to make sufficient concessions to vindicate non-violent opposition, would probably be wise enough in the first place to read the signs of the times and change things. There would be no need for any freedom movement outside the law, violent or non-violent. Otherwise, the gloomy law holds—normally, non-violent protest only gets results when it is seen by those in power as a desirable alternative to violence, and it only becomes desirable when the other alternative is being spelled out in blood.

# 5. 'COMBATIVE PACIFISM' AGAINST PATRIARCHY: FEMINIST CRITIQUES OF MOVEMENT-BUILDING

*As* Insurrectionary Uprisings *works to present an introduction to the historical roots of the concepts of revolution and nonviolence, we are struck by the necessity of a feminist critique within the conversation if we are to adequately address new strategic visions for the future.*

*This section of the book, then, focuses on the vital role which we believe feminism must play in any reconfiguration of movements for radical social change. If we seek a lasting end to war and all the causes of war, making these cross-sectional connections is long over-due.*

—The Editors

# ECOFEMINISM AND NONVIOLENCE

Ynestra King

Feminism and Nonviolence is a vast topic—it encompasses analyses of violence as it relates to gender, a history of women's (and feminist) nonviolent activism and political innovation, and ingenious forms of resistance. We are at a very dynamic moment in history, where the emergence of a philosophy and practice of 'revolutionary nonviolence' urges daring and creativity.

In the midst of the Covid-19 pandemic, every kind of planetary inequity is on glaring display. The effects of the pandemic mirror the disparities in wealth and power that were already evident to the most vulnerable peoples. Gender-based violence has increased worldwide as financial stressors and the curtailment of movement created new levels of pressure at home and in relationships contained in small physical spaces. But radical feminist activism has also increased. New feminist, nonviolent political imaginaries are emerging all around us, germinating new forms of care-based, horizontally-organized activism.

There is also a new awareness of the depth and perniciousness of white supremacy, as a movement to combat it and to link colonialism and slavery as interconnected systems of power that emerged worldwide. Women are in the leadership of Black Lives Matter, the Movement for Black Lives, and the many grassroots formations inspired by the unprecedented mass uprisings of 2020. And women are in the leadership of the intensifying anti-extractive, place-based, nonviolent direct actions protecting water, land, and sacred spaces. Some of the most recent centers of these campaigns are at Standing Rock of the Lakota/Dakotas, the White Earth Stop Line Three campaign of Minnesota. Women are in the leadership of struggle to protect the health and integrity of women's bodies, as in the successful Argentinian feminist campaign to legalize abortion and launch an international Women's Day Strike. Feminists throughout Latin America, in fact, have been at the forefront of pro-democracy and human rights movements in Chile, Peru, Bolivia, Ecuador, Mexico and elsewhere over the past decade. Scholars and activists of the Global North have barely begun to learn from and understand these change-making movements.

As we were developing the field of ecofeminism decades ago, my writings about the convergences between feminism and ecology included a grounding in praxis which is relevant to the rethinking of revolutionary nonviolence which we are working on today. Theory never converts simply or easily into practice, with our scholarship often lagging behind the work of organizers. As the unity of theory and practice, praxis is fundamental to any attempt at something new. During the 1970's and 80's feminist anti-war activists faced the sexism and racism of too much of the left as well as that of the state.

Grace Paley, a prominent writer and political leader of our movement, liked to call herself a 'combative pacifist', emphasizing the necessity of nonviolent militant resistance (the restraining hand) as well as our commitment to creating beloved communities (the hand of connection, see the Women's Pentagon Action statement in this section).

Another visionary leader of our movement, Barbara Deming, first articulated a 'two-handed practice' in her essay 'On Revolution and Equilibrium'.[1] Barbara Deming, who spent the last decade of her life in feminist anti-violence and anti-militarist movements, also spent decades working at the frontline of white alliance-building with the Southern and Northern, Black-led freedom movements. It was here that she studied and practiced nonviolent direct action, including civil disobedience and numerous jail sentences. Barbara was a prolific writer, and her thoughts on revolution and strategic unarmed resistance, honed in both the civil rights and anti-war movement, led her to argue that nonviolence is an experiment still in its earliest stages. Feminist nonviolence is personal and political, ferocious and gentle, oppositional and loving. It requires an ability to balance a practice of opposition to all forms of oppression with a recognition of the humanity of all people, including that of the oppressor. It may be that one of the most vital summary lessons of Deming, Paley, and ecofeminism is that we must maintain a fidelity to feminism as an understanding of the breadth and depth of patriarchal violence as it relates to militarism, the devastation of the planet and everyday exploitation of human beings of all genders. Feminist nonviolence not only opposes violence but mobilizes our hearts and our imaginations toward a nonviolent world beyond patriarchy.

---

1. See pp 178-189 in this volume.

# GRACE

Leora Skolkin-Smith

2016[1]

Grace Paley was a known pacifist and, also, a famous short story-writer. She enjoyed being referred to as a 'combative pacifist and a cooperative anarchist.'

Grace Paley was not extreme in either her pacifism or her sense of government as reliably unreliable in the governing of the *Little Disturbances of Man* (the title of her most famous short story collection). She lived within the law, gracefully and with moral direction, though she protested and therefore refused to pay war taxes at times.

Grace Paley was a member of the War Resisters League, a pacifist organization, from the 1950s to her death in August, 2007. Started in the 1920's, The War Resisters League is one of the oldest antiwar organizations in the country and is renowned for its conscientious and peaceful protests. The declaration of the War Resisters League 'affirms that all war is a crime against humanity. We are determined not to support any kind of war, international or civil, and to strive nonviolently for the removal of all causes of war, including racism, sexism, and all forms of exploitation.' These words describe Grace Paley's pacifism as well.

The journalist Judith Mahoney Pasternak wrote about Paley in her tribute after the author's death:

Grade Paley's place in the history books is hers alone, and unlikely ever to be matched. In the canon of U.S. literature, no writer has ever risen so high while compiling such a long and honorable arrest record in the cause of peace in the history of the U.S. resistance, no activist has reaped nearly as many literary honors.'

Interviewed in 1985, Paley said she wasn't an activist-she was only doing her 'ordinary, citizenly duty.' It was a concept she repeated often to describe what was clearly her other career, a career of virulent, persistent nonviolence she began by demonstrating against the presence of buses in Washington Square. (Her baby daughter was almost hit by a bus there, she said, so how could she not protest?) Not long afterward, she began working against the Vietnam War with the Greenwich Village Peace Center and the War Resisters League. Ultimately, she was involved in protesting every aspect of militarism and U.S. aggression across the globe.

Paley traveled to Hanoi in 1969; she was arrested at protest after protest, including an anti-nuclear demonstration on the White House lawn in 1978, the

---

1. Source: Skolkin-Smith, Leora. 2016. 'Grace'. *Pacifism for the 21st Century*. Pacifism21.org.

Women's Pentagon Action in 1980, and War Resisters League's 'A Day Without the Pentagon' in 1998. But she wasn't 'an arrest freak,' Paley said. She got arrested only 'when there's a good reason to get arrested, to show we're serious about something, we're not going to go away ... [or] to actually stop something, like destroying a [missile] nose cone.'

It's fascinating to explore the ways Grace Paley's background helps to define her enigmatic, charismatic personality. Her father, Isaac Goodside, had spent time in prison in Russia as a political dissenter, and her mother, Manya Ridnyik Goodside, had been sent into exile in the Ukraine. Her parents came to America as many Russian Jews did, escaping the pogroms and jailing, surviving the journey on crowded refugee ships. Paley's mother went to work in the garment shops of lower Manhattan, and her father taught himself English by reading Charles Dickens, finishing medical in night school and eventually leading her family from working class to middle-class. After settling in America, Isaac anglicized the family name from Gutseit to Goodside. The author and pacifist was born to these parents as Grace Goodside in the Bronx in 1922.

Her family spoke Russian and Yiddish along with English, which is why Paley's later stories brim over with the Yiddish of socialist immigrant New York City, the raw shouts and street conversations of her lower Manhattan neighborhood and the Bronx of her childhood. Her writing was a melting pot of immigrant gene pools, swirling with upward and downward social mobility, as if her characters were caught in a speeding, giant elevator of social changes, wondering what floor they can get off on.

In 1942, Grace married Jesse Paley. They had two children: Nora, born in 1949, and Danny, born in 1951. Grace and Jesse separated in the late 1960s and divorced in 1972, and later that year she married Robert Nichols, a family friend and political ally. Grace Paley's life as a pacifist and political activist, was a role that began, as it might have for many of the characters she has created in her stories, as an extension of PTA activities in her children's school. She also studied in these early years with W. H. Auden at the New School for Social Research in the 1940s, and later spoke of being influenced by Auden's social concern and sense of conscience in his poetry.

By the 1950s, Paley had joined protests against nuclear proliferation and American militarization across the globe. She also worked with the American Friends Service Committee to establish neighborhood peace groups. The combination of neighborhood and, increasingly, global concerns led her to a prominent role in the peace movement of the 1960s and a series of often controversial trips to some of the world's most troubled nations, among them North Vietnam in 1969, and Chile in 1972. Her famous essay, 'The Man in an Airplane in the Sky is a Killer' was an early literary protest against the Vietnam War.

Grace Paley demonstrated regularly in New York's Washington Square and in Washington D.C against the Vietnam War, and particularly against the napalming of children in South Vietnam. Besides being a pioneer for the War Resisters League and the eco-feminist group Women's Pentagon Action, she was also an early yarn bomber. Kjerstin Johnson, a fellow member of Paley's anti-war/feminist group, wrote an essay called 'Adventure in Feministory: Grace Paley' that includes this intriguing memory: 'One of the ways the WPA protested the arms race was to weave the doors of the Pentagon shut.'

Paley gained national recognition as an activist when she accompanied a 1969 peace mission to Hanoi to negotiate the release of prisoners of war. By the time her second short story collection, *Enormous Changes at the Last Minute* was published in 1974, Paley was serving as a delegate to the 1974 World Peace Conference in Moscow. She was arrested as one of 'The White House Eleven' for unfurling an anti-nuclear banner (that read 'No Nuclear Weapons-No Nuclear Power-USA and U.S.SR') on the White House lawn in 1978. When, many years later, she published poems and stories illustrated by a long-time friend from childhood who also had joined the War Resister's League, Paley wrote: 'Vera and I came from the same neighborhood in the Bronx, separated by two elevators (a linguistic trick but a fact). We have worked together in and out of War Resister's League, Women's Pentagon Action, women's affinity groups, mobilization, Central American actions. I had heard of her and never forgotten her *Liberation* magazine cover designs-the Vietnamese child's head that rolled across our conscience, a marble of pain.'

Grace's literary works poignantly articulated a sense of 'deep politics', an interest in 'the daily life of black, white, brown children in the grown-up world'. This cannot be reduced to a political icon's missive or slogan, and in her fiction Paley's voice is rich with bold humor and irony. The theme of mothers and housewives petitioning as ordinary women in communities and being belittled for their actions is abundantly present in her stories. In 'Faith in a Tree', Paley has a male passerby stare up at a woman named Faith who is stuck in a tree in the middle of Washington Square Park:

> The ladies of the PTA
> Wear baggies in their blouses
> They talk on telephones all day.

In another story, called 'Politics,' Paley wrote:

> A group of mothers from our neighborhood went downtown to the board estimate hearing and sang a song. They had contributed the facts and the tunes but the idea for that kind of political action came from the clever head of a media man floating on the ebb tide of our Lower West Side culture because of the housing shortage. He was from the far middle plains and loved our well-known tribal organization. He said it was the coming thing Oh! How he loved our old moldy pot New York!
>
> He was also clean-cut and attractive. For that reason, the first mother stood up straight when the clerk called her name. She smiled, said excuse me, jammed past the knees of her neighbors, and walked proudly down the aisle of the hearing room. Then she sang, according to some sad melody learned in her mother's kitchen, the following lament requesting better playground facilities:

Oh oh oh
Will someone please put a high fence up
Around the children's playground
They are playing a game and have only one more year of childhood
Won't the city come
Or their daddies to keep the bums and the tramps out of the yard
They are too little now to have the old men wagging their
Crocker pricks at them or feeling their
Knees and saying to them
Sweetheart, sweetheart, sweetheart,
Can't the cardinal keep all these creeps out-

Though immensely entertaining, Paley's playfulness came from a place of creative depth and never sacrificed layered, complex, and serious social and historical meanings. She loosely defined herself as a 'combative pacifist' and 'cooperative anarchist.' I believe she sought to adhere to the kind of Western and once Eastern European 'spirituality' that Milan Kundera describes in his *Art of the Novel* as being, for the writer: 'the passion to know'; to 'scrutinize man's concrete life' and 'protect it against the forgetting of being,' to hold 'the world of life' under a 'permanent light.'

For Paley, writing stories from the Western side of the Cold War's barriers and walls, the literary task was the opposite of Milan Kundera's. Paley's writing involved not a rescue of who was lost and unremembered as time buried them, but a recognition of marginalized communities whom she felt compelled to put on the literary stage, as for the first time.

Her characters were more organically swept up and absorbed in the chaotic swirl of events and political protests during the Cold War and its aftermath than those of her colleagues on both sides of the globe. They are resonant with the 'screaming rhetoric' from groups begging for visibility for the first time in a classist but potentially socially mobile America, the voices and stories of the marginalized 'other' on New York City street corners, minorities, single mothers, women and men sitting on city stoops of walking through the park with their baby carriages, sharing pieces of their lives, gossiping, living urban lives.

I had the gift of studying with Grace Paley as an undergraduate at Sarah Lawrence and later as a graduate student. She emphasized as a teacher a rite of passage that built the inner strength a writer needs. Grace was the master of telling stories about the marginalized, so that for me 'marginalized' became not an awful word, but a special place of privilege.

At times Grace Paley's work feels flown in from a storm far away in the sky, fragments of tales depicting lives filled with life's interruptions and desertions, its marital heartbreaks, illicit lusts and itches, and Paley's inimitable offhanded but brilliant remarks, true to the dialect of her own family's Yiddish and a medley of other ethnic tongues; her wild one-sentence wordplays with their breath-taking twists of irony and absurdity.

My own mother was born a Jew in Palestine as were my grandmother and great grandmother in the 1920s. The news about Israel and the war there was constant throughout my lifetime, but after the first Intifada in the 1980s, bombings and death were graphically shown on TV in monotonous, bloody, relentless, and repeated reportage. Grace Paley was always interested in Israel. By this time I was phoning her daily, telling her stories, sharing the intimate scenes of sitting around the dinner table in 1963, in early Jerusalem when my mother took me there to visit as a child. These stories seemed to illuminate a forgotten Jerusalem, not so besieged and terrifying.

On September 11, 1991, Grace Paley wrote on my behalf to the United Nations. Through her support, I was able to meet and interview the UN Mandate representatives of Palestine. From there, the chaotic birth of my first novel *Edges: O Israel, O Palestine* began.

In the last conversation I had with Grace before she died, I told her that my novel had been optioned for feature film, to be shot on location in my mother's native city, a now-divided Jerusalem. Grace and I decided that what we wanted to do with some of the proceeds was start an archive at the Jerusalem museum of first person accounts from other families, Arabs and Jews, whose lives, like mine, were full of erased stories of friendship and affinity. It was my greatest privilege to dedicate this book to her, my literary mother, mento, and friend who will, for me and so many others continue to teach us that our ears are smarter than we think, and out eyes can forever embrace that light she left glowing for us in the dark. It is now my hope that her unique sense of pacifism will serve as a vital model for the times we live in now, as more and more ordinary lives are pulled into the gun violence that now dominates our culture. She gifted us with an antidote and with solutions through her action. Her voice has been a special privilege and responsibility. She brought the very large word 'pacifism' into the realm of community activism and family. I think she still has much to tell and teach us.

# UNITY STATEMENT OF WOMEN'S PENTAGON ACTION

Women's Pentagon Action

---

1980[1]

We are gathering at the Pentagon on November 17 because we fear for our lives. We fear for the life of this planet, our Earth, and the life of our children who are our human future...

We have come here to mourn and rage and defy the Pentagon because it is the workplace of imperial power which threatens us all. Every day while we work, study, love, the colonels and generals who are planning our annihilation walk calmly in and out the doors of its five sides. To carry out their plans they have been making 3-6 nuclear bombs every day. They have accumulated over 30,000. They have invented the neutron bomb which kills people but leaves property and buildings like this one intact. They will produce the MX Missile and its billion dollar subway system which will scar thousands of miles of our western lands and consume its most delicate resource—water. They are creating a technology called Stealth- the invisible- the invisible, unperceivable arsenal. The have just appropriated 20 million dollars to revive cruel old killer nerve gas. They have proclaimed Directive 59 which asks for 'small nuclear wars, prolonged but limited'. They are talking about a first strike...

We are in the hands of men whose power and wealth have separated them from the reality of daily life and from the imagination. We are right to be afraid. At the same time our cities are in ruins, bankrupt; they suffer the devastation of war. Hospitals are closed, our schools are deprived of books and teachers. Our young Black and Latino youth are without decent work. They will be forced, drafted to become the cannon fodder for the very power that oppresses them...

The lands of the Native American people have been turned to radioactive rubble in order to enlarge the nuclear warehouse. The uranium of South Africa, necessary to the nuclear enterprise enriches the white minority and encourages the vicious system of racist oppression and war...

**There is a fear among the people, and that fear, created by the industrial militarists is used as an excuse to accelerate the arms race. 'We will protect you...' they say, but we never have been so endangered, so close to the end of human**

---

time.

**We women are gathering because life on the precipice is intolerable.**

We want to know what anger in these men, what fear which can only be satis-fied through destruction, what coldness of heart and ambition drives their days.

We want to know because we do not want that dominance which is exploita-tive and murderous in international relations, and so dangerous to women and children at home–we do not want that sickness transferred by the violent society through the fathers to sons.

What is it that we women need for our ordinary lives, that we want for our-selves and also for our sisters in new nations and old colonies who suffer the white man's exploitation and too often the oppression of their own countrymen?

We want enough good food, useful work, decent housing, communities with clean air and water, good care for our children while we work. We expect equal pay for work of equal value.

We want health care which respects and understands our bodies. We want an education for children which tells the true history of our women's lives, which describes the earth as our home to be cherished, to be fed as well as harvested.

We want to be free from violence in our streets and in our houses. The perva-sive social power of the masculine ideal and the greed of the pornographer have come together to steal our freedom, so that whole neighborhoods and the life of the evening and night have been taken away from us. For too many women the dark country road and the city alley have concealed the rapist. We want the night returned, the light of the moon, special in the cycle of female lives, the stars and the gaiety of the city streets.

We have the right to have or to not have children, we do not want gangs of politicians and medical men to say we must be sterilized for the country's good. We know that this technique is the racist's method of controlling populations. Nor do we want to be prevented from having an abortion when we need one. We think that this freedom should be available to poor women as it has always been available to the rich. We want to be free to love whomever we choose. We will live with women or with men or we will live alone. We will not allow the oppression of lesbians. One sex or one sexual preference must not dominate another.

We do not want to be drafted into the army. We do not want our young broth-ers to be drafted. We want them equal with us.

We want to see the pathology of racism ended in our time. There can be no peace while one race dominates another, one nation dominates the others.

We want the uranium left in the earth and the earth given back to the people who tilled it. We want a system of energy which is renewable, which does not take resources out of the earth without returning them. We want those systems to belong to the people and their communities not to the corporations which invariably turn knowledge in to weaponry. We want the sham of Atoms for Peace ended, all nuclear plants decommissioned and the construction of new plants stopped. That is another war against the people and the child to be born in fifty years.

We want an end to the arms race. No more bombs. No more amazing inven-tions for death.

We understand that all is connected. The earth nourishes us as we with our bodies will eventually feed it. Through us, our mothers connected the human past to the human future.

With that sense, that ecological right, we oppose the financial connections between the Pentagon and the multinational corporations and banks that the Pentagon serves.

These are connections made of gold and oil.

We are connections made of blood and bone, we are made of the sweet and finite resource, water.

We will not allow these violent games to continue. If we are here in our stubborn hundreds today, we will certainly return in the thousands and hundreds of thousands in the months and years to come.

We know there is a healthy sensible loving way to live and we intend to live that way in our neighborhoods and on our farms in these United States and among our sisters and brothers in all the countries of the world.

# COME SEPTEMBER

Arundhati Roy

2002[1]

Writers imagine that they cull stories from the world. I'm beginning to believe that vanity makes them think so. That it's actually the other way around. Stories cull writers from the world. Stories reveal themselves to us. The public narrative, the private narrative—they colonize us. They commission us. They insist on being told. Fiction and nonfiction are only different techniques of storytelling. For reasons I do not fully understand, fiction dances out of me. Nonfiction is wrenched out by the aching, broken world I wake up to every morning.

The theme of much of what I write, fiction as well as nonfiction, is the relationship between power and powerlessness and the endless, circular conflict they're engaged in. John Berger, that most wonderful writer, once wrote: "Never again will a single story be told as though it's the only one."[2]

There can never be a single story. There are only ways of seeing. So when I tell a story, I tell it not as an ideologue who wants to pit one absolutist ideology against another but as a storyteller who wants to share her way of seeing. Though it might appear otherwise, my writing is not really about nations and histories, it's about power. About the paranoia and ruth- lessness of power. About the physics of power. I believe that the accumulation of vast unfettered power by a state or a country, a corporation or an institution—or even an individual, a spouse, friend, or sibling—regardless of ideology, results in excesses such as the ones I will recount here.

Living as I do, as millions of us do, in the shadow of the nuclear holocaust that the governments of India and Pakistan keep prom- ising their brainwashed citizenry, and in the global neighborhood of the war on terror (what President Bush rather biblically calls "the task that does not end"), I find myself thinking a great deal about the relationship between citizens and the state.[3]

In India, those of us who have expressed views on nuclear bombs, Big Dams, corporate globalization, and the rising threat of communal Hindu fascism—views that are at variance with the Indian government's—are branded "antinational." While this accusation does not fill me with indignation, it's not an accurate

---

1. Source: Arundhati Roy: My Seditious Heart: Collected Nonfiction, Chicago: Haymarket Books, 2019. 187-204, for which permission to reproduce has been granted by Arunhati Roy and Haymarket Books. First presented as a lecture in Santa Fe, New Mexico, at the Lensic Performing Arts Center, September 18, 2002. Sponsored by Lannan Foundation: www.lannan.org.
2. See John Berger, G. (New York: Vintage International, 1991), 123.
3. See Damon Johnston, "U.S. Hits Back Inspirations," Advertiser, September 22, 2001, 7.

description of what I do or how I think. An antinational is a person who is against her own nation and, by inference, is pro some other one. But it isn't necessary to be antinational to be deeply suspicious of all nationalism, to be antinational*ism*. Nationalism of one kind or another was the cause of most of the genocide of the twentieth century. Flags are bits of colored cloth that governments use first to shrink-wrap people's minds and then as ceremonial shrouds to bury the dead. When independent, thinking people (and here I do not include the corporate media) begin to rally under flags, when writers, painters, musicians, filmmakers suspend their judgment and blindly yoke their art to the service of the nation, it's time for all of us to sit up and worry. In India we saw it happen soon after the nuclear tests in 1998 and during the Kargil War against Pakistan in 1999.

In the US we saw it during the Gulf War and we see it now, during the war on terror. That blizzard of made-in-China American flags.[4]

Recently those who have criticized the actions of the US government (myself included) have been called "anti-American." Anti-Americanism is in the process of being consecrated into an ideology.

The term *anti-American* is usually used by the American establishment to discredit and—not falsely, but shall we say inaccurately—define its critics. Once someone is branded anti-American, the chances are that he or she will be judged before they're heard and the argument will be lost in the welter of bruised national pride.

What does the term *anti-American mean*? Does it mean you're anti-jazz? Or that you're opposed to free speech? That you don't delight in Toni Morrison or John Updike? That you have a quarrel with giant sequoias? Does it mean you don't admire the hundreds of thousands of American citizens who marched against nuclear weapons, or the thousands of war resisters who forced their government to withdraw from Vietnam? Does it mean that you hate all Americans?

This sly conflation of America's culture, music, literature, the breathtaking physical beauty of the land, the ordinary pleasures of ordinary people, with criticism of the US government's foreign policy (about which, thanks to America's "free press," sadly, most Americans know very little) is a deliberate and extremely effective strategy. It's like a retreating army taking cover in a heavily populated city, hoping that the prospect of hitting civilian targets will deter enemy fire.

There are many Americans who would be mortified to be associated with their government's policies. The most scholarly, scathing, incisive, hilarious critiques of the hypocrisy and the contradictions in US government policy come from American citizens. When the rest of the world wants to know what the US government is up to, we turn to Noam Chomsky, Edward Said, Howard Zinn, Ed Herman, Amy Goodman, Michael Albert, Chalmers Johnson, William Blum, and Anthony Arnove to tell us what's really going on.

Similarly, in India, not hundreds but millions of us would be ashamed and offended if we were in any way implicated with the present Indian government's

---

4. See John Pomfret, "Chinese Working Overtime to Sew U.S. Flags,"*Washington Post*, September 20, 2001, A14.

fascist policies, which, apart from the perpetration of state terrorism in the valley of Kashmir (in the name of fighting terrorism), have also turned a blind eye to the recent state-supervised pogrom against Muslims in Gujarat.[5] It would be absurd to think that those who criticize the Indian government are "anti-Indian"—although the government itself never hesitates to take that line. It is dangerous to cede to the Indian government or the American government, or *anyone* for that matter, the right to define what "India" or "America" is or ought to be.

To call someone anti-American, indeed, to *be* anti-American (or for that matter anti-Indian, or anti-Timbuktuan), is not just racist, it's a failure of the imagination. An inability to see the world in terms other than those that the establishment has set out for you: If you're not a Bushie, you're a Taliban. If you don't love us, you hate us. If you're not Good, you're Evil. If you're not with us, you're with the terrorists.

Last year, like many others, I too made the mistake of scoffing at this post–September 11 rhetoric, dismissing it as foolish and arrogant. I've realized that it's not foolish at all. It's actually a canny recruitment drive for a misconceived, dangerous war. Every day I'm taken aback at how many people believe that opposing the war in Afghanistan amounts to supporting terrorism or voting for the Taliban. Now that the initial aim of the war—capturing Osama bin Laden (dead or alive)—seems to have run into bad weather, the goalposts have been moved.[6] It's being made out that the whole point of the war was to topple the Taliban regime and liberate Afghan women from their burqas. We're being asked to believe that the US marines are actually on a feminist mission. (If so, will their next stop be America's military ally Saudi Arabia?) Think of it this way: In India there are some pretty reprehensible social practices, against "Untouchables," against Christians and Muslims, against women. Pakistan and Bangladesh have even worse ways of dealing with minority communities and women. Should they be bombed? Should Delhi, Islamabad, and Dhaka be destroyed? Is it possible to bomb bigotry out of India? Can we bomb our way to a feminist paradise? Is that how women won the vote in the United States? Or how slavery was abolished? Can we win redress for the genocide of the millions of Native Americans, upon whose corpses the United States was founded, by bombing Santa Fe?

None of us need anniversaries to remind us of what we cannot forget. So it is no more than coincidence that I happen to be here, on American soil, in September—this month of dreadful anniversaries. Uppermost on everybody's mind of course, particularly here in America, is the horror of what has come to be known

5. See "Democracy: Who Is She When She's at Home?" Arundhati Roy: My Seditious Heart: Collected Nonfiction, Chicago: Haymarket Books, 2019.

6. See David E. Sanger, "Bin Laden Is Wanted in Attacks, 'Dead or Alive,' President Says," *New York Times*, September 18, 2001, A1; John F. Burns, "10-Month Afghan Mystery: Is Bin Laden Dead or Alive?" *New York Times*, September 30, 2002, A1.

as "9/11." Three thousand civilians lost their lives in that lethal terrorist strike.[7] The grief is still deep. The rage still sharp. The tears have not dried. And a strange, deadly war is raging around the world. Yet each person who has lost a loved one surely knows secretly, deeply, that no war, no act of revenge, no daisy-cutters dropped on someone else's loved ones or someone else's children will blunt the edges of their pain or bring their own loved ones back. War cannot avenge those who have died. War is only a brutal desecration of their memory.

To fuel yet another war—this time against Iraq—by cynically manipulating people's grief, by packaging it for TV specials sponsored by corporations selling detergent or running shoes, is to cheapen and devalue grief, to drain it of meaning. What we are seeing now is a vulgar display of the *business* of grief, the commerce of grief, the pillaging of even the most private human feelings for political purpose. It is a terrible, violent thing for a state to do to its people.

It's not a clever enough subject to speak of from a public platform, but what I would really love to talk to you about is loss. Loss and losing. Grief, failure, brokenness, numbness, uncertainty, fear, the death of feeling, the death of dreaming. The absolute, relentless, endless, habitual unfairness of the world. What does loss mean to individuals? What does it mean to whole cultures, whole peoples who have learned to live with it as a constant companion?

Since it is September 11 that we're talking about, perhaps it's in the fitness of things that we remember what that date means, not only to those who lost their loved ones in America last year but to those in other parts of the world to whom that date has long held significance. This historical dredging is not offered as an accusation or a provocation. But just to share the grief of history. To thin the mist a little. To say to the citizens of America, in the gentlest, most human way: Welcome to the World.

Twenty-nine years ago, in Chile, on the eleventh of September 1973, General Pinochet overthrew the democratically elected government of Salvador Allende in a CIA-backed coup. "I don't see why we need to stand by and watch a country go Communist due to the irresponsibility of its own people," said Henry Kissinger, Nobel Peace laureate, then President Nixon's national security adviser.[8]

After the coup President Allende was found dead inside the presidential palace. Whether he was killed or whether he killed himself, we'll never know. In the regime of terror that ensued, thousands of people were killed. Many more simply "disappeared." Firing squads conducted public executions. Concentration camps and torture chambers were opened across the country. The dead were buried in mine shafts and unmarked graves. For more than sixteen years, the peo-

---

7. See the Associated Press list, available on the website of the *Toledo Blade*, of those confirmed dead, reported dead, or reported missing in the September 11 terrorist attacks, www.toledoblade.com/Nation/2011/09/11/list-of-2977-victims-of-Sept-11-2001-terror-attacks.html.
8. Quoted in Seymour M. Hersh, *The Price of Power: Kissinger in the Nixon White House* (New York: Summit Books, 1983), 265.

ple of Chile lived in dread of the midnight knock, of routine disappearances, of sudden arrest and torture.[9]

In 2000, following the 1998 arrest of General Pinochet in Britain, thousands of secret documents were declassified by the US government.[10] They contain unequivocal evidence of the CIA's involvement in the coup as well as the fact that the US government had detailed information about the situation in Chile during General Pinochet's reign. Yet Kissinger assured the general of his support: "In the United States, as you know, we are sympathetic with what you are trying to do," he said. "We wish your government well."[11]

Those of us who have only ever known life in a democracy, however flawed, would find it hard to imagine what living in a dictatorship and enduring the absolute loss of freedom really means. It isn't just those who Pinochet murdered, but the lives he stole from the living that must be accounted for, too.

Sadly, Chile was not the only country in South America to be singled out for the USgovernment'sattentions. Guatemala, Costa Rica, Ecuador, Brazil, Peru, the Dominican Republic, Bolivia, Nicaragua, Honduras, Panama, El Salvador, Peru, Mexico, and Colombia—they've all been the playground for covert—and overt—operations by the CIA.[12] Hundreds of thousands of Latin Americans have been killed, tortured, or have simply disappeared under the despotic regimes and tin-pot dictators, drug runners, and arms dealers that were propped up in their countries. (Many of them learned their craft in the infamous US government–funded School of the Americas in Fort Benning, Georgia, which has produced sixty thousand graduates.)[13] If this were not humiliation enough, the people of South America have had to bear the cross of being branded as a people who are incapable of democracy—as if coups and massacres are somehow encrypted in their genes.

This list does not of course include countries in Africa or Asia that suffered US military interventions—Somalia, Vietnam, Korea, Indonesia, Laos, and Cambodia.[14] For how many Septembers for decades together have millions of Asian people been bombed, burned, and slaughtered? How many Septembers have gone

---

9. See Pilar Aguilera and Ricardo Fredes, eds., *Chile: The Other September 11* (New York: Ocean, 2002); Amnesty International, "The Case of Augusto Pinochet."

10. Clifford Krauss, "Britain Arrests Pinochet to Face Charges by Spain," *New York Times*, October 18, 1998, 1; National Security Archive, "Chile: 16,000 Secret U.S. Documents Declassified," press release, November 13, 2000, nsarchive.gwu.edu/news/20001113/; and selected documents on the National Security Archive website, nsarchive.gwu.edu/news/20001113/#docs.

11. Kissinger told this to Pinochet at a meeting of the Organization of American States in Santiago, Chile, on June 8, 1976. See Lucy Kosimar, "Kissinger Covered Up Chile Torture," *Observer*, February 28, 1999, 3.

12. Among other histories, see Eduardo Galeano, *Open Veins of Latin America: Five Centuries of the Pillage of a Continent*, trans. Cedric Belfrage, 2nd ed. (New York: Monthly Review Press, 1998); Noam Chomsky, *Turning the Tide: U.S. Intervention in Central America and the Struggle for Peace*, 2nd ed. (Boston: South End, 1985); Noam Chomsky, *The Culture of Terrorism* (Boston: South End, 1983); and Gabriel Kolko, *Confronting the Third World: United States Foreign Policy, 1945–1980* (New York: Pantheon, 1988).

13. n a public relations move, the SOA renamed itself the Western Hemisphere Institute for Security Cooperation (WHINSEC) on January 17, 2001. See Jack Nelson-Pallmeyer, *School of Assassins: Guns, Greed, and Globalization*, 2nd ed. (New York: Orbis Books, 2001); Michael Gormley, "Army School Faces Critics Who Call It Training Ground for Assassins," Associated Press, May 2, 1998; and School of the Americas Watch, www.soaw.org.

14. On these interventions, see, among other sources, Noam Chomsky, *American Power and the New Mandarins*, 2nd ed. (New York: New Press, 2002); Noam Chomsky, *At War with Asia* (New York: Vintage Books, 1970); and Howard Zinn, *Vietnam: The Logic of Withdrawal*, 2nd ed. (Cambridge, MA: South End, 2002).

by since August 1945, when hundreds of thousands of ordinary Japanese people were obliterated by the nuclear strikes in Hiroshima and Nagasaki? For how many Septembers have the thousands who had the misfortune of surviving those strikes endured the living hell that was visited on them, their unborn children, their children's children, on the earth, the sky, the wind, the water, and all the creatures that swim and walk and crawl and fly? Not far from here, in Albuquerque, is the National Atomic Museum, where Fat Man and Little Boy (the affectionate nicknames for the bombs that were dropped on Hiroshima and Nagasaki) were available as souvenir earrings. Funky young people wore them. A massacre dangling in each ear. But I am straying from my theme. It's September that we're talking about, not August.

September 11 has a tragic resonance in the Middle East, too. On the eleventh of September 1922, ignoring Arab outrage, the British government proclaimed a mandate in Palestine, a follow-up to the 1917 Balfour Declaration, which imperial Britain issued, with its army massed outside the gates of the city of Gaza.[15] The Balfour Declaration promised European Zionists "a national home for Jewish people."[16] (At the time, the empire on which the sun never set was free to snatch and bequeath national homes like the school bully distributes marbles.) Two years after the declaration, Lord Arthur James Balfour, the British foreign secretary, said, "In Palestine we do not propose even to go through the form of consulting the wishes of the present inhabitants of the country ... Zionism, be it right or wrong, good or bad, is rooted in age-long tradition, in present needs, in future hopes, of far profounder import than the desires and prejudices of the 700,000 Arabs who now inhabit that ancient land."[17]

How carelessly imperial power decreed whose needs were profound and whose were not. How carelessly it vivisected ancient civilizations. Palestine and Kashmir are imperial Britain's festering, blood-drenched gifts to the modern world. Both are fault lines in the raging international conflicts of today.

In 1937 Winston Churchill said of the Palestinians:

> I do not agree that the dog in a manger has the final right to the manger, even though he may have lain there for a very long time. I do not admit that right. I do not admit, for instance, that a great wrong has been done to the Red Indians of America, or the black people of Australia. I do not admit that a wrong has been done to these people by the fact that a stronger race, a higher grade race, a more worldly-wise race, to put it that way, has come in and taken their place.[18]

That set the trend for the Israeli state 's attitude toward Palestinians. In 1969 Israeli prime minister Golda Meir said, "Palestinians do not exist." Her successor, prime minister Levi Eshkol, said, "Where are Palestinians? When I came here

15. See Samih K. Farsoun and Christina E. Zacharia, *Palestine and the Palestinians* (Boulder, CO: Westview, 1997), 10.
16. The Balfour Declaration is included in ibid., appendix 2, 320.
17. Quoted in Noam Chomsky, *Fateful Triangle: The United States, Israel, and the Palestinians*, 2nd ed. (Cambridge, MA: South End, 2000), 90.
18. Quoted in "Scurrying towards Bethlehem," editorial, *New Left Review* 10 (July/August 2001), 9n5.

[to Palestine] there were 250,000 non-Jews, mainly Arabs and Bedouins. It was desert, more than underdeveloped. Nothing." Prime minister Menachem Begin called Palestinians "two-legged beasts." Prime minister Yitzhak Shamir called them "'grasshoppers' who could be crushed."[19] This is the language of heads of state, not the words of ordinary people. In 1947 the UN formally partitioned Palestine and allotted 55 percent of Palestine's land to the Zionists. Within a year they had captured more than 76 percent.[20] On May 14, 1948, the State of Israel was declared. Minutes after the declaration, the United States recognized Israel. The West Bank was annexed by Jordan. The Gaza Strip came under the military control of Egypt.[21] Formally, Palestine ceased to exist except in the minds and hearts of the hundreds of thousands of Palestinian people who became refugees.

In the summer of 1967, Israel occupied the West Bank and the Gaza Strip. Settlers were offered state subsidies and development aid to move into the occupied territories. Almost every day more Palestinian families are forced off their lands and driven into refugee camps. Palestinians who continue to live in Israel do not have the same rights as Israelis and live as second-class citizens in their former homeland.[22]

Over the decades there have been uprisings, wars, intifadas. Thousands have lost their lives.[23] Accords and treaties have been signed. Ceasefires declared and violated. But the bloodshed doesn't end. Palestine still remains illegally occupied. Its people live in inhuman conditions, in virtual Bantustans, where they are subjected to collective punishments and twenty-four-hour curfews, where they are humiliated and brutalized on a daily basis. They never know when their homes will be demolished, when their children will be shot, when their precious trees will be cut, when their roads will be closed, when they will be allowed to walk down to the market to buy food and medicine. And when they will not. They live with no semblance of dignity. With not much hope in sight. They have no control over their lands, their security, their movement, their communication, their water supply. So when accords are signed and words like *autonomy* and even *statehood* are bandied about, it's always worth asking: What sort of autonomy? What sort of state? What sort of rights will its citizens have?

Young Palestinians who cannot contain their anger turn themselves into human bombs and haunt Israel's streets and public places, blowing themselves up, killing ordinary people, injecting terror into daily life, and eventually hardening both societies' suspicion and mutual hatred of each other. Each bombing invites merciless reprisals and even more hardship on Palestinian people. But then suicide bombing is an act of individual despair, not a revolutionary tactic. Although Palestinian attacks strike terror into Israeli civilians, they provide the perfect cover for the Israeli government's daily incursions into Palestinian terri-

---

19. Quoted in Farsoun and Zacharia, *Palestine and the Palestinians*, 10, 243.
20. Ibid., 111, 123.
21. Ibid., 116.
22. See Chomsky, *Fateful Triangle*, 103–07, 118–32, 156–60.
23. From 1987 to 2002 alone, more than two thousand Palestinians were killed. See statistics from B'Tselem (Israeli Information Center for Human Rights in the Occupied Territories) at www.btselem.org/statistics.

tory, the perfect excuse for old-fashioned nineteenth-century colonialism, dressed up as a new-fashioned twenty-first-century war. Israel's staunchest political and military ally is and always has been the US government. The US government has blocked, along with Israel, almost every UN resolution that sought a peaceful, equitable solution to the conflict.[24] It has supported almost every war that Israel has fought. When Israel attacks Palestine, it is American missiles that smash through Palestinian homes. And every year Israel receives several billion dollars from the United States.[25]

What lessons should we draw from this tragic conflict? Is it really impossible for Jewish people who suffered so cruelly themselves—more cruelly perhaps than any other people in history—to understand the vulnerability and the yearning of those whom they have displaced? Does extreme suffering always kindle cruelty? What hope does this leave the human race with? What will happen to the Palestinian people in the event of a victory? When a nation without a state eventually proclaims a state, what kind of state will it be? What horrors will be perpetrated under its flag? Is it a separate state that we should be fighting for, or the rights to a life of liberty and dignity for everyone regardless of their ethnicity or religion?

Palestine was once a secular bulwark in the Middle East. But now the weak, undemocratic, by all accounts corrupt, but avowedly nonsectarian Palestinian Liberation Organization (PLO) is losing ground to Hamas, which espouses an overtly sectarian ideology and fights in the name of Islam. To quote from its manifesto: "We will be its soldiers and the firewood of its fire, which will burn the enemies."[26]

The world is called upon to condemn suicide bombers. But can we ignore the long road they have journeyed on before they arrived at this destination? September 11, 1922, to September 11, 2002—eighty years is a long, long time to have been waging war. Is there some advice the world can give the people of Palestine? Some scrap of hope we can hold out? Should they just settle for the crumbs that are thrown their way and behave like the grasshoppers or two-legged beasts they've been described as? Should they just take Golda Meir's suggestion and make a real effort to not exist?

In another part of the Middle East, September 11 strikes a more recent chord. It was on the eleventh of September 1990 that George W. Bush Sr., then president of the United States, made a speech to a joint session of Congress announcing his government's decision to go to war against Iraq.[27]

---

24. See Naseer H. Aruri, *Dishonest Broker: The United States, Israel, and the Palestinians* (Cambridge MA: South End, 2003); Noam Chomsky, *World Orders Old and New*, 2nd ed. (New York: Columbia University Press, 1996).
25. In addition to more than $3 billion annually in official Foreign Military Financing, the US government supplies Israel with economic assistance, loans, technology transfers, and arms sales. See Nick Anderson, "House Panel Increases Aid for Israel, Palestinians," *Los Angeles Times*, May 10, 2002, A1; Aruri, *Dishonest Broker*; and Anthony Arnove and Ahmed Shawki, foreword to *The Struggle for Palestine*, ed. Lance Selfa (Chicago: Haymarket Books, 2002), xxv.
26. Article 27 of the Charter of the Islamic Resistance Movement (Hamas), quoted in Farsoun and Zacharia, *Palestine and the Palestinians*, appendix 13, 339.
27. George H. W. Bush, "Text of Bush's Speech: 'It Is Iraq against the World'", *Los Angeles Times*, September 12, 1990, A7.

The US government says that Saddam Hussein is a war criminal, a cruel military despot who has committed genocide against his own people. That's a fairly accurate description of the man. In 1988 he razed hundreds of villages in northern Iraq and used chemical weapons and machine guns to kill thousands of Kurdish people. Today we know that that same year the US government provided him with $500 million in subsidies to buy American agricultural products. The next year, after he had successfully completed his genocidal campaign, the US government doubled its subsidy to $1 billion.[28] It also provided him with high-quality germ seed for anthrax, as well as helicopters and dual-use material that could be used to manufacture chemical and biological weapons.[29]

So it turns out that while Saddam Hussein was carrying out his worst atrocities, the US and the UK governments were his close allies. Even today the government of Turkey, which has one of the most appalling human rights records in the world, is one of the US government's closest allies. The fact that the Turkish government has oppressed and murdered Kurdish people for years has not prevented the US government from plying Turkey with weapons and development aid.[30] Clearly it was not concern for the Kurdish people that provoked President Bush's speech to Congress.

What changed? In August 1990, Saddam Hussein invaded Kuwait. His sin was not so much that he had committed an act of war but that he acted independently, without orders from his masters. This display of independence was enough to upset the power equation in the Gulf. So it was decided that Saddam Hussein should be exterminated, like a pet that has outlived its owner's affection.

The first Allied attack on Iraq took place in January 1991. The world watched the prime-time war as it was played out on TV. (In India those days, you had to go to a five-star hotel lobby to watch CNN.) Tens of thousands of people were killed in a month of devastating bombing.[31] What many do not know is that the war did not end then. The initial fury simmered down into the longest sustained air attack on a country since the Vietnam War. Over the last decade, American and British forces have fired thousands of missiles and bombs on Iraq. Iraq's fields and farmlands have been shelled with three hundred tons of depleted uranium.[32] In their bombing sorties, the Allies targeted and destroyed water treatment plants, aware of the fact that they could not be repaired without foreign assistance.[33] In southern Iraq there has been a fourfold increase in cancer among children. In the decade of economic sanctions that followed the war, Iraqi civilians have been denied food, medicine, hospital equipment, ambulances, clean water—the basic essentials.[34]

---

28. See Glenn Frankel, "Iraq Long Avoided Censure on Rights," *Washington Post*, September 22, 1990, A1.
29. See Christopher Dickey and Evan Thomas, "How Saddam Happened," *Newsweek*, September 23, 2002, 35–37.
30. See Anthony Arnove, introduction to *Iraq under Siege*, 20.
31. Arnove, *Iraq under Siege*, 221–22.
32. Ibid., 17, 205.
33. See Thomas J. Nagy, "The Secret behind the Sanctions: How the U.S. Intentionally Destroyed Iraq's Water Supply," *Progressive* 65, no. 9 (September 2001).
34. See Arnove, *Iraq under Siege*, 121, 185–203. See also Nicholas D. Kristof, "The Stones of Baghdad," *New York Times*, October 4, 2002, A27.

About half a million Iraqi children have died as a result of the sanctions. Of them, Madeleine Albright, then US ambassador to the United Nations, famously said, "I think this is a very hard choice, but the price—we think the price is worth it."[35] "Moral equivalence" was the term that was used to denounce those who criticized the war on Afghanistan. Madeleine Albright cannot be accused of moral equivalence. What she said was just straightforward algebra.

A decade of bombing has not managed to dislodge Saddam Hussein, the "Beast of Baghdad." Now, almost twelve years on, president George Bush Jr. has ratcheted up the rhetoric once again. He's proposing an all-out war whose goal is nothing short of a "regime change." The New York Times says that the Bush administration is "following a meticulously planned strategy to persuade the public, the Congress and the allies of the need to confront the threat of Saddam Hussein." Andrew Card, the White House Chief of Staff, described how the administration was stepping up its war plans for the fall: "From a marketing point of view," he said, "you don't introduce new products in August."[36] This time the catchphrase for Washington's "new product" is not the plight of Kuwaiti people but the assertion that Iraq has weapons of mass destruction. Forget "the feckless moralising of 'peace' lobbies," wrote Richard Perle, chairman of the Defense Policy Board; the United States will "act alone if necessary" and use a "pre-emptive strike" if it determines it's in US interests.[37]

Weapons inspectors have conflicting reports about the status of Iraq's "weapons of mass destruction," and many have said clearly that its arsenal has been dismantled and that it does not have the capacity to build one.[38] However, there is no confusion over the extent and range of America's arsenal of nuclear and chemical weapons. Would the US government welcome weapons inspectors? Would the UK? Or Israel?

What if Iraq *does* have a nuclear weapon, does that justify a preemptive US strike? The United States has the largest arsenal of nuclear weapons in the world. It's the only country in the world to have actually used them on civilian populations. If the United States is justified in launching a preemptive attack on Iraq, why then any nuclear power is justified in carrying out a preemptive attack on any other. India could attack Pakistan, or the other way around. If the US government develops a distaste for the Indian prime minister, can it just "take him out" with a preemptive strike?

Recently the United States played an important part in forcing India and Pakistan back from the brink of war. Is it so hard for it to take its own advice? Who is guilty of feckless moralizing? Of preaching peace while it wages war? The United

35. Leslie Stahl, "Punishing Saddam," produced by Catherine Olian, *60 Minutes*, CBS, May 12, 1996.
36. Elisabeth Bumiller, "Bush Aides Set Strategy to Sell Policy on Iraq," *New York Times*, September 7, 2002, A1
37. Richard Perle, "Why the West Must Strike First against Saddam Hussein,"*Daily Telegraph* (London), August 9, 2002, 22.
38. See Alan Simpson and Glen Rangwala, "The Dishonest Case for a War on Iraq," September 27, 2002, www.grassroots-peace.org/counter-dossier.html; Glen Rangwala, "Notes Further to the Counter-Dossier," September 29, 2002, grass-rootspeace.org/archivecounter-dossierII.html.

States, which George Bush calls "a peaceful nation," has been at war with one country or another every year for the last fifty years.[39]

Wars are never fought for altruistic reasons. They're usually fought for hegemony, for business. And then of course, there's the business of war. Protecting its control of the world's oil is fundamental to US foreign policy. The US government's recent military interventions in the Balkans and Central Asia have to do with oil. Hamid Karzai, the puppet president of Afghanistan installed by the United States, is said to be a former employee of Unocal, the American-based oil company.[40] The US government's paranoid patrolling of the Middle East is because it has two-thirds of the world's oil reserves.[41] Oil keeps America's engines purring sweetly. Oil keeps the free market rolling. Whoever controls the world's oil controls the world's markets. And how do you control the oil? Nobody puts it more elegantly than the *New York Times* columnist Thomas Friedman. In an article called "Craziness Pays," he says, "[T]he U.S. has to make clear to Iraq and U.S. allies that . . . America will use force, without negotiation, hesitation, or UN approval."[42] His advice was well taken. In the wars against Iraq and Afghanistan, as well as in the almost daily humiliation the US government heaps on the UN. In his book on globalization, *The Lexus and the Olive Tree,* Friedman says, "The hidden hand of the market will never work without a hidden fist. McDonald's cannot flourish without McDonnell Douglas And the hidden fist that keeps the world safe for Silicon Valley's technologies to flourish is called the U.S. Army, Air Force, Navy, and Marine Corps."[43]

Perhaps this was written in a moment of vulnerability, but it's certainly the most succinct, accurate description of the project of corporate globalization that I have read.

After September 11, 2001, and the war on terror, the hidden hand and fist have had their cover blown, and we have a clear view now of America's other weapon—the free market—bearing down on the developing world, with a clenched unsmiling smile. The Task That Does Not End is America's perfect war, the perfect vehicle for the endless expansion of American imperialism. In Urdu, the word for profit is *fayda*. *Al-Qaeda* means The Word, The Word of God, The Law. So in India some of us call the war on terror *Al-Qaeda versus Al Fayda*—The Word versus The Profit (no pun intended). For the moment it looks as though *Al Fayda* will carry the day. But then you never know . . .

In the last ten years of unbridled corporate globalization, the world's total income has increased by an average of 2.5 percent a year. And yet the number of the poor in the world has increased by 100 million. Of the top hundred biggest

39. George Bush, "Bush's Remarks on U.S. Military Strikes in Afghanistan," *New York Times*, October 8, 2001, B6
40. See Paul Watson, "Afghanistan Aims to Revive Pipeline Plans," *Los Angeles Times*, May 30, 2002, A1; Ilene R. Prusher, Scott Baldauf, and Edward Girardet, "Afghan Power Brokers," *Christian Science Monitor*, June 10, 2002, 1.
41. See Lisa Fingeret et al., "Markets Worry That Conflict Could Spread in Area That Holds Two-Thirds of World Reserves," *Financial Times* (London), April 2, 2002, 1.
42. Thomas L. Friedman, "Craziness Pays," *New York Times*, February 24, 1998, A21.
43. Thomas L. Friedman, *The Lexus and the Olive Tree: Understanding Globalization* (New York: Farrar, Strauss, and Giroux, 1999), 373.

economies, fifty-one are corporations, not countries. The top 1 percent of the world has the same combined income as the bottom 57 percent, and the disparity is growing.[44] Now, under the spreading canopy of the war on terror, this process is being hustled along. The men in suits are in an unseemly hurry. While bombs rain down on us and cruise missiles skid across the skies, while nuclear weapons are stockpiled to make the world a safer place, contracts are being signed, patents are being registered, oil pipelines are being laid, natural resources are being plundered, water is being privatized, and democracies are being undermined.

In a country like India, the "structural adjustment" end of the corporate globalization project is ripping through people's lives. "Development" projects, massive privatization, and labor "reforms" are pushing people off their lands and out of their jobs, resulting in a kind of barbaric dispossession that has few parallels in history. Across the world as the free market brazenly protects Western markets and forces developing countries to lift their trade barriers, the poor are getting poorer and the rich richer. Civil unrest has begun to erupt in the global village. In countries like Argentina, Brazil, Mexico, Bolivia, and India, the resistance movements against corporate globalization are growing. To contain them, governments are tightening their control. Protesters are being labeled "terrorists" and then being dealt with as such. But civil unrest does not only mean marches and demonstrations and protests against globalization. Unfortunately, it also means a desperate downward spiral into crime and chaos and all kinds of despair and disillusionment, which, as we know from history (and from what we see unspooling before our eyes), gradually becomes a fertile breed- ing ground for terrible things—cultural nationalism, religious bigotry, fascism, and of course terrorism.

All these march arm in arm with corporate globalization.

There is a notion gaining credence that the free market breaks down national barriers and that corporate globalization's ultimate destination is a hippie paradise where the heart is the only passport and we all live together happily inside a John Lennon song (*Imagine there's no countries ...*). This is a canard.

What the free market undermines is not national sovereignty but *democracy*. As the disparity between the rich and poor grows, the hidden fist has its work cut out for it. Multinational corporations on the prowl for sweetheart deals that yield enormous profits cannot push through those deals and administer those projects in developing countries without the active connivance of state machinery—the police, the courts, sometimes even the army. Today corporate globalization needs an international confederation of loyal, corrupt, authoritarian governments in poorer countries to push through unpopular reforms and quell the mutinies. It needs a press that pretends to be free. It needs courts that pretend to dispense justice. It needs nuclear bombs, standing armies, sterner immigration laws, and watchful coastal patrols to make sure that it's only money, goods, patents, and services that are globalized—not the free movement of people, not a respect for

---

44. Statistics from Joseph E. Stiglitz, *Globalization and Its Discontents* (New York: W. W. Norton, 2002), 5; Noam Chomsky, *Rogue States: The Rule of Law in World Affairs* (Cambridge, MA: South End, 2000), 214; and Noreena Hertz, "Why Consumer Power Is Not Enough," *New Statesman*, April 30, 2001.

human rights, not international treaties on racial discrimination, or chemical and nuclear weapons, or greenhouse gas emissions, climate change, or, god forbid, justice.[45] It's as though even a *gesture* toward international accountability would wreck the whole enterprise.

Close to one year after the war on terror was officially flagged off in the ruins of Afghanistan, freedoms are being curtailed in country after country in the name of protecting freedom, civil liberties are being suspended in the name of protecting democracy.[46] All kinds of dissent is being defined as "terrorism." All kinds of laws are being passed to deal with it. Osama bin Laden seems to have vanished into thin air. Mullah Omar is said to have made his escape on a motorbike.[47] (They could have sent Tin-Tin after him.) The Taliban may have disappeared, but their spirit, and their system of summary justice, is surfacing in the unlikeliest of places. In India, in Pakistan, in Nigeria, in America, in all the Central Asian republics run by all manner of despots, and of course in Afghanistan under the US-backed Northern Alliance.[48]

Meanwhile down at the mall there's a midseason sale. Everything's discounted—oceans, rivers, oil, gene pools, fig wasps, flowers, childhoods, aluminum factories, phone companies, wisdom, wilderness, civil rights, ecosystems, air—all 4.6 billion years of evolution. It's packed, sealed, tagged, valued, and available off the rack (no returns). As for justice—I'm told it's on offer, too. You can get the best that money can buy.

Donald Rumsfeld said that his mission in the war on terror was to persuade the world that Americans must be allowed to continue their way of life.[49] When the maddened king stamps his foot, slaves tremble in their quarters. So, standing here today, it's hard for me to say this, but The American Way of Life is simply not sustainable. Because it doesn't acknowledge that there is a world beyond America.

Fortunately, power has a shelf life. When the time comes, maybe this mighty empire will, like others before it, overreach itself and implode from within. It looks as though structural cracks have already appeared. As the war on terror casts its net wider and wider, America's corporate heart is hemorrhaging. For all the endless empty chatter about democracy, today the world is run by three of the most secretive institutions in the world: the International Monetary Fund, the World Bank, and the World Trade Organization, all three of which, in turn, are dominated by the United States. Their decisions are made in secret. The peo-

---

45. Among the many treaties and international agreements the United States has not signed, ignores, violates, or has broken are the UN International Covenant on Economic, Social and Cultural Rights (1966); the UN Convention on the Rights of the Child (CRC); the UN Convention on the Elimination of All Forms of Discrimination Against Women (CEDAW); agreements setting the jurisdiction for the International Criminal Court (ICC); the 1972 Anti-Ballistic Missile Treaty with Russia; the Comprehensive Test Ban Treaty (CTBT); and the Kyoto Protocol regulating greenhouse gas emissions.
46. See David Cole and James X. Dempsey, *Terrorism and the Constitution: Sacrificing Civil Liberties in the Name of National Security* (New York: New Press, 2002).
47. Luke Harding, "Elusive Mullah Omar 'Back in Afghanistan,'" *Guardian* (London), August 30, 2002, 12.
48. See Human Rights Watch, "Opportunism in the Face of Tragedy: Repression in the Name of Anti-terrorism," http://www.hrw.org/legacy/campaigns/september11/opportunismwatch.htm.
49. See "Power Politics," 76–105, and related notes.

ple who head them are appointed behind closed doors. Nobody really knows any-thing about them, their politics, their beliefs, their intentions. Nobody elected them. Nobody said they could make decisions on our behalf. A world run by a handful of greedy bankers and CEOs whom nobody elected can't possibly last.

Soviet-style communism failed, not because it was intrinsically evil, but because it was flawed. It allowed too few people to usurp too much power. Twenty-first-century market capitalism, American style, will fail for the same reasons. Both are edifices constructed by human intelligence, undone by human nature.

The time has come, the Walrus said. Perhaps things will get worse and then better. Perhaps there's a small god up in heaven readying herself for us. Another world is not only possible, she's on her way. Maybe many of us won't be here to greet her, but on a quiet day, if I listen very carefully, I can hear her breathing.

# USES OF ANGER

Audre Lorde

1981[1]

*Racism.* The belief in the inherent superiority of one race over all others and thereby the right to dominance, manifest and implied.

*Women respond to racism.* My response to racism is anger. I have lived with that anger, on that anger, beneath that anger, on top of that anger, ignoring that anger, feeding upon that anger, learning to use that anger before it laid my visions to waste, for most of my life. Once I did it in silence, afraid of the weight of that anger. My fear of that anger taught me nothing. Your fear of that anger will teach you nothing, also.

Women responding to racism means women responding to anger, the anger of exclusion, of unquestioned privilege, of racial distortions, of silence, ill-use, stereotyping, defensiveness, misnaming, betrayal, and coopting.

My anger is a response to racist attitudes, to the actions and presumptions that arise out of those attitudes. If in your dealings with other women your actions have reflected those attitudes, then my anger and your attendant fears, perhaps, are spotlights that can be used for your growth in the same way I have had to use learning to express anger for my growth. But for corrective surgery, not guilt. Guilt and defensiveness are bricks in a wall against which we will all perish, for they serve none of our futures.

Because I do not want this to become a theoretical discussion, I am going to give a few examples of interchanges between women that I hope will illustrate the points I am trying to make. In the interest of time, I am going to cut them short. I want you to know that there were many more.

For example:

- I speak out of a direct and particular anger at a particular academic conference, and a white woman comes up and says, 'Tell me how you feel but don't say it too harshly or I cannot hear you.' But is it my manner that keeps her from hearing, or the message that her life may change?
- The Women's Studies Program of a southern university invites a Black woman to read following a week-long forum on Black and white women.

---

1. Source: https://www.blackpast.org/african-american-history/speeches-african-american-history/1981-audre-lorde-uses-anger-women-responding-racism/

'What has this week given to you?' I ask. The most vocal white woman says, 'I think I've gotten a lot. I feel Black women really understand me a lot better now; they have a better idea of where I'm coming from.' As if understanding her lay at the core of the racist problem. These are the bricks that go into the walls against which we will bash our consciousness, unless we recognize that they can be taken apart.

- After fifteen years of a women's movement which professes to address the life concerns and possible futures of all women, I still hear, on campus after campus. 'How can we address the issues of racism? No women of Color attended.' Or, the other side of that statement, 'We have no one in our department equipped to teach their work.' In other words, racism is a Black women's problem, a problem of women of Color, and only we can discuss it.

- After I have read from my work entitled 'Poems for Women in Rage' a white woman asks me, 'Are you going to do anything with how we can deal directly with our anger? I feel it's so important.' I ask, 'How do you use *your* rage?' And then I have to turn away from the blank look in her eyes, before she can invite me to participate in her own annihilation. Because I do not exist to feel her anger for her.

- White women are beginning to examine their relationships to Black women, yet often I hear you wanting only to deal with the little colored children across the roads of childhood, the beloved nurse-maid, the occasional second-grade classmate; those tender memories of what was once mysterious and intriguing or neutral. You avoid the childhood assumptions formed by the raucous laughter at Rastus and Oatmeal, the acute message of your mommy's handkerchief spread upon the park bench because I had just been sitting there, the indelible and dehumanizing portraits of Amos and Andy and your Daddy's humorous bedtime stories.

- I wheel my two-year-old daughter in a shopping cart through a supermarket in Eastchester in 1967 and a little white girl riding past in her mother's cart calls out excitedly, 'Oh look, Mommy, a baby maid!' And your mother shushes you, but she does not correct you. And so, fifteen years later, at a conference on racism, you can still find that story humorous. But I hear your laughter is full of terror and dis-ease.

- At an international cultural gathering of women, a well-known white American woman poet interrupts the reading of the work of women of Color to read her own poem, and then dashes off to an 'important panel.'

- Do women in the academy truly want a dialogue about racism? It will require recognizing the needs and the living contexts of other women. When an academic woman says, for instance, 'I can't afford it,' she may mean she is making a choice about how to spend her available money. But when a woman on welfare says, 'I can't afford it,' she means she is surviving on an amount of money that was barely subsistence in 1972, and she often does not have enough to eat. Yet the National Women's Studies Association here in 1981 holds a Convention in which it commits itself to responding to racism, yet refuses to waive the registration fee for poor women and women of Color who wished to present and conduct workshops. This has made it impossible for many women of Color-for instance, Wilmette Brown, of Black Women for Wages for Housework-to participate in this Convention. And so I ask again: Is this to be merely another situation of the academy discussing life within the closed circuits of the academy?

To all the white women here who recognize these attitudes as familiar, but most of all, to all my sisters of Color who live and survive thousands of such encounters—to my sisters of Color who like me still tremble their rage under harness, or who sometimes question the expression of our rage as useless and disruptive ( the two most popular accusations), I want to speak about anger, my anger, and what I have learned from my travels through its dominions.

*Everything can be used, except what is wasteful. You will need to remember this, when you are accused of destruction.*

Every woman has a well-stocked arsenal of anger potentially useful against those oppressions, personal and institutional, which brought that anger into being. Focused with precision it can become a powerful source of energy serving progress and change. And when I speak of change, I do not mean a simple switch of positions or a temporary lessening of tensions, nor the ability to smile or feel good. I am speaking of a basic and radical alteration in all those assumptions underlining our lives.

I have seen situations where white women hear a racist remark, resent what has been said, become filled with fury, and remain silent, because they are afraid. That unexpressed anger lies within them like an undetonated device, usually to be hurled at the first woman of Color who talks about racism.

But anger expressed and translated into action in the service of our vision and our future is a liberating and strengthening act of clarification, for it is in the painful process of this translation that we identify who are our allies with whom we have grave differences, and who are our genuine enemies.

Anger is loaded with information and energy. When I speak of women of Color, I do not only mean Black women. We are also Asian American, Caribbean, Chicana, Latina, Hispanic, Native American, and we have a right to each of our names. The woman of Color who charges me with rendering her invisible by assuming that her struggles with racism are identical with my own has something to tell me that I had better learn from, lest we both waste ourselves fighting the truths between us. If I participate, knowingly or otherwise, in my sister's oppression and she calls me on it, to answer her anger with my own only blankets the substance of our exchange with reaction. It wastes energy I need to join with her. And yes, it is very difficult to stand still and to listen to another woman's voice delineate an agony I do not share, or even one in which I myself may have participated.

We speak in this place removed from the more blatant reminders of our embattlement as women. This need not blind us to the size and complexities of the forces mounting against us and all that is most human within our environment. We are not here as women examining racism in a political and social vacuum. We operate in the teeth of a system for whom racism and sexism are primary, established, and necessary props of profit. Women responding to racism is a topic so dangerous that when the local media attempt to discredit this Convention they choose to focus upon the provision of Lesbian housing as a diversionary device—as if the Hartford *Courant* dare not mention the topic chosen for discussion here, racism, lest it become apparent that women are in fact attempting to examine and to alter all the repressive conditions of our lives.

Mainstream communication does not want women, particularly white women, responding to racism. It wants racism to be accepted as an immutable given in the fabric of existence, like evening time or the common cold.

So we are working in a context of opposition and threat, the cause of which is certainly not the angers which lie between us, but rather that virulent hatred leveled against all women, people of Color, Lesbians and gay men, poor people—against all of us who are seeking to examine the particulars of our lives as we resist our oppressions, moving toward coalition and effective action.

Any discussion among women about racism must include the recognition and the use of anger. It must be direct and creative, because it is crucial. We cannot allow our fear of anger to deflect us nor to seduce us into settling for anything less than the hard work of excavating honesty; we must be quite serious about the choice of this topic and the angers entwined within it, because, rest assured, our opponents are quite serious about their hatred of us and of what we are trying to do here.

And while we scrutinize the often painful face of each other's anger, please remember that it is not our anger which makes me caution you to lock your doors at night, and not to wander the streets of Hartford alone. It is the hatred which lurks in those streets, that urge to destroy us all if we truly work for change rather than merely indulge in our academic rhetoric.

This hatred and our anger are very different. Hatred is the fury of those who do not share our goals, and its object is death and destruction. Anger is the grief of distortions between peers, and its object is change. But our time is getting shorter. We have been raised to view any difference other than sex as a reason for destruction, and for Black women and white women to face each other's angers without denial or immobilization or silence or guilt is in itself a heretical and generative idea. It implies peers meeting upon a common basis to examine difference, and to alter those distortions which history has created around difference. For it is those distortions which separate us. And we must ask ourselves: Who profits from all this?

Women of Color in America have grown up within a symphony of anguish at being silenced, at being unchosen, at knowing that when we survive, it is in spite of a whole world out there that takes for granted our lack of humanness, that hates our very existence, outside of its service. And I say 'symphony' rather than 'cacophony' because we have had to learn to orchestrate those furies so that they do not tear us apart. We have had to learn to move through them and use them for strength and force and insight within our daily lives. Those of us who did not learn this difficult lesson did not survive. And part of my anger is always libation for my fallen sisters.

Anger is an appropriate reaction to racist attitudes, as is fury when the actions arising from those attitudes do not change. To those women here who fear the anger of women of Color more than their own unscrutinized racist attitudes, I ask: Is our anger more threatening than the woman—hatred that tinges all the aspects of our lives?

It is not the anger of other women that will destroy us, but our refusals to stand still, to listen to its rhythms, to learn within it, to move beyond the manner of presentation to the substance, to tap that anger as an important source of empowerment.

I cannot hide my anger to spare you guilt, nor hurt feelings, nor answering anger; for to do so insults and trivializes all our efforts. Guilt is not a response to anger; it is a response to one's own actions or lack of action. If it leads to change then it can be useful, since it becomes no longer guilt but the beginning of knowledge. Yet all too often, guilt is just another name for impotence, for defensiveness destructive of communication; it becomes a device to protect ignorance and the continuation of things the way they are, the ultimate protection for changelessness.

Most women have not developed tools for facing anger constructively. CR [consciousness-raising] groups in the past, largely white, dealt with how to express anger, usually at the world of men. And these groups were made up of white women who shared the terms of their oppressions. There was usually little attempt to articulate the genuine differences between women, such as those of race, color, class, and sexual identity. There was no apparent need at that time to examine the contradictions of self, woman, as oppressor. There was work on expressing anger, but very little on anger directed against each other. No tools were developed to deal with other women's anger except to avoid it, deflect it, or flee from it under a blanket of guilt.

I have no creative use for guilt, yours or my own. Guilt is only another way of avoiding informed action, of buying time out of the pressing need to make clear choices, out of the approaching storm that can feed the earth as well as bend the trees. If I speak to you in anger, at least I have spoken to you; I have not put a gun to your head and shot you down in the street; I have not looked at your bleeding sister's body and asked. 'What did she do to deserve it?' This was the reaction of two white women to Mary Church Terrell's telling of the lynching of a pregnant Black woman whose baby was then torn from her body. That was in 1921, and Alice Paul had just refused to publicly endorse the enforcement of the Nineteenth Amendment for all women—excluding the women of Color who had worked to help bring about that amendment.

The angers between women will not kill us if we can articulate them with precision, if we listen to the content of what is said with at least as much intensity as we defend ourselves from the manner of saying. Anger is a source of empowerment we must not fear to tap for energy rather than guilt. When we tum from anger we turn from insight, saying we will accept only the designs already known, those deadly and safely familiar. I have tried to learn my anger's usefulness to me, as well as its limitations.

For women raised to fear, too often anger threatens annihilation. In the male construct of brute force, we were taught that our lives depended upon the good will of patriarchal power. The anger of others was to be avoided at all costs, because there was nothing to be learned from it but pain, a judgment that we had been bad girls, come up lacking, not done what we were supposed to do. And if we accept our powerlessness, then of course any anger can destroy us.

But the strength of women lies in recognizing differences between us as creative, and in standing to those distortions which we inherited without blame but which are now ours to alter. The angers of women can transform differences through insight into power. For anger between peers births change, not destruction, and the discomfort and sense of loss it often causes is not fatal, but a sign of growth.

My response to racism is anger. That anger has eaten clefts into my living only when it remained unspoken, useless to anyone. It has also served me in classrooms without light or learning, where the work and history of Black women was less than a vapor. It has served me as fire in the ice zone of uncomprehending eyes of white women who see in my experience and the experience of my people only new reasons for fear or guilt. And my anger is no excuse for not dealing with your blindness, no reason to withdraw from the results of your own actions.

When women of Color speak out of the anger that laces so many of our contacts with white women, we are often told that we are 'creating a mood of hopelessness,' 'preventing white women from getting past guilt,' or 'standing in the way of trusting communication and action.' All these quotes come directly from letters to me from members of this organization within the last two years. One woman wrote, 'Because you are Black and Lesbian, you seem to speak with the moral authority of suffering.' Yes, I am Black and Lesbian, and what you hear in my voice is fury, not suffering. Anger, not moral authority. There is a difference.

To turn aside from the anger of Black women with excuses or the pretexts of intimidation, is to award no one power—it is merely another way of preserving racial blindness, the power of unaddressed privilege, unbreached, intact. For guilt is only yet another form of objectification. Oppressed peoples are always being asked to stretch a little more, to bridge the gap between blindness and humanity. Black women are expected to use our anger only in the service of other people's salvation, other people's learning. But that time is over. My anger has meant pain to me but it has also meant survival, and before I give it up I'm going to be sure that there is something at least as powerful to replace it on the road to clarity.

What woman here is so enamoured of her own oppression, her own oppressed status, that she cannot see her heelprint upon another woman's face? What woman's terms of oppression have become precious and necessary as a ticket into the fold of the righteous, away from the cold winds of self-scrutiny?

I am a Lesbian woman of Color whose children eat regularly because I work in a university. If their full bellies make me fail to recognize my commonality with a woman of Color whose children do not eat because she cannot find work, or who has no children because her insides are rotted from home abortions and sterilization; if I fail to recognize the Lesbian who chooses not to have children, the woman who remains closeted because her homophobic community is her only life support, the woman who chooses silence instead of another death, the woman who is terrified lest my anger trigger the explosion of hers; if I fail to recognize them as other faces of myself, then I am contributing not only to each of their oppressions but also to my own, and the anger which stands between us then must be used for clarity and mutual empowerment, not for evasion by guilt or for further separation. I am not free while any woman is unfree, even when her shackles are very different from my own. And I am not free as long as one person of Color remains chained. Nor is any one of you.

I speak here as a woman of Color who is not bent upon destruction, but upon survival. No woman is responsible for altering the psyche of her oppressor, even when that psyche is embodied in another woman. I have suckled the wolfs lip of anger and I have used it for illumination, laughter, protection, fire in places where there was no light, no food, no sisters, no quarter. We are not goddesses or matriarchs or edifices of divine forgiveness; we are not fiery fingers of judgment or instruments of flagellation; we are women always forced back upon our woman's power. We have learned to use anger as we have learned to use the dead flesh of animals; and bruised, battered, and changing, we have survived and grown and, in Angela Wilson's words, we *are* moving on. With or without uncolored women. We use whatever strengths we have fought for, including anger, to help define and fashion a world where all our sisters can grow, where our children can love, and where the power of touching and meeting another woman's difference and wonder will eventually transcend the need for destruction.

For it is not the anger of Black women which is dripping down over this globe like a diseased liquid. It is not my anger that launches rockets, spends over sixty thousand dollars a second on missiles and other agents of war and death, pushes opera singers off rooftops, slaughters children in cities, stockpiles nerve gas and chemical bombs, sodomizes our daughters and our earth. It is not the anger of Black women which corrodes into blind, dehumanizing power, bent upon the annihilation of us all unless we meet it with what we have, our power to examine and to redefine the terms upon which we will live and work; our power to envision and to reconstruct, anger by painful anger, stone upon heavy stone, a future of pollinating difference and the earth to support our choices.

We welcome all women who can meet us, face to face, beyond objectification and beyond guilt.

# ON ANGER

Barbara Deming

1971[1]

I have been asked to write about the relation between war resistance and resistance to injustice. There are many points to be made that I need hardly labor. I don't have to argue at this date that if we resist war we must look to the causes of war and try to end them. And that one finds the causes of war in any society that encourages not fellowship but domination of one person by another. We must resist whatever gives encouragement to the will to dominate.

I don't think you would object to my stating the relationship between the two struggles in another way; restating it, for it has been often said: Bullets and bombs are not the only means by which people are killed. If a society denies to certain of its members food or medical attention, or a political voice, the sense of their own worth, the freedom to exercise their talents — this, too, is waging war of a kind.

I can remember a time when there was lively debate over whether or not the two struggles, against war and against injustice, were one struggle. But that debate is past history. Now another question troubles our minds and divides us among ourselves: what should our relation be to the very many people we find struggling alongside us against social injustice and against a particular war, comrades who are not committed, as we are, to nonviolence? That's what I am going to try to write about.

It is relevant to go back for a moment to the time when we were still arguing over whether or not the two struggles were one.

I remember the first, London, Peacemaker conference I ever attended, in 1960. At the time, there were very few activists in the field, but almost all of them professed a faith in nonviolence. Rev. Fred Shuttlesworth attended the conference and talked about his experience of nonviolent discipline, while struggling in Birmingham, Alabama, for integration. The question as to whether or not pacifists should take part in civil rights actions began to be discussed. Many pacifists who were present said that we shouldn't. Because there were so few of us and disarmament was such a pressing priority, they were afraid that we would dissipate our energies. I remember one man making the point: 'If we all blow up, it's not going to matter whether we blow up integrated or segregated.' That fight was for later. Many disagreed, of course.

1. Deming, Barbara. 2014. 'On Anger'. *Peace News*. Issue 2568-2569

At the time a center of action was set up in England without council or committee. Day after day we wrote letters, long letters, telling not merely of a theory, but telling facts of how people had resisted World War II in many countries. The response to our letters reached us from all parts of the world, telling how the same idea had had birth in the minds of men and women living under the most varied conditions.

I remember, too, all the discussion we had before setting out on the first peace walk through the South — the 1962 Nashville to Washington Walk; a walk this time that spoke to disarmament. We had endless discussions about whether or not to talk about race relations as we went. One black man, Bob Gore, was walking with us, so the subject was sure to come up. Should we pursue it, or should we try to get the talk quickly back to disarmament? Almost everyone who advised us — including James Farmer, then head of CORE [Congress of Racial Equality]—advised us not to try to mix the two issues. It was hard enough to talk about either; it would be harder if we linked them. And we wouldn't be helping black people by associating ourselves with their struggle; we would just be dumping on them the added burden of that association.

Most of us who were actually on the walk felt very uncomfortable about the advice being given, and felt in our bones that the two issues had to be joined. And what happened is that in the course of the walk itself, we just naturally, inevitably, did join forces with the civil rights people.

But no, it wasn't inevitable, and we almost spoiled it. The very first day, walking out of Nashville, we walked right past a Simple Simons fast food restaurant, where several black students were sitting in. Walked right past, although it felt so wrong that we talked about it at Scarritt College [Neosho, Missouri], and learned that the students felt it made no sense either. A dialogue between us had begun. And black people began walking with us for stretches near their hometowns, turning it by that act into a walk for integration as well as disarmament. We began to stay at black churches. And our causes were joined. Our encounter with each other was the main happening on that walk. We gave each other added strength and insight. I think we learned more from them than they from us; but it worked both ways.

As I look back now at the discussions before the walk started, I find them a little hard to believe. Here we were, two groups, pitifully small in numbers, both committed to nonviolence, and we were wondering whether we should link forces. It hardly seems real. But I think it is very important to look back and remind ourselves that it was real indeed. The obvious did not seem obvious to us at the time. So it may not now.

What did seem obvious to a lot of pacifists then was that a black man who professed belief in nonviolence was inconsistent in his thought, was fooling himself that he was nonviolent, unless he came out against war. I remember at that 1960 Peacemaker conference one young pacifist flinging that challenge at Shuttlesworth, who had been risking his life daily, remaining nonviolent under the most extreme provocation: 'The key to whether you have really adopted nonviolence or not is: How many of your men refuse to go into the army?' But it wasn't obvious to a lot of pacifists that they were inconsistent in their nonviolence if they didn't act against racism. I remember a good editorial at the time in *Liberation*, entitled 'Are Pacifists willing to be Negroes?'[2]

Well the problem back then seems simple to us now; it was then the problem of how we were going to relate to others who profess the same nonviolent faith. Now the question seems all the more complex: How are we going to relate to those who don't profess that faith?

But I submit that the answer is basically the same. We are in one struggle. There is, moreover, a sense in which we can say that we do share the same faith. When we define the kind of world that we want to bring into being, our mutual vision is of a world in which no person exploits another, abuses, or dominates another — in short, a nonviolent world. We differ about how to bring this world into being; and that's a very real difference. But we are in the same struggle and we need each other. We need to take strength from each other, and we need to learn from each other. And the question I most want to discuss is: What kind of thinking on our part is likely to result in our learning the most that we can from others in the nonviolent and pacifist movements, and their learning the most that they can from us?

To address this, I want to speak particularly about our relation to anger, because I think that lies at the heart of the question. A lot of people next to whom we find ourselves struggling are very angry people. Black people are angry. Welfare mothers are angry. Women are furious, as one of the buttons claims. In spite of that name, gay people are angry. Veterans, GI's, prisoners are angry. How do we relate to their anger? And how do we relate to our own anger? Because that has a lot to do with how we relate to them.

I started thinking about this most especially after a recent experience I had with a friend, a sister, a young woman who has been very deeply touched and changed by the women's liberation movement. When I first met her she was much involved in the anti-war movement and committed to nonviolence. Now she has concentrated above all on resistance to her own oppression and that of her sisters; and she was no longer sure that she was committed to nonviolence, although she had remained nonviolent in the most extreme situations. She had been jailed and beaten, and told me that she could now all too easily imagine killing a man.

We had a long talk. I spoke of what seems to me the deep, deep need for the women's movement to be a nonviolent movement if we want to make the changes that we need swiftly and surely as we can, and if we want to see the fewest possible people hurt in the struggle. For I can more and more see this struggle becoming a very bloody one.

I spoke with her of the need I see for us to reassure men continually as we take from them the privileges they have had so long, take from them the luxury of not having to be weaned from their mothers' care, because they can count on wives,

---

2. Dave Dellinger, Robert Franklin Williams, Rev. Dr. Martin Luther King Jr., and Dorothy Day: Are Pacifists Willing to Be Negroes? A 1950s Dialogue on Fighting Racism and Militarism, Using Nonviolence and Armed Struggle. In Elizabeth Betita Martínez, Mandy Carter & Matt Meyer: *We Have Not Been Moved: Resisting Racism and Militarism in 21st Century America*, PM Press, Oakland CA, 2012

mistresses to play mother to them still; spoke of the need to convince them that this loss will not be as grievous as they fear, that the pleasures of relating to others as equals may really prove greater than the pleasure of relating to others as merely shadows of themselves, second selves. I spoke with her too of the inevitability of panic on most men's part; they are so used to the present state of things. I had a long talk with her. I wasn't at all sure how persuasive I was. As it happened, some time later a mutual friend reported to me that my sister felt estranged from me. Here is how she summed it up: She didn't feel that I sufficiently respected her anger.

This took me by surprise. For I feel that I do indeed respect it. I have often enough felt very deep anger myself, about the roles in which women and men are cast.

I told myself, at first, that someone who was giving up a faith in nonviolence must feel, in spite of herself, jealous of the person who still holds it. And I think there is some truth in this. But I began to think, too, that I shouldn't be sure that this was the whole answer. I had better question my relation to her anger more deeply, meaning, really, my relation to my own kindred anger.

Perhaps I had withheld from her a full description of my anger, because it was so painful to describe it to someone else, to have to look at it. I think that I could not kill anyone. But when I study myself I have to acknowledge that in many moments of anger I have, in effect, wished a man dead, wished he wasn't there for me to have to cope with him. So I should have acknowledged precisely this to her, during our talk.

I think of a chapter in Erik Erikson's book, *Gandhi's Truth: On the Origins of Militant Nonviolence* [New York: Norton, 1963], in which he writes a letter to Gandhi as though he were still alive, and offers certain criticisms of him —in the light of insights introduced by psychoanalysis. Erikson writes of certain things that Gandhi wrote in his Autobiography, 'I seemed to sense the presence of . . . something unclean, when all the words spelled out an unreal purity.' [Erikson's italics] He charges Gandhi with seeming to be unaware of — or wanting to wish or pray away — a coexistence of love and hate, an ambivalence, which, he says, 'must become conscious in those who work for peace.' He found this especially when Gandhi wrote of very close relationships.

Erikson says, 'If, in order to fathom the truth, we must hold on to the potential of love in all hate, so must we become aware of the hate which is in all love.' He submits that only if we accept the presence of ambivalence in the most loving encounters does truth become just what Gandhi means by it, that which supports evolving human nature in the midst of antagonisms, because these antagonisms call for conscious insight rather than for moralistic repression. Erikson says that of course Gandhi could not possibly have known of the power of ambivalence. But contemporary Gandhians do know it, or should.

This is a chapter all pacifists should read and muse about. Because I believe that the response he describes is a response to us experienced by many of our comrades. They sense in us an unreal purity. It is a response that puts a fatal distance between us, and makes them feel that they have nothing to learn from us. They feel too often that they can't learn from us and can't count on us because we don't really know ourselves, don't dare know ourselves.

There is a terrible irony here. Because we want above all to be able to persuade people that truth is a powerful weapon, the most powerful weapon if, to use Gandhi's phrase, one clings to the truth and not only speaks it out, but also acts it out, and stubbornly. (The truth, above all, that every human being deserves respect. We assert the respect due ourselves, when it is denied, through non-cooperation; we assert the respect due all others, through our refusal to be violent.) But how can we communicate the power there is in acting out truth, if we give the impression of not daring to be truthful to ourselves about our own deep feelings?

Let me quote from a letter from quite another sister, in response to a pacifist mailing. She ascribes to middle class hangups what she, too, clearly feels to be purity on our part:

> 'It's a rotten shame that middle class people get so uptight and uneasy about so called violence. Y'all, in fact, seem not to understand that often the most healthy, beautiful thing to happen is for people to have a knock-down, drag out fight. It's just another form of communication for ghetto folk ... All I hear is peace, peace, love, love, Barbara, that is not what I want. I want friction, confusion, confrontation, violent or not, it doesn't matter. People grow when they are agitated, put up against the wall, at war. All the peace talk is merely a cover up for weakness, or unwillingness to wage total struggle ... This I have learned from experience.'

It's easy enough to point out that she fails to make certain distinctions. She is right that for people to grow there has to be confrontation, agitation. The charge is often 'disturbance of the peace'. Whether it's violent or nonviolent it's almost always called violent. But no, she doesn't distinguish clearly between the so-called violence of many such confrontations (including, I for one would grant her, certain knockdown fights) and the very real violence of those that actually harm or kill. If someone ends up dead, then the confrontation hasn't been just a form of communication, and certainly can't be said to have been healthy for that person.

So it may seem easy to distance ourselves from her letter. But I think that we shouldn't. I think we should pay close attention to the evidence in this letter, and other statements like it, that many people feel that we fear so-called violence quite as much as violence itself. That we fear any stark confrontation or communication; fear telling it like it is. And fear the emotions roused in us at such moments and don't want to have to look at them.

[All] anger is not in itself violent, even when raising its voice, which it sometimes does; when it brings about agitation, and confrontation, which it always does. It contains both respect for oneself and respect for the other. To oneself it says: 'I must change for I have been playing the part of the slave.' To the other it says: 'You must change for you have been playing the part of the tyrant.' It contains the conviction that change is possible for both sides; and it is capable of transmitting this conviction to others, touching them with the energy of it, even one's antagonist. This is the anger the sister who wrote me that first letter speaks of: it communicates.

Why do we who believe in nonviolence shy away from the word? Because there is another kind of anger, very familiar to us, that is not healthy, that is an affliction, which, by the way, is the first synonym for anger that is given in Webster's International Dictionary.

This anger asserts to another not: 'you must change and you can change' but: 'your very existence is a threat to my very existence.' It speaks not hope but fear. The fear is: 'you can't change, and I can't change if you are still there.' It asserts not: 'change!' but: 'drop dead!' The one anger is healthy, concentrates all one's energies; the other leaves one trembling, because it is murderous. Because we dream of a new society in which murder has no place, and it disturbs that dream.

Our task, of course, is to transform the anger that is affliction into the anger that is determination to bring about change. I think, in fact, that this transmutation might serve as a definition of revolution.

◊

Anger at deep oppression can be seen as a pride in one's own fundamental worth; the anger is an affirmation. But when this anger, this pride, is under the duress of oppression, and when it feels alone, helpless to work the change its nature demands, it can exist only in hiding. And there it becomes less than itself.

It does sometimes find ways of keeping itself in relative health. In Julius Lester's *To Be a Slave* [New York: Dial Press, 1968] he describes how slaves on plantations would meet in secret in the woods and there hold meetings, dances in which they could be themselves. He quotes from a song from the time: 'Got one mind for the boss to see, Got another mind for what I know is me.' In secret, they would be themselves, keep those selves precariously intact.

I think of the severely suppressed anger of the Chinese peasants William Hinton writes of in *Fanshen* [New York: Vintage, 1966] when, during the revolution, the property they had always been denied began at last to be divided among them; and they were encouraged, after a lifetime of oppression by the landlords, to speak out what they felt to be due to them from those men — speak out their anger. As they began to let it out, it would overwhelm them and they would often beat the landlords to death on the spot. In a passion, in part, of uncertainty that their new rights were really theirs. It is of course precisely when some real hope is born at last, when a movement for change begins to gain momentum, that anger pushes up; it has to be contended with.

I have experienced this in the context of the women's movement in a way that took me very much by surprise, because I thought my own anger as a woman was quite known to me. I thought I had noted the situation women are born to, disapproved of it, and found my own way to face it. I had, for example, long ago made an instinctive decision not to marry. Given the obvious power relationship between the two sexes, I was afraid that my life would never be my own if I lived with a man. I recall James Bevel at Birmingham talking about the relation of blacks to whites: 'We love our white brothers; but we don't trust them.' I didn't dare trust even a man who loved me enough to let me be myself, and not merely an extension of himself, his second self. I was afraid that I wouldn't be able to live in comradeship with a man, as a woman can live with a woman.

And so, as I say, I thought I knew my anger. I didn't think of it as suppressed anger, as it had to be in the case of women who led married lives. Yet, as the women's movement began to gain some momentum, I found that expressions of the male will to dominate began to rouse in me anger in a new degree, an anger rising from my toes with a force that startled me at first. Even when the man would be a very young man and obviously under great pressure to act as he thought a man must, and I would know this and with part of myself forgive him, part of me couldn't forgive him. It was very painful for me to look at this new anger; and it is only gradually that I am learning to transmute it into determination. For a while I felt helpless in its grip.

Now one way, of course, that we avoid looking at the anger that most afflicts us, one way we find of affirming our pride without facing its anger (which we sense can overwhelm us) is by resisting the oppression of that pride, as it were by analogy.

I remember some years ago being asked why I walked through the South; and I questioned myself and decided that perhaps the deepest explanation was my relation to a black woman who worked for my family for many years, and my growing painful awareness that she led too little of her own life, too much simply of ours. I think my love for her certainly had something to do with my walking through the South, but I think now that the more fundamental explanation is that I was protesting against any such classification as second class citizen —protesting it in my own name.

I am sure this is true for many of you who are white and who joined the struggle against racism. You didn't do it out of altruism; you did it because you knew in your souls something of what it is to be a 'nigger'. If you were gay, and known to be, you even knew what it was to receive the hate stare. And as pacifists it was much easier to control the anger that was in you, to transmute, to be nonviolent, in this struggle, where you could deal with that anger by analogy.

Some of us are perhaps tempted to continue to deal with it always by analogy; and I guess one of the main recommendations I would make is that we all resist that temptation. I am not suggesting that we abandon any of the struggles that we have been taking part in. I am suggesting that if we will take upon ourselves the further struggle of confronting our own most particular, own personal oppression, we will find ourselves better able to wage those struggles in a more conscious solidarity. Confronting our personal oppression in the company of others is in truth deeply political.

I find myself very much in agreement with Shulamith Firestone when she writes, in *The Dialectic of Sex*, [New York: William Morrow, 1970] that the sexual class system is the model for all other systems of oppression, and that until we resist this, until we eliminate this, we will never succeed in truly eliminating any of the others.

For those of us who are women, or gay, it is probably clear enough what anger I mean should be faced. Though it is often hard enough to admit to, even so. But

I would very much include, among those who have a personal anger to confront, the men among you. For if women are oppressed by men, and cannot fully be themselves, men in succumbing to all the pressures put upon them from an early age to dominate, lose the chance to be freely themselves. I cannot believe that there is not in men a deep, buried anger about this.

Apparently, there are now men's liberation groups springing up. I had been going to suggest that, as War Resisters' has played an important role in counseling men who are unwilling to commit aggression in wars, it might consider playing a comparable role in counseling men who would like to know how to resist committing aggression at home against women. I do recommend this.

I could have entitled this essay, perhaps: 'Are Pacifists Willing to be Angry?' I suggest that if we are willing to confront our own raw anger, and take upon ourselves the task of translating this raw anger into the disciplined anger of the search for change, we will find ourselves in a position to speak much more persuasively to comrades about the need to root out from our anger the spirit of murder.

# WELFARE IS A WOMAN'S ISSUE

Johnnie Tillmon

1972[1]

I'm a woman. I'm a black woman. I'm a poor woman. I'm a fat woman. I'm a middle-aged woman. And I'm on welfare.

In this country, if you're any one of those things poor, black, fat, female, middle-aged, on welfare you count less as a human being. If you're all those things, you don't count at all. Except as a statistic.

I am a statistic.

I am 45 years old. I have raised six children.

I grew up in Arkansas, and I worked there for fifteen years in a laundry, making about $20 or $30 a week, picking cotton on the side for carfare. I moved to California in 1959 and worked in a laundry there for nearly four years. In 1963 I got too sick to work anymore. Friends helped me to go on welfare.

They didn't call it welfare. They called it A.F.D.C. Aid to Families with Dependent Children. Each month I got $363 for my kids and me. I pay $128 a month rent; $30 for utilities, which include gas, electricity, and water; $120 for food and nonedible household essentials; $50 for school lunches for the three children in junior and senior high school who are not eligible for reduced-cost meal programs.

There are millions of statistics like me. Some on welfare. Some not. And some, really poor, who don't even know they're entitled to welfare. Not all of them are black. Not at all. In fact, the majority about two- thirds of all the poor families in the country are white.

Welfare's like a traffic accident. It can happen to anybody, but especially it happens to women.

And that is why welfare is a women's issue. For a lot of middle-class women in this country, Women's Liberation is a matter of concern. For women on welfare it's a matter of survival.

Forty-four percent of all poor families are headed by women. That's bad enough. But the *families* on A.F.D.C. aren't really families. Because 99 percent of them are headed by women. That means there is no man around. In half the states there really can't be men around because A.F.D.C. says if there is an 'able-bodied' man around, then you can't be on welfare. If the kids are going to eat, and the man can't get a job, then he's got to go. So his kids can eat.

1. Source: https://msmagazine.com/2021/03/25/welfare-is-a-womens-issue-ms-magazine-spring-1972/

The truth is that A.F.D.C. is like a supersexist marriage. You trade in a man for *the* man. But you can't divorce him if he treats you bad. He can divorce you, of course, cut you off anytime he wants. But in that case, *he* keeps the kids, not you.

*The* man runs everything. In ordinary marriage, sex is supposed to be for your husband. On A.F.D.C., you're not supposed to have any sex at all. You give up control of your own body. It's a condition of aid. You may even have to agree to get your tubes tied so you can never have more children just to avoid being off welfare.

*The* man, the welfare system, controls your money. He tells you what to buy, what not to buy, where to buy it, and how much things cost. If things, rent for instance, really cost more than he says they do, it's just too bad for you.

There are other welfare programs, other kinds of people on welfare: the blind, the disabled, the aged. (Many of them are women too, especially the aged.) Those others make up just over a third of all the welfare caseloads. We A.F.D.C. are two-thirds.

But when the politicians talk about the 'welfare cancer eating at our vitals,' they're not talking about the aged, blind, and disabled. Nobody minds them. They're the 'deserving poor.' Politicians are talking about A.F.D.C. Politicians are talking about us the women who head up 99 percent of the A.F.D.C. families and our kids. We're the 'cancer,' the 'undeserving poor.' Mothers and children.

In this country we believe in something called the 'work ethic.' That means that your work is what gives you human worth. But the work ethic itself is a double standard. It applies to men and to women on welfare. It doesn't apply to all women. If you're a society lady from Scarsdale and you spend all your time sitting on your prosperity paring your nails, well, that's okay.

The truth is a job doesn't necessarily mean an adequate income. A woman with three kids—not twelve kids, mind you, just three kids—that woman earning the full federal minimum wage of $2.00 an hour, is still stuck in poverty. She is below the Government's own official poverty line. There are some ten million jobs that now pay less than the minimum wage, and if you're a woman, you've got the best chance of getting one.

The President keeps repeating the 'dignity of work' idea. What dignity? Wages are the measure of dignity that society puts on a job. Wages and nothing else. There is no dignity in starvation. Nobody denies, least of all poor women, that there is dignity and satisfaction in being able to support your kids through honest labor.

We wish we could do it.

The problem is that our country's economic policies deny the dignity and satisfaction of self-sufficiency to millions of people the millions who suffer every day in underpaid dirty jobs and still don't have enough to survive.

People still believe that old lie that A.F.D.C. mothers keep on having kids just to get a bigger welfare check. On the average, another baby means another $35 a month barely enough for food and clothing. Having babies for profit is a lie that only men could make up, and only men could believe. Men, who never have to bear the babies or have to raise them and maybe send them to war.

There are a lot of other lies that male society tells about welfare mothers; that A.F.D.C. mothers are immoral, that A.F.D.C. mothers are lazy, misuse their welfare checks, spend it all on booze and are stupid and incompetent.

If people are willing to believe these lies, it's partly because they're just special versions of the lies that society tells about all women....

On TV, a woman learns that human worth means beauty and that beauty means being thin, white, young and rich.

She learns that her body is really disgusting the way it is, and that she needs all kinds of expensive cosmetics to cover it up.

She learns that a 'real woman' spends her time worrying about how her bathroom bowl smells; that being important means being middle class, having two cars, a house in the suburbs, and a minidress under your maxicoat. In other words, an A.F.D.C. mother learns that being a 'real woman' means being all the things she isn't and having all the things she can't have.

Either it breaks you, and you start hating yourself, or you break it.

There's one good thing about welfare. It kills your illusions about yourself, and about where this society is really at. It's laid out for you straight. You have to learn to fight, to be aggressive, or you just don't make it. If you can survive being on welfare, you can survive anything. It gives you a kind of freedom, a sense of your own power and togetherness with other women.

Maybe it is we poor welfare women who will really liberate women in this country. We've already started on our welfare plan.

Along with other welfare recipients, we have organized together so we can have some voice. Our group is called the National Welfare Rights Organization (N.W.R.O.). We put together our own welfare plan, called Guaranteed Adequate Income (G.A.I.), which would eliminate sexism from welfare.

There would be no 'categories' men, women, children, single, married, kids, no kids just poor people who need aid. You'd get paid according to need and family size only $6,500 for a family of four (which is the Department of Labor's estimate of what's adequate), and that would be upped as the cost of living goes up.

If I were president, I would solve this so-called welfare crisis in a minute and go a long way toward liberating every woman. I'd just issue a proclamation that 'women's' work is *real* work.

In other words, I'd start paying women a living wage for doing the work we are already doing child-raising and house-keeping. And the welfare crisis would be over, just like that. Housewives would be getting wages too, a legally determined percentage of their husband's salary instead of having to ask for and account for money they've already earned.

For me, Women's Liberation is simple. No woman in this country can feel dignified, no woman can be liberated, until all women get off their knees. That's what N.W.R.O. is all about—women standing together, on their feet.

# HOW ANTI-VIOLENCE ACTIVISM TAUGHT ME TO BE A PRISON ABOLITIONIST

Beth E. Richie

2014[1]

Sometimes we learn our most profound political lessons in the contours of our everyday activism. This is certainly the case for me as I recount my journey as a Black feminist activist working to end gender violence for the past 20 years, during which the United States was engaged in building itself up as the world's leading prison nation. My journey began in Harlem, the renowned community in New York City that was at the center of struggles for racial and economic justice. The on-the-ground work at the time included organizing for material changes (safe and affordable housing, better schools, accessible health care, jobs that offered a future, political representation, neighborhood businesses that support the local economy, and the end to growing expansion of the prison industrial complex). The organizing work was sustained by rhetoric about the 'liberation of our people' and the vision of what our community would look like if we could sustain grassroots activism in the service of broad-based social change.

As many Black and other feminists of color will remember, the promise of liberation within racial justice formations was critically hampered by the lack of an analysis of how gender oppression figured into the work. Indeed, despite our demands that the analysis include: 1) how women experience injustice (like poverty or incarceration) in particular ways 2) that the particular oppression that women suffer (like sexual assault by individuals or state agencies) be included into the activist agenda and 3) that women's leadership be recognized and supported as critical to political advancement, we were disappointed.

This disappointment was part of what propelled me to immerse myself in the anti-violence movement against rape, battering, sexual harassment, emotional abuse, and economic exploitation of women and the non-gender conforming. These activist organizations provided a temporary relief, and my commitment to feminist ideas was rejuvenated. But the respite provided by local and national anti-violence organizations was brief; very quickly I became aware of the political limitations that a gender-essentialized notion of violence held for a truly trans-

---

1. Source: https://thefeministwire.com/2014/01/how-anti-violence-activism-taught-me-to-become-a-prison-abolitionist/

formative agenda related to women of color. Indeed, substituting a gender analysis that did not include a very well articulated position regarding racial or class hierarchy was as much a roadblock as a racial justice project that does not include gender. In particular, an analysis of gender oppression that did not include state violence excluded a large part of the abuses that Black and other women of color experienced because of their position as racialized bodies in a heteropatrichal society. A second major disappointment.

The ongoing work of trying to find the political crossroads that link racial and economic justice with an analysis of gender oppression became more difficult in the 1980s and 1990's when the United States deepened its commitment to building itself up as a prison nation. The complications looked something like this. First, both the public and private sector committed more and more resources to the prison industrial complex while at the same time elite leaders advanced an ideological campaign to frame public 'risk' in racialized terms. Second, neoliberal policy decisions lead to the divestment of economic resources from already disadvantaged communities who suffer deepening degrees of material and political liabilities that turned social problems into 'crimes'. Third, political organizing strategies used by both anti-violence organizations and racial justice groups got coopted by a 'not-for-profit/social service' mentality that served as a distraction from the root causes of structural inequality and the violence that results from it. Groups organized to resist racialized oppression *or* class exploitation *or* gender violence *or* other monolithic formulations, treating them as separate issues. And they lost focus on how the state colludes to construct a hierarchy of oppression that cannot be agreed upon or changed.

On the ground today, it looks something like this. The anti-violence movement buys into the carceral state by advancing 'anti-violence' campaigns that rely on arrest, prosecution, and punishment as ways to solve the problem of gender violence. The focus of the problem is individual incidents of abuse rather than public policies that result in state violence against women and queer communities, which are ignored by feminist groups who invest in or accept resources that are tied to the growing punishment industry. Those racial justice organizations that do resist state violence and the concomitant crises that result from mass incarceration see their work in mansculinist terms. Some even point to anti-violence activism as one of the culprits in the mass incarceration of poor men of color. Many fail to understand that the criminal legal system is not only racist, it relies on heteropatriarcal assumptions that narrate a kind of social order that is based on domination.

So how do anti-violence activism and prison abolition politics get politically reconciled when the movements have been so set apart from one another? Angela Davis, Ruthie Gilmore, Alicia Beira, Andrea Smith and other members of the INCITE national organizing committee articulate this more fully. We are learning collectively that the way out is not to simply keep pushing back against each of those policies, strategies, and movement organizations that have disappointed us, but rather to adopt a feminist political strategy that embraces the possibility of Prison Abolition. This is where we would bring together attention to state violence as an essential aspect of ending violence against women of color and non-gender conforming communities. *All people would be safer.* It means investing in a new kind of community, especially within communities of color, where those who are most disadvantaged are in leadership of sustained, base-building activities for justice. *Concerns about gender justice and sexuality liberation would necessarily be included.* Strategies to address the harm caused by violence would be grounded in these stronger, more equitable communities. *Safety would come from communities, and, therefore, prisons could eventually become obsolete.* Here, in a feminist prison abolition project is where I find the best possibility of the kind of liberation that I have been working towards for so long.

# THE WOUNDS OF AFRIN, THE PROMISE OF ROJAVA: AN INTERVIEW WITH NAZAN ÜSTÜNDAĞ

An Interview

Nazan Üstündağ

2018[1]

**Nazan Üstündağ (NÜ):** I visited Rojava four times. Twice I visited the canton of Jazeera and twice that of Kobane. Three of these were as part of a research project I am pursuing concerning the transformation of the Kurdish Liberation Movement, its ideas and practices. In the canton of Jazeera I went to different cities and interviewed government representatives, freedom fighters, representatives of neighborhood assemblies, individuals responsible for transforming the justice system, the education system and the university, women from the women's movement and self-defense units and women's houses where crimes against women are addressed and problems of women solved. I went to Kobane once to show solidarity with the fighters of Kobane against ISIS attacks. The second time I was there it was again for purposes of research, but my interviews and observations occurred under conditions of post-war devastation. All of these occurred in the years 2015 and 2016. So, although I still watch it carefully, I must admit that some of my comments may be outdated.

The nature of governance in Rojava is inspired by the ideas of Abdullah Öcalan, the leader of the PKK, who is in the prison of the island of Imralı in Turkey since 1999. The interesting thing about Rojava is that while the YPG and YPJ are lauded worldwide for their struggle against the Islamic State, the fact remains that the solidarity shown for the Syrian Kurds is based on a notion of a common enemy rather than shared truths. While ISIS was globally understood in the terms of science fictional apocalypse, the city of Kobane became a metaphor for secularism, heroism, anti-terrorism and patriotism, all values assumed to prevent the arrival of the doomsday and behind which, the world, specifically the western world, would securely stand. Ironically however, the ideas that inspire

1. Source: https://lefteast.org/nazan-ustundag-interview/

what's happening in Rojava developed from a critique of western paradigms of capitalism, positivism, individualism and professionalism. Therefore, it is urgent to become informed about the ideals of the Kurdish Liberation Movement and what it does on the ground so that now a larger support can be mobilized for it as it is dealing with Turkish attacks and its abandonment by the U.S., Russia and Europe.

Abdullah Öcalan, who is one of the main authors of Syrian Kurds' ideals in Rojava, is neither a nativist nor an anti-modernist. On the contrary, he is fond of critical western thought and concepts as much as he is of myth and Islamic history. While adhering to a Marxist critique of capitalism, he nevertheless couples it with a radical critique of the state and patriarchy informed by anarchist, deconstructionist, poststructuralist and feminist theory. In the simplest form one could argue that in his view the problem of capitalist modernity is that the means by which societies produce and reproduce themselves have been usurped by men, the state and the bourgeoisie and, it is by reclaiming and democratizing those means that society and individuals will be emancipated and liberated. A (women's) revolution in epistemology, ethics and aesthetics is fundamental to such a project. So is a new conception of self-defense: A web of relations, which will empower societies against the state.

For Öcalan, the Kurdish Liberation Movements in particular and Kurds in general have the potential of being pioneers in the construction of a new society and subjectivities, because they have no state and they are dispersed in at least four countries in the Middle East and as such what they construct will have consequences for the whole geography. Their partially traditional character and experience of colonization are both obstacles and opportunities. They are obstacles because these make Kurds conservative and at times supportive of ruling regimes. But in other ways, they are capable of wanting other social forms than those of capitalism and colonialism because they suffer from it and they can draw on their memory and traditional skills to imagine new forms. In Syrian Kurdistan, the process of constructing a new society had already begun before the 2011 Revolution, albeit underground and at the risk of imprisonment and severe punishment. When the Syrian Revolution started, the Kurdish Liberation Movement's ideals represented by the political party PYD were already popular among the inhabitants of Rojava.

Given that PYD did not appeal to sovereignty and operated with the assumption that the Syrian state will continue existing in one form or another under the rule of Assad or the opposition, PYD did not participate in an armed war to overthrow the regime but instead chose to organize its model in a peaceful fashion. It called this the third way and negotiated with different actors in Syria to deepen democracy and autonomy under the conditions of what transformed itself from a people's revolution to a civil war. In 2012, the Rojava revolution occurred and the autonomy of the cantons were declared. That was followed by a Constitution that was defined as a voluntary agreement between people and groups with no unified identity. In certain parts of Rojava where there was still a population loyal to the state, the state's presence remained intact in the form of universities, hospitals or schools. Conversation and struggle with these however, continued. Then of course it also became affected directly by the war as ISIS became a primary actor in Syria.

In discussing the new institutions of Rojava, a number of people emphasized the creation of People's Parliaments as the primary means of democracy and discussed them in the framework of 21st-century socialism. While this is a very important dimension of the revolution, the transformation that occurred in Rojava is not restricted to the democratization of decision-making processes. I would describe what I have observed in the period I stayed Rojava as a revolution that democratizes governance (law, security, education) and decision making all at once.

Öcalan defines the primary needs of any society as nutrition, reproduction and defense. In order to meet these needs a society must organize its sociability, economy and knowledge without letting the means by which these are organized be appropriated by a centralized power. The Rojava Revolution involves the creation of gender equal-ist communes, cooperatives and academies at every level of society so that these means can be taken back by people and women and protected from the state, capitalism and patriarchy. While communes are the main social and political units that will define problems, come up with solutions and make decisions, cooperatives are economic units that are responsible for production and exchange. Academies on the other hand, accumulate and disseminate knowledge and struggle against hierarchization and monopolization of information. Communes have co-presidencies consisting of one woman and man and form committees as the need arises. Almost every commune has defense units and peace committees that protect people from violence and solve conflicts. Diplomacy, economy and ecology are examples of other topics around which committees are established. In each residential unit, along with mixed gender communes there are also all-women communes, which have the right to veto decisions made by the former.

In Rojava while younger people go to fight the Islamic State and join YPJ and YPG, it is their fathers, mothers, brothers and sisters who become responsible for public peace and safety. As with everything in Rojava, it was only when the need arose that public defense units were formed, and this happened when ISIS began a campaign of suicide bombings against Kurds. However today, defense units have a number of sections that for example, fight against organized crime. Just like communes, each district has two defense units. One mixed gender and one all women. Women's defense units are exclusively responsible for crimes against women. All units have rules, regulations and bylaws that would impress most of HR NGOs since people who have suffered human rights violations have prepared these and since these defense units have themselves signed several humanitarian conventions. When I was in Rojava, defense unit members were working on innovating new 'techniques of rehabilitation' such as reducing years of sentence if the person learns a new language, reads or writes a book.

Officials who will work in defense units must go through a short period of training before taking their post. This training is given by academies of security run by wounded fighters some of whom have not only witnessed war in Syria but also participated in the guerilla warfare against Turkey. One third of the trainees are women who will take posts in all-women security points. In the academy only half of the lessons involve 'real' police or military business. The rest are about 'how not to sacrifice the revolution to your feelings of anger, revenge and despair' as one of the teachers had said to me. There are poetry sessions and discussions of crimes the PKK committed in its early years, all of which aim at cultivating a consciousness of humanity and forgiveness as opposed to one of militarism and security.

Still, tensions develop. While defense units ideologically aim to get rid of any centralized understanding of defense and to return the means of defense to people themselves, an increasingly sophisticated and regulated system is being created as a result of the ongoing war. At times comparing one's system to a less democratic and more oppressive one becomes enough reason to celebrate one's self-created institutions. At other times, utopia becomes distanced as more dead bodies culminate in the war-stricken spaces of Rojava.

**Is it possible to build a democratic society at a time of war, when the battle front as well as the home front need utmost mobilization, centralization, and discipline?**

NÜ: This is a very important question. I think one thing that is specific to Rojava is that it is divided into cantons. On the one hand, there is a push to centralization during war in terms of resource allocation, decision-making, recruitment and security. On the other hand, because each canton is very different in terms of population composition, geography, resources, accessibility, alliances etc., there is a space for autonomy and diversity. Also, because of war and because cantons are developing democracy and autonomy within an existing state, everything is very fragile. This forces the government and the revolutionaries to be extremely careful while adapting to the wishes of people against PYD or ethnic groups other than Kurds. They know very well because of their experience in Turkey that they can only survive by appealing to people who are not like them and that forces them to become democratic as well apart from the fact their ideology commands them to be.

When I was in Rojava there were two important debates. One was what to do with...mandatory military service. Of course, many people did not want that. Yet, not only does YPG need soldiers but also the government feels that voluntary military duty creates inequality. Those whose sons or daughters get killed during war believe they paid a price for Rojava and hence deserve more. How is this going to be solved? I think at this point it is only in some regions that there is a mandatory military duty...War pushes for control, security, homogeneity and centralization. However, the built-in structures of democratic autonomy checks and balances these demands, although not necessarily with results that make everyone happy.

**PYD started as the (illegal) political party of a Kurdish minority struggling for basic rights. Over the course of the war, its reach has extended beyond traditionally Kurdish areas and it has tried to represent Arab, Syriac, Turkmen, etc., etc.,**

etc. people, as reflected in the name change of the political entity, from Rojava (a Kurdish name meaning West) to 'Democratic Federation of Northern Syria.' Was this transformation of PYD/ Rojava from a Kurdish nationalist project to a multi-cultural, pan-Syrian one purely a function of war exigency? Do you have a sense of how its expansion has worked out beyond the traditional Kurdish core?

NÜ: Definitely not an exigency of war. I am not saying that Kurds are not patriotic or have no prejudices against other people. Surely, they do. But the ideology of the Kurdish Liberation Movement defines itself to be against prioritizing any identity and in Turkey and Syria it proposed the democratic autonomy project always for everyone in the nation-state. The alliance with other minorities did not only occur in Rojava but also in Turkey where HDP included Armenians, Alevis, LGBTQ and other oppressed people. In response to your first question I also mentioned the new electoral system that is fashioned to increase the representation of Arabs and Assyrians and others.

Also, the Rojava Constitution appeals to no singular ethnic identity and binds all people who voluntarily agree to live in a non-ethnic, autonomous and democratic society. We must remember, that in northern Syria all the diversity for the Middle East is represented, Circassians, Chechens, Turkmens, Assyrians, Arabs, Kurds and Armenians. Of course, some of these are more willing to participate in the new institutions than others and in different capacities. Assyrian women are more active for example. Assyrians, Arab , Yazidis and Alevites have their own defense units under the umbrella of the YPG. The co-president of the Jazeera canton is an Arab sheikh who controls the 30% of an *ashiret* (tribe) that reaches out from Yemen to Iraq. But when we talked, he was enthusiastic about ethnic diversity but not gender equality. I heard he thinks differently now.

**Rojava has existed under conditions of civil war, state collapse, and economic blockade. Can you tell us a little bit about life in the places you saw—what is the economy like? Is there any provision of electricity, water, phone and internet connections, or basic state services such as trash collection, etc.**

NÜ: When I was there, consultants of the Jazeera canton government explained to me that currently three different economies exist in Rojava: a 'war economy,' an 'open economy' and a 'commune economy.' The war economy finances the war. I would assume that this is a largely an informal economy given that the cantons are not recognized internationally and have no legal standing. Also, what the canton governments produce (for example, they have workshops where the uniforms of the fighters are made) is oriented towards the war. The open economy is regulated by the ministry of economy, which sets consumer taxes and prices. The commune economy on the other hand, is only slowly created and is based on the cooperatives. Most of these cooperatives are agricultural cooperatives that are formed in the land that was previously state owned and now distributed to the communes by the canton government. The canton government plays an important role in the economy as buyer of the goods produced by cooperatives and individual wheat cultivators and also as producer specifically of oil.

I must say that the open economy is a very difficult area for PYD to interfere with. People quickly become alienated by radical transformations since their habits were formed in a national, capitalist, patriarchal economy. Still, the canton governments win the trust of people by providing them with free electricity and water. Internet connection depends on Turkish and Syrian firms.

**What meaningful forms of solidarity with Rojava exist for those of us located outside of it?**

**NÜ:** When the war of ISIS over Kobane was waged, the YPG and YPJ were in a very, very bad condition until people all over the world organized rallies in their support. That's how the coalition became convinced to interfere and supported the fighters on the ground with air bombing. Magazines were then showing YPJ women every day as if they were the elves. I think that support has to be renewed not because Turkey is evil–it is,–but I guess that a state is evil is something usual that calls for no response,–but because the Kurds in northern Syria along with other populations are struggling to create something new and beautiful that should and could inspire all of us. I cannot forget the picture of the Kurdish female commander with her all-women unit addressing the world when ISIS was defeated in Raqqa. She spoke in Arabic and she said she was doing this out of respect for the heroic Arab women who endured ISIS occupation and dedicated their glory against ISIS to women in the world. How can women now remain silent when it is once again women who are being killed by the Turkish army, who fight against occupation and whose bodies are mutilated, filmed and tweeted by Turkish mercenaries? There is a lot that people outside of Afrin can do. It is only people's alliance, rallies, slogans, writings, petitions that can mobilize their states to do something about this atrocity. Moreover, that would not only be a win for Afrin but a win for those who rallied and generated civil power to affect world politics.

I count myself lucky to have been a witness to the perseverance and struggle of the Kurdish Liberation Movement and the Kurdish people and their allies. Their resistance and creativity bring magic to the world (as a very good friend of mine who died in Kobane while fighting against ISIS would say). They force us to think in new ways, to develop new concepts and theories. They demand that we be much more tuned with what's happening on the ground.

What more can a feminist, a sociologist, a communist want?

# TRANS LIBERATION: A MOVEMENT WHOSE TIME HAS COME

Leslie Feinberg

---

1992[1]

Who decides what the 'norm' should be? Why are some people punished for their self-expression?

...[A]ncient communal societies held transgendered people in high esteem. It took a bloody campaign by the emerging ruling classes to declare what had been considered natural to be its opposite. That prejudice, foisted on society by its ruling elite, endures today.

Yet even in a society where there are harsh social penalties for not fitting, a large part of the population can't or won't change their nature. It is apparent that there are many ways for men and women to be; everything in nature is continuum.

It was gay transvestites who led the 1969 battle at the Stonewall Inn in New York City that gave birth to the modern lesbian and gay movement.

But just as the lesbian and gay movement had to win over the progressive movement to the understanding that struggling shoulder to shoulder together would create a more powerful force for change, the transgendered community is struggling to win the same understanding from the lesbian and gay movement.

While the oppression within these two powerful communities are not the same, we face a common enemy. Gender-phobia—like racism, sexism and bigotry against lesbians and gay men—is meant to keep us divided. Unity can only increase our strength.

Solidarity is built on understanding how and why oppression exists and who profits from it. It is our view that revolutionary changes in human society can do away with inequality, bigotry and intolerance.

Transgendered women and men have always been here. They are oppressed. But they are not merely products of oppression. It is *passing* that's historically new. Passing means hiding. Passing means invisibility. Transgendered people should be able to live and express their gender without criticism or threats of violence. But that is not the case today.

---

1. Source: https://www.workers.org/book/transgender-liberation-a-movement-whose-time-has-come/

Transgender is a very ancient form of human expression that pre-dates oppression. It was once regarded with honor. A glance at human history proves that when societies were not ruled by exploiting classes that rely on divide-and-conquer tactics, 'cross-gendered' youths, women and men on all continents were respected members of their communities.

'Strange country, this,' a white man wrote of the Crow nation on this continent in 1850, 'where males assume the dress and perform the duties of females, while women turn men and mate with their own sex.

Randy Burns, a founder of the modern group Gay American Indians, wrote the GAI's History Project documented these alternative roles for women and men in over 135 North American Native Nations.

The high incidence of transgendered men and women in Native societies on this continent was documented by the colonialists who referred to them as *berdache*.

Perhaps the most notable of all berdache Native women was Barcheeampe, the Crow 'Woman Chief,' the most famous war leader in the history of the upper Missouri nations. She married several wives and her bravery as a hunter and warrior was honored in songs. When the Crow nations council was held, she took her place among the chiefs, ranking third in a band of 160 lodges.

Today transgender is considered 'anti-social' behavior. But amongst the Klamath nations transgendered women were given special initiation ceremonies by their societies.

Among the Cocopa, Edward Gifforn wrote, 'female transvestites were called war'hameh, wore their hair and pierced their noses in the male fashion, married women and fought in battle alongside men.

Osh-Tische (Finds Them Kills Them), a Crow berdache or badé who was also born a man, fought in the Battle of Rosebud. When a colonial agent tried to force Osh-Tisch to wear men's clothing, the other Native people argued with him that it was against her nature and they kicked the agent off their land. They said it was a tragedy, trying to change the nature of the badé.

A Jesuit priest observed in the 1670s of the berdach, 'They are summoned to the Councils, and nothing can be decided without their advice.'

But the missionaries and colonialist military reacted to the Native berdache in this hemisphere with murderous hostility. Many berdache were tortured and burnt to death by their Christian conquerors.

Ancient religions, before the division of society into classes, combined collectively held beliefs with material observations about nature. Christianity as a mass religion really began in the cities of the Roman Empire among the poor, and incorporated elements of the collectivism and hatred of the rich ruling class. But over several hundred years, Christianity was transformed from a revolutionary movement of the urban poor into a powerful state religion that served the wealthy elite.

Transgender in all its forms became a target. In reality it was the rise of private property, the male-dominated family and class divisions [that] led to narrowing what was considered acceptable self-expression. What had been natural was declared its opposite.

As the Roman slave-based system of production disintegrated it was gradually replaced by feudalism. Laborers who once worked in chains were now chained to the land.

Even after the rise of feudalism, remnants of the old pagan religion remained. It was joyously pro-sexual—lesbian, gay, bisexual and straight. May women were among its practitioners. Many shamans were still transvestites. And tranvestism was still a part of virtually all rural festivals and rituals.

But in order for the land-owning Catholic church to rule, it had to stamp out the old beliefs that persisted from pre-class communal societies, because they challenged private ownership of the land.

Ancient respect for transgendered people still had roots in the peasantry. Transvestism played an important role in rural cultural life. Many pagan religious leaders were transgendered. So it was not surprising that the Catholic church hunted down male and female transvestites, labeling them as heretics, and tried to ban and suppress transvestism from all peasant rituals and celebrations.

By the 11th Century, the Catholic church—by then the largest landlord in Western Europe—gained the organizational and military strength to wage war against the followers of the old beliefs. The campaign was carried out under a religious banner—but it was a class war against the vestiges of the older communal societies.

[By the 13th century, the Catholic church] was the only powerful institution that cemented all of feudal Western Europe into one political system. More important, the church was by far the most powerful feudal lord, claiming ownership of one-third of the soil of the Catholic world.

The Inquisition, and later the witch trials, were weapons of terror and mass murder that took a staggering toll in human life—from Ireland to Poland. Many peasant women, including many lesbians, who followed the older rural-based religions were accused of being witches and tortured and burned. Transgendered people, gay men, Arabs, Jews, scientists, herbalists, healers—anyone who challenged or questioned the ruling class and the church was considered a threat and exterminated.

Torture was the rule. The Inquisitors didn't come armed with just the Bible—they arrives with swords and fire to put down peasant uprisings.

Our focus has been on European history, and consciously so. The blame for anti-transgender laws and attitudes rests squarely on the shoulders of the ruling classes [of Europe]. The seizures of lands and assests of the 'accused' during the witch trials and the Inquisition helped the ruling classes acquire the capital to expand their domination over Asia, Africa and the Americas. The European elited then tried to force their ideology on the peoples they colonized around the world.

But despite the colonialists' racist attempts at cultural genocide, tranvestism and other transgendered expression can still be observed in the rituals and beliefs of oppressed peoples.

The civil rights and national liberation movements of the 1950s and 1960s, and the massive resistance to the Vietnam war, rocked the world and helped give rise to the women's liberation struggle as well.

In 1969, militant young gay transvestites in New York City's Greenwich Village led a fight against cops who tried to raid the Stonewall Inn. The battles lasted for four nights running. The Stonewall Rebellion gave birth to a modern lesbian and gay rights movement that will never again be silenced behind closet doors.

From peasant uprisings against feudalism in the Middle ages to the Stonewall Rebellion in the 20th century, transvestites and other transgendered people have figured in many militant struggles, both in defense of the right of personal expression and as a form of political rebellion.

But from the violence on the streets to the brutality of the police, from job discrimination to denial of health care and housing—survival is still a battle for the transgendered population.

This institutionalized bigotry and oppression we face today have not always existed. They arose with the division of society into exploiter and exploited. Divide-and-conquer tactics have allowed the slave-owners, feudal landlords and corporate ruling classes to keep for themselves the lions share of wealth created by the laboring class.

Like racism and all forms of prejudice, bigotry toward transgendered people is a deadly carcinogen. WE are pitted against each other in order to keep us from seeing each other as allies.

Genuine bonds of solidarity can be forged between people who respect each other's differences and are willing to fight their enemy together. We are the class that does the work of the world, as can revolutionize it. WE can win true liberation.

The struggle against intolerable conditions is on the rise around the world. And the militant role of transgendered women, men and youths in today's fight-back movement is already helping to shape the future.

# 6. RESISTANCE AGAINST EMPIRE

*The words of six women and one man that comprise this section of* Insurrectionary Uprisings *strengthen our resistance to U.S. empire, presage its defeat, and foreground the imbrications of decoloniality and nonviolence.*

—The Editors

# WE ARE OUT OF TIME

Wende Marshall

At the heart of this section are Berta Cáceres' brilliant words which clearly and simply delineate what it means to resist U.S. empire in the 21st century. Berta urges us to wake up and recognize that we are out of time, that 'giving our lives... for the protection of the river' is our highest calling as humans, and that allowing 'rapacious capitalism, racism and patriarchy' to continue means that we are allowing ourselves to be destroyed.

Haunani-Kay Trask's searing critique of the written history of Hawai'i reminds us that the hegemony of Western scholarship is deadly. As she deconstructs Western views on Hawaiian history and culture, Trask reads the West back on itself. 'When historians wrote ... that our chiefs were despotic, they were telling of their own society, where hierarchy always results in domination... And when they wrote that we were promiscuous, they meant that lovemaking in the Christian West is a sin. And when they wrote that we were racist because we preferred our own ways to theirs, they meant that their culture needed to dominate other cultures.'

Citing Trask, Lilikalā Kameʻeleihiwa, and Manu Aluli Meyer, among other Indigenous Hawaiian scholars, Wende Marshall explores the meaning of the Hawaiian concept of mana in the context of late twentieth century struggles for decolonization and sovereignty. She weaves together the conception of mana with analysis of the brutal processes of dis-commoning in Europe and Africa at the origins of capitalism, arguing that liberatory aspirations, drawing on memories in which humans are contained within and not opposed to nature are possible, even for African Americans in urban settings on the U.S. mainland.

Maria Lugones and Aníbal Quijano wrote from a framework of decoloniality, which is less a structural process and more of an inter-subjective practice. Lugones, through an analysis of gender, race and colonialism, and Quijano through and analysis of race and colonialism argued together that the future requires that we transcend the constraints of Euro/America as ideology, epistemology and ontology.

Aimee Carillo Rowe asserts the need to transcend the politics of the nation-state by centering the struggle against U.S. settler-colonialism in LGBTQ politics. Lolita Lebron's moving letter to Catholic Worker founder Dorothy Day reminds us of the imperative of love in our resistance to empire.

As we were completing the work on this book Maria Lugones and Haunani-Kay Trask joined Berta Cáceres and Aníbal Quijano in the realm of the ancestors. Thus, this section of Insurrectionary Uprisings, is a tribute to those ancestors whose lives and work continues to light the path forward.

Berta *presente!* Haunani-Kay *presente!* Maria *presente!* Aníbal *presente!*

# GOLDMAN PRIZE ACCEPTANCE SPEECH

Berta Cáceres

---

2015[1]

'In our worldview, we are beings who come from the earth, from the water and from the corn. The Lenca people are ancestral guardians of the rivers, in turn protected by the spirits of young girls, who teach us that giving our lives in various ways, for the protection of the river is giving our lives for the well-being of humanity and of this planet. COPINH, walking alongside people struggling for their emancipation validates this commitment to continue protecting our waters, the rivers, our shared resources and nature in general as well as our right as a people. Let us wake up! Let us wake up, humankind. We are out of time. We must shake our conscience free of the rapacious capitalism, racism and patriarchy that will only assure our own self-destruction. The Gualcarque River has called upon us, as have other gravely threatened rivers. We must answer their call. Our Mother Earth—militarized, fenced-in, poisoned, a place where basic rights are systematically violated—demands that we take action. Let us build societies that are able to coexist in a dignified way in a way that protects life. Let us come together and remain hopeful as we defend and care for the blood of this earth and of its spirits. I dedicate this award to all the rebels out there, to my mother, to the Lenca people, to Río Blanco and to the martyrs who gave their lives is the struggle to defend our natural resources. Thank you very much.'
—Berta Cáceres

## Goldman Environmental Prize Foundation: Rationale for Awarding Berta Cáceres

*In a country with growing socioeconomic inequality and human rights violations, Berta Cáceres (d. 2016) rallied the Indigenous Lenca people of Honduras and waged a grassroots*

---

1. Source: https://www.goldmanprize.org/recipient/berta-caceres/

*campaign that successfully pressured the world's largest dam builder to pull out of the Agua Zarca Dam.*

Since the 2009 coup, Honduras has witnessed an explosive growth in environmentally destructive megaprojects that would displace Indigenous communities. Almost 30 percent of the country's land was earmarked for mining concessions, creating a demand for cheap energy to power future mining operations. To meet this need, the government approved hundreds of dam projects around the country, privatizing rivers, land, and uprooting communities.

Among them was the Agua Zarca Dam, a joint project of Honduran company Desarrollos Energéticos SA (DESA) and Chinese state-owned Sinohydro, the world's largest dam developer. Agua Zarca, slated for construction on the sacred Gualcarque River, was pushed through without consulting the Indigenous Lenca people—a violation of international treaties governing Indigenous peoples' rights. The dam would cut off the supply of water, food and medicine for hundreds of Lenca people and violate their right to sustainably manage and live off their land.

Berta Cáceres, a Lenca woman, grew up during the violence that swept through Central America in the 1980s. Her mother, a midwife and social activist, took in and cared for refugees from El Salvador, teaching her young children the value of standing up for disenfranchised people.

Cáceres grew up to become a student activist and in 1993, she cofounded the National Council of Popular and Indigenous Organizations of Honduras (COPINH) to address the growing threats posed to Lenca communities by illegal logging, fight for their territorial rights and improve their livelihoods.

In 2006, community members from Rio Blanco came to COPINH asking for help. They had witnessed an influx of machinery and construction equipment coming into their town. They had no idea what the construction was for or who was behind the project. What they knew was that an aggression against the river—a place of spiritual importance to the Lenca people—was an act against the community, its free will, and its autonomy.

With mandates from local community members at every step of the way, Cáceres began mounting a campaign against the Agua Zarca Dam. She filed complaints with government authorities, bringing along community representatives on trips to Tegucigalpa. She organized a local assembly where community members formally voted against the dam, and led a protest where people peacefully demanded their rightful say in the project.

The campaign also reached out to the international community, bringing the case to the Inter-American Human Rights Commission and lodging appeals against the project's funders such as the International Finance Corporation (IFC), the private sector arm of the World Bank.

Ignoring these appeals, the national government and local mayors forged ahead. They doctored minutes from a community meeting to paint a false picture of unanimous approval for the dam, and offered cash to local people in exchange for their signature on documents declaring their support.

In April 2013, Cáceres organized a road blockade to prevent DESA's access to the dam site. Using a carefully organized system of alerts to keep everyone in the loop, the Lenca people maintained a heavy but peaceful presence, rotating out friends and family members for weeks at a time. For well over a year, the blockade withstood multiple eviction attempts and violent attacks from militarized security contractors and the Honduran armed forces.

Honduras' violent climate is well known to many, but few understand that environmental and human rights activists are its victims. Tomas Garcia, a community leader from Rio Blanco, was shot and killed during a peaceful protest at the dam office. Others have been attacked with machetes, discredited, detained, and tortured. None of the perpetrators have been brought to justice.

Against these odds, Cáceres and the Lenca community's efforts successfully kept construction equipment out of the proposed dam site. In late 2013, Sinohydro terminated its contract with DESA, publicly citing ongoing community resistance and outrage following Tomas' death. Agua Zarca suffered another blow when the IFC withdrew its funding, citing concerns about human rights violations. To date, construction on the project has effectively come to a halt.

Death threats to Cáceres continued until March 3, 2016, when she was killed by gunmen in her home in La Esperanza, Honduras. Her death, followed by the killing of her colleague and fellow COPINH member Nelson García just 12 days later, sparked international outrage. Dutch development bank FMO and FinnFund have since suspended their involvement in the Agua Zarca project.

A Honduran court ruled in 2018 that executives of DESA ordered the killing of Cáceres. Seven men were found guilty of the murder and sentenced to 30 to 50 years. The president of DESA has been arrested and the case is ongoing. Cáceres' family continues to seek justice through a thorough investigation of the intellectual authors of her murder. COPINH and fellow activists continue her enduring legacy, fighting irresponsible development and standing up for the rights of the Lenca people in Honduras.

# NOTES FROM A NATIVE DAUGHTER

Haunani-Kay Trask

1993[1]

*Aloha kakou.* Let us greet each other in friendship and love. My given name is Haunaniokawēkiu o Haleakala, native of *Hawai'i Nei.* My father's family is from the *'aina* (land) of Kaua'i, my mother's family from the *'aina* of Maui. I reside today among my native people in the community of *Waimanalo.* I have lived all my life under the power of America. My native country, Hawai'i, is owned by the United States. I attended missionary schools, both Catholic and Protestant, in my youth, and I was sent away to the American mainland to receive a 'higher' education at the University of Wisconsin. Now I teach the history and culture of my people at the University of Hawai'i. When I was young the story of my people was told twice: once by my parents, then again by my schoolteachers. From my *'ohana* (family), I learned about the life of the old ones: how they fished and planted by the moon; shared all the fruits of their labors, especially their children; danced in great numbers for long hours; and honored the unity of their world in intricate genealogical chants. My mother said Hawaiians had sailed over thousands of miles to make their home in these sacred islands. And they had flourished, until the coming of the *haole* (whites). At school, I learned that the 'pagan Hawaiians' did not read or write, were lustful cannibals, traded in slaves, and could not sing. Captain Cook had 'discovered' Hawai'i and the ungrateful Hawaiians had killed him. In revenge, the Christian god had cursed the Hawaiians with disease and death.

I learned the first of these stories from speaking with my mother and father. I learned the second from books. By the time I left for college, the books had won out over my parents, especially since I spent four long years in a missionary boarding school for Hawaiian children.

When I went away, I understood the world as a place and a feeling divided in two: one *haole* (white), and the other *kanaka* (native). When I returned ten years later with a Ph.D., the division was sharper, the lack of connection more painful. There was the world that we lived in – my ancestors, my family, and my people – and then there was the world historians described. This world, they had written, was the truth. A primitive group, Hawaiians had been ruled by bloodthirsty

---

1. See: https://uhpress.hawaii.edu/title/from-a-native-daughter-colonialism-and-sovereignty-in-hawaii-revised-edition/

priests and despotic kings who owned all the land and kept our people in feudal subjugation. The chiefs were cruel, the people poor.

But this was not the story my mother told me. No one had owned the land before the haole came; everyone could fish and plant, except during sacred periods. And the chiefs were good and loved their people.

Was my mother confused? What did our *kūpuna* (elders) say? They replied: did these historians (all haole) know the language? Did they understand the chants? How long had they lived among our people? Whose stories had they heard?

None of the historians had ever learned our mother tongue. They had all been content to read what Europeans and Americans had written. But why did scholars, presumably well-trained and thoughtful, neglect our language? Not merely a passageway to knowledge, language is a form of knowing by itself; a people's way of thinking and feeling is revealed through its music.

I sensed the answer without needing to answer. From years of living in a divided world, I knew the historian's judgment: There is no value in things Hawaiian; all value comes from things haole.

Historians, I realized, were very like missionaries. They were a part of the colonizing horde. One group colonized the spirit: the other, the mind. Frantz Fanon had been right, but not just about Africans. He had been right about the bondage of my own people: 'By a kind of perverted logic, [colonialism] turns to the past of the oppressed people, and distorts, disfigures, and destroys it' (1968:210)[2]. The first step in the colonizing process, Fanon had written, was the deculturation of a people. What better way to take our culture than to remake our image? A rich historical past became small and ignorant in the hands of Westerners. And we suffered a damaged sense of people and culture because of this distortion.

Burdened by a linear, progressive conception of history and by an assumption that Euro-American culture flourishes at the upper end of that progression, Westerners have told the history of Hawai'i as an inevitable if occasionally bitter-sweet triumph of Western ways over 'primitive' Hawaiian ways. A few authors – the most sympathetic–have recorded with deep-felt sorrow the passing of our people. But in the end, we are repeatedly told, such an eclipse was for the best.

Obviously, it was best for Westerners, not for our dying multitudes. This is why the historian's mission has been to justify our passing by celebrating Western dominance. Fanon would have called this missionizing, intellectual colonization. And it is clearest in the historian's insistence that pre-haole Hawaiian land tenure was 'feudal' – a term that is now applied, without question, in every monograph, in every schoolbook, and in every tour guide description of my people's history.

From the earliest days of Western contact my people told their guests that no one owned the land. The land – like the air and the sea – was for all to use and

---

2. Frantz Fanon: French West Indian psychiatrist, author, and political leader. Fanon (1925-1961) is perhaps best known for his psychoanalytic study of Black life in a white dominated world, *Black Skin, White Masks*. His *The Wretched of the Earth* called for an anticolonial revolution by peasants; he anticipated that such a struggle would produce a new breed of modern people of color.

share as their birthright. Our chiefs were stewards of the land; they could not own or privately possess the land any more than they could sell it.

But the haole insisted on characterizing our chiefs as feudal land lords and our people as serfs. Thus, a European term which described a European practice founded on the European concept of private property – feudalism – was imposed upon a people halfway around the world from Europe and vastly different from her in every conceivable way. More than betraying an ignorance of Hawaiian culture and history, however, this misrepresentation was malevolent in design.

By inventing feudalism in ancient Hawai'i, Western scholars quickly transformed a spiritually-based, self-sufficient economic system of land use and occupancy into an oppressive, medieval European practice of divine right ownership, with the common people tied like serfs to the land. By claiming that a Pacific people lived under a European system – that the Hawaiians lived under feudalism–Westerners could then degrade a successful system of shared land use with a pejorative and inaccurate Western term. Land tenure changes instituted by Americans and in line with current Western notions of private property were then made to appear beneficial to the Hawaiians. But in practice, such changes benefited the haole, who alienated the people from the land, taking it for themselves.

The prelude to this land alienation was the great dying of the people. Barely half a century after contact with the West our people had declined in number by eighty percent. Disease and death were rampant. The sandalwood forests had been stripped bare for international commerce between England and China. The missionaries had insinuated themselves everywhere. And a debt-ridden Hawaiian king (there had been no king before Western' contact) succumbed to enormous pressure from the Americans and followed their schemes for dividing up the land.

This is how private property land tenure entered Hawai'i. The common people, driven from their birthright, received less than one percent of the land. They starved while huge haole-owned sugar plantations thrived.

And what had the historians said? They had said that the Americans 'liberated' the Hawaiians from an oppressive 'feudal' system. By inventing a false feudal past, the historians justify – and become complicitous in – massive American theft.

Is there 'evidence' – as historians call it – for traditional Hawaiian concepts of land use? The evidence is in the sayings of my people and in the words they wrote more than a century ago, much of which has been translated. However, historians have chosen to ignore any references here to shared land use. But there is incontrovertible evidence in the very structure of the Hawaiian language. If the historians had bothered to learn our language (as any American historian of France would learn French) they would have discovered that we show possession in two ways: through the use of an 'a' possessive, which reveals acquired status, and through the use of an 'o' possessive, which denotes inherent status. My body (ko 'u kino) and my parents (ko'u makua), for example, take the 'o' form; most material objects, such as food (ka'u mea'ai) take the 'a' form. But land, like one's body and one's parents, takes the 'o' possessive (ko'u 'aina). Thus, in our way of speaking, land is inherent to the people; it is like our bodies and our parents. The people cannot exist without the land, and the land cannot exist without the people.

Every major historian of Hawai'i has been mistaken about Hawaiian land tenure. The chiefs did not own the land: they could not own the land. My mother was right and the haole historians were wrong. If they had studied our language, they would have known that no one owned the land. But was their failing merely ignorance, or simple ethnocentric bias?

No, I did not believe them to be so benign. As I read on, a pattern emerged in their writing. Our ways were inferior to those of the West, to those of the historians' own culture. We were 'less developed,' or 'immature,' or 'authoritarian.' In some tellings we were much worse. Thus, Gavan Daws (1968), the most famed modern historian of Hawai'i, had continued a tradition established earlier by missionaries Hiram Bingham (1848) and Sheldon Dibble (1909), by referring to the old ones as 'thieves' and 'savages' who regularly practiced infanticide and who, in contrast to 'civilized' whites, preferred 'lewd dancing' to work. Ralph Kuykendall (1938), long considered the most thorough if also the most boring of historians of Hawai'i, sustained another fiction— that my ancestors owned slaves, the outcast *Kauwā*. This opinion, as well as the description of Hawaiian land tenure as feudal, had been supported by respected sociologist Andrew Lind (1938)[3]. Finally, nearly all historians had refused to accept our genealogical dating of over one hundred generations in Hawai'i. They had, instead, claimed that our earliest appearance in Hawai'i could only be traced to A.D. 700. Thus at least seven hundred years of our history were repudiated by 'superior' Western scholarship. Only recently have archeological data confirmed what Hawaiians had said these many centuries (Tuggle 1979).

Suddenly the entire sweep of our written history was clear to me. I was reading the West's view of itself through the degradation of my own past. When historians wrote that the king owned the land and the common people were bound to it, they were saying that ownership was the only way human beings in their world could relate to the land, and in that relationship, some one person had to control both the land and the interaction between humans. And when they said that our chiefs were despotic, they were telling of their own society, where hier-

---

3. See also Fornander (1878-85), Lest one think these sources antiquated, it should be noted that there exist only a handful of modern scholarly works on the history of Hawai'i. The most respected are those by Kuykendall (1938) and Daws (1968), and a social history of the twentieth century by Lawrence Fuchs (1961). Of these, only Kuykendall and Daws claim any knowledge of pre-haole history, while concentrating on the nineteenth century. However, countless popular works have relied on these two studies which, in turn, are themselves based on primary sources written in English by extremely biased, anti-Hawaiian Westerners such as explorers, traders, missionaries (e.g., Bingham (1848) and Dibble [1909]), and sugar planters. Indeed, a favorite technique of Daws's - whose *Shoal of Time* is the most acclaimed and recent general history - is the lengthy quotation without comment of the most racist remarks by missionaries and planters. Thus, at one point, half a page is consumed with a 'white man's burden' quotation from an 1886 Planter's Monthly article ('It is better for the colored man of India and Australia that the white man rules, and it is better here that the white man should rule ... ,.. etc., p, 213). Daws's only comment is 'The conclusion was inescapable.' To get a sense of such characteristic contempt for Hawaiians, one has but to read the first few pages, where Daws refers several times to the Hawaiians as 'savages' and 'thieves' and where he approvingly has Captain Cook thinking, 'It was a sensible primitive who bowed before a superior civilization' (p. 2). See also - among examples too numerous to cite - his glib description of sacred hula as 'frivolous diversion,' which, instead of work, the Hawaiians 'would practice energetically in the hot sun for days on end ... their bare brown flesh glistening with sweat' (pp. 65-66), Daws, who repeatedly displays an affection for descriptions of Hawaiian skin color, taught Hawaiian history for some years at the University of Hawai'i, he now holds the Chair of Pacific History at the Australian National University's Institute of Advanced Studies. [Author's note]

archy always results in domination. Thus, any authority or elder is automatically suspected of tyranny. And when they wrote that Hawaiians were lazy, they meant that work must be continuous and ever a burden. And when they wrote that we were promiscuous, they meant that lovemaking in the Christian West is a sin.

And when they wrote that we were racist because we preferred our own ways to theirs, they meant that their culture needed to dominate other cultures.

And when they wrote that we were superstitious, believing in the mana of nature and people, they meant that the West has long since lost a deep spiritual and cultural relationship to the earth.

And when they wrote that Hawaiians were 'primitive' in their grief over the passing of loved ones, they meant that the West grieves for the living who do not walk among their ancestors.

For so long, more than half my life, I had misunderstood this written record, thinking it described my own people. But my history was nowhere present. For we had not written. We had chanted and sailed and fished and built and prayed. And we had told stories through the great blood lines of memory: genealogy.

To know my history, I had to put away my books and return to the land. I had to plant taro in the earth before I could understand the inseparable bond between people and 'aina. I had to feel again the spirits of nature and take gifts of plants and fish to the ancient altars. I had to begin to speak my language with our elders and leave long silences for wisdom to grow. But before anything else, I had to learn the language like a lover so that I could rock within her and lay at night in her dreaming arms.

There was nothing in my schooling that had told me of this, or hinted that somewhere there was a longer, older story of origins, of the flowing of songs out to a great but distant sea. Only my parents' voices, over and over, spoke to me of a Hawaiian world. While the books spoke from a different world, a Western world.

And yet, Hawaiians are not of the West. We are of *Hawai'i Nei*, this world where I live, this place, this culture, this 'aina.

What can I say, then, to Western historians of my place and people? Let me answer with a story. A while ago I was asked to share a panel on the American overthrow of our government in 1893. The other panelists were all haole. But one was a haole historian from the mainland who had just published a book on what he called the American anti-imperialists. He and I met briefly in preparation for the panel. I asked him if he knew the language. He said no. I asked him if he knew the record of opposition to our annexation to America. He said there was no real evidence for it, just comments here and there. I told him that he didn't understand and that at the panel I would share the evidence. When we met in public and spoke, I said this:

There is a song much loved by our people. It was sung when Hawaiians were forbidden from congregating in groups of more than three. Addressed to our imprisoned Queen, it was written in 1898, and tells of Hawaiian feelings for our land against annexation. Listen to our lament:

> Famous are the children of
> Hawai'i

Who cling steadfastly to the land
Comes the evil-hearted with
A document greedy for plunder
Hawai'i, island of Keawe,
answers
The bays of Pi'ilani [of Maui, Moloka'i, and Lana'i] help
Kaua'i of Mano assists
Firmly together with the sands of
Kakuhihewa
Do not put the signature
On the paper of the enemy
Annexation is wicked sale
Of the civil rights of the
Hawaiian people
We support Lili'uokalani
Who has earned the right to the
land
The story is told
Of the people who love the land

This song, I said, continues to be sung with great dignity at Hawaiian political gatherings. For our people still share the feelings of anger and protest that it conveys.

But our guest, the haole historian, answered that this song, although beautiful, was not evidence of either opposition or of imperialism from the Hawaiian perspective.

Many Hawaiians in the audience were shocked at his remarks, but, in hindsight, I think they were predictable. They are the standard response of the historian who does not know the language and has no respect for its memory.

Finally, I proceeded to relate a personal story, thinking that surely such a tale could not want for authenticity since I myself was relating it. My *tutu* (grandmother) had told my mother who had told me that at the time of annexation (1898) a great wailing went up throughout the islands, a wailing of weeks, a wailing of impenetrable grief, a wailing of death. But he remarked again, this too is not evidence.

And so, history goes on, written in long volumes by foreign people. Whole libraries begin to form, book upon book, shelf upon shelf. At the same time, the stories go on, generation to generation, family to family.

Which history do Western historians desire to know? Is it to be a tale of writings by their own countrymen, individuals convinced of their 'unique' capacity for analysis, looking at us with Western eyes, thinking about us within Western philosophical contexts, categorizing us by Western indices, judging us by Judeo-Christian morals, exhorting us to capitalist achievements, and finally, leaving us an authoritative because- Western record of their complete misunderstanding?

All this has been done already. Not merely a few times, but many times. And still, every year, there appear new and eager faces to take up the same telling, as if the West must continue, implacably, with the din of its own disbelief.

But there is, as there has been always, another possibility. If it is truly our history Western historians desire to know, they must put down their books, and take up our practices. First, of course, the language. But later, the people, the 'aina, the stories. Above all, in the end, the stories. Historians must listen, they must hear the generational connections, the reservoir of sounds and meanings.

They must come, as American Indians suggested long ago, to understand the land. Not in the Western way, but in the Indigenous way, the way of living within and protecting the bond between people and 'aina.

This bond is cultural, and it can be understood only culturally. But because the West has lost any cultural understanding of the bond between people and land, it is not possible to know this connection through Western culture. This means that the history of Indigenous people cannot be written from within Western culture. Such a story is merely the West's story of itself.

*Our* story remains unwritten. It rests within the culture, which is inseparable from the land. To know this is to know our history. To write this is to write of the land and the people who are born from her.

# TASTING EARTH: HEALING, RESISTANCE KNOWLEDGE, AND THE CHALLENGE TO DOMINION

Wende Marshall

2012[1]

> In Hawai'i, at the turn of the twentieth century, [a] deeper meaning of decolonization was occurring at the intimate level of the body and soul and collectively at the level of community...Native Hawai'ians in the late twentieth century grasped the concept that decolonization was based upon healing, and they revived ways of understanding health and disease that had been outlawed and suppressed by colonial rule. Most significantly, they understood that decolonizing and healing meant recovering historical and ancestral memory and reasserting the primacy of mana, love, and dependence between humans, the environment, and the divine. But the assertion of ancestra land historical memory in Hawai'i was not simply about understanding the past, it was about creating the means for a different, decolonized future.
> —Potent Mana, Marshall, 2011

This article explores an Indigenous Hawaiian perspective on health in which nature is accorded the status of healing agent.[2] This perspective, which reemerged in the Native Hawaiian decolonization struggle of the 1990s, contains an explicit critique of Western sociocultural and political–economic forces, and the effects of these forces on the bodies and souls of colonized and neo-colonized Hawaiians. The origins of this understanding of healing derive from the ancestors of present-day Indigenous Hawaiians and from enduring ways of knowing and being that survived the onslaught of colonial power. Conceptions of the interdependency of human beings and the earth, which lie at the core of this perspective on healing, are expressed through the Polynesian principle of *mana*. To understand how mana is a basis for resistance knowledge, we will contrast it with the Judeo-Christ-

---

1. See: https://anthrosource.onlinelibrary.wiley.com/doi/abs/10.1111/j.1548-1409.2012.01109.x
2. During fieldwork in the 1990s, the majority of my collaborators and informants identified as Native Hawaiian. They were also ethnically mixed with Chinese, Japanese, Portuguese, and Puerto Ricans, among others. While the culture and ethos that defines mana is Hawaiian, those for whom the concept is meaningful may be themselves ethnically mixed, since the transmission of culture is not limited by biological notions of race. Native Hawaiians are a statistical minority in terms of statewide population, with various Asian groups (including Japanese, Chinese, and Filipinos) and whites predominating. In the 2010 U.S. Census, Native Hawaiians comprised 10 percent of the state's population.

ian-Islamic theology of dominion. While mana stresses the interconnection of all living things and human love for and dependence on nature, the dominion of Genesis 1:28, in contrast, posits that humans are separable from and dominant over nature—a theology at the root of the 20th-century politics of human dispossession and environmental degradation.

My analytic frame lies at the intersections of health disparities, environmental injustice, and political power. Through these lenses it is clear that the planet has been degraded by the global spread of capitalism. It is less clear, however, how humanity will survive the mortal and moral dilemmas of climate instability, eroding global reserves of petroleum, food and water scarcity, and the spread of new epidemics and chronic disease.

## Resistance Knowledge

To confront these critical issues it is necessary to reach toward alternative horizons and stretch our sense of the possible. To do this work as scholars requires that we reinterpret the past in order to re-imagine the future and that we breach the borders of canonical wisdom to engage with peripheral, subaltern, and resistance knowledge and practices. To grasp the relationship between health disparities, environmental degradation, and social inequality and understand mana, we must draw on multiple sources from both non scholarly and scholarly disciplines and traditions. Such resistance knowledge is critically important precisely because it is constantly delegitimized in the process of normalizing the world we now inhabit.

In arguing that a focus on peripheral knowledge and past wisdom can be a guide to present and future possibilities, I realize I open myself up to the charge of uncritically accepting golden myths of origins that reify a non-European past. However, I follow Aníbal Quijano and others, who argue that unless we challenge a horizon 'totally and exclusively occupied by the predatory needs of financial capital' (2002:82), we will have no future. Quijano argues that in emerging forms of Latin American social action it is not inevitable that 'conventional Eurocentric versions' of the future will prevail. Rather, Quijano asserts that 'people begin to act not only in response to their problems and needs, but also by appealing to their memory to define' their liberatory aspirations (2002:84). This opens the possibility for 'parallel horizon[s]' of knowing and 'non-Eurocentric rationalit[ies]' that can also redefine the future (2002:85).

In Hawai'i during the 1990s the long struggle against U.S. conquest was invigorated under a cohort of leaders who remembered and reinterpreted ancestral knowledge. As the scholar Noenoe Silva (2004:2,16) has argued, Hawaiian resistance to foreign intrusion, which began with the first landing of Europeans, was evident throughout the 19th century and continues today. Through a careful exegesis of the Hawaiian language press from the mid-nineteenth to the mid-20th century, Silva brought to light the history of Native Hawaiian written resistance to U.S. conquest. From the moment of the first encounter with British and U.S. foreigners, the struggle for Hawaiian political and cultural integrity has not ceased. The form of struggle changed with historical circumstances, since the violent structural and cultural realities of being colonized meant that resistance was often expressed indirectly. Clearly, however, the resurgence in political and cultural activism that was evident in Hawai'i in the late 20th century was in a historical tradition of resistance.[3] My research on this struggle focused on conceptions of health and on the resurgence of knowledge, which had been demoted and delegitimized in the process of colonization (Marshall 2011:2, 57, 78, 84, 95). Here the concept of health is broad and encompassing and rather than addressing specific illnesses, it connotes the sense of well-being. In the theories and practices that made up the decolonization movement in Hawai'i, nature was understood as a catalyst for healing the physical and psychic wounds of colonialism. Healing depended on reinterpretations of ancestral knowledge about the connection between humans and the earth and remembrance of specifically Hawaiian definitions of well-being, knowledge that the colonizer claimed was merely superstition. Decolonization, as a form of social and cultural healing, depended on dreaming, imagining, and remembering before and beyond the times of Western rule. And healing depended on recognition of mana, a cosmology at the core of Hawaiian life signifying the inseparability of land and people.

While I begin with the chain of islands called Hawai'i, I will end with reflections on resistance knowledge among struggling communities on the U.S. mainland and with possibilities for African American healing, remembering, and recovery.

## Kinship between Humans and Earth

The islands of Hawai'i rise from the depths of the dark blue waters of the mid-Pacific, 4,000 miles east of Japan and 2,500 miles from the western edge of North America. This is the most isolated archipelago on earth. In the poetic language of the Kumulipo, the Hawaiian creation story, the islands emerge from the heat of the earth, the unfolding of heavens, and the eclipse of the sun by a round bright moon. In this origin story, the ancestors of Hawaiians were born from a 'deep darkness, darkening' (Kame'eleihiwa 1992:1–2).

These ancestors of present-day Hawaiians were self-governing, self-sufficient, and complete.[4] Before the land was alienable, before sandalwood and whales were rendered nearly extinct, before the onslaught of settlers with desires to own the land, the islands overflowed with geotheological significance. In this world, the 'āina (or land) was comprised of conscious elements that communicated and interacted in relationships of mutuality, reciprocity, and familiarity across a spec-

3. In the 1990s the sovereignty and cultural revitalization movements in Hawai'i contained an array of positions, politics and tactics, fraught with internal critiques, debates about strategy and meaning, and divisions about the ultimate goals of the movement. Various strands of the movement, however, shared a commitment to the revitalization of Indigenous Hawaiian culture, even while they disagreed about acceptable forms of political autonomy.
4. To claim that the world of Hawai'i before the arrival of Europeans was 'complete' is to hermeneutically challenge the implied teleology of Western conquest and disarrange the sense that Indigenous people were less than complete before collision with Western societies.

trum of divinity, humanity, and nature. According to Luciano Minerbi, a professor of urban and regional planning,

In traditional Hawaiian thinking nature and land are considered sacred and animate. The world is a conscious entity and people can communicate with all species in nature and interact in a mutual relationship of rights and responsibilities. The Kumulipo (creation chant) implies that the universe is alive and conscious and that its evolutionary development comes from within. This evolution explains how man is related and is kin to nature. [1994:103]

Although the islands of Hawai'i were overwhelmed beginning in the late 18th century by Western economics, religion, and politics, the beliefs and practices of Indigenous Hawaiians were never extinguished. Hawaiians endured. They survived deadly epidemics. They persisted through lethal narratives that portrayed their history, culture, language, and society as diseased and degenerate. And they also retained cosmologies centered on the reciprocity of humans and the land, even when these ways of understanding were driven underground by Western religion and economics. In the late 20th century, a burgeoning Hawaiian movement and an intense focus on reclamation of land, language, and health as a basis of decolonization demonstrated the potent mana of a people determined to thrive.

## Dominion and Discommoning

In order to grasp the meaning of the Polynesian concept of mana, we must attend to the foundations of Western thinking about the land–human relationship. The notion that humans were separable from and dominant over nature was clearly articulated in the Hebrew Bible in Genesis 1:28, which reads: 'Be fruitful and multiply, and fill the earth and *subdue it*; and *have dominion* over the fish of the sea and over the birds of the air, and over every living thing that moves upon the earth' (NRSV:2).

As dominion sundered human kinship from the land, in favor of mastery and subjugation, its disruption of human love for and dependence on nature, remained key to understanding the rise of capitalism as a social order and cosmology. Indeed, Quijano wrote about a sundering between mind and body, best articulated by Descartes, who replaced alternative notions in which 'the two dimensions are always co-present, co-acting, never separated' (2007:53). Quijano argued that it is impossible to understand either the construction of race or of gender without attending to this radical dualism in which the nature– culture divide becomes a map of social hierarchies of difference.

Karl Marx began the analysis that led to his critique of political economy when he wrote 'Debates on the Law on the Theft of Woods' in 1842 about the criminalization of the woodland commons of the Moselle Valley Peasants in Germany (Linebaugh 2008:144–145). In *Capital*, Marx identified the violence of land dispossession as the original sin of primitive capital accumulation (1977:873, 874). Primitive accumulation centered on brutal processes of discommoning, the expulsion of people from the land, and the conversion of common and collective property into private property; it meant the violent suppression of Indigenous forms of production and consumption in the West and in the colonies in order to ensure a labor force for commodity production (Harvey 2005:145). As the historian Peter Linebaugh argues, European 'communing' was a practice expressive of 'relationships in society that are inseparable from relations to nature' (2008:279). Linebaugh cites a late-16th-century exposition on the multiple meanings of 'common,' which included communitas, community, participation, and fellowship (2008:279).

At the end of the 14th century, English peasants possessed lands in common. But by the end of the 15th century, they had been forcibly removed from the land (Marx 1977:878). Driven by the rise of wool manufacturing, land that had been used for subsistence farming was transformed into enclosures for sheep (1977:879). In the course of the 18th century, in a process that foreshadows the colonial theft of land in Hawai'i and elsewhere, laws were written that became instruments through which 'the people's land [was] stolen' (1977:885). Primitive accumulation, the enclosure of nature meant that land and people were no longer engaged in reciprocal processes. Indeed, it meant that the very meaning of humanity, of nature, and of well-being was transformed. Once the land was owned, the people followed. Linebaugh has argued that industrial capitalism in the Atlantic world rode into modernity on the backs of land enclosures and the slave trade. He wrote:

Together the expelled commoners and the captured Africans provided the labor power available for exploitation in the factories of the field (tobacco and sugar) and the factories of the towns (woolen and cottons). Whether.. . [Europeans or Africans], the lords of humankind looked upon them indifferently as laboring bodies to produce surplus value... which entirely depended upon a prior discommoning. [Linebaugh 2008:94]

By the end of the 18th century, the last traces of common land had disappeared in Europe (1977:883) and one hundred years later, Marx wrote, 'the very *memory* of the connection between' people and the land 'had . . . vanished' (1977:889). Marx described how the people were 'forcibly expropriated from the soil, driven from their homes, turned into vagabonds, and then whipped, branded, and tortured by grotesquely terroristic laws into accepting the discipline necessary for the system of wage-labor' (1977:899). The roots of capital-ism's health, and environmental crisis lie in this dispossession, in this sundering of earth and people.

## The Meaning of Mana

This Western concept of dominion, of land enclosure, and of private ownership starkly contrasts with the Polynesian concept of mana. Based on notions of reciprocity, kinship, and love between gods, humans, and the land, mana is an Indigenous ontology (Kame'eleihiwa 1992:31; Shore 1989:142; Valeri 1985:99). More than a theory, mana is a relationship and a practice that in precolonial times was the source of health, vitality, and abundance, in which a thriving world was the co-creation of divinity, humanity, and nature: fractal and indivisible.

The anthropological literature on mana sometimes misconstrued its meaning, beginning with Mauss who viewed it as a sign of social superiority, a quality accruing to powerful individuals rather than a result of proper social relations. The work of the anthropologists Raymond Firth, Valerio Valeri, and Bradd Shore, however, explored mana as a foundational social principle. Firth learned from his informants that the fecundity of the land and the people was 'not merely a concatenation of physical forces but depend[ed] on the maintenance of a *relationship* between man and spiritual beings' (1940:505). Valeri's analysis of mana stressed relational reciprocity as central to the meaning of the term. He hypothesized that in Hawaiian cosmology, 'god is clearly treated as a commensal who eats with his worshippers and is fed by them as they are fed by him' (1985:104). Following Firth and Valeri, Shore posited that mana was based on 'the possibilities of exchange' between gods, humans, and nature. Mana, Shore argued, was a generative potency especially linked 'to the two primary sources of human life: food and sex' (1989:165).

At the same time, the anthropological mana literature also reflected what Mignolo and Tlostanova (2006:206) have characterized as an 'epistemology of imperial expansion' in which a Western scholarly observer makes 'the rest of the world an object of observation.' Through this imperializing lens, mana was cast as an artifact. Little scholarly work concerned itself with the meaning and currency of mana in late 20th century Polynesian societies (see Tomlinson 2006), and, until recently, the perspective of Indigenous scholars on the significance of mana did not circulate in the global political economy of academic knowledge.

Late in the 20th century, though, scholars writing from a perspective that recognized the searing impact of colonialism reinterpreted the meaning of mana and demonstrated its relevance in a neo-colonial context.

The historian Lilikalā Kame'eleihiwa,, for example, argued that 'the lack of the Native point of view' in scholarship on Hawai'i resulted in Eurocentric understandings of historical changes (1992:3). Following Dening's 1980 work in *Islands and Beaches*, Kame'eleihiwa placed the concepts and metaphors central to the worldview of Hawaiians in the time before the arrival of Westerners at the core of her historical analysis (1992:6). In *Native Land and Foreign Desires*, she defined the Māhele—the law allowing privatization of Hawaiian land that occurred in the mid-19 century—as a catastrophic moment for Native Hawaiians (1992:8, 11). In particular she analyzed the clusters of meaning around the concept of *Āina* (land) and demonstrated that decenter-ing European metaphors for land created the possibility for different historical interpretations.

Kame'eleihiwa posited that the privatization of land in Hawai'i was a profound disruption to Hawaiian life.[5] Although commoner Hawaiians petitioned against the Māhele, their voices were not heard. A petition from three hundred Native Hawaiian citizens in 1845 urged the King to refuse both land and citizenship to

---

5. See also Merry (2000:95) who argued the Māhele transformed land use that was based on reciprocal relations between the commoner Hawaiians and the ruling elite. In place of this relationship based on genealogy and rank, the Māhele introduced relations of inequality based on property ownership and the market.

foreigners. 'If the Chiefs are to open this door of the government as an entrance way for the foreigners to come into Hawaii,' the petition argued, 'then you will see the Hawaiian people going from place to place in this world like flies' (Petition 1845, cited in Kame'eleihiwa 1992:331). The petitioners were prescient: the damage of the Māhele was sure and swift. The minimal bits of land commoners retained were soon lost, since these bits and pieces could not provide subsistence (Herman 1999:85; Levy 1975:857). These plots were soon purchased by foreigner plantation owners (Levy 1975:861) producing an abundance of dispossessed and impoverished Hawaiians. Landlessness and the inability to grow subsistence crops created widespread malnutrition, which exacerbated the spread of multiple epidemics (see Inglis 2005:238).

Native Hawaiian scholar–activists have analyzed the on-going experience of colonialism through lenses privileging the ethics and worldview of their ancestors. In the view of legal activist, Mililani Trask, dispossession was a key metaphor for colonialism. 'Hawaiians were evicted from their land' she wrote,

> that was genocide. Their ability to fish certain waters and cultivate land so that they could eat and live was taken away at the very time that Western diseases were taking a terrible toll. ...The appropriate healing practices were almost lost because people who were oral keepers of those traditions died. Genealogies were lost, so people no longer knew who their families were. They were dispossessed of the land, they wandered, and they were not able to find their own families again. [1996:392]

## Mana as Resistance

Beyond such historical considerations, however, the poet, political scientist, and Native rights activist, Haunani Trask, has asserted how the relevance of mana persists for Hawaiians in the current moment. She powerfully expresses the centrality of mana to the practices and aspirations of a people engaged in decolonization. In an essay titled 'Writing in Captivity,' Trask observed that 'resistance to the strangulation of our people and culture is interwoven with a celebration of the magnificence of our nation: the lavish beauty of our delicate islands; the intricate relationship between our emotional ties to each other and our ties to the land; the centuries-old ways of caring for the land, the sea, and, of course, the mana that is generated by human beings in love with and dependent upon the natural world' (Trask 2000:52).

Manu Aluli Meyer, a scholar of education, has explored enduring differences between current Hawaiian and Western ways of learning and knowing. She has argued that the 'ontological premise' of Hawaiian empiricism is the conception of the world as 'alive and filled with meaning... and metaphor' (Meyer 1998a:39). For Meyers, the *relational* is a fundamental mode of Hawaiian knowing; it organizes experience, trains the senses, and establishes relevance. The land, the gods, and the people form a foundational web through which knowledge is drawn and made meaningful (Meyer 2001:127). In Hawaiian cosmology, taro is a fruit of the 'a¯ina, the historic staple food, and a synonym for the bonds of siblinghood. Thus,

Meyer explores how a complex notion of 'feeding' is a metaphor for contemporary Hawaiian knowing and understanding (1998b:23) based on the imperative of interdependence between people and land.

Scholars of mana have recognized the centrality of the concept of 'ai (usually translated into English as *to eat, to feed, to consume*), and of its elaboration in the term 'a¯ina (land, sea, earth) in Hawaiian cosmology. In translation, the English words *food, eat,* and *land,* however, do not begin to approach the multivalent depth of the cluster of Hawaiian concepts centered on the root word 'ai. Valeri (1985:104) uses the term *commensal* as way to translate the meaning of 'ai. *Commensal* is defined as 'eating together at the same table'; 'living with, on, or in another, without injury to either'; and as a sociological term which connotes a person or group 'not competing while residing in or occupying the same area as another individual or group having independent or different values or customs.'6 'Eat,' in contrast, means to 'take into the mouth and swallow for nourishment' and to 'consume by or as if by to devour gradually.'7 There is vast conceptual distance between 'ai and *eat* and between concepts of commen-sality and of consumption that clearly mark differences in ontology and practice. These distinctions reflect the incommensurability of 'dominion' and 'mana.'8

From the perspective of scholars writing toward the goal of decolonization, mana remained an ontological exchange between the ancestors and their late 20th-century descendants, despite centuries of Western demotion of Indigenous knowledge. This sustaining knowledge, this recognition of the 'reciprocal code-termination' (Lewontin and Levins 2007:12) of all living things is exigent to the health of Native Hawaiians and is a foundational goal of decolonization (see Trask 1993, 2000). Colonialism in Hawai'i is an injustice that occurred in the political–economic and sociocultural realms. But the injustices—the trauma of land dispossession, of political disenfranchisement, of changes in agricultural production and diet, and the community-wide disorientation that ensued from the enforcement of foreign practices and ideologies—were not experienced only as formal, abstract, and structural. The effects of these processes were etched deeply

---

6. http://dictionary.reference.com/search?q=commensality. Accessed on March 26, 2009.
7. http://dictionary.reference.com/browse/eat. Accessed on March 26, 2009.
8. The philosopher John Patterson's (2000) exploration of the meaning of mana in Maori culture argues for the possibility of mana as the ontology of an environmental philosophy suitable to Western cultures. He argued that in order to understand mana, Westerners must grasp the 'web of relationships' between the natural and the supernatural, between the past and the present, and between Oceania and the rest of the globe (2000:233). The relational web implied in the concept of mana, the notion that kinship encompasses all things living and divine, however, has not been grasped in the power centers of global capitalism. Western adoption of mana as a basis of environmental philosophy would require a thorough understanding of the theological, sociocultural and political-economic implications of the vast epistemological difference between the concept of 'ai and the concept of 'eat.' Deleuze's (2006) concept of 'incompossibility' articulates the skepticism with which we might view Patterson's desire for the Western adoption of mana as ontology. Deleuze (2006:60) cited Leibniz's notion that the Christian God chooses from 'infinity of possible worlds.' God, Deleuze wrote, chooses the world 'that has the most possible reality.' Alternative worlds are 'incompossible.' Dimakopoulou's (2006:81–82) elucidates Deleuze's notion of incompossibility with reference to the transition from the European baroque period to the neo-Baroque era, and from modernity to postmodernity. According to Dimakopoulou: Deleuze writes that the transition from the baroque to the neo-baroque is marked by the absence of the principle of convergence according to principles of preestablished harmony and the incompossibles enter the arena of fragmentation... . The dissonant coexistence of incompossible 'events,' can be read as an allegory of the transition from modernity onto postmodernity: a cultural and historical condition in which more than one [virtuality is] actualized... a world that witnesses the transition from 'harmonic closure' to ...'polyphony of polyphonies.' [Dimakopoulou 2006:81–82]

into the bodies and souls of the colonized. The long-term effects of colonialism and neocolonialism on the health and well-being of Native Hawai'i in the late 20th century meant that reclaiming mana was urgent.

The effects of colonialism and neocolonialism were evident in the health status of Native Hawaiians, who had higher rates of morbidity and mortality from chronic and infectious disease when compared with other ethnic groups in the Islands and in the United States as a whole. The effects are seen on the land, which suffers inundation by tourists, by the U.S. military controlling a quarter of the land base on O'ahu, by diversion of streams for corporate food processing, and by the threat of unexploded military ordnance in places like Makaha Valley. This distribution of harm was a visible manifestation of centuries of colonial rule and of the sundering of Indigenous Hawaiians from the land.

Native Hawaiians have developed theories about what makes them sick that are distinct from causal models in biomedicine and social epidemiology. Beyond a focus on pathology originating in the temporal, organic body and beyond the analytics of race, class, and gender in the spread of epidemic, Native Hawaiians offer an Indigenous critique of health and disease in Western societies. From this perspective the etiology of disease can be located in Western economic and cultural practices.

## Land as Healing Agent

Native Hawaiian understandings of health and disease emerged through aspirations for land reclamation, cultural integrity, sovereignty, and decolonization. This epistemology is fundamentally rooted in the mana cosmology, the traditions of ancestors, and in the history and memory of a colonized people.

The land as a place of healing and transformation was a major theme in the stories of staff and clients at Ho'o Mo⁻hala, a Native Hawaiian-run drug treatment clinic that was the principal site of my Hawai'i research. These transformation narratives contradicted Western notions about treating disease as a process that should occur indoors, under professional supervision, and through purely biochemical processes, or about the individual as the unit of analysis and treatment. In narratives of transformation at Ho'o Mo⁻hala, the 'a⁻ina (land) was understood as a catalyst for the achievement of well-being, clearly drawing on conceptions of mana in pre-European Hawaiian cosmology.

Alaka'i Ono, the clinical director, was an ex-convict, a recovering alcoholic, and drug addict. When I met him, he had been five years sober. He told me that when he was a teenager, he and a group of buddies would travel around O'ahu and break into tourists' rental cars. When he reflected on his past, he believed that his heavy drug and alcohol use cut off any other viable life options. Alaka'i told me that as a Hawaiian he was angry at all of the 'rich tourists' and used that as a justification for his crimes. After spending time in prison, Alaka'i began the process of recovery—he was a client at Ho'o Mo⁻hala in its first year of operation. In recovery he 'learned other ways of being Hawaiian besides robbing tourists,' including attending rallies and demonstrations supporting the sovereignty movement. But for Alakaʻi, the most profound expression of 'being Hawaiian' involved nature as catalyst for healing.

Shortly after joining the staff at Hoʻo Mōhala, Alakaʻi attended a staff immersion in Hawaiian language and culture at Waipiʻo, a lush, verdant valley, surrounded by the precipitous heights of the Kohala Mountain Range. The steep, nearly vertical cliffs limited access, thus Waipiʻo was by-passed by most of the tourist trade.[9] Ten Hoʻo Moʻhala staff members traveled to Waipiʻo and met with a small group of Hawaiians, who deliberately spoke only the Hawaiian language, cultivated taro with irrigation canals, hunted, pounded poi (a traditional dish of fermented taro), and lived in thatch dwellings. The Hoʻo Moʻhala staff had to communicate in Hawaiian, although none of them were fluent. They slept in tents, pulled weeds in the taro ponds, and bathed in the ocean. For Alakaʻi the trip was transformative. He explained to me that sleeping under the stars, communicating in Hawaiian, plunging his hands into muddy taro ponds, and eating poi made him feel proud to be Hawaiian. He decided then that he would eat poi at home and send his children to Hawaiian language-immersion school.

Susan Miller, a Filipino woman, and graduate of Hoʻo Moʻhala, told me how cynical she was when she was paroled from prison to drug treatment:

> And how I got into Hoʻo Moʻhala ... was, at that time they had a contract with the Department of Public Safety. And so Public Safety was paying for my treatment. So what the hell; you know? This is free. And I am going to stay here for t'ree months and clean up little bit and come back out and [keep on using drugs]. . . that's how I thought. ... And I was there my first week and I was up at the [taro ponds] and it just overwhelmed me ... I went through some kind of grieving. My first time being clean, I think. Clear of mind... the loʻi (or taro ponds) are so, . . . I don't know how to explain it. It is so spiritual up there. I felt at ease. I felt comfortable, I felt so relaxed. And I never felt that way for a long time. And I think that's what it was, that feeling of being free.

The taro ponds at Mt. Kaʻala Cultural Learning Center were part of a community garden, a sprawling series of ponds fed by irrigation canals that predate European contact. Located high in the valley, surrounded by the Waiʻanae range, and with a stunning view of the sea, volunteering at Mt. Kaʻala was a regular part of the treatment program at Hoʻo Moʻhala. Susan's experience at Mt. Kaʻala was not uncommon; many people who worked or volunteered at the Center spoke of its intense beauty, spirituality, and ability to heal.

Kili Simmons was a middle-age Hawaiian woman diagnosed with bipolar disorder and substance addiction. In a Native Hawaiian women's support group, Kili told stories of violence and disease going back to the time of her grandparents. Sometimes Kili would wail and cry and rock; her pain was immense. She told sto-

---

9. In Kiana Davenport's 1995 novel *Shark Dialogues*, Waipiʻo valley is represented as a refuge for armed sovereignty movement revolutionaries who are waging guerilla warfare against the tourist industry.

ries about incest: she was raped by her grandfather, molested by her uncle, and she told stories about her father beating her mother and then turning his anger towards her. As a child, when she felt threatened, Kili would run away seeking refuge. 'In small kid times, I was an abused child. My father fought my mother and then he fought me. I used to hide in the space under the house to get away from them, but when I really wanted to get far away, I would run up into the mountains. Up in the mountains there were birds and guava trees and I always felt safe. I would lie on the ground and I remember the smell of the [taro pond], it was a certain sweet earthy smell. ... . And I remember the leaves of the taro, which are shaped like a heart, bending as they were blown by the wind. It was like the taro leaves were waving to me.'

## Nurturing the Body–Soul

Taro, the basis of poi, was once the staple food of Indigenous Hawaiians, but in the industrial food system that now dominates, taro became scarce and expensive and Hawaiians were forced to consume less nutritious white rice and white potatoes. The theological origins of food and food's kinship with humanity are core principles of mana and a basis of Native Hawaiian critiques of Western models of health and disease. The taro plant is understood both as a means of nourishment and as an elder sibling: a metaphor for origins and belonging. In the cosmology of Hawai'i, the origins of taro are the origins of humanity. The Hawaiians I worked with expressed their reverence for taro in a locally produced cookbook written for those who were engaged in returning to more traditional diets. The cookbook told the story of taro's origins as the shape-shifting, stillborn, first child of Waʻkea (sky father) and Papa (earth mother). In the space where the baby was buried, a plant sprouted and soon produced many offshoots, becoming bountiful. Thus, taro is the firstborn child of the gods, humans are the second. The cookbook states, Ka poʻe kahiko or the ancestors said that it was the will of God that taro was born first, for he provided the necessary food for all those who came later (Wai'anae Coast Comprehensive Health Center 1995:10, see also Handy et al. 1991:80).

In this Hawaiian view, the natural, spiritual, and human worlds are irrevocably enmeshed. The gods and ancestral spirits are evoked and incarnated in and through food and the land. Identity, kinship, and place are then thoroughly interconnected. The vitality of each individual is transmitted genealogically, but also through substances that dwell in the land. According to Davianna McGregor, who conducted research on the persistence of traditional customs and practices in late 20th century Hawai'i, 'the land is not a commodity to [Hawaiians]...The land is a part of their [family] and they care for it as they do the other living members of their families' (1996:16).

In Hawaiian cosmology, then, both humans and nutritional food share the same origins, the same substance. Indeed, the primogeniture of taro illustrates the dependence and love between humanity and sanctified land. But what happens to kinship and identity, when transnational corporations become the source of nutrients? How does an exploited labor force and mass cruelty to animals affect health? What mana dwells in a Big Mac or a Whopper with cheese? From the perspective of Hawaiian cosmology (one informed by an epistemological critique of what the Western world lacks), the danger of ingesting fast foods is not simply about sodium, fat, cholesterol, and the risks of physical degradation but, rather, the risk in the danger of cultural and spiritual extinction, since being Hawaiian depends on nurturing the body with food produced on ancestral lands.

Drawing the link between Native Hawaiian political powerlessness, disease, landlessness, and poverty was a central project of the decolonization movement. At the end of the 20th century, Native Hawaiians struggled with hunger, homelessness, joblessness, diabetes, heart disease, cancer, and a land base overwhelmed by the tourist economy and the military. In Wai'anae, the site of my research, a cohort of leaders sought to mobilize the community by involving them in projects that addressed their immediate needs, as well as the larger issues of power, cultural integrity, and decolonization. The community of Wai'anae is a semisuburban, semi-rural space on the periphery of Honolulu. Farrington Highway was the only public road in Wai'anae that connected with Honolulu and the rest of the O'ahu. The highway hugged the coastline and was punctuated by Burger Kings, McDonalds, Taco Bells, and convenience stores. Near the highway, built on lands specifically set aside for Native Hawaiians, several suburban-style tract-housing settlements contrasted with the rural scene in the upland valleys. In the upland valleys of Wai'anae (where the sounds of exploding ordnance from a nearby U.S. military base could be heard echoing off the mountains), families still lived in Quonset huts (sold by the military as surplus after World War II), and the land was zoned for agriculture.

The executive director of the Opelu⁻ Project (a Wai'anae organization focused on community gardening and aquaculture), Puanani Burgess told me that what drew people into larger political processes were not theories about oppression. 'In poor communities like Wai'anae,' she said, 'projects and programs are based on questions like: 'why can't we feed ourselves,' 'why can't we heal ourselves,' or just simply, 'why can't we?' It is these questions which encouraged involvement.'[10] 'Political activism,' she said, 'and the language of 'issues' often obscured what was most important. Issued words like racism, injustice, and oppression 'masked' the simple reality of 'my babies only have the worst food.'' For Burgess a focus on health and food held the potential of bringing even the most marginal Native Hawaiian women into the political process because, she said, 'food… [and] health... so touch the lives of everyone.'

## Coda

These stories from Hawai'i illustrate how resistance knowledge, circulating as theories and practices of healing form the basis for real challenges to Western

---

10. Interview with Puanani Burgess. Wai'anae, Hawai'i. January 7, 1997.

notions about health, nature, and the constitution of power. Stuart Kirsch, who conducted research on social and environmental relations in New Guinea, has similarly argued for a 'reverse anthropology' meant to 'enhance recognition of Indigenous modes of analysis. . . and interpretive capacities. ... and to acknowledge and benefit from the resulting insight(s)' (Kirsch 2006:222). But it is not just in places like Hawai'i and New Guinea where resistance epistemologies and modes of interpretation are being produced and exercised. There are thriving, though beleaguered, health justice movements based in poor communities of color in the mainland United States. The scholar Giovanna Di Chiro persuasively argued that in contrast with mainstream health and environmental justice organizations, local grassroots groups have different understandings about human health and the environment. Many grassroots organizations start with the assumption that the 'daily realities and conditions of people's lives' should be at the center of any health justice discourse and practice. They problematize the hostile nature–culture dichotomy and insist that struggling communities of color are also 'endangered species' (Di Chiro 1996:299, 301– 02). This merging of health, environmental, and social justice issues opens different possibilities for transformation and catalyzes processes of remembering and redefinition (Di Chiro 1996:303). Environmental health scholar Jason Corburn has argued that 'political power hinges in part on the ability to manipulate knowledge and to challenge evidence presented in support of particular policies' (Corburn 2005:201). 'Ultimately,' he wrote, 'expertise, whether called professional or local, is a political resource exploited to justify political decisions; it is not an objective truth' (Corburn 2005:201). Coburn's book *Street Science: Community Knowledge and Environmental Health Justice* explored how residents of Brooklyn draw on rich contextualized knowledge often unattainable by outsiders to solve the environmental health problems in deindustrialized urban neighborhoods. Street science, he argued, improves academic scientific information, provides a method for community organizing, and a way of intervening that is contextually relevant (2005:216). Most importantly, Corburn argued that community-based knowledge production is a basis for resistance, action, and intervention by urban residents disenfranchised by a neoliberal state regime that personalizes and depoliticizes inequality.

Statistics on African American health and mortality indicate significant disparities when compared with the health and mortality of white Americans. Black babies, for example, are four times as likely to die from complications of low birth weight than non-Hispanic white babies.[11] African Americans are twice as likely to have diabetes as non-Hispanic whites, and one and a half times as likely to have hypertension.[12] Food related illnesses such as diabetes and hypertension flourish in the absence of sources of nutritious food. In Detroit, a city with a population that is over 80 percent black, it is estimated that half the population lives

---

11. Office of Minority Health, 'Infant Mortality and African Americans,' U.S. Department of Health and Human Services (2011).
12. Office of Minority Health (2010).

in neighborhoods 'either lacking or far away from conventional supermarkets.'[13] Furthermore, African Americans and other people of color are disproportionately affected by environmental degradation. African Americans are 79 percent more likely than whites to live in neighborhoods where industrial pollution is suspected of causing the gravest health dangers.[14] While the concept of mana and contemporary Indigenous Hawaiian understandings of the term depend on access to a deep well of cultural–historic and community knowledge, the meaning of mana as a relationship between humans, earth, and the divine productive of social health and well-being has correlates across cultures and historical epochs. By weaving together current understandings of mana with Marx's analysis of the brutal processes of discommoning in Europe and Africa during the origins of capitalism, I am suggesting that liberatory aspirations, drawing on memories in which humans are contained within and not opposed to nature are possible, even for African Americans in urban settings on the U.S. mainland.

The urban garden movement in the United States, situated at the juncture of health, environment, and community organizing, holds great promise. At an urban garden in Charlottesville, Virginia, children were surprised by the sweet, crunchiness of a freshly harvested carrot, since few had tasted carrots that had not come out of a can. Their grandmothers embraced the sautéing of Swiss chard and recalled meals plucked fresh from family plots in their rural, Southern childhoods. Addressing health disparities and environmental degradation in low wealth communities, urban farming encourages remembering and reinterpreting, and seeing beyond the limits of private control over the means of sustenance, in order to relearn and reclaim alternative cultural and political meanings of food, land, and health.

I end with a passage from Alice Walker's essay 'The Black Writer and the Southern Experience,' because it suggests the potency of *African American* memory and knowledge in the struggle for health justice. Implicitly, Walker argued that dominion is an ideology of city dwellers that fails to recognize the love and reciprocity between humans and the earth that sustains rural communities. Walker writes:

> Perhaps my northern brothers will not believe me when I say that there is a great deal of positive material I can draw from my 'underprivileged' background. But they have never lived, as I have, at the end of a long road in a house that was faced by the edge of the world on one side and nobody for miles on the other. They have never experienced the magnificent quiet of a summer day when the heat is intense and one is so very thirsty, as one moves across the dusty cotton fields, that one learns forever that water is the essence of all life. In the cities it cannot be so clear to one that he is a creature of the earth, feeling the soil between the toes, smelling the dust

---

13. Steven Gray, 'Can America's Urban Food Deserts Bloom?' (2009).
14. United Church of Christ (2007).

thrown up by the rain, loving the earth so much that one longs to taste it and sometimes does. [1983:21]

Health and environmental justice projects in the United States, particularly urban gardening, suggest it is becoming clearer that even in cities, one is a creature of the earth, and even on the U.S. mainland, memories of kinship with nature survive.

# References

Corburn, Jason (2005): *Street Science: Community Knowledge and Environmental Health Justice*. Cambridge: MIT Press.

Davenport, Kiana (1995): *Shark Dialogues*. New York: Penguin.

Deleuze, Giles (2006): *The Fold*. New York: Continuum.

Dening, Greg: (1980): *Islands and Beaches: Discourse on a Silent Land: Marquesas 1774–1880*. Chicago: Dorsey.

Di Chiro, Giovanna (1996): Nature as Community: The Convergence of Environment and Social Justice. *In*
*Uncommon Ground: Rethinking the Human Place in Nature*. William Cronen, ed. pp 298–320. New York: W. W. Norton & Company.

Dimakopoulou, Stamatina (2006): Remapping the Affinities between the Baroque and the Postmodern: the Folds of Melancholy and the Melancholy of the Fold. *Revue Électronique d'Études sur le Monde Anglophone* 41:75–82.

Firth, Raymond (1940): An Analysis of Mana: An Empirical Approach. *Journal of the Polynesian Society* 49(196):482–510.

Gray, Steven (2009): Can America's Urban Food Deserts Bloom? *Time*. May 26, 2009.    http://www.time.com/time/nation/article/0,8599,1900947,00.html, accessed on January 6, 2012.

Handy, E. S. Craighill, Elizabeth Green Handy, and Mary Kawena Pukui (1991): *Native Planters in Old Hawai'i: Their Life, Lore and Environment*. Honolulu: Bishop Museum Press.

Harvey, David (2005): *A Brief History of Neoliberalism*. New York: Oxford University Press.

Herman, R. D. K. (1999): The Aloha State: Place Names and the Anti-Conquest of Hawai'i. *Annals of the Association of American Geographers* 89(1):76–102.

Inglis, Kerri A. (2005): 'A *Land Set Apart': Disease, Displacement, and Death at Makanalua, Moloka'i*. Ph.D. dissertation, Department of Anthropology, University of Hawai'i.

Kame'eleihiwa, Lilikala (1992): *Native Land and Foreign Desires: Ko Hawai'i' Āina a me NaKoi Pu'umake a ka Po'e Haole: A History of Land Tenure Change in Hawai'i from Traditional Times until the 1848 Māhele, including an Analysis of Hawaiian Ali'i Nui and American Calvinists*. Honolulu: Bishop Museum Press.

Kirsch, Stuart (2006): *Reverse Anthropology: Indigenous Analysis of Social and Environmental Relations in New Guinea*. Stanford: Stanford University Press.

Levy, Neil M. (1975): Native Hawaiian Land Rights. *California Law Review* 63(4):848–885.

Lewontin, Richard, and Richard Levins (2007): *Biology Under the Influence: Dialectical Essays on Ecology, Agriculture, Health*. New York: Monthly Review.

Linebaugh, Peter (2008): *The Magna Carta Manifesto: Liberties and Commons for All*. Berkeley: University of California Press.

Marshall, Wende Elizabeth (2011): *Potent Mana: Lessons in Power and Healing*. Albany: SUNY Press.

Marx, Karl (1977[1867]) *Capital. Vol. 1*. Ben Fowkes. Trans. New York: Vintage.

McGregor, Daviana Pomaika'i (1996): An Introduction to the Hoa'aina and Their Rights. *Hawaiian Journal of History* 30(1):1–27.

Merry, Sally Engle (2000): *Colonizing Hawai'i: The Cultural Power of Law*. Princeton: Princeton University Press.

Meyer, Manu Aluli (1998a): Native Hawaiian Epistemology: Exploring Hawaiian Views of Knowledge. *Cultural Survival Quarterly* 22(1):38–40.

Meyer, Manu Aluli (1998b): Native Hawaiian Epistemology: Sites of Empowerment and Resistance. *Equity and Excellence in Education* 31(1):22–28.

Meyer, Manu Aluli (2001) Our Own Liberation: Reflections on Hawaiian Epistemology. *The Contemporary Pacific* 13(1):124–148.

Mignolo, Walter D., and Madina V. Tlostanova (2006): Theorizing from the Borders: Shifting to Geo- and Body-Politics of Knowledge. *European Journal of Social Theory* 9(2):205–221.

Minerbi, Luciano (1994) Sanctuaries, Places of Refuge, and Indigenous Knowledge in Hawai'i. *In Science of Pacific Island Peoples*. John Morrison et al. eds. Pp. 89–129. Honolulu: Institute of Pacific Island Studies.

Office of Minority Health (2010): Heart Disease Data/Statistics. U.S. Department of Health and Human Services. http://minorityhealth.hhs.gov/templates/browse.aspx?lvl=3&lvlid=6, accessed on January 6, 2012.

Office of Minority Health (2011): Infant Mortality and African Americans, U.S. Department of Health and Human Services. http://minorityhealth.hhs.gov/templates/content.aspx?ID=3021, accessed on January 6, 2012.

Patterson, John (2000): Mana: Yin and Yang. *Philosophy East and West*. 50(2):220–241.

Quijano, Aníbal (2002): The Return of the Future and Questions about Knowledge. *Current Sociology*. 50(1):75–87.

Quijano, Aníbal (2007): Questioning 'Race.' *Socialism and Democracy* 21(1):45–53.

Shore, Bradd (1989) Mana and Tapu. *In Developments in Polynesian Ethnology*. Alan Howard and Robert Borofsky, eds. Pp. 137–174. Honolulu: University of Hawai'i Press.

Silva, Noenoe K. (2004): *Aloha Betrayed: Native Hawaiian Resistance to American Colonialism*. Durham, NC: Duke University Press.

Tomlinson, Matt (2006): Retheorizing Mana: Biblical Translation and Discourse of Loss in Fiji. *Oceania* 76(2):173–85.

Trask, Haunani-Kay (1993) *From a Native Daughter: Colonialism and Sovereignty in Hawai'i*. Monroe, ME: Common Courage Press.

Trask, Haunani-Kay (2000): Writing in Captivity: Poetry in a Time of De-Colonization. *In Navigating Islands and Continents: Conversations and Contestations in and around the Pacific.* Cynthia Franklin, Ruth Hsu, and Suzanne Kosanke, eds. Pp. 51–55. Honolulu: University of Hawai'i Press.

Trask, Mililani (1996): Mililani Trask. *In Autobiography of Protest in Hawai'i.* Robert H. Mast and Anne B. Mast, eds. Honolulu: University of Hawai'i Press.

United Church of Christ (2007): Environmental Racisms Indisputable Facts. *United Church News Archives.* http://www.ucc.org/ucnews/octnov07/environ-mental-racisms.html, accessed January 6, 2012.

Valeri, Valerio (1985) *Kingship and Sacrifice: Ritual and Society in Ancient Hawaii.* Chicago: University of Chicago Press.

Wai'anae Coast Comprehensive Health Center (1995): *Wai'anae Diet Cookbook 'Elua. vol. 2.* Wai'anae, Hawai'i: Waianae Coast Comprehensive Health Center.

# TOWARD A DECOLONIAL FEMINISM

Maria Lugones

2007[1]

*In "Heterosexualism and the Colonial/Modern Gender System" (Lugones 2007), I proposed to read the relation between the colonizer and the colonized in terms of gender, race, and sexuality. By this I did not mean to add a gendered reading and a racial reading to the already understood colonial relations. Rather I proposed a rereading of modern capitalist colonial modernity itself. This is because the colonial imposition of gender cuts across questions of ecology, economics, government, relations with the spirit world, and knowledge, as well as across everyday practices that either habituate us to take care of the world or to destroy it. I propose this framework not as an abstraction from lived experience, but as a lens that enables us to see what is hidden from our understandings of both race and gender and the relation of each to normative heterosexuality.*

Modernity organizes the world ontologically in terms of atomic, homogeneous, separable categories. Contemporary women of color and third-world women's critique of feminist universalism centers the claim that the intersection of race, class, sexuality, and gender exceeds the categories of modernity. If *woman* and *black* are terms for homogeneous, atomic, separable categories, then their intersection shows us the absence of black women rather than their presence. So, to see non-white women is to exceed "categorial" logic. I propose the modern, colonial, gender system as a lens through which to theorize further the oppressive logic of colonial modernity, its use of hierarchical dichotomies and categorial logic.

I want to emphasize categorial, dichotomous, hierarchical logic as central to modern, colonial, capitalist thinking about race, gender, and sexuality. This permits me to search for social organizations from which people have resisted modern, capitalist modernity that are in tension with its logic. Following Aparicio and Blaser,[2] I will call such ways of organizing the social, the cosmological, the

---

1. This is an abridged version of the original. Source: Lugones, María. 'Toward a Decolonial Feminism'. *Hypatia* 25, no. 4 (2010): 742–59. http://www.jstor.org/stable/40928654.
2. Juan Ricardo Aparicio and Mario Blaser present this analysis and the relation between knowledge and political practices that focuses on politically committed research in indigenous communities in the Americas, including both acade-

ecological, the economic, and the spiritual *non-modern*. With Aparicio and Blaser and others, I use non-modern to express that these ways are not premodern. The modern apparatus reduces them to premodern ways. So, non-modern knowledges, relations, and values, and ecological, economic, and spiritual practices are logically constituted to be at odds with a dichotomous, hierarchical, "categorial" logic.

# I. The coloniality of gender

I understand the dichotomous hierarchy between the human and the nonhuman as the central dichotomy of colonial modernity. Beginning with the colonization of the Americas and the Caribbean, a hierarchical, dichotomous distinction between human and non-human was imposed on the colonized in the service of Western man. It was accompanied by other dichotomous hierarchical distinctions, among them that between men and women. This distinction became a mark of the human and a mark of civilization. Only the civilized are men or women. Indigenous peoples of the Americas and enslaved Africans were classified as not human in species—as animals, uncontrollably sexual and wild. The European, bourgeois, colonial, modern man became a subject/agent, fit for rule, for public life and ruling, a being of civilization, heterosexual, Christian, a being of mind and reason.

The European bourgeois woman was not understood as his complement, but as someone who reproduced race and capital through her sexual purity, passivity, and being homebound in the service of the white, European, bourgeois man. The imposition of these dichotomous hierarchies became woven into the historicity of relations, including intimate relations. In this paper I want to figure out how to think about intimate, everyday resistant interactions to the colonial difference. When I think of intimacy here, I am not thinking exclusively or mainly about sexual relations. I am thinking of the interwoven social life among people who are not acting as representatives or officials.

I begin, then, with a need to understand that the colonized became subjects in colonial situations in the first modernity, in the tensions created by the brutal imposition of the modern, colonial, gender system. Under the imposed gender framework, the bourgeois white Europeans were civilized; they were fully human. The hierarchical dichotomy as a mark of the human also became a normative tool to damn the colonized. The behaviors of the colonized and their personalities/souls were judged as bestial and thus non-gendered, promiscuous, grotesquely sexual, and sinful. Though at this time the understanding of sex was not dimorphic, animals were differentiated as males and females, the male being the perfection, the female the inversion and deformation of the male.[3] Hermaphrodites,

---

mics and activists, insiders and outsiders to the communities in their forthcoming work. This is an important contribution to understanding decolonial, liberatory processes of knowledge production.

3. Since the eighteenth century the dominant Western view "has been that there are two stable, incommensurable, opposite sexes and that the political, economic, and cultural lives of men and women, their gender role, are somehow based

sodomites, viragos, and the colonized were all understood to be aberrations of male perfection.

The civilizing mission, including conversion to Christianity, was present in the ideological conception of conquest and colonization. Judging the colonized for their deficiencies from the point of view of the civilizing mission justified enormous cruelty. I propose to interpret the colonized, non-human males from the civilizing perspective as judged from the normative understanding of "man," the human being par excellence. Females were judged from the normative understanding of "women," the human inversion of men.[4] From this point of view, colonized people became males and females. Males became not-human-as-not-men, and colonized females became not-human-as-not-women. Consequently, colonized females were never understood as lacking because they were not men-like, and were turned into viragos. Colonized men were not understood to be lacking as not being women-like. What has been understood as the "feminization" of colonized "men" seems rather a gesture of humiliation, attributing to them sexual passivity under the threat of rape. This tension between hypersexuality and sexual passivity defines one of the domains of masculine subjection of the colonized.

It is important to note that often, when social scientists investigate colonized societies, the search for the sexual distinction and then the construction of the gender distinction results from observations of the tasks performed by each sex. In so doing they affirm the inseparability of sex and gender characteristic mainly of earlier feminist analysis. More contemporary analysis has introduced arguments for the claim that gender constructs sex. But in the earlier version, sex grounded gender. Often, they became conflated: where you see sex, you will see gender and vice versa. But, if I am right about the coloniality of gender, in the distinction between the human and the non-human, sex had to stand alone. Gender and sex could not be both inseparably tied and racialized. Sexual dimorphism became the grounding for the dichotomous understanding of gender, the human characteristic.

One may well be interested in arguing that the sex that stood alone in the bestialization of the colonized, was, after all, gendered. What is important to me here is that sex was made to stand alone in the characterization of the colonized. This strikes me as a good entry point for research that takes coloniality seriously and aims to study the historicity and meaning of the relation between sex and gender.

---

on these 'facts'" (Laqueur 1992, 6). Thomas Laqueur also tells us that historically, differentiations of gender preceded differentiations of sex (62). What he terms the "one-sex model" he traces through Greek antiquity to the end of the seventeenth century (and beyond): a world where at least two genders correspond to but one sex, where the boundaries between male and female are of degree and not kind (25). Laqueur tells us that the longevity of the one-sex model is due to its link to power. "In a world that was overwhelmingly male, the one-sex model displayed what was already massively evident in culture: *man* is the measure of all things, and woman does not exist as an ontologically distinct category" (62). Laqueur sums up the question of perfection by saying that for Aristotle and for "the long tradition founded on his thought, the generative substances are interconvertible elements in the economy of a single-sex body whose higher form is male" (42).

4. There is a tension between the understanding of procreation central to the one-sex model and the Christian advocacy of virginity. Instead of seeing the working of sex as related to the production of heat leading to orgasm, St. Augustine sees it as related to the fall. Idealized Christian sex is without passion (see Laqueur 1992, 59-60). The consequences for the coloniality of gender are evident, as the bestial, colonized males and females are understood as excessively sexual.

The colonial "civilizing mission" was the euphemistic mask of brutal access to people's bodies through unimaginable exploitation, violent sexual violation, control of reproduction, and systematic terror (feeding people alive to dogs or making pouches and hats from the vaginas of brutally killed indigenous females, for example). The civilizing mission used the hierarchical gender dichotomy as a judgment, though the attainment of dichotomous gendering for the colonized was not the point of the normative judgment. Turning the colonized into human beings was not a colonial goal. The difficulty of imagining this as a goal can be appreciated clearly when one sees that this transformation of the colonized into men and women would have been a transformation not in identity, but in nature. But turning the colonized against themselves was included in the civilizing mission's repertoire of justifications for abuse. Christian confession, sin, and the Manichean division between good and evil served to imprint female sexuality as evil, as colonized females were understood in relation to Satan, sometimes as mounted by Satan.

The civilizing transformation justified the colonization of memory, and thus of people's senses of self, of intersubjective relation, of their relation to the spirit world, to land, to the very fabric of their conception of reality, identity, and social, ecological, and cosmological organization. Thus, as Christianity became the most powerful instrument in the mission of transformation, the normativity that connected gender and civilization became intent on erasing community, ecological practices, knowledge of planting, of weaving, of the cosmos, and not only on changing and controlling reproductive and sexual practices. One can begin to appreciate the tie between the colonial introduction of the instrumental modern concept of nature central to capitalism, and the colonial introduction of the modern concept of gender, and appreciate it as macabre and heavy in its impressive ramifications. One can also recognize, in the scope I am giving to the imposition of the modern, colonial, gender system, the dehumanization constitutive of the coloniality of being. The concept of the coloniality of being that I understand as related to the process of dehumanization was developed by Nelson Maldonado Torres (2008).

I use the term *coloniality* following Anibal Quijano's analysis of the capitalist world system of power in terms of "coloniality of power" and of modernity, two inseparable axes in the workings of this system of power. Quijano's analysis provides us with a historical understanding of the inseparability of racialization and capitalist exploitation[5] as constitutive of the capitalist system of power as anchored in the colonization of the Americas. In thinking of the coloniality of

---

5. Anibal Quijano understands the coloniality of power as the specific form that domination and exploitation takes in the constitution of the capitalist world system of power. "Coloniality" refers to: the classification of the world's populations in terms of races—the racialization of the relations between colonizer and colonized; the configuration of a new system of exploitation that articulates in one structure all forms of control of labor around the hegemony of capital, where labor is racialized (wage labor as well as slavery, servitude, and small commodity production all become racialized forms of production; they were all new forms as they were constituted in the service of capitalism); Eurocentrism as the new mode of production and control of subjectivity; a new system of control of collective authority around the hegemony of the nation-state that excludes populations racialized as inferior from control of collective authority (see Quijano 199; 1995; and Quijano and Wallerstein 1992).

gender, I complicate his understanding of the capitalist global system of power, but I also critique his own understanding of gender as only in terms of sexual access to women.[6] In using the term *coloniality* I mean to name not just a classification of people in terms of the coloniality of power and gender, but also the process of active reduction of people, the dehumanization that fits them for the classification, the process of subjectification, the attempt to turn the colonized into less than human beings. This is in stark contrast to the process of conversion that constitutes the Christianizing mission.

## II. Theorizing resistance / Decolonizing gender

The semantic consequence of the coloniality of gender is that "colonized woman" is an empty category: no women are colonized; no colonized females are women. Thus, the colonial answer to Sojouner Truth is clearly, "no."[7]

Unlike colonization, the coloniality of gender is still with us; it is what lies at the intersection of gender/class/race as central constructs of the capitalist world system of power. Thinking about the coloniality of gender enables us to think of historical beings only one-sidedly, understood as oppressed. As there are no such beings as colonized women, I suggest that we focus on the beings who resist the coloniality of gender from the "colonial difference." Such beings are, as I have suggested, only partially understood as oppressed, as constructed through the coloniality of gender. The suggestion is not to search for a non-colonized construction of gender in indigenous organizations of the social. There is no such thing; "gender" does not travel away from colonial modernity. Resistance to the coloniality of gender is thus historically complex.

When I think of myself as a theorist of resistance, it is not because I think of resistance as the end or goal of political struggle, but rather as its beginning, its possibility. I am interested in the relational subjective/intersubjective spring of liberation, as both adaptive and creatively oppositional. Resistance is the tension between subjectification (the forming/informing of the subject) and active subjectivity, that minimal sense of agency required for the oppressing← →resisting relation being an active one, without appeal to the maximal sense of agency of the modern subject (Lugones 2003).[8]

Resistant subjectivity often expresses itself infra-politically, rather than in a politics of the public, which has an easy inhabitation of public contestation. Legitimacy, authority, voice, sense, and visibility are denied to resistant subjectivity. Infra-politics marks the turn inward, in a politics of resistance, toward liberation. It shows the power of communities of the oppressed in constituting

---

6. For my argument against Quijano's understanding of the relation of coloniality and sex/gender, see Lugones 2007.

7. "Ain't I a Woman."; speech given at the Women's Convention in Akron, Ohio, May 29, 1851.

8. In Lugones 2003 I introduce the concept of "active subjectivity" to capture the minimal sense of agency of the resister to multiple oppressions whose multiple subjectivities is reduced by hegemonic understandings/colonial understandings/racist-gendered understandings to no agency at all. It is her belonging to impure communities that gives life to her agency.

resistant meaning and each other against the constitution of meaning and social organization by power. In our colonized, racially gendered, oppressed existences we are also other than what the hegemon makes us be. That is an infra-political achievement. If we are exhausted, fully made through and by micro and macro mechanisms and circulations of power, "liberation" loses much of its meaning or ceases to be an intersubjective affair. The very possibility of an identity based on politics (Mignolo 2000) and the project of de-coloniality loses its peopled ground.

As I move methodologically from women of color feminisms to a decolonial feminism, I think about feminism from and at the grassroots, and from and at the colonial difference, with a strong emphasis on ground, on a historicized, incarnate intersubjectivity. The question of the *relation* between resistance or resistant response to the coloniality of gender and de-coloniality is being set up here rather than answered.[9] But I do mean to understand resistance to the coloniality of gender from the perspective of the colonial difference.

Decolonizing gender is necessarily a praxical task. It is to enact a critique of racialized, colonial, and capitalist heterosexualist gender oppression as a lived transformation of the social. As such it places the theorizer in the midst of people in a historical, peopled, subjective/intersubjective understanding of the oppressing resisting relation at the intersection of complex systems of oppression. I call the analysis of racialized, capitalist, gender oppression "the coloniality of gender." I call the possibility of overcoming the coloniality of gender "decolonial feminism."

The coloniality of gender enables me to understand the oppressive imposition as a complex interaction of economic, racializing, and gendering systems in which every person in the colonial encounter can be found as a live, historical, fully described being. It is as such that I want to understand the resister as being oppressed by the colonizing construction of the fractured locus. But the coloniality of gender hides the resister as fully informed as a native of communities under cataclysmic attack. So, the coloniality of gender is only one active ingredient in the resister's history. In focusing on the resister at the colonial difference I mean to unveil what is obscured.

The process of colonization invented the colonized and attempted a full reduction of them to less than human primitives, satanically possessed, infantile, aggressively sexual, and in need of transformation. The process I want to follow is the oppressing resisting process at the fractured locus of the colonial difference. That is, I want to follow subjects in intersubjective collaboration and conflict,

---

9. It is outside the scope of this article, but certainly well within the project to which I am committed, to argue that the coloniality of gender is constituted by and constitutive of the coloniality of power, knowledge, being, nature, and language. They are crucially inseparable. One way of expressing this is that the coloniality of knowledge, for example, is gendered and that one has not understood the coloniality of knowledge without understanding its being gendered. But here I want to get ahead of myself in claiming that there is no de-coloniality without de-coloniality of gender. Thus, the modern colonial imposition of an oppressive, racially differentiated, hierarchical gender system permeated through and through by the modern logic of dichotomizing cannot be characterized as a circulation of power that organizes the domestic sphere as opposed to the public domain of authority and the sphere of waged labor (and access and control of sex and reproduction biology) as contrasted to cognitive/epistemic intersubjectivity and knowledge, or nature as opposed to culture.

fully informed as members of Native American or African societies, as they take up, respond, resist, and accommodate to hostile invaders who mean to dispossess and dehumanize them. The invasive presence engages them brutally, in a pre-possessing, arrogant, incommunicative and powerful way, leaving little room for adjustments that preserve their own senses of self in community and in the world. But, instead of thinking of the global, capitalist, colonial system as in every way successful in its destruction of peoples, know-ledges, relations, and economies, I want to think of the process as continually resisted, and being resisted today. And thus I want to think of the colonized neither as simply imagined and constructed by the colonizer and coloniality in accordance with the colonial imagination and the strictures of the capitalist colonial venture, but as a being who begins to inhabit a fractured locus constructed doubly, who perceives doubly, relates doubly, where the "sides" of the locus are in tension, and the conflict itself actively informs the subjectivity of the colonized self in multiple relation.[10]

The gender system is not just hierarchical but racially differentiated, and the racial differentiation denies humanity and thus gender to the colonized.[11] Irene Silverblatt (1990; 1998), Carolyn Dean (2001), Maria Esther Pozo (Pozo and Ledezma 2006), Pamela Calla and Nina Laurie (2006), Sylvia Marcos (2006), Paula Gunn Allen (1992), Leslie Marmon Silko (2006), Felipe Guaman Poma de Ayala (2009), and Oyeronke Oyewumi (1997), among others, enable me to affirm that gender is a colonial imposition, not just as it imposes itself on life as lived in tune with cosmologies incompatible with the modern logic of dichotomies, but also

---

10. A further note on the relation of intersectionality and categorical purity: intersectionality has become pivotal in U.S. women of color feminisms. As said above, one cannot see, locate, or address women of color (U.S. Latinas, Asians, Chicanas, African Americans, Native American women) in the U.S. legal system and in much of institutionalized U.S. life. As one considers the dominant categories, among them "woman," "black," "poor," they are not articulated in a way that includes people who are women, black and poor. The intersection of "woman" and "black" reveals the absence of black women rather [than] their presence. That is because the modern categorial logic constructs categories as homogenous, atomic, separable, and constituted in dichotomous terms. That construction proceeds from the pervasive presence of hierarchical dichotomies in the logic of modernity and modern institutions. The relation between categorical purity and hierarchical dichotomies works as follows. Each homogeneous, separable, atomic category is characterized in terms of the superior member of the dichotomy. Thus "women" stands for white women. "Black" stands for black men. When one is trying to understand women at the intersection of race, class, and gender, non-white black, mestiza, indigenous, and Asian women are impossible beings. They are impossible since they are neither European bourgeois women, nor indigenous males. Intersectionality is important when showing the failures of institutions to include discrimination or oppression against women of color. But here I want to be able to think of their presence as being both oppressed and resisting. So, I have shifted to the *coloniality of gender* at and from the *colonial difference* to be able to perceive and understand the fractured locus of colonized women and agents fluent in native cultures.
11. I agree with Oyeronke Oyewumi, who makes a similar claim for the colonization of the Yoruba (Oyewumi 1997). But I complicate the claim, as I understand both gender and sex as colonial impositions. That is, the organization of the social in terms of gender is hierarchical and dichotomous, and the organization of the social in terms of sex is dimorphic and relates the male to the man even to mark a lack. The same is true of female. Thus, Mesoamericans who did not understand sex in dimorphic, separable terms, but in terms of fluid dualisms, became either male or female. Linda Alcoff sees the contribution of sperm and egg in the reproductive act as in some way entailing the sexual division and the gender division. But the contribution of sperm and egg is quite comparable with intersexuality. From "contributes the ovum" or "contributes sperm" to a particular act of conception, it does not follow that the sperm contributor is either male or a man, nor does it follow that the egg contributor is female or a woman. But nothing about the meaning of *male* or *man*, would unequivocally point to a sperm contributor who is markedly intersexed as a male man, except again as a matter of normal logic. It the Western modern, gender dichotomy is conceptually tied to the dimorphic sexual distinction, and production of sperm is the necessary and sufficient condition of maleness, then of course the sperm donor is male and a man. Hormonal and gonadal characteristics are notoriously insufficient in determining gender. Think of the dangerous misfit of male-to-female transexuals being housed in male prisons to get a feel for this perception embedded in language and popular consciousness.

that inhabitations of worlds understood, constructed, and in accordance with such cosmologies animated the self-among-others in resistance from and at the extreme tension of the colonial difference.

The long process of subjectification of the colonized toward adoption/internalization of the men/women dichotomy as a normative construction of the social—a mark of civilization, citizenship, and membership in civil society—was and is constantly renewed. It is met in the flesh over and over by oppositional responses grounded in a long history of oppositional responses and lived as sensical in alternative, resistant socialities at the colonial difference. It is movement toward coalition that impels us to know each other as selves that are thick, in relation, in alternative socialities, and grounded in tense, creative in-habitations of the colonial difference.

I am investigating emphasizing the historicity of the oppressing-resisting relation and thus emphasizing concrete, lived resistances to the coloniality of gender. In particular, I want to mark the need to keep a multiple reading of the resistant self in relation. This is a consequence of the colonial imposition of gender. We see the gender dichotomy operating normatively in the construction of the social and in the colonial processes of oppressive subjectification. But if we are going to make another construction of the self in relation, we need to bracket the dichotomous human/non-human, colonial, gender system that is constituted by the hierarchical dichotomy man/woman for European colonials the non-gendered, non-human colonized. As Oyewumi makes clear, a colonizing reading of the Yoruba reads the hierarchical dichotomy into the Yoruba society, erasing the reality of the colonial imposition of a multiply oppressive gender system. Thus it is necessary for us to be very careful with the use of the terms *woman* and man and bracket them when necessary to weave the logic of the fractured locus, without causing the social sources woven into the resistant responses to disappear. If we only weave man and woman into the very fabric that constitutes the self in relation to resisting, we erase the resistance itself. Only in bracketing [ ] can we appreciate the different logic that organizes the social in the resistant response.

## III. The colonial difference

The colonial difference is the space where coloniality of power is enacted. (Mignolo 2000, ix). Once coloniality of power is introduced into the analysis, the "colonial difference" becomes visible, and the epistemological fractures between the Eurocentric critique of Eurocentrism is distinguished from the critique of Eurocentrism, anchored in the colonial difference...(37)

I have prepared us to hear these assertions. One can look at the colonial past and, as an observer, see the natives negotiating the introduction of foreign beliefs and practices as well as negotiating being assigned to inferior positions and being found polluting and dirty. Clearly, to see this is not to see the coloniality. It is rather to see people—anyone, really—pressed under difficult circumstances to occupy demeaning positions that make them disgusting to the social superiors. To see the coloniality is to see the powerful reduction of human beings to animals, to inferiors by nature, in a schizoid understanding of reality that dichotomizes the human from nature, the human from the non-human, and thus imposes an ontology and a cosmology that, in its power and constitution, disallows all humanity, all possibility of understanding, all possibility of human communication, to dehumanized beings.

To see the coloniality is to see both the *jaqi,* the persona, the being that is in a world of meaning without dichotomies, and the beast, both real, both vying under different powers for survival. Thus to see the coloniality is to reveal the very degradation that gives us two renditions of life and a being rendered by them. The sole possibility of such a being lies in its full inhabitation of this fracture, of this wound, where sense is contradictory and from such contradiction new sense is made anew.

[The colonial difference] is the space where *local* histories inventing and implementing global designs meet *local* histories, the space in which global designs have to be adapted, adopted, rejected, integrated, or ignored. (Mignolo 2000, ix)

[The colonial difference] is, finally, the physical as well as imaginary location where the coloniality of power is at work in the confrontation of two kinds of local histories displayed in different spaces and times across the planet. If Western cosmology is the historically unavoidable reference point, the multiple confrontations of two kinds of local histories defy dichotomies. Christian and Native American cosmologies, Christian and Amerindian cosmologies, Christian and Islamic cosmologies, Christian and Confucian cosmologies among others only enact dichotomies where you look at them one at a time, not when you compare them in the geohistorical confines of the modern/ colonial world system. (ix)

Thus, it is not an affair of the past. It is a matter of the geopolitics of knowledge. It is a matter of how we produce a feminism that takes the global designs for racialized female and male energy and, erasing the colonial difference, takes that energy to be used toward the destruction of the worlds of meaning of our own possibilities. Our possibilities lie in communality rather than subordination; they do not lie in parity with our superior in the hierarchy that constitutes the coloniality. That construction of the human is vitiated through and through by its intimate relation with violence.

The colonial difference creates the conditions for dialogic situations in which a fractured enunciation is enacted from the subaltern perspective as a response to the hegemonic discourse and perspective. (Mignolo 2000, x) The transcending of the colonial difference can only be done from a perspective of subalternity, from decolonization, and, therefore, from a new epistemological terrain where border thinking works. (45)

I see these two paragraphs in tension precisely because if the dialogue is to be had with the modern man, his occupation of the colonial difference involves his redemption but also his self-destruction. Dialogue is not only possible at the colonial difference but necessary for those resisting dehumanization in different and intermingled locals. So, indeed, the transcending can only be done from the perspective of subalterity, but toward a newness of being.

I am proposing a feminist border thinking, where the liminality of the border is a ground, a space, a borderlands, to use Gloria Anzaldua's term, not just a split, not an infinite repetition of dichotomous hierarchies among de-souled specters of the human. The reading I want to perform sees the coloniality of gender and rejection, resistance, and response. It adapts to its negotiation always concretely, from within.

## IV. Reading the fractured locus

What I am proposing in working toward a decolonial feminism is to learn about each other as resisters to the coloniality of gender at the colonial difference, without necessarily being an insider to the worlds of meaning from which resistance to the coloniality arises. That is, the decolonial feminist's task begins by her seeing the colonial difference, emphatically resisting her epistemological habit of erasing it. Seeing it, she sees the world anew, and then she requires herself to drop her enchantment with "woman," the universal, and begins to learn about other resisters at the colonial difference.[12] The reading moves against the social-scientific objectifying reading, attempting rather to understand subjects, the active subjectivity emphasized as the reading looks for the fractured locus in resistance to the coloniality of gender at a coalitional starting point. In thinking of the starting point as coalitional because the fractured locus is in common, the histories of resistance at the colonial difference are where we need to *dwell*, learning about each other. The coloniality of gender is sensed as concrete, intricately related exercises of power, some body to body, some legal, some inside a room as indigenous female-beasts-not-civilized-women are forced to weave day and night, others at the confessional. The differences in the concreteness and intricacy of power in circulation are not understood as levels of generality; embodied subjectivity and the institutional are equally concrete.

As the coloniality infiltrates every aspect of living through the circulation of power at the levels of the body, labor, law, imposition of tribute, and the introduction of property and land dispossession, its logic and efficacy are met by different concrete people whose bodies, selves in relation, and relations to the spirit world do not follow the logic of capital. The logic they follow is not countenanced by the logic of power. The movement of these bodies and relations does not repeat itself. It does not become static and ossified. Everything and everyone continues to respond to power and responds much of the time resistantly—which is not to say in open defiance, though some of the time there is open defiance—in ways that may or may not be beneficial to capital, but that are not part of its logic. Part of what I see is tense movement, people moving: the tension between the dehumanization and paralysis of the coloniality of being, and the creative activity of be-ing.

One does not resist the coloniality of gender alone. One resists it from within a way of understanding the world and living in it that is shared and that can

---

12. Learning each other's histories has been an important ingredient in understanding deep coalitions among U.S. women of color. Here I am giving a new turn to this learning.

understand one's actions, thus providing recognition. Communities rather than individuals enable the doing; one does with someone else, not in individualist isolation. The passing from mouth to mouth, from hand to hand of lived practices, values, beliefs, ontologies, space-times, and cosmologies constitutes one. The production of the everyday within which one exists produces one's self as it provides particular, meaningful clothing, food, economies and ecologies, gestures, rhythms, habitats, and senses of space and time. But it is important that these ways are not just different. They include affirmation of life over profit, communalism over individualism, "estar" over enterprise, beings in relation rather than dichotomously split over and over in hierarchically and violently ordered fragments. These ways of being, valuing, and believing have persisted in the resistant response to the coloniality.

Finally, I mark here the interest in an ethics of coalition-in-the-making in terms of both be-ing, and be-ing in relation that extends and interweaves its peopled ground (Lorde 2007). I can think of the self in relation as responding to the coloniality of gender at the colonial difference from a fractured locus, backed by an alternative communal source of sense that makes possible elaborate responses. The direction of the possibility of strengthening the affirmation and possibility of self in relation lies not through a rethinking of the relation with the oppressor from the point of the oppressed, but through a furthering of the logic of difference and multiplicity and of coalition at the point of difference (Lorde 2007). The emphasis is on maintaining multiplicity at the point of reduction—not in maintaining a hybrid "product," which hides the colonial difference—in the tense workings of more than one logic, not to be synthesized but transcended. Among the logics at work are the many logics meeting the logic of oppression: many colonial differences, but one logic of oppression. The *responses from the fragmented loci can be creatively in coalition,* a way of thinking of the possibility of coalition that takes up the logic of de-coloniality, and the logic of coalition of feminists of color: the oppositional consciousness of a social erotics (Sandoval 2000) that takes on the differences that make be-ing creative, that permits enactments that are thoroughly defiant of the logic of dichotomies (Lorde 2007). The logic of coalition is defiant of the logic of dichotomies; differences are never seen in dichotomous terms, but the logic has as its opposition the logic of power. The multiplicity is never reduced.

So, I mark this as a beginning, but it is a beginning that affirms a profound term that Maldonado Torres has called the "decolonial turn." The questions proliferate at this time and the answers are difficult. They require placing, again, an emphasis on methodologies that work with our lives, so the sense of responsibility is maximal. How do we learn about each other? How do we do it without harming each other but with the courage to take up a weaving of the everyday that may reveal deep betrayals? How do we cross without taking over? With whom do we do this work? The theoretical here is immediately practical. My own life-ways of spending my time, of seeing, of cultivating a depth of sorrow—is animated by great anger and directed by the love that Lorde (2007), Perez (1999), and Sandoval (2000) teach us. How do we practice with each other engaging in dialogue at the colonial difference? How do we know when we are doing it?

Isn't it the case that those of us who rejected the offer made to us over and over by white women in consciousness-raising groups, conferences, workshops, and women's studies program meetings saw the offer as slamming the door to a coalition that would really include us? Isn't it the case that we felt a calm, full, substantial sense of recognition when we asked: "What do you mean "We," White Woman?" Isn't it the case that we rejected the offer from the side of Sojourner Truth and were ready to reject their answer? Isn't it the case that we refused the offer at the colonial difference, sure that for them there was only one woman, only one reality? Isn't it the case that we already know each other as multiple seers at the colonial difference, intent on a coalition that neither begins nor ends with that offer? We are moving on at a time of crossings, of seeing each other at the colonial difference constructing a new subject of a new feminist geopolitics of knowing and loving.

# References

Aparicio, Juan Ricardo, and Mario Blaser. [unpublished manuscript.] La "CiudadLetrada" y la insurreccion de saberes subyugados en America Latina.

Calla, Pamela, and Nina Laurie. 2006. Desarrollo, poscolonialismo y teoria geografica politica. In *Las displicencias de genero en los cruces del siglo pasado al nuevo milenio en los* Andes, ed. Nina Laurie and Maria Esther Pozo. Cochabamba, Bolivia: CESU-UMSS.

Dean, Carolyn. 2001. Andean androgyny and the making of men. In *Gender in pre-Hispanic* America, ed. Cecilia Klein. Washington, D.C.: Dumbarton Oaks.

Guaman Poma de Ayala, Felipe. 2009. *The* first new *chronicle and good government:* On *the* history *of the* world and *the Incas up* to 1615. Austin: University of Texas Press.

Gunn Allen, Paula. 1992. *The sacred hoop: Recovering the feminine in American Indian* traditions. Boston: Beacon Press.

Laqueur, Thomas. 1992. *Making sex: Body and gender* from *the Greeks to* Freud. Cambridge, Mass., and London: Harvard University Press.

Lorde, Audre. 2007. *Sister outsider: Essays and speeches.* Berkeley: The Crossing Press.

Lugones, Maria. 2003. Street walker theorizing. In *Pilgrimages/peregrinajes: Theorizing coalition against multiple oppression,* ed. Maria Lugones. Lanham, Md.: Rowman & Littlefield Publishers, Inc.

Lugones, Maria. 2007. Heterosexualism and the colonial/modern gender system. *Hypatia* 22 (1): 186-209.

Maldonado Tones, Nelson. 2008. *Against war: Views* from *the underside of modernity.* Durham, N.C.: Duke University Press.

Marcos, Sylvia. 2006. *Taken from the lips:* Gender *and eros in mesoamerican religions.* Leiden and Boston: Brill.

Mignolo, Walter D. 2000. *Local histories/global designs:* Coloniality, , *subaltern knowledges* and border *thinking.* Princeton: Princeton University Press.

Oyewumi, Oyeronke. 1997. *The invention of women: Making African sense of Western discourses.* Minneapolis: University of Minnesota Press.

Perez, Emma. 1999. *The decolonial imaginary: Writing chicanas into history.* Bloomington: Indiana University Press.

Pozo, Maria Esther, and Jhonny Ledezma. 2006. Genero: trabajo agricola y tierra en Raqaypampa. In *Las displicencias de genero en los cruces del siglo pasado al nuevo mile-nio en los Andes,* ed. Nina Laurie and Maria Esther Pozo. Cochabamba, Bolivia: CESU-UMSS.

Quijano, Anibal. 1991. *Colonialidad, modernidad/racialidad. Peru Indigerna* 13 (29): 11-29.

Quijano, Anibal. 1995. Modernity, identity, and utopia in Latin America. In *The postmodernism debate in Latin America,* ed. J. Beverley, M. Aronna, and J. Oviedo. Durham, N.C.: Duke University Press.

Quijano, Anibal, and Immanuel Wallerstein. 1992. Americanity as a concept, or the Americas in the modern world-system. ISSA1 134:549-47.

Sandoval, Chela. 2000. *Methodology of the oppressed.* Minneapolis: University of Minnesota Press.

Silko, Leslie Marmon. 2006. *Ceremony.* New York: Penguin Books.

Silverblatt, Irene. 1990. Taller de historia oral Andina. La Mujer *Andina en la historia.* Chukiyawu: Ediciones del THOA.

————. 1998. Moon, *sun, and witches.* Princeton: Princeton University Press.

# COLONIALITY OF POWER

Aníbal Quijano

2000[1]

What is termed globalization is the culmination of a process that began with the constitution of America and colonial/modern Eurocentered capitalism as a new global power. One of the fundamental axes of this model of power is the social classification of the world's population around the idea of race, a mental construction that expresses the basic experience of colonial domination and pervades the more important dimensions of global power, including its specific rationality: Eurocentrism. The racial axis has a colonial origin and character, but it has proven to be more durable and stable than the colonialism in whose matrix it was established. Therefore, the model of power that is globally hegemonic today presupposes an element of coloniality.

## America and the New Model of Global Power

America[2] was constituted as the first space/time of a new model of power of global vocation, and both in this way and by it became the first identity of modernity. Two historical processes associated in the production of that space/time converged and established the two fundamental axes of the new model of power. One was the codification of the differences between conquerors and conquered in the idea of 'race,' a supposedly different biological structure that placed some in a natural situation of inferiority to the others. The conquistadors assumed this idea as the constitutive, founding element of the relations of domination that the con-

1. Editor's note: This is an abridged version of the original (Quijano, 2000, 'Coloniality of Power, Eurocentrism and Latin America,' *Nepantla: Views from the South*, V. 1, I. 3: 533-580). We are well aware that this vital excerpt makes no mention of the words 'violence', 'nonviolence', or even 'revolution.' However, as we approach a contemporary view of the modern world ahead of us, it is clear that no conception of peace and/or justice can exist without a sharp confrontation of the structural violence which pervades all aspects of all society. In that sense, this essay contextualizes all of the intersectional points of our current realities: a colonized, gendered, whiteness which secures capitalism as the defining space of modern 'being.' As is poignantly noted here, we cannot become who we really are meant to be without fully dismantling these defining systems of oppression.
2. Even though for the imperialist vision of the United States of America the term 'America' is just another name for that country, today it is the name of the territory that extends from Alaska in the North to Cape Horn in the South, including the Caribbean archipelago. But from 1492 until 1610, America was exclusively the time/space under Iberian (Hispanic Portuguese) colonial domination. This included, in the northern border, California, Texas, New Mexico, Florida (conquered in the nineteenth century by the United States), the Spanish-speaking Caribbean area, up to Cape Horn in the South—roughly, the time/space of today's Latin America. The Eurocentered, capitalist, colonial/modern power emerged then and there. So, though today America is a very heterogeneous world in terms of power and culture, and for descriptive purposes could be better referred to as the Americas, in regards to the history of the specific pattern of world power that is discussed here, 'America' is still the proper denomination.

quest imposed. On this basis, the population of America, and later the world, was classified within the new model of power. The other process was the constitution of a new structure of control of labor and its resources and products. This new structure was an articulation of all historically known previous structures of control of labor, slavery, serfdom, small independent commodity production and reciprocity, together around and upon the basis of capital and the world market.[3]

## Race: A Mental Category of Modernity

The idea of race, in its modern meaning, does not have a known history before the colonization of America... However, what matters is that soon it was constructed to refer to the supposed differential biological structures between those groups.

Social relations founded on the category of race produced new historical social identities in America—Indians, blacks, and mestizos—and redefined others. Terms such as *Spanish* and *Portuguese,* and much later *European,* which until then indicated only geographic origin or country of origin, acquired from then on, a racial connotation in reference to the new identities. Insofar as the social relations that were being configured were relations of domination, such identities were considered constitutive of the hierarchies, places, and corresponding social roles, and consequently of the model of colonial domination that was being imposed. In other words, race and racial identity were established as instruments of basic social classification.

In America, the idea of race was a way of granting legitimacy to the relations of domination imposed by the conquest. After the colonization of America and the expansion of European colonialism to the rest of the world, the subsequent constitution of Europe as a new identity needed the elaboration of a Eurocentric perspective of knowledge, a theoretical perspective on the idea of race as a naturalization of colonial relations between Europeans and non-Europeans. Historically, this meant a new way of legitimizing the already old ideas and practices of relations of superiority/inferiority between dominant and dominated. From the sixteenth century on, this principle has proven to be the most effective and long-lasting instrument of universal social domination, since the much older principle—gender or intersexual domination—was encroached upon by the inferior/superior racial classifications. So the conquered and dominated peoples were situated in a natural position of inferiority and, as a result, their phenotypic traits as well as their cultural features were considered inferior.[4] In this way, race became the fundamental criterion for the distribution of the world population into ranks, places, and roles in the new society's structure of power.

---

3. See Quijano and Wallerstein 1992.
4. The idea of race is literally an invention. It has nothing to do with the biological structure of the human species. Regarding phenotypic traits, those that are obviously found in the genetic code of individuals and groups are in the specific sense biological. However, they have no relation to the subsystems and biological processes of the human organism, including those involved in the neurological and mental subsystems and their functions. See Mark 1994 and Quijano 1999.

## Capitalism, the New Structure for the Control of Labor

In the historical process of the constitution of America, all forms of control and exploitation of labor and production, as well as the control of appropriation and distribution of products, revolved around the capital-salary relation and the world market. These forms of labor control included slavery, serfdom, petty-commodity production, reciprocity, and wages. In such an assemblage, each form of labor control was no mere extension of its historical antecedents. All of these forms of labor were historically and sociologically new: in the first place, because they were deliberately established and organized to produce commodities for the world market; in the second place, because they did not merely exist simultaneously in the same space/time, but each one of them was also articulated to capital and its market. Thus, they configured a new global model of labor control, and in turn a fundamental element of a new model of power to which they were historically structurally dependent. That is to say, the place and function, and therefore the historical movement, of all forms of labor as subordinated points of a totality belonged to the new model of power, in spite of their heterogeneous specific traits and their discontinuous relations with that totality. In the third place, and as a consequence, each form of labor developed into new traits and historical-structural configurations.

Insofar as that structure of control of labor, resources, and products consisted of the joint articulation of all the respective historically known forms, a global model of control of work was established for the first time in known history. And while it was constituted around and in the service of capital, its configuration as a whole was established with a capitalist character as well. Thus emerged a new, original, and singular structure of relations of production in the historical experience of the world: world capitalism.

## Coloniality of Power and Global Capitalism

The new historical identities produced around the foundation of the idea of race in the new global structure of the control of labor were associated with social roles and geohistorical places. In this way, both race and the division of labor remained structurally linked and mutually reinforcing, in spite of the fact that neither of them were necessarily dependent on the other in order to exist or change.

In the course of the worldwide expansion of colonial domination on the part of the same dominant race (or, from the eighteenth century onward, Europeans), the same criteria of social classification were imposed on all of the world population. As a result, new historical and social identities were produced: yellows and olives were added to whites, Indians, blacks, and mestizos. The racist distribution of new social identities was combined, as had been done so successfully in Anglo-America, with a racist distribution of labor and the forms of exploitation of colonial capitalism. This was, above all, through a quasi-exclusive association of whiteness with wages and, of course, with the high-order positions in the colonial administration. Thus, each form of labor control was associated with a particular race. Consequently, the control of a specific form of labor could be, at the same time, the control of a specific group of dominated people. A new technology of domination/exploitation, in this case race/labor, was articulated in such a way that the two elements appeared naturally associated. Until now, this strategy has been exceptionally successful.

## Coloniality and the Eurocentrification of World Capitalism

The privileged positions conquered by the dominant whites for the control of gold, silver, and other commodities produced by the unpaid labor of Indians, blacks, and mestizos (coupled with an advantageous location in the slope of the Atlantic through which, necessarily, the traffic of these commodities for the world market had to pass) granted whites a decisive advantage to compete for the control of worldwide commercial traffic. The progressive monetization of the world market that the precious metals from America stimulated and allowed, as well as the control of such large resources, made possible the control of the vast preexisting web of commercial exchange that included, above all, China, India, Ceylon, Egypt, Syria—the future Far and Middle East. The monetization of labor also made it possible to concentrate the control of commercial capital, labor, and means of production in the whole world market.

The fact is that from the very beginning of the colonization of America, Europeans associated nonpaid or non-waged labor with the dominated races because they were 'inferior' races. The vast genocide of the Indians in the first decades of colonization was not caused principally by the violence of the conquest nor by the plagues the conquistadors brought, but took place because so many American Indians were used as disposable manual labor and forced to work until death. The elimination of this colonial practice did not end until the defeat of the *encomenderos* in the middle of the sixteenth century. The subsequent Iberian colonialism involved a new politics of population reorganization, a reorganization of the Indians and their relations with the colonizers. But this did not advance American Indians as free and waged laborers. From then on, they were assigned the status of unpaid serfs. The serfdom of the American Indians could not, however, be compared with feudal serfdom in Europe, since it included neither the supposed protection of a feudal lord nor, necessarily, the possession of a piece of land to cultivate instead of wages. Before independence, the Indian labor force of serfs reproduced itself in the communities, but more than one hundred years after independence, a large part of the Indian serfs was still obliged to reproduce the labor force on its own.[5] The other form of unwaged or, simply put, unpaid labor, slavery, was assigned exclusively to the 'black' population brought from Africa.

The racial classification of the population and the early association of the new racial identities of the colonized with the forms of control of unpaid, unwaged labor developed among the Europeans the singular perception that paid labor was the whites' privilege. The racial inferiority of the colonized implied that they were not worthy of wages. They were naturally obliged to work for the profit of their owners. It is not difficult to find, to this very day, this attitude spread out among the white property owners of any place in the world. Furthermore, the lower wages 'inferior races' receive in the present capitalist centers for the same work as done by whites cannot be explained as detached from the racist social classification of the world's population—in other words, as detached from the global capitalist coloniality of power.

The control of labor in the new model of global power was constituted thus, articulating all historical forms of labor control around the capitalist wage-labor relation. This articulation was constitutively colonial, based on first the assignment of all forms of unpaid labor to colonial races (originally American Indians, blacks, and, in a more complex way, mestizos) in America and, later on, to the remaining colonized races in the rest of the world, olives and yellows. Second, labor was controlled through the assignment of salaried labor to the colonizing whites.

Coloniality of labor control determined the geographic distribution of each one of the integrated forms of labor control in global capitalism. In other words, it determined the social geography of capitalism: capital, as a social formation for control of wage labor, was the axis around which all remaining forms of labor control, resources, and products were articulated. But, at the same time, capital's specific social configuration was geographically and socially concentrated in Europe and, above all, among Europeans in the whole world of capitalism. Through these measures, Europe and the European constituted themselves as the center of the capitalist world economy.

When Raul Prebisch coined the celebrated image of center and periphery to describe the configuration of global capitalism since the end of World War II, he underscored, with or without being aware of it, the nucleus of the historical model for the control of labor, resources, and products that shaped the central part of the new global model of power, starting with America as a player in the new world economy.[6] Global capitalism was, from then on, colonial/modern and Eurocentered. Without a clear understanding of those specific historical characteristics of capitalism, the concept of a 'modern world-system' itself...cannot be properly or completely understood.

---

5. This is precisely what Alfred Métraux, the well-known French anthropologist, found at the end of the fifties in southern Peru. I found the same phenomenon in 1963 in Cuzco: an Indian peon was obliged to travel from his village, in La Convención, to the city in order to fulfill his turn of service to his patrons. But they did not furnish him lodging, or food, of, of course, a salary. Métraux proposed that the situation was closer to the Roman colonato of the fourth century.
6. See Prebisch 1959, 1960. On Prebisch, see Baer 1962.

# The New Model of World Power and the New World Intersubjectivity

[The colonized peoples] were not in the same line of continuity as the Europeans, but in another, naturally different category. [They were considered] inferior races and in that manner were the past vis-à-vis the Europeans.

That perspective imagined modernity and rationality as exclusively European products and experiences. From this point of view, inter-subjective and cultural relations between Western Europe and the rest of the world were codified in a strong play of new categories: East-West, primitive-civilized, magic/mythic-scientific, irrational-rational, traditional-modern —Europe and not Europe. Even so, the only category with the honor of being recognized as the other of Europe and the West was 'Orient'—not the Indians of America and not the blacks of Africa, who were simply 'primitive.' For underneath that codification of relations between Europeans and non-Europeans, race is, without doubt, the basic category'.[7] This binary, dualist perspective on knowledge, particular to Eurocentrism, was imposed as globally hegemonic in the same course as the expansion of European colonial dominance over the world.

It would not be possible to explain the elaboration of Eurocentrism[8] as the hegemonic perspective of knowledge otherwise. The Eurocentric version is based on two principal founding myths: first, the idea of the history of human civilization as a trajectory that departed from a state of nature and culminated in Europe; second, a view of the differences between Europe and non-Europe as natural (racial) differences and not consequences of a history of power. Both myths can be unequivocally recognized in the foundations of evolutionism and dualism, two of the nuclear elements of Eurocentrism.

## The Question of Modernity

The fact that Western Europeans will imagine themselves to be the culmination of a civilizing trajectory from a state of nature leads them also to think of themselves as the moderns of humanity and its history, that is, as the new, and at the same time, most advanced of the species.

If the concept of modernity refers to the ideas of newness, the advanced, the rational-scientific, the secular, then there is no doubt that one must admit that it is a phenomenon possible in all cultures and historical epochs. With all their respective particularities and differences, all the so-called high cultures (China,

---

7. Around these categories produced during European colonial dominance of the world, there exist a good many lines of debate: Subaltern studies, postcolonial studies, cultural studies, and multiculturalism are the current ones. There is also a flourishing bibliography, too long to be cited here, lined with famous names sucah as Ranajit Guha, Gayatri Spivak, Edward Said, Homi Bhabha, and Stuart Hall.

8. On the theoretical propositions of this conception of power, see Quijano n.d. 'Coloniality of power and its Institutions.' Paper presented at conference Coloniality and Its Disciplinary Sites, April 1999, Binghamton University, Binghamton, NY.

India, Egypt, Greece, Maya-Aztec, Tawantin-suyo) prior to the current world-system unequivocally exhibit signs of that modernity, including rational science and the secularization of thought. In truth, it would be almost ridiculous at these levels of historical research to attribute to non-European cultures a mythic-magical mentality, for example, as a defining trait in opposition to rationality and science as characteristics of Europe. Therefore, apart from their symbolic contents, cities, temples, palaces, pyramids or monumental cities (such as Machu Picchu or Borobudur), irrigation, large thoroughfares, technologies, metallurgy, mathematics, calendars, writing, philosophy, histories, armies, and wars clearly demonstrate the scientific development in each one of the high cultures that took place long before the formation of Europe as a new id-entity.

In the first place, the current model of global power is the first effectively global one in world history in several specific senses. First, it is the first where in each sphere of social existence all historically known forms of control of respective social relations are articulated, configuring in each area only one structure with systematic relations between its components and, by the same means, its whole. Second, it is the first model where each structure of each sphere of social existence is under the hegemony of an institution produced within the process of formation and development of that same model of power. Thus, in the control of labor and its resources and products, it is the capitalist enterprise; in the control of sex and its resources and products, the bourgeois family; in the control of authority and its resources and products, the nation-state; in the control of intersubjectivity, Eurocentrism.'? Third, each one of those institutions exists in a relation of interdependence with each one of the others. Therefore, the model of power is configured as a system.'9 Fourth, finally, this model of global power is the first that covers the entire planet's population.

In this specific sense, humanity in its totality constitutes today the first historically known global *world-system,* not only a world, as were the Chinese, Hindu, Egyptian, Hellenic-Roman, Aztec-Mayan, or Tawantin-suyan. None of those worlds had in common but one colonial/imperial dominant. And though it is a sort of common sense in the Eurocentric vision, it is by no means certain that all the peoples incorporated into one of those worlds would have had in common a basic perspective on the relation between that which is human and the rest of the universe. The colonial dominators of each one of those worlds did not have the conditions, nor, probably, the interest for homogenizing the basic forms of social existence for all the populations under their dominion. On the other hand, the modern world-system that began to form with the colonization of America, has in common three central elements that affect the quotidian life of the totality of the global population: the coloniality of power, capitalism, and Eurocentrism... Its globality means that there is a basic level of common social practices and a

---

9. I mean 'system' in the sense that the relations between parts and the totality are not arbitrary and that the latter has hegemony over the parts in the orientation of the movement of the whole. But not in a systematic sense, as the relations of the parts among themselves and with the whole are not logically functional. This happens only in machines and organisms, never is social relations.

central sphere of common value orientation for the entire world. Consequently, the hegemonic institutions of each province of social existence are universal to the population of the world as intersubjective models, as illustrated by the nation-state, the bourgeois family, the capitalist corporation, and the Eurocentric rationality.

From this perspective, it is necessary to admit that the colonization of America, its immediate consequences in the global market, and the formation of a new model of global power are a truly tremendous historical change and that they affect not only Europe but the entire globe. This is not a change in a known world that merely altered some of its traits. It is a change in the world as such. This is, without doubt, the founding element of the new subjectivity: the perception of historical change. It is this element that unleashed the process of the constitution of a new perspective about time and about history. The perception of change brings about a new idea of the future, since it is the only territory of time where the changes can occur. The future is an open temporal territory. Time can be new, and so not merely the extension of the past. And in this way history can be perceived now not only as something that happens, something natural or produced by divine decisions or mysteries as destiny, but also as something that can be produced by the action of people, by their calculations, their intention, their decisions, and therefore as something that can be designed, and consequently, can have meaning (Quijano 1988a).

With America an entire universe of new material relations and intersubjectivities was initiated. It is pertinent to admit that the concept of modernity does not refer only to what happens with subjectivity (despite all the tremendous importance of that process), to the individual ego, to a new universe of intersubjective relations between individuals and the peoples integrated into the new world-system and its specific model of global power. The concept of modernity accounts equally for the changes in the material dimensions of social relations (i.e., world capitalism, coloniality of power). That is to say, the changes that occur on all levels of social existence, and therefore happen to their individual members, are the same in their material and intersubjective dimensions. And since 'modernity' is about processes that were initiated with the emergence of America, of a new model of global power (the first world-system), and of the integration of all the peoples of the globe in that process, it is also essential to admit that it is about an entire historical period. In other words, starting with America, a new space/time was constituted materially and subjectively: this is what the concept of modernity names.

Capitalist determinations, however, required also (and in the same historical movement) that material and intersubjective social processes could not have a place but within social relations of exploitation and domination. For the controllers of power, the control of capital and the market were and are what decides the ends, the means, and the limits of the process. The market is the foundation but also the limit of possible social equality among people. For those exploited by capital, and in general those dominated by the model of power, modernity generates a horizon of liberation for people of every relation, structure, or institution linked to domination and exploitation, but also the social conditions in order to advance toward the direction of that horizon. Modernity is, then, also a question of conflicting social interests. One of these interests is the continued democratization of social existence. In this sense, every concept of modernity is necessarily ambiguous and contradictory (Quijano 1998a; 2000b).

## Coloniality of Power and Eurocentrism

The intellectual conceptualization of the process of modernity produced a perspective of knowledge and a mode of producing knowledge that gives a very tight account of the character of the global model of power: colo-nial/modern, capitalist, and Eurocentered. This perspective and concrete mode of producing knowledge is Eurocentrism.[10]

Eurocentrism is, as used here, the name of a perspective of knowledge whose systematic formation began in Western Europe before the middle of the seventeenth century, although some of its roots are, without doubt, much older. In the following centuries this perspective was made globally hegemonic, traveling the same course as the dominion of the European bourgeois class. Its constitution was associated with the specific bourgeois secularization of European thought and with the experiences and necessities of the global model of capitalist (colonial/modern) and Eurocen-tered power established since the colonization of America.

This category of Eurocentrism does not involve all of the knowledge of history of all of Europe or Western Europe in particular. It does not refer to all the modes of knowledge of all Europeans and all epochs. It is instead a specific rationality or perspective of knowledge that was made globally hegemonic, colonizing and overcoming other previous or different conceptual formations and their respective concrete knowledges, as much in Europe as in the rest of the world.

## Capital and Capitalism

First, the theory of history as a linear sequence of universally valid events needs to be reopened in relation to America as a major question in the social-scientific debate. More so when such a concept of history is applied to labor and the control of labor conceptualized as modes of production in the sequence precapitalism-capitalism. From the Eurocentric point of view, reciprocity, slavery, serfdom, and independent commodity production are all perceived as a historical sequence prior to commodification of the labor force. They are precapital. And they are considered not only different, but radically incompatible with capital. The fact is, however, that in America they did not emerge in a linear historical sequence; none of them was a mere extension of the old precapitalist form, nor were they incompatible with capital.

---

10. The literature on the debate about Eurocentrism is growing rapidly. See Amin 1989 for a different (although somewhat related) position than the one that orients this article.

Slavery, in America, was deliberately established and organized as a commodity in order to produce goods for the world market and to serve the purposes and needs of capitalism. Likewise, the serfdom imposed on Indians, including the redefinition of the institutions of reciprocity, was organized in order to serve the same ends: to produce merchandise for the global market. Independent commodity production was established and expanded for the same purposes. This means that all the forms of labor and control of labor were not only simultaneously performed in America, but they were also articulated around the axis of capital and the global market. Consequently, all of these forms of labor were part of a new model of organization and labor control. Together these forms of labor configured a new economic system: capitalism.

Capital, as a social relation based on the commodification of the labor force, was probably born in some moment around the eleventh or twelfth century in some place in the southern regions of the Iberian and/or Italian peninsulas and, for known reasons, in the Islamic world.[11] Capital is thus much older than America. But before the emergence of America, it was nowhere structurally articulated with all the other forms of organization and control of the labor force and labor, nor was it predominant over any of them. Only with America could capital consolidate and obtain global predominance, becoming precisely the axis around which all forms of labor were articulated to satisfy the ends of the world market, configuring a new pattern of global control on labor, its resources, and products: world capitalism. Therefore, capitalism as a system of relations of production, that is, as the heterogeneous linking of all forms of control on labor and its products under the dominance of capital, was constituted in history only with the emergence of America. Beginning with that historical moment, capital has always existed, and continues to exist to this day, as the central axis of capitalism. Never has capitalism been predominant in some other way, on a global and worldwide scale, and in all probability it would not have been able to develop otherwise.

## The New Dualism

For the sake of my argument, it is pertinent to revisit the question of the relations between the body and the non-body in the Eurocentric perspective, because of its importance both in the Eurocentric mode of producing knowledge and to the fact that modern dualism has close relations with race and gender. My aim here is to connect a well-known problematic with the coloniality of power.

The differentiation between body and non-body in human experience is virtually universal in the history of humanity. It is also common to all historically known 'cultures' or 'civilizations,' part of the copresence of both as unseparable dimensions of humanness. The process of the separation of these two elements (body and nonbody) of the human being is part of the long history of the Christian world founded on the idea of the primacy of the soul above the body. But

---

11. See Wallerstein 1983; and Arrighi 1994.

the history of this point in particular shows a long and unresolved ambivalence of Christian theology. The soul is the privileged object of salvation, but in the end, the body is resurrected as the culmination of salvation. The primacy of the soul was emphasized, perhaps exasperated, during the culture of the repression of Christianity, as resulted from the conflicts with Muslims and Jews in the fifteenth and sixteenth centuries, during the peak of the Inquisition. And because the body was the basic object of repression, the soul could appear almost separated from the intersubjective relations at the interior of the Christian world. But this issue was not systematically theorized, discussed and elaborated until Descartes's writing (1963-67) culminated the process of bourgeois secularization of Christian thought.[12]

With Descartes the mutation of the ancient dualist approach to the body and the nonbody took place.[13] What was a permanent copresence of both elements in each stage of the human being, with Descartes came a radical separation between reason/subject and body. Reason was not only a secularization of the idea of the soul in the theological sense, but a mutation into a new entity, the reason/subject, the only entity capable of rational knowledge. The body was and could be nothing but an object of knowledge. From this point of view the human being is, par excellence, a being gifted with reason, and this gift was conceived as localized exclusively in the soul. Thus the body, by definition incapable of reason, does not have anything that meets reason/subject. The radical separation produced between reason/subject and body and their relations should be seen only as relations between the human subject/reason and the human body/nature, or between spirit and nature. In this way, in Eurocentric rationality the body was fixed as object of knowledge, outside of the environment of subject/reason.

Without this objectification of the body as nature, its expulsion from the sphere of the spirit, the 'scientific' theorization of the problem of race... would have hardly been possible. From the Eurocentric perspective, certain races are condemned as inferior for not being rational subjects. They are objects of study, consequently bodies closer to nature. In a sense, they became dominable and exploitable. According to the myth of the state of nature and the chain of the civilizing process that culminates in European civilization, some races—blacks, American Indians, or yellows—are closer to nature than whites.[14] It was only within this peculiar perspective that non-European peoples were considered as an object of knowledge and domination/exploitation by Europeans virtually to the end of World War II.

---

12. I have always wondered about the origin of one of liberalism's most pernicious propositions: Ideas should be respected, but the body can be tortured, crushed, and killed. Latin Americans repeatedly cite with admiration the defiant phrase spoken while a martyr of the anticolonial battles was being beheaded: 'Barbarians, ideas cannot be beheaded!' I am now sure that the origin of the idea can be found in the new Cartesian dualism that made the body into mere nature'.
13. Bousquié (1994) asserts that Cartesianism is a new radical dualism.
14. The fact that the only alternative category to the Occident was, and still is, the Orient, while blacks (Africa) or Indians (American before the United States) did not have the honor of being other to Europe, speaks volumes about the processes of Eurocentered subjectivity.

This new and radical dualism affected not only the racial relations of domination, but the older sexual relations of domination as well. Women, especially the women of inferior races ('women of color'), remained stereotyped together with the rest of the bodies, and their place was... inferior for their race, so that they were considered much closer to nature or (as was the case with black slaves) directly within nature. It is probable (although the question remains to be investigated) that the new idea of gender has been elaborated after the new and radical dualism of the Eurocentric cognitive perspective in the articulation of the coloniality of power.

Furthermore, the new radical dualism was amalgamated in the eighteenth century with the new mystified ideas of 'progress' and of the state of nature in the human trajectory: the foundational myths of the Eurocentric version of modernity. The peculiar dualist/evolutionist historical perspective was linked to the foundational myths. Thus, all non-Europeans could be considered as pre-European and at the same time displaced on a certain historical chain from the primitive to the civilized, from the rational to the irrational, from the traditional to the modern, from the magic-mythic to the scientific. In other words, from the non-European/pre-European to something that in time will be Europeanized or modernized. Without considering the entire experience of colonialism and coloniality, this intellectual trademark, as well as the long-lasting global hegemony of Eurocentrism, would hardly be explicable. The necessities of capital as such alone do not exhaust, could not exhaust, the explanation of the character and trajectory of this perspective of knowledge.

## Eurocentrism and Historical Experience in Latin America

The Eurocentric perspective of knowledge operates as a mirror that distorts what it reflects, as we can see in the Latin American historical experience. That is to say, what we Latin Americans find in that mirror is not completely chimerical, since we possess so many and such important historically European traits in many material and intersubjective aspects. But at the same time we are profoundly different. Consequently, when we look in our Eurocentric mirror, the image that we see is not just composite, but also necessarily partial and distorted. Here the tragedy is that we have all been led, knowingly or not, wanting it or not, to see and accept that image as our own and as belonging to us alone. In this way, we continue being what we are not. And as a result we can never identify our true problems, much less resolve them, except in a partial and distorted way.

## The Nation-State in America: The United States

In the Anglo-American area, the colonial occupation of territory was violent from the start. But before independence, known in the United States as the American Revolution, the occupied territory was very small. The Indians did not inhabit occupied territory—they were not colonized. Therefore, the diverse Indigenous peoples were formally recognized as nations, and international commercial relations were practiced with them, including the formation of military alliances in the wars between English and French colonists. Indians were not incorporated into the space of Anglo-American colonial domination. Thus when the history of the new nation-state called the United States of America began, Indians were excluded from that new society and were considered foreigners. Later on, they were dispossessed of their lands and were almost exterminated. Only then were the survivors imprisoned in North American society as a colonized race. In the beginning, then, colonial/racial relations existed only between whites and blacks. This last group was fundamental for the economy of the colonial society, just as during the first long moment of the new nation. However, blacks were a relatively limited demographic minority, while whites composed the large majority.

At the foundation of the United States as an independent country, the process of the constitution of a new model of power went together with the configuration of the nation-state. In spite of the colonial relation of domination between whites and blacks and the colonial extermination of the Indigenous population, we must admit, given the overwhelming majority of whites, that the new nation-state was genuinely representative of the greater part of the population. The social whiteness of North American society included the millions of European immigrants arriving in the second half of the nineteenth century. Furthermore, the conquest of Indigenous territories resulted in the abundance of the offer of a basic resource of production: land. Therefore, the appropriation of land could be concentrated in a few large states, while at the same time distributed in a vast proportion of middling and small properties. Through these mechanisms of land distribution, the whites found themselves in a position to exercise a notably democratic participation in the generation and management of public authority. The coloniality of the new model of power was not cancelled, however, since American Indians and blacks could not have a place at all in the control of the resources of production, or in the institutions and mechanisms of public authority.

About halfway through the nineteenth century, Tocqueville (1835, chaps. 16-17) observed that in the United States people of such diverse cultural, ethnic, and national origins were all incorporated into something that seemed like a machine for national reidentification; they rapidly became U.S. citizens and acquired a new national identity, while preserving for some time their original identities. Tocqueville found that the basic mechanism for this process of nationalization was the opening of democratic participation in political life for all recently arrived immigrants. They were brought toward an intense political participation, although with the choice to participate or not. But Tocqueville also saw that two specific groups were not allowed participation in political life: blacks and Indians. This discrimination was the limit of the impressive and massive process of modern nation-state formation in the young republic of the United States of America. Tocqueville did not neglect to advise that unless social and political discrimination were to be eliminated, the process of national construction would be limited. A century later, another European, Gunnar Myrdall (1944), saw these same limitations in the national process of the United States when the source of immigration changed and immigrants were no longer white Europeans but, for the most part, nonwhites from Latin America and Asia. The colonial relations of the whites with the new immigrants introduced a new risk for the reproduction of the nation. Without doubt, those risks are increasing this very day insofar as the old myth of the melting pot has been forcefully abandoned and racism tends to be newly sharpened and violent.

In sum, the coloniality of the relations of domination/exploitation/ conflict between whites and nonwhites was not, at the moment of the constitution of a new independent state, sufficiently powerful to impede the relative, although real and important, democratization of the control of the means of production and of the state. At the beginning control rested only among the whites, true, but with enough vigor so that nonwhites could claim it later as well. The entire power structure could be configured in the trajectory and orientation of reproducing and broadening the democratic foundations of the nation-state. It is this trajectory to which, undoubtedly, the idea of the American Revolution refers.

## Latin America: The Southern Cone and the White Majority

At first glance, the situation in the countries of the so-called Southern Cone of Latin America (Argentina, Chile, and Uruguay) was similar to what happened in the United States. Indians, for the most part, were not integrated into colonial society, insofar as they had more or less the same social and cultural structure of the North American Indians. Socially, both groups were not available to become exploited workers, not condemnable to forced labor for the colonists. In these three countries, the black slaves were also a minority during the colonial period, in contrast with other regions dominated by the Spanish or Portuguese. After independence, the dominants in the countries of the Southern Cone, as was the case in the United States, considered the conquest of the territories that the Indigenous peoples populated, as well as the extermination of these inhabitants, necessary as an expeditious form of homogenizing the national population and facilitating the process of constituting a modern nation-state 'a la europea.' In Argentina and Uruguay this was done in the nineteenth century, and in Chile during the first three decades of the twentieth century. These countries also attracted millions of European immigrants, consolidating, in appearance, the whiteness of the societies of Argentina, Uruguay, and Chile and the process of homogenization.

Land distribution was a basic difference in those countries, especially in Argentina, in comparison with the case of North America. While in the United States the distribution of land happened in a less concentrated way over a long period, in Argentina the extreme concentration of land possession, particularly in lands taken from Indigenous peoples, made impossible any type of democratic social relations among the whites themselves. Instead of a democratic society capable of representing and politically organizing into a democratic state, what was constituted was an oligarchic society and state, only partially dismantled after World War II... Its rapid transformation in the last quarter of the eighteenth century as one of the more prosperous areas in the world market was one of the main forces that drove a massive migration from southern, eastern, and central Europe in the following century. But this migratory population did not find in Argentina a society with a sufficiently dense and stable structure, history, and identity to incorporate and identify themselves with it, as occurred in the United States. At the end of the nineteenth century, immigrants from Europe comprised more than 80 percent of Buenos Aires's population. They did not immediately enforce the national identity, instead preferring their own European cultural differences, while at the same time explicitly rejecting the identity associated with Latin America's heritage and, in particular, any relationship with the Indigenous population.[15]

The process of the racial homogenization of a society's members, imagined from a Eurocentric perspective as one characteristic and condition of modern nation-states, was carried out in the countries of the Southern Cone not by means of the decolonization of social and political relations among the diverse sectors of the population, but through a massive elimination of some of them (Indians) and the exclusion of others (blacks and mestizos). Homogenization was achieved not by means of the fundamental democratization of social and political relations, but by the exclusion of a significant part of the population, one that since the sixteenth century had been racially classified and marginalized from citizenship and democracy.

> [I]n certain Ibero-American societies, the small white minority in control of the independent states and the colonial societies could have had neither consciousness nor national interests in common with the American Indians, blacks, and mestizos.

On the contrary, their social interests were explicitly antagonistic to American Indian serfs and black slaves, given that their privileges were made from precisely the dominance and exploitation of those peoples in such a way that there was no area of common interest between whites and nonwhites and, consequently, no common national interest for all of them. Therefore, from the point of view of the dominators, their social interests were much closer to the interests of their European peers, and consequently they were always inclined to follow the interests of the European bourgeoisie.

In reality, each category used to characterize the Latin American political process has always been a partial and distorted way to look at this reality. That is an inevitable consequence of the Eurocentric perspective, in which a linear and one-directional evolutionism is amalgamated contradictorily with the dualist vision of history, a new and radical dualism that separates nature from society, the body from reason, that does not know what to do with the question of totality (simply denying it like the old empiricism or the new postmodernism) or under-

15. Even in the 1920s, as in the whole twentieth century, Hector Murena, an important member f the Argentinean intelligentsia, proclaimed, 'We are Europeans exiled in these savage pampas.' See Imaz 1964. During Argentina's social, political, and cultural battles in the 1960s, cabecita negra was the nickname for racial discrimination.

stands it only in an organic or systemic way, making it, thus, into a distorted perspective, impossible to be used, except in error.

It is not, then, an accident that we have been defeated, for the moment, in both revolutionary projects, in America and in the entire world. What we could advance and conquer in terms of political and civil rights in a necessary redistribution of power (of which the decolonization of power is the presupposition and point of departure) is now being torn down in the process of the reconcentration of the control of power in global capitalism and of its management of the coloniality of power by the same functionaries. Consequently, it is time to learn to free ourselves from the Eurocentric mirror where our image is always, necessarily, distorted. It is time, finally, to cease being what we are not.

# References

Amin, Samir. 1989. *Eurocentrism*. New York: Monthly Review Press.

Arrighi, Giovanni. 1994. *The Long Twentieth Century*. London: Verso.

Baer, Werner. 1962. 'The Economics of Prebisch and ECLA'. *Economic Development and Culture Change* 10.

Bousquié, Paul. 1994. *Les corps, cet inconnu*. Paris: Harmattan.

Imaz, Eugenio. 1964. *Nosotros mañana*. Buenos Aires: Editorial Sudamericana.

Mark, Jonathan. 1994. *Human Biodiversity, Genes, Race, and History*. New York: Aldyne de Gruyter.

Prebisch, Raúl. 1959. 'Commercial Policy in the Underdeveloped Countries'. *American Economic Review, Papers and Proceedings*. 49: 251-273.

_____. 1960. *The Economic Development in Latin America and Its Principal Problems*. New York: ECLA, United Nations.

Quijano, Aníbal. 1999. ¡Que Tal Raza!' In *Familia y cambio social*. Lima: CECOSAM.

_____. 2000. 'Coloniality of Power, Eurocentrism and Latin America.' *Nepantla: Views from the South*. V. 1. I. 3: 533-580.

_____. n.d. 'Coloniality of Power and Its Institutions'. Paper presented at conference Coloniality and Its Disciplinary Sites. April 1999. Binghamton University, Binghamton, NY.

Quijano, Aníbal and Immanuel Wallerstein. 1992. 'Americanity as a Concept, or the Americas in the Imaginary of the Modern World-System'. *International Journal of Social Science*. V. 134: 549-559.

Wallerstein, Immanuel. 1983. *Historical Capitalism*. London: Verso.

# QUEER INDIGENOUS MANIFESTO

Aimee Carillo Rowe

2017[1]

Wander with me a bit as I tack between my moving locations, grounded intersectionalities, and activist theories and practices to name and claim forms of queer resistance, inspired by Indigenous knowledges of life and land. Let this move mobilize a manifesto of queer Indigenous futurity. I feel it like moving between inhale and exhale: inhaling, I share experience of my engagement with queer family across recent Trump protest activities; exhaling, I reflect on the settler consciousness that informs forms of resistance. The breath is the constant reminder that we are literally constituted through our relations as with every breath we are 'becoming-other.'[2] We inhale particles of dust, earth, stone; oxygen from trees and plants; the breath and bodily scents of humans, birds, reptiles, four-leggeds; exhaust from vehicles and industry. We exhale ourselves, our particles, water, our $CO_2$ that become part of 'all our relations,' those connectivities that 'in Native thought, place and the four elements of life—water, fire, earth, wind' as 'relatives to the Indigenous human world.'[3] This observation about breath intends to set an Indigenous frame on this writing and invite readers to join me in breathing and becoming-in-relation, through the pulp of the page, the glow of the computer, and an engagement with the animacy of the life within and around you.

A manifesto is a 'published verbal declaration of the intentions, motives, or views of . . . an individual, group, political party or government,'[4] which draws on previously published documentation to promote changes and state the commitments of a community. I call this writing a manifesto with the intent that the queer *QED* community declare its intentions to align our vision, actions, and interventions with Indigenous struggles for life and land. *QED*, the journal's editors explain, references 'that which had to be demonstrated'[5]—a connotation that accentuates the journal's commitment to praxis. In creating a queer Indigenous manifesto, I merge theory and activist practice to mobilize such an emphasis on

1. Source: Rowe, Aimee Carillo. 'A Queer Indigenous Manifesto'. *QED: A Journal in GLBTQ Worldmaking* 4, no. 2 (2017): 93–99. https://doi.org/10.14321/qed.4.2.0093.
2. Elspeth Probyn's sense of 'becoming-other'—placing oneself at the edge of 'subjectivity' that arises not so much through the desire for an-other, but through recognition of the self one must become in this striving. Elspeth Probyn, Outside Belongings(New York: Routledge, 1996).
3. Patrisia Gonzales, *Red Medicine: Traditional Indigenous Rites of Birthing and Healing*(Tempe: University of Arizona Press, 2012), xxi.
4. Wikipedia, accessed March 6, 2017, https://en.wikipedia.org/wiki/Manifesto. [End Page 97]
5. QED: A Journal of GLBTQ Worldmaking, accessed March 6, 2017, http://msupress.org/journals/qed/.

praxis that sees reversing the ongoing processes of Indigenous erasure—and foregrounding Indigenous theory and activism—as its central project.

What kind of decolonial politics might we imagine and mobilize at this historic juncture, in which we find the mask of the U.S. settler nation state torn from its hinges? I want to expand the metaphorical and material grounds of a queer Indigenous politics that works through radical and alternative forms of relationality, land, and family. This work, in part, entails interrogating and remaking our various relationships to land and its dis/possession. As I reckon with my identity as a queer settler Indigenous-identified Xicana, I wrangle with the incommensurate forces, affective and material investments, and commitments that shape all-my-relations. This labor leads me to practice ways of being in the world that are organized through alternative relational structures and in aligning my political praxis with Native political projects and sensibilities.

When we stepped onto the Metro with 100,000 others to protest this regime of hate under Trump, the passengers began a round of Woody Guthrie's, 'This Land is Your Land.' It was January 23, 2017, the day a Million Women Marched in Los Angeles, Washington, DC, Chicago, New York—and countless medium and small cities around the country. And this doesn't even count the actions around the globe, like the thousands who poured into the dusty streets of Granada, Nicaragua, where our queer kin live. The song rose and then faded, like a passing gust of wind. It might have become a more sustained gale, like the Santa Ana winds that sweep through the Los Angeles basin; instead it just tickled the hair of my five-year-old daughter, who heard it and tucked her head into the wing of my neck and hair. 'This Land is Your Land, this land is my land, from California to the New York Island. From the redwood forest, to the gulf stream waters. This land was made for you and me.' Perhaps the song lost steam because of its vexed history as a protest that was revised to acquiesce to the threat of the McCarthy regime's gag tactics, but you'd think protestors would sense the alignments between our struggles and those Guthrie named.[6] I think perhaps it was something else that took the wind from our song.

I grew up with folk songs like this. I have always found it moving when my mom and her eight-woman folk group, The Why Nots, would harmonize their voices, mandolins, and guitars around the curves, dips, and trills of This Land, among others. The other children would sit at the feet of our mothers and sway to their music, play games, sing along, eat snacks. Songs like these taught me that this land is MY land. Countless images, stories, movies, TV shows, the patriotic songs we sang in school—all of these cultural narratives confirmed my place on this land. Never once did it cross my mind that this land is Indigenous land. I was raised in the womb of a settler consciousness that has confirmed—through the heart-felt repetition of songs, shows, stories and images—my firm emplacement on and rightful ownership of these Native lands.

---

6. The lyrics that Guthrie was forced to cut marked the privatization of land. 'There was a big high wall there that tried to stop me. The sign was painted, said 'Private Property.' But on the backside, it didn't say nothing. This land was made for you and me.' https://en.wikipedia.org/wiki/This_Land_Is_Your_Land, accessed February 24, 2017.

How is it that I grew up running wild in the hills of Southern California—reeling as developers overtook more and more of our playground—and never thought about the people from whom the land was/is continually expropriated? How had I, a young queer Chicanita with my own buried Native ancestry, failed to learn the stories of how this land came/comes to be my land? This story of emplacement is contingent upon Native extraction, dispossession, and extinction, organized through a settler logic constituted through Indigenous erasure.[7] This pervasive invisibility works to naturalize the supremacy of settler identity through repeated affirmations of settler belonging on occupied Indigenous land through its attendant erasure of Indigenous existence—the production of the Native as always-already 'disappearing.'

As we sat at the feet of our mothers singing, 'this land is my land,' my mind drifted to forests, beaches, hills and mountains, places I liked to play. Never did my imagination glimpse the genocide of Native peoples through which my land was/is secured. This is because 'uninhabited wilderness had to be created before it could be preserved, and this type of landscape became reified in the first national parks.'[8] And the 'creation' of this land was made possible through the creation of, in the words of Oglala Lakota Sioux elder, Black Elk, 'islands' that incrementally and increasingly separated Native people from the four-leggeds through the construction of Indian reservations and nature preserves. The conversion of this land mobilized settler conceptions of 'Indian wilderness' as 'an uninhabited Eden' that would be the playground of 'vacationing Americans.'[9] This is how this land is my land.

The gust of 'This Land Is Your Land' that rose and fell on the day of the Million Woman March reveals both the possibilities and limit points of left-liberal activism in this historical moment of orange-on-brown-and-black-and-queer-and-Muslim-and-undocumented neofascism. This moment provides a point of entry for reflections on how queer Indigenous praxis might interrupt the ongoing cycle of dispossession and disappearance through which 'my land' has been secured. How might we take responsibility for restoring our own 'right relationships' to land?[10] This labor the settler must undertake to participate in decolonization is complex, contradictory, and painful, grounded in the 'incommensurate' investments settler, slave, and Native place in life and land. A queer Indigenous praxis transforms possessive and privatized relationships to land, grounded 'in belief that 'this land is your land, this land is my land,'' to dismantle settler expansion.[11] Perhaps the rise and fall of the song gestures toward the vexed quality and affective structures that animate, consciously or not, such a politics of decolonization. Is there a subconscious recognition that 'this land' is actually

---

7. Andrea Smith, Conquest: Sexual Violence and American Indian Genocide(Cambridge, MA: South End Press, 2005).
8. Mark David Spence, Dispossessing the Wilderness: Indian Removal and the Making of the National Park(Oxford: Oxford University Press, 1999), 5.
9. Ibid., 2.
10. Aman Sium, Chandni Desai, and Eric Ritskes Ontario, 'Towards the 'tangible unknown': Decolonization and the Indigenous Future,' Decolonization: Indigeneity, Education and Society1, no. 1 (2012): 3.
11. Ibid.

not 'my land,' but is Indigenous land? How might queer left activists consciously and actively engage a decolonial politics as central to our strategy for a sustained response to and reworking of the insidious systemization of hate under a Trump regime?

A queer Indigenous Manifesto calls for decolonizing our activism by foregrounding the role of Native sovereignty and land struggles, lifeways, and treaties in cultivating our political strategies and visions for the material and metaphorical grounds of our movement. In this historic moment in which undocumented, Muslim, and LGBTQ communities are under attack, we must continue to link the struggles to protect people's basic humanity with those of Indigenous communities who are now enduring aggressive dispossession. So, we must be aware of what these struggles are. In his first week as 'president,' Donald Trump signed an executive order to continue construction of Dakota Access Pipeline (DAPL), which violates treaties with the Dakota Sioux to modernize and improve U.S. infrastructure. The White House website promises their efforts will 'Transform America's crumbling infrastructure into a golden opportunity for accelerated economic growth and more rapid productivity.'[12] The quote reifies a long history of Native dispossession under Manifest Destiny, like the gold rush, which created a twentyfold increase in settler populations (from 10,000 to 220,000) as Native populations plummeted (from 275,000 prior to Spanish settlement to just 30,000 after the gold rush). Such projects create 'golden opportunities' for capitalists to gain wealth through ongoing Native genocide, displacement, and dispossession. Audra Simpson describes the larger Keystone dam project as a for-private-profit 'compact' between big oil and local and federal governments.[13]

As queer allies to Indigenous struggles, then, our work is to align our political action and consciousness to fight settler colonial expansion. The Pipeline is just one example of countless large and small affronts on Indigenous land that marks the formation of settler nation states, for 'territoriality is settler colonialism's irreducible element.'[14] Land for settlers is a resource to be exploited, a 'golden opportunity' for generating wealth. Land for Indigenous peoples is life, a 'field of 'relationships of things to each other,'' a way of 'knowing, experiencing, and relating with the world.'[15] So the erosion of Native land holdings through settler expansion like the Dakota Access Pipeline is an affront to Indigenous lifeways. Native dispossession is secured through ongoing treaty violations denoted through the figure of the 'x-mark'—a 'sign of consent in a context of coercion'

---

12. Donald Trump, accessed February 1, 2017, https://www.donaldjtrump.com/policies/an-americas-infrastructure-first-plan.
13. Audra Simpson, 'The State is a Man: Theresa Spence, Loretta Saunders and the Gender of Settler Sovereignty,' Theory and Event19, no. 4 (2016): 8.
14. Patrick Wolfe, 'Settler Colonialism and the Elimination of the Native' Journal of Genocide Research, 8, no. 4 (2006): 387–409.
15. Glen Coulthard, 'From Wards of the State to Subjects of Recognition? Marx, Indigenous Peoples, and the Politics of Dispossession in Denendeh,' in Theorizing Native Studies, eds. Audra Simpson and Andrea Smith (Durham, NC: Duke University Press, 2014), 70.

that denotes Indian agency in a context of 'little choice.'[16] The DAPL, according to the Standing Rock Tribe, violates the Sioux Treaty of 1868.[17]

It seems that at this historic moment in which a president seeks to unravel the democratic elements of our government, while people pour into the streets in unprecedented numbers, might be a most productive time to imagine a futurity in which Indigenous frameworks and land, human, and relational practices guide our steps forward. Indigenous futurities decenter the role of the U.S. nation-state in its politics and imaginary to focus on the reassertion of Native sovereignties that empower Native peoples to care for their people and their lands—on their own terms.[18] At this moment, in which the U.S. nation-state comes under radical scrutiny, let us imagine all-our-relations beyond the limiting liberal politics of nationalism.

When I reflect on the round of 'This Land' that rose and fell on the Metro as we protesters rode to the Million Woman March, I take heart in both the rise and the fall. In this moment, I was with the protestors, holding my daughter then passing her along to my friends, a network my mother refers to as 'Mothers and Others.' These women are family to us. And all of these Metro riders are kin in some form, all of us here to protest the inauguration, alternative facts, and the barrage of Executive Orders that have ensued. We might read the rise of 'This Land' as some kind of recognition, conscious or not, that this struggle really is about this land. This stolen land is the condition of possibility for all the horrors that follow. This land, twisted into resource through the violence of the drill, the bulldozer, the jackhammer. When the round of 'This Land' fell, perhaps it marked our recognition of the untenable logics of childlike settler innocence and a glimmer of the fact that this land is Red—and so not really free at all.

---

16. Scott Richard Lyons, X-Marks: Native Signatures of Assent(Minneapolis: University of Minnesota Press, 2010), 1.

17. Lauren Kimmel, 'Does the Dakota Access Pipeline Violate Treaty Law?' Michigan Journal of International Law38 (2016), http://www.mjilonline.org/does-the-dakota-access-pipeline-violate-treaty-law.

18. Hōkūani K. Aikau, 'Following the Alaloa Kīpapa of Our Ancestors: A Trans-Indigenous Futurity without the State,' American Quarterly67, no. 3 (2015): 659.

# CORRESPONDENCE WITH DOROTHY DAY

Lolita Lebron

1969-1976[1]

*In a series of dozens of handwritten letters, Puerto Rican patriot Lolita Lebron and North American Catholic pacifist Dorothy Day exchanged news, thoughts about the Gospel, and personal message of appreciation and solidarity. Day, now being considered for beatification (sainthood) by the Vatican, was the founder of the Catholic Worker movement, a significant base for progressive and leftist Catholic thought and organization. In the wobbly script of an elderly woman, Day noted in the margins of an early letter that Lolita was 'a Puerto Rican Independence activist' who was serving 'many years behind bars for shooting at the Visitors Gallery in the U.S. House of Representatives.' Lebron's militant act in Congress made worldwide headlines in 1954; in addition to the dramatic tactics which carefully resulted in no loss of life, Lebron also became a global icon as the first female commander of a Latin American revolutionary movement. Day and Lebron met during one of many prison visits which the Catholic Worker movement saw as part of their regular calling. The two women became close friends.*

*These excerpts from the never-before-published exchange between Day and Lebron contain Lolita's writings to Dorothy. They begin here following commentary by Lebron of Puerto Rico's nationalist-oriented newspaper* Claridad.

Dear Dorothy,

Your Catholic Worker is a jewel of Christian love and dedication to the cause of the Oppressed, to Peace, to a better world. As a member of this world, I thank you and love you and wish to express my best wishes and my love and gratitude to you and to all the Catholic Workers there with you.

Thank you for your wonderful letter, for those so warm and loving handwritten lines you so kindly wrote to me. Please forgive me Dorothy if you'd rather not hear my words, but they are short of expressing my humble but true and profound sentiments towards you, in whom Jesus delights. I love Jesus and in the love of

---

1. Including portions of notes from March 28, 1969; August 1, 1970; April 13, 1971; and May 4, 1976. https://www.marquette.edu/library/archives/Mss/DDCW/cw-sc.php

this, Dorothy, the world grows and flourishes and I become emotional and mystical – which is to say deeply moved by God in here.

I am feeling fine. I would appreciate any book or books you might send me. I love your books and look forward to reading all of your works. I like history, literature, philosophy. I like all serious books...and enjoy your books especially because they teach Love, Peace, Beauty, and – through loving courage and sacrifice – they give us Christ in your life, and His eternal caress in your heart...

You are my most admired woman. Don Pedro Albizu Campos – my teacher – is my most admired man. He loved the good that Christ revealed to mankind. He sacrificed himself for our country's sovereignty and had the charisma and the light to awaken us to our nation's being—as a People, Sovereign, a People called to be free as all others are called. He never had material things; he lived a poor and most beautiful – though tragic – life. He was tortured and suffered the unbearable at the hands of the oppressors. He never wanted violence for God's people whether on our land or in other countries; his becoming a part of violence was imposed upon him as it was imposed upon the country and people of Puerto Rico. His disciples have proven that he taught love and beauty, valor and sacrifice; he is with Jesus in heaven, his life for us never ceases toward the independence of our nation.

It was through the way of National Freedom that this great man enlightened for me—that my title bearing a Message from God to the Atomic age for the cause: situating Puerto Rico in a very special place among the People and the Nations of Mankind...

Of course, I think you know that Peace without Freedom for my country or any other nation or people cannot be obtained. Pacifists, am sure, cannot forsake my country's right to liberation!...

Dorothy, I am profoundly touched by your sublime gesture in giving me 'your most precious possessions.' This is one of the greatest graces God has bestowed on this unworthy servant. For though I represent my captive nation, I am aware of my unworthiness. God has given Puerto Rico a mission in this age, so He made Puerto Rico very great. But I? I am the most unworthy penitent of his Kingdom.

Eternal love and gratitude,

Lolita Lebron

# 7. REVOLUTIONARY NONVIOLENCE IN THE 21ST CENTURY

*It's hard now to think back now on any 21st century event more internationally significant than the pandemic which shook the world—not only in shockingly numerous and fast deaths but in its stark spotlighting of the capitalist, imperialist, white supremacist, and patriarchal nature of oppressions and dominations which determine to a significant degree who lives and who dies. That some actually profit from this disease, as well as from the continued pillage of the earth and the people—despite the devastation which climate crisis brings in the immediate as well as long term—seems par for the course. It is the 'same old, same old', at a time when people are crying out to never 'return to normal'. Rather people are calling for building new normalcies which will be people-centered and justice-based. Even the cataclysmic events of 9/11 are shadowed by these later, truly global phenomena.*

*It is therefore logical that the final section of this book, looking to encourage and develop new thinking about the praxis in building peaceful and wholly decolonized futures, begins with creative responses. Cooperation Jackson, centered in the poorest part of the U.S. south, led by a new generation of Black radicals and visionary, multi-tactical organizers, writes of the need for a general strike. This is followed by a dialogue by Peoples Strike, a new coalition Cooperation Jackson helped to create to agitate for cross-industry, globally diverse boycotts, work stoppages, and militant actions of all sorts. Here, the south meets the north in stark contrast: the poorest of the poor within the richest nation in history seek leadership from and provide engagement with advanced thinkers and actors in Latin America, Africa, and Asia/Pacific. Thus, a classic European Marxist fits easily into a Zapatista framework, understanding that the way forward must cross old ideological constructs in order to, in the words of Subcomandante Moisés from the jungles of Chiapas, create a beautiful world that 'is only possible if everyone, everyone, everything, struggles to raise it.'*

*Indigenous resistance is central to this beauty, and as Nick Estes, co-founder of The Red Nation and Standing Rock activist, teaches us elsewhere: 'Our history is the Future.' The question of sovereignty here corresponds directly to the still-colonized peoples of the world, who not only include UN-recognized entities such as Western Sahara or Puerto Rico, but also West Papua, Kashmir, Tibet, and the lesser-known Ambazonia[1] in central Africa. Palestinian resistance therefore follows in perfect harmony, as the adage 'our exis-*

---

1. The self-declared state constituting the Northwest Region and Southwest Region of Cameroon.

tence is resistance' rings true for a growing number of displaced of every land. We bring this anthology to a close with a final chapter by Wende Marshall challenging white workers: 'the possibilities for nonviolent revolution rest largely in your hands'.

If a new nonviolence, a decolonized, justice-driven peacemaking, is to emerge from the rubble of contemporary disasters, it must be because the lessons of the wretched of the earth, the most dispossessed who are also the best architects of ingenious social change, are learned and headed by those who must give up privileges while fighting for a complete reallocation of power as we know it. Insurrectionary uprising must become more common and more global than infectious diseases, and our healing must be universal—for all humankind and for the earth.

—The Editors

# POSSIBILITIES OF INSURRECTIONARY NONVIOLENCE

Matt Meyer

---

History is always hardest to grasp in the moment. This is why, in part, poorly taught young students mistake history as having only to do with the deep past. And it is also why so much money and time is spent trying to mold historical interpretations into one or another walled silo which prohibits creative thought and action. The greater the power of a myth—for example, that the most important and effective social change is made by brilliant, saint-like individuals—the greater the chances for any given status quo (no matter how oppressive) to curtail and contain future movements.

This entire book is about breaking down the walls between decades, ideas, and ideologies to reveal useful lessons for the present and the future. And the test of whether these lessons are learned, or are in fact useful, cannot be gleaned from the score on any abstract test. Only in the praxis of insurrectionary uprisings—including street actions, rethinking revolution and nonviolence, destroying colonialism, imperialism, and all forms of oppression in all their varied forms, and the leading of transgressive lives—can we determine our success. This final section of the book, therefore, is our last chance as editors to bring the reader some contemporary tools to help build the path towards a better day.

Wende Marshall and I spent the better part of 2020 struggling to survive the global COVID-19 pandemic as people whose bodies are especially 'vulnerable' to the severest forms of the disease. We also worked to finish this book while at the same time serving as founding members of the U.S.-based People's Strike coalition[1] and members of its National Organizing Committee — an ambitious attempt to unite broad sectors of people under the leadership of radical Black workers. Whatever the strengths or weaknesses of any given organization, we maintain a strong belief that only through massive, general (non-industry specific), economic disruptions will those of us in the belly of the U.S. imperial beast ever see anything close to liberty, democracy, justice or peace. Thus, we include here for your review some of the founding documents of this bold initiative.

We remain struck by the visionary thinking and action of the work of the Indigenous peoples of Mexico and South America that have occurred for well

---

1. See: https://peoplesstrike.org/

over 25 years, especially under the leadership of the Zapatista movement. John Holloway has long written of their significance globally, and this recent piece by John brings up-to-the-moment perspectives on what is to be done. Zapatista Subcommander Moisés summarizes some of the current work of the movement. And Red Nation leader Nick Estes, who has reminded us that Indigenous history *is* the future, adds a northern perspective to life in and without empire.

We gain insight and hope from the continued creative resistance of the Palestinian people. While we quote the great Edward Said and recommend books of related investigations, the ongoing Palestinian uprisings and resistance have so much to teach us about a future we would be proud to live in. It was intentional, therefore, that we are proud to have a Foreword written by a prominent Palestinian educator; and that we close with a recent piece by Palestinian author-academic Mark Muhanned Ayyash, whose writings about violence and resistance continue to inform and inspire.

The afterword is by the visionary pan-African, pan-American, pan-sexual comrade and colleague Hakim Mohandas Amani Williams. But this is preceded by a piece by my life-long friend and co-editor Wende Marshall, an important radical scholar and organizer. Wende reminds us, as few have done before, of the deep complexities surrounding the ideals of revolutionary practice. These include the parameters of a nonviolent ethic and tactic, pursued during perhaps the most structurally violent and heinous period in modern times. The burden of revolutionary nonviolence is, indeed, not merely on those most oppressed who are struggling to breathe, but also on those more privileged who are committed to think, dream, support and build alternatives to the intensifying quagmire in which we find ourselves.

Any volume of this magnitude should contain some wonderful surprises. At the same time, there will inevitably be shortcomings in areas which we wish could have been explored further. We trust the reader will forgive us for any omissions. We hope that the essays in this volume will stimulate debate and discussion about the possibilities of insurrectionary nonviolence.

# A CALL TO ACTION: TOWARDS A GENERAL STRIKE TO END THE COVID-19 CRISIS AND CREATE A NEW WORLD

Cooperation Jackson

2020[1]

Greetings Comrades,

COVID-19 pandemic is changing the world before our very eyes. In less than three months, it has exposed the grotesque nature of the capitalist system to millions, ground the world economy to a halt, and revealed how truly interconnected our little planet really is.

As bad as this crisis is on its own terms, it is made considerably worse by the misleadership from the White House, Congress and many state and local governments. President Trump not only failed to heed the advice of the state's intelligence services regarding the potential threat of the coronavirus, he downplayed its severity for months, and has refused to mobilize the vast resources at the disposal of the U.S. government to address the crisis. He continues to deny the science and proven medical advice and is now threatening to retract social distancing orders and call for everyone to return to work by the end of April. A bipartisan Congress just passed the largest corporate bailout in history, that provided paltry relief to most working people in the form of a one time payoff that won't cover most people's rent and utilities for a month. The Governors of Mississippi, Florida, and Georgia have refused to shut their states down and give clear stay at home orders to halt the spread of the virus. And the Federal Reserve is doing everything it can to protect Wall Street, in total disregard of the real time needs of millions of people. If Trump and his political alliies in government, Wall Street, and the corporations are successful in forcing a considerable number of workers to go back to work before the pandemic has been brought under control, it will turn into an outright calamity in the U.S.. We cannot afford to let this happen.

---

1. Source: https://cooperationjackson.org/announcementsblog/towardsageneralstrike

This is just the tip of the iceberg. Disaster capitalism and white supremacy are running amok. The Trump alliance of the neo-fascist right, combined with sectors of finance capital, the fossil fuel industry and the religious right are exploiting this crisis to accelerate climate change, reshape society and redefine the geopolitical order. In the midst of this pandemic they have eliminated critical environmental protection standards (reducing already poor air quality giving new horrible life to the Black Lives Matter slogan borne of Eric Garner's murder, 'I can't breathe' as millions struggle for air). Trump has eliminated various health and safety standards to protect workers and consumers, undermining unions and other working class organizations. He has allowed genetically modified plants to be unleashed in protected lands, expanded roundup and deportation operations, and refused to provide adequate medical treatment of federal prisoners. Brutal bipartisan sanctions on Iran and Venezuela prevent millions of poor and working class from accessing critical life saving resources, and U.S. intervention has blocked Venezuela from receiving an IMF loan to address the COVID-19 pandemic. Right now the federal response is being driven by finance ministers and corporations, rather than the medical experts and front line workers directly addressing the response to the pandemic, abandoning the potential power of a coordinated federal response. All this is just a sample of the crimes against humanity unfolding daily at the hands of the White House.

Despite the asymmetry of power between ourselves in the left and the organized working class and the forces of right, we have to do everything we can to intervene. We must stop the worst most deadly version of this pandemic from becoming a reality, and we have to ensure that we never return to the society that enabled this pandemic to emerge and have the impact it is having in the first place. We must do everything that we can to create a new, just, equitable and ecologically regenerative economy.

The question is how? To fight back we have to use the greatest power we have at our disposal – our collective labor.

We can shut the system down to break the power of the state and capitalist class. We must send a clear message that things cannot and will not go back to normal. In order to do this, we need to call for collective work and shopping stoppages, leading to a general strike that is centered around clear, comprehensive demands. We must make demands that will transform our broken and inequitable society, and build a new society run by and for us – the working class, poor, oppressed majority.

A general strike cannot be organized through online campaigns alone, or as the result of the mere expression of a desire or even great need for a general strike. A general strike is not organized through a list of demands, though demands are necessary

In order for a general strike to not only take place right now, but also be effective, we need to develop a broad united front organized around short-term and long-term aims. We need to assess connections between unions of all sorts and organized labor, and begin reaching out to other poor and working-class people from within our places of work, our places of living, our places of worship, and our places of leisure.

A general strike will also take resources to sustain. We cannot count on capital to support this effort; they will attack and undermine us at every turn. So, we are going to have to call for and reply upon our collective resources. This includes our own individual purchasing power, but also the mobilization of the collective resources at the disposal of our unions, civic organizations, mutual aid, and spiritual institutions. We need to make sure that we can provide aid to workers on the frontlines of the health struggle and the frontlines of the supply chain struggles. This means providing mutual aid where warranted, as well as strike funds to support workers from losing their homes, cars, medical care, and other essential expenses.

Those with the most experience in organizing strikes of all sorts – both young and old – must step up in this moment and provide general insights and strategies that can be utilized by the united front in tandem with organized labor groups that are on the same page, and these insights in addition to strategy must inform an open information campaign that not only brings attention to strike efforts, but brings in supporters from outside of our organized formations who can then employ a wide range of strategies to begin initiating mass actions without feeling isolated.

The capitalists and landlords win when we are divided, fearful, and/or fighting our own battles in isolation. All it takes is enough of us breaking for them to have their way. We stand a much better chance coordinating nationally and internationally, and with organizing networks and infrastructure that are fortified with centuries' worth of cumulative experience between the organizers who comprise them. We also stand a better chance with global attention.

Those who control the land, the property, and the businesses want you to believe that this COVID-19 crisis is going to blow over soon, and that everyone will simply go back to work. They want you to believe that things will return to 'normal' within a matter of months, and even weeks. Right now, poor and working-class people have an opportunity to make it clear to the ruling classes that not only was 'normal' abnormal to begin with, but that we are not going to settle for a return to the social and economic conditions that created this pandemic to begin with.

We should take inspiration in that we are not alone in calling for and acting upon a call for a general strike. Workers throughout the country and the world are spontaneously taking matters into their own hands. Auto workers, chicken factory workers, nurses, drivers, grocery store workers, and more are all taking independent action. Calls for a rent strike are going viral, as working poor and homeless workers are starting to occupy hundreds of vacant homes to meet their needs and practice the necessary social distancing to ensure their survival. Things are in motion and we need to build upon this momentum, quickly.

*This crisis changes everything.*

*We have an opportunity to take control now, and we are ready to fight for a society in which all people can live with full autonomy without having to worry about survival.*

Below is the basic framing and list of preliminary demands that we think are essential to call for and act upon at this time.

## *General Strike! No Work, No Shopping Friday, May 1st*

*People over Profit: Tell the Government and Wall Street that their priority must be to Save Lives, Not Profits. Returning to Work under this Pandemic is a threat to our Collective Health and Safety.*

*We Need Systems Change, Not Just Relief and Reform. The Capitalist System Can't Resolve this Crisis.*

## *Our Demands:*

- *Protect All Frontline Workers in the Hospitals, the Supply Chains, and the Farms and Fields to ensure that they have all of the equipment and disinfectant materials that they need to keep themselves and the general public healthy*
- *Protect Asians and other vulnerable communities, including the homeless, migrants, and refugees from discrimination and attack in this time of crisis*
- *Democratize the Means of Production, Convert the Corporations and Workplaces into Cooperatives to produce what we need and distribute equitably according to need*
- *Institute Universal Health Care Now*
- *Institute Universal Basic Services Now (Education, Childcare, Elderly Care, Water, Electricity, Internet, etc.) based on Economic, Social and Cultural rights guidelines*
- *Institute Universal Basic Income Now*
- *Democratize the Finance, Credit and Insurance Industries – Bailout the People, Not the Corporations and Wall Street*
- *Decarbonize the Economy, Institute a Green New Deal based on a Just Transition, End the Fossil Fuel and Extractive Industries Now*
- *Housing is a Human Right, Decommodify Housing Now, Open all available housing stock to those who need it now*
- *Ensure there is clean drinking water for all communities, decommodify water now*
- *Cancel Our Debts, Institute a Debt Jubilee Now*
- *Close the Jails, Close the Prisons, Release the Prisoners*
- *Close the Detention Centers, Reunite the Families, Stop the Raids and Deportations*
- *Close all of the Overseas Military Bases, Cut the Military (Defense) and Spy (Surveillance) Budgets and Redirect these funds to Health Care, Social Services, Universal Basic Income and Greening Public Infrastructure and the Economy*

We are calling upon all who agree with this call to join us in calling for militant action to shut the system down. This is what we are asking you to do immediately:

1. Let us know if you agree with this call and this list of demands, or how you would add upon or strengthen them.
2. Let us know if you would be willing to participate in a coordinating body to help organize and advance this call. This coordinating body would take on the task of building out the base of the united front, help facilitate community between its constituent parts, and facilitate the calls to action.
3. Join us for our first zoom call on Monday, April 6th at 12 pm est/11 am cst/ 10 am mst/9 am pst to start building this front and advancing this call to action.
4. To participate in the call and communicate your alignment and willingness help coordinate a broad, united front initiative email us at mayday2020generalstrike@gmail.com.

Finally, this initiative is not intended to negate any of the calls already issued for a rent strike, a people's bailout, etc. We hope to unite all who can be united, while respecting the independence of initiative of the various forces that would comprise the front. We have to apply ceaseless, unyielding pressure on the system and the forces that enable it. Let's do so with any eye towards employing maximum unity to end this crisis and create a new world in its aftermath.

*Cooperation Jackson*
Tuesday, March 31, 2020

# A DEEPER UNDERSTANDING OF WHAT WE'RE TRYING TO ACCOMPLISH: A PEOPLE'S STRIKE DIALOGUE

Kali Akuno; Rose Brewer; Saki Hall; Wende Marshall; and Matt Meyer

2021

**Wende**: What is the relationship between a strategy of dual power and a revolutionary conception of nonviolence? How can we build mutual aid into revolutionary processes and concrete revolutionary projects? What are the lessons of the Black Panther Party and post 1960s movements, especially in terms of mutual aid, self-defense, and community ties? How do we balance militancy and militarism, the idea that nonviolence is always reformist, that 'by any means necessary' equals armed struggle? How do we understand and deal with the violence generated by this white supremacist capitalist patriarchy, and ours?

**Kali**: I think we have to do a lot more work of dispelling this notion that nonviolence is inherently reformist, because it's not. Now we know that many of examples which people cite, or the ones that they know best, those narratives tend to lean in that direction. But in actual practice, both from a theoretical from a practical standpoint, the powerful unarmed strategy we can use, to the extent that we can organize it, is a general strike. When one organizes all those who labor in one form or another, primarily for the means of livelihood and survival, to act in accord with one another you have a formula for massive and radical social change. In this scenario, we could first shut the system down, but then also move away from existing system. Transformation of society could actually be done, and in some cases has been done, through nonviolent means.

There are just some conceptions which have come down, particularly within the Black Liberation framework, in terms of dichotomies. 'Malcolm is the revolutionary and Martin was a reformer.' These actually don't fit our own history in the larger narrative. They play into a particularly dangerous narrative that we see in the here-and-now between 'the good progress' and 'the bad protester,' which only benefits our enemies.

That type of thinking doesn't help us form a deeper understanding of what it is we're trying to accomplish and what it will take. We always need to have clarity that those who own the means of production, those who control the state, are not going to give up their power without a struggle and are not going to accept even the most basic of democratic practices without a struggle. At the end of the day, we can and should control all strategies and tactics, but not do so blindly. I think there's more of a merging of those two past dichotomies. Those issues have to fit into a larger context around strategy, and what it will take to get to that point of mass insurrection and general strike.

Our strategic analysis of the moment is what should dictate and determine tactical considerations. When our enemies strike back, and we know at some points that they will strike back , they will surely use the violent apparatuses of the state. The question for us, then, is: What should be our collective response?

And if there's a limited response, it's typically going to mean more of a self-defense kind of struggle. If it is a more collective response, then we could use more of the nonviolent tactics. It is important to understand that when we talk about some of the dynamics of a general strike, we must be prepared for the fact that the opposition is always going to be extracting penalties and making life unbearable. The people's power is in making it so that nothing can move, no production or work or schooling or business as usual can proceed, because there's a heightened sense of universal solidarity that everybody would act on the same core principles and frameworks. That General Strike scenario is going to take a whole hell of a lot of political understanding and unity building over an extended period of time. But I think it's something that we should always keep in mind.

This also goes back to the piece which Saki raised and elevated, about the sanctity of life which must remain our aim and objective. We understand that not everybody is going to come along or want to come along with that viewpoint. There are fascist elements who would much rather see the planet burn and everything be destroyed than see life preserved. We shouldn't walk into anything blindly. We need to be clear about all our articulations about the sanctity of life.

At the same time, we must also be clear that half measures are not going to do it. We can't mediate our way to liberation through a series of compromises with Capital or the institutions of reaction! Thinking that this is possible will actually be a barrier to the change that we're trying to seek. We must constantly and strategically reflect up how we build within an overall dialectic of where we will make compromises and where we won't. And that's a big piece because that is where our enemies best utilize divide and conquer tactics. They push to know what our breaking points are.

Following the Summer 2020 Black Liberation uprisings, we saw a trend very illustrative of this point, in how much money was being pumped into a certain kind of social justice reformism. We have to really figure out how to move those who are within that that kind of reformist orbit so as not to get lost in their narratives or their games. We do need to do the work of actually reaching out to the large mass of the people in this country who are not in formal organizations, but who are feeling the pain. And there are still tons of spaces to reach people to build bases within the U.S., building an infrastructure and relying on our own resources.

That's where I think that this larger piece around mutual aid fits in, because there's a level of mutual aid which revolutionaries in the U.S. context really have to reinvent.

**Saki:** I think we have to figure out how to bring together people who see themselves as revolutionaries, especially those who are tied and connected to organizations or projects. There are disconnects even just between people who are paid organizers and unpaid deep community organizers with ties to the grassroots. There are lessons here from the post-1960s era, with mutual aid and self-defense work and the deeply rooted relationships which directly engaged people to be able to develop strong ties.

Unfortunately, part of what makes the gap is folks who are doing paid organizing work conforming to the very nature of the nonprofits. They create a certain dynamic that's different; the conversation is more about how people get paid to do the work, compared to how we get back to a voluntary responsibility and something we're doing to sustain ourselves. I think we've seen that gap widening instead of decreasing, but now—dealing with mutual aid—we may be coming back to thinking about 'how do you build the new society' while also increasing accountability and fightback, and community defense work.

Another big issue around balancing militancy and militarism and the violence that is meted against us is how our own relationship to violence repeats within our communities. I advocate for us paying great attention to the problem, which we fuel just by repeating militarized thinking even in language we use and how we talk about strategy. There is a repetition of military thinking and language that is deeply patriarchal and violent and lends itself to perpetuating (or at least leaving the door open) to the kind of tactics which have repeatedly been used against us.

**Kali** (*gently laughing*): Saki's on a campaign to change movement language! She doesn't want anything referred to based on military roots; and this is this is a long-standing battle between us!

**MattM:** There are echoes here of contemporary Mozambican reflections on their post-independence conflicts with apartheid and U.S.-supported counterrevolutionaries. FRELIMO militants have been consistent in their self-critiques of how militarized their education and propaganda was, and how that propaganda did not do well to prepare the next generation of revolutionaries. As Amilcar Cabral of Guinea-Bissau warned, 'we must be militants but never militarists.'

**Saki:** I don't see how we can want to shift away from how we relate to one another and how we struggle for change while still maintaining these ideas and concepts and language which has successfully put us at odds with each other! Because the language does impact our practice!! So, yeah, I am an advocate for changing how we speak to one another, and I've even questioned the way we've used the language of having 'enemies.' People aren't always clear about who the enemy is, and there is a spectrum right now as we deal with tactical and strategic differences within the movement. But those differences don't necessarily mean that you're my enemy, compared to people who actually are at odds with our entire Black community attaining self-determination!

# A CASCADE OF ANGERS... ALONG THE ROAD TO HOPE

John Holloway

2020[1]

The doors open. You can feel the pent-up energy even before the faces appear. The lockdown is over. A dam is burst. Out pours a torrent of angers, anxieties, frustrations, dreams, hopes, fears. It is as if we cannot breathe.

We have all been locked in. Cut off physically from the outside world, we have been trying to understand what is happening. A strange virus has changed our lives, but where did it come from? It first appeared in Wuhan, China, but the more we read, we realize that it could have been anywhere. Experts have been warning for years of the likelihood of a pandemic, even if they did not understand how quickly it might spread. It is not that it comes from any particular place, it comes rather from the destruction of our relationship with the natural environment. From the industrialization of agriculture, the destruction of the peasantry in all the world, the growth of cities, the destruction of the habitats of wild animals, the commercialization of these animals for profit. And we learn from the experts that if there is not a radical change in our relation to other forms of life, then it is quite likely that more pandemics will follow. It is a warning: get rid of capitalism or advance on the road to extinction. Get rid of capitalism: a fantasy indeed. And there grows in us a fear and an anger and maybe even a hope that there might be some way we could do it.

And as the lockdown proceeds, our attention shifts, moves beyond the illness to what we are told are the economic consequences. We are moving into the worst economic crisis since at least the 1930s, the worst for 300 years in Britain, they say. Over a hundred million people will be tipped into extreme poverty, the World Bank tells us. Another lost decade for Latin America. Millions and millions of people unemployed in all the world. People starving, people begging, more crime, more violence, hopes broken, dreams shattered. There will be no fast recovery, any recovery is likely to be fragile and weak. And we think: all this because we had to stay at home for a couple of months? And we know it cannot be so. Of course, we will be a bit poorer if people stop working for a couple of months, but millions and millions unemployed, people dying of starvation? Surely not. A

---

1. Source: https://duepublico2.uni-due.de/servlets/MCRFileNodeServlet/duepublico_derivate_00073378/08_Holloway_Cascade_of_Angers.pdf; see also: https://darajapress.com/2020/06/17/john-holloway-a-cascade-of-angers-my-covid-19-fantasy

break for a couple of months cannot have that effect. Just the contrary, we should go back refreshed and full of energy to do all the things that need to be done. And we think a bit more and we realize that of course the economic crisis is not the consequence of the virus, though it may well have been triggered by it. In the same way as the pandemic was predicted, the economic crisis was predicted even more clearly. For thirty years or more, the capitalist economy has literally been living on borrowed money: its expansion has been based on credit. A house of cards ready to collapse. It almost collapsed, with the most awful effects, in 2008, but a renewed and enormous expansion of credit propped it up again. The economic commentators knew it could not last. 'God gave Noah the rainbow sign, no more water, the fire next time': the financial crisis of 2008 was the flood, but the next time, which would not be long delayed, it would be fire.[2] This is what we are living: the fire of capitalist crisis. So much misery, hunger, shattered hopes, not because of a virus, but in order to restore capitalism to profitability. And what if we just got rid of the system based on profit? What if we just went out with our renewed energy and did what needs to be done without worrying about profit: clean the streets, build hospitals, make bicycles, write books, plant vegetables, play music, whatever. No unemployment, no starvation, no broken dreams. And the capitalists? Either hang them from the nearest lamppost (always a temptation) or just forget about them. Better just forget about them. Another fantasy, but more than a fantasy: an urgent necessity. And our fears and our angers and our hopes grow inside us.

And there is more, much much more, to feed our angers in the lockdown. The whole coronavirus event has been a huge unmasking of capitalism. It stands exposed as rarely before. In so many ways. The enormous difference in the experience of lockdown, to start with, depending on how much space you have, whether you have a garden, whether you have a second home that you can retreat to. Related to this, the hugely different impact of the virus on rich and poor, something that has become clearer and clearer with the advance of the disease. Connected to that, the great difference in the rates of infection and death among whites and blacks. And the appalling inadequacy of medical services after thirty years of neglect. And the terrible incompetence of so many states. And the glaring expansion of surveillance and police and military powers in nearly all countries. And the discrimination in educational provision between those who have access to internet and those who do not, not to mention the complete insulation of educational systems from the changes that are taking place in the world in which the children live. And the exposure of so many women to situations of terrible violence. All this, and much more, at the same time as the owners of Amazon and Zoom and so many other technological companies reap amazing profits and the stock market, buoyed by the action of the central banks, continue with the barefaced transfer of wealth from poor to rich. And our angers grow and our fears

---

2. See the last chapter of Martin Wolf's The Shifts and the Shocks, Penguin Press, New York, 2014: 'Conclusion: Fire Next Time'.

and our desperation and our determination that it must not be so, that we MUST NOT LET THIS NIGHTMARE COME TRUE.

And then the doors are opened and the dam is burst. Our angers and hopes burst out on the streets. We hear of George Floyd, we hear his last words, 'I cannot breathe'. The words go round and round in our heads. We do not have the knee of a murdering policeman on our neck, but we too cannot breathe. We cannot breathe because capitalism is killing us. We feel vialence, vialence burstin out of us.[3] But that is not our way, it is theirs. Yet our angers-hopes, hopes-rages have to breathe, have to breathe. And they do, in the massive demonstrations against police brutality and racism in all the world, in the throwing of the statue of the slave trader, Edward Colston, into the river in Bristol, in the creation of the Capital Hill Autonomous Zone in Seattle, in the burning of the police precinct in Minneapolis, in so many fists raised to the sky.

And the torrent of angers-hopes-fears-hungers-dreams-frustrations goes cascading onwards, from one anger to another, living each anger, respecting each anger and overflowing on to the next. The angers burning inside us are not just against police brutality, not just against racism, not just against the slavery that created the basis for capitalism, but also against the violence against women and all forms of sexism, and so the enormous marches of 8M surge again singing. The Chileans come out on the streets again and continue their revolution. And the people of Kurdistan push back the states that cannot tolerate the idea of a stateless society. And the people of Hong Kong inspire all the Chinese in their repudiation of the mockery of communism: no more communism, they cry, let's communize. And the Zapatistas create the world of many worlds. And the peasants leave their slums and go back to the land and start to heal the relationship with other forms of life. And the bats and wild animals go back to their habitats. And the capitalists crawl back to their natural habitats, under the stairs. And labor, capitalist labor, that awful machine that generates richness and poverty and destroys our lives, comes to an end and we start to do what we want to do, we start to create a different world based on the mutual recognition of dignities. And then there will be no lost decade and no unemployed and no hundreds of millions pushed into extreme poverty and no one starving. And then, yes, then we can breathe.

◊

## Along the Way to Hope: A Conversation with John Holloway, by Suren Moodliar and Matt Meyer

**Suren Moodliar**: I can imagine both Matt and I will have several detours that we'd want to take along the way to HOPE, but beginning with *Change The World*

---

3. See Linton Kwesi Johnson, 'Time Come': 'now yu si fire burning in mi eye/ smell badness pan mi breat/ feel vialence, vialence, /burstin outta mi;/ look out!' *Dread Beat and Blood*, Bogle-L'Ouverture Publications, London, 1975.

*Without Taking Power*, it's not an exaggeration to say that it was a seminal text. It provoked a whole seminar series, counter books, and constant references to the phrase 'You're up to the present.' How would you describe the context in which you wrote that book? What was the conjuncture?

**John Holloway**: I think two things. The conjunction in which—the moment in which—it came out was pretty important. The book itself was something that I had been working on for years. I was involved in the old debates of the Conference of Socialist Economists in Britain, in the '70s and '80s, around the state, and really developing the idea, which also connected with the German State Derivation Debate. So the central idea there was how we understand the state as a capitalist state. If we understand the state as a capitalist state, then it seemed to me obvious. Well, obviously that means we can't think of changing the world through the state. And I just took that for granted as being obvious.

By the time I finally formulated all this is a book it was 2002, which was a very lively time. Especially in Latin America, especially in Argentina. The book was published in Spanish in Argentina, just after the uprising of December 2001 and the whole movement that stretched into 2002. So it just connected perfectly there with all the discussions that were going on, and also connected obviously with the whole Zapatista and post Zapatistas alter-globalization movement.

In that sense, the timing was very fortunate, I think. And partly because of that it sparked off loads and loads of discussions. It was translated into 11 languages, I think. When I first finished the book, I thought, 'Well, maybe a few of my friends will understand what I'm trying to say.' But the reaction was just fantastic.

**Suren Moodliar**: I appreciate the context of the alter-globalization movement events in Argentina, but this was also the time when the pink tide seemed to be coming in, and there were many state-based projects, including the Bolivarian project in Venezuela. So it seemed very credible at the time. What was the chemistry between these two?

**John Holloway**: I think with Venezuela there really was not so much connection. My contact in Venezuela is the absolutely fabulous cooperative known as CECOSESOLA, which has existed for nearly 50 years. They are a center of cooperatives and their main activity is what they call, peculiarly, a festival of consumption. But their festival of consumption is actually the organization of a popular supermarket each weekend, where [food is provided to the community]. This is in the town of Barquisimeto, and a huge proportion of the town's population go there every week.

The amazing thing is that if you go there and visit them, you discover that they spend a big part of their time just sitting around in circle, with children. They discuss their problems, personal problems, communal problems. And in this way, they're trying to build a different world.

Their argument, which was really a critical argument already at that time of the Bolivarian government, was that 'if you really want to change things, you can't just bring in a decree that now there are going to be lots of cooperatives.' You need a process of years and years of work together, developing different social relations, different ways of doing things, different ways of thinking about things.

I suppose the three things that had a big impact in Latin America were the whole movement in Argentina, which was just amazing, the War of Water in Bolivia in the 2000, and—all the time— the background of the Zapatista movement here in Mexico, which has just been an amazing source of inspiration.

**Matt Meyer:** I'm curious as to whether you've had contact with the folks in Venezuela who helped develop the First Eco-Socialist International. I am not aware of them particularly citing you, but there's no question that part of the conversations among the eco-socialists has been along similar lines. Obviously in Venezuela they have a Ministry of Eco-socialism, but those who founded the International are grassroots folks who led the movement to get rid of Monsanto, as well as the movement being called 'Trueke'—bartering and trade—mainly rooted in the Afro-Venezuelan centers of the country.

It seems to me fairly inevitable that some of concepts which you have put forward, like the idea of ceasing to 'create' capitalism, are integrated into that mindset, whether because of an overt understanding of those concepts or just because of the evolutionary way in which it's become clear that the state is not necessarily the only, or perhaps the major, way of making revolution.

**Suren Moodliar:** To follow up on that, and to move in a more conceptual direction; you famously challenged the idea of social movements as an emancipatory category, preferring instead the idea of movements in opposition. You've cite positively the anti-privatization water movement in Bolivia. Can you say a little bit more about the distinction between social movements and the oppositional movements that you have in mind?

**John Holloway:** It is not so much a distinction...There's a question of vocabulary in conceptualization. It's really in the last 20, 30 years that the notion of social movements has arisen. And I think to some extent, initially it was a conscious attempt to get away from the language of class struggle. This may be wrong, but the idea of the social movements suggests an infinite number of movements struggling against particular injustices.

But the peculiar thing is that if you've got an infinite or this huge number of disparate movements, then you're in fact killing the notion of hope. Because [these movements form] a permanent thing. Of course, you're going to win one struggle, lose another. You'll lose most of them and you'll win some of them, and it'll go on and on. There is no longer any revolutionary perspective. There's no longer any perspective, except in the most general terms. There's no direct fighting against capitalism as a coherent social system.

If you look at all of these movements, they're not social. I mean, they're social movements in one sense, but they're actually movements of resistance. They are movements that arise from some sort of aggression, which can be understood normally as a capitalist depression. So they are in fact movements of resistance, and in the best, most active cases, they're movements of resistance and rebellion.

What really annoys me is the degree to which this notion of social movements has become established: convenient enough, but actually very destructive, both theoretically and politically.

**Suren Moodliar**: If one looks at Alain Touraine's overall trajectory, he first began to write extensively about social movements after looking at the 1968 student movements, and then discovered movements like Solidarity in Poland or the Corsican nationalist movement. In that period he also developed the idea of the sociological intervention, in which he brought together movement activists of various parts of the movement, and seemed to have a notion that by understanding the interaction between the activists in different parts of the movement, we get an overall sense of their developmental potential, and their transformational capacity.

Of course, by the late 1990s, he almost arrives at the end of history, and as you say, at the end of Hope. So I find your argument about the way in which social movements are conceptualized back then as quite credible. Although I do want to recognize that there are many sociologists who still use the vocabulary and see it in emancipatory terms as well.

**John Holloway**: That's right. It's quite difficult to avoid the vocabulary completely, and of course, as you're saying, many sociologists and students do want to do something radical. The easiest way to think about it is that if we focus solely on social movements something important is lost.

**Suren Moodliar**: This brings me to another dichotomy, the proletariat against the working class. Can you tell us a little bit about that?

**John Holloway**: I take this from Katherina Nasyoka, a PhD student of mine whose thesis was later published as a book. She focused on the uprising in Oaxaca in 2006, and the uprising in Athens, and Greece as a whole, in 2010. She's Greek herself and her argument is that the best way to understand what was happening is as a result of the proletariat against the working class.

If you look at Greece, especially at that time, there were very big conflicts within the radical left. There are few who don't want to be called left, the radical anti-capitalists or rebels on the one hand, and the powerful structure of the trade unions, still dominated by the old Communist Party, on the other.

In that context, I remember there was one occasion in 2011 when the organized workers, the 'working class' in that sense, actually physically defended the Parliament from an assault by the rebels. I have another Greek former PhD student, Panagioti Stulos, who says that we probably shouldn't attach the name 'rebels' to the opposition. We should think of them as some 'movement without name' against the organized and named working class.

**Matt Meyer**: It seems to me we're stuck in some ways, in part in the naming of things. Because parts of what they're talking about are old left versus new left and newer left. Some of this may just be different ways of attacking the problem. But part of it is a conceptual one: whether social movements can be a form building more radical or revolutionary movements.

As we've talked about the 'end of history' and the end of hope, you've written about 'shattering the continuum of history', which I think is a much more interesting concept. In fact, it's not about the end of history, it's about the end of conceptualizing things in a particular way, especially about (re)creating capitalism in a particular way and replacing it by something else.

John, you've written some years ago that we want a moment or we need a moment of terrible social intensity. Are we at that moment today? Have we reached that moment? If we have, if this is that moment, then what do people need to be doing to shatter the continuum of history and build new forms?

**John Holloway**: The easy answer is I don't know!

I would say we're possibly on the edge of such a moment. Okay, this is silly, but you remember the musical West Side Story and the song 'Something's Coming!'? It's only at the beginning, but kind of on the edge. Somethings going to happen, maybe something good, but we don't know what.

I think there are moments when you can actually feel that. In Argentina in December 2001, you could really feel kind of an excitement and tension and anger in the air. I also happened to be in Athens in 2011, just before the occupation of the squares began. Are we in that moment now? It is always fairly hard to judge. What I would say is that yes, but probably not within a week.

I think that it is very likely, or very possible rather, that within one or two years we will be in a really explosive situation in different parts of the world. And I suspect different cities of the world in particular. I think that we're in a situation of suspense at the moment. It's just not clear how things are going to come out. It's not just the U.S.; it's not clear what's going to happen with the whole situation of capitalism in the next couple of years.

One real possibility is that we're in a situation rather like the 1930s, but possibly much worse. We might see a period of huge unemployment, of real impoverishment, of growing nationalism, of a growing push towards the possibility of war. How do we prepare for that? How do we think of that? That's really the question you're posing.

I suppose in terms of anger, there's kind of a reasoning that says we should win with periods of great anger, but there are also historical experiences which suggest that we tend to lose in periods of great anger. If we think obviously of the 1930s, but also just back to 2008 and all that followed, I think that led to a huge upsurge in social anger throughout the world. But that social anchor was then expressed in the rise of people like Trump, Johnson or Bolsanaro.

It may be that what's going to happen over the next couple of years is a similar and much greater surge of social anger. How do we say that this is anger is ours? Is it anger against capital? This anger has to come in our direction. How do we do that? How do we intervene in an angry world, an angry and also fairly diffuse world? I don't have a clear answer at all. Obviously we try to make the connections between people's anger and the failure of capital. I suppose that is what's happening at the moment, in a way, with the pandemic.

But it seems really important to say: 'look, this is the failure of a system.' It's the failure of capitalism, that's what we're living now. Lots of people are saying that I suppose, but how do we use that, and think in terms of change through that. Obviously, I don't think it's a question of electoral politics. Maybe one could use some electoral politics in terms of opposing things, but not in terms of proposing things.

**Matt Meyer**: As part of reconceptualizing and rethinking or rebuilding revolution, are there ways that blow apart old and sometimes false dichotomies? Are there tactical, strategic, and sometimes philosophical conceptions of violence and nonviolence, for example, which need to be reworked, the idea of only being able to make revolution one way and not the other. How can we not get stuck in dogmas, in old dichotomies, possibly like violence/nonviolence.

The recent piece that you wrote about the world post-COVID speaks a little bit to hope beyond the current crises. Part of what you wrote says: 'Well, what do we do with the capitalists? Maybe we should just hang them by the nearest lamppost. Or maybe just forget about them. Yeah, better to just forget about them.' What is your thinking about getting past these dichotomies?

**John Holloway**: I'd forgotten about that thing! But yes, people got annoyed with that.

I think it's what I was saying a moment ago. We have to start from or at least certainly respect people's anger. The Zapatistas have this fantastic phrase, 'La Digna Rabia'—Righteous rage! And that seems to me absolutely the right way to think about it. We have to think of change, we have to think of movements, not starting from rational argument but in terms of respect for the anger that people feel.

From that anger, I suppose my feeling is that the best way, without wanting to be completely pacifist, would be to say that violence seemed to be a mistake. It was and is the wrong way to express our anger for two reasons.

Firstly, because we're just not very good at it! We're not violent people. If I took up and matched guns against the Mexican state, obviously I would lose. I mean, it'd be ridiculous.

And the other thing is it's not part of the society we want to create. Whereas I wouldn't rush to condemn somebody for being violent—it's not a kind of principled pacifism—but the important thing really is to find how to express our anger in dignified, worthy, righteous ways. And that is something else. That is not shooting people, and it is not hitting people.

**Suren Moodliar:** John, you have also considered the challenge of identity politics, and in some ways respected dignity is at the core. In talking about a many-headed Hydra, which expresses itself in the traditional race, class, gender kinds of distinctions, you written that we need to go back to the notion of capital, and capital as a transitory phenomenon. Can you say a little bit more about capital? The way we treat conceptualized capital in order that we may transcend it and how this relates to your critique of identity.

**John Holloway**: This really goes back to my involvement in the state derivation debate in the 1970s. The question there really was: how do we derive the particularization of the state from the nature of capitalist social relations? In other words, the question is, how do we derive the existence of the political as something distinct from the economic? How do we conceptualize this from the base, from the nature of capitalist social relations? That leads us then to the idea that capital is characterized by this separation into the political and the economic. In other words, when we are talking about capital, we're talking about the totality of social relations.

Capital is not just an economic category. It's a way of talking about the totality of social obligations and saying that this totality of social relations has a certain structure, a certain form. This is how Marx analyzes things in *Capital*. It's based on the fact that richness or wealth exists in the form of commodities. When I talk about the importance of capital, I'm not talking just about the importance of the economic, okay? There is importance in trying to understand the structure and dynamic of social relations in society.

Secondly, what I've been thinking more and more about over the past year or so is that this concept of capital is crucial for thinking about hope. We tend to think of capital as a form of domination, which of course it is. But the idea of an overall structure of society is crucial for thinking about hope. We need this in order to understand that yes, we really can transform society as a whole. If we lose the overall concept of capital, if everything dissolves into a multitude of social movements, then the idea of a fundamental transformation of society gets lost completely. And I think that is what's been happening with many contemporary protest movements.

There is a loss of the concept of capital. There are fewer and fewer students reading *Capital*, for example. Fewer are understanding or using that language. It may be that more students are working on social movements, or women's movements, or studying gender; I don't know. But there is a loss of this overall concept of a social structure which can be transformed.

Identity comes into it because I think that these losses are part of the growth of particularistic politics, divorced from some sort of conception of a universal or totalizing structure. Whereas if we think about political capital, then we're thinking of society as being antagonistic, constitutively antagonistic, to things that don't penetrate into all of us. If political capital penetrates into all of us, then it's silly to think that we have some sort of identity separated from that antagonism. Does that make sense?

**Matt Meyer**: I think it's not a coincidence that these contradictions have emerged so strikingly at a time when we talk a lot about the nonprofit industrial complex, the 'professionalization' of social change. We talk a lot more about social change and a lot more about individualized or personalized depression, and a lot less about revolution—a lot less about liberation.

**John Holloway**: I think that's right.

**Suren Moodliar**: Thinking about how we oppose capital as a whole, you've proposed anti-power. Where does the historical notion of pure power fit in, if at all? In other words, how can we go about building another form of power within the capitalist society, in order to transcend it?

**John Holloway**: You're asking where the notion of dual power fits in?

The notion of dual power, I suppose, is usually associated with the traditional state-centered idea of revolutions. It's a situation of dual power in Russia in 1917, no? How should we think about it at this moment? I suppose, I don't know. If we're talking about cracks, for example, then we have to talk about the development of more and more attempts to create spaces or times that go against capital. There are different ways of developing things. Do you call that a situation of dual power? Perhaps.

**Suren Moodliar**: In some ways my question is a bit of an anachronism in the sense that we don't really talk about dual power anymore. However, there are many projects, especially here in the United States, which don't quite reject electoral politics but are involved in building large regional systems of power as it were. There is some coordination between political projects and more community-based cooperatives, like Cooperation Jackson or Cooperation Humboldt.

**John Holloway**: I think that these questions are definitely important. It connects with something that we've been discussing here—the increasing use of alternatives. But in Mexico and Latin America, instead of talking about revolution people are talking about the construction of alternatives. The construction of alternatives obviously could be seen in terms of dual power. And when we go on creating alternatives, we are creating a different world.

On the one hand, I find the growth of all these movements trying to do things in a different way quite exciting. But I also find it disturbing in the sense that some of these are not actually alternatives at all. But some of what is developing are in fact movements against capitalist organization or capitalist imposition. We have to theorize this way and understand a certain negative grammar. Negative grammar may say, okay, these are exciting movements, but they're movements against—movements against capital, rather than just movements for the creation of something else. We must wonder, why? Why insist on this negative grammar?

I think it's a little bit like raising a flag. What are we trying to do? If we're writing a thesis or a book, if we're organizing around something, we want to raise a black and red flag on top of it! Sometimes we don't want to say it and sometimes it doesn't make sense to say it. But perhaps it's important for us to at least have that flag in our minds!

I suppose that comes back to question of dual power. We must understand dual power as part of a fundamental antagonism, and not just the proliferation of different things. Because the proliferation of different things is fairly easily integrate-able back into capital.

**Suren Moodliar**: So we must keep in mind the idea of a break; the antagonism has to be central to any use of a euphemistic term 'alternative.'

**John Holloway**: I think so, yes. It's a kind of protection, giving 'alternatives' some clear direction against capital.

**Suren Moodliar**: Against the totalization of capital, you're proposing the idea of many worlds. So one can see the idea of alternatives, of tax shelters as it were, as being quite consistent with at least the ambition of a future world or many worlds. How are these many worlds supposed to relate to one another? What are the forms of communication and negotiation that have to happen between these many worlds?

**John Holloway**: It's not me who's proposing the many worlds, it's the Zapatistas who say 'we want to create a world of many worlds.' And the Zapatistas are extremely important in all these discussions. This growth of emphasis on alternatives, for example—certainly in Latin America, is very much connected with Indigenous movements. But the way I understand the Zapatistas is that they saying 'absolutely not.' We are anti-capitalist. They're far too diplomatic and far too clever to simply say 'we are not an alternative.' But especially with the EZLN Sixth Declaration in 2005, they say explicitly for the first time: We are Anti-Capitalist.

There are two new communiques which came out in October 2020 that are absolutely astonishing, brilliant. They're saying: look, we're going to go to all the continents of the world, to set sail in April. This isn't a question of an Indigenous movement, they assert. We need every color, every people from all over the world to think about breaking with the catastrophe that we're living. It seems to me they're breaking completely with this kind of 'alternative' picture. ['A Mountain in the High Seas' http://enlacezapatista.ezln.org.mx/2020/10/05/sexta-parte-una-montana-en-alta-mar/]

The Zapatista idea of a world of many worlds is terrific but it's not now. In order to get to the world of many worlds, we have to break with a single capitalist imposition of a logic of destruction. We must think about how we would organize or build organization and interconnection between different worlds or different communities. This thinking and organizing may be growing, with many different experiments. But some things will have to be left for when it comes.

**Matt Meyer**: So what should we do now, as we look towards the edge of the cliff we're on now?

**John Holloway:** I am trying to write a book on hope. My starting point in all this was Ernst Bloch's *Principle of Hope*, which took me into Marx and all the discussions. He starts off saying that when he comes back to Germany after the war, after exile in the States, that now is the time to learn hope. My argument is that in this situation we are again in a time to learn hope. We're no longer in the same context as Bloch. He was still thinking in terms of a traditional concept of revolution led by the Communist Party. Today, there aren't any significant revolutionary parties in the world. Things seem to be getting darker and darker in many ways. And yet there's a real need for hope.

People actually relate to this idea all the time. It's the one cliche that is used by every single politician. For us, the only way we can think about hope is by thinking about the crisis of capital, the crisis of the existing system. How do we connect hope to our notion of the crisis, and what this crisis means?

We want to think of hope in relation to crisis. There has to be some way in which a breakdown of the system is part of the transition to a different world. I think possibly that's what we're living or what we're going to be living in the next few years. We must figure out how to think about this in a way that isn't Armageddon-ist. It does seem to me likely that we will be in a social crisis within a year or two that we just have no experience of. We don't really have a clear conception of what it might mean politically and socially to have that level of great crisis in the current world. On the one hand, that prospect is very frightening but on the other hand, perhaps not. Perhaps we have to think of hope in that context.

# A MOUNTAIN IN A HIGH SEA

Subcommander Moisés

---

2020[1]

Communique from the Indigenous Revolutionary Clandestine Committee
General Command of the Zapatista Army for National Liberation

To the National Indigenous Congress-Indigenous Government Council:
To the Sixth National and International:To the Networks of Resistance and Rebellion:
To the honest people who resist in all corners of the planet:

Sisters, brothers, siblings:
Compañeras, companeros and campanions:

The Indigenous peoples of Mayan and Zapatista roots salute them and tell them what came of our common thought, according to what we look at, hear and feel.

First. —We look and listen to a sick world in its social life, fragmented into millions of people alien to each other, bent on their individual survival, but united under the oppression of a system willing to do anything to quench its thirst for profit, even when it is clear that his path goes against the existence of planet Earth.

The aberration of the system and its stupid defense of 'progress' and 'modernity' crashes against a criminal reality: *femicides*. The murder of women has no color or nationality, it is worldwide. If it is absurd and unreasonable for someone to be persecuted, disappeared, killed because of their skin color, their race, their culture, their beliefs; It cannot be believed that being a woman amounts to a sentence of marginalization and death.

In a foreseeable escalation (harassment, physical violence, mutilation and murder), with the endorsement of structural impunity ('she deserved it', 'she had tattoos', 'what was she doing in that place at that time?', 'with those clothes, it was to be expected '), the murders of women have no criminal logic other than that of the system. Of different social strata, different races, ages ranging from early childhood to old age, and in distant geographies, gender is the only constant. And the system is unable to explain why this goes hand in hand with its 'development'

---

1. https://enlacezapatista.ezln.org.mx/2020/10/07/part-six-a-mountain-on-the-high-seas/

and 'progress.' In the outrageous statistics of deaths, the more 'developed' a society is, the greater the number of victims in this authentic gender war.

And 'civilization' seems to say to native peoples: 'the proof of your underdevelopment is in your low rate of *femicides*. Have your *megaprojects*, your trains, your thermoelectric plants, your mines, your dams, your shopping centers, your appliance stores -with a television channel included-, and learn to consume. Be like us. To pay off the debt of this progressive aid, their lands, their waters, their cultures, their dignities are not enough. They must complete with the lives of women'.

Second.—We look and listen to nature wounded to death, and that, in its agony, warns humanity that the worst is yet to come. Each 'natural' catastrophe announces the next and conveniently forgets that it is the action of a human system that causes it.

Death and destruction are no longer a distant thing, which is limited to borders, respects customs and international conventions. Destruction in any corner of the world, affects the entire planet.

Third.— We watch and listen to the powerful retreating and hiding in the so-called National States and their walls. And, in that impossible leap back, revive fascist nationalisms, ridiculous chauvinisms and deafening verbiage. In this we warn of the wars to come, those that feed on false, hollow, lying stories and that translate nationalities and races into supremacies that will be imposed by way of death and destruction. In different countries there is a dispute between foremen and those who aspire to succeed them, hiding that the boss, the master, the boss, is the same and has no nationality other than that of money. Meanwhile, international organizations languish and become mere names, like museum pieces ... or not even that.

In the darkness and confusion that precede those wars, we listen and watch the attack, siege, and pursuit of any hint of creativity, intelligence, and rationality. Faced with critical thinking, the powerful demand, demand and impose their fanaticism. The death they plant, cultivate and harvest is not just physical; it also includes the extinction of humanity's own universality -intelligence-, its advances and achievements. New esoteric currents, secular and not, are reborn or created, disguised as intellectual fashions or *pseudo* sciences; and the arts and sciences seek to be subjugated to political militancy.

Fourth.—The COVID 19 Pandemic not only showed the vulnerabilities of the human being, but also the greed and stupidity of the different national governments and their supposed oppositions. Measures of the most elementary common sense were despised, always betting that the Pandemic would be short-lived. As the disease progressed more and more, the numbers began to replace tragedies. Death thus became a figure that is lost daily amid scandals and statements. A gloomy comparison between ridiculous nationalisms. The batting and earned run percentage that determines which team, or Nation, is better or worse.

As detailed in one of the previous texts, in Zapatismo we opted for prevention and the application of sanitary measures that, at the time, were consulted with scientists who guided us and offered, without hesitation, their help. The Zapatista peoples are grateful to them and that is how we wanted to show it. After 6 months of the implementation of these measures (mouth covers or its equivalent, distance between people, closure of direct personal contacts with urban areas, 15-day quarantine for those who may have been in contact with infected people, frequent washing with soap and water ), we regret the death of 3 colleagues who presented two or more symptoms associated with Covid 19 and who had direct contact with those infected.

Another 8 companions and a companion, who died in that period, presented one of the symptoms. As we lack the possibility of proof, we assume that all 12 comrades died from the so-called Corona virus (scientists recommended us to assume that any respiratory difficulty would be Covid 19). These 12 absences are our responsibility. They are not the fault of the 4T or the opposition, of neoliberals or neoconservatives, of chairos or fifís, of conspiracies or plots. We think that we should have taken even more precautions.

Currently, with the lack of those 12 comrades, we are improving prevention measures in all communities, now with the support of Non-Governmental Organizations and scientists who, individually or collectively, guide us in how to cope with more strength a possible regrowth. Tens of thousands of mouth covers (specially designed to prevent a probable carrier from infecting other people, inexpensive, reusable and adapted to the circumstances) have been distributed in all communities.

Tens of thousands more are being produced in the *insurgents'* sewing and embroidery workshops as well as those in the communities. The measures we have recommended to our own communities as well as to our party-affiliated brothers and sisters—the widespread use of masks, a 2-week quarantine for those potentially infected, physical distance, continual hand and face washing with soap and water, and avoidance of the cities to the greatest extent possible—are all oriented toward containing any spread of contagion as well as permitting the maintenance of community life.

The details of what was and is our strategy may be consulted in due course. For now we say, with life beating in our bodies, that, according to our assessment (in which we can probably be wrong), facing the threat as a community, not as an individual matter, and directing our main effort to prevention. It just allows us to say, as Zapatista peoples: here we are, we resist, we live, we fight.

And now, all over the world, big capital wants to return to the streets so that people can resume their status as consumers. Because it is the problems of the market that concern him: the lethargy in the consumption of merchandise.

You have to take back the streets, yes, but to fight. Because, as we have said before, life, the struggle for life, is not an individual matter, but a collective one. Now it is being seen that it is not a matter of nationalities, it is global.

◊

Many of these things we look at and hear. And we think about them a lot. But not only...

Fifth.—We also listen and look at the resistances and rebellions that, not because they are silenced or forgotten, cease to be key, clues of a humanity that refuses to follow the system in its hasty passage to collapse: the mortal train of progress that advances, superb and flawless, towards the cliff. While the machinist forgets that he is just another employee and believes, naively, that he decides the way, when he is only following the prison of the rails towards the abyss.

Resistance and rebellion that, without forgetting the cry for absences, insist on fighting for -who would say-, the most subversive thing that exists in those worlds divided between neoliberals and neoconservatives-: life.

Rebellions and resistances that understand, each one in their own way, their time and their geography, that the solutions are not in faith in national governments, that they are not gestated protected by borders or wear different flags and languages.

Resistances and rebellions that teach us, we, *nosotroas*, Zapatistas, that solutions could be down, in basements and corners of the world. Not in government palaces. Not in the offices of large corporations.

Rebellions and resistances that show us that, if those from above break the bridges and close the borders, it remains to navigate rivers and seas to find ourselves. That the cure, if there is one, is worldwide, and has the color of the earth, of the work that lives and dies in streets and neighborhoods, in seas and skies, in the mountains and in its entrails. That, like the original corn, many are its colors, its tones and sounds.

◊

All this, and more, we watch and listen. And we look at each other and listen to each other for what we are: a number that does not count. Because life does not matter, it does not sell, it is not news, it does not enter the statistics, it does not compete in polls, it has no valuation on social networks, it does not provoke, it does not represent political capital, party flag, fashion scandal. Who cares that a small, very small group of natives, Indigenous people, lives, that is, they fight?

Because we happen to live. That despite paramilitaries, pandemics, *megaprojects* , lies, slander and forgetfulness, we live. I mean, we fight.

And we think about this: that we continue to fight. That is, we continue to live. And we think that during all these years, we have received the brotherly embrace of people from our country and the world. And we think that if life resists here and, not without difficulties, flourishes, it is thanks to those people who challenged distances, procedures, borders, and cultural and language differences. Thanks to them, they, *they* – but above all them-, who challenged and defeated calendars and geographies.

In the mountains of the Mexican southeast, all the worlds of the world found, and find, heard in our hearts. His word and action was food for resistance and rebellion, which are but a continuation of those of our predecessors.

People with the sciences and the arts as a way, they found the way to embrace and encourage us, even if it was from a distance. Journalists, fifis and no, who reported misery and death before, dignity and life always. People of all professions and trades who, a lot for us, maybe a little for them, were, are.

And all this we think of our collective heart, and arrived in our thinking that it is time now that we, us, *nosotroas* , Zapatistas us respond to the ear, the word and the presence of those worlds. The near and far in geography.

Sixth.—And this we have decided:

That it is time again for hearts to dance, and that their music and their steps are not those of lament and resignation.

That various Zapatista delegations, men, women and *others* of the color of our land, we will go out to travel the world, we will walk or sail to remote soils, seas and skies, seeking not difference, not superiority, not affront, much less forgiveness and the pity.

We will go to find what makes us equal.

Not only humanity that animates our different skins, our different ways, our different languages and colors. Also, and above all, the common dream that, as a species, we have shared since, in Africa that seems distant, we started walking on the lap of the first woman: the search for freedom that animated that first step … and that continues to walk.

That the first destination of this planetary journey will be the European continent.

That we will sail to European lands. That we will leave and that we will set sail, from Mexican lands, in the month of April of the year 2021.

That, after traveling through various corners of Europe below and to the left, we will arrive in Madrid, the Spanish capital, on August 13, 2021 -500 years after the supposed conquest of what is now Mexico. And that, immediately afterwards, we will continue on the path.

That we will speak to the Spanish people. Not to threaten, reproach, insult or demand. Not to demand that you ask us for forgiveness. Not to serve you or to serve us.

We are going to tell the people of Spain two simple things:

One: They didn't win us over. That we continue in resistance and rebellion.

Two: They don't have to ask us to forgive them anything. Enough of playing with the distant past to justify, with demagoguery and hypocrisy, current and ongoing crimes: the murder of social fighters, such as brother Samir Flores Soberanes; the genocides hidden behind *megaprojects*, conceived and carried out for the joy of the powerful – the same one that is scourging every corner of the planet-; monetary encouragement and impunity for the paramilitaries; the purchase of consciences and dignities with 30 coins.

We, we, *nosotroas*, Zapatistas do not want to go back to the past, either alone, much less than the hand of those who want to sow racial hatred and aims to feed their nationalism trasnochado with the splendor course of an empire, the Aztec, which grew cost of the blood of their fellow men, and who wants to convince us that, with the fall of that empire, the original peoples of these lands were defeated.

Neither the Spanish State nor the Catholic Church have to ask us for forgiveness of anything. We will not echo the phonies who ride on our blood and thus hide that their hands are stained with it.

What is Spain going to apologize for? Of having given birth to Cervantes? To José Espronceda? Leon Felipe? Federico García Lorca? To Manuel Vázquez Montalbán? Miguel Hernández? Pedro Salinas? Antonio Machado? Lope de Vega? To Bécquer? Almudena Grandes? To Panchito Varona, Ana Belén, Sabina, Serrat, Ibáñez, Llach, Amparanoia, Miguel Ríos, Paco de Lucía, Víctor Manuel, Aute always? Buñuel, Almodóvar and Agrado, Saura, Fernán Gómez, Fernando León, Bardem? Dalí, Miró, Goya, Picasso, El Greco and Velázquez? Some of the best of world critical thinking, stamped with the libertarian ' *A* ' ? To the republic? To exile? To the Mayan brother Gonzalo Guerrero?

What is the Catholic Church going to apologize for? From the passage of Bartolomé de las Casas? From Don Samuel Ruiz García? From Arturo Lona? From Sergio Méndez Arceo? From Sister Chapis? From the steps of the priests, religious and secular sisters who have walked alongside the natives without directing or supplanting them? Of those who risk their freedom and life to defend human rights?

◊

The year 2021 will mark the 20th anniversary of the March of the Color of the Earth, which we carry out, together with the brother peoples of the National Indigenous Congress, to claim a place in this Nation that is now crumbling.

20 years later we will sail and walk to tell the planet that, in the world that we feel in our collective heart, there is room for everyone, everyone, *everything* . Simply and simply because that world is only possible if everyone, everyone, *everything*, struggles to raise it.

The Zapatista delegations will be made up mainly of women. Not only because they intend to return the hug they received in previous international meetings. Also, and above all, so that we Zapatista men make it clear that we are what we are, and we are not what we are not, thanks to them, for them and with them.

We invite the CNI-CIG to form a delegation to accompany us and thus make our word richer for the other that fights far away. We especially invite a delegation from the peoples that raise the name, image and blood of brother Samir Flores Soberanes, so that his pain, his anger, his struggle and resistance reach further.

We invite those whose vocation, commitment and horizon, the arts and sciences, to accompany, from a distance, our navigations and steps. And so they help us to spread that in them, sciences and arts, there is the possibility not only of the survival of humanity, but also of a new world.

In short: we left for Europe in April 2021. The date and time? We don't know... yet.

◊

Companions, companions, *companions* :
Sisters, brothers and *sisters* :

This is our commitment:

In front of the powerful trains, our canoes.

In front of the thermoelectric plants, the little lights that the Zapatistas gave in custody to women who fight all over the world.

Facing walls and borders, our collective sailing.

In front of the great capital, a common cornfield.

Faced with the destruction of the planet, a mountain sailing at dawn.

We are Zapatistas, carriers of the virus of resistance and rebellion. As such, we will go to the 5 continents.

That's all for now.

From the mountains of the mexican southeast.

On behalf of the Zapatista women, men and *other* women.

**Insurgent Subcommander Moisés**
Mexico, October 2020.

PS- Yes, it is the sixth part and, like the trip, it will continue in the opposite direction. That is, the fifth part will follow, then the fourth, then the third, it will continue in the second and end with the first.

# THE EMPIRE OF ALL MALADIES: COLONIAL CONTAGIONS AND INDIGENOUS RESISTANCE

Nick Estes

2020[1]

One of the most potent myths of mainstream U.S. historiography concerns what Indigenous archaeologist Michael V. Wilcox calls 'terminal narratives': an obsession with the death, disappearance, and absence of Indigenous people rather than their continued, visible presence and challenge to colonialism. The most obvious example of this tendency are historical models that assign blame for the mass killing of the Indigenous to invisible, chance forces—above all, the diseases colonizers unwittingly carried with them—rather than to calculated warfare and theft over centuries of relentless European invasion.

Debates about the epidemiological vulnerability of Indigenous people first came to prominence in the 1970s as historians backed away from narratives of European cultural superiority in search of more scientific explanations. This biological turn identified microbes as a primary culprit in the mass death of the Indigenous, suggesting that the depopulation of the Americas was an inevitable result of Native communities' contact with diseases from the old world. In a 1976 essay, the historian Alfred W. Crosby put forth the 'virgin-soil epidemics' thesis, which posited that Europeans brought diseases—in particular, smallpox and measles—that wiped out 70 percent or more of Native people in the Western Hemisphere because they lacked immunity. In what was framed as the most extreme demographic disaster in human history, the most affected regions experienced a 90 percent depopulation rate, including deaths related to disease, which is estimated to have reduced the population of the Americas from one hundred million to ten million.

Crosby's thesis soon gained wide traction in the academy. In his classic 1991 study *The Middle Ground*, the historian Richard White wrote that Indigenous people, cut off from European pathogens, 'had not been selected over time for resistance to such diseases' and were therefore 'doomed to die.' Indigenous people had 'no opportunity to build up immunological resistance,' Colin Calloway similarly argued in his 1997 book *New Worlds for All*; they 'were doomed to die in one of

1. Source: https://thebaffler.com/salvos/the-empire-of-all-maladies-estes

the greatest biological catastrophes in human history.' That same year, Jared Diamond published his Pulitzer Prize-winning book, *Guns, Germs, and Steel*, in which he endorsed the 'virgin-soil epidemics' thesis, thereby bringing it into the popular consciousness.

Indigenous scholars have long contested this thesis—though few were paying attention to their rebuttals. Disease as a result of colonial policy and actions 'was rarely called genocide until the rise of Indigenous movements in the mid-twentieth century,' writes historian Roxanne Dunbar-Ortiz in *An Indigenous Peoples' History of the United States*. For the Lenape historian Jack D. Forbes, it was not so much the Indigenous who were suffering affliction, but the Europeans who had been infected with what he called *wétiko*, the Algonquin word for a mind-virus associated with cannibalism. The overriding characteristic of *wétiko*, as he recounted in his 1979 book *Columbus and Other Cannibals*, is that 'he consumes other human beings' for profit. This concept is nearly synonymous with the European psychosis of domination and plunder.

Today, it is clear that the disease thesis simply doesn't hold up. From where I write, in what is now New Mexico, recent archaeological evidence suggests that a population decline among the Pueblo nations of the Southwest didn't occur until a century after Spanish invasion in the mid-sixteenth century. The Jemez people of New Mexico, for example, didn't start abandoning their villages until after 1620. It was around this time that Spanish colonization took hold. Catholic missions began crowding the Pueblo people together, removing them from their lands and taking away their livelihoods, providing the critical conditions for the spread of disease. By 1680, the Pueblo of Jemez had lost an estimated 87 percent of their population: most to war, famine, and disease. This was no doubt a key inspiration of the Pueblo Revolt of the same year, which led to the successful expulsion of the Spanish.

A similar situation unfolded along the Upper Missouri River, where I was born and raised. When Lewis and Clark led a military expedition upriver, Missouri River Indigenous nations had already experienced several rounds of smallpox epidemics as a result of increased contact with British and French trappers. But none were as apocalyptic as the smallpox epidemic of 1837, by which time the United States dominated the river trade. U.S. trading led to the utter annihilation of furbearing animals through over-hunting, the ecological destruction of the river, and its increased militarization (the U.S. presence heightened conflict between Indigenous nations engaged in trading). Under these adverse conditions, the Mandans were nearly wiped out by smallpox. From 1780 to 1870, Indigenous river nations experienced an 80 percent population decline, with some experiencing rates higher than 90 percent, mostly due to disease.

The forced diet proved to be one of the deadliest diseases imposed by colonizers. Diabetes was almost non-existent among the Missouri River tribes, even during the reservation period. But after the Pick-Sloan plan dammed the Upper Missouri River with a series of five earthen-rolled dams in the mid-twentieth century for hydroelectricity and irrigation, 75 percent of wildlife and native plants on the area's reservations disappeared, and hundreds of thousands of acres of Indigenous farms were destroyed. In total, 550 square miles of Native land were affected across nine different Indigenous reservations: Santee, Yankton, Crow Creek, Lower Brule, Cheyenne River, Standing Rock, Fort Berthold, and Fort Peck. What was once a subsistence economy based on wild harvesting and small-scale agriculture was transformed almost overnight into dependency on U.S.DA commodities. White flour, milk, white sugar, and canned foods replaced formerly protein- and nutrient-rich diets. Diabetes rates skyrocketed, and its spread can be contact-traced to a single public works project.

## Who CARES?

Fast forward half a century, and the situation remains eerily similar. On May 17, Trump's health secretary Alex Azar told CNN that the high coronavirus death rate in the United States had less to do with government inaction than it did with certain people being unhealthier than others. 'Unfortunately, the American population is very diverse,' Azar explained, noting that, 'in particular,' Black people and 'minority communities' have 'significant underlying . . . health disparities and disease comorbidities.'

His statement was only a small part of the immense deceit and distortion surrounding the U.S. government's shameful response to coronavirus, which has already claimed over one hundred thousand lives. The government has once again made clear that the lives of the poor—especially the Black and Indigenous poor—are less sacred than private property. White America has only driven this point home. Since late April, after statistics revealed that the virus had a greater impact on Black, Latinx, and Indigenous communities, so-called anti-lockdown protests surged. Men armed with assault rifles and donning military-grade body armor stormed state capitol buildings, demanding haircuts and the reopening of beaches and ice cream parlors. That is why the Cheyenne River Sioux Tribe and the Oglala Sioux Tribe have set up health checkpoints. 'We will not apologize for being an island of safety in a sea of uncertainty and death,' Cheyenne River chairman Harold Frazier wrote to the governor of South Dakota, one of five states to issue no stay-at-home order in response to the pandemic.

Native nations have been hit the hardest by the virus. The Navajo Nation, whose lands helped make the United States the world's largest oil producer, now faces some of the worst rates of infection and death—not only compared to other states, but to entire countries. About 30 percent of its reservation population lives without running water, and about 10 percent without electricity, while coal from its lands fuels power plants, and the water from its rivers soaks golf courses in Phoenix. The United States created the first nuclear bomb on a sacred Tewa mesa with uranium mined from Navajo lands, poisoning generations. For the Navajo people, the real pandemic is—and has always been—resource colonization.

What 'help' the government has provided Indigenous people so far has been unsatisfactory, if not downright harmful. On paper, it seems that the Department of Interior, which is charged with gifting U.S. freedom and democracy to the Indigenous (curiously, it also manages wildlife and natural resources), is currently in the process of allocating the $8 billion of CARES Act money reserved for tribal coronavirus relief. But a closer look at the department's response reveals something more akin to a land-grab, graft, and slow-motion Indian massacre.

On May 20, five tribal organizations signed a letter to David Bernhardt, the secretary of the interior (and a former oil lobbyist), calling for the resignation of assistant secretary of Indian affairs Tara Sweeney, an Inupiaq Alaskan Native (also a former oil lobbyist) for what she had set into motion during the pandemic. In late February, as coronavirus swept through the country, a federal court denied the Mashpee Wampanoag the right to restore their homeland in Massachusetts, a process set into motion by Sweeney in 2018 that was overturned by a federal judge in June. Her office also failed to protect the Tohono O'odham Nation's burial and sacred sites from being destroyed with explosives to build Trump's border wall, the construction of which continued unabated as large sectors of the economy were shut down. Meanwhile, the Interior Department allowed for-profit Alaskan Native corporations, many of which have investments in the oil and gas industry, to seek payouts from the Covid-19 relief money reserved for tribal governments. It is still unclear how this determination was made. While pandering to for-profit Alaskan Native corporations, Sweeney's office restricted Alaskan Natives from restoring their homelands through a fee-to-trust process.

The pandemic has also thrown into relief the way that mass incarceration affects Indigenous communities. According to a report compiled by the Lakota People's Law Project, American Indian men are incarcerated at four times the rate of white men, and American Indian women are incarcerated at six times the rate of white women. Police kill American Indians and African Americans at the highest rates. On April 28, three weeks after giving birth while in custody, Andrea Circle Bear, a thirty-year-old citizen of the Cheyenne River Sioux Tribe, became the first woman to die of coronavirus in federal prison. She was five months pregnant when sentenced to twenty-six months for a minor drug charge. Prison officials said the new mother had 'a pre-existing medical condition,' making her more susceptible to severe symptoms, such as shortness of breath. It's not clear what that condition was, but her pregnancy was also noted as a risk factor. In truth, the 'pre-existing condition' that removed Andrea Circle Bear from the 'island of safety' her nation had created with health checkpoints, that exposed her to her a deadly virus, wasn't just inequality. (Five years earlier, on July 6, Andrea's twenty-four-year-old sister-in-law Sarah Lee Circle Bear, a mother of two whose family claimed she was pregnant at the time, died in jail after being picked up for a bond violation following a traffic accident.)

Last month was the three-year anniversary of the killing of Zachary Bearheels, a twenty-nine-year-old citizen of the Rosebud Sioux Tribe. After suffering a mental breakdown and being kicked off a bus in Omaha while on his way back to Oklahoma City, police were filmed tasing Bearheels twelve times and punching him thirteen times in the head. 'I can't fucking breathe,' he told officers as he sat in the back of the cruiser. A coroner later found his cause of death to be 'excited delirium,' a condition that supposedly leads to aggressiveness, incoherence, and 'superhuman strength,' often after taking cocaine or methamphetamines. (Bearheels, however, had no drugs or alcohol in his system at the time of his death.) This diagnosis is controversial; it is frequently cited when people die in police custody. Three of the officers involved in Bearheels's death were reinstated in April.

As it happens, the Minneapolis police officers who murdered George Floyd this Memorial Day also had 'excited delirium' on their minds. As Floyd laid face down on the pavement with Derek Chauvin's knee on his neck, one officer asked if they should turn their victim over onto his side. 'I am worried about excited delirium or whatever,' he told Chauvin, according to a court statement. 'That's why we have him on his stomach,' Chauvin responded. 'I can't breathe,' Floyd told the police. 'No physical findings support a diagnosis of traumatic asphyxia or strangulation,' a preliminary medical examiner's report later claimed; it was 'underlying health conditions' such as heart disease that got him.

## The Humane Condition

The United States has a long history of sacrificing or killing off groups of people—through war or disease or both—in the name of its self-proclaimed destiny. This belief in the country's violent superiority was already evident among the early Puritans, who attributed the mass die-off of Indigenous peoples to divine intervention. 'God hath so pursued them' John Winthrop, the Puritan leader of the Massachusetts Bay Colony, wrote of the Indigenous to the King of England in 1634. 'The greatest part of them are swept away by smallpox ... God hath thereby cleared our title to this place.' Winthrop and his fellow colonists later consummated their possession by mixing blood and soil in the Pequot War of 1637, which set the stage for subsequent Indian campaigns that concluded in the total or near-total extermination of their enemies.

To blind themselves to the destruction they wrought, colonizers wove cultural fictions about the 'vastness' of a continent devoid of human civilization—*terra nullius*—and thus open for white European settlement. (This was an early ideological ancestor of the Zionist phrase, 'a land without a people for a people without a land,' that has come to justify the expulsion and colonization of Palestinians.) General Henry Knox, the revolutionary war hero and the United States' first secretary of war, was less confused about how the land was emptied. He recalled 'the utter extirpation of all the Indians in the most populous parts of the Union' by measures 'more destructive to the Indian natives than the conduct of the conquerors of Mexico and Peru.' No small feat.

The imperial project wasn't confined to what became the continental United States. It soon turned outward, as the settler state exported the horrors it had committed against the Indigenous to the rest of the planet. Most historians have failed to draw what are obvious connections between heightened rates of infection and conditions of war, invasion, and colonialism. We need only look at the cholera outbreak in Yemen to see the relationship of disease to U.S. foreign policy. No one is disputing the fact that the infection of millions and the deaths of thousands there at the hands of this preventable disease are the result of a U.S.-backed, Saudi-led war, which has destroyed Yemen's health care infrastructure. It shouldn't surprise us to learn that one in four surgical amputations conducted at Red Cross centers in Iraq, Syria, and Yemen are the result of diabetes. These three countries have been the staging ground for U.S.-backed military interventions and invasions that have disrupted critical food and medical supply chains.

Economic sanctions, frequently hailed by politicians of all stripes as a 'humane' alternative to war, are simply war by another means. U.S. sanctions currently hit hard in thirty-nine countries—one-third of humanity—causing currency inflation and devaluation and upsetting the distribution of medicine, food, power, water treatment, and other human needs. A 2019 report by the Center for Economic and Policy Studies found that U.S. sanctions on Venezuela accounted for an estimated forty thousand deaths and a loss of $6 billion in oil revenue between 2017 and 2018. As Iran began to experience increased rates of coronavirus infection, the country faced medical supply shortages because of sanctions. While countries like China and Cuba, themselves both sanctioned by the United States, provided international aid to other countries suffering from the pandemic, Trump actively prevented other countries from adequately responding to the crisis. To top things off, this May, he withdrew from the WHO in protest, shifting the blame to China for his own country's failure to stop the virus's spread.

## The Tribe They Cannot See

'The United States operates on incredibly stupid premises,' the Standing Rock intellectual Vine Deloria Jr. wrote half a century ago in *Custer Died for Your Sins*. 'It always fails to understand the nature of the world and so does not develop policies that can hold the allegiance of people.' Put simply, the United States only knows violence. It convinces through force. It is numb to suffering and indifferent to the welfare of people.

When confronted with science and hard facts that deny its mythology, the United States chooses hallucination. It sees Indigenous genocide unfold before its very eyes and blames 'pre-existing conditions.' It sees police murdering and torturing Black people every day and describes that as law and order. It sees global warming coming and does nothing. (In fact, it speeds it up, renaming fossil fuels 'freedom molecules' and natural gas 'freedom gas,' emitted to liberate the atmosphere.) It sees a pandemic approaching months in advance and chooses not to act.

Perhaps the starkest illustration of the intoxicating power of Manifest Destiny is America's latest flirtation with space. In February 2019, President Trump issued an executive order to begin the process of creating the sixth branch of the military, the Space Force, 'to organize, train, and equip military space forces . . . to ensure unfettered access to, and freedom to operate in, space.' (By December it was formally established.) 'America has always been a frontier nation,' he remarked in his most recent State of the Union address. 'Now we must embrace the next frontier, America's manifest destiny in the stars.' Two months later, amid the chaos of the surging pandemic, the president signed an executive order granting the United States the preemptive right—the first monopoly of claims—to start mining the moon and asteroids. And as more than thirty U.S. cities erupted in open rebellion over racist police terror, Trump and Vice President Mike Pence went to Florida to watch Elon Musk's SpaceX launch an astronaut. Trump has elevated U.S. belligerence to the cosmos.

If he trained his eyes back on earth, he would realize that after living through two economic recessions, endless war, and cascading ecological destruction, Americans still act like antibodies to the virus called capitalism. Yet a new world is coming into existence, even as fires burn in the Amazon or on the streets of Minneapolis. It has always been here. It was present at Standing Rock, in the chants of 'water is life'; it could be heard among the Wet'suwet'en calls to 'heal the people, heal the land'; and it resounded once again as hundreds of thousands took to the street to demand that 'Black lives matter.'

Yes, this world has been here all along, but as the late Dakota poet John Trudell once said, 'We are the tribe they cannot see.' His message was clear: colonialism is not only a contest over territory, but over the meaning of life itself. The sonic vibrations of the words 'Indian' or 'Native American'—make-believe vocabularies—never penetrated the airwaves of the lands now called America until European invasion. 'We have been called many names,' Trudell remarked, listing other labels—hostile, Pagan, militant—that have become synonymous with Indigenous in the grammar of colonialism. 'The callers of names cannot see us, but we can see them,' he says. 'We are the Halluci Nation.'

# BUILDING FROM THE RUBBLE: PALESTINIAN RESISTANCE AND THE ROAD TO LIBERATION

Mark Muhannad Ayyash

2021[1]

The Palestinian literary critic and anti-colonial theorist, Edward Said, taught us that 'The native point of view... is not an ethnographic fact only... it is in large measure a continuing, protracted, and sustained adversarial resistance' to academic, cultural, and political discourses of empire.

Critical to underscore is how the position, standpoint, and perspective of the native Palestinian is not only an ethnic, racial, or nationalist one. It is first and foremost the position of the dominated, oppressed, and colonized. It is the standpoint of bodies that are marked for maiming, killing, and erasure. It is the perspective that launches a committed, grounded, and adversarial resistance to empire.

The Indigenous Palestinian resistance to Israeli settler colonialism is the embodiment of a decolonial alternative to the world of colonial modernity, which is based on an instrumental rationality that drives and maximizes absolute domination, control, and supremacy over all life forms. European colonial projects since the fifteenth century have ravaged the majority of the world's population through slavery and the slave trade, direct and indirect colonialism, destructive resource extraction, labor exploitation, race and racism, and the transfer of massive wealth from the world's colonized spaces into the colonizing Euro-American spaces. Particularly destructive in colonial modernity is the erection of the modern nation-state, built on race and racism, resting on absurd notions of ethnic and racial purity.

The Israeli state is a form of modern nationalist settler colonialism that asserts exclusive Jewish sovereignty over the land of historic Palestine. Israel is built on the displacement and ethnic cleansing of the native Palestinian population. But despite the suffering, devastation, and loss, for over one hundred years, Palestinians have resisted their displacement from their lands. Since the Nakba of 1948

---

1. Source: Ayyash, Mark Muhannad. 'Building from the Rubble: Palestinian Resistance and the Road to Liberation.' *The Baffler*. May 19. https://thebaffler.com/latest/building-from-the-rubble-ayyash

and the creation of the Israeli state, Palestinians have resisted an advanced Israeli military apparatus mostly with just their bare bodies.

Given the Euro-American laser-focused gaze on Palestinian armed resistance, it is easy to understand why many American readers might find this usage of 'bare bodies' controversial or new. In fact it is neither of those things. This statement is simply the insertion of the colonized's reality into the empire's orgy of narratives—narratives that serve to conceal that reality: 'democracy vs. theocracy,' 'civilized vs. savage,' 'enlightenment vs. mysticism,' 'Western values vs. the backward Orient,' and so on.

Over its long history, Palestinian resistance practices have included labor strikes, boycotts, marches, demonstrations, general strikes, popular memorialization and commemorations, sit-ins, resistance art: the list is indeed too large to enumerate. It is a list full of ingenuity, courage, and humanity. Decade after decade, these practices have stood and continue to stand in the face of Israeli settler colonial violence, which seeks to eliminate and replace the native Palestinians. Two features of this violence stand out: fragmentation and dehumanization.

In order to defeat and derail Palestinian resistance, Israel has long separated Palestinians from each other physically, symbolically, and experientially.

Divided and contained within manageable fragments in Gaza; East Jerusalem; the West Bank; '48 Palestine (the lands within what became Israel, where Palestinians managed to remain); refugee camps; or in exile across the world, Israel believed that Palestinians would no longer be able to resist in unison. Many commentators have been observing this fragmentation for decades, concluding that the Israeli plan has in fact worked. But once again, as we are witnessing today, the Palestinian people have proven all such political analyses and calculations wrong.

It is perhaps most glaringly in Gaza that we see both elements of fragmentation and dehumanization. In what is a cruel, vicious, and brutal form of collective imprisonment and punishment, the dehumanization of Palestinians in Gaza is difficult for Palestinians like myself to write about and describe. In fact, it is impossible for anyone to fully capture and understand.

A population of largely 1948 refugees and their descendants crammed into a tiny, isolated, besieged space. Nothing comes in or out of that space without Israeli regulation and approval. Clean water, electricity, medical equipment and facilities, jobs, housing, safety from Israeli military onslaughts, dignity, freedom, liberty, movement, food, and much more are all desperately lacking for the majority of the people in Gaza. Most have never been able to leave that place. Most have never seen Jerusalem.

The dehumanization of Gazans does not only happen when the cameras of the world—at least those not being blown to smithereens by the Israeli war machine—are fixated on a wave of military attacks. Dehumanization is always happening in Gaza, and it began long before the onset of besiegement in 2007, when Israel imposed the ongoing blockade. From the very first years of childhood, Palestinians in Gaza receive a clear message from Israel and indeed from the world: you are not human, and we do not care.

But just as Frantz Fanon taught is the case in all contexts of colonialism and settler colonialism, the colonized never forget that they are in fact human.

Despite all of the censorship and propaganda in Euro-America, many heart wrenching and devastating images, videos, and words from Palestinians in Gaza are reaching the world to communicate this very fact. One example is a photo of two young Palestinian children. In the background, their homes have been reduced to rubble. But amid all of the unbearable death and brutal odds, the two stand smiling, holding a small jar of water with their fish inside. In their smiles, they're clinging to contentment, maybe even happiness that their fish is still alive. That they rescued from their devastation this small creature, this small life form, allows them to stand firm and as affirmative of life. Of a human life that still reaches out to all life forms, and connects with them, as one precious life to another.

Some children in this world get to gaze at the stars, kickstarting their sense of wonderment and discovery. The children in Gaza are forced instead to gaze at stones, at the rubble. But instead of descending into the nonhuman, of breaking down into a rubble among the rubbles, of losing themselves in the rubble, they find the beauty in the rubble. They stand on top of the rubble carrying in their small hands the life they saved, enmeshed as they are in their harmonious connection to all life forms, engendering a sense of wonderment, belonging, and exploration of all the human potentialities that lie deep within them.

Their defiance to live as humans, on top of the rubble and the death, in the face of horrendous dehumanization, is in fact the very core of something grander than colonial modernity's depraved notion of the human. They bring life from underneath the rubble, transforming the meaning of the rubble away from death and back to a harmonious life. Not the instrumentalizing homo-economicus of colonial modernity. A human life properly connected to all life forms with care, dignity, contentment, and happiness in the face of all that threatens life. The rubble becomes the building blocks of the rejuvenation of a new life.

Today, we are witnessing this rejuvenation in Palestine. On May 18, Palestinians across all of Palestine and in exile heeded the call for a general strike. In their call for the strike, activists from '48 Palestine signed the statement with the following words, "Ashat Falastin Waheda / 'Ashat Intifada Al-Wahda': 'Long Live a United Palestine / Long Live the Intifada of Unity.'

As Palestinian activist Salem Barahmeh describes the strike in a tweet: 'The scenes across Palestine are breathtaking, Ramallah chanting for Gaza, Haifa singing to Ramallah, the Palestinian flag being raised in Jerusalem. It is an incredible day, led by the people for their liberation from the subjugation of a tyrannical regime. Long live Palestine.'

This Intifada of Unity has been on display from the very beginning of these recent events. Despite all Israeli efforts to block them, '48 Palestinians—who are the Palestinian second class citizens of Israel—worked with Palestinians in Jerusalem to ensure that they were able to reach al-Aqsa Mosque and stand in solidarity with Sheikh Jarrah. When Israeli mobs, supported and protected by Israeli soldiers, attacked Palestinians in Lydd, Palestinians from Jerusalem and the Naqab drove there in buses to protect them by sheer numbers. From Lebanon and Jordan, children of Palestinian refugees who were displaced in 1948 managed to temporarily cross back into their historic lands. Despite their brief stay, the images were powerful: for a brief moment, they rejected the reality of empire and colonization that has been imposed on them, and in doing so, revealed the depth of their yearning for return.

This is but a small taste of the incredible unity that Palestinians have communicated and shared with each other over the last week, which suggests that underneath their fragmentation, that unity never disappeared. If you are not stirred into action by the images, videos, and words reaching you from colonized Palestine, then you are part of the problem of colonial modernity and its uninhibited brutality. And so perhaps you need to gaze at the rubble instead of the stars. Do not look away from the images and videos, and hear them in accordance with their voice, not the voice of empire.

And if you are stirred, or become stirred, then you already know, implicitly or explicitly, that Palestinian resistance is not just the story of Palestinians and Palestine, but the story of all those who are dominated, colonized, enslaved, oppressed—who are being crushed like rubble under the weight of the world of empire. Let's build from that rubble, from our shattered and fragmented selves, a new humanity and a new world.

This is why empire fears Palestinian resistance; because it excites the revolutionary spirit, reinvigorates the revolutionary soul, and points us towards a new world, a better and more just world for all of us. A decolonial world.

# TO BE BLACK, TO SIMPLY LIVE: THE BURDEN OF REVOLUTIONARY NONVIOLENCE

Wende Marshall

2020[1]

This is a message to white workers:

The possibilities for nonviolent revolution rest largely in your hands.

You made a bargain with capital that W.E.B. Du Bois described as a 'psychological wage.' The deal stipulated that you lower your expectations and present yourself for quotidian exploitation in exchange for status as *Not Black*. Status as *Not Black* meant that you would accrue the wages of whiteness, a set of relatively paltry social and economic benefits that both obscured your class interests and cemented you to the cause of the capitalist overlords. But pay attention: the chimera of your white privilege and social status were nothing more than a cheap trick executed by the bloody hands of Euro/American capital. The wages and prestige you earned in this transaction depended entirely upon the debasement of Black life. The mechanisms holding this bargain together were unremitting physical and structural violence against my people, 'organized abandonment[2]' of our communities, the carceral state, the metaphorical knee on our neck.

To procure free, cheap, and degraded labor white capital propped you up with myths of your superiority. They created a vortex of violence that undergird your white civil society and your white American dreams.

Your white picket fence obscured barbed wire. Your apple pie was poisoned by pesticides and the trauma of slave and near slave farm labor. Your excessive desire for things choked the rivers with filth and smothered the air with toxic dirt. Still, you persisted in your myths. You clung to the apotheosis of your mediocrity, hoarding that meager wealth allowed to you—wealth that was created by my ancestors—turning a blind eye to the systematic genocide, state-sanctioned and extra-legal murder, and the maelstrom of quotidian violence.

But now they are coming for you. Now, in the 21st Century, capital has eschewed the bargain and turned against you. Many more of you are on now on

---

1. Adapted from a keynote plenary speech delivered at the 2018 Peace and Justice Studies Association conference, Arcadia University, Philadelphia, PA
2. Ruth Wilson Gilmore etc. find cite

the economic precipice. More of you are experiencing dehumanization, degradation, premature death, and soteriological insecurity. You are made redundant by robots and workers in the global south, your factories are shuttered, your labor unions are feeble and ineffective. You are overdosing on meth, heroin, and pharma-peddled opioids, causing a startling rise in your white mortality rates. You rally behind a cheap slogan about making America great again, your rage is stoked by white demagogues whose job it is to distract you from the realities of white working-class life in a dying empire.

What do you do at this juncture? Do you cling to your whiteness, to your false and shaky privilege? Or do you lay your body on the line to learn and resist? Will you remain distracted from the reality that white supremacy is an elaborate game to subvert the power of working-class unity across race and class? Or will you rise to the occasion and practice the actual solidarity and sacrifice needed, for white folks to make on behalf of Black lives?

White workers need to get clear that white supremacy and capitalism were joined from the beginning, that Euro/American wealth begins at the nexus of the enclosure of peasant lands in Europe, the rape of the African continent, the forced transportation of some 12 million Black bodies and the genocidal theft of these Indigenous lands.

The white men who wrote the U.S. Constitution evaded recognition that slavery was foundational to the U.S.—politically, economically, and socio-culturally. They told lies about white superiority that served as an alibi for the violence of accumulation. Nevertheless, it was enslaved Africans, brought in chains, that provided the labor which enabled the United States to grow into a capitalist economic power. Thoroughly dehumanized and defined as chattel, my ancestors produced cotton, sugar, tobacco, and rice. They were bought and sold yielding profit for slave owners and a host of allied industries including Southern merchants, who supplied food and clothing to slave owners, railroad and ship owners who transported slaves, Northern banks that handled the exchange of money, and Northern insurance companies covering slave owners' investments.

The slave trade was the foundation of the entire economy.[3] The entire economy rested on the backs of slaves. The New England textile industry, for example, was fueled by the labor of enslaved Blacks picking cotton. Indeed, according to the scholar Garakai Chengu: '[c]otton was to the early 19th century what oil was to the 20th century: the commodity that determined the wealth of nations. Cotton amounted to a staggering fifty per cent of U.S. exports and ignited the economic boom that America experienced. America owes its very existence as a first world nation to' the degradation of my enslaved ancestors.[4]

From the beginning, white supremacy and capitalism depended upon terror. It was terror and violence that attended the Atlantic slave trade and opened the

3. Maurie D. McInnis, 'How the Slave Trade Built America,' *The New York Times*, April 3, 2015, accessed at http://opinionator.blogs.nytimes.com/2015/04/03/how-the-slave-trade-built-america/?_r=0 on 8/31/2016.
4. Garakai Chengu, 'How Slaves Built American Capitalism,' *Counterpunch*, December 18, 2015, accessed at http://www.counterpunch.org/2015/12/18/how-slaves-built-american-capitalism/ on 8/31/2016.

possibility for generations of great/white/wealth. And it is terror and violence today that attends the Black incarcerated bodies of the 21st century. On one end, in the 15th and 16th centuries, Black death fueled the accumulation of capital. On this end in the 21st century, Black death and warehousing are tools for solving the endemic crisis of overaccumulation.[5] The point is this: white culture, society and political economy only rises upon the dead and debilitated bodies of Black, Indigenous, and Brown people. Your lifestyle is enabled by terror, violence, and death. Your civil society, with all its hypocrisy and denial, is based upon the death and degradation of my people.

Ruth Wilson Gilmore, the Marxist geographer, defines racism as 'the state-sanctioned or extra-legal production and exploitation of group-differentiated vulnerability to premature death.' Black, Brown and Indigenous people are under constant attack, legally and extra-legally, and the result is terror, violence and the looming reality of early death. This is true in terms of police violence, mass criminalization, deportation, and the abject failure to protect. But it is also true everywhere, every day through the most intimate details our lives. The bodies of Black women and Black children have no value. A Black woman is 22 percent more likely to die from heart disease than a white woman, 71 percent more likely to perish from cervical cancer and 243 percent more likely than white women to die from pregnancy or child-birth related causes.[6] 243 percent! Black babies are two or three hundred percent more likely to die in infancy than white babies.[7] In cities like Baltimore, Philadelphia and Chicago there is a 20-year gap in life expectancy between people living in Black neighborhoods and those living in wealthier white ones.[8] An entire generation. Twenty years.

Eric Garner was confronted by police for selling loosies. 'I'm minding my business, officer. Please just leave,' he said. And then a policeman grabbed him in a choke hold while five others pinned him down on the sidewalk and forced his arms behind his back. 'I can't breathe,' Eric Garner said eleven times. And then he died. Three years later, Eric Garner's warrior daughter, Erica Garner, died.[9] She died of heart failure after a severe asthma attack and after three years of waging intense battle seeking justice for her father. Why have no police been convicted or sent to jail for killing Black men, she demanded? Why do police departments possess tactical military equipment that make community protest routes resem-

5. Thoughts in this paragraph were informed by Frank Wilderson, III, (2003) 'Gramsci's Black Marx: Whither the Slave in Civil Society,' *Social Identities*, Vol. 9. No. 2: 225-240.

6. Sheela Nimishakavi, 'Racial Health Disparities are Well Documented,' *Nonprofit Quarterly*, December 12, 2014. https://nonprofitquarterly.org/2017/12/12/racial-health-disparities-well-documented/ , Nina Martin and Renee Montagne, 'Black Mothers Keep Dying After Giving Birth,' NPR.com, December 7, 2017. https://www.npr.org/2017/12/07/568948782/black-mothers-keep-dying-after-giving-birth-shalon-irvings-story-explains-why

7. Qing Wai Wong, 'The Black-White Infant Mortality Gap,' *Public Health Post*, January 18, 2018. https://www.publichealthpost.org/research/black-white-infant-mortality-gap/

8. Olga Khazan, 'Being Black in America Can be Hazardous to Your Health,' *The Atlantic*, July/August 2018. https://www.theatlantic.com/magazine/archive/2018/07/being-black-in-america-can-be-hazardous-to-your-health/561740/

9. Vivian Wang, 'Erica Garner, Activist and Daughter of Eric Garner, Dies at 27,' *The New York Times*, December 30, 2017. https://www.nytimes.com/2017/12/30/nyregion/erica-garner-dead.html

ble war zones?[10] In an interview two days before she died, Erica Garner said this: 'My father died on national TV. I had to see him die on national TV... I felt the same pain my father felt on that day when he was screaming 'I can't breathe.' He was sayin' he was tired of bein' harassed, tired of bein' arrested, his money bein' stole from him... I'm not givin' up and this is the fight. I'm in this fight forever. We deserve justice.'[11] Forever was short, though, because Erica died. Death at the hands of police, death by the weight of oppression and grief, either way Erica and her father died prematurely, caught in the vortex of terror and violence that completely defines this space called America.

I turn to George Jackson, author, theorist, and revolutionary who thought and wrote brilliantly about what it means to be human in a world that wants you dead. Jackson was very clear that white supremacist monopoly capital would not be defined away with peaceful protest. 'The argument that the prestige of power will let itself be educated away is too idiotic to be allowed to stand. Waiting for power to move to its inevitable collapse is suicidal for all concerned,' he wrote.[12] Jackson's exploration of the meaning of revolutionary violence centered on exposing the brutality and repression that keep the U.S. intact. To expose the terms that white supremacist monopoly capital rule is predicated on, Jackson believed in the sacrifice of an armed revolutionary vanguard. What he so clearly articulated was that armed revolution or not, we are sacrificed. 'Born to a premature death,' he wrote, 'a menial, subsistence wage worker, odd-job man, the cleaner, the caught, the man under the hatches, without bail... Anyone who can pass the civil service examination today can kill me tomorrow. Anyone who passed the civil service examination yesterday can kill me today with complete immunity. I've lived with repression every moment of my life, a repression so formidable that any movement on my part can only bring relief, the respite of a small victory or the release of death.'[13] Since I am already dead as a slave, Jackson is arguing, the only redeeming course, the only way possible for us to claim our humanity and survive is the sacrifice of armed struggle.

I am a product of violence: a deep and searing violence that shapes my ontology, the contours of my history, the dimensions of my future. I did not make the violence. The violence made me, and it will unmake me. I wept as I quoted George Jackson. I wept as I faced the dilemma, the truth that the desire to be Black and survive, to simply live, requires a confrontation with repression and violence that consists of bloody sacrifice and more violence. I do not see a way out of this dilemma, because I cannot trust you.

But this is what I know and what I want to say to you: being human requires you to recognize that your life depends upon savage brutality and murder. Being human requires that you confront the terror and violence upon which rests the

---

10. Julie Hirschfeld Davis, 'Obama Faces Growing Expectations on Race and Policing,' *The New York Times*, July 21, 2016. https://www.nytimes.com/2016/07/22/us/politics/obama-police-race.html

11. Benjamin Dixon interview with Erica Garner, December 28, 2017. https://twitter.com/BenjaminPDixon/status/946436687588192257

12. George Jackson, *Blood in my Eye*, Baltimore: Black Classic Press: 51.

13. Ibid, 7.

foundation of your white lives. For us to simply live, to express our humanity, the possibility of nonviolence it is ultimately up to you.

This is the truth. Revolutionary nonviolence is up to you.

# AFTERWORD

Hakim Mohandas Amani Williams

---

*...colonialism is not only a contest over territory, but over the meaning of life itself.*
—Nick Estes

*This is what true revolutions are about. They are about redefining our relationships with one another, to the Earth and to the world.*
—Grace Lee Boggs

These two epigraphs that I have excerpted from this compendium encapsulate my thoughts on revolutionary nonviolence: those lingering colonialities (Williams, 2016), with their necrophilic inclination, will subsume everything if we allow them; resistances to them urge us to remember and re-envision sustainable relationalities. I perceive revolutionary nonviolences as significant parts of our pluriversal toolkit of resistances. I am intentionally using nonviolence in the plural because the amalgam of beautiful and thought-provoking writings in this volume represent old and new wisdoms. They remind us that as we theorize and strategize anew that we must give plenteous nods to that which is still relevant and generative from our past (without puritanically deifying all things pre-colonial); in other words, Sankofa as symbol, signpost, and praxis!

I grew up in the twin island republic of Trinidad & Tobago, just off the coast of Venezuela. It is purported that on his third trip to the Caribbean, Columbus took a more southernly trip, and as his ship sailed up between Venezuela and what was then called Iere (an Indigenous name for Trinidad meaning Land of the Hummingbird) he spotted three mountain peaks which reminded him of La Trinidad, the Holy Trinity. With the zeal and hubris that accompanies the term *terra nullius* (Latin for 'nobody's land'), Columbus renamed Iere to Trinidad, and the name stuck. When I utter the name of my country, it is a signification for colonialism, slavery, indentureship, and myriad hybridities emergent therefrom. As an example of the connection between coloniality and modernity (Mignolo, 2009, 2011; Quijano, 2007), the name and the State itself are imbued with lingering colonialities such as hierarchization, violence as disciplinary technology, exploitation, exclusion, and marginalization. One of the sinews that connects coloniality and modernity is a logic that impels us to invade, seize and own. This logic to own and thingify (Césaire, 2000) humans and the Earth itself, in the parlance of dynamical systems theory, has become a negative attractor. Vallacher et al (2010) describe an attractor:

> as a subset of potential states or patterns of change to which a system's behavior converges over time. Metaphorically, an attractor 'attracts' the

system's behavior, so that even very different starting states tend to evolve toward the subset of states defining the attractor... When a system's dynamics are governed by an attractor... the system is resistant to perturbing influences that would otherwise move it to a different state or pattern of changes. An external factor might promote a temporary change in the state of a system, but over time the system will return to its attractor (p. 265).

This logic to thingify persists and has warped human relationality (with each other and with the Earth). However, imprisonment of the human spirit can be and has been fodder for revolution! The spirit to live and be free is perhaps a positive attractor, informing patterns of transgressive and liberatory behaviors in the face of dehumanization. So when I utter the name of Trinidad, it also is a signification for both the many un-remembered peoples who, in small and large ways,[1] fought against the grips of oppression, and as well as for the likes of Claudia Jones, Eric Williams, Stokely Carmichael, George Padmore, and CLR James. There is perhaps a vibrant dynamism in the interstices of the dialectical relationship between the negative attractor of the logic of coloniality and the positive attractor of the revolutionary spirit to live and be free; may this dynamism be nourished by the ancestral power of maroonage.

I am from Laventille,[2] a socioeconomically disadvantaged community that brims with creativity. Laventille, a much smaller, but very similar version of the favelas of Rio de Janeiro, sits atop a hill rimming the Trinbagonian capital city of Port of Spain. When I see those hills of Laventille, and similar hills across the Caribbean and South America, I imagine the enslaved–once-plantation-property—escaping with revolutionary vigor, into the wild hills, to reclaim not only their freedom but also their subjectivity. These maroons did this all across the putative 'New World'; the Haitian Revolution being one of the most seismic consequences of maroonage. Maroons—despite the pernicious, white supremacist attempts at inculcating inferiority—knew that they were not born for enslavement, so they delinked from that odious apparatus, and set about creating a life for themselves outside that ontologically-narrowing, ethically-emaciated sphere. The Black Lives Matter movement is contemporarily an example of insurrectionary maroonage. With this spirit of maroonage, of abolitionism, we must delink from today's entrenched and violent apparatuses of oppression, and re-envision radical alternatives. As Kali Akuno stated (in this volume) 'we can't mediate our way to liberation through a series of compromises with capital'.

---

1. When I use the words 'small' and 'large', I do not mean a hierarchy of importance, but moreso to note that some actions are, for varied reasons, more legible to wider and diverse audiences. I do believe in the power of micro-revolutionary actions; that is, the often quiet, under-the-radar defiances (both inadvertent and intentionally strategic), the amalgam of which can build pressure, create fissures, and over time, render corrosive impacts on larger structural hindrances to social change.
2. Laventille, said by many, is the birthplace of the steelpan. The first steelpans invented were made from old oil drums. The steel pan, according to Caribbean intellectual Lloyd Best (2001), is an incarnation of the ingenuity of a denigrated people accustomed to taking the discarded and crafting something of purpose; I aver that that is perhaps at once our ancestral fight for life *and* a sublimation of some of the prolonged violences rendered upon us.

Ergo, we need alternatives to capitalism, to the exclusionary bureaucratic modern nation state, and to practices of individuals privatizing and harming the Earth. Actuating revolutionary nonviolences is a form of maroonage, and as we enact them *in the now* for a world that we (re)envision, they become prefigurative praxes (C. Boggs, 1977) and, in so doing, become life-giving attractors.

I do think that consciously enacting revolutionary nonviolences as a positive attractor presupposes deliberate preparation, and since I am in the field of education, my aforementioned postulations necessarily beget the question: what does education for *and* of revolutionary nonviolence look like? It is a nascent thought experiment in which I am currently engaged, therefore, I have few solidified thoughts. But definitiveness isn't my final goal because such singular-self-directed conclusions are the hallmark of coloniality, exclusion, and ego. Guided by Dr. MLK Jr.'s injunction that moral means are requisite for moral ends, an education for and of revolutionary nonviolence must be concerned with content, form, values, *and* ends. I concur with Grace Lee Boggs' assertion that we need a revolution of values, because I think that as space exploration/colonialism advances, as anthropogenic global warming imperils livelihoods, as artificial intelligence further blurs the boundaries between human and machine, values and praxes (such as revolutionary nonviolences) will hopefully help us navigate fast-changing topographies (social and otherwise). An education for and of revolutionary nonviolence has to be iterative (because of inevitably constant attempts to co-opt), holistic (i.e. intentionally re-tethering cartesianized mind-body-spirit-Earth), community-oriented, substantively intersectional, planetary in scope, and pluriversal in implementation.

As we continue to sketch, strategize, trial-run and course correct our revolutionary nonviolences, may our imaginations be not restricted or our energies blunted by the myopic dictates of realpolitik that charge us as naïve. Many of us are still here because of the audacity of our ancestors; dare to summon them!

## References

Best, L. (2001). Jagan Lecture: Race, Class, Ethnicity: A Caribbean Interpretation. Retrieved from https://www.yorku.ca/wp-content/uploads/sites/259/2021/01/Best.pdf.

Boggs, C. (1977). Marxism, prefigurative communism and the problem of workers' control. Radical America, 11(6), 99–122. Retrieved from: https://library.brown.edu/pdfs/1125404123276662.pdf Bohm, D. (2005). Wholeness and the implicate order. (1st edition, 1980)

Césaire, A. (2000). Discourse on colonialism. (1st edition, 1955). Monthly Review Press.

Mignolo, W. (2009). Epistemic Disobedience, Independent Thought and Decolonial Freedom. Theory, Culture and Society, 26(7/8), pp. 159–181. http://dx.doi.org/10.1177/0263276409349275

Mignolo, W. (2011). The darker side of Western modernity: Global futures, decolonial options. Duke University Press.

Quijano, A. (2007). Coloniality and Modernity/rationality, Cultural Studies, 21 (2): 168-178).

Vallacher, R., Coleman, P., Nowak, A, & Bui-Wrzosinska, L. (2010). Rethinking Intractable Conflict: The Perspective of Dynamical Systems. American Psychologist, 65(4), 262 278.

Williams, H. M. A. (2016). Lingering Colonialities as Blockades to Peace Education; School Violence in Trinidad. In M. Bajaj & M. Hantzopoulos (Eds.), Peace Education: International Perspectives (141-156). London: Bloomsbury Publishing.

# CONTRIBUTOR BIOGRAPHIES

**Joyce Ajlouny** has served as the General Secretary of the American Friends Service Committee (the 1947 Nobel Peace laureate), since September of 2017. A Quaker leader who is committed to help bring peace and justice to oppressed and vulnerable communities globally, Joyce is a Palestinian American who started her career working in international development in Palestine, focusing on minority and refugee rights, gender equality, economic development, and humanitarian support. She served as the country director for Palestine and Israel with Oxfam-Great Britain, chaired the Association of International Development Agencies, and worked as a program manager at various United Nations agencies. Prior to joining AFSC, Joyce served as the director of the Ramallah Friends School in Palestine for 13 years, where she led a diverse staff to transform the school academically, physically and financially.

**Kali Akuno** is a co-founder and co-director of Cooperation Jackson in Mississippi, and previously served as the Director of Special Projects and External Funding in the Jackson Mayoral Administration of the late Chokwe Lumumba. Kali has also served as the Co-Director of the U.S. Human Rights Network, the Executive Director of the Peoples' Hurricane Relief Fund (PHRF) based in New Orleans, Louisiana after Hurricane Katrina. He was a co-founder of the School of Social Justice and Community Development (SSJCD), a public school serving the academic needs of low-income African American and Latino communities in Oakland, California and a leader of the Malcolm X Grassroots Movement.

**Hannah Arendt** (1906-1975) was a German-born U.S. political theorist. She is widely considered one of the most important political thinkers of the 20th century; many of her books and articles – on topics ranging from the nature of power and evil, politics, direct democracy, authority, and totalitarianism – have had a lasting influence on political theory and philosophy.

**Mark Muhannad Ayyash** was born and raised in Silwan, Al-Quds (Jerusalem), before immigrating to Canada, where he is now an Associate Professor of Sociology at Mount Royal University. He is the author of *A Hermeneutics of Violence* (UTP, 2019). He teaches and writes in the areas of social and political theory, postcolonial theory, the study of violence, exiling writing, Canada-Palestine relations, and decolonial movements, particularly focusing on the Palestinian struggle. He has published several academic articles in journals such as *Interventions*, the *European Journal of International Relations*, *Comparative Studies of South Asia, Africa and the Middle East*, and the *European Journal of Social Theory*. He also has a co-edited book on Protests and Generations in the MENA and the Mediterranean, and has written opinion pieces for *Middle East Mon-*

*itor, Middle East Eye,* and *Al-Jazeera*. He is currently writing a book on settler colonial sovereignty in Palestine-Israel.

**Ella Josephine Baker** (1903-1986) was an African-American civil rights and human rights activist. She was a largely behind-the-scenes organizer whose career spanned more than five decades. In New York City and the South, she worked alongside some of the most noted civil rights leaders of the 20th century, including W. E. B. Du Bois, Thurgood Marshall, A. Philip Randolph, and Martin Luther King Jr. She also mentored many emerging activists, such as Diane Nash, Stokely Carmichael, Rosa Parks, and Bob Moses, whom she first mentored as leaders in the Student Nonviolent Coordinating Committee (SNCC). Baker criticized professionalized, charismatic leadership; she promoted grassroots organizing, radical democracy, and the ability of the oppressed to understand their worlds and advocate for themselves. She realized this vision most fully in the 1960s as the primary advisor and strategist of the SNCC. Baker has been called 'one of the most important American leaders of the twentieth century and perhaps the most influential woman in the civil rights movement.' She is known for her critiques not only of racism within American culture, but also of sexism within the civil rights movement.

**Sally Bermanzohn** was a professor of political science and department chair at Brooklyn College, City University of New York. Author of Through Survivors' Eyes: From the Sixties to the Greensboro Massacre, she and her husband are survivors of the 1979 Greensboro Massacre, when members of the Klu Klux Klan supported by local North Carolina law enforcement killed and wounded anti-Klan protesters. An ally of Indigenous rights, she was active in the Two Row Wampum Renewal Campaign, and is a is a member of Native Resistance Network.

**Steve Bloom** is a life-long political activist who lives in Brooklyn NY and works as a decorative painter and faux finisher. A strategist and essayist active with the Green Party and independent left movement-building, Steve is also an accomplished and published poet as well as a musician and composer. He has worked for the freedom of U.S. political prisoners and in support of liberation movements across the world and within the U.S..

**Grace Lee Boggs** (1915-2015) was a U.S.-born author, social activist, philosopher and feminist, co-founder of the National Organization for an American Revolution and an iconic figure in the Asian American and Black Liberation movements. Her classic writings, including collaborations with CLR James, Raya Dunayevskaya, and her husband James Boggs, include *The Next American Revolution: Sustainable Activism for the Twenty-First Century*.

**Amilcar Cabral** (1924-1973) was the founder and leader of the African Party for the Independence of Guinea-Bissau and the Cape Verde Islands (PAIGC). A Marxist and trained agronomist, Cabral emphasized Pan-Africanism, with a focus on organizing the rural peasantry into a nationalist movement. Under his leadership the PAIGC succeeded in ousting Portugal from sixty percent of the land in Guinea-Bissau. On the eve of the declaration of formal independence for Guinea-Bissau, Cabral was assassinated.

**Berta Cáceres** (1971-2016) was a leader of the Indigenous Lenca people of Honduras. She co-founded the National Council of Popular and Indigenous Organizations of Honduras (COPINH) and devoted her life to the fight for human and environmental rights. She was assassinated while leading the opposition to the Agua Zarca dam on a river that is sacred to the Lenca people. A former executive of the dam company and an ex-army intelligence officer was convicted of Carceres murder.

**Kassahun Checole** is a leading Eritrean entrepreneur and intellectual, the founder, publisher, and CEO of Africa World Press and Red Sea Press. A renowned Pan Africanist and Pan American scholar he is a long-time associate of the Association of Concerned African Scholars and the African Studies Association

**James Cone** (1938-2018) was the preeminent theologian of Black Liberation in the U.S.. His many books argued unapologetically that in preaching a theology of white supremacy the white church abjured the gospel of Jesus Christ and had blood on its hands. In *The Cross and the Lynching Tree*, Cone analyzed the lynching tree as a symbol of white power and black death in contrast to the cross, as a symbol of divine power and Black lfe overcoming the power of sin and death. Cone wrote that the image of Jesus dying on a tree grounded the faith of blacks during the lynching era.

**Dave Dellinger** (1915-2004) was a prominent U.S. nonviolent activist and coalition builder, author of *Revolutionary Nonviolence* (1970), and member of the famed Chicago Seven 1969 conspiracy trial. As a World War Two conscientious objector, leader of the Vietnam anti-war movement, and justice advocate till the time of his death, he was in many ways the preeminent force in the 20th Century U.S. peace movement.

**Barbara Deming** (1917-1984) was a leading racial justice activist, feminist, nonviolent theoretician and practitioner, and author. An open lesbian since the 1930's, Deming founded *The Money for Women Fund* to support female artists, was a leader of the Women's Pentagon Action, and was an editor and contributor to the influential *Liberation* magazine.

**Nick Estes** is a citizen of the Lower Brule Sioux Tribe and works as an Assistant Professor in the American Studies Department at the University of New Mexico. In 2014, he co-founded *The Red Nation*, an Indigenous resistance organization. From 2017-2018, Estes was the American Democracy Fellow at the Charles Warren Center for Studies in American History at Harvard University. He is the author of the book *Our History Is the Future: Standing Rock Versus the Dakota Access Pipeline, and the Long Tradition of Indigenous Resistance* (2019).

**Frantz Fanon** (1925-1961) was a Martinique-born psychiatrist, political philosopher and activist, noted as the author of the classic anti-colonial reader The Wretched of the Earth (1961). An influential intellectual in the fields of postcolonial studies, critical theory, and Marxism, Fanon was also a leading Pan-Africanist and solidarity activist campaigning for the Algerian independence movement against France.

**Leslie Feinberg** (1949-2014) was a butch lesbian, trans activist, communist and the author of *Stone Butch Blues*. Feinberg used the pronouns she/zie and her/

hir. According to her partner, Minnie Bruce Pratt, Feinberg's last words were 'remember me as a revolutionary communist.'

**Ela Gandhi** is a South African peace and justice activist, former African National Congress Member of Parliament from 1994-2004. Daughter of Manilal and granddaughter of Mohandas Gandhi, she keeps her family's legacy alive as the Director of the Gandhi Development Trust and as a leading patron of the Phoenix Settlement, an early community space set up by her grandfather. Gandhi also served as Chancellor of the Durban Institute of Technology.

**Mohandas Gandhi** (1869-1948) was a leading force of the Indian independence movement against British colonialism, is considered by many as the most important modern practitioner of nonviolent social change and is referred to as 'Mahatma' – a 'great soul' – by most who cite his work.

**Fannie Lou Hamer** (1917-1977) was born into a Mississippi share-cropping family and worked in the fields in her early life. She lost her job in the fields when she succeeded in registering to vote. In 1962 she became a community organizer with the Student Nonviolent Coordinating Committee to register other black voters. In 1964 she founded the Mississippi Freedom Democratic Party and challenged the seating of the all-white regular delegates to the 1964 National Democratic Convention.

**Vincent Harding** (1931-2014) was an activist, historian, and author, with a focus on religion and society and an emphasis on what he termed 'the Black-led, southern-based U.S. freedom movement.' Noted for his friendship and speech-writing for Rev. Dr. Martin Luther King, Jr., including the historic speech critiquing U.S. military involvement in Vietnam, Harding was also author of the books *There Is A River, Hope and History*, and *Martin Luther King: The Inconvenient Hero*. He served as co-chairperson of the social unity group Veterans of Hope Project and as Professor of Religion and Social Transformation at Colorado's Iliff School of Theology.

**John Holloway** is a lawyer, philosopher, and sociologist, professor at Mexico's Institute for Humanities and Social Sciences at the Autonomous University of Puebla, and close associate of the Zapatista movement. Among his influential and noted books are *Open Marxism: Emancipating Marx, Zapatista!: Reinventing Revolution in Mexico, Change the World Without Taking Power*, and *Crack Capitalism* Pluto Press.

**Natalie Jeffers** is a specialist in communications and the repurposing of research for new and non-academic audiences. She is director of Matters of the Earth, a company which develops engaging and creative educational products, including web-based learning platforms, interactive learning resources, curriculums, policy briefings, synthesis reports, eBooks, info-graphics, films, animations, comic books and outreach programmes.

**Colin Kaepernick** is a former football quarterback who played for the San Francisco 49ers. In 2016 Kaepernick remained seated during the national anthem at an NFL per-season game to protest racial inequality and police brutality. After speaking with an army veteran, Kaepernick later chose to kneel, rather than sit, as a sign of respect for military personnel. Following his example, other NFL players began to kneel and raise fists at NFL games. In 2018, Kaepernick won Amnesty International's Ambassador of Conscience award.

**Kenneth Kaunda** (1924-2021) was the founding President of independent Zambia, serving from 1964-1991. In that time, he was a leader of the frontline states in support of the anti-colonial and anti-apartheid freedom movements, and served as a strong supporter of the Non-Aligned Movement and as chair of the Organization of African Unity. A Christian humanist, he authored several books including *The Riddle of Violence* based on his reflection as a statesman on the possibilities of unarmed defence and lasting change.

**Martin Luther King, Jr.** (1929-1968) was a U.S. Baptist minister whose impressive oratory, writing, and coalition-building skills and commitment to civil disobedience and nonviolent direct action propelled him to the leadership of the 1950's-1960's movements for racial equality, economic justice, and peace. Awarded the Nobel Peace Prize in 1964, King founded and served as first president of the Southern Christian Leadership Conference, and authored five books in his lifetime including *Why We Can't Wait*.

**Ynestra King** has been an activist, teacher, and writer since the 1970's, widely credited for helping develop and popularize theories of 'ecofeminism' as a founder of the Women and Life on Earth group. Also a member of the Committee on Women, Population and the Environment, the Women's Pentagon Action, and the AJ Muste Institute, King has been a Visiting Scholar at the Barnard Center for Research on Women and an independent scholar at Massachusetts' Five College Women's Studies Research Center. She is author, editor, and contributor to numerous books, including the recent *Rocking the Ship of State: Towards a Feminist Peace Politics*.

**Lolita Lebron** (1919-2010) was a Puerto Rican nationalist and supporter of independence who served twenty-five years in prison for actions taken in 1954 at the U.S. Capitol Building in Washington DC. She was a follower of independence leader Pedro Albizu Campos, becoming part of the movement following the Ponce Massacre which saw members of the Puerto Rican Nationalist Party killed while leading a peaceful protest. Thought to be the first female commander of a Latin American armed movement, Lebron led several others into the visitor's gallery while Congress was in session, eventually firing shots from their semi-automatic pistols into the ceiling of the building. Proclaiming 'I did not come to kill anyone, I came to die for Puerto Rico,' Lebron became a lifelong symbol of the indomitable Puerto Rican spirit. She and her colleagues were released in 1979 following a commutation of their sentences by President Jimmy Carter.

**Audre Lorde** (1934-1992) described herself as a 'black, lesbian, mother, warrior, poet.' Her poems and essays confronted the injustices of racism, sexism, classism and homophobia. Affirming her own and others 'collective identities,' her poems and prose largely deal with issues related to civil rights, feminism, lesbianism, illness and disability, and the exploration of black female personhood. Her extensive influences include her part in developing the Combahee River Collective (and it's essay asserting that 'until Black women are free, none of us are free') as well as Kitchen Table: Women of Color Press. She was the first

Black and first female Poet Laureate of the State of New York, and author of numerous important works including *The Black Unicorn*; *The Cancer Journals*; *Zami: A New Spelling of My Name*; and *Sister/Outsider*.

**Maria Lugones** (1944-2020) was an Argentine feminist philosopher, activist, and Professor of Comparative Literature and of women's studies at Carleton College in Northfield, MN and at Binghamton University in New York State. She identified as a U.S.-based woman of color and theorized this category as a political identity forged through feminist coalitional work. Known for her theory of multiple selves and work on decolonizing feminism, she theorized various forms of resistance against multiple oppressions in Latin America, the U.S. and elsewhere – including through the concept of the 'coloniality of gender' which posits that gender is a colonial imposition.

**Graça Machel** is a Mozambican humanitarian and former Minister of Education who is a noted international advocate for women's and children's rights. As former first lady of both Mozambique (widow to Samora Machel) and South Africa (widow to Nelson Mandela), Machel has been a distinguished figure serving on the African Progress Panel, the Elders group, and as a leader of both UNESCO and the UN. From 1999 to 2019, she served as Chancellor of the University of Cape Town.

**Nozizwe Madlala-Routledge** is a lifelong South African activist for justice, first joining the movement as a young follower and friend of Steve Biko. The founding chair of the Natal Organization of Women and a part of the United Democratic Front, Madlala-Routledge was a part of the negotiations for an end to apartheid, serving as a representative of the South African Communist Party and a member of the African National Congress (ANC). Following South Africa's first open elections in 1994, Madlala-Routledge was elected as a Member of Parliament, eventually serving as both Deputy Minister of Defence and Deputy Minister of Health. Given her outspoken commitment to nonviolence and practicing Quaker (Friends) faith beliefs, she is likely the first pacifist to serve as second-in-command of a country's armed forces. After many years in Parliament, including a term as the Deputy Speaker of the National Assembly. Retiring from politics in 2007 following controversies regarding the President's denialist policies on AIDS and Nozizwe's staunch support of people with AIDS, she co-founded the human rights organization Embrace Dignity, dedicated to fighting sex trafficking and sexual exploitation of all forms. In 2021, she was named Director of the Quaker United Nations Office in Geneva.

**Wende Marshall** worked as a student and community organizer in Central Harlem, New York City during the 1980s and graduated with an M.A. in religious studies from Union Theological Seminary in 1992. In 1999 she received a Ph.D. in anthropology from Princeton University. Her book (*Potent Mana: Lessons in Power and Healing*) explores the effects of colonialism on the physical, mental, and spiritual health of Native Hawaiians. Marshall was a leader of Stadium Stompers, an anti-gentrification movement of North Philadelphia-based community members, students, and workers that forced Temple University to scrap its plans to build a football stadium in the neighborhood. As an adjunct at Temple University, Marshall was a leader in the efforts to unionize adjuncts, resulting in their joining the Temple Association of University Professionals, for which she served as Chair of the Adjunct Constituency Council and member of the Executive Committee. Marshall is currently serving on the National Organizing Committee of People's Strike, is a member of the Circle on Revolutionary Nonviolence, and of RAFT, the rank and file caucus of Temple's faculty union focused on contingent faculty issues.

**Mireille Fanon Mendès-France** is a prominent professor and activist, and the former Chair of the United Nations Working Group on People of African Descent. A Judge with the Permanent Peoples Tribunal (following in the history of the Bertrand Russell Tribunals), she is also a former Commissioner of the 2020 International Commission on Inquiry of Systemic Racist Police Violence against U.S. People of African Descent). She is Co-Chair of the Frantz Fanon Foundation, dedicated to the legacy of her father.

**Matt Meyer** is an internationally noted author, historian, and organizer, reelected in 2021 as Secretary-General of the International Peace Research Association (IPRA, the world's leading consortium of university-based professors, scholars, students, and community leaders). Meyer is the Senior Research Scholar of the University of Massachusetts/Amherst's Resistance Studies Initiative, a position he has held since retiring from 30+ years as a tenured educator and teacher-trainer for the New York City Department of Education. He is also active with the International Fellowship of Reconciliation (IFOR) and the War Resisters' International (WRI), serving as Chair of IFOR's Financial Advisory Committee, and Africa Support Network Coordinator for WRI. Meyer is the author or editor of over a dozen books and one hundred chapters and articles, including *White Lives Matter Most and other 'little' white lies*. His first book, *Guns and Gandhi in Africa* (co-authored with Bill Sutherland), included a Foreword by South African Nobel Peace laureate Archbishop Desmond Tutu, noting that Sutherland and Meyer 'have looked beyond the short-term strategies and tactics which too often divide progressive peoples...They have begun to develop a language which looks at the roots of our humanness.' Fellow Nobel Peace laureate Adolfo Perez Esquivel of Argentina, in his Introduction to Meyer's encyclopedic anthology on political imprisonment *Let Freedom Ring*, added that 'Meyer is a coalition-builder,' one who 'provides tools for today's activists' in his writings and his work.

**Mel Paisley** is transmasculine author, illustrator, and general loudmouthed inkslinger based out of Savannah, GA. He writes a lot about pre-Stonewall herstory, schizophrenia, and being mixed and queer in the Deep South.

**Peoples Strike**, convened by Kali Akuno, of Cooperation Jackson, in April of 2020, is a black-led anti-capitalist, anti-white supremacist, anti-heteropatriarchal formation committed to general strike as a tactic and strategy for winning a world based on love and justice

**Aislinn Pulley** is an organizer with Black Lives Matter Chicago. She was an organizer with We Charge Genocide, a founding member of Insight Arts, a cultural non-profit that used art for social change, and a member of the performance ensemble, End of the Ladder. She is a founder of the young women's performance ensemble dedicated to ending sexual assault, Visibility Now, as well as the founder and creator of urban youth magazine, Underground Philosophy.

**Aníbal Quijano** (1930-2018) was a Peruvian sociologist and radical intellectual whose work on coloniality and power reshaped understanding of race in Latin America. Arguing that identity as well as domination are based upon race, he viewed race as key to the construction of the coloniality of power. His work theorized the work of external domination through colonialism, but he attended as well to internal domination by a ruling elite based upon whiteness and race.

**David Ragland** is a co-founder and co-executive director of the Truth Telling Project, and director of the Grassroots Reparations Campaign. A writer, scholar, and activist, Ragland has taught at the Pacifica Graduate Institute and was inducted into the Rev. Martin Luther King Jr. Collegium of Scholars at Morehouse College. Ragland served as the Senior Bayard Rustin Fellow of the Fellowship of Reconciliation and as a board member for the Peace and Justice Studies Association.

**Milan Rai** is a British writer and anti-war activist, part of the British Plowshares Movement, the Campaign for Nuclear Disarmament, Voices in the Wilderness UK, and Justice Not Vengeance. Rai is the author of numerous books, including *Regime Unchanged: Why the War on Iraq Changed Nothing* and *7/7: The London Bombings, Islam and the Iraq War*.

**Beth Richie** is Head of the Department of Criminology, Law and Justice and Professor of Black Studies at The University of Illinois at Chicago. The emphasis of her scholarly and activist work has been on the ways that race/ethnicity and social position affect women's experience of violence and incarceration, focusing on the experiences of African American battered women and sexual assault survivors. Dr. Richie is the author of *Arrested Justice: Black Women, Violence and America's Prison Nation* which chronicles the evolution of the contemporary anti-violence movement during the time of mass incarceration in the United States and numerous articles concerning Black feminism and gender violence, race and criminal justice policy, and the social dynamics around issues of sexuality, prison abolition, and grassroots organizations in African American Communities. She is a co-editors of *The Long Term: Resisting Life Sentences, Working Towards Freedom*, author of *Compelled to Crime: the Gender Entrapment of Black Battered Women*, and is currently working on a new book titled *Abolition. Feminism. Now.* with Angela Y. Davis, Gina Dent and Erica Meiners. She has been awarded the Audre Lorde Legacy Award from the Union Institute, The Advocacy Award from the U.S. Department of Health and Human Services, and The Visionary Award from the Violence Intervention Project and the UIC Woman of the Year Award. Dr. Richie is a board member of The Institute on Domestic Violence in the African Community, The National Network for Women in Prison, A Call To Men and a founding member of INCITE!: Women of Color Against Violence.

**Raquel Salas Rivera** is a bilingual Puerto Rican poet who writes in Spanish and English, focusing on the experience of being a migrant to the United States, the colonial status of Puerto Rico, and of identifying as a queer Puerto Rican and Philadelphian of non-binary gender.

**Aimee Carrillo Rowe** is a memoirist, feminist theorist, culture critic, and professor of Communication Studies at California State University, Northridge. Her books include *Power Lines: On the Subject of Feminist Alliances, Answer the Call: Virtual Migration in Indian Call Centers*, and *Queer Xicana: Performing the Sacred* (in progress). Her writing appears in *GLQ (A Journal of Gay and Lesbian Studies), Cultural Studies/Critical Methods, American Quarterly, Biography*, and elsewhere. She received her Ph.D. in Communication Studies from The University of Washington and MFA in Creative Writing at UCR, Palm Desert. Her memoir about queer single motherhood is entitled, *After Birth: Memoir of a Queer Family*.

**Arundhati Roy** is an Indian political activist and author involved in human rights and environmental work, best known for her best-selling novel The God of Small Things. Her critiques of the Indian government, including support for Kashmiri independence, contributed to her 2010 arrest on sedition charges.

**Sacajawea 'Saki' Hall** is a radical Black feminist activist, mother, birth-worker, educator and journalist who loves crafting. She sees her life's work as engaging in the collective struggle for African liberation, human rights and social transformation. She is a native Lower East Side New Yorker who migrated to Jackson, Mississippi, in December 2013 to help advance the Jackson--Kush Plan. She is a founding member of Cooperation Jackson.

**Ruby Sales** is a nationally recognized human-rights activist, public theologian, and social critic, whose articles and work appear in many journals, online sites, and books. Sales joined the Student Nonviolent Coordinating Committee (SNCC) in the 1960's as a teenager at Tuskegee University and went to work as a student freedom fighter in Lowndes County, Alabama. Sales has preached around the country and spoken at national conferences on race, class, gender, and reconciliation. Her groundbreaking work on community and non-violence formation included serving as a national convener of the *Every Church A Peace Church* Movement. Sales has earned degrees from Tuskegee Institute, Manhattanville College, and Princeton University, as well as a Masters of Divinity from the Episcopal Divinity School (EDS) in Cambridge, Massachusetts, where she specialized in Feminist, African-American, and Liberation Theologies, with an emphasis on race, class, and gender issues. Sales is the founder and director of the SpiritHouse Project, a national nonprofit organization that uses the arts, research, education, action, and spirituality to bring diverse peoples together to work for racial, economic, and social justice, as well as for spiritual maturity.

**Russell Maroon Shoatz** is a political prisoner who has been held unjustly for over thirty years, including two decades in solitary confinement. He was active as a leader in the Black Liberation Movement in Philadelphia, both above and underground. As a dedicated community activist, Maroon was a founding member of the Black Unity Council, a former member of the Black Panther Party, and a soldier in the Black Liberation Army. He is serving multiple life sentences as a U.S.-held prisoner of war. His successful escapes from maximum-security prisons earned him the title 'Maroon.' Many of his writings are included in the book *Maroon the Implacable.*

**Gwendolyn Zoharah Simmons** is a human rights activist, a scholar of women in Islam and a retired member of the faculty in the Department of Religion at the University of Florida, Gainesville. A former leader of the Student Non-violent Coordinating Committee (SNCC) in Laurel, Mississippi and Atlanta, Georgia, Simmons helped found a number of independent Black political organizations throughout the 1970's and 1980's. Simmons, a Sufi Muslim, draws on the compassion and inclusiveness of her faith in her work as community organizer, scholar and writer; she also served as a national staffperson for the American Friends Service Committee. In 2016, at the invitation of the Fellowship of Reconciliation, she lectured in four European countries about the history and meaning of the African American freedom movement.

**Leora Skolkin-Smith** is an Israeli-American novelist whose first novel, *Edges: O Israel, O Palestine,* was selected and edited by Grace Paley for Glad Day Books.

**Starhawk** is an author, activist, permaculture designer and teacher, and a prominent voice in modern earth-based spirituality and ecofeminism. She is the author or co-author of thirteen books, including *The Spiral Dance: A Rebirth of the Ancient Religion of the Great Goddess* and the ecotopian novel *The Fifth Sacred Thing,* and its sequel *City of Refuge.* Her most recent non-fiction book is *The Empowerment Manual: A Guide for Collaborative Groups,* on group dynamics, power, conflict and communications. Starhawk founded Earth Activist Training, teaching permaculture design grounded in spirituality and with a focus on activism. She travels internationally, lecturing and teaching on earth-based spirituality, the tools of ritual, and the skills of activism.

**Student Nonviolent Coordinating Committee** was formed in 1960 following the lunch counter sit-in movement in the U.S. South. SNCC played a leading role in organizing the Freedom Rides, a direct challenge to segregationist Jim Crow laws and the failure of the U.S. government to uphold the Supreme Court decision banning segregation on public buses. SNCC evolved as first chairman John Lewis (later to become a Georgia congressperson) was replaced by Stokley Carmichael, whose popularization of the slogan 'Black Power' led to a widespread shift in the movement and organization, including changing the name to Student National Coordinating Committee.

**Subcommander Moisés** is a spokesperson, writer, and organizer with Mexico's Ejército Zapatista de Liberación Nacional (EZLN), known popularly and simply as the Zapatistas.

**Bill Sutherland** (1918-2010) was a U.S.-based World War II conscientious objector until his 1953 departure to Africa, where he lived most of his life as an unofficial ambassador and Pan African bridge between the anti-colonial and independence movements of the continent and the peace movements of the global north. Host to both Rev. Dr. Martin Luther King Jr. in Ghana and Minister Malcolm X in Tanzania, Sutherland was committed to an unorthodox nonviolence strictly adhering to people's self-determination rights as to how they should wage their own struggles. Active with both the War Resisters International and as a staff person for the American Friends Service Committee,

Sutherland's life and work is in part portrayed in his book, co-authored with Matt Meyer, *Guns and Gandhi in Africa: Pan African Insights on Nonviolence, Armed Struggle, and Liberation.*

**Henry David Thoreau** (1817-1862) was an American naturalist, essayist, poet, and philosopher. A leading transcendentalist, he is best known for his book *Walden*, a reflection upon simple living in natural surroundings, and his essay 'Civil Disobedience', an argument for disobedience to an unjust state.

**Johnnie Tillmon** (1926-1995) was a U.S. welfare rights activist. A migrant sharecropper's daughter, she later worked as a union shop steward in a California laundry. Tillmon became ill in 1963 and was advised to seek welfare. She soon learned how welfare recipients were harassed by caseworkers. To fight this treatment, Tillmon organized people in the housing project and founded one of the first grassroots welfare mothers' organizations called ANC (Aid to Needy Children) Mothers Anonymous, in 1963. ANC Mothers later became a part of the National Welfare Rights Organization (NWRO). Tillmon became a chairperson of the NWRO. Together with other welfare mothers, she struggled for adequate income, dignity, justice and democratic participation.

**Haunani-Kay Trask** (1949-2021) was a leader in the Native Hawaiian Sovereignty Movement, a scholar, poet and founder of the discipline of Hawaiian Studies at the University of Hawai'i. She was a fierce critic of U.S. imperialism, of the presence of the U.S. military on the islands of Hawai'i, and of the tourism industry.

**Nazan Üstündağ** is an Academy in Exile and IIE-Scholar Rescue Fund Fellow at the Forum Transregionale Studien. Nazan's dissertation examined different forms of subjectivities and belongings of rural-to-urban women in Istanbul and the life stories they craft in the intersection of the violence of state, capital, and patriarchy. Aside from writing on urban belongings in the era of neoliberalism, Nazan writes extensively on social policy, gendered subjectivities, and state violence in Kurdistan; she is also a member of Women for Peace and Academics for Peace.

**Hakim Mohandas Amani Williams**, a native of Trinidad & Tobago, is the inaugural Daria L. & Eric J. Wallach Professor & Director of Peace and Justice Studies, Associate Professor of Africana Studies, Affiliate of Education, and Advisory Committee Member for International & Global Studies, Public Policy, and Civil War Era Studies at Gettysburg College in Pennsylvania. He is the founder of the Consortium of North American Peace Programs, and was a Visiting Scholar (2015-2016) at the Advanced Consortium on Cooperation, Conflict and Complexity at Columbia University's Earth Institute. A noted speaker, author, educator and trainer, he is the co-coordinator of the planned 2023 International Peace Research Association conference and assembly.

**Robert Franklin Williams** (1925-1996) came to national attention within the U.S. as president of the Monroe, North Carolina chapter of the National Association for the Advancement of Colored People. A promoter of armed self-defense, he set up a rifle club with a charter from the National Rifle Association to help defend the Black community from Klu Klux Klan attacks, and authored the popular Negroes with Guns. To avoid arrest or worse, he and his wife left the U.S. in 1961 and became unofficial representatives of the Black Liberation movement of that time in newly socialist states of Cuba, China, and later Tanzania. He served as the first president of the Republic of New Afrika.

**Women's Pentagon Action** was an all-women gathering which took place in November of 1980 and again in 1981, in the words of historian and participant Pam Macallister 'a pageant-like demonstration that combined rational thought with deep emotion.' With defiance, rage, mourning and a sense of empowerment, the Action centered around a jargon-free manifesto penned by Grace Paley and friends following an Amherst, Massachusetts conference on Women and Life on Earth. It combined guerilla theater, poetry, civil disobedience, and ritual, with input from over 200 women. Organizer Ynestra King noted: *'For weeks Grace took phone calls, read the statement to women in her kitchen, on the subway, in New York, Vermont, Massachusetts. The spirit of unity...and the process of writing the statement and reaching consensus on it...told our politics and brought us together. We all listened to each other, everyone was heard and satisfied, and we took this statement home with us to organize...All of us were the theater, the actors, there were no speakers, no stage, no leaders.'*

# ACKNOWLEDGEMENTS

We thank our editor and publisher, Firoze Manji, for meticulous attention, unflagging enthusiasm, and comradely understanding.

We are grateful to our partners Kelley Collings and Meg Starr, whose political work in Working Educators Caucus (PFT), and Resistance in Brooklyn (RnB) inspires us and whose patient support was crucial to completing the book.

We exist in a whirlwind of political struggle with comrades who inspire and challenge us every day and with whom collectively we develop our revolutionary practice. We are especially grateful to the Circle of Revolutionary Nonviolence, a new and still fairly internal formation, which nevertheless helped inform the creation and development of this book, and to Peoples Strike, whose vision and struggle for mass action helped frame our thinking during this past pandemic and crisis-laden years. A special thanks to Dean Johnson, whose early thinking and work around a compendium of writings on revolution and nonviolence helped start the project which has become this book. Many other groups and individuals can also be named, but we will err on the side of brevity so as not to exclude any of the many.

For financial assistance toward finishing the book, we thank the International Peace Research Association.

We appreciate all the authors and contributors to this book but convey a special thanks to all those who provided new contributions and commentaries, especially for this volume: Joyce Ajlouny, Kassahun Checole, Mireille Fanon Mendès-France, Ela Gandhi, Ynestra King, Ruby Sales, and Hakim Williams.

For kind permission to republish their work, we thank the following: Dr. Mark Muhannad Ayyash, Dr. Sally Bermanzohn, Nick Estes, John Holloway, Mel Paisley, Aislinn Pulley, Dr. Beth E. Richie, Dr. Aimee Carillo Rowe, Russell Maroon Shoatz and Steve Bloom, Leslie Skolkin-Smith, Starhawk, and Nazan Nazan Üstündağ.

We also acknowledge with appreciation permissions from the University of Arizona Press, for x/ex/exis, by Raquel Salas Rivera; HarperCollins Publishers, for excerpts from Hannah Arendt's "On Violence"; *Phylon*, for permission to reprint James Cone's "Martin and Malcolm on Nonviolence and Violence"; Duke University Press, for permission to reprint Anibal Quijano's "Coloniality of Power"; Cambridge University Press, for permission to reprint Maria Lugones "Toward a Decolonial Feminism"; University of Hawa'i Press for permission to reprint Haunani-Kay Trasks' "From a Native Daughter'; the Charlotte Sheedy Literary Agency for permission to reprint excerpts of Audre Lorde's *Sister Outsider: Essays and Speeches* (originally published by Crossing Press/Penguin Random House, Copyright © 1984, 2007). Our thanks also to Arundhati Roy and Haymarket Books for permission to reproduce "When the Saints Go Marching Out:

The Strange Fate of Martin, Mohandas, and Mandela" and "Come September" originally published in Arundhati Roy: *My Seditious Heart: Collected Nonfiction*, Chicago: Haymarket Books, 2019; to the estate of Leslie Feinberg for "Trans Liberation"; and to the James and Grace Lee Boggs Foundation for permission to publish Grace Lee Boggs' "The Beloved Community."

# INDEX